OMNIBUS II

Omnibus II

Church Fathers through the Reformation

General Editor **DOUGLAS WILSON**
Managing Editor **G. TYLER FISCHER**
Associate Editor **CARL L. PETTICOFFER**

Veritas Press, Lancaster, Pennsylvania
www.VeritasPress.com
©2005, 2010 by Veritas Press
ISBN 978-1-932168-94-5
Second edition 2010

All rights reserved. No part of this book may be reproduced without permission from Veritas Press, except by a reviewer who may quote brief passages in a review; nor may any part of this book be reproduced, stored in a retrieval system or transmitted in any form by any means, electronic, mechanical, photocopying, recording or otherwise, without prior, written permission from Veritas Press.

Printed in the United States of America.

For my grandchildren, in the hope that they will read many of these books to their grandchildren.

—Douglas Wilson

For Emily, whose love, support and longsuffering made this work possible. May your children rise up and call you blessed, adding their voices of praise to mine. *Amore fidelis.*

—G. Tyler Fischer

Table of Contents

Foreword

One of the most obvious questions that Christians might ask about a curriculum like this one is, "Why study this stuff?" The question can be asked for different reasons. Perhaps a concerned parent is attracted to the rigor of a "classical and Christian approach," and yet has thumbed through a couple of the texts and is taken aback by some of the material. "It was this kind of gunk," he thinks, "that chased us out of the government school." Or perhaps the question is asked by the student himself when he "hits the wall." The rigor that is built into this course of study is significant, and about a third of the way through the year, a student might be asking all sorts of pointed questions. "Why are you making me do this?" is likely to be one of them. The student may be asking because of his workload, but if he points to the nature of the material, the question still needs a good answer. It is a good question, and everyone who is involved in teaching this course needs to have the answer mastered.

G.K. Chesterton said somewhere that if a book does not have a wicked character in it, then it is a wicked book. One of the most pernicious errors that has gotten abroad in the Christian community is the error of *sentimentalism*—the view that evil is to be evaded, rather than the more robust Christian view that evil is to be conquered. The Christian believes that evil is there to be fought, the dragon is there to be slain. The sentimentalist believes that evil is to be resented.

My wife and I did not enroll our children in a classical Christian school so that they would never come into contact with sin. Rather, we wanted them there because we wanted to unite with like-minded Christian parents who had covenanted together to deal with the (inevitable) sin in a consistent, biblical manner. We fully expected our children to encounter sin in the classroom, on the playground and in the curriculum. We also expected that when they encountered it, they would see it dealt with in the way the Bible says sin should be dealt with.

A classical Christian school or a home school following the classical Christian curriculum must never be thought of as an asylum. Rather, this is a time of basic training; it is boot camp. Students are being taught to handle their weapons, and they are being taught this under godly, patient supervision. But in order to learn this sort of response, it is important that students learn it well. That is, setting up a "straw man" paganism that is easily demolished equips no one. All that would do is impart a false sense of security to the students—until they get to a secular college campus to encounter the real thing. Or, worse yet, if they continue the path into a soft, asylum-style Christian college and then find themselves addressing the marketplace completely unprepared.

If this basic training is our goal, and it is, then we should make clear what one potential abuse of the Omnibus curriculum might be. This curriculum was written and edited with the assumption that godly oversight and protection would accompany the student through his course of work. It was written with the conviction that children need teachers, flesh and blood teachers, who will work together with them. It was also written with the assumption that many of these teachers need the help and the resources that a program like this can supply. But we also believe that, if a seventh-grader is simply given this material and told to work through it himself, the chances are good that the student will miss the benefit that is available for those who are taught.

The Scriptures do not allow us to believe that a record of sinful behavior, or of sinful corruption, is inherently corrupting. If it were, then there are many stories and accounts in the Bible itself that would have to be excluded. But if we ever begin to think our children need to be protected "from the Bible," this should bring us up short. Perhaps we have picked up false notions of holiness somewhere. In short, there is no subject that this curriculum will raise in the minds of seventh-grade students that would not *also* be raised when that student reads through his Bible, cover to cover. It is true that this curriculum has accounts of various murders, or examples of prostitution, or of tyranny from powerful and cruel kings. But we can find all the same things in the book of Judges.

So the issue is not the *presence* of sin, but of the *response* to that sin. What we have sought to do throughout—in the introductory worldview essays, the questions and exercises, and in the teachers' materials—is provide a guideline for responding to all the various worldviews that men outside of Christ come up with. This program, we believe, will equip the student to see through pretences and lies that other Christian children, who have perhaps been too sheltered, are not able to deal with.

Of course, there is a limit to this, as we have sought to recognize. There *are* certain forms of worldliness and corruption that would overwhelm a student's ability to handle it, no matter how carefully a parent or teacher was instructing them. And while children differ in what they can handle, in our experience with many students of this age, we believe that the content of this curriculum is well within the capacity of Christian children of this age group. But again, this assumes godly oversight and instruction. The challenge here is two-fold. The rigor of the curriculum can seem daunting, but we have sought to provide direction and balance with regard to the demands of the material. The second concern is the question of false worldviews, paganism and just plain old-fashioned sin, which we have addressed above.

As our students work their way through this material, and in the years of the Omnibus program that will follow, we want them to walk away with a profound sense of the *antithesis.* What we mean by this is that right after Adam and Eve fell in the Garden, God gave His first messianic promise (Gen. 3:15). But along with this promise, He also said that there would be constant antipathy between the seed of the woman and the seed of the serpent. This is what we mean by the antithesis, and we want our students to come to share in that godly antipathy. The fear of the Lord is to hate evil (Ps. 97:10; Prov. 8:13). In every generation, in all movements (whether of armies or philosophies), in all schools of literature, the men and women involved are either obeying God or disobeying Him. They are either trusting Him or they are not trusting Him. All students are learning to love God, or they are not learning to love God.

But when they love and trust Him, they must do so in the face of conflict. Jesus was the ultimate Seed of the woman, and yet when He came down and lived among us, He faced constant opposition from "broods of vipers." It is not possible to live in this world faithfully without coming into conflict with those who have no desire to live faithfully. The task of every Christian parent bringing children up to maturity in such a world is to do it in *a way that equips.* False protection, precisely because it does not equip, leaves a child defenseless when the inevitable day comes when that artificial shelter is removed. True protection equips. We do not want to build a fortress for our students to hide in; we want to give them a shield to carry—along with a sword.

Students who have faithfully worked through this course of study will not be suckers for a romanticized view of ancient paganism offered up by Hollywood. They have read Suetonius, and they have worked through a Christian response to true paganism. They are grateful that Christ came into this dark world, and they know *why* they are grateful.

—Douglas Wilson

Preface

In the grip of unbelief, some cultures are truly blind. The Bible describes what it is like to live without God and without hope in the world. Before the gospel came to them, the Gentiles of the first century were caught in the grip of "vanity of mind" and "blindness of heart." This was their way of life, their culture of futility. When a people do not know Christ, they are dead in their trespasses and sin, and God gives them over to the logical consequences of their unbelief. The twisted results of this can be seen clearly in St. Paul's description in Romans 1.

This does not mean that the depravity of unbelievers is absolute, or that they are as wicked as they could possibly be. We know that by God's common grace, He restrains cultures from getting to the end of the road, and such cultures can still produce poems, stories, engravings and statues that are quite beautiful. Christians can study such things, and profit by them, but they have to be very careful in this. This was the kind of task we had before us in the first *Omnibus* text—we were dealing with many texts from the ancient classical world, and this meant that we had to take their cultural blindness into account and learn to bring the revelation of Jesus Christ to bear.

This second *Omnibus* text is covering the medieval period, and as a result we must adjust what we are doing. We are *not* adjusting our commitment to Jesus Christ and His Word, but rather recognizing that we are working with quite a different period. It is possible to move from one task to another while retaining the same work ethic. The reason our task in this year of readings is so different is that we must take account of the conversion of Europe to the Christian faith. And in the history of our people during the medieval period, one of the most striking things about us at that time is that we were unashamed of Jesus Christ. This entire and complete confidence in Him

is largely missing today, even in many churches.

However, after the gospel comes to a people, this does not mean that they automatically have the cultural equivalent of perfect 20/20 vision. This side of the resurrection, all believing cultures, even the best of them, will still have their blind spots. This certainly includes our medieval fathers, and it means that we will perhaps see some things more clearly than they did. But it is very tempting for us to simply assume this as a given across the board, and part of the reason for having our students study this period with deep appreciation is so that we might come to learn the dangers in this self-serving approach.

The reason for this is that the reverse is also true; *they* saw certain things far more clearly than we do. We may be permitted to see their blind spots, and, being alive, we can talk about them. But they can see our blind spots also, and if we want to hear their critique, we will have to read some books from another era. In a famous essay on the reading of old books, C.S. Lewis makes the very important point that reading such old books prevents us from falling into what might be described as a chronological provincialism. The people in one village, who don't get out much, can easily believe that the people in that *other* village fifty miles down the road don't pronounce some of their words right. And the more we are limited to just our own village, the more likely it is that we will believe this kind of thing. But someone who has traveled extensively around the world is unlikely to get caught up in such a mistake. Travel broadens the mind, and reading old books is a form of travel.

Most students today are living in the chronological equivalent of a village. They don't read all that much, and, of what they read, over ninety percent of it was written within a small fraction of their lifetime. When it comes to history, literature, poetry, art and architecture, this robs such students and makes them the temporal equivalent of rubes and cornpones.

The students working through the *Omnibus* program this year will be reading many glorious texts. And these texts will of course have blind spots and errors, like all human productions—but they won't be the errors that are characteristic of *our* age. That being the case, we are likely to be able to identify them. By the same token, we will also be able to see some of their statements of the *truth* that are not characteristic of our age either. And those statements of the truth will bring us up short and make us reflect on the practices of our "small village." The period in which we live is also a "period," and five hundred years from now students will be struggling over it, trying to make sense of some of our practices. Nothing is better for clearing our minds of the vanity that afflicts us than to begin seeing ourselves as others will see us. And since we are currently living in the future's "past," a good way of coming to an understanding of ourselves is by studying and appreciating and *understanding* that which is past to us now.

And so this is why we are inviting the student reader to exult in *The Song of Roland,* to learn the shrewd insights of *The Canterbury Tales,* to see the connections between Anglo/Saxon culture and the world of Middle-earth in *The Lord of the Rings,* to rejoice with Arthur in *Sir Gawain and the Green Knight,* to grasp the similarities between David the future king and Robin Hood, to learn to alliterate with joy in *Beowulf,* and to enjoy history in the same way that Geoffrey of Monmouth did. The writers of this textbook have enjoyed the process thoroughly, and we invite you to now join us.

—Douglas Wilson

Publisher's Preface

Have you ever stopped to think what the President of the United States in the year 2040 is doing right now? What about the next Martin Luther or John Calvin? I'll tell you what I hope they are doing. I hope they just finished reading this sentence!

There is no doubt in my mind that classical Christian education and the rigorous study of the greatest works of Western Civilization is a tool to create leaders like no other—godly leaders who understand that this is God's world, Christ inherited it, and we are to take dominion of it to His glory.

Many have begun down the path of studying this material and have not persevered—in their minds it was too hard, too salacious for Christian ears, too unrealistic, too much to grasp, the books were too old or some other "too." Be assured, like the Scriptures say in the Parable of the Sower, the work you do will *bear fruit a hundredfold* if you stick with it. In the lives of our own children we have already seen tremendous benefit and really have just barely scratched the surface.

Our goal with this text is to make the work easier for you. This text should make approaching *Omnibus*, and other material not previously encountered, come alive in a way that instills confidence, and it should convey a sense that young students (and teachers) can handle it.

We have done all we could to make this text a stand-alone guide for reading, studying and understanding these great books. A couple reference books will prove beneficial as resources for this year as well as the following years. *Western Civilization* by Jackson Spielvogel and *History of Art for Young People* by H.W. Janson and Anthony F. Janson are the two main ones. If you have previously used our *Veritas Press History and Bible Curriculum*, you will want to keep the flashcards from them handy, too.

May you be blessed as you dig in and study the hand of God at work in the past and prepare for His use of you in the future.

—*Marlin Detweiler*

ADVISORY TO TEACHERS AND PARENTS

In the course of history there has been much fluctuation on what has been deemed age appropriate for young students. And for those of us alive today, there remains great variation as to what is considered age appropriate. The material we have created and the books we have assigned address numerous subjects and ideas that deal with topics (including sex, violence, religious persuasion and a whole host of other ideas) that have been the subject of much discussion of whether they are age appropriate. The judgment we applied in this text has been the same as we apply to our own children.

In the creation of this program we have assumed that it will be used by students in seventh grade and above. Furthermore, we have assumed that there is no part of the Bible deemed inappropriate to discuss with a seventh-grade student. Therefore, the material assumes that the student knows what sex is, that he understands the existence of violence, that he understands there are theological and doctrinal differences to be addressed and that he has the maturity to discern right and wrong.

The worldview we hold and from which we write is distinctly protestant and best summarized in the *Westminster Confession of Faith.* The Bible is our only ultimate and infallible rule of faith and practice.

We encourage you to become familiar with the material that your students will be covering in this program in order to avoid problems where you might differ with us on these matters.

Introduction

Knock, knock, knock.

Who could that be?

Knock, knock, knock!

Unfortunately, my wife is away at choir practice, and so I have to go and find out. Hadn't I turned the lights off outside?

KNOCK, KNOCK, KNOCK!

I swing the door open to find Frankenstein, Spiderman, some sort of zombie-looking creature and someone with a knife sticking out of his head. He is carrying a chain saw. (*I hope that it is not real.*) Out from among them steps the prince of darkness himself—not looking too fearsome.

"Trick or Treat!" they scream (which might be translated in some neighborhoods as "bribe us with candy or we will show you what this chain saw is for," but in the quiet, rolling fields of Lancaster County it still means something like "please"). I reach for the candy.

They thank me and scurry down the driveway. I switch off the lights. I have got to get some work done—no more distractions.

As I settle into my chair, I think back to the devil (or facsimile of a devil) that I just bribed with candy and wonder how our culture got so messed up—so comfortable with the Devil.

Today, we seem to have two competing cultural attitudes toward Satan: fear or adoration. Part of our culture seems to almost admire the Devil as the leader of all rebels. We see the fringe of this in the hard core Rock and Rollers, but as the first generation of Dark Lord-worshiping metal heads mumbles incoherently into a permanent stupor, who can argue that this is a good life? Still, our modern culture will not be persuaded by the evidence and still follows in the spirit of rebellion, even when it seems increasingly clear that we are running out of things to rebel against.

Often the Christian attitude is one of fear. In some circles of Christians where divine worship has become increasingly light and airy, I have even seen the odd paradox of Christians who seem to fear and respect the Devil more than they do God. *Jesus is my pal, but the Devil, yikes!*

Thankfully, as in most things, the medieval world both explodes and informs our sad, modern outlook. They did neither fear Satan nor admire him. They mocked him. In fact, it is quite possible that the original celebrations on the Eve of All Saints Day—or All Hallow's Eve, a.k.a., Halloween—were done for this purpose.[1] Some have pointed to celebrations that centered on Christian children chasing a few men dressed as demons and devils out of town—usually with sticks. The children were learning to chase the Devil out because he is a vanquished foe. Whether these stories are true or apocryphal, this sort of celebration certainly fits with the medieval mentality concerning the Devil. They treated him like a vanquished foe because that is what they knew him to be.

I will supply two examples of this attitude. The first comes from no less eminent a source than Martin Luther himself—who claimed to have often seen the Devil. When Luther thought that he saw Satan, he did not cower in fear, but instead threw ink bottles and other things at him. He is also said to have claimed that the Devil could be chased away by, among other things, prayer and laughter.[2] St. Boniface, the great missionary to the Germans, supplies the other example. He faced down the pagans who were in spiritual slavery to the demonic forces. They lived dark lives eating each other and worshiping a grove of gigantic, sacred oaks. These pagans feared the devil. St. Boniface did not. One night, with the fearful pagans still clinging to their tree-gods, a sound echoed through the forest. CHOP, CHOP, CHOP! The pagans rushed out, and, as the story goes, they warned Boniface that the pagan gods would surely destroy him if he continued this folly. Boniface's answers can be paraphrased: "Bring it on." CHOP, CHOP, CHOP! They say that the pulpit of Boniface's first church among the Christian Germans was made of oak. The power of the pagan gods had been shattered. There was a new *Man* in town, *the Man Christ Jesus.* Before the gospel came Satan and his forces looked invincible. The light of the gospel revealed them for what they really were: petty, defeated tyrants whose time was over. He was a foe whose head had been crushed, and for the medieval world this meant that it was time to celebrate.

Perhaps this will be the most shocking aspect of the Middle Ages for those who are studying it anew this year. The medieval world was one of great beauty, joy and celebration. They rejoiced because they knew the horror of what they had been freed from and the joy of serving a new, glorious master. In light of the great wisdom and joy that we will explore in the Middle Ages, I thought it was appropriate to address in this Introduction how to use the Omnibus wisely and joyfully.

One of the chief ideas to remember is that Omnibus is a path of renewal and remembrance. In it, we are attempting to rediscover the wisdom of our forefathers that we have, as a culture, cast aside in derision—to our own destruction. What we are seeking to recover is a pearl of great value and complexity. We should not hope to recover everything overnight—in fact, if we could "get up to speed" overnight, we should recognize that what is being recovered is cheap.

At Veritas Academy, we do a better and more comprehensive job of teaching Omnibus every year. When we started doing this, we did not read as much or as deeply as we do now. We could not for a number of reasons, the main one being that our teachers were learning material with which they were unfamiliar. We are getting to know our fathers through the books they have left to us. We know them better now, so we can teach our students to know them better. In those days we read less and not as deeply.

As you work through *Omnibus II,* there are three variables to consider: the teacher, the student and the material. Go as close to the recommended rate as these three allow, keeping in mind the ultimate purpose of this material and of all Christian education: that our training should end with our students taking joyful dominion of our culture for the glory of Christ.

Just as our teachers went more slowly at the beginning, so will you. Do not be afraid to omit a book or books or to take more time on a session (maybe spending an extra day or two on something that is recommended to be one day), particularly if you are just starting out.

Failing to "ramp up" to doing all or most of the books, or doing the program for the first time in a home school situation, can lead to a couple of catastrophic problems. The first problem is burnout—which feels something like living death. I have made acquaintances with some who have done this with Omnibus and with other material. A few have even claimed—usually tearfully—that I, or others at Veritas Press, are trying to destroy their lives! Of course, nothing could be further from the truth. The fact of the matter is, however, that this material—like any other curriculum—can become a cruel taskmaster if mishandled or followed woodenly instead of wisely.

As a general rule of thumb, the teacher can only take the student as far as he, the teacher, can inspire him. This means that teachers might need to limit the amount of material that can be effectively pursued in a year. Perhaps this fact will make you downcast, but recognize that this is the way it has always been. Unwise teachers push ahead when no learning is occurring. This is usually an issue of pride, but there can be other motives that lead a teacher to burn out or to exasperate their students. Perhaps the temptation to burn out is even greater with this approach than with others because of the glory of the content. I have met few who claimed that the reading proposed in this book is not worth doing. For most classical Christian school teachers and home educators, I do not even have to argue the point. We all know that we should do it. We must, however, learn to pace ourselves wisely. The end goal of reading the Great Books and entering into the Great Conversation is that we would get to know our fathers, learn from their wisdom and mistakes and thereby be enabled to take dominion presently for Christ and to do this joyfully. If you are not headed toward this end, stop and realign. If you are not headed there joyfully, you are really not headed there at all. The love of learning is, in fact, a love. Instructors should seek to wisely gauge their own ability to lead students through the books, recognizing that their ability should grow each year.

The ability of the student or students will limit what you can accomplish. If you are in a school setting, you might recognize that from year to year the classes might not move forward at the same rate. I have met those who are befuddled by this—the medieval educator would not be, however. He would recognize that we are training children and that children—like most humans—are unique individuals. When you join them together in a class of ten or twelve, this tendency seems to me to be multiplied rather than diluted. (Of course, if you increase your class size greatly—as many schools in our culture do—you can round the edges and create a system that works mechanically. The only drawback to this is that anything that works like this should hardly be called an education.) So the ability of the students must also be accounted for when a teacher is considering what he can accomplish with them in a year, and this is certainly the case in a home school setting as well.

This advice must be balanced with a goad. Learning is hard work, however joyful it may be. You should get to the end of the year of Omnibus and feel like you need to take a week or two off. In fact, teachers *and* students should probably take a week or two off after your school year is complete. The more we pour into the education of our children the more we should expect to see them and their descendents gaining ground in our culture. If you are a teacher, you should usually expect to move more quickly and effectively through the material as you become more familiar with it. But do not expect Dante to deliver up all his glories immediately. At first, he might seem extraordinarily complicated—almost opaque—to both you and the student. By no means give up! Have patience, simmer on the material, ponder it as you drive to the store where you encounter a child or adult racing from one popular brand name to another. Does this remind you of the Vestibule of Hell? It should.

So, this is how you can use *Omnibus II* wisely—or should we say *medievally?* Using it in this manner will prepare your sons and daughters to take dominion joyfully—as many did in the Middle Ages. For unlike what we read about the Middle Ages in stale and unreadable volumes of "enlightened" history, the Middle Ages were not dark ones. Medieval people were staggeringly wise at some points, and to them we owe much of the good that exists in the world—and some of the bad as well. Something in them calls us back. We yearn like Dante to see Beatrice. We long for leaders like Aragorn or Beowulf. We desire to be noble like Arthur or Gawain and courageous like Boniface. We long to worship in cathedrals and dance as we celebrate Epiphany. To see women dressed as if they meant to be feminine and to meet men who do not remind us of our modern rootless, chestless species. We can not go back and would not want to in many ways—only the most desperate fools want to experience the word *medieval* as it is attached to words like *medicine* or *transportation.* We must, however, be driven forward to a future that learns from much that is presently ignored or forgotten. We must create a culture that remembers and builds on the beauty and glory of this most Christian age.

Knock, knock, knock.

Maybe we just want the ghouls to stop knocking at the front door. *I know the lights are off now.*

KNOCK, KNOCK, KNOCK!

Wait! Was that a *KNOCK* or a *Chop?*

Perhaps if I just close my eyes I can imagine that the rapping at my chamber door is the swing of St. Boniface's ax.

CHOP, CHOP, CHOP!

There, that's better.

—*G. Tyler Fischer*
All Hallow's Eve, A.D. 2005

NOTES

1 I do not intend to settle all of the debates that go on among Christians concerning the roots of and propriety of celebrating Halloween. I would only note that both sides of the debate, the *This-Is-the-Devil's-Holiday* crowd and the *Halloween-is-Essentially-Christian* group, tend to base their opinions on conjecture about the origin of traditions, and neither side is immune from the charge of pseudo-scholarship.

2 He mentioned one other method, but I can not and will not mention it here. If you go and do the historical research, however, you will be either fascinated or scandalized.

Using Omnibus

Students throughout the ages have read the books that you are about to read. These books have been their teachers and have done a lot to make them the great men and women that they became. Now, you are being welcomed to come along and join with them and to learn from them. It is important to realize that some of these books are not to be learned from uncritically—some of them we learn from by the problems they caused. Before you get started, however, there are a few terms you need to understand. First among them is the word *omnibus.* This Latin word means "all encompassing" or "everything." So, in a very loose sense, the Omnibus curriculum is where we talk about everything. All of the important ideas are set on the table to explore and understand. In a more technical sense, however, this Omnibus focuses our attention on the ideas, arguments and expressions of the Western Canon, which have also become known as the Great Books of Western Civilization.

The Great Books are those books that have guided and informed thinking people in Western Civilization. They are the books that have stood the test of time. They come from many sources, starting with the Hebrews and Greeks and extending to their Roman, European and Colonial heirs. These books represent the highest theological and philosophical contemplations, the most accurate historical record and the most brilliant literary tradition that have come down to us from our forefathers. The Great Books lead us into a discussion of the *Great Ideas,* which are the ideas that have driven discussion and argument in Western Civilization throughout its illustrious history.

The Omnibus takes students on a path through the Great Books and the Great Ideas in two cycles. It follows the chronological pattern of Ancient, Medieval and Modern periods. The first cycle is Omnibus I-III, and focuses on sharpening the skills of logical analysis. The second is *Omnibus IV-VI,* focusing on increasing the rhetorical skills of the student.

TITLE	PERIOD	YEARS	EMPHASIS
Omnibus I	Ancient	Beginning–A.D. 70	Logic
Omnibus II	Medieval	70–1563	Logic
Omnibus III	Modern	1563–Present	Logic
Omnibus IV	Ancient	Beginning–A.D. 70	Rhetoric
Omnibus V	Medieval	70–1563	Rhetoric
Omnibus VI	Modern	1563–Present	Rhetoric

Two kinds of books are read concurrently in the Omnibus, *Primary* and Secondary. The list of Primary Books for each year is what might be termed the traditional "Great Books." On this list are authors like Homer, Dante and Calvin. The Secondary Books are ones that give balance to our reading (balance in the general areas of Theology, History and Literature). The secondary list contains works such as *The Chronicles of Narnia* and *The Lord of the Rings.* These books are usually easier, and less class time is devoted to them. Each year is similarly organized. There are thirty-seven weeks' worth of material. Each week is divided into eight sessions of roughly seventy minutes each, optimally. The time estimate is approximate. Home schooling situations might vary greatly from student to student. Five of these sessions are committed to the study of the Primary Books. The other three are dedicated to the Secondary Books.

Kinds of Sessions

Prelude

Each chapter is introduced with a session called a Prelude. In each Prelude we seek to stir up the interest of the students by examining a provoking question that is or could be raised from the book. This is done in the section called A Question to Consider. When the teacher introduces this question he should seek to get the students' initial reaction to the question. These questions might range from "Can you teach virtue?" to "Are all sins equally wicked?" Usually, a student in the Logic years will love to argue his answers. Generally, it will prove helpful for a student to read the introductory essay in the student text ***before*** tackling A Question to Consider. Sometimes a teacher may want to introduce the question first to stir up interest. This "introductory material" will give the students both the general information on the work and a worldview essay which will unpack some of the issues that will be dealt with in the book. After reading this section, the student will be asked to answer a few questions concerning the chapter. These questions are based only on the introductory material they have just read, not on the reading of the book itself.

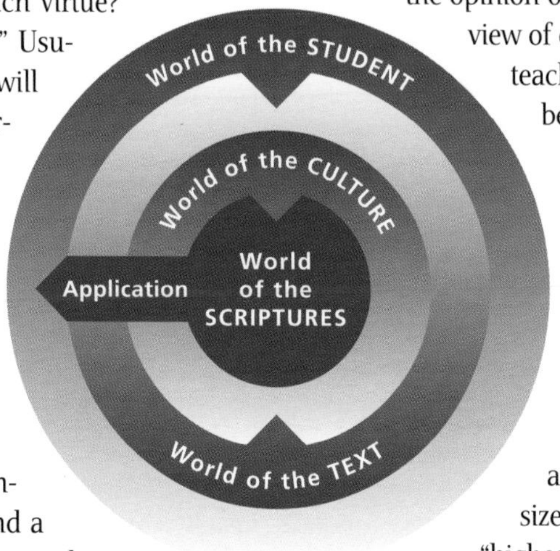

Discussion

The Discussion is the most frequently used class in the Omnibus. It has five parts. The Discussion seeks to explore a particular idea within a book from the perspective of the text itself, our culture and the Bible. It begins, like the Prelude, with A Question to Consider, which is the first of "four worlds" that will be explored, the *world of the student.* The *world of the text* is discovered through the Text Analysis questions. These questions unlock the answer that the book itself supplies for this question (e.g., when reading the *Aeneid,* we are trying to find out how the author, Virgil, would answer this question). After this, in the Cultural Analysis section, the student examines the world of the culture, how our culture would answer the same question. Many times this will be vastly different from the answer of the student or the author. The Biblical Analysis questions seek to unearth what God's Word teaches concerning this question. We can call this discovering the world of the Scriptures. So the progression of the questions is important. First, the students' own opinions and ideas are set forth. Second, the opinion of the text is considered. Next, the view of our culture is studied. Finally, the teaching of the Scriptures is brought to bear. All other opinions, beliefs and convictions must be informed and corrected by the standard of God's Word. Often, after hearing the Word of God, the material seeks to apply the discovered truth to the life of the students. Finally, the students are challenged to think through a Summa Question which synthesizes all they have learned about this "highest" idea from the session.

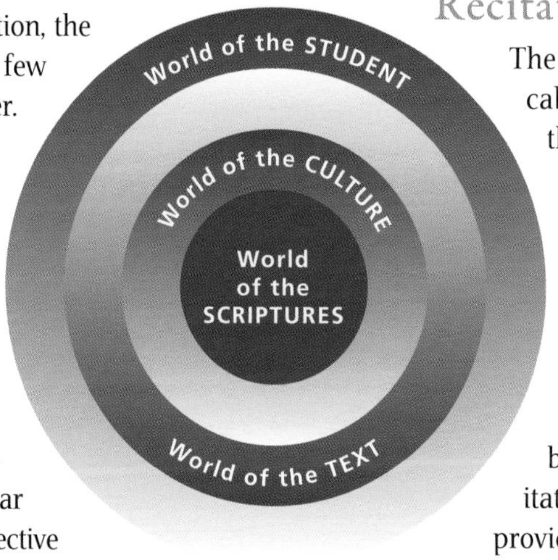

Recitation

The Recitation is a set of grammatical questions that helps to reveal the student's comprehension of the facts or ideas of the book. This can be done in a group setting or individually with or by students. The Recitation questions can also be answered in written form and checked against the answers, but we encourage doing the Recitation orally whenever possible. It provides great opportunity for wandering down rabbit trails of particular interest or launching into any number of discussions. Of course, we cannot predict what current events are occurring when your students study this material. Recitations can prove a great time to direct conversation that relates to the questions and material being covered in this type of class.

Analysis

This session of worldview analysis is focused on comparing a character, culture or author you are studying to some other character, culture or author. This might be done by comparing two or three characters' or authors' answers to the same questions. This type of session effectively helps students to understand the differences between cultures and characters, especially in the arena of worldview.

Writing

There are a variety of writing assignments all focusing on expanding a student's ability to write effectively and winsomely. In the earlier years the focus is on the basics. This includes exercises of the *progymnasmata,* beginning writing exercises used by Greek and Roman students in antiquity and by their medieval and colonial counterparts. Also, essay writing and argument is at the forefront. The assignments in these sessions will progress each year from teaching the basics to including composition in fiction and poetry.

Activity

These classes are focused on bringing creative ideas into the mix. Activities might include debates, trials, sword fights, board games and dramatic productions. Music and art appreciation are also included in this category. These classes are harder to prepare for, but are quite important. Often, the student will remember and understand (and love) the material only if our discussions and recitations are mixed with these unforgettable activities. There are also a number of field trips that are recommended. Often, these are recommended in two categories: ones that most people can do and ones that are "outside the box" experiences that only some will be able to do. The first category might send you to the local museum or planetarium. The latter will recommend ideas like chartering a boat at Nantucket to experience what Ishmael felt on the *Pequod.* Careful pre-planning is important to be able to take advantage of these opportunities.

Review and Evaluation

Weekly testing is not recommended. Students will weary of it and will spend all of their time preparing for tests instead of learning. Choose your tests carefully. Even if a chapter has an evaluation at the end, know that you can use it as a review. The test and the review both work toward the same goal of demonstrating the knowledge of the students and cementing the material into their minds.

Evaluations are divided into three sections. The first section tests the student's *grammatical* knowledge of the book. Answers to these questions should be short, consisting of a sentence or two. The second section is the *logic* section. In this section students are asked to answer questions concerning the ideas of the book and to show that they understand how ideas connect with each other within the book. The final section is called *lateral thinking.* This section asks students to relate ideas in one book with the ideas that they have studied in other books . For instance, the student might be asked to compare Homer's ideal heroes (Achilleus and Odysseus) with Virgil's character Aeneas to discover how the Roman conception of the hero was different from the Greek idea. Finally, students often will be asked to compare and contrast these pagan ideas with a biblical view. So, students might be asked to contrast Homer and Virgil's teaching on what is heroic with the ultimate heroic work of Christ. In this way students demonstrate that they can set ideas in their proper biblical context, showing the relationship between the writing of one author and another. Students should be allowed to have their books and Bibles available during testing. If they are having to do extensive reading during the tests, they are not going to be able to finish or do well anyway. Students should not be permitted to have notes of any kind during the test.

Optional Sessions and Activities

For each chapter there are also some optional classes included. These allow the teacher to be flexible and to add to, or omit classes as they think wise. Usually the number of optional classes is approximately one optional class for every week that the book is taught. There are also a number of optional activities included. These activities allow you to spend addition time on ideas that your students might find fascinating.

Midterms and finals have been provided on the *Omnibus* Teacher's Edition CD. These tests are optional, but can be a helpful gauge of how much the student is retaining. Usually midterms are given around the ninth week of the semester, and finals are given during the last week of the semester. Midterm exams are designed to be completed in a class period. (You might want to give the students slightly more time if possible.) The finals, however, are made to be completed over two class periods (or roughly two and a half hours). Most students will finish more quickly, but some might need all of the time. If possible, give the finals when the student has no time limit. These tests, as well, are given with open books and Bibles, but no notes, and they feature the same sections as the review and evaluation (i.e., grammar, logic and lateral thinking).

For those getting ready to teach this curriculum, preparation should be carefully considered. The material has been designed so that it can be taught with little preparation, but this is not recommended. If you want your students to get the most out of this program, you should prepare carefully. First, make sure you are familiar with the book being studied. Also, consult the Teaching Tips on the Teacher's Edition CD before teaching. Knowing where you are going in the end will help you to effectively move through the material and interact with your students effectively.

What's on this CD?

Teacher's Edition of the Text

The teacher text includes 300 additional pages of material, with an expanded Introduction and suggested answers for all the questions, writing assignments and activities in the daily sessions.

Lesson Plans

Session-by-session lesson plans for each chapter.

Midterms and Exams

Tests with answer keys for both semesters. Three versions are provided for each test (labeled A, B and C).

Grading Tools

An explanation of our suggested grading routine, including sample and blank grading charts, as well as a grading calculator in a popular spreadsheet format.

Requirements and Use

The CD is Windows and Macintosh compatible. Requires free Acrobat Reader. Installer for the latest version is right on the CD or may be downloaded for free at http://get.adobe.com/reader.

Windows OS

If the main application does not appear automatically, double-click the file named "VP.exe".

Macintosh OS

Double-click the file named "Omnibus II (Double-click)" to launch the main application. *Macintosh OS 9 and earlier—double-click the individual files you wish to view.*

PRIMARY BOOKS

First Semester

The Church History

Have you ever wondered what it must have been like for the first generation of pioneers who migrated to the Oregon Territory in the Northwest United States? As a resident of the state of Washington, I have sporadic opportunities to meditate on this question. I wander into the wilderness and wonder, "How in the world did they do it?"

Recently I learned that the earliest settlers in the Northwest arrived under the leadership of David Thompson, a Canadian explorer and fur trapper. He established a trading post near my hometown of Spokane, Washington, and appointed two men, Finan McDonald and Jaco Finlay, to oversee its operation. As I read about their adventures, I marvel at their fortitude, strength, courage, and tenacity. Finan and Jaco picked up their shipment of trading goods at the mouth of the Columbia River, rowed them 600 miles up the river—past portages, hostile Indians, and swift currents—to the mouth of the Spokane River where they transferred the goods to pack animals and hiked the remaining distance to the fort.

Such endurance stuns me. I'm winded by the time I get to the top of my stairs— after all, ten is a pretty big number! But these men did what seems to me nearly impossible. And yet there they are, larger than life. They came and did it, and I'm living off their legacy. So why can't I get up those stairs more easily?

The book that you are preparing to read is a pioneering book. The history recorded tells us about the earliest members, the pioneers, of Christ's church following the death and resurrection of our Lord Jesus. The men and women who hallow and stain these pages are pioneers of the likes of Finan McDonald, Martin Luther, John Winthrop, and Romulus. Not only does this book record the doings of pioneers, it also explores new territory. For this book is the first record we have of the church's history since Luke penned the book of Acts in the New Testament more than *two hundred years* earlier.

And so, as you pick up this book and read it through, envision the pioneers throughout history who have given and sacrificed that we might enjoy the fruit of their labors.

"I am the good shepherd; and I know My sheep, and am known by My own. As the Father knows Me, even so I know the Father; and I lay down My life for the sheep." Artwork of the Good Shepherd became common after the third century, usually with the shepherd bearing a sheep across his shoulders, while other sheep stand by his side. In this fifth-century mosaic from Galla Placidia Mausoleum, Ravenna, Italy, we do not find Jesus depicted with a red sash and beard as most Protestants expect, but as a young farm laborer dressed in a Roman toga, clean shaven and using a cross as a shepherd's staff.

General Information

Author and Context

The author of our book is Eusebius (c. 265–c. 339). While Eusebius is not a very common name today (What would we nickname him? Sebi?), it was a common name in the early church. Indeed, it was so common that our Eusebius is sometimes called *Eusebius of Caesarea* to distinguish him from the others.

Eusebius was born around the year 265 and likely lived and was educated in the eastern portion of the Roman Empire. After witnessing and experiencing the vicious results of the Diocletian persecution, including the death of his good friend Pamphilius[1], he was appointed Bishop of Caesarea in 313. In this role he served for the remainder of his life.

Because of his vast learning and prolific pen, Eusebius was highly esteemed by the emperor Constantine, the first Christian emperor. After the persecution of Christians was terminated by the Edict of Milan in 313, Eusebius became one of Constantine's chief advisors. He is most famous for his role in the Arian controversy,[2] serving as one of the leading bishops at the Council of Nicea, which Constantine convened in 325 to bring peace and unity to the church.

It was around the time of the Nicene Council that Eusebius finished *The Church History*[3] at the request of Paulinus, the Bishop of Tyre. As Eusebius glanced back over the three hundred years separating him from the death and resurrection of the Lord Jesus, he could not help but marvel at the overriding hand of Providence and see in the conversion of Constantine the realization of Isaiah's prophecy:

> "Kings will see and arise,
> Princes will also bow down,
> Because of the Lord who is faithful,
> The Holy One of Israel who has chosen You"
> (Isaiah 49:7b).

A sarcophagus from Adelphia bears this carving of The Triumphal Entry.

Significance

Without Eusebius's book our knowledge of the early history of the church would be scant. One problem with reconstructing the history of pioneering days is that the pioneers were often so busy building, planting, and just surviving that they did not have the leisure to sit and write about what they were doing. So it was in the early church. Our fathers were so busy articulating the Gospel, preserving it from false teachers, and maintaining a consistent witness before their pagan rulers, that they did not have the leisure to look at the big picture and consider what God was accomplishing through them.

By God's good providence, this situation changed with the conversion of Constantine. Christians were suddenly freed from the impending sense of doom. Perceiving the significance of this moment, Eusebius wrote the first history of our people—becoming in the process the Father of Church History.

Eusebius's work did not remain in obscurity. It was copied and recopied, read and reread, imitated and re-imitated throughout history. While there are no church historians prior to Eusebius, there are many after him: Socrates (not the famed hemlock drinker), Sozomen, Theodotus, Augustine. One thing characterizes them all—they start with Eusebius.

Main Characters

The main character in *The Church History*, who occasionally pops out from behind the screen to reveal that He is the real mover and shaker in this period, is God Himself. Eusebius clearly understands that God is the author of history, and he interprets the changing fortunes of the church through the lens of God's sovereign control.

But God orchestrates this story through the lives of men and women, and so Eusebius is careful to include their names. He discusses heroes of the faith like the apostles and their successor bishops, the presbyters (elders) who strove to protect biblical doctrine from false teachers and the confessors and martyrs who endured torture and oftentimes death for the sake of their Master. There are, for instance, great teachers and writers like Origen and Dionysius of Alexandria who defended the church from false teaching. There are apologists like Justin Martyr and Quadratus who risked personal harm to defend their brethren in writing. There are martyrs like Polycarp and Blandina who endured unimaginable cruelties for the sake of the Name.

Eusebius's story includes not only heroes but also villains. There are emperors who set themselves against God, Jews who reject the Messiah, and false teachers who endeavor to lead the church astray. They include vile men like Nero, Galerius, and Maximin Daia; weak men like Pilate; deceptive men like Simon Magus, Valentinus, and Paul of Samosata. Each plays his role in the story which God has orchestrated for the ultimate good of His people.

Summary and Setting

The basic purpose of *The Church History* is to record the history of God's people from the life of our Lord through Eusebius's own day. More particularly, Eusebius states in the opening paragraph of the book that it is his intent to record (1) the names and deeds of the apostles and their successor bishops in the most famous churches, (2) the major historical events which occurred in this period, (3) the writings of those shepherds who strove to teach and defend Christian doctrine, (4) the names of the heretics who endeavored to corrupt apostolic teaching, (5) the fate of the Jews who rejected their Messiah, and (6) the glorious achievements of the confessors and martyrs who suffered for the sake of Christ.

Eusebius accomplishes this purpose by organizing his material in a series of ten books (what we would call chapters). The books are arranged chronologically, beginning with the life, death and resurrection of our Lord Jesus, proceeding through the reigns of the Roman emperors, and closing with the victories of Constantine over Maxentius, Maximin Daia and Licinius.

BOOK 1: The historicity of the Christian faith and the life of our Lord
BOOK 2: The labors of the apostles up to the destruction of Jerusalem (A.D. 70)
BOOK 3: The destruction of Jerusalem by the Romans and the labors of the apostles and first leaders through the reign of Trajan
BOOK 4: Bishops, heretics, martyrs and apologists from Trajan to Marcus Aurelius

BOOK 5: From Marcus Aurelius to Septimius Severus
BOOK 6: Origen's life and deeds; from Septimius Severus to Decius
BOOK 7: Dionysius of Alexandria; from Gallus to Diocletian
BOOK 8: The persecution of Diocletian; from Diocletian to Galerius
BOOK 9: The victories of Constantine
BOOK 10: Reestablishment of the churches; final victory of Constantine

Worldview

Pioneers are frequently criticized. Later generations look back and are prone to question every move, every decision made. Why did they do it *that* way? Why didn't they think of that problem? Why didn't they tell us what happened on that occasion? Hindsight is always 20/20.

Eusebius has not escaped this type of criticism. As the first man to compose a history of the early church, he has been the object of numerous criticisms. "He relies too much on other sources." "He doesn't give us sufficient detail about the heretical movements he mentions." "He is too triumphalistic." "He is not sufficiently critical of Constantine." The list goes on.

One of the most persistent criticisms leveled against Eusebius as historian is the first—he relies too much on other sources. As you read you will quickly discover that he quotes freely and liberally from previous writers. His style of writing history (*historiography*) is not attuned to modern standards which do not value such extensive borrowing.

His use of other sources, however, does not detract from Eusebius's accomplishment or mar our knowledge of his own understanding of the events he covers. Eusebius's quotations and excerpts are joined together in a masterful way such that the material reads as a cohesive story. He didn't simply cut and paste; rather, he carefully organized his material and added explanatory notes and chapters to unite it in a single tale. What emerges is a stirring saga of the earliest years of the church.

The Creator of All

This saga begins with the God of heaven and earth as He has revealed Himself in Christ. Apart from Christ, as Eusebius himself remarks, there would be no Christians. Therefore, if we are to compose a history of the Christians, it follows that we must start with Christ (1.1).

So who is Christ? Where did He come from? Is He merely an ordinary man or is He something more? Is He God? Is He God and man? Is He a creature or is He, in fact, the Creator? Is He different from the Father or absolutely the same? And is His Father also the Creator of the universe, the God of the Old Testament, or is He a completely new deity?

Most Christians today answer these questions rapidly and without a great deal of contemplation. However, in the early history of the church, these basic questions had to be carefully considered in light of the Word of God and the worship of God's people. Who exactly is Christ?

Every pioneer has to stake out the limits of the territory he is claiming. Whether it is Romulus plowing the Palatine Hill or Finan McDonald stacking the logs of Spokane House, one of the pioneer's first tasks is to build fences or place boundary stones which declare, "This is mine." The pioneer needs to know what land is rightfully his so he can improve the land without fear of losing it when the next settler arrives and so he can defend it from invaders and thieves.

Likewise early Christians had to articulate their understanding of God and Christ and stake out, as it were, what teachings were acceptable and unacceptable in referring to Him. Jesus himself had warned that false Christs would appear and attempt to lead his people astray. Sure enough, this happened. Heretics like Simon Magus, Menander, Marcion, Valentinus, Mani and Paul of Samosata arose and endeavored to lead the people of God astray from the truth. The leaders in the church had to counter such men and preserve "the faith once for all delivered to the saints" (Jude 3).

One of the first stakes that our fathers had to pound in the ground was the relationship between Jesus and the God of the Old Testament. Heretics like Marcion, Valentinus, and other Gnostics denied that the Creator and the Father were one and the same God. They maintained that the Father revealed by Jesus is different from the Creator who fashioned the earth. They even held that, while the Father is good and loving, the Creator is a harsh and judgmental being unworthy of our worship (cf. 4.11). Is this what our Lord Jesus and the apostles taught?

According to Eusebius and the other early fathers of the church, the answer is most emphatically, "No!" The God of the Old Testament who created heaven and earth is the Father of our Lord Jesus Christ. As the Nicene Creed would later declare, "We believe in one God, the Father Almighty, Maker of heaven and earth . . ." Eusebius fully embraced this understanding of the Father. He repeatedly uses the Psalms as hymns of praise to God, quotes the prophets who anticipated the coming of the Lord, and criticizes those who reject the Old Testament. He urges his hearers, "Let us then sing the new song to the Doer of wonders, the Lord of the universe, Creator of the world, the almighty, the all-merciful, the one and only God" (10.4).

The first thing we learn, then, about our Lord Jesus Christ is that He is the Son of the Living God, the Creator of heaven and earth. Jesus did not come to introduce some new deity, but the same Lord who sent a flood upon the earth, called Abraham out of Ur of the Chaldees, and led the Israelites out of Egypt. Contrary to Marcion and his pals, it is this God who is the Father of our Lord Jesus.

The Sovereign Creator

As Eusebius relates the early history of the church, he not only confesses that God is the Creator of all, he also recognizes God's providential direction of every event in the saga that he writes. Eusebius repeatedly gives praise to God, acknowledging His goodness,

BONE POLITICS

An ancient limestone burial box (called an *ossuary*) with an inscription "James, son of Joseph, brother of Jesus" was found in Israel in 2002. As one noted scholar explained, "The James ossuary is testimony to the fact that the people of the time had a strong belief in the resurrection of Jesus. In antiquity, crucifixion was the most humiliating and dishonorable way to die, and people believed that how you die was a reflection on your character. If Jesus's life had simply ended in crucifixion, no one in their right mind would include his name—in a place of honor—on the box." Previously, the ossuary of the high priest Caiaphas, who orchestrated Judas's betrayal of Jesus, was uncovered by archaeologists in 1990.

This limestone box is about 20x10x12 inches and bears the inscription "James, son of Joseph, brother of Jesus."

James's Bone Box came to public light when the Biblical Archaeology Society (BAS) published the findings of a French scholar and the Geological Survey of Israel that the box and its inscription were authentic. The publication set off a media frenzy and a series of charges and counter-charges about whether the box or inscription are authentic or fraudulent. It seems that the box was not dug up by professional archaeologists but was originally bought by an Israeli engineer from an antiquities dealer. This engineer obtained the services of a French scholar, who became convinced the box was authentic, and the Geological Survey confirmed authenticity. Subsequently the Royal Ontario Museum also confirmed authenticity. Still, some archaeologists questioned the finding because the box was not professionally excavated under controlled conditions.

Then in 2003 the Israeli Antiquities Authority reported their conclusion that, based on their analysis of the patina, the inscription was a recent forgery. It had been made to look old by adding a chalk solution. It is wise to remember that faith is not based on archaeological evidence. Many times Christians grasp at archaelogical findings to prove the Bible's veracity. We must instead insist that the Bible is the standard for all truth and not what we might dig up in the ground.

crediting Him with miraculous wonders and praising His power. Eusebius is constantly aware of God's sovereignty.

Nearly all of us, no doubt, would be willing to confess that God is sovereign. But how far are we willing to take this? As we look at the church around us and see her divided into factions, do we confess that this is according to God's plan? When we see unbelievers mocking Christ and placing crucifixes in jars of urine,[4] do we see this as God's chastisement upon the church for our unbelief and lack of love? When nations suffer civil strife and upheaval, do we view this as evidence of God's governance of the nations?

Eusebius would have answered, "Yes," to all these questions. God's sovereignty means that nothing happens apart from His determination. "Our God is in the heavens; He does whatever He pleases" (Ps. 115:3).

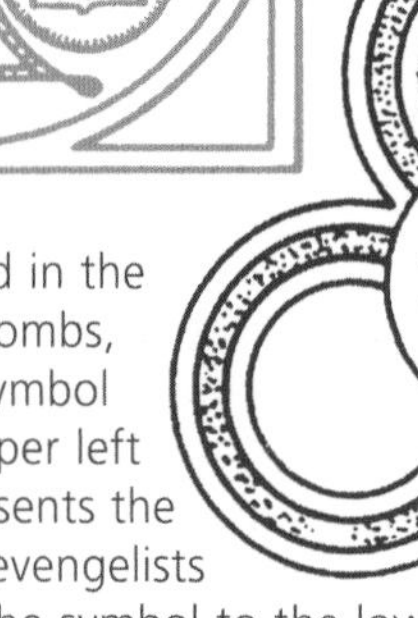

Found in the catacombs, the symbol at upper left represents the four evengelists and the symbol to the lower right is a representation of the Trinity.

Eusebius's confession of God's sovereignty is robustly biblical. First, Eusebius acknowledges time and time again that God is the one permitting the horrendous persecutions being perpetrated against the church. God brings it about and brings it to an end in His time and for His good purposes. "[T]he rulers of this life," writes Eusebius, "would never find it easy to attack the churches of Christ, unless the hand that champions us allowed this as a divine judgment to punish and reform us at chosen times" (7.30). It is God, not man, who orchestrates the trials through which the church passes (cf. Phil. 1:29–30; 1 Pet. 4:12–14).

Second, Eusebius emphasizes the close connection between piety toward God and blessings and curses in this life, both for the church and for the world. God is the one who governs history, and we can expect that if we rebel against Him, He will chastise us. In self-conscious imitation of the book of Deuteronomy (cf. Deut. 28), Eusebius traces the rise of the Diocletian persecution to the unbelief and wickedness of God's people during the time of peace which preceded it (8.1; 9.8). God is faithful and will always, with His "accustomed mercy", discipline His people when they turn away from Him.

While God disciplines the church out of mercy as a father does his son, His judgment on the wicked—both individuals and communities—is a result of His justice. As an example of individuals who faced God's judgment, consider the emperors who persecuted the Christians. They share a remarkable thing in common: nearly all of them died miserably. Herod was eaten by worms, Pontius Pilate committed suicide, Herod Agrippa was racked by stomach pains, Galerius was transformed into a great blob of flabby fat, Maxentius sank to the bottom of the Tiber and Maximin Daia withered away. Why? Because God "attacked the perpetrator[s] of these crimes, angry with [them] as the prime instigator[s] of the whole evil persecution" (8.16).

God's judgment confronts communities of people no less than individuals. Communities suffer from plague, famine and war as a result of their warfare against God's people. These sufferings are not simply a matter of natural consequences—God visits these consequences upon them. "In response [to human rebellion], God sent them floods and conflagrations, famines and plagues, wars and thunderbolts—punishments progressively drastic—in order to restrain the noxious illness of their souls" (1.2). This is particularly evident in God's judgment upon those Jews who rejected Jesus as the Messiah (cf. 3.5–7). However, it is also evident in the history of Rome (8.13). God is not mocked. What a man or community sows, that will he also reap. Eusebius sees this with crystal clarity and interprets the history he records within this framework. God is sovereign and rules over the affairs of both men and nations.

Since God is sovereign, what cause could there possibly be for Christians to despair? Remember the horrendous things Eusebius is recording—cruel deaths, vicious tortures, heartless sentences. Do these things cause Eusebius to write without hope? To mourn the hard fortunes of the church? By no means! God is in control. He knows precisely what He is doing at every moment and the people of God can rest in His sovereign disposal of all events. At the end of the Great Persecution, Eusebius declares:

> After all this, God, the great, heavenly Champion of the Christians, having displayed his wrath to all men in return for their brutal assaults against us, restored his providence to us again and caused the light of peace to shine on us out of black darkness, as it were, making it clear to all that God himself had constantly been overseeing our affairs. Sometimes he scourged his people and in due time corrected them through trials, but after enough chastening he showed mercy and kindness to those who had hope in him (9.8).

God's sovereignty, therefore, is not some abstract idea for Eusebius—it is a teaching of immense practical comfort and application. No matter how much Satan may rage against the people of God (cf. 4.7), no matter how many enemies rise up and persecute them, God is in control. He does all things, and He does all things well.

The God-Man

But there was other ground to stake out in addition to Jesus' relation to the God of the Old Testament, the Sovereign Creator of all things. Even if it is agreed that he revealed the same God mentioned in Genesis, we still have not answered our original question—who is Jesus? The answers to this question varied widely in Eusebius's day.. Some heretical groups began to teach that Jesus was just a man.[5] Others insisted that He was only God and had merely appeared to be man.[6] Still others maintained that, while He was more than man, He was less than God.[7] The options seemed limitless.

Eusebius is careful to criticize all these false views of Christ. Christ is no ordinary man. He is the Word of God, "who existed before the world and assisted the God of the universe in the fashioning of all created things" (1.2). In ages past He appeared as the Angel of the Lord but now has finally revealed Himself by taking on human nature and dwelling among us. He is the divinely anointed Christ of God, serving as our Prophet, Priest and King (1.3).

But neither did Christ only appear or seem to be a man. He really and truly became flesh in order to redeem us from our sin and rescue us from our bondage to Satan. Eusebius spends considerable time harmonizing the genealogies in Matthew and Luke not only to vindicate the trustworthiness of Scripture but also to emphasize Christ's human lineage (1.7). According to Eusebius, Christ appeared "in the form of a man, [with] a nature like ours" (1.2); as "the only Son of the Father, [he] willingly assumed our corrupt nature" (10.4). Christ was a man with a nature like ours.

How then can Christ be no ordinary man and yet simultaneously be a man? The full answer to this question is not given by Eusebius, nor the rest of the church until the Council of Chalcedon. Remember that pioneers don't always answer every question. Nevertheless, Eusebius embraces the mysterious reality that the Christ who was clearly man was just as clearly God. "Thus Jesus Christ our Savior is the only person in history to be acknowledged—even by earth's most exalted—not as an ordinary human king but worshiped as the true Son of the God of the universe and as himself God" (10.4). Jesus shares "in the unbegotten divinity of the Father" (1.3) and "to this day is honored by his worshipers throughout the world as King, held in greater awe than a prophet, and glorified as the true and only High Priest of God and above all as the preexistent Word of God, having his being before all ages and worshiped as God" (1.3).

Despite these clear statements of Christ's deity, there are moments when Eusebius's comments about the Lord Jesus should make us squirm—even more than when we read that the original pioneers ate cow tongue. As a disciple of Origen, Eusebius at times comes perilously close to *subordinationism,* the teaching that Christ was less than the Father. On a couple occasions, for instance, he remarks that Christ should be accorded "second place" in relation to the Father (1.2; 10.4). However, on the whole, Eusebius's comments about Christ in *The Church History* appear remarkably orthodox.

A New Race of Men

Prior to the coming of the God-man, mankind was divided into two basic ethnic groups—Jews and

Gentiles. While both were created in the image of God, God bestowed certain blessings upon the Jews which He did not give to the rest of humanity. That exclusivity changed when Christ came. The saga that Eusebius records bears testimony to this transformation. In Christ, Jew and Gentile cease to be relevant categories (cf. Gal. 3:28). Christ came to create a "new people" with a new name—Christian (1.4).

Eusebius articulates this transformation throughout *The Church History*. At the very beginning of Book One he notes that, though Adam was created in the image and likeness of God, he rebelled against God and plunged humanity into ruination and distress (1.2). This rebellion had horrendous consequences for humanity. We have become dead in our sin, we wander in darkness and we labor as slaves for the Prince of Darkness. Our lives are no longer our own and, apart from Christ, we are without hope in the world. But the good news is that while we were in this state of despair, God sent Christ to redeem and rescue us. "But God demonstrates his own love for us, in that while we were yet sinners, Christ died for us" (Rom. 5:8). Eusebius explains:

> Like the best doctor . . . so [Jesus] saved us, who were not merely sick or afflicted with terrible ulcers and festering wounds but lying among the dead, for no one else in heaven could undertake the salvation of so many. He alone endured our sorrows, taking on himself the penalty for our sins when we were not half dead, but decaying in tombs, and he raised us up and saves us now, as in the days of old, out of ardent love for humankind, sharing with us the Father's blessings—our lifegiver, enlightener, great physician, king, and lord, the Christ of God. When he saw the whole human race sunk in demon-inspired darkness, his appearance alone tore apart the chains of sin as easily as wax melts in the sun (10.4).

Christ came to deliver all men, Jew and Gentile, from their natural bondage to sin. In so doing he destroyed these ethnic boundaries. "For He Himself is our peace, who made both groups into one and broke down the barrier of the dividing wall, by abolishing in His flesh the enmity, which is the Law of commandments contained in ordinances, so that in Himself He might make the two into one new man, thus establishing peace" (Eph. 2:14–15). Christ has made a new race of men called Christians.

Men at War

Though Christ has eliminated the ethnic boundaries which separated Jew and Gentile, He has not eliminated all boundaries. Because all men by nature are lost in sin and in need of salvation, Eusebius clearly embraces the idea of *antithesis*. There are those who reject Christ and refuse to join the "new people" which God has created in Him. There is therefore a fundamental divide in humanity. There are those for Christ and those against Him. There are the sheep and the goats, believers and unbelievers, friends and enemies. The story which God is orchestrating involves conflict.

Eusebius understands that the church is at war. God's people are fighting for their own salvation and for the deliverance of all humanity from Satan's clutches. While the biggest danger that the modern church faces is pretending as though she does not have enemies, in Eusebius's day the threat was more direct. The enemies were banging down the doors, burning the churches, killing the bishops and torturing the laymen. In his day the enemies were not trying to lull God's people into complacency—they were endeavoring to obliterate the church from the earth. And so Eusebius makes sharp distinctions between the church and her enemies. He calls rulers who oppress God's people "tyrants." He labels unbelievers "wicked." He even christens a certain heretic a "conceited crackbrain!" But behind all these labels is his firm conviction that the church is at war with her enemies. In order to prevail, she must recognize them as such.

Triumphant Men

While calling a spade a spade, Eusebius perceives that all the machinations of these tyrants, oppressors and heretics are inspired by that foe of humanity, the devil. These men are merely his instruments. It is he who holds mankind in his clutches and who recognizes in the death and resurrection of Christ his own impending doom. He would like nothing more than to see the light of the gospel put out and God's people crushed (10.4). And so he strives in every way possible to undermine the truth.

But try as he might, he is ultimately doomed to failure because Christ is at the head of His church and shall lead her in triumph over all her foes. For Eusebius the idea that the church will ultimately fail in her mission to disciple the nations is nonsense. Christ has entrusted the truth to the church—how could she possibly fail? In contrasting the outcome of heretical movements in his day with the course of the true church, Eusebius remarks:

> . . . the earlier [heresies] continually fragmented and disappeared. But the universal and only true church, remaining ever the same, continued to grow in greatness, shedding on Greeks and non-Greeks alike the free, sober, and pure light of the divine teaching for conduct and thought. The passage of time, then, squelched the defamations against our teaching so that it stands alone, victorious and supreme, and no one today dares to resume the vile slanders of past enemies against our faith (4.7).

Despite opposition from outside and corruption from inside, the church is destined to prevail—not because of any inherent goodness in her but because her Savior is sovereign and "leads his armies after death, puts up trophies over his foes, and fills every place, district, and city, both Greek and foreign, with votive [free will] offerings" (10.4). As the book of Esdras, an apocryphal tale about the biblical Ezra, declares, *Magna est veritas et praevalebit,* "The truth is great and will prevail."

Transformed Men

This sense of optimism and triumph permeates Eusebius's vision for the church and the people of God. The same Christ who will eventually cause the church to triumph over her foes is the One who currently causes his people to triumph by transforming them with his Word. God's people possess the truth in the Scriptures—and as God's story unfolds this truth must change them. "And do not be conformed to this world, but be transformed by the renewing of your mind, that you may prove what is that good and acceptable and perfect will of God" (Rom. 12:2).

How should the truth transform the people of God? First, it should make them bold and courageous. "The wicked flee when no one is pursuing, but the righteous are bold as a lion" (Prov. 28:1). Eusebius tells story after story of men, women, and children who endured unspeakable torments because they knew whom they served. They were so confident of the grace, mercy, and truth found in Christ, that no danger could dissuade them from clinging to him. The result of their uncommon boldness was that many were converted to the faith. "At first," Dionysius of Alexandria reports, "we were persecuted and stoned, but then some of the heathen abandoned their idols and turned to God. Through us the Word was sown among them for the first time, and it seems that for this God exiled us to them and returned us when we had finished our mission" (7.11). As Tertullian, another early church father, declares, "The blood of the martyrs was the seed of the church." The truth of God should make us bold.

The truth should also inspire us to fight for the purity and unity of the church. When the pioneers came out west, they frequently had to defend their homes from Indian attack. Supposedly the famous frontiersman Kit Carson developed his keen eye from helping his father defend their home when a mere lad of ten years old. Just as the pioneers were passionate to defend their homes, Christians must be passionate to defend the church.

First, we should preserve the unity of the church. "Let us not become conceited, provoking one another, envying one another" (Gal. 5:26). We see in our own day how difficult it is for the church to maintain a godly witness when divided into many camps. The same was no less true in Eusebius's day. "[T]he very people who ought to be unified in fraternal concord are separated from each other in a disgraceful, no, abominable manner, providing those who are strangers to this most holy religion a pretext for scoffing" (10.5 cf. 6.45). To provide such a pretext is shameful, and God's people should long for the unification of the church around the truth.

Second, we should safeguard the purity of the church both morally and doctrinally. One of Eusebius's greatest heroes is Origen whose leadership in the church was as remarkable as some of his ideas were odd and even misguided. He was greatly affected by Plato's philosophy and even made himself a eunuch for the sake of the kingdom. At the remarkably young age of 18 he was appointed a teacher in Alexandria and was so brilliant that men paid to have others transcribe his lectures. Origen had an immense impact on his generation—instructing Christians in the way of truth, converting unbelievers from their paganism, and even recovering heretics from their error. What was the secret of his success? "His deeds matched his words and his words his deeds, as the saying goes, which explains why, under God, he led so many to share his enthusiasm" (6.3). Origen hungered to defend the church, and Eusebius reckoned him a model for generations to come.

Not only should the truth of God make his people bold and courageous; not only should it inspire us to uphold the unity and purity of the church; it should also infuse us with compassion for others—whether believer or unbeliever. One of the pressing problems that confronted the church following periods of persecution was what to do with those who had denied their faith under torture (called the *lapsi*). Novatus and his disciples insisted that the *lapsi* should be permanently excluded from the church—the church should consist only of the pure who had withstood torture without abandoning Christ in any way. Eusebius contrasts the harshness of the Novatians with the mercy and forgiveness expressed by many confessors who had themselves endured the persecutions. "They did not boast over the fallen but shed tears in their behalf to the Father, praying for life, and he gave it to them" (5.2).

The compassion of Christians should be directed not only internally but externally. One of the most remarkable testimonies in Eusebius is the behavior of Christians during the periods of hunger and famine which God sent upon the Romans for their sin. While the pagans frequently abandoned their own relatives who were struck with the plague, Christians ministered to their former persecutors—tending their wounds, slaking their thirst, and often contracting their disease themselves (cf. 9.8). It was through this ministry of mercy that the Word of God spread among the unbelieving communities and a taste of the gospel's eventual triumph was experienced.

The saga that Eusebius records—beginning with the Creator of all, centering in the life, death and resurrection of the God-man, ending in the triumph of the God-man over his enemies through his transformed people—should stir our souls and fire our imaginations. Eusebius wrote his history to awaken us from our lethargy and give us a sense of what God can accomplish through us today. The remarkable deeds that Eusebius relates need not be confined to the early days of the church. The same God who led our pioneering fathers is the God who leads the church today.

And so, in the same way that we marvel at the deeds of the pioneers who traversed deserts, streams and mountains to settle the Northwest, and are moved by them to greater feats of self-discipline and achievement, we ought to marvel at the conviction and fortitude of our fathers and mothers in the faith and be inspired to see the church grow and prosper in our own day. As Eusebius himself looked back at the faith of Old Testament saints and was encouraged to righteousness, we can look at the lives of the men and women in the early church and be inspired to serve Christ with unflagging zeal. Let us excel "in self-control and righteousness, in discipline and virtue, and in the confession of the one and only God over all, and in all this [let us show] no less zeal than [them]" (1.4).

—Stuart W. Bryan

A carving in an ivory casket depicting the death of Judas and the Crucifixion, c. 420 A.D.

For Further Reading

Bruce, F.F. *The Spreading Flame.* Grand Rapids, Mich.: Eerdmans, 1980.

Shelley, Bruce L. *Church History in Plain Language.* Chicago: Nelson, 1996. 1–123.

Spielvogel, Jackson J. *Western Civilization.* Seventh Edition. Belmont, Calif.: Thomson Wadsworth, 2009. 168–177.[8]

Veritas Press History Cards: New Testament Greece and Rome. Lancaster, Pa.: Veritas Press. 26, 27, 29, 30.

Session I: Prelude

A Question to Consider

Would you hand the Scriptures over to the authorities to be burned?

From the General Information above answer the following questions:

1. Who was Eusebius, and when did he live?
2. Why is *The Church History* considered a pioneering book?
3. Why did Eusebius write *The Church History?*
4. What does Eusebius say about God's sovereignty?
5. Why does Eusebius call folks tyrants, oppressors, heretics and crackbrains?
6. What is Eusebius's vision for the future of the church?

Reading Assignment:
Book 1.1–1.13

SESSION II: DISCUSSION

Book 1.1–1.13

A Question to Consider

Who is Christ?

Discuss or list short answers to the following questions:

Text Analysis

1. How does Eusebius describe the nature of Christ (1.2)?
2. Eusebius offers some proofs that Christ existed *prior* to His earthly advent. List these proofs (1.2).
3. Briefly explain Eusebius's argument reconciling the two different genealogies of Christ (1.7).
4. Should holy men of old be called Christians according to Eusebius? Why or why not (1.4)?
5. According to Eusebius, what does it mean to be a Christian? What strikes you about his summary (1.4)?

Cultural Analysis

1. What do most people think about Christ?
2. Do all Christians today agree with Eusebius's statement that Abraham and his forebears should be called Christians?
3. How does our culture define *Christian?*

Biblical Analysis

1. What do the following passages reveal about the deity of our Lord Jesus Christ: John 1:1; Col. 2:9; Heb. 1:3–13?
2. What do the following passages reveal about the humanity of our Lord Jesus Christ: Luke 2:1–40; Phil. 2:5–11; Heb. 2:14–18?
3. Compare Eusebius's summary of what it means to be a *Christian* with the following biblical summaries: Deut. 10:12–13; Mic. 6:6–8; Mark 12:28–34. How do they compare?
4. What do the following Scriptures reveal about the relationship between Old Testament saints who served the Lord and Christ: Acts 7:51–53; 1 Cor. 10:1–13; Heb. 11:1–40 (esp. v. 26)?

SUMMA

Write an essay or discuss this question, integrating what you have learned from the material above.
Who is Christ?

READING ASSIGNMENT:
Book 2.1–2.26

SESSION III: DISCUSSION

Book 2.1–2.26

A Question to Consider

Are there apostles today?

Discuss or write short answers to the following questions:

Text Analysis

1. To whom did Christ give the name *apostles* (1.10)?
2. Does Eusebius use the word *apostle* in a broader sense than just the Twelve (1.12)?
3. What role did the apostles serve in determining correct doctrine (2.14)?
4. Does Eusebius distinguish between the time when the apostles were alive and the time after (3.32)?

Cultural Analysis

1. What authority do the Declaration of Independence and the United States Constitution have in American society?
2. How does our society tend to look upon past authorities in our culture?

Biblical Analysis

1. What metaphor does Paul use to describe the function of Christ and the apostles in Ephesians 2:19–22?
2. How might this metaphor assist us in answering the question about whether there are apostles today? (When you are building a house how many times do you lay the foundation [cf. Rev. 21:14]?)
3. What offices were established by the apostles to guide and direct the church following their deaths? (See Acts 20:17–35; 1 Tim. 3:1–13; Titus 1:5–9.)

4. What were the requirements placed upon the man chosen to succeed Judas as one of the Twelve Apostles (cf. Acts 1:15–26)? Can any man now meet these requirements?

Summa

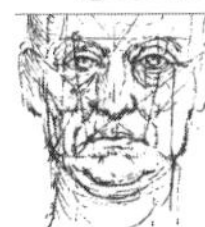

Write an essay or discuss this question, integrating what you have learned from the material above.
Are there apostles today?

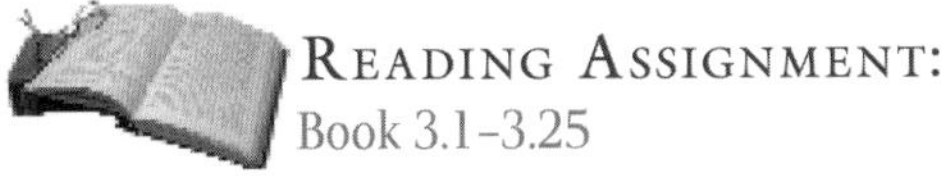

Reading Assignment:
Book 3.1–3.25

Session IV: Discussion

Book 3.1–3.25

A Question to Consider

What is the Canon?

Discuss or write short answers to the following questions:

Text Analysis

1. Summarize Eusebius's opinions on the *accepted, disputed, rejected* and *heretical* books of the New Testament canon (3.25).
2. Make a list from this section of the connection between the various books of the New Testament and the apostles (2.15, 2.23, 3.3, 3.4, 3.24).
3. What did Josephus say about the respect which was shown by the Jews toward the Old Testament Scriptures? Does he think that the Old Testament apocryphal books have equal weight with the other Old Testament books (3.10)? On this last question, you may also consult the Old Testament canon listed in 4.26.
4. To be a part of the canon, a book had to have been written by an apostle or one closely associated with an apostle. What other clues does Eusebius cite to determine which were canonical (2.23; 3.24–25)?

Cultural Analysis

1. What is the attitude toward the Bible in our culture at large?
2. In our culture, who or what determines what is true or good?

Biblical Analysis

1. Where do we discover the will of God for us today (John 17:17; 2 Tim. 3:14–17; 2 Pet. 1:19–21)?
2. Did the apostles expect their teachings to be obeyed by the church (cf. 1 Cor 11:2; 2 Thess. 2:15; 2 Pet. 3:14–18)?
3. What is the relationship between the church and the truth (cf. 1 Tim. 3:15)?

Summa

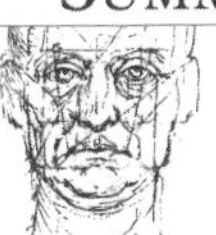

Write an essay or discuss this question, integrating what you have learned from the material above.
What is the Canon?

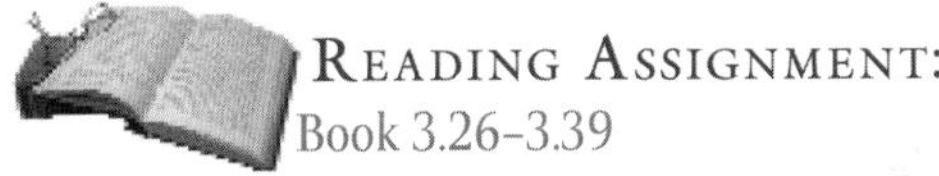

Reading Assignment:
Book 3.26–3.39

Session V: Recitation

Books 1.1–3.39

Comprehension Questions

Answer the following questions for factual recall:

1. Was Eusebius aware that he was the first man to write a history of the church (1.1)?
2. How did Herod die? What did "wise onlookers" declare about the manner of his death (1.8)?
3. According to tradition, how did the city-state of Edessa come to profess the Christian faith (1.13)?
4. According to tradition, who was the original author of all heresies (2.13–2.14)?
5. Who was James the Just? How did he die (2.23)?
6. Which three emperors who persecuted the church are recorded in this section (2.25, 3.13, 3.17–20; 3.33)?
7. Why and when was Jerusalem destroyed? Which historian gives us the most detailed account of its destruction (3.5–3.8)?
8. Who were the Ebionites, and what did they teach about the Lord Jesus (3.27)?
9. How did Eusebius decide whether to write about someone who succeeded the apostles? In other words, what was his principle of selecting whom to include (3.37)?

Hippolytus, a third-century scholar, likened the ark to the church—keeping the people of God in safety, carrying them above the chaotic waters of a sinful world apart from God. And to the early believers, Noah's ark quickly became a sign of baptism, through which a believer enters the church.

Session VI: Recitation

Polycarp

Some events recorded by Eusebius have massive importance historically and inspirationally. One of the most inspiring stories is that of the martyrdom of Polycarp.

Today, you are going to do a recitation on this passage. Answer the questions as you read the passage. Reading it aloud is encouraged. Read The Church History *4.14–15 about Polycarp of Smyrna and answer the following questions:*

1. Who was Polycarp?
2. What vision preceded Polycarp's martyrdom?
3. How does Polycarp demonstrate his trust in Christ's word in Matt. 5:10–12?
4. What miracles occurred when Polycarp was martyred? Do you accept these as legitimate or legendary? Why?
5. How should we assess the miracle stories we find in non-biblical literature?

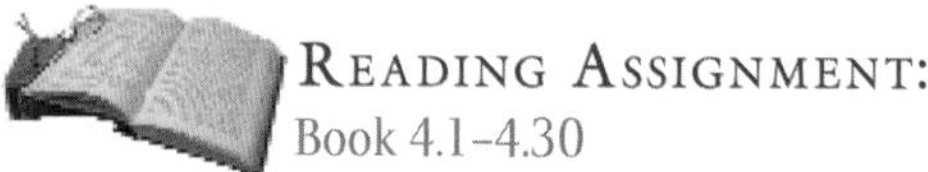

Reading Assignment:
Book 4.1–4.30

Session VII: Discussion

Book 4.1–4.30

A Question to Consider

Was the created world considered good by the early church?

Discuss or write short answers to the following questions:

Text Analysis

1. What did Cerdo and his student Marcion teach about God (4.11)?
2. How did the Encratites apply this teaching to the material world (4.29)?
3. How did Clement of Alexandria refute those who rejected marriage (3.30)?
4. How did Attalus convince Alcibiades that he should give up his practice of consuming only bread and water (5.3)?

Cultural Analysis

1. Does the American obsession with dieting grow out of a hatred for the material world?
2. Was the temperance movement in America a reflection of biblical values?

Biblical Analysis

1. What is God's evaluation of the created world and of marriage (cf. Gen. 1:10, 12, 18, 21, 25, 31; 2:18-25)?
2. What does Paul say about those who forbid marriage and treat the material world as though it is evil (cf. Col. 2:16-19; 1 Tim. 4:1-5)?
3. What will happen to creation at the end of time (cf. John 5:28-29; Rom. 8:18-25; 1 Cor. 15:50-57)?
4. What does John mean when he tells us not to "love the world nor the things in the world" (1 John 2:15-17)?

Summa

Write an essay or discuss this question, integrating what you have learned from the material above.

Is the created world good?

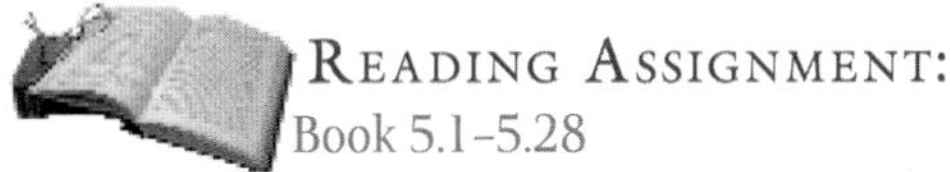

Reading Assignment:
Book 5.1-5.28

Session VIII: Discussion

Book 5.1-5.28

A Question to Consider

What would you do if the government mandated the way you were to worship?

Discuss or write short answers to the following questions:

Text Analysis

1. What were three accusations commonly brought against Christians (4.7; 4.15; 5.1)?
2. What were some of the things Christians were ordered to do by their persecutors (4.15)?
3. Did Eusebius take martyrdom as an automatic sign of piety (5.16)?
4. What did the heretic Basilides teach about denying the faith in times of persecution (4.7)? Read ahead and compare this with the Helkasites in 6.38.
5. Is it appropriate to defend oneself when accused (4.3; 4.12; 4.26)?
6. How did the church deal with those who lapsed during times of persecution (5.2)?

Cultural Analysis

1. For what does our culture say it is worth dying?
2. Why do most newspapers choose not to report the many instances of persecution of Christians that happen daily throughout the world—particularly in Islamic countries?

Biblical Analysis

1. Did Christ and the apostles think that Christians would suffer persecution (Matt. 10:16-39; John 15:18-25; Acts 14:21-22)?
2. Should we be surprised by or fear persecution (Matt. 10:26-31; 1 Pet. 4:12-16)?
3. How should we respond to persecution (Matt. 5:10-12, 43-48; Heb. 10:32-39)?
4. Is it permissible for Christians to flee persecution (Matt. 10:23)? To protest against unjust treatment (Acts 16:35-40; 22:25-29)? To deny Christ with their mouths but confess him inwardly (Matt. 10:32-33; Luke 12:8-9; 2 Tim. 2:11-13)?

Summa

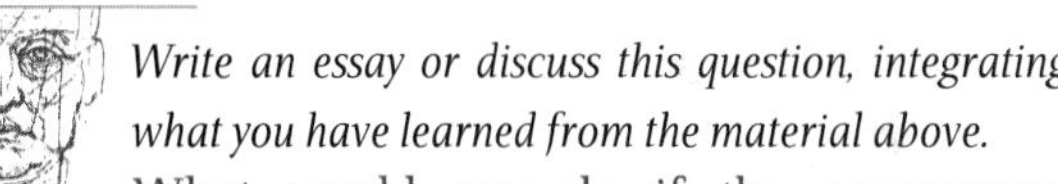

Write an essay or discuss this question, integrating what you have learned from the material above.

What would you do if the government mandated the way you were to worship?

Session IX: Writing

Progymnasmata

Classical training in rhetoric included preparatory writing exercises called the *progymnasmata.* These exercises in composition introduced the beginning student to basic forms and techniques that would then be used and combined when practicing more advanced exercises and speeches. One of these progymnasmata was called an *impersonation.* The impersonation seeks to imitate the style and characteristics of the person making the speech. To compose an impersonation:

- Discuss or think through the characteristics of the person whose speech you are emulating.
- Read carefully through the speech or event that you are impersonating (in many cases you will be asked to write an impersonation of a speech that a person has not given, but could have made at a certain time).
- Put the book away and write the speech yourself.
- Read it to someone else.
- After reading it, explain how different personal characteristics of this person come through in your impersonation.

Be careful to remember what has happened in the personal history of the character on which you are writing, and also remember what will happen in the future. You must remember to keep everything in the proper setting (e.g., you can not make the young George Washington say, "I will be the first president under the new Constitution of the United States," because when he was a boy, of course, neither the Constitution nor the office existed, let alone the country itself).

Write an impersonation of a Christian defending himself against the false charges of cannibalism, incest and atheism.

I. Exordium
- Give appropriate honor
- Claim innocence

II. Narratio
- Answer each charge in turn
- Describe absurdity of the charge in light of Christian teaching and practice

III. Exhortation or Prayer
- Appeal to the justness of your case
- Restate innocence

Session X: Recitation

Books 4.1-5.28

Comprehension Questions

Answer the following questions for factual recall:

1. Who utilized the various heretical teachers to try to destroy the church (4.7)?
2. Who was Justin Martyr (4.11; 4.16–18)?
3. What did many of the heretical groups endeavor to do with the Scriptures (4.23; 4.29; 5.18; 5.28)?
4. Identify two of the most notable martyrs of the churches of Lyons and Vienne (5.1).
5. Who were the Montanists and what did they teach (5.16–19)?
6. Briefly explain the controversy over the date of Easter. How did Irenaeus respond to the Bishop of Rome's attempt to excommunicate the Asian churches (5.24)?
7. What was the heresy of Artemon (5.28)?
8. Which emperor was responsible for the persecutions in this section (4.14–15; 5.1)?

Session XI: Discussion

A Question to Consider

What is heresy?

Discuss or write short answers to the following questions:

Text Analysis

1. Who is the instigator of all heresies (4.7)?
2. Make a list of as many heretics/heresies as you can find mentioned in *The Church History*, books 1-5.
3. What makes a teaching heretical (5.28)?
4. How did churches deal with false teachers that arose in their midst (4.11, 24; 5.16)?
5. How seriously did the early church leaders take their obligation to protect the church from false teaching (5.20)?
6. How did the various heretics tend to handle Scripture (4.29; 5.28)?
7. What does Eusebius claim about the ultimate destiny of heresy (4.7)?

Cultural Analysis

1. What beliefs are considered "unacceptable" (heretical) in our culture?
2. How does our culture "excommunicate" these heretics?

Biblical Analysis

1. How did Paul try to prepare the elders in Ephesus to combat heresy? (Acts 20:28–32)
2. Why do divisions (heresies) arise in the church (1 Cor. 11:19)?
3. What did Paul urge Titus to do with divisive men

(heretics) who refused to repent (Titus 3:10)?

4. What requirements did Paul place upon those who aspired to leadership in the church (Titus 1:9)?

Summa

Write an essay or discuss this question, integrating what you have learned from the material above.
What is heresy?

Reading Assignment:
Book 6.1-6.46

Session XII: Activity

Book 6.1-6.46

Identifying Modern Heresies

Using the Nicene Creed, *included below as a summary of the foundational doctrines of the Christian faith, spend some time identifying modern day heresies.*

We believe in one God, the Father Almighty, maker of heaven and earth, and of all things visible and invisible;

And in one Lord Jesus Christ, the only begotten Son of God, begotten of His Father before all worlds, God of God, Light of Light, very God of very God, begotten, not made, being of one substance with the Father; by whom all things were made; who for us men and for our salvation came down from heaven, and was incarnate by the Holy Ghost of the Virgin Mary, and was made man; and was crucified also for us under Pontius Pilate; He suffered and was buried; and the third day He rose again according to the Scriptures, and ascended into heaven, and sitteth on the right hand of the Father; and He shall come again, with glory, to judge both the quick and the dead; whose kingdom shall have no end.

And we believe in the Holy Ghost the Lord, and Giver of Live, who proceedeth from the Father and the Son; who with the Father and the Son together is worshiped and glorified; who spake by the Prophets.

And we believe in one holy catholic and apostolic church; we acknowledge one baptism for the remission of sins; and we look for the resurrection of the dead, and the life of the world to come. Amen.

The heretic Joseph Smith claimed he had received inscribed gold plates from the angel Moroni and used them for the English translation of *The Book of Mormon.* In this work Smith wrote that the Native American indians were descendants of the lost tribes of Israel in the Americas.

Optional Further Reading

House, H. Wayne. *Charts of Cults, Sects, and Religious Movements.* Grand Rapids, Mich.: Zondervan, 2000.

Martin, Walter. *The Kingdom of the Cults.* Minneapolis, Minn.: Bethany House, 1992.

Wilson, Douglas, ed. *Bound Only Once.* Moscow, Idaho: Canon Press, 2001.

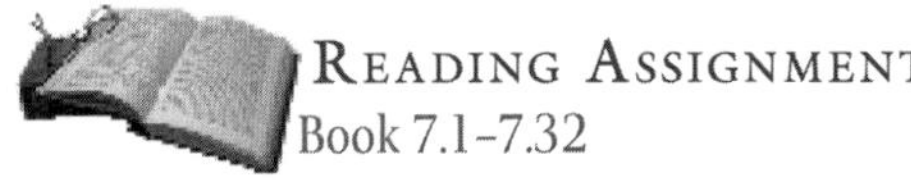

Reading Assignment:
Book 7.1-7.32

Session XIII: Discussion

Book 7.1–7.32

A Question to Consider

What would be the result if Jesus were a mere man and not God and man?

Discuss or write short answers to the following questions:

Text Analysis

1. Which heretics maintained that Jesus was just a man (3.27, 5.28, 7.27)?
2. How did the churches of Antioch counteract the teaching of Paul (7.28–29)?
3. Briefly describe the behavior of Paul of Samosata (7.30).
4. What action of Paul was a direct consequence of his belief that Christ was a mere man (7.30)?
5. Briefly describe the character of the worship services led by Paul. How does Eusebius say one ought to worship in "God's house" (7.30)?

Cultural Analysis

1. Do most Christian worship services display the type of orderly reverence which Eusebius encourages?
2. Does the nature of our worship reveal anything about the God we serve?

Biblical Analysis

1. Is it lawful to worship anyone or anything other than God (Ex. 20:3; Deut. 6:13–15; Rom. 1:21–23)?
2. During His earthly ministry, did Jesus receive worship (Matt. 8:1–4; John 9:35–38; Rev. 5:11–14)?
3. What did the apostles do when people tried to worship them (Acts 10:24–26; 14:11–18)?
4. What happened to Herod when he accepted worship that was not due him (Acts 12:21–23)?

Summa

Write an essay or discuss this question, integrating what you have learned from the material above.

What would be the result if Jesus were a mere man and not God and man?

Session XIV: Writing

Progymnasmata

This session introduces another of the writing exercises called the *progymnasmata.* Recall that these exercises in composition introduced the beginning student to basic forms and techniques that would then be used and combined when practicing more advanced exercises and speeches. One of these progymnasmata was called the *encomium,* a composition written to praise an individual. Its opposite exercise (which condemns an individual) is called a *vituperation* (or an *invective*). This writing exercise expounds the virtues or condemns the vices of a specific person (e.g., Joe is a strong warrior), but does not talk about virtue in a general sense (e.g., strength in war is admirable). The encomium and the vituperation each have six parts. The *Prologue* comes first. It introduces the topic and, at the end of the paragraph, states or implies the opinion of the writer. The second part of this exercise is a paragraph called *Description of Heritage.* In this paragraph the writer looks for ways to praise or condemn the person on account of his family history. For instance, if a person comes from righteous parents, then highlight the fact that he learned his righteous habits at home and added to the glory of the family name. A vituperation would emphasize that he comes from a family or nation that taught him wrong beliefs or bad habits. Next comes a paragraph called *Description of Upbringing.* The point is to show how the person profited from a good education or overcame a bad one (this is for the encomium). For the vituperation you should attempt to show how he failed to profit from a good education or learned well the lessons of a bad education. The most powerful part of the encomium comes next: the *Description of Deeds.* In this section the writer praises the excellencies of the mind, body and fortune of the subject. For example, the writer praises the practice of philosophical virtue, the way the person looked and his wealth, influence or social stature. Since Christianity has transformed our society it seems out of place to dwell on physical appearance or possessions (e.g., he was evil because he was quite homely, or it is obvious that he was a good man because he was fabulously rich), so instead the paragraph should concentrate on the actions and motives of the subject. This can be especially powerful if his life demonstrates a pattern. Next is a *Comparison* of the subject to someone else to portray him in a favorable light (if it is an encomium). An unfavorable comparison is best for vituperation. The final paragraph is an *Exhortation* or *Prayer* in which others are called on to imitate this person's example or a proclamation to everyone telling them not to go down the wicked path that this person did.

Write an encomium on Origen or a vituperation on Paul of Samosata.

I. Prologue
   - Introduce the topic
   - State your opinion
II. Description of Heritage
   - Praise or condemn the person on account of his family history
III. Description of Upbringing
   - Show how the person profited or failed to profit from his education
IV. Description of Deeds
   - Praise or condemn the excellencies or deficiencies of his actions and motives
V. Comparison
   - Portray the person favorably or unfavorably in comparison to someone else
VI. Exhortation or Prayer
   - Call upon others to either imitate or shun this person's example

LIBERATOR OR OPPORTUNIST?

Constantine was the first Roman emperor to become a Christian. From his famous victory in the Battle of Milvian Bridge in October 312, when he defeated his major challenger for control of the Roman Empire, till his death in 337, he regularly supported the church and took actions against those who persecuted Christians. Because not all of Constantine's actions were consistent with the Faith, some historians contend that he was never really converted to Christianity and that he cynically used the church to serve his own political ambitions. Eusebius was a close advisor to Constantine in his later years and wrote a panegyric (biography extolling his greatness) that fails to mention some of Constantine's faults.

In evaluating historical figures like Constantine, we must understand his times and circumstances. From the perspective that Constantine was the very first major ruler to become a Christian, living in the transition time between pagan and Christian-based cultures, his failure to always conform to Biblical standards in his life and actions is not surprising. Nevertheless, his actions on behalf of the church were constant and faithful, and he always saw himself as the converter of the Roman Empire to Christianity. Most importantly, he effectively stamped out the horrendous persecution of the church. This feat alone was enough to make Constantine a hero to Eusebius and to Christians throughout the Empire.

While Constantine was not the ideal Biblical ruler, we should nevertheless acknowledge and be grateful for how God used him in his time to end the major persecution of Christians and bring about the downfall of paganism.

Optional Activity

Ask at least one other person to listen as you deliver orally the speech you have written. Don't tell them beforehand whether your speech is in praise of the individual or in judgment of him. At the conclusion, ask your audience to evaluate your speech and identify it as either an *encomium* or a *vituperation.* The best of these should praise the person effectively without making the person seem angelic or condemn the person without making the writer (that's you) look like a browbeating ogre. Listen carefully to the feedback that you get, and see if you can strike the right balance. Evaluate your own success based on their answer.

Session XV: Recitation

Books 6.1-7.32

Comprehension Questions

Answer the following questions for factual recall:

1. During which emperor's reign was Leonides, the father of Origen, martyred (6.1)?
2. What did Leonides insist form the foundation for Origen's education (6.2)?
3. Why did Origen encourage the study of secular philosophy (6.18)?
4. What method of interpretation did Origen learn from Chaeremon the Stoic (6.19)?
5. Compare the opinions of Clement of Alexandria and Origen on the authorship of Hebrews. With whom do you agree (6.14, 25)?
6. What did the Novatian heresy maintain (6.43)?
7. How did Christians respond to their neighbors during the time of plague and hardship in Alexandria (7.22)?
8. How did Dionysius endeavor to convince those who had embraced the opinion of Nepos of their error (7.24)?
9. Summarize Dionysius's argument against John the Apostle as author of Revelation (7.25).
10. List the persecuting emperors mentioned in these two books (6.1, 28, 39; 7.10, 30).

Session XVI: Discussion and Writing

A Question to Consider

The state should be religiously neutral.

Discuss or briefly answer the questions that follow. Begin to write a one-page synopsis of your position either in favor of or against the Question to Consider *in preparation for a debate in Session XVIII.*

Text Analysis

1. According to tradition, who was the first ruler to convert to the Christian faith (1.13)?
2. How does Lucius defend his Christian brother who had been sentenced to die (4.17)? What does this reveal about Lucius's attitude toward the duties of the state?
3. What was Dionysius ordered to do by his persecutor, Aemilianus (7.11)? What does this reveal about the religious basis of the Roman state?
4. When Paul of Samosata refused to depart from his church after he was convicted of heresy, how did Christians respond (7.30)?

Cultural Analysis

1. How does the United States Constitution answer the question of the relation between religion and state? (See Amendment 1 of the Bill of Rights)[9]

Biblical Analysis

1. Were church and state united in Old Testament Israel (Num. 3:10; 16:1–40; 2 Chron. 26:16–21)? Religion and state (Deut. 6:24–25; 1 Chron. 28:5–10; Prov. 16:12)?
2. Does Scripture call upon rulers to submit to Christ (Ps. 2:10–12; Prov. 8:12–17; Rev. 19:11–16)?

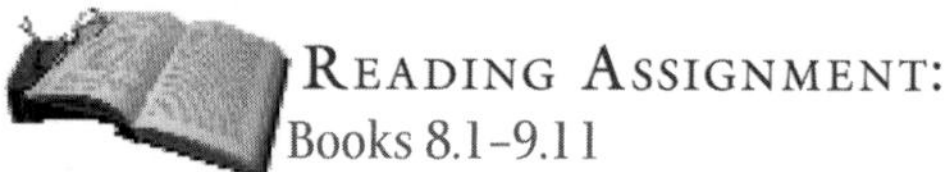

Reading Assignment:
Books 8.1–9.11

Session XVII: Discussion and Writing

Books 8.1–9.11

A Question to Consider

The state should be religiously neutral.

Discuss or briefly answer the questions that follow. Finish writing the one-page synopsis of your position either in favor of or against the Question to Consider.

Text Analysis

1. What happened to the town in Phrygia that confessed Christ (8.11)?
2. What religious beliefs and practices formed the basis of Maxentius's and Maximin Daia's policies and decisions (8.14)?
3. Maximin accuses of outright stupidity those who refuse to recognize what simple truth (9.7)?
4. Why did the Armenians go to war against the Romans (9.8)?
5. What happened to the Roman state as a result of the persecution of Christians (8.13; 9.8)?

Cultural Analysis

1. What does our culture believe about the relationship between one's religious beliefs and the adoption of public policies?

Biblical Analysis

1. Are rulers required to rule justly (Deut. 16:18–20; Is. 32:1–8; Mic. 6:8)?
2. Where do we discover what is just (Deut. 4:5–8; 1 Tim. 1:8–11; Heb. 2:2)?
3. What happens to nations who do or do not practice justice? Does private morality have an affect on the corporate life of a people (Deut. 28:1–68; Rom. 13:1–7; Rev. 14:6–8)?

Session XVIII: Activity

Books 8.1–9.11

Debate

The state should be religiously neutral.

Students should use the synopses that they have written to argue either in favor of or against the proposition. In a group setting, listen to the arguments from both sides, alternating between the two, and then have other students or parents and family members decide on the winner.

Reading Assignment:
Book 10.1–10.9

Session XIX: Review

Books 8.1–10.9

Comprehension Questions

Discuss or list short answers to the following questions:

1. Many emperors are mentioned in this section. Provide a brief description of each of the following emperors:
   Constantine
   Constantius [Chlorus]
   Diocletian
   Galerius
   Licinius
   Maxentius
   Maximian
   Maximin Daia

Christ and the Twelve Apostles, from the catacomb of St. Domitilla in Rome. The catacomb is named after one of the two martyrs named Domitilla, most likely Flavia Domitilla.

2. What happened in the church during the many years of peace she enjoyed prior to the Diocletian Persecution (8.1)?
3. What were the so-called *Acts* or *Memoirs of Pilate* (9.5, 9.7)?
4. Which two books of the Bible does Eusebius primarily use in his speech of praise (10.4)?
5. What did the Edict of Milan say about religious worship (10.5)?

Session XX: Evaluation

The Church History

All tests and quizzes are to be given with an open book and a Bible available.

Grammar

Answer each of the following questions in complete sentences. Some answers may be longer than others. (2 points per answer)

1. Who was Eusebius, and when did he write *The Church History?*
2. Who was Constantine?
3. Who was Origen?
4. What is the story of Polycarp's martyrdom?
5. What was the Edict of Milan?
6. Who were the *lapsi?*
7. What did Marcion teach about the deity?

Logic

Demonstrate your understanding of Eusebius's worldview as set forth in The Church History. *Answer the following questions in complete sentences; your answer should be a paragraph or so. Answer two of the four questions. (10 points per answer)*

1. According to Eusebius, who rules human history?
2. What is heresy?
3. What happens to those who oppress the people of God?
4. Is the created world good?

Lateral Thinking

Answer one of the following questions. These questions will require more substantial answers. (16 points per answer)

1. Utilizing your knowledge of the persecutions endured by God's people as recorded in *The Church History*, in what ways was the blood of the martyrs the seed of the church?
2. Using your knowledge of the story which Eusebius records, is the future of the church bright or dull?
3. According to Eusebius, who is Christ, and why is His identity important?

Optional Session A: Activity

Historical Tales: Roman

Read Aloud from Historical Tales: Roman *by Charles Morris.*[10] *Read the chapters that discuss two of the most notorious emperors in this section, Caligula and Nero. These chapters include "An Imperial Monster," "The Murder of an Empress," "Rome Swept by Flames," and "The Doom of Nero." Answer the following questions:*

1. Which of these emperors do you consider the worst?
2. How did these emperors die?
3. Utilizing what you know about the overthrow of the Tarquin dynasty and the establishment of the Roman Republic (from Livy's *Early History of Rome* or other sources), how do the lives of these emperors justify the early Roman distrust of monarchy?

Optional Session B: Activity

Debate

Invite a Mormon to class for a debate on, "Is Mormonism Christian?" Examine the Mormon view of: God, Christ, Man, Scripture.

Optional Session C: Discussion

A Question to Consider

Should Christians rejoice in the deaths of their persecutors?

Discuss or write short answers to the following questions:

Text Analysis

1. Does Eusebius rejoice in the deaths of the persecutors (2.10; 8.16; 9.9; 10.1)?
2. To what does Eusebius ascribe the deaths of the persecutors (8.16; 9.10)?
3. Does Eusebius make use of the imprecatory psalms—those psalms that ask God to judge His enemies—in his analysis of history (10.4)?

Cultural Analysis

1. Do most Christians today think it is appropriate to rejoice in the deaths of persecutors?
2. Does your church sing the imprecatory psalms—those psalms that ask God to judge His enemies—of the Old Testament? Why or why not?

Biblical Analysis

1. Is it appropriate to pray that God would judge His and our enemies (Ps. 137:7–9; 139:19–22; 2 Tim. 4:14–15; Rev. 6:9–11)?
2. Is it appropriate to rejoice when God executes judgment on those who have set themselves against the church of God (Is. 14:3–11; Prov. 16:4; Rev. 18:20)?
3. How does God go about conquering (judging) his enemies (Ps. 83:16–18; Acts 9:1–9; 12:21–23)?
4. How should we treat our enemies while waiting for God to act (Matt. 5:43–48; Rom. 12:14–21)?

A fourth-century mosaic depicting Christ with a chi-rho "halo."

SUMMA

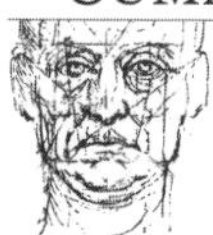

Write an essay or discuss this question, integrating what you have learned from the material above.

Should Christians rejoice in the deaths of their persecutors?

ENDNOTES

1 Eusebius is sometimes also called *Eusebius Pamphili*, "Eusebius [the friend of] Pamphilius," because of their close friendship.

2 Arius (c. 250–c. 336) was a presbyter in Alexandria who taught that Jesus was not God but the first creation of God. In 318 he was accused of heresy by his bishop, Alexander, was examined, and was eventually excommunicated. However, the controversy continued and Constantine convened the Council of Nicea to bring resolution to the matter. Eusebius feared that orthodox churchmen like Athanasius were denying the distinction between the Father and the Son (a position known as *Sabellianism*) and so frequently appeared on the side of Arius and his defenders. Nevertheless, he did adopt the Nicene Creed and rejected the Arian doctrine that there was a time when the Son did not exist. Opinions on his orthodoxy vary.

3 More frequently called the *Ecclesiastical History*, from the Greek *ekklesia*, meaning "church."

4 This refers to the infamous "art work" by Andres Serrano in which a cross submerged in urine was presented as a piece of art. Sadly, American tax dollars were used to support this work.

5 The Ebionites, Paul of Samosata, Beryllus.

6 The Docetists.

7 This would include the Arians about whom Eusebius says nothing in *The Church History*—likely because he had some sympathy with their teaching and because the issue had not yet been completely resolved.

8 Note, however, that Spielvogel misunderstands some critical aspects of Christianity, so do not trust him as a reliable guide in doctrinal matters.

9 A copy of the Bill of Rights may be found by clicking Link 1 for this chapter at www.VeritasPress.com/OmniLinks.

10 You may view this work by clicking Link 2 for this chapter at www.VeritasPress.com/OmniLinks.

Confessions

There is no better place to be than at the pool on a hot summer's day, so I was really excited when my mom decided that she was going to take my little sister, my brother and me to the big pool in Harmonie State Park. This was the nicest and cleanest pool in the area. What made it even better was that my cousin Jeff was in town from Kentucky, and he was going to go along. It was going to be a perfect day.

I was probably ten or twelve and Jeff was about five years older than I, but he and I and my brother loved playing in the pool that was so large that it seemed like an ocean. Of course, we wanted to play all the games that the narrow-minded life guards were forbidding: running, showering unsuspecting people with a well placed "cannon ball" and dunking each other endlessly. (Who made these rules anyway?).

While this was fun, it had one distinct drawback. Jeff was five years older than I. I compensated for my lack of age by wearing husky-sized trunks, but still, when we locked up and tried to dunk each other, I usually got the short end of the stick. Every so often, however, and with great effort, I dunked him. This felt wonderful. Stealthily, we would sneak around the pool looking for an opportunity to dunk each other. What could be better?

As our strategies became more advanced, I discovered that I was at another tactical disadvantage. Jeff was of a lean, athletic build. I was, at the time, more—shall we say—full figured. He could outrun and outswim me. I could not get close enough to grab him and use my physical mass to take over. He would simply paddle away and laugh at me.

After wearing myself out with the frontal assault, I had to come up with "Plan B." Different areas of the pool were different depths. I was a little over five feet tall, so I usually stayed in the area that was five feet

Pears are not usually one of the first things we associate with sin. Yet Augustine spends six pages in his *Confessions* lamenting over his theft of pears from a neighbor's orchard when he was sixteen years old! Why did he do this? Because Augustine learned that the real extent of evil is not how gross or bloody or bold our wrong actions are but how deliberate or purposeful our heart's rebellion against God is when we do them. Augustine stole the pears, not because he needed food or desired to taste them, but simply because it was wrong: a perverse, pathetic attempt to stick his tongue out at God, so to speak, under the delusion that he didn't need to heed his Creator.

The Creation from a Bible printed by Anton Koberger in Nuremberg in 1483. About the Creation, Augustine said: "Seven days by our reckoning, after the model of the days of creation, make up a week. By the passage of such weeks time rolls on, and in these weeks one day is constituted by the course of the sun from its rising to its setting; but we must bear in mind that these days indeed recall the days of creation, but without in any way being really similar to them."

deep. I was, however, a good swimmer, so I would even venture to the "deep end" which was eight feet deep and the diving well which was thirteen feet deep. I decided that if I could not catch my cousin, I would have to get him to come close to me. I would go to the six-foot-deep area and bob up and down, pretending to be in trouble. Jeff, being the helpful but gullible cousin that he was, would come to the rescue, only to find himself with a mouthful of over-chlorinated water.

At first, the plan did not go nearly as well as I hoped. I got into the six-foot area and began to bob up and down, waving my arms and acting mildly distressed. Jeff looked on with disdain. Perhaps he was not as gullible as I thought! I had to up the ante. I started yelling louder and waving my arms wildly. He began to swim in my direction. I thought: "I love it when a plan comes together.". Little did he know, I was only faking it.

Just as he got close enough to grab, I realized that something had gone horribly wrong. As I wrapped my arm around his head in a sort of headlock, I was raised a couple of inches out of the water. In an instant I realized that I had attracted *slightly* more attention than I had intended. Everyone in the entire pool was looking in my direction. The life guards were springing from their chairs. Jeff, in fact, was the only one in the entire pool that knew what I was doing. His sly grin gave away the fact that he also knew that I was going to get a lot more than I had bargained for. He took me to the side of the pool. I climbed out. People started poking and prodding me as if I had almost drowned. My worried and embarrassed mother took me in her arms. She was probably having a vision of my funeral. She was really worried.

At that point, I should have made a confession: "I was just fooling around." But I could not. I claimed to have gulped down some water and became disoriented. What a cowardly way out! My punishment of being banned from all of the fun areas of the pool for fear that I would die was well deserved. As I sulked in the six inches of water in the baby pool, I realized a great lesson: Real men confess their sins. Confession is difficult to do, and the older you get the more difficult it becomes. This is probably because you are supposed to be smarter and wiser (but usually you just get more proud).

In *Confessions,* Augustine, one of the greatest minds of the ancient and medieval worlds (in a way he ends one world and begins the other—now *that* is an accomplishment!) makes his confession. For him confession means two things, one negative and one positive. In this book he tells us all the things that he has done wrong: stupid things he believed, immoral things he did, even the cowardly vacillation of his stubborn heart. He tells about himself, warts and all. He confesses his sin, but he also confesses his faith. *Confessions* is the story of Augustine's journey from his rough and rowdy youth to his conversion. In it he does not excuse, glorify or rationalize his sin (like some people do who make their confessions on the talk shows of our day). Instead he confesses that God has redeemed him and saved him from his own utter futility. *Confessions* does this in such an interesting and charismatic way that it has become a classic for the ages. I hope you enjoy it.

General Information

Author and Context

Aurelius Augustine is probably the most important Christian teacher since the time of Christ (excluding the apostles, of course). With Augustine, the story of a pagan's surrender to Christianity is played out on a personal level. His conversion, however, did not take place until later in life. He was born in Roman North Africa in A.D. 354 to a pagan father, Patrick, and devout Christian mother, Monica. He was not baptized as an infant, because his mother feared that he might stray from the faith, making his baptism a curse for him.

Augustine grew into a man of great stature. His father sought to give him a classical education, and Augustine showed immense gifts in the field of rhetoric. His skill and hard work in this area brought him from Africa to Rome and Milan.

Confessions is the story of Augustine's life from the time of his youth to shortly after his conversion. Before he was converted, Augustine wallowed in many sins. He had a number of mistresses and fathered a child out of wedlock. He had wealth, power, women and security. In all of this, however, Augustine found that his heart could not find peace. Still, in the end, God's mercy called down by his mother's ceaseless prayers took this wicked man and turned him into a great church father.

His great struggle with the faith and his eventual surrender to it have become part of the history of the West. His charisma and straightforward honesty (evident throughout this work) made him one of the most influential thinkers in history.

Significance

The significance of Augustine's *Confessions* can hardly be overestimated because Augustine's contribution to the life of the church and the life of the West can hardly be overvalued. In some ways, Augustine is the father of both Roman Catholicism and Protestantism. He taught that the sacraments are outward and visible signs of inward and spiritual grace. He stood against the erroneous monk, Pelagius, and championed God's sovereignty in salvation—those who read *Chosen by God* in Omnibus I will remember this discussion.

Augustine in his study, painted in the early sixteenth century by Vittore Carpaccio. When shown in his study, Augustine is conventionally depicted as dispensing the rule of his order.

The church fathers often are difficult to get to know because one must infer or read between the lines in their stories. This is not the case with Augustine. *Confessions* is an introduction to one of the most powerful minds in history.

Augustine's life and thoughts continued their broad influence later in church history. The rulers and missionaries of the Middles Ages who fought against and Christianized the invading barbarians had few books. Other than the Bible, the two that were probably most read and influential were Augustine's *City of God* and *Confessions.* In Augustine, one can see a believer, but also a person who struggled with and still fights against sin. He is certainly not like the plastic, pseudo-spiritual Christian "heroes" of our day when he prays "Lord, make me chaste . . . but not yet."

Main Characters

Augustine is one of the main characters in *Confessions* and the book is interesting and enjoyable because Augustine is Augustine. He is a larger-than-life character who is not afraid to bare his soul (and his dirty laundry) before the watching world. Augustine, however, is not doing this because he wants attention (like so many of our modern "confessors" who happily trot their lurid behavior out on national TV so that some sap will cry for them or at least pay attention to them). Augustine describes himself and his sin with a steady and unflattering hand. He lived a rough and rowdy youth, but instead of reminiscing about his "glory days," Augustine shows us his own deep-seated emptiness and loss. He sought pleasure with women and material goods, but found them unsatisfying and vain.

The other great character of the *Confessions* is God. Silently, stealthily, God brings Augustine to his knees before Christ. He empties all of the pleasures out of Augustine's sin. He calls Monica to cry out for the lost soul of her son. He attracts Augustine to the preaching of St. Ambrose. Initially, Augustine, the rhetoric teacher, goes to church simply because Ambrose is such a gifted speaker. In all this, God is the final harbor for the wayward boat of Augustine's soul, and in the end God's truth becomes Augustine's confession.

Finally, Monica, Augustine's mother, is a major character of *Confessions.* She suffers much at the hands of her husband, and her son often breaks her heart, but she never gives up on him and always keeps praying.

Summary and Setting

Confessions divides nicely into two parts. The first nine books of *Confessions* recount the story of Augustine's childhood, his teenage years and his young adulthood. This section ends with his conversion and baptism and the death of his faithful mother. In these books Augustine confesses his sins. The last three books of *Confessions* focus on what man is and on the meaning of Genesis chapter one. In this part of the book, Augustine makes a confession of his faith.

In the life of Augustine, one can see the final defeat of paganism in the West and the rise of the Christian West. His life sets the stage for the Middle Ages. Augustine possesses all that a pagan could ever want: pleasure, women, growing fame, power and ability. As a rhetoric teacher (the most sought after aspect of education in those days), the keys to power and influence were in his hand. All of this, however, he eventually sets aside gladly for the sake of Christ. In him, the world of unbelief sees its ultimate futility and the rest and peace that come with submission to Christ. As Augustine is washed with the waters of baptism, one can see the coming of Christendom.

Worldview

Sometimes only one thing can satisfy us. Have you ever been really thirsty—maybe during a sports practice or mowing the lawn on a scorching day in the midst of July? During other times of the year or under other circumstances, any sort of drink will do. You might prefer a Coke or iced tea or coffee, but if you are drop-dead thirsty, your body longs for water. Nothing else is quite as good. At moments like that when you are sweaty and your parched throat feels like sandpaper, you do not want a hot cup of coffee or a syrupy soda. Even a sports drink with all of its potassium and electrolytes is not quite right (almost, but not quite). You need water.

Augustine faced a situation much like this. He had a longing. With this longing, his book begins crying out to God: "You made us for Yourself and our souls are restless until they find their rest in You."

The fulfillment of this longing and the discovery of rest, however, takes a long time for Augustine because of the type of person that he was. Most of us are limited in many ways. We might not have the gifts or abilities that others have. We might be excellent with numbers, but not be able to relate well to people. We might be a good basketball player, but struggle when it comes to spelling. Not so with Augustine. He was gifted in most every way. He was an incredible speaker and writer. He got along well with others (too well when it came to women). His family loved him and his father provided him with an excellent classical education. He had gained quite a reputation even at an early age because of his many gifts.

Still, Augustine found no satisfaction, even though he displayed a measure of tenacity or work ethic. He rose quickly in popularity and importance through teaching rhetoric, which was the hallmark of a good Roman education. He moved from North Africa to Italy, teaching rhetoric in both Rome and Milan. His fame and reputation as a teacher grew, and students sought him out.

None of these seemingly wonderful characteristics helped him to fulfill his restless longing. They did, however, give him the ability and imagination to try to find many things to fill the empty void of his soul. *Confessions* is particularly interesting because Augustine has the courage to recount all the ways in which he tried to satisfy this great longing. It would be like coming in from the blistering sun on a hot summer's day, dipping up a bowl of steaming chili covered with melted cheese, then washing it down with a cup of boiling hot coffee. All of us do unwise things like this at some point in our lives. Most of us, however, do not have the courage to write it down. Augustine did.

"Make me chaste . . . but not yet."

As a pagan Augustine sought to satisfy his longing with false gods. We see some people today following unusual beliefs and practices. They search for answers, but move only into stranger and increasingly weird practices. Augustine, trying to satisfy his longing, joined up with a bizarre group called the *Manicheans.* These followers of the teacher Mani believed that no one should marry or have children. Eventually, this odd group died out (imagine that). They also taught that the only food their more spiritual members would eat was fruit. These "elect" Manicheans, however, could not pick the fruit, so novice, or new, Manicheans would have to go out and pick the fruit for the initiated ones. While these beliefs might seem comical to us, Augustine was serious about it for a while. His parched throat continued to burn even though the Manicheans promised him fulfillment.

Augustine of *Hippo?* Was that a jab at the weight of the scholar saint? No, Hippo was the name of where he lived—Hippo Regius (now called Annaba, in Algeria). In 396 he was made coadjutor bishop of Hippo (assistant with the right of succession on the death of the current bishop), and remained as bishop in Hippo until his death in 430.

He also looked to philosophy to cure his ills. The words of philosophers like Plato and Cicero echoed through his mind, but none of it satisfied him.

Augustine admits that, as an unbeliever, he had some strange ideas about God that kept him back from belief in the God of the Bible. He exposes his own amusement at some of his false beliefs when he recounts his idea that God must have a huge material body.

Augustine also sought all sorts of pleasure to fill the void in his soul. Early in his life, when he was your age, he hung out with the "cool" crowd of local ruffians. He tried to satisfy his longings with the acceptance of others or with the thrill that one can have by stealing. They called themselves the Wreckers. These are the sort of kids that have fun vandalizing cars or stealing pears and feeding them to pigs instead of eating them. All of this, he recounts, was empty. Later he rose on the corporate ladder. He gained the trust of many. His fame grew. And yet it was all empty. As he grew up Augustine sought to fill his soul with the love of women. He had a number of mistresses and even fathered a child out of wedlock. He never married. This, however, proved even more unsatisfying in the end, because Augustine found himself not only unsatisfied, but also addicted to something that would not satisfy him. With everything that a pagan could want, he found himself trapped, enslaved and increasingly restless.

He was so desperate that he turned to the religion that his pious mother had always prayed he would follow. Still, he could not let go of his sin. He prayed, "Lord, make me chaste . . . but not yet." He longed to give up sexual immorality and serve Christ, but he could not. He was trapped. It was as if his throat felt like it was full of cotton from being parched and, rather than drinking water to quench his thirst he actually filled his mouth with more cotton. He even came to realize that Christ is, in fact, the "true drink." But he could not run to the fountain because he was addicted to things that would not satisfy.

When it comes to the pleasures of sin, Augustine's diminishing returns teach us an important lesson. Sin might seem and even feel very satisfying for a while. God, however, does not let this satisfaction continue. The world that God has made is not ultimately satisfying outside of Him. Many in our day blame God for this. Why would He ever take joy from us, or, even worse, send sickness and even death? Why not indulge our immorality and let us live in perpetual satisfaction and peace? Why does God make us restless? This characteristic of the world and of our God must be viewed as one of His greatest mercies. We cannot function properly without God alone at the root of our souls. All of it feels empty. As one of our own poets has said, "I can't get no satisfaction."

As he languishes, vacillating between belief and unbelief, we also learn that God uses many means to move us along the way to salvation. In the life of Augustine, He used tragedy, example, strong teaching and faithful prayer to move Augustine toward His kingdom. Tragedy touched Augustine when one of his friends died. His friend's illness was so severe that for a long time he was unconscious. During this period of unconsciousness, he was baptized. Later he recovered slightly and awoke from his coma. Augustine, who was still a pagan, made light of the baptism that was performed on his friend while he slept, but was shocked to find that his friend rejected his advice and was whole-heartedly unwilling to renounce Christ. Soon after, the illness returned, and his friend died. Augustine's paganism was challenged both by the fear of death and by the change that he witnessed in this converted friend.

Examples of Christian devotion helped to dislodge Augustine's reticence to follow Christ. Two of the main examples that helped him were Victorinus and St. Anthony. Victorinus was a studied pagan philosopher in Rome who argued against Christianity. Eventually, however, he saw the emptiness of his ways and turned to Christ. In this Augustine perceived a path that he could follow. Through a book on the life of St. Anthony, Augustine saw a way of complete devotion that was attractive to him. The book presented the story of Anthony, one of the founders of Christian Monasticism, who left worldly living and retreated to the desert to give himself whole-heartedly to war against the flesh and to devote himself to Christ. God used these examples to batter the walls of unbelief surrounding Augustine's heart.

Providentially, Augustine also was exposed to excellent teachers who both instructed him in the faith and helped him deal with many of his objections to Christianity. Chief among these teachers was Ambrose of Milan. Augustine moved to Milan to accept a position teaching rhetoric and was exposed to Ambrose's teaching. Augustine went to hear Ambrose preach, not because Augustine was a believer at the time but because Ambrose was such a good speaker and rhetorician. Even though Augustine was perhaps attracted for the "wrong reasons," he learned much truth from Ambrose's powerful preaching. Increasingly, Augustine came to see that the longings of his heart were ones that only Christ could satisfy.

Finally, God used faithful prayers to convert Augustine. Monica, his mother, never gave up on her son. While Augustine focused on and achieved worldly success, this did not satisfy his mother. Her desire was to see her son safely in the church. To this end she prayed.

All of this demonstrates to us a tremendous truth about God. He is the Master of history and of means. He used a multi-faceted attack to win the heart of Augustine, humbling his pride, destroying his objections and finally bringing him to his knees.

"Take up and read!"

Augustine's conversion also demonstrates God's providence and great truths about regeneration, or being born again. The story of Augustine's faith is a classic of Christian history. This proud and powerful pagan is finally reduced to distressed weeping because he finds all of life to be empty without Christ. Yet he seems unable to let go of his sin. God pushes him over the edge using a combination of His word, a child's game and a seeming random coincidence—but we know there are no "random" coincidences in God's world! God's sovereign hand in salvation is clearly presented in the story of Augustine's conversion.

Augustine's conversion shows the proper relationship between God's sovereignty and man's faith. It would be ridiculous to argue that God did not choose or predestine Augustine's conversion. The circumstances have God's fingerprints all over them. Those who would say that salvation rests chiefly in the choice of man should be dismayed as they see God dragging Augustine to conversion, battering down Augustine's defenses and destroying his pleasure in sin. In salvation sinners initially are completely passive. Only God's power can free Augustine from his slavery to sin and free him to declare his faith in Christ.

As God's word and Spirit overwhelm Augustine and bring him to life spiritually, his conversion shows that newborn Christians become active *after* God's Spirit changes their heart. As a newborn babe in the faith, Augustine places his trust in Christ. This is not implanted in him. He is no longer passive. Augustine's restored will chose Christ because God's Spirit has made Augustine's spirit new.

Augustine's life also helps us understand the proper relationship between conversion and the sacraments. He is converted to Christianity as he reads God's word. His family and friends rejoice, and he has irrevocably moved from the kingdom of darkness to the realm of light. His baptism waits until the next Easter. This clearly shows that baptism and participation in the rest of the sacraments are the natural reactions of a believing heart to God's grace, but that conversion is not tied to the moment of the sacrament's application. His story corrects anyone who would claim that conversion happens only when a sinner is baptized.

Augustine also corrects our often weak view of the sacraments. Today many churches treat the sacraments as unnecessary or superfluous. This is certainly not Augustine's view. For him, they are the official recognition of the existing relationship. In and through the sacraments we enter into a covenant relationship with God.

Although marriage is not a sacrament, it does supply a good example at this point because it is a covenant. Imagine a man, Jerry, and a woman, Sally, who are contemplating marriage. Jerry gets to know her family; Sally gets to know his. They spend time together, and Jerry goes through the godly (and often fearful) process of winning her heart and getting the blessing of her family. Eventually, Jerry and Sally commit themselves to each other. This happens when Jerry proposes to Sally. When she says yes, great joy erupts.[1] A relationship has been inaugurated. Promises have been made. If Jerry is flirting with another girl the day after he and Sally make this commitment,

AUGUSTINIAN FIRSTS

Augustine was not only one of the greatest theologians and philosophers in history. He was one of the few people in history who significantly changed the way people understand God's world, and he has many "firsts" to his credit—including being the first saint to have an internet site devoted to him! *Confessions* is the first autobiography and the first profound study of memory. And fifteen hundred years before Sigmund Freud made psychology a fashionable study in the early twentieth century, Augustine studied the idea of the self and the soul from a biblical perspective, arriving at many profound insights.

One of Augustine's profound insights about memory is its Trinitarian structure. Augustine understood how so much of God's world reflects the Trinitarian nature of our Creator God. He recognized that our memory, our understanding and our will are three-in-one aspects of ourselves that are distinctive yet equal and interpenetrating: I *remember* that I have memory, understanding and will; I *understand* that I have understanding, and memory, and will; and I *will* that I will, and remember, and understand. Commentator Garry Wills summarizes Augustine's insight in *Saint Augustine's Memory:* "Since any of the three (aspects—that is memory, understanding and will) contains any of the other two, or all of them, they must be equal to any of the others, or to all of them, each to all and all to each—yet these three are one life, one mind, one substance."

he is in a whole new sort of trouble. He has made a commitment to Sally and her family that he is going to devote himself to her and her alone. Both Sally and Jerry, however, do not yet enjoy all of the rights and privileges of marriage. That waits for a day when they have a ceremony to recognize officially and formally the commitment that they have made to one another. After this ceremony the covenant between them is recognized by all, and they can enter into the joys and privileges of marriage. If the two of them entered into a sexual relationship before the marriage ceremony, we would say that they had committed the sin of fornication. After the ceremony, they are not only encouraged but are charged to enter into this aspect of their relationship. If they don't, they are being unfaithful. In the same way, the covenant relationship with God has reality when God acts to change the heart of a sinner, but is only formally recognized and entered into when a believer participates in the sacraments.

A person who claims to be a believer but is unwilling to be baptized and brought into the church should be looked on with suspicion and eventually be treated like someone who pretends to be married. If a group of kindergarteners are pretending to "play house," with one taking the role of Mommy, another playing Daddy and the rest filling the role of children, we might think that this is quaint and cute. If two adults are pretending marriage by living together, it is ghastly and proves that they do not understand the gravity of the commitment they are pretending to make. They are still acting like infants and are proving that the relationship they claim is so dear is one they are truly unwilling to protect and to commit to. The same is true of someone who says that he believes and yet refuses baptism. This fellow is, through his failure to act, proving that he doesn't really believe what he claims to believe. In a similar way, those who are baptized but live sinful lives proclaim that they despise the covenant relationship they are claiming. In a marriage this faithlessness often leads to divorce; in our covenant with God it leads to apostasy (when a baptized Christian rejects the faith and falls into unbelief) and excommunication (when the church officially recognizes that the apostate person no longer should be treated like a believer).

A fresco of Augustine teaching Rhetoric and Philosophy, painted by Benozzo Gozzoli as part of a series of seventeen images in the Apsidal Chapel of Sant'Agostino in San Gimignano, Italy.

"Give grace to do as You ask, and ask whatever You will."

Augustine's conversion shows us that God's grace is the key to understanding Him rightly. After his conversion, Augustine's heart is pliable and trusts God's word. His objections to Christianity melt as he hears God's word explained. The problems that he had with falsely thinking God had a large physical body fade into the background. Thus, we see that faith is demanded if one wants to rightly understand God.

This mature faith, however, allows for mystery and differences between fellow Christians. Much of the second section of *Confessions* (books 10–13) deals with the interpretation of Genesis 1 and 2. This passage tells of the creation of the world. It was controversial in Augustine's day and continues to be in our day. Augustine confesses his own views on creation but admits that some things are hard to understand and are even mysterious. When it comes to these difficult issues, Augustine recognizes that other believers may disagree with him, and that he might be wrong. While we might not agree with some of his interpretations (I don't—it seems to me that there are some ideas here that should remind us of our reading in Plato last year), we should admit that it is refreshing to hear one of the greatest Christian minds in history admit that he might be totally wrong about what he is writing.

Although Augustine's interpretations of some passages may strike us as fanciful and wrong-headedly allegorical, they are a nice corrective to our modern "scientific" view of the Bible. Augustine treats the Bible as if there are a lot of hidden and secret meanings. In creation, Augustine speculates that the dry land represents faith and the sea points to unbelief. Later, he claims that the fish and the sea monsters represent the sacraments. At points we might scratch our heads and wonder how Augustine is getting all of these strange interpretations out of the text. At other times, we might notice that some of the meanings he is drawing out sound a lot like Plato. Augustine was attempting to mine every bit of truth that God sent us in His Word. Sometimes this truth has many layers full of allegory, symbol and metaphor. At times, Augustine saw these meanings in places where he shouldn't have. We, however, err in the opposite direction by trying to turn all the Bible into a book of scientifically verifiable, logical propositions. We think that if we can just prove that all of these propositions are true, unbelief will crumble. While we see that Augustine's interpretations might be far-fetched at some points, his view is certainly closer to the interpretations made by the writers of the New Testament when *they* look back at and interpret the Old Testament. In Matthew 13:35, Christ tells us that Psalm 78:2— "I will open my mouth in a parable; I will utter dark sayings of old"—is a prophecy about Him. As we look back at the Psalm, however, it might initially appear that Jesus is mistaken. In Psalm 78, these words are clearly referring to Asaph, the writer of Psalm 78—not Jesus. (One good rule of thumb when you are interpreting the Bible, however, is that any time you think that Jesus is making the wrong interpretation, perhaps you need to rethink your own interpretation!) How, then, can Jesus be correct? Clearly, Jesus' interpretation is correct because God is prophesying through Asaph in a manner that is not obvious on the surface of the text. To put it succinctly, Asaph was saying more than he knew. He was talking about himself, but his words were also describing and prophesying about Jesus. While we might disagree (and should) with some of Augustine's interpretations, we must not deny that sometimes God communicates to us in ways that don't fit easily within our "modern" scientific definitions of the truth.[2]

Augustine's new life in Christ shows the power of God's grace in overcoming temptation. He knew the cruel slavery of sin. For years these chains of lust and pride had kept him from faith. Now, as God releases him, we see a man who is able to stand against temptation. The old Augustine was always vacillating between sin and belief. Now, however, he is a humble, useful weapon in God's hand.

This newfound strength, however, does not imply some sort of perfectionism, or teaching that Christians do not sin after conversion. Augustine was too wise about his own heart to fall into this error. He freely admits that all his works are still polluted by sin and that his heart is often wayward. In all of this, he looks to Christ for grace (X.31).

He shows us that all Christian endeavors rely completely on God's grace. In a famous line, he sets forth the way believers should live, "Give me the grace to do as You command, and command me to do what

You will" (X.29). In this we see that in everything Augustine sees our need of grace. He teaches that believers should whole-heartedly follow where God leads, trusting that God has the power to give us grace to overcome any obstacle that sits in our way.

This reliance on God's grace should lead us to holy boldness. It did for Augustine. He faced huge battles in his life against popular heretics like Pelagius, but he faced them with the confidence that God can accomplish anything through us by his grace. We see this same truth affirmed in the Old Testament when Jonathan and his armor bearer go to fight the Philistines in 1 Samuel 14. Jonathan expects God to accomplish his will and defeat his enemies. Instead of looking at the odds, he goes to fight the enemy and a great victory is accomplished through him.

In Christ, Augustine finally finds rest for his soul, and he drinks deeply of the one drink that can truly satisfy a thirsty soul. In Christ, Augustine discovers what eluded him or was missing from him in the lies of the Manicheans or the pomp and power of wealth or in the adulation and love from others; in Christ, Augustine's weary soul finds rest. This rest erupts throughout *Confessions* into prayers of thanksgiving and praise. Augustine, who has seen the hopeless end of all that the world has to offer, pours out his soul without reserve and serves his Lord in the same manner.

One can also see in Augustine's conversion a precursor or an allegory of the final destruction of ancient paganism. Having been born in A.D. 354, he lives during a period in which Christianity, suppressed until the time of Constantine (whose great Edict of Milan was written in 313), was quickly spreading through the Roman Empire. But the pagan hold on society was still sizable. In Augustine, we see the final and irrevocable fall of ancient paganism. Augustine was all that a pagan could hope to be. He was powerful, winsome, well educated, affluent and beloved. All of this, however, does not satisfy. It is worthless compared to Christ. Augustine's thirst drove him to discard everything that failed to satisfy. In the end, he was left with Christ alone as the only spring of living water. The rest of the ancient pagan world would eventually follow Augustine into the waters of baptism. The reasons for this were many, but in Augustine we see that paganism has no power to stand against the gospel and cannot offer anything that will satisfy our thirst for life. The light of Christ will overcome the darkness of the world.

Augustine's life and teachings tell us much about a Christian worldview, but more than anything else they point us to Christ as the only source of true rest. In life we might be tempted to look to other things for comfort and hope. Augustine tried them all and teaches us that none of them will ever fill the gaping need that you have. Nothing but Jesus can quench your thirst. So, one can be reminded of the imperative words that Christ uttered during the first Lord's Supper, "Take, drink . . ."

—*G. Tyler Fischer*

For Further Reading

Cowan, Louise and Guinness, Os. *Invitation to the Classics.* Grand Rapids, Mich.: Baker Books, 1998. 81–84.

Gonzalez, Justo. *The Story of Christianity. Vol. 1.* San Francisco: HarperCollins, 1984, 206–216.

Spielvogel, Jackson J. *Western Civilization.* Seventh Edition. Belmont, Calif.: Thomson Wadsworth, 2009, 192–193.

Veritas Press History Cards: Middle Ages, Renaissance and Reformation. Lancaster, Pa.: Veritas Press. 1.

Session I: Prelude

A Question to Consider

What is your plan to find satisfaction?

From the General Information above answer the following questions:

1. What were Augustine's mother and father like?
2. How did Augustine's conversion set the stage for the fall of western classical paganism?
3. What are some of the ways in which Augustine sought to satisfy the longing of his soul?
4. How does Augustine's conversion help us to see how the sacraments are related to salvation?
5. Why is Augustine's allegorical interpretation of Scripture sometimes more biblical than ours?

Reading Assignment:
Confessions, Book I

Session II: Discussion

Confessions, Book I

A Question to Consider

How does an infant learn to sin?

Discuss or list short answers to the following questions:

Text Analysis

1. Is it wrong for a child to cry when it wants food (I.7)?
2. What evidence does Augustine give that children can be jealous (I.7)?
3. Why does Augustine say that babies are sometimes thought of as more innocent (I.7)?
4. To what sort of sins do the sins of infancy give birth (I.8–10, 19)?
5. What was the first cause of prayer in Augustine's life (I.9)?

Cultural Analysis

1. Where does our culture say children learn to sin (what causes them to turn out bad)?
2. Is our culture all wrong in this?

Biblical Analysis

1. When did David believe that he became a sinner (Ps. 51:5)?
2. When does God say is the first point where people demonstrate wickedness (Ps. 58:1–5)?
3. What is God's reaction to this wickedness as it grows and matures (Ps. 58:6–11)?

Summa

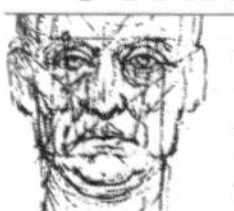

Write an essay or discuss this question, integrating what you have learned from the material above.

We come out of the womb wayward. Who does this to us and is it fair?

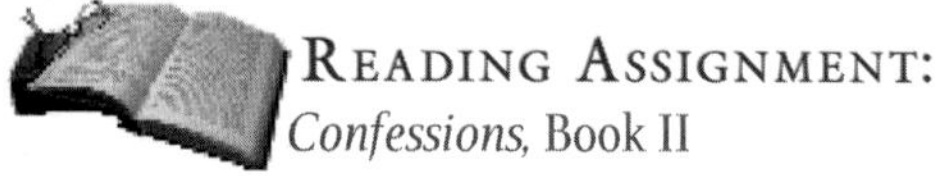

Reading Assignment:
Confessions, Book II

Session III: Writing

Confessions, Book II

Making Your Own Confession, *Part One*

One of the reasons for the enduring nature of Augustine's *Confessions* is that he does such a wonderful job confessing his sins and praising God for showing him grace and mercy. He does this without glorifying his sin or making it seem fulfilling. He does this because he can see his sin for what it really is and he is honest about the motives of his heart. He is also truthful about the horrible results of sin.

Today, we are going to start working on writing our own confession. Ours is going to be different from Augustine's, but we do need to learn a little about the "art of confession" from him. Augustine tells us all about his life; we are only going to confess one of our sins. You might have noticed that Augustine introduces each chapter of his book by praising God for His goodness and mercy. He goes on to tell the circumstances of his life and the sins that he committed. He also tears down any defenses that he could make concerning why he sinned. In my experience of both making and hearing confessions, this is one of the greatest problems that we have. We are reluctant to confess our sins unless we can explain our motives so that we do not look like what we really are: sinners. This usually comes out in the lives of children in almost comical ways: "I punched him three times in the head . . . by accident," or "I did not know it was cheating to look at the answers during the test." We must guard ourselves from this sin and follow Augustine's more biblical pattern of accepting responsibility for our actions.

Finally, we are going to explain the outcome of our sin. This should contain two parts. First, we should tell of the bad results that happened because of our sin. Second, we should return to praising God for the forgiveness He has extended to us in Jesus Christ.

Today we are going to outline our confession. We will write and edit it later, so do not lose your work. There are a couple of problems that come up with this exercise (they come up in the Christian life as well). The first problem is that people often "confess" their sins and end up making themselves seem *cool* in doing so. This is not confession. It is the sin of pride (and is *another* sin needing confession). If your confession starts something like this: "I was the meanest, toughest, strongest kid in the fourth grade. I used to beat up everyone at recess and take their lunch money. I was the *bomb,*" then you are not confessing. The word *confession* comes from Latin and means "to speak with" or "to agree with." When we confess our sins, we are agreeing with God that our sins are the horrible thing that He says they are. If you were a fourth grade bully, God did not think you were the *bomb.*[4] The Greek word for confession is *homologeo,* and literally means "to speak the same." When we confess our sins, we should be saying the same thing about them that God says.

The second problem is the opposite. Some of you might have been born into a Christian home and you have always been reckoned a Christian. Perhaps, like me, you cannot remember a time when you did not believe. I remember once being in a group of Christian men and having to give my testimony. Unfortunately, the guy before me had one of those "I used to be a drug dealer and sold military secrets to aliens on a UFO" testimonies that was bound to make my testimony seem bland by comparison. Remember, however, that God's greatest grace does not extend to the jail cell, but to the nursery. Further, remember that although your sins might not be as

A fresco of Augustine painted by Botticelli for the Vespucci family in the church of Ognissanti. The scene depicts the saint at the point when he is seeing a vision of the death of Saint Jerome.

spicy, they are real sins, and if you dig deep into the motive of your heart, they are equally nasty (perhaps even nastier).

Below is a pattern for you to follow. Work through the following outline form and remember to save your work so that we can return to it later as we study this book.

Outline

Exordium

Introduce your topic by telling of God's grace and goodness. I was born into a Christian home.

I was brought up in the nurture and admonition of the Lord.

Partitio

Tell of the parts of your confession.

I deceived a classmate in a first grade coloring contest by tricking him into voting for my picture, and then I did not follow through on our agreement to vote for his.

Narratio

Give any background information that you need so that people can understand the circumstances of your sin.

First grade: Our teacher was trying to get us to carefully practice our coloring and to develop our fine motor skills.

When we would color a picture, she would tape them on the board, and we would vote for the best one.

Many of the girls were better at coloring than I, so they would usually win.

Confirmatio

Tell of your sin and the motives of your heart.

I made a deal with a classmate, Alan. He would vote for mine and I, in turn, would vote for his.

Alan was less skilled at coloring and did not stay in the lines (he was even worse than me).

I knew that just an extra vote or two could secure victory.

When it came time, he voted for mine.

Embarrassed of his, I did not reciprocate, but pretended that I could not clearly see which one was his.

I voted for another and broke our agreement.

My heart yearned for victory, and I was willing to lie and deceive in order to achieve it.

Refutatio

Tell of any defenses that someone might make for you and explain why they should not be listened to.

I claimed at the time that I could not see—this was a lie.

I could say that Alan's was not as good, so I was only acting in fairness—this also is untrue. I was thinking of myself the entire time, not him. I wanted to be thought well of, and voting for his would have made me look like I did not know good coloring. My pride caused me to break my word

Peroratio

Tell of the result of your sin (how did it effect you?) and return to the praise of God for bringing you to the point of confession and forgiveness.

I was immediately ashamed of the lie that I had told.

I lost anyway.

I remember the look on his face when he realized that I had lied to him.

I have thought about it often over the years.

Thank God for forgiveness.

Reading Assignment:
Confessions, Book III

Session IV: Discussion

Confessions, Books II & III

A Question to Consider

Why do we sin?

Discuss or list short answers to the following questions:

Text Analysis

1. Why does Augustine recount the sins of his youth (II.1)?
2. What did Augustine long for, and what two things were mixed in his "murky" mind (II.2)?
3. How did Augustine sin with the pears? Why did he do it (II.4–6)?
4. What effect did Augustine's friends have on him (II.8–9)?
5. Do lust and the emotion of the theater lead Augustine to satisfaction or frustration? (How does he

describe his life?) (III.2)

6. How do Augustine and his friends become even worse sinners (III.3)?

Cultural Analysis

1. Our culture often denies the reality of sin, but at times (after suicide bombings or mass murders) they are forced to admit the reality of evil. When they do acknowledge evil, on what do they blame it?
2. In Augustine's day, students of your age were given over to sin for sins' sake. Where do we see examples of this in the behavior of young people today?

Biblical Analysis

1. According to James 4:1–3, why do we sin?
2. Does the reason that James gives for our sinning mean that God wants our lives to be devoid of enjoyment (James 4:4–10)?

Summa

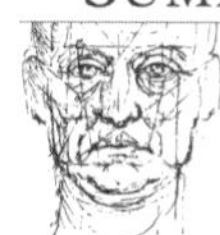

Write an essay or discuss this question, integrating what you have learned from the material above.

How can we overcome sin?

Reading Assignment:
Confessions, Book IV

Session V: Recitation

Confessions, Book IV

Comprehension Questions

Answer the following questions for factual recall:

1. At the beginning of Confessions, what does Augustine say is the only way to find peace and contentment (I.1)?
2. In Augustine's youth what was mixed with the desire for love in his mind? What effect did this have (II.2)?
3. Why didn't Monica want Augustine to marry when he was a young man (II.3)?
4. What did Augustine and his friends do with the pears they stole? Why did they do this? (II.4–6)
5. To what big city was Augustine sent to continue his education (III.1)?
6. As a student, whose writings did Augustine prefer to the Scriptures? Why? (III.4–5)
7. What is Monica doing for Augustine while he is wandering in darkness (III.11–12)?
8. Why does Augustine call his young adult life "empty and void" (IV.1)?
9. What happens to his young friend that Augustine finds disturbing (IV.4)?
10. With what does Augustine try to fill his life in order to find meaning (IV.1, 2, 13, 16)?

Reading Assignment:
Confessions, Book V

Session VI: Discussion

Confessions, Book V

A Question to Consider

What are the strangest religious teachings that you have heard people believe? Why do they believe them?

Discuss or list short answers to the following questions:

Text Analysis

1. What were the teachings of the Manicheans concerning fruit (III.10)?
2. How does Augustine compare the Manicheans to "scientists" (V.4)?
3. What did the Manicheans claim concerning their leader Manes (V.5)?
4. How does Faustus, the Manichean leader, answer Augustine's questions (V.6–7)?
5. What objections did Augustine have that kept him from trusting in Christ (V.10)?
6. Whose teaching helps Augustine leave the Manicheans once and for all (V.13–14)?

Cultural Analysis

1. What is the main question that our culture asks when it considers a person's religion? (Hint: It is not "Is it true?" It has more to do with personal feelings.)

In this famous portrayal, Augustine is shown as a scholarly saint (notice halo effect), probably in the act of writing his *Confessions.* Virtually all the paintings of Augustine over the centuries show him writing or contemplating a book.

2. What is the only claim that a religion can make that causes our culture to vehemently reject it?

Biblical Analysis

1. What are some things that attract people to false religions (Acts 19:23–28; Isaiah 44:9–20)?
2. How can people be won from false religions (Ruth 1:6–16; 1 Peter 3:1; Jonah 3:1–7)?

Summa

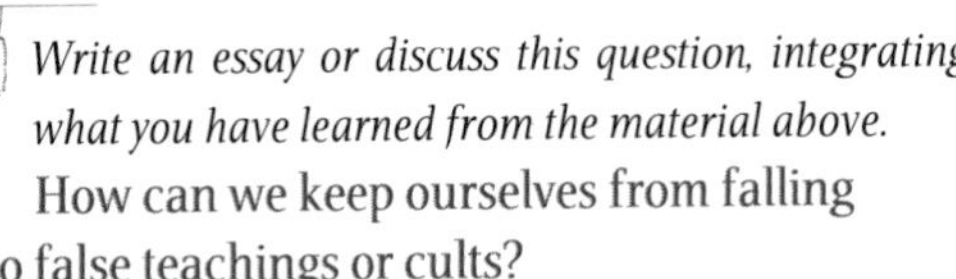

Write an essay or discuss this question, integrating what you have learned from the material above.

How can we keep ourselves from falling into false teachings or cults?

Reading Assignment:
Confessions, Book VI

Session VII: Discussion

Confessions, Book VI

A Question to Consider

When do you know that someone is an addict?

Discuss or list short answers to the following questions:

Text Analysis

1. What "addiction" does Augustine recount that Monica struggled with (VI.1–2)?
2. How does Augustine seek to fill the void of his soul in VI.6?
3. To what does Augustine compare ambition? Does ambition compare favorably or unfavorably to this vice (VI.6)?
4. In what sin was Augustine's friend Alypius trapped? How did this happen (VI.7–8)?
5. To what sin was Augustine in bondage (VI.12)?
6. What proved this bondage (VI.13–14)?

Cultural Analysis

1. How does our culture treat addictions?
2. How does our culture treat addicts?
3. How should the church treat addicts?

Biblical Analysis

1. How does the Bible picture our slavery to sin (Prov. 26:11)?
2. Who can free us from our slavery? (John 8:34–36)

Summa

Write an essay or discuss this question, integrating what you have learned from the material above.

Can believers become addicts?

Reading Assignment:
Confessions, Book VII

Session VIII: Logic Activity[5]

Confessions, Book VII

The Problem of Evil

The Problem of Evil is an argument that has been used by unbelievers to question the Christian faith through the years. It takes the form of an argument called the Dilemma. It goes something like this:

If God exists, then He is all good and all powerful.
If God is all good, then He would want to put a stop to evil.
If God is all powerful, then He would be able to put a stop to evil.
Evil exists.
Therefore, God does not exist.

This argument held Augustine back from the faith for a time, and if you go to a college or a job in which unbelief is rampant, you will encounter this argument. Usually, it will be spouted by some smug, liberal, atheistic philosophy professor who wants to demonstrate how he can shake the faith of hayseed Christians in a matter of minutes. If you pay attention to this session, you should be able to resist such foolish devices.

If you have studied logic you know that, when considering an argument, two things must be taken into account: validity and soundness. First, we must discern whether an argument is valid. The technical definition of validity is that a valid argument is one in which, if all of the premises are true, then the conclusion must be true. Validity has to do with the structure of an argument. Some arguments are set up in a structure that yields logical arguments. Many are not. If something is not valid, it does not matter how convincing it sounds. It is not a good argument. One example of an invalid form is the following argument:

If it rains tonight, then your car will be wet in the morning.
Your car is wet in the morning.
Therefore, it must have rained last night.

While initially this might seem like a good argument, if you consider it closely you can see that it does not work. Think about it. If your car is wet in the morning, does it definitively prove that it rained last night? Is there anything else that could have caused your car to be wet? You might have slept in and someone washed it. A fire hydrant might have burst, or the lawn sprinklers came on. This argument is so common that it has received its own special name. It is called *affirming the consequent*, and it is always invalid.

The second consideration when we analyze an argument is whether it is sound or not. This consideration asks: are the parts of the argument actually true. You can put something in the right form, but if you do not have sound premises, your argument is worthless. Take this argument for example:

If someone eats all of the candy, then we will have none.
Someone ate all the candy.
Therefore, we will have none.

This argument is in it proper form, so it is valid. This form of argument is actually used very often, and it has been given the name *modus ponens*. There can, however, be a problem with it. What if your brother came in and told you this argument claiming that someone had eaten all of the candy. You might fly into a rage, because you wanted some of the candy and it was yours. When you go to check for clues, however, you discover that no one has, in fact, eaten the candy. The argument is valid, but one of the premises is a lie, namely:

Someone ate all the candy.

This means that the argument is unsound.

Today, we are going to evaluate both the validity and soundness of the argument called the Problem of Evil. (If you have not studied Logic yet, you may not be able to analyze the argument for validity, but you can still analyze each premise for soundness.

Step #1: Testing the Validity of the Problem of Evil

To test validity we use something called a truth table. (If you have not studied testing validity with shorter truth tables in logic, skip to step two.) This is done by breaking the argument up into a symbolic language and testing its form. (Remember, even if we find that the Problem of Evil passes this test, that still does not mean it is true—only that it is in a proper format or form.)

In the following form these symbols represent the following:

B = God exists
G = God is all good
W= God would want to put a stop to evil
P = God is all powerful
A = God would be able to put a stop to evil
E = Evil exists
~ = Not
⊂ = If then
• = And
∨ = Or
∴ = Therefore

So, the Dilemma

If God exists, then He is all good and all powerful.
If God is all good, then He would want to put a stop to evil.
If God is all powerful, then He would be able to put a stop to evil.
Evil exists.
Therefore, God does not exist.

can be translated into the following symbolic language:

B⊂(G•P) G⊂W P⊂A E E⊂(~G∨~P) ∴ ~B

We can use the shorter truth table method to analyze this argument: pretend that all the premises are true and the conclusion is false. In a valid argument this cannot occur and should produce a contradiction. Thus:

B⊂(G•P)	G⊂W	P⊂A	E	E⊂(~G∨~P)	∴ ~B
T	T	T	T	T	F

Now, using what you know about the terms, see if you are led into a contradiction at this point. If so, the argument is valid.[6]

Step #2: Consider the Soundness of the Problem of Evil

When we consider the soundness of an argument, we have to consider whether each premise of the argument is actually true. Consider the questions below to tell if the Problem of Evil consists of sound premises. For each premise, state whether it is sound and why or why not.

If God exists, then He is both all good and all powerful.

B⊂(G•P)

If God is all good, then He would want to stop evil.

G⊂W

If God is all powerful, then He is able to stop evil.

P⊂A

E

If evil exists, then God is either not all good or not all powerful.

E⊂(~G ∨ ~P)

Reading Assignment:
Confessions, Book VIII

Session IX: Recitation

Confessions, Book VIII

Comprehension Questions

Answer the following questions for factual recall:

1. According to Augustine, which are better, scientists or Manicheans? Why? (V.3)
2. What does Augustine learn from the venerable Manichean scholar Faustus (V.6–7)?
3. When Augustine moves to Milan, under whose influence does he begin to fall? Why? (V.13)
4. Which is better, drunkenness or ambition? Why? (VI.6)
5. What sins hold Augustine and his friend Alypius in bondage (VI.6–16)?
6. One of the road blocks in the way of Augustine's faith was that he conceived of evil as a substance that God must have created. To what understanding about evil does Augustine eventually come (VII.12–13)?
7. What two examples encourage Augustine (VIII.2 and 6)?
8. What sin is Augustine enslaved to, and how does this cause him to pray (VIII.7)?
9. How is Augustine converted (VIII.12)?

Reading Assignment:
Confessions, Book IX

Session X: Discussion

Confessions, Book IX

A Question to Consider

What has to happen for someone to be saved?

Discuss or list short answers to the following questions:

Text Analysis

1. What sin was Augustine clinging to that kept him from faith in Christ (VIII.5–7)?
2. Did Augustine find this sin fulfilling? If not, why did he continue in it? (VI.12–15; VIII.5)
3. How was God's Word instrumental in Augustine coming to faith in Christ (VIII.12)?
4. How was God's providential control of the world and its circumstances (particularly the game that the children picked that day and the placement of the Scriptures) useful in Augustine's conversion?
5. As we see Augustine repenting and believing, where do we see regeneration or effectual calling?

Cultural Analysis

1. Where does our culture look for salvation?
2. Why is looking to God for salvation and recognizing that we are totally unable to save ourselves something that our culture is unwilling to do?
3. What practices in the modern church might lead people to think that salvation is a work of man at its root and not a work of God?

Biblical Analysis

1. Why is man unable to save himself (Rom. 3:1–10, Eph. 2:1–2)?
2. Who is the ultimate cause of salvation (John 8:34–36, Rom. 9:16, Acts 16:14)?
3. What part then do we have in salvation (Eph. 2:8–10)?

Summa

Write an essay or discuss this question, integrating what you have learned from the material above.

Sometimes in the modern church, people make it seem as if salvation is something that the sinner controls. How would you answer someone who claims that your salvation is up to you alone?

Reading Assignment:
Confessions, Book X

Session XI: Writing

Confessions, Book X

Making Your Own Confession, *Part Two*

Today, we are going to write out our confessions. Please refer to the instructions that were given in Session III for background. Your confession should start and end giving glory to God, and it should agree with God concerning the nature of your sin and should not glorify or excuse sin in any way. Your final product will, of course, differ from the example given (if it does not, you might want to start over and confess the sin of plagiarism):

> Heavenly Father and God of all blessings and light, how gracious you were to me! How you showered blessings on the head of one so undeserving. You, by the mystery of your providence, caused me to be born into a family that feared and honored Your holy name. Every week we sat under the preaching of Your word and I believed on You from early days, having passed through the waters of baptism in my infancy.
>
> Also, you gave me the extraordinary blessing of having two wonderful, Christian parents. My father worked diligently to provide for my family, and my mother loved and cared for me and my siblings, teaching us Your ways. When I sinned, they disciplined me, and although I dreaded it then, how I thank you for it now. Still, I often sinned and wandered far from the way of righteousness. I recall how I deceived a classmate in a first-grade coloring contest by tricking him into voting for my picture and then I did not follow through on our agreement to vote for his.
>
> While at times I try to forget these youthful sins, they demonstrate my own weakness and lack of character. Help me, O Lord, to recall these things clearly. This sin happened when I was six or seven. My teacher had given us a coloring assignment. She instructed us to be careful coloring, because we still struggled to stay within the lines of the drawing. As a young man, I wanted desperately to win, but many of the girls were better at coloring than I was.

To motivate us she let us know that we were going to vote for the best one after we were all finished, and the winner was to receive some trifle of a prize. This contest brought out the worst in me. I was competitive, Lord, and the desire to do my best was, no doubt, from You. My lust for victory, however, caused me to lie and deceive my classmates.

I deceived a student named Adam. I made an agreement with him, offering to vote for his picture if he would in turn vote for mine. (None of us were allowed to vote for our own.) In a small class like this the turning of a vote or two could make the difference. Neither of us should have made an agreement like this, bending the truth to gain victory, for neither of our pictures deserved the award. Alan was not good at coloring and had more trouble staying within the lines than I did. When the time came, he faithfully voted for my poor drawing. When my turn came to vote for his, I was embarrassed and voted instead for another students' drawing.

Pride led me to these sins. First, I wanted to win so badly that I was willing to bend the truth and to encourage others to bend it with me in hopes that I could win and lord it over my classmates. Their opinion of me guided my actions more than Your word; I feared them more than You. My pride also caused me to break my agreement with Alan. As I contemplated voting for his drawing, I knew that this would cause me to look foolish in the eyes of my classmates; knowing that Alan had already cast his vote for mine, I knew that I could protect my own reputation and have his vote as well. Thus, I deceived him.

The manner in which I lied was contrived and vile. Instead of being man enough to be open about my sin, I hid it by pretending that I did not recognize his picture. Instead, I pretended confusion and voted for a better drawing. I, however, was not confused, but was thinking only of myself and what my classmates would think of me. Alan was crestfallen and rightly trusted me less because of my deception. What deceit and falsehood an unbridled lust for victory brings!

Some might seek to excuse my actions for various reasons, but You, O Lord, know the truth. Because I sat in the back of the class, some might think that I could not see clearly, but I admit that I clearly understood the agreement and knew the picture that I had agreed to vote for. The confusion that I pretended was yet another lie. Others could claim that I was motivated only by fairness. Alan's work was not worthy of my vote, so, one could argue, I was only failing to execute a plan that was based on twisting the truth. While it is true that I was twisting the truth, my motives were not pure, but sinful. I was looking out for myself, and was in no way yearning for the truth. It was pride and not virtue that motivated my failure to do what I had agreed to do.

Gracious Lord, You made my sin bitter to me. Immediately, my conscience was troubled by my action and the victory that I sought was kept from me as well. The look on Alan's face when he recognized that I had lied to him is etched into my memory. Often I have seen it in my mind's eye over the years, and this sin has kept me from lying to others. Father, you are gracious and kind; forgive, O Lord, the sins of youth even though they are riddled with bad motives and deceit.

READING ASSIGNMENT:
Confessions, Book XI

SESSION XII: DISCUSSION

Confessions, Book XI

A Question to Consider

How can you avoid temptation?

Discuss or list short answers to the following questions:

Text Analysis

1. What sort of career move does Augustine's conversion cause him to make? Was this necessary or wise (IX.4)?
2. What memories from his past trouble Augustine?

How does he fight them? (X.30)

3. How does Augustine seek to bring his appetites into subjection (X.31)?
4. How are sights and sounds temptations to him (X.33–34)?
5. According to Augustine, is mental curiosity a good thing or a bad thing (X.35)?
6. Whose benediction does Satan want us to seek? How does Augustine seek to battle this? (X.36–37)

Cultural Analysis

1. What does our culture think of the pursuit of holiness through discipline?
2. What does our culture think of fasting? Is fasting to be practiced in our churches?

Biblical Analysis

1. What is at the root of temptation (James 1:12–15)?
2. How does God use temptation in our lives (1 Cor. 10:13, James 1:12)?
3. In light of passages like Revelation 19:1–10 and Deuteronomy 14:22–26, is Augustine's view of food biblical?

Summa

Write an essay or discuss this question, integrating what you have learned from the material above.

How can you fight against the world, the flesh and the devil and avoid temptation?

Optional Activity

The Bible calls on us to be disciplined in the way that we use everything. Food is part of everything. The Bible also calls on us to feast and enjoy the bounty of all the good things that God has given us. We must affirm both of these truths and work to apply them wisely.

If you accept this mission, you are probably going to have to get some help from Mom or some funds from Dad, or maybe both (tell them it is for a school project and that the whole family can join in).

STEP #1: A Day of Fasting: Plan a day of fasting for everyone in your family who is able. Your might plan it out for only one meal, but perhaps for the whole day. You might want to start the fast on Friday night. Take the extra time that you have at dinner, breakfast and lunch and meet as a family to pray toward a certain end. This might have to do with the plan that you have laid out in the Summa question for this section. It might also be a concern in the life of your family or a concern of our nation (abortion, cultural acceptance of perversion, etc.). During the day, your stomach will start to ache; let this remind you to call out again to the Lord.

STEP #2: The Feast: At sundown on Saturday night begin your Sabbath with a feast. If you have fasted for a day, the turkey or filet will taste even better, and the wine will gladden the hearts (Ps. 104:15) of all who partake—this might be just Mom and Dad. Either have Mom cook up the best meal she can or head out to a local restaurant and get a nice meal. Celebrate and thank God for the good food that He gives.

Reading Assignment:
Confessions, Book XII

Session XIII: Discussion

Confessions, Book XII

A Question to Consider

How was the world created?

Discuss or list short answers to the following questions:

Text Analysis

1. How does Augustine connect the work of the Father and the Son in creation (XI.5–7)?
2. How are some overly curious people made into laughing stocks by the answer to the question: "What was God doing before He created the world?" (XI.13)?
3. What important truth does Augustine affirm that separates Christians from Pantheists such as Hindus (XII.7–8)?
4. What is the "Heaven of heavens" (XII.13–15)?
5. What is Augustine's attitude toward other Christians whose interpretation of Scripture differs from his? How does this differ from his attitude toward those that teach that Moses was wrong? (XII.14, 18, 23, 30)

Cultural Analysis

1. What is our culture's beliefs concerning creation?
2. Some have argued that Intelligent Design is a

good way to make sure that students in public schools learn the truth about creation (or at least are not lied to as badly). What should our opinion of this be?

Biblical Analysis

1. Where do you see the Trinity in Genesis 1?
2. What difficulties do you see with Augustine's Day-Age View in light of Romans 5:12?

SUMMA

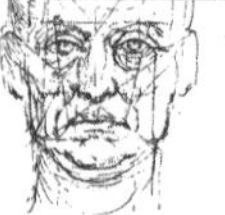

Write an essay or discuss this question, integrating what you have learned from the material above.

How can we recognize other Christians whose views of Genesis 1 differ with our view (which is the correct view—right?) and focus our fight on destroying unbelief?

READING ASSIGNMENT:
Confessions, Book XIII

SESSION XIV: ACTIVITY

Confessions, Book XIII

The Confessions Game

DIRECTIONS

This game may be played using a game piece on lined paper, or the students themselves may serve as game pieces and move up and down a room divided into spaces (a tiled floor works well).

RULES FOR THE GAME

TO START

Place the game piece at one end of the "board" (the lined paper). The teacher or game leader reads a true or false statement (provided in the teacher's edition).

THE DECISION PHASE

Each player decides whether the statement is true or false. If he believes it is true, he (or his game piece) moves forward one space. If he believes it is false, he does not move. After each player decides to move or stay, the leader reveals whether it is true or false.

THE REWARD PHASE

If a player guessed true, and is correct, he stays on his new space. If he is incorrect, he must back up two spaces.

If a player guessed false, and is correct, he moves forward one space. If he is incorrect, he must back up one space and is not eligible for the bonus. As a bonus, a correct player may attempt to explain how the statement is false, and if his explanation is correct, he may move forward two additional spaces. (In group settings the explanation may need to be whispered to the leader or written down by each individual.)

The leader continues in like manner with more statements, the players proceeding through the Decision and Reward phases. The teacher's edition contains statements for seven rounds. Do as many rounds as time or space allows. After the last round, see who has advanced the farthest, or alternatively, establish a goal line and proclaim the first to cross it as the winner.

SESSION XV: EVALUATION

Evaluation

All tests and quizzes are to be given with an open book and a Bible available.

Grammar

Answer each of the following questions in complete sentences. Some answers may be longer than others. (2 points per answer)

1. At the beginning of the Confessions what does Augustine say is the only way to find peace and contentment?

This is a bust of the famous Greek philosopher Plato (427–347 B.C.), whose writings and philosophy influenced Augustine for good and ill. Although some of Plato's ideas were used by God to bring Augustine closer to the truth before his conversion, other Platonic ideas infected Augustine's theology thereafter like an unbiblical virus.

2. Which are better, scientists or Manicheans? Why?
3. When Augustine moved to Milan, under whose influence did he begin to fall? Why?
4. What two examples encouraged Augustine?
5. How was Augustine converted?
6. How did Augustine react to Monica's death?
7. What is Augustine's attitude toward those who differ with his interpretation of Genesis 1 and 2. What is his attitude toward those who think Moses was wrong?

Logic

Answer two of the following questions in complete sentences; your answer should be a paragraph or so. (10 points per answer)

Analyze the Problem of Evil: State the argument, tell if it is valid and if it is sound. How would you attack this argument if it were brought against you in a debate?

2. What is essential for a sinner to be saved? Where do we see this in Augustine's conversion?
3. How does James 4:1–3 explain Augustine's pre-conversion life?

Lateral Thinking

Answer one of the following questions. These questions will require more substantial answers. (16 points per answer)

1. Compare and contrast the Christian view of sin in *Confessions* with the Greek view of sin that we find in the writings of Sophocles and Plato. (What causes Augustine to do wrong and what causes Oedipus or Socrates' opponents to do wrong?)
2. How does the life and conversion of Augustine prove Jesus' words in John 8:34–36?

Remember the pears that the young Augustine pilfered from his neighbor for no reason other than that it was wrong? With his delinquent "friends" Augustine shook down a whole tree full of pears. Then, to show their contempt for the fruit of God's good creation, they didn't eat the pears or sell them or give them away—they threw them to some pigs! In the ancient world, pigs (like dogs) were symbols of uncleanness and filth. Ironically, as people who treated what is valuable and good (the pears) as worthless and contemptible, Augustine and his hoodlum friends played the role of the swine in Matthew 7:6, which admonishes Christians not to "throw your pearls before swine, or they will trample them under foot."

Chart 1: **COMPARING AUGUSTINE TO PLATO**

QUESTION	PLATO'S ANSWER	AUGUSTINE'S ANSWER	SCRIPTURE'S ANSWER
What is sin?	Plato taught that sin is mainly a matter of ignorance and that, if man simply understood things correctly, he would act righteously. (Euthyphro, 1–11a)		
What is man?		Augustine says that he is a soul that has sense experience through a physical body. (X.7)	
What is God like? Does the idea of Christ's incarnation cause any problems?			The Bible is God's story about Himself and portrays Him not as some distant spirit but as a covenant-making and -keeping God. To save His people, He took on flesh and died for them. This view fits with Augustine's. (Gen. 12; Matt. 27–28)

Optional Session A: Discussion

A Question to Consider

How should someone grieve when someone close dies?

Discuss or list short answers to the following questions:

Text Analysis

1. What kind of wife was Monica to Patrick (IX.9)?
2. How did Monica face death (IX.10–11)?
3. How did Augustine react to Monica's death internally (IX.12)?
4. Why did he temper his external response in the presence of his friends (IX.12)?
5. In what did Augustine take comfort (IX.13)?

Cultural Analysis

1. In the past people have worn black after the death of a loved one or even put the tears shed at the funeral into a special bottle.[10] What practices do we have in our culture to define grieving?
2. Are we better off or worse off by having fewer set patterns of grief?

Biblical Analysis

1. What was the biblically prescribed period of mourning for a national leader (Num. 20:29; Deut. 34:8)?
2. Did David mourn Saul, Jonathan or Absalom with restraint or with passion (2 Sam. 1:11–27; 2 Sam. 18:29–19:4)?
3. How did Jesus mourn the death of Lazarus (John 11:34–36)?

Chart 1: **COMPARING AUGUSTINE TO PLATO** *continued*

QUESTION	PLATO'S ANSWER	AUGUSTINE'S ANSWER	SCRIPTURE'S ANSWER
What is righteousness?	Plato taught that righteousness was gained through the contemplation of the eternal forms. Thinking about this eternal and unchangeable world made someone less connected to this "shadowy" material world. (Phaedo 100b–102a)		
How is man saved?			The Bible presents sin as a master that rules over sinners; they can only be saved by the power of God through the work of Christ applied by the power of the Holy Spirit. (John 8:34–36)
What is the view of the material world (e.g., food, sex)?			

Summa

Write an essay or discuss this question, integrating what you have learned from the material above.
How should we mourn?

Optional Session B: Analysis

Comparing Augustine to Plato

At some points, Augustine was influenced by Plato's philosophy. He even claims in *Confessions* Book V that the philosopher led him away from Manichaeism and toward Christianity. At other points, however, did Augustine let Plato affect his own philosophy and biblical interpretation too much? Some have thought so. In Chart 1 we examine some of Augustine's teaching and compare it to Plato's philosophy and to the Bible. Fill in the blank sections.

Optional Session C: Discussion

A Question to Consider

Should Christians be baptized immediately or is putting off the time of baptism acceptable?

Discuss or list short answers to the following questions:

Text Analysis

1. When was Augustine freed from the chains of slavery to sin (VIII.12–13; IX.1)?
2. Why did Augustine wait to be baptized (IX.2)?
3. When was the normal time for baptism (according to Augustine) (IX.2)?
4. Where was Augustine baptized? Why did he go there? (Think of who would have been doing the baptizing.) (IX.6)
5. Who was Augustine baptized with (IX.6)?

Cultural Analysis

1. Does our culture think that ceremonies like weddings and baptisms are important?
2. Does our culture connect status and ceremony (i.e., what does our culture think changes when a ceremony occurs)?

Biblical Analysis

1. When was the most normal time for the baptism of converts during the time of the apostles (Acts 8:12, 16:33)?
2. Is immediate baptism wrong? Why is the Ethiopian eunuch baptized immediately (Acts 8:27–40)?

SUMMA

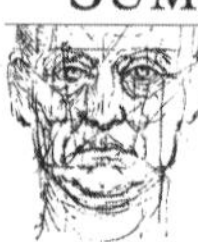

Write an essay or discuss this question, integrating what you have learned from the material above.

What should determine whether you wait to be baptized or not?

ENDNOTES

1 For my wife and I, we smiled so long and so often that a few days later our faces were actually sore. Let this be a lesson to you. Practice smiling diligently if you are contemplating marriage.

2 This is not meant to deny that there are propositions in the Bible or that we need not defend them. It is, however, affirming that sometimes the Bible communicates in a way that is true on levels that do not fit neatly within our surface interpretations of Scripture. It is almost as if a being much smarter than us communicated in ways that are amazingly meaningful and deep. Go figure!

3 *This endnote appears only in the teacher's edition.*

4 This temptation has been so great that, from time to time, Christian leaders have actually confessed sins that they never, in fact, committed just to seem like they had an interesting testimony.

5 This class is heavily indebted to Jim Nance, whose logic books and videos have benefited many. He works through an exercise like this one in his informative videos.

6 As we analyze this argument, we find that the Problem of Evil is a valid argument. This does not mean that it should be persuasive to us, but we must admit that it is in a form where, if all the premises are true, then the conclusion must also be true. For it to be a convincing argument, however, the premises have to be sound, and, as we shall see, this is not the case.

7 *This endnote appears only in the teacher's edition.*

8 *This endnote appears only in the teacher's edition.*

9 *This endnote appears only in the teacher's edition.*

10 These bottles were called *lachrymatories.* In Victorian times the tradition was that you mourned the dead for a period as long as it took the tears in this bottle to evaporate. The more you cried the longer the mourning period. More information about this practice may be found at Link 1 for this chapter at www.VeritasPress.com/OmniLinks.

11 *This endnote appears only in the teacher's edition.*

ON THE INCARNATION

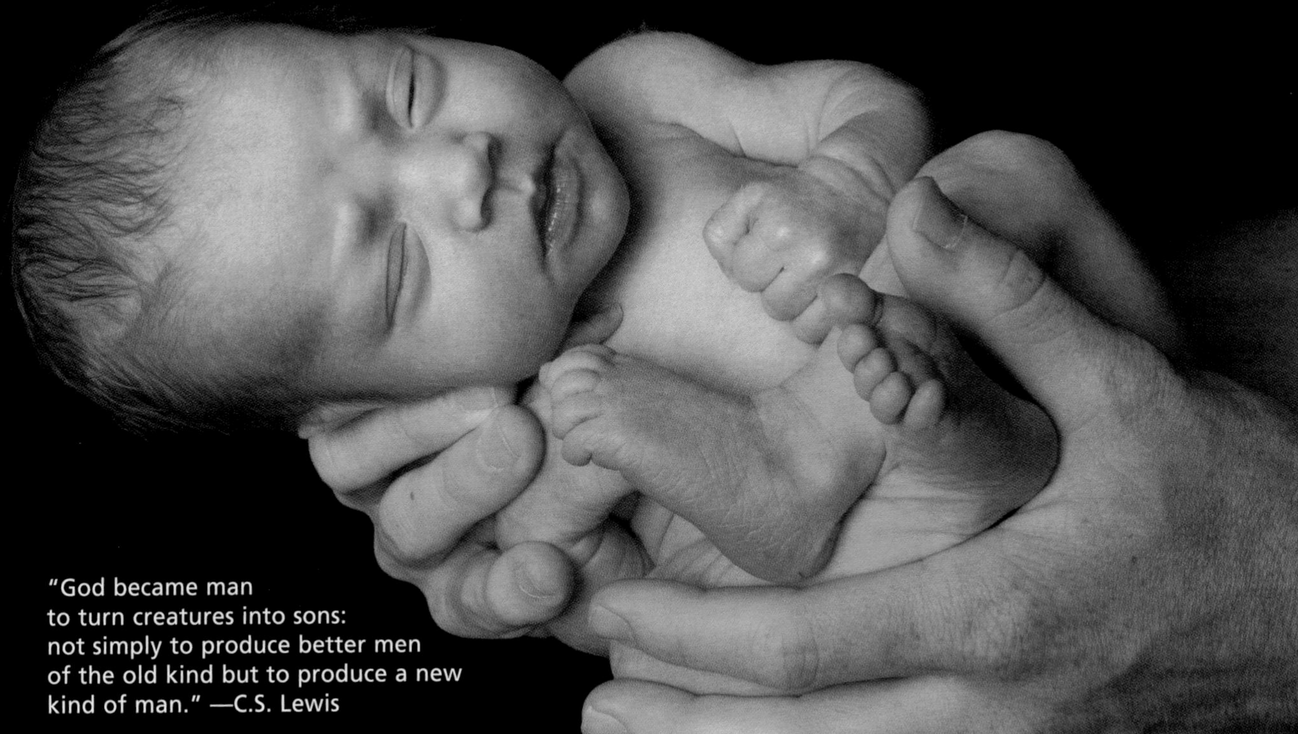

"God became man to turn creatures into sons: not simply to produce better men of the old kind but to produce a new kind of man." —C.S. Lewis

For in [Christ] all the fullness of God was pleased to dwell, and through Him to reconcile to Himself all things, whether on earth or in heaven, making peace by the blood of His cross. And you, who once were alienated and hostile in mind, doing evil deeds, He has now reconciled in His body of flesh by His death, in order to present you holy and blameless and above reproach before Him. . .. [This is] the mystery hidden for ages and generations but now revealed to His saints.

Colossians 1:19–22, 26

Let us not mock God with metaphor,
Analogy, sidestepping, transcendence;
Making of the event a parable, a sign painted in the
Faded credulity of other ages;
Let us walk through the door.

Let us not seek to make it less monstrous,
For our own convenience, our own sense of beauty,
Lest, awakened in one unthinkable hour, we are
Embarrassed by the miracle,
And crushed by remonstrance.

John Updike, *Seven Stanzas at Easter*

A small, determined man moved quickly, quietly through the wharves and back streets of Alexandria, Egypt, his alert eyes darting furtively. Dressed in a dark, tattered monk's cowl, the middle-aged man silently passed by two seedy wharves, eerily quiet in the middle of the night except for the slow rhythmic lapping of Mediterranean Sea water against the hulls of docked grain ships, motionless like beached whales. Only a few strands of fine gold thread, unintentionally peering out from beneath the edges of his robe, indicated that this might not be an ordinary thief in the night.

The shadowy fugitive crossed the canal near the docks, briefly turned east on royal Canopic Street, then south onto a dark alley in the direction of Pompey's Pillar and the old Temple of Serapis, briefly crouching behind each cart and barrel in his path to quickly assess his situation. Halfway through the alley he heard two Roman soldiers on Canopic Street exclaim, "There he is!" He dashed across the alley into an abandoned building, the two soldiers in close pursuit.

Inside the building he attempted to bolt the front

door shut, but the latch was broken. He quickly ran to the back room facing another street. Securely bolting the door to the back room just as his pursuers entered the building, he frantically piled a few pieces of old furniture against the door, then leaned against the back wall next to a small open window to catch his breath and plan his next move.

Within the minute, his pursuers pounded on the bolted door. "Bishop! We know you're in there," one of the pursuers shouted authoritatively. "Give yourself up now and Emperor Julian will show you mercy." His heart racing, the fugitive considered his options, few and unsatisfactory as they were. He had been in similar situations before, too many times as far as he was concerned. Being a churchman, his thoughts involuntarily veered to the Gospels. How did Jesus suffer the constant hounding of His enemies and escape their murderous designs? he wondered. Suddenly a big, brawny arm shot through the open window, grabbed the bishop around the chest and pulled him through the window into a grain cart. The hand of the body snatcher immediately covered the bishop's mouth as a pair of horses pulled the cart away. Only when the terrified bishop finally focused on the face of his abductor did he realize that he had been saved by friends. By the time the two soldiers broke into the empty back room, the cart was several blocks away, the bishop hidden under a pile of wheat.

The bumpy cart sped along, making several twisting turns, until it abruptly stopped at the canal several blocks farther south. "Hurry, hurry," said the hushed voice of his abductor as the bishop hopped out of the cart and into a waiting rowboat. After a silent signal the cart disappeared and the bishop began rowing south quickly but quietly. As he looked up from under his hood he saw a Roman naval boat following him down the canal at some distance. He continued to row as fast as possible without drawing attention to himself. As he rounded a bend in the canal heading east he lost sight of the naval boat. The bishop quickly analyzed his situation. He had to assume the naval boat was searching for him. There was no way he could outrun it. He quickly made his decision. Abruptly turning his boat around, he started rowing *back* around the bend. As he boldly approached the slowing naval boat, Roman soldiers on board yelled out, "Have you seen the bishop recently?" "Yes, you're quite close to him," replied the hooded bishop as he calmly rowed past them. The naval boat sped on around the bend after its quarry. The bishop looked skyward, smiled for the first time all night and quickly rowed to shore. He tied up his boat and made his way to the safety of Alexandria's secret catacombs as the first rays of morning light came over the horizon. He had successfully defied yet another Roman emperor. Soon Julian the Apostate would die and the bishop would return to his great work of defending the gospel against its enemies.

Who was this clever little man with the big heart who risked life and limb in defense of the gospel? His name was Athanasius, and he was Bishop of Alexandria during the pivotal fourth century A.D. He writes faithfully about the biggest event in history in the little book you are about to read, *On the Incarnation.*

General Information

Author and Context

Athanasius (A.D. 296–373) was bishop of the great city of Alexandria, Egypt, for 45 years, 17 of which were spent in exile for his faith. He lived during the time of the transition of Rome from an officially pagan empire to an officially Christian empire. Before Constantine, the empire was the major enemy of the church. After the conversion of Constantine in A.D. 312, the empire generally supported Christianity, and the major threat to the church came from false teachers in her midst who, influenced by Greek and Eastern philosophy, attacked the key doctrines of the Trinity and the Incarnation. One of these false teachers, the Alexandrian priest Arius, taught that Jesus was created by, and not equal to, God the Father. The "Arian" teaching became widespread in the church.

Emperor Constantine called for a church council at Nicea to decide the Arian issue. After much bitter debate, Arianism was declared heresy and the church approved the famous Nicene Creed. Shortly after Nicea, Athanasius became the bishop of Alexandria, but the Arians gained political influence in Constantine's court and were permitted back in the church. When Athanasius vigorously objected, he was banished from his office. He was exiled a total of five times by four different emperors. One time he escaped death by hiding out for four months in his father's tomb. Another time he hid in the Egyptian desert for several years from killers paid to murder him. During the worst years the future looked very bleak for the gospel as Arianism gained the upper hand in the church. Yet Athanasius stood firm, and ever since has been known by the famous Latin epithet *Athanasius Contra Mundum,* "Athanasius against the world." In his last years he was reinstalled as the bishop of Alexandria, and shortly after his death the church finally defeated the Arians for good.

Significance

Stop and think for a moment. If someone asked you what is the most important event in the history of the world, or in your personal life, how would you respond? Incredible as it may sound, the event which far surpasses all the great events of world history and your own personal life is the Incarnation of Jesus Christ. It is the one indispensable (can't do without it) event in all history (including *your* history), the one and only event that eternally transforms the meaning and destiny of all other events and relationships from the beginning to the end of history and beyond. Have you ever seen food coloring dropped into a pitcher of clear water? The color penetrates the water in every direction so that every molecule of water changes color. The Incarnation has had the same effect on the world—except that as the Incarnation "coloring" spreads throughout the world it does not get increasingly diluted, but rather grows stronger.

The English word *incarnation* comes from the Latin *in* and *caro,* meaning "in the flesh." *Incarnate* means clothed or embodied in flesh. The *Incarnation* refers specifically to the mystery of the second person of the Trinity uniting Himself with a human nature and body: "and so [He] was and continues to be God and man in two distinct natures and one person, forever" (*Westminster Shorter Catechism* Q. 21).

There are three unique, unrepeatable, foundational events in history: Creation, Incarnation and Final Judgment. The pivotal event is the Incarnation. Without the Incarnation there is no Christmas, no sinless life of

The Madonna of the Chair (Madonna della Stedia) c. 1514, is one of the most popular of all Raphael madonnas, and was likely painted for Pope Leo X. Much may be said for the skillful accommodation with which Raphael consolidated these three figures into the restricting circular design. Mary's torso, like that of Christ, is set in profile in order to appear less crowded, while her legs are thrust up to provide a comfortable place for the child. In the foreground the corner of a chair establishes the outer limit of the compressed space of the painting, which suggests the form of a sphere or globe, especially through the curvature of the Madonna's right arm and the child's left arm.

Jesus, no cross, no resurrection, no binding of Satan and ascension of Christ, no church. There is no final revelation of the Trinity, no new covenant securing God's people forever, no kingdom of God growing on earth as it is in heaven, no incarnation of the ultimate love of God, no reconciliation between God and men, no reconciliation among men, no salvation of men, no redemption of the world, no future resurrection of the body, no future new heavens and new earth where every tear shall be wiped away—in short, no hope.

Setting and Summary

By the early fourth century God was in the process of dismantling the Roman Empire and beginning to establish His never-ending kingdom, initiated in the life of Jesus. The *Pax Romana* was built on the universal but futile pagan desire for salvation and peace through political power. After more than two hundred years of Roman persecution of the growing Christian community, Emperor Constantine's official recognition of Christianity signaled the beginning of the end of Roman paganism. However, just at this point of the transition the focus of the church's spiritual warfare shifted from the external battle with paganism to an internal battle against false teaching. With the coming of the kingdom and the establishment of the church, the enemies of God sought to attack the very heart of the gospel by denying or perverting the reality of the Incarnation. Power-seeking church leaders, especially in the eastern empire and the imperial court, were attracted especially to the Arian heresy because it seemed to justify the empire's unified power that the gospel was in the process of destroying. In this hostile environment God raised up the diminutive Athanasius to defend the truth of the gospel. It was the glory of the fourth century church, including the council of Nicea, and its subsequent defenders Athanasius and Ambrose, to grasp the biblical vision of the kingdom of God regenerating society through the propagation of the gospel of the incarnate Messiah.

On the Incarnation addresses the goodness of Christ's creation; the necessity of the Incarnation in response to the divine dilemma caused by man's sinful rebellion; and the triumph of Christ in destroying death, recreating man, and redeeming the world. It concludes with a refutation of the Jews and pagans who oppose the gospel.

Worldview

The beautiful but proud and overbearing daughter of a great king scornfully rejected all the young kings and noblemen who asked for her hand in marriage, mocking them all. She made special sport of a very tall king with a distinguished chin. "Only look," cried she, laughing, "he has a chin like a thrush's beak!" From then on they called him "King Thrushbeard."

The scornful rejection of all her suitors so angered the great king that he swore that his daughter should wed the first beggar that came to the castle door. Soon a poor traveling ballad-singer sang under the window in hopes of a small gift of alms. The great king told the ballad-singer, "I will give thee my daughter to wife." The daughter was horrified but the king had sworn an oath, and it was done.

After the ceremony the great king informed his daughter, "Since you are a beggar wife, you can no longer stay in my castle, so off with you and your husband." On the long journey to the beggar's home they came in turn to a great wood, a large meadow, and a prosperous town. After the beggar told her that each of these fine places belonged to King Thrushbeard and might have been hers, she cried, "I'm a silly young thing, I'm afeared, would I have taken that good King Thrushbeard!" Then said the beggar, "It does not please me to hear you always wishing for another husband. Am I not good enough for you?"

At last they came to a little shack. "Oh, dear me!" she said, "What poor little house do I see?" "That is where we must live together," he answered. "Where are the servants?" asked the great king's daughter. "What servants? What you want to have done you must do yourself. Make a fire quick, put on water and cook me some food; I am very tired."

But the great king's daughter understood nothing about cooking and cleaning, and the beggar had to constantly help her. Soon they came to the end of their food. So the beggar set about having his wife make baskets to sell, but her tender hands could not manage the trick. So he set her to spinning thread, but the harsh thread cut her soft fingers. "You are no good at any sort of work; I made a bad bargain when I took you," he said. So he made her sell clay pots in the market square. Her very first day, a drunken soldier rode his horse straight into the midst of her pots, breaking them into a thousand pieces.

Distraught, she ran home and told the beggar. "Now leave off crying," he said, "I see you are not fit for any regular work. Your father's kitchen help has agreed to take you on; at any rate you will get our victuals for free." So the great king's daughter became a kitchen maid. In each of her pockets she fastened a little pot, to carry home leftover scraps for the beggar.

One day, when the wedding of the great king's eldest prince was celebrated, the poor kitchen maid went upstairs and stood by the parlor door to see what was going on. All was brilliancy and splendor, and she thought of her own fate with a sad heart, bewailing her former pride and haughtiness which had brought her so low. Every now and then servants would throw her a few fragments of rich food which she put in her pockets for home. Suddenly an elegant prince seized her hand and urged her to dance with him. Ashamed and trembling, she refused, for she saw it was King Thrushbeard whom she had earlier spurned. Nevertheless, he drew her into the room; and all at once the band to which her pockets were fastened broke spilling soup and scraps everywhere. In horror she fled, but King Thrushbeard caught her at the door and said to her in a kind tone, "Do not be afraid, I and the beggar with whom you lived in the wretched little hut are one. For love of you, I disguised myself, and it was I who broke your pots in the guise of the drunken soldier. I did all that to bring down your proud heart and to punish your haughtiness which caused you to mock me."

Weeping bitterly, she said, "I have done great wrong, and am not worthy to be your wife." But he said, "Take courage, the evil days are gone over; now let us keep our wedding day." Then came her father, the great king, and his whole court, and wished her joy on her marriage with King Thrushbeard, and the merrymaking began in good earnest.

Like King Thrushbeard in the Grimm's fairytale of the same name, who humbled himself and became a beggar to save his proud and arrogant wife, the eternal Son of the Father, second person of the Trinity, creator and sustainer of the universe, "made Himself of no reputation, taking the form of a bondservant, and coming in the likeness of men" (Phil. 2:7) in order to

"My soul magnifies the Lord, and my spirit has rejoiced in God my Savior. For He has regarded the lowly state of His maidservant; for behold, henceforth all generations will call me blessed. For He who is mighty has done great things for me, and holy is His name."

save His proud and disobedient bride, the church, and redeem the whole world. Thanks to the Incarnation, we too can "take courage" because "the evil days are gone over," and therefore look forward to the great wedding day feast when the people of God are presented as the pure and spotless bride to our Lord and Savior Jesus Christ.

The humiliation of the Son of God in the Incarnation far exceeded that of King Thrushbeard. But the exaltation of the Son of God also far, far exceeded that of King Thrushbeard. The distance between God and man is infinitely greater than the distance between king and beggar, and Jesus not only experienced the sufferings of our fallen world and an excruciating death on the cross, but bore the full fury of God's righteous wrath in taking upon Himself the sins of the whole world. Equally significant, the humiliation of the Messiah, unlike that of King Thrushbeard, was not just a story—it actually happened. Unlike people who make up stories to tell or to sell in books and TV and movies, God creates stories through His word that become reality. We are living, breathing characters in God's reality story, our lives being individual episodes within and intimately connected to His story. And the crucial event that penetrates, connects, and determines the outcome of each of our stories and their relationship to God's master story is the Incarnation. Through this enduring event our Lord suffers in loving obedience to the Father, dies on the cross as atonement for the sins of the world, is resurrected as the first fruits of the new humanity (God's people) and new creation, and ascends to the right hand of the Father where He rules with His people until all His enemies are put under His feet and the whole world is redeemed.

This nativity scene comes from the *Tres Belles Heures de Bruxelles*, a Parisian manuscript illuminated mainly by Netherlandish artists and begun about 1382.

Unlike fairytales, where only the prince and princess "live happily ever after," at the end of God's story all God's people will live happily ever after. As Athanasius shows us, through the Incarnation Jesus became the new Adam (succeeding where the old Adam failed), initiated the kingdom of God on earth, created a new covenant with all people and nations that repent and follow Him, reconciling them to the Father and to each other so they can be adopted into the Father's kingdom, and guaranteed the victory of His kingdom and the redemption of the entire world at the culmination of history.

Over 1,600 years ago Athanasius came to understand the centrality of the Incarnation, both for our salvation and for the entire course of history, because he faithfully heard God's word, the true story of how our world came to be, why things are the way they are, and where things are headed. Because God and His world are personal and infinitely complex, history and reality are more like a drama or story than a philosophical treatise or mathematical equation. The story progresses, develops, and incorporates the stories of men, unfolding like a great spreading oak tree from a small acorn. Contrary to pagan Greek speculations, God is not a philosophical idea or "prime mover" which we discover by our "reason." Nor is He the mystical, impersonal "force" of Eastern pagan imaginations, in which we seek to lose ourselves. Although Athanasius's vocabulary is sometimes unduly influenced by his Greek philosophical education, he is aware that we can only understand God, ourselves, history and reality through God's revelation of Himself and His story. And the Incarnation is at the heart of both God's revelation and story, for it was through the Incarnation that the love and goodness of the Father was shown for the salvation of men. The "renewal of creation has been wrought by the Self-same Word who made it in the beginning," explains Athanasius. That is, the God who created the whole world and everything in it and said it was good, is the same God who through the Incarnation now begins the renewal of that same creation previously corrupted and cursed because of man's rebellion. Our Father has effected the salvation of the world "through the same Word Who made it in the beginning."

God

Athanasius's understanding of God rightly assumes the centrality of the Trinity, the Father, Son and Holy Spirit who mutually love and serve one another. Although his language has been influenced by abstract, impersonal philosophical concepts like *essences* and *non-existence,* he nevertheless demonstrates an understanding that God is fundamentally personal when he asserts that the "love and goodness of [Jesus'] Father" is the reason behind the Incarnation itself. There is no such thing as love in the abstract. Love can only be known through the actions of living persons. For example, when a husband tells his wife that he loves her, it means nothing unless he shows her love through his actions. Athanasius sees that the Father, Son and Holy Spirit are continually loving and serving one another, and therefore constantly reminds us that God is love, as well as good, holy, all-powerful, all-knowing, sovereign and infinite.

Athanasius also affirms the Bible's teaching that, in accordance with God's preordained plan from the beginning, and motivated by His honor and His love, the Father, through the Son and Spirit, created all things out of nothing by the word of His power and sustains all things that exist. God communicates through His creation and His word. God's words are not hazy, sterile, philosophical concepts groping to describe or explain the world, but words of power through which He acts and makes sacrificial commitments in the real, physical world He created. God reveals Himself to us not through impersonal, scientific propositions about Himself but actually reveals Himself through His actions in covenantal faithfulness to His people and His creation. Over and over, God reminds His people to remember how He has kept His covenant promises to Abraham, Isaac and Jacob and to the people of Israel by bringing them safely out of Egypt to the promised land, and finally to the peoples of every nation in the coming of the promised Messiah and Savior, Jesus.

Athanasius asserts that although God created and sustains all things, always being present in them, there is a permanent distinction between His creatures and the Creator. "For His being in everything does not mean that He shares the nature of everything, only that He gives all things their being and sustains them in it," he explains. Unlike pagan concepts of god that assume there is no permanent chasm between the nature of man and the nature of god, the only difference being that god has greater powers and knowledge, Athanasius understands that even the uniting of the Son with a human nature in Jesus did not breach this permanent distinction. The Son is two distinct natures, divine and human, united but never confused, in one person. Thus, through the deep mystery of the Incarnation, followers of Christ are united in fellowship with God, becoming adopted sons of the Father through Christ, but never gods themselves.

Man

Man is made in the image of God, acknowledges Athanasius. Contrary to Greek or Eastern thinking, man is a unified entity of body and soul, the physical and spiritual aspects of his person being two sides of the same coin. Man is totally dependent on God, not only for his life but for true knowledge. It is because God made us in His image and revealed Himself to us that we are capable of knowing love and personally relating to God and each other (rather than using *or* fighting each other to get what we want), as well as cultivating and caring for the creation. We reflect the image of the Trinity in our personal relationships such as marriage, family, race, and nation. But unlike the Trinity, we are not self-sufficient: that is, we cannot have fellowship and love by ourselves.

When man rebelled against God in the garden, his whole being, spiritual and physical, was corrupted, shattering his relationship with God, and consequently with himself, his neighbor and the creation. Rebellion also made him blind to the truth of God's revelation and he began a futile search for fulfillment and glory apart from fellowship with God. But there is no substitute for Godly fellowship, the ultimate absence of which can only lead to death. Thus, before the Incarnation, death reigned in man and "the human race was in the process of destruction." Deceived and self-deceived, now living in a world cursed by sin, man was in no position to save himself from this tragedy. Although man desperately desired to avoid the consequences of sin, he had no desire to submit to God's authority. As Athanasius notes, "having rejected what is good, [men] have invented nothings instead of the truth, and have ascribed the honor due to God and the knowledge concerning Him to demons and men in the form of stones." Even if he had a desire to submit to his Creator, man had no way to meet the requirements of God's justice and pay for his rebellion and sin, other than by his own death and damnation! In other words, man in Adam was doomed. Not a good situation!

Incarnation

Man's deplorable situation created what Athanasius aptly calls the "divine dilemma." God cannot repeal man's death sentence for treason because God's judgment is perfectly just. Yet this very judgment means the destruction of those who were created out of divine love, in the image of God, to take dominion of God's creation. Repentance alone is insufficient, for if God in His mercy simply forgave man without more, His justice in the form of the required death penalty would then be thwarted. This is unthinkable, since all the justice in the universe depends on the just character of God Himself.

Yet this dilemma did not take God by surprise, nor was it out of God's control. Athanasius quotes the apostle Paul in 1 Corinthians 1:21: "For since, in the wisdom of God, the world through wisdom did not know God, it pleased God through the foolishness of the message preached to save those who believe." From the very foundation of the world God decreed the most astonishing solution to the dilemma that would set in motion the amazing drama of the Incarnation. And He was rightly motivated to do so not only by His great love, but also for His honor and glory. Athanasius compares God to "a king who has founded a city," who does not neglect the city when it is on the verge of destruction because of the carelessness and misbehavior of its people, but rather "saves it from destruction, having regard rather to his own honor rather than to the people's neglect."

"O, that You would rend the heavens! That You would come down! . . . to make Your name [of *Savior*] known to Your adversaries, that the nations may tremble at Your presence!" cried the prophet Isaiah (Isa. 64:1–2). In the fullness of time God answered Isaiah's cry and solved the divine dilemma. The Father sent His Son, who "taking the form of a bondservant, and coming in the likeness of men . . . humbled Himself and became obedient to the point of death, even the death of the cross" (Phil. 2:7–8). The Son, who created and sustains the world and all things in it, humbled Himself immeasurably more than King Thrushbeard by permanently taking on a body and human nature, spilling His blood and surrendering His body to death in place of all humanity. Out of sheer love for us, He offered Himself as a "sacrifice free from every stain, that He forthwith abolished death for His human brethren." But the story does not end at the cross. His resurrection sealed forever the defeat of death "and freely graced us all with incorruption through the promise of the resurrection." In so doing God magnificently solved the divine dilemma, and established both His justice and His mercy. Above all it is the story of God's incomparable love that is revealed to us in the Incarnation. "Therefore God also has highly exalted [Christ] and given Him the name which is above every name, that at the name of Jesus every knee should bow, of those in heaven, and of those on earth, and of those under the earth, and that every tongue should confess that Jesus Christ is Lord, to the glory of God the Father" (Phil. 2:9–11).

One of Athanasius's most important insights is that God could not be true to Himself, nor bring about the actual redemption of the world, by simply waving His all powerful arm, so to speak, and dismissing our sin by saying to men "I forgive you." Imagine how tempted we would be to choose such a seemingly easy solution rather than take the difficult and arduous road that Christ took. This "let's just pretend" or "let's just forget about it" approach, however, fails to take reality seriously. It's a cheap and easy, but illusory, solution to a profoundly real problem that is ultimately contemptuous of God and His creation.

Most of us enjoy movies or video games or amusement rides which simulate or give the illusion of reality. One of the reasons is that we vicariously experience the thrill of some aspect of reality that, given the actual consequences, we would not really want to experience (like being shot at by real soldiers). But we really want (and need) to be saved, and it is impossible to be "virtually" saved from our sins. In a real war we are looking for a real solution, and illusory bullets would be worse than a useless defense. The real world involves real actions, real rights and wrongs, and real consequences—do not be fooled, says the apostle Paul in Galatians: whatever you sow you shall reap. True forgiveness is never a matter of saying "It's okay; it doesn't matter." It is the most costly thing in the world. And the real sin of men required as an antidote the real incarnation, suffering, death and resurrection of the Son of God, not some "philosophical truths" or "theological stories" about a dying and rising god which didn't really happen (a sort of virtual incarnation). The death and resurrection of Christ happened publicly, in history, for real ("[it] was not done in a corner," Paul tells King Agrippa), so that we might be saved.

Not only would the "let's just forget about it" approach have been no solution, it would have made man's situation even worse, if that were possible. On a much smaller scale, when parents take this approach with bad behavior, children end up behaving even worse. Similarly, when society fails to appropriately punish criminal behavior, criminals further victimize society with repeat offenses. In the case of the divine dilemma, the "let's just forget about it" approach repudiates the very foundation of all justice in the universe, the holy and just character of God Himself. Fortunately for the world, the God of Abraham, Isaac and Jacob is not a "virtual god" like the gods of the pagans, but the real God who did not and cannot repudiate His own holy and just character and so He sent His Son to suffer and pay the just price for the

The Virgin and Child in an Interior, c. 1430, from the workshop of Robert Campin.

sins of the real world on a real cross.

We only have space to mention a few of the momentous consequences of God's new humanity (the new Adam who inaugurates and fulfills the new covenant), assuring His people's bodily resurrection.

of this ultimate act of God's love for us. Through the Incarnation God has forever bound Himself with His people and confirmed the goodness of His creation. When God uses "good" to describe His actions and creation, He always means it in two complementary ways—good in what it is and good in its purpose in God's redemptive plan for the world. Jesus came to reconcile the world to Himself and thereby reunite the broken and shattered relationships between heaven and earth, man and himself, man and woman in marriage, man and his neighbor and man and creation. In so doing He is recreating the world, bringing freedom and order out of slavery and chaos. By conquering death through His bodily resurrection, Jesus became the first fruits

"The Word became Flesh" is relevant to us today only if God died on the cross for sinners. The Nativity has power because of the Crucifixion, as depicted in *The Sacrifice*, an 11′ x 16′ painting by Edward Knippers.

He also became the first fruits of the new creation, assuring the redemption and transformation of the whole world.

Not only was reconciliation and salvation accomplished in the Incarnation, but also the full disclosure of the Trinitarian God who reconciles and saves. This profound good news turned the ancient cultures of despair upside down. Athanasius himself witnessed the powerful effect of the gospel on ancient pagan peoples. It is hard for us, living in the aftermath of two thousand years of gospel influence, to fathom the despair and pessimism of pagan culture, although the current resurgence of neo-paganism coupled with the church's unfaithfulness has given us a small taste of such pessimism in our own culture. A favorite pagan Greek and Roman epitaph expressing this despair, so common it was often seen on tomb-stones in its initial letters, was: "I wasn't, I was, I am not, I don't care" (eerily, this sounds a lot like our own "Whatever . . .

never mind"). Now the great "I Am" has fully revealed Himself in love, forever banishing the despair of all those who place their hope in the Lord. Man is now freed by God's grace to understand the true story of the world and his place in it, be reconciled to his creator, and through the power of Christ's spirit act in concert with Christ to bring about the redemption of the whole world.

The Incarnation also inaugurated the never-ending kingdom of God that continues to grow and will eventually supplant all other kingdoms of this world. The church, as the bride of Christ and the visible expression on earth of the heavenly hosts, has a special role to play in the drama of the growing kingdom. Even as God is in the process of purifying and making His church more Christlike (as He does over the life of individual believers), His Spirit works through His imperfect people to fulfill the Great Commission. The church has been empowered by Christ's all-encompassing authority to "make disciples of all the nations" (literally, "disciple the nations," not just individuals), "baptizing them in the name of the Father and of the Son and of the Holy Spirit, teaching them to observe all things that I have commanded you" (Matt. 28:19–20). This is a command to spread Christ's kingdom, not by force like the Islamic parody of Christianity, but by the proclamation of the Word of Christ and by faithful obedience. Jesus tells us to take up our cross and follow Him because sometimes faithfulness will require self-sacrifice and suffering for the sake of the truth, just as it did throughout the life of Athanasius.

Christians today need to hear again Athanasius's message and take to heart the great privilege we have through Christ to be a part of God's kingdom work in history. The kingdom vision, the central focus of the Lord's Prayer, has largely been lost in the modern West due to the church's shriveled, distorted vision of Christianity and its failure to incarnate its faith in the real world. Just as Christ accomplished His greatest of works through the Incarnation, and just as Athanasius himself not only wrote about the Incarnation but incarnated his own faith in his life and works, so we have the great privilege and responsibility of incarnating *our* love for Christ in history by not just hearing His word but doing it in real life. God calls us to seek first the kingdom of God and His righteousness. Only then will we receive God's blessing. Only then can we hope for that unsurpassable reward of hearing our Lord and Savior say to us "well done, good and faithful servant." Let us pray that God will give us the courage he gave Athanasius in fulfilling His kingdom work in history.

—*William S. Dawson*

For Further Reading:

Anatolios, Khaled. *Athanasius: The Coherence of His Thought.* New York: Routledge, 1998.

Barnes, Timothy D. *Athanasius and Constantius: Theology and Politics in the Constantinian Empire.* New York: Routledge, 1993.

Pettersen, Alvyn. *Athanasius.* New York: Morehouse, 1996.

Session I: Prelude

A Question to Consider

What do you think is the most important event in history and why?

From the General Information above answer the following questions:

1. Describe the false teaching in the church that Athanasius fought against his entire life.
2. What is the Incarnation that is referred to in Athanasius's book?
3. What was the divine dilemma described in the book?
4. How did the Incarnation solve the divine dilemma?
5. Why is it important to understand the nature of creation in understanding the Incarnation?
6. Why is the Incarnation the most important event in history?

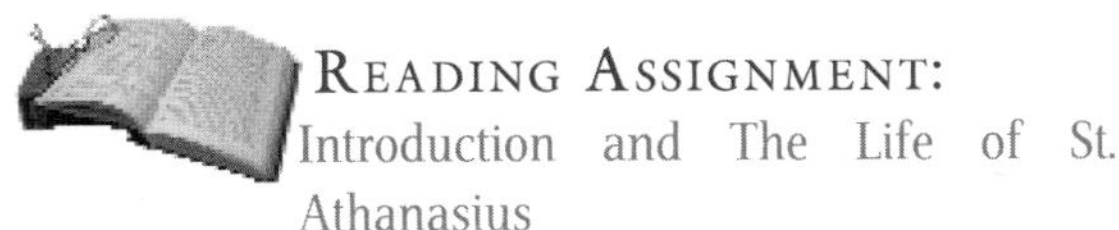

Reading Assignment:
Introduction and The Life of St. Athanasius

SESSION II: RECITATION

Introduction and The Life of St. Athanasius

Comprehension Questions

Answer the following questions for factual recall:

1. What is the "strange idea abroad" about reading books that C.S. Lewis refers to in the Introduction, and what is the cause of this "error?"
2. Why is it better to read the old books directly, according to Lewis?
3. If you must read only the new books or only the old books, which does Lewis advise that you read?
4. Why does Lewis say the old books are more important to read than the new books?
5. How many old books does Lewis recommend reading?
6. How can we see the unity in the core of Christianity according to Lewis?
7. Lewis says that when it looked like the whole of the civilized world was slipping back from Christianity into Arianism, Athanasius stood firm for what?
8. Why does Lewis think Athanasius's approach to miracles is needed especially in our time?
9. According to Lewis, what was it that Athanasius could point to confidently in his time regarding the life of Christians that we need to recover in our own time?
10. According to The Life of Athanasius, why was Athanasius so aware of the history of Christian martyrdom?
11. What had those persecutions done to many Alexandrian Christians?
12. Athanasius later wrote the life of the most famous of these early monastics, who was a great friend to Athanasius. What was his name?
13. "Athanasius always knew the real thing when he saw it" (Life of Athanasius). What is "the real thing?"

READING ASSIGNMENT:
Chapter 1

SESSION III: DISCUSSION

Chapter 1

A Question to Consider

Have you ever wished you could be recreated or remade and start your life all over? Why did you wish that?

Discuss or list short answers to the following questions:

Text Analysis

1. Who is responsible for the creation, order and sustenance of the world (sections 1 & 3)?
2. What were the various Greek views of creation about in the time of Athanasius (section 2)?
3. What was the status of man at the time of creation (section 3)?
4. What does the creation have to do with the Incarnation of the Son of God, which is the topic of our book (sections 1 & 4)?
5. What does Athanasius say about man's knowledge after the fall into sin (section 4)?
6. What did the dominion of death caused by sin unleash in the world (section 5)?
7. Why did the unbelieving Greeks deride the Incarnation (section 1)?

Cultural Analysis

1. What do most people in our culture believe about creation?
2. Why do so many people in our culture reject the Incarnation?
3. What does the modern church in our culture say about creation and the Incarnation?

Biblical Analysis

1. What does 1 John 4:1–6 say about how we know whether a person's spirit is of God?
2. Given this test, are persons or churches who claim to be Christian but deny the historical Incarnation of Christ, such as many liberal churches and Unitarians, Christian at all (1 John 4:1–6)?
3. For those who are "of God" and do confess the historical Incarnation of Christ, what does the apostle John promise (1 John 4:1–6)?
4. Athanasius explains that as a result of sin, man "lost the knowledge of God... [and thus] lost exis-

tence with it; for it is God alone Who exists, evil is non-being, the negation and antithesis of good." Is this a biblical explanation (Rom. 1)?

Summa

Write an essay or discuss this question, integrating what you have learned from the material above.

How should we understand the history of the Incarnation and its relationship to creation?

Optional Activity

Read more about the life of Athanasius from the internet or other resources and write a short essay of two to three paragraphs summarizing how Athanasius incarnated his faith in the real world.[1]

Reading Assignment:
Chapter 2

Pieter Bruegel the Elder was the greatest Flemish painter of the sixteenth century. He developed a unique style of oil painting that uniformly holds narrative together, as seen here in *The Adoration of the Kings*.

Session IV: Recitation

Chapter 2

Comprehension Questions

Answer the following questions for factual recall:

1. What "law" does Athanasius cite as following inevitably from man's rebellion in the fall (section 6)?
2. How did Athanasius describe the divine dilemma caused by man's fall (section 6)?
3. Why was repentance not sufficient to take care of the problem (section 7)?
4. Who was the only person who could restore humanity *and* meet the requirements of God's justice (section 7)?
5. What is the sense in which the Son of God had been and is always near and involved in the world (section 8)?
6. What was the new way in which the Son entered the world (section 8)?
7. What did the incarnate Son of God do on earth in His human body (section 8)?
8. How did Christ's death and resurrection abolish death for all believers (sections 9 & 10)?
9. What would have happened had the Son not become incarnate and dwelt among men (section 9)?

10. In Athanasius's analogy of the king who has founded a city, what is the primary motivation for the king to avenge the city and save it from destruction (section 10)?
11. Since Christ died for us, in what sense do all His followers die (section 10)?
12. How was Christ perfected for us and subsequently glorified by the Father (section 10)?
13. Who had the power of death and was subsequently conquered by the Incarnation of Christ (section 10)?

READING ASSIGNMENT:
Chapter 3

SESSION V: DISCUSSION

Chapter 3

A Question to Consider

Have you ever "incarnated" any thoughts, ideas or plans you had by making them happen in the real world?

Discuss or list short answers to the following questions:

Text Analysis

1. According to Athanasius, why was the state of man's knowledge of God in such deplorable condition after the fall (sections 11 & 12)?
2. What is the connection between man's problems related to the knowledge of God and the Incarnation of Jesus Christ (section 14)?
3. How did the Son of God reveal Himself as both a man and the ruler of all creation (sections 17 & 18)?
4. Why was the Son of God not defiled by taking on a human body and nature in the Incarnation (section 17)?

Cultural Analysis

1. How does our culture view the current state of man's knowledge about God?
2. How does our culture view the Incarnation of Jesus Christ?

Biblical Analysis

1. Why does our culture have such a difficult time understanding the truth of God and the Incarnation (Rom. 1)?
2. How do men become enlightened about the truth of God and the Incarnation (Rom. 1; 2 Cor. 1:21–22)?

SUMMA

Write an essay or discuss this question, integrating what you have learned from the material above.

How can we know that we are understanding the truth of God and the Incarnation in our lives?

READING ASSIGNMENT:
Chapters 4 & 5

SESSION VI: DISCUSSION

Chapters 4 & 5

A Question to Consider

Have you ever paid a debt that someone else owed? Or has someone else ever paid a debt you had? How is this like and unlike what Christ did for us in paying off our death penalty for sin?

Discuss or list short answers to the following questions:

Text Analysis

1. How does Athanasius understand Christ's atonement for us in His death and resurrection (section 20)?
2. What was so astounding and marvelous about Christ's death and resurrection? What happened to death because of it (section 20)?
3. For those who place their trust in Christ, what is the consequence from His death and resurrection (section 21)?
4. Why does Athanasius say there is no room for doubt concerning the effects of the resurrection of Christ (section 32)?

Cultural Analysis

1. Although our modern culture often denies the reality of sin, the reality creates continuous attempts

(conscious and unconscious) by society to atone for sin. What are some ways our culture attempts to atone for sin?
2. What is wrong with these attempts at atonement?

Biblical Analysis

1. Describe some key elements of Christ's atonement from the following passages: John 1:29, 3:16–18; 1 Peter 2:21–25; 2 Corinthians 5:17–21; Romans 3:23–25, 5:8–11.
2. How was Christ's atonement a sacrifice (Heb. 9:6–16, 13:9–13)?

Summa

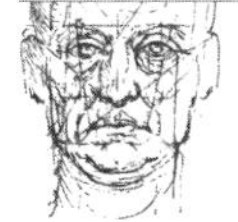

Write an essay or discuss this question, integrating what you have learned from the material above.

How did the death and resurrection of Christ atone for the sins of the world?

Optional Activity

Read about the different Old Testament sacrifices in Leviticus 1–7 and 16, and then read in Hebrews 9 and 10 about how Christ fulfilled these all. Write a short essay comparing the Old Testament sacrifices with Christ's final sacrifice, or make a chart comparing them.

Reading Assignment:
Chapter 6

Session VII: Activity

Chapter 6

In refuting the Jews of his time who denied Christ, Athanasius pointed to the Old Testament scriptures as proof that Jesus is the Messiah. He referenced the prophet Isaiah especially. Listen to George F. Handel's *Messiah* and identify the passages from the book of Isaiah and other biblical books about aspects of the Incarnation of Jesus Christ.[2]

1. In an early recitative of the *Messiah* the lines are from Isaiah 7:14. What does this verse foretell?
2. The King James Version of Isaiah 53:3 is sung in the *Messiah*. What does this verse tell us about Jesus' life during His ministry on earth?
3. A famous chorus entitled "Surely He Hath Borne Our Griefs" is taken from where in Isaiah?
4. In the "All we like sheep" chorus from Isaiah 53:6, what does the Lord do?
5. The famous "Hallelujah" chorus is taken from what biblical text?
6. The chorus that begins "Since by man came death" comes from what Pauline text?
7. "O Death, where is thy sting" begins a duet in Part Three of *Messiah*. This famous line is from where in the Bible? What famous English poet wrote a poem on this line?
8. The final chorus of *Messiah* is from what biblical text?

Reading Assignment:
Chapters 7 & 8

Session VIII: Recitation

Chapters 7 & 8

Comprehension Questions

Answer the following questions for factual recall:

1. Athanasius says the unbelief of the Jews of his day is refuted by what (section 33)?
2. What prophet foretold the virgin birth (section 33)?
3. From whose seed shall the Messiah come, according to the prophets (section 33)?
4. What amazing sign demonstrated Christ's rule of the universe even as He was humbling Himself and being born of a woman in a stable (section 37)?
5. What Old Testament prophet signifies the actual time of Christ's incarnation (sections 39 & 40)?
6. To what does Athanasius compare the Jews in their denial of Christ (section 39)?
7. Why are the Gentile unbelievers, especially the Greeks who pride themselves on their "reason," so unreasonable when "they deny that there is a Word of God at all" (section 41)?
8. Why is it not incredible that God the Son is capable of becoming incarnated as a man (section 42)?
9. What is the only creature in creation to have "erred from the path of God's purpose for it" (section 43)?

10. Why didn't God save man the same way He created Him, simply by "the mere signification [word] of His will" (sections 44 & 45)
11. According to Athanasius, how has Christ manifested Himself as God so as to drive all other gods out of consideration (section 45)?

READING ASSIGNMENT:
Chapter 9

SESSION IX: RECITATION

Chapter 9

Comprehension Questions

Answer the following questions for factual recall:

1. What does Athanasius recommend that Macarius (and by implication all his readers) do after reading *On the Incarnation* (section 56)?
2. What does Athanasius claim about the Scriptures (section 56)?
3. Who does Athanasius say he learned from (section 56)?
4. What does Athanasius say about Christ's "second manifestation to us" (section 56)?
5. What will Christ's final bodily manifestation to us in history entail (section 56)?
6. What does the apostle Paul say about the final judgment (section 56)?
7. What has Christ in store for His faithful when the redemption is complete (section 57)?
8. What does Athanasius say is a requirement for the "right understanding" of the Scriptures (section 57)?
9. If we cleanse our own lives, and copy the lives of the saints, what will be the result, according to Athanasius (section 57)?

"And this will be a sign for you: you will find a babe wrapped in swaddling cloths and lying in a manger."

SESSION X: EVALUATION

All tests and quizzes are to be given with an open book and a Bible available.

Grammar

Answer each of the following questions in complete sentences. Some answers may be longer than others. (2 points per answer)

1. What is the Incarnation referred to in Athanasius's book?
2. How did Athanasius describe the divine dilemma caused by man's fall?
3. What did the incarnate Son of God do on earth in His human body?
4. Since Christ died for us, in what sense do all his followers die?
5. What amazing sign demonstrated Christ's rule of the universe even as He was humbling Himself and being born of a woman in a stable?
6. To what does Athanasius compare the Jews in their denial of Christ?
7. Why is the Incarnation the most important event in history?

Logic

Answer the following question in complete sentences; your answer should be a paragraph or so. Answer two of the three questions. (10 points per answer)

1. What does the creation have to do with the Incarnation of the Son of God, which is the topic of our book?
2. How did the Son of God reveal Himself as both a man and the ruler of all creation?
3. What was so astounding and marvelous about Christ's death and resurrection?

Lateral Thinking

Write up to a thousand-word essay on one of the two questions below. (16 points)

1. In what ways do the actions of the early martyrs described in Eusebius's *Church History* reveal the incarnation of faith in history?
2. What is the relationship of the destruction of Jerusalem in A.D. 70 with the Incarnation of Christ?

Optional Session A: Analysis

Foreshadowing the Incarnation

The entire Old Testament scriptures point to and foreshadow the Incarnation of our Lord Jesus. Athanasius especially focuses on Isaiah's foretelling of the Incarnation of Christ. Another prophet who foretold and foreshadowed the Incarnation of Christ was Jeremiah. Read the following excerpts about Jeremiah from the *Omnibus I* essay on the Book of Jeremiah.

[Jeremiah] begins his ministry at [a time of great crisis in Judah] . . .. All kinds of moral and religious wickedness were caused by Manasseh, Judah's most evil king (686–643 B.C.). King Josiah made great reforms (641–609 B.C.) with the rediscovery of a scroll of the Law (perhaps Deuteronomy) (2 Kings 22–23). Still, the reforms lasted only a short time and were somewhat external. Then Jehoiakim (609–597 B.C.), Josiah's son, returned to idolatry and even practiced child sacrifice. Jehoiakim disregarded the warnings of the Lord spoken by Jeremiah (Jer. 36). He even burned the written prophecies of Jeremiah. Then Jehoiachin, son of Jehoiakim, acted wickedly, too. When Nebuchadnezzar attacked Jerusalem in 597, Jehoiachin was taken captive along with the nobility of Jerusalem, as the city was largely plundered (2 Kings 24:1–17). In 2 Kings 24:17, the text says, "Then the king of Babylon made Mattaniah, Jehoiachin's uncle, king in his place, and changed his name to Zedekiah." Despite Jeremiah's warnings, Zedekiah rebelled against Nebuchadnezzar in 589 B.C. because he listened to false prophets promising deliverance. He heard the message that he wanted to hear: "Peace, peace." Then Nebuchadnezzar attacked Jerusalem, and after eighteen months of breaking into the walls, destroyed it, along with the palace and the Temple. Most of the people of Judah were taken into captivity in Babylon (586 B.C.) . . .. Jeremiah 1:9–10 records the very mission of Jeremiah:

Then the LORD put forth His hand and touched my mouth, and the LORD said to me: "Behold, I have put My words in your mouth.
See, I have this day set you over the nations and over the kingdoms,
To root out and to pull down,
To destroy and to throw down,
To build and to plant."

. . . Therefore thus says the LORD
God of hosts:
"Because you speak this word,
Behold, I will make My words in
your mouth fire,
And this people wood,
And it shall devour them.
Behold, I will bring a nation
against you from afar,
O house of Israel . . .(5:14–15)".

Jeremiah provides a very direct picture of man in Adam, the human condition. In the very well-known words of Jeremiah 17:9, "The heart is deceitful above all things, And desperately wicked; Who can know it?"

. . . Jeremiah condemns many sins of idolatry, including the sacrifice of children to the honor of Baal–Molech (7:31; 19:5; 32:35) and the worship of "the queen of heaven" (7:18; 44:19). Jeremiah denounces sins of immorality, such as dishonesty, injustice, oppression of the helpless, and slander. These violations of God's law become a covenant lawsuit against the representatives of the people, the priests and prophets.

Thankfully, Jeremiah shows us the Savior of such sinful people. In many cases Jeremiah parallels the actions of Jesus Christ in His earthly ministry. Words from Jeremiah (chapter 7) are spoken by Christ in the "cleansing of the temple" when He attacked the money-changers. When Jesus attacked false religious practices in Jerusalem, He was saying what Jeremiah had said: this place will be destroyed. This is what had already happened in Jeremiah's day (to Shiloh, 7:12). Christ's words parallel this with the promised judgment of the destruction of Jerusalem.

> Assuredly, I say to you, all these things will come upon this generation. O Jerusalem, Jerusalem, the one who kills the prophets and stones those who are sent to her! How often I wanted to gather your children together, as a hen gathers her chicks under her wings, but you were not willing! See! Your house is left to you desolate (Matt. 23:36–38).

Just as Jeremiah was rejected, so Christ was rejected. The Scriptures say of our Lord, "He came to His own, and His own did not receive Him" (John 1:11). Jesus gave the same message and acted like Jeremiah warning that Jerusalem would be destroyed. In the center of Jeremiah's book of warnings and weeping, he links the covenant-breaking people of Judah with the promised hope of a new covenant. This new covenant is central for the people of God today, since Christ is the mediator of the new covenant (Heb. 8:6). The very name of the second portion of the Scriptures proclaiming Christ's actions is the New Testament (an older term sometimes used for covenant).

Discuss or write a short essay on how Jeremiah's ministry foreshadowed and paralleled the earthly ministry of Christ.

Optional Session B: Activity

Look up these passages from the Gospel of John, where Christ says He has, is, or will do things in obedience to the Father. For each passage, identify the obedience being shown by the Son, and what the passage tells us about the relationship of the Father and the Son, using your answers to fill in chart 1.

Chart 1: **CHRIST'S OBEDIENCE AND RELATIONSHIP TO THE FATHER**

PASSAGE IN JOHN	OBEDIENCE SHOWN BY THE SON	WHAT THIS TELLS US ABOUT THE RELATIONSHIP BETWEEN THE FATHER AND THE SON
John 5:30		
John 6:38–40		
John 8:28		
John 10:17–18		
John 10:37–38		
John 12:49–50		
John 14:10		
John 14:24		
John 14:31		
John 15:9		
John 15:15		
John 20:21		

Endnotes

1 Find more biographical information about Athanasius through Links 1 and 2 for this chapter at www.VeritasPress.com/OmniLinks.

2 If you don't have access to a recording, some websites with audio clips of Handel's *Messiah* may be found through Links 3 and 4 for this chapter at www.VeritasPress.com/OmniLinks. Veritas Press also has the CD available at Link 5.

The Creeds

Once upon a time there were three chickens named Pete, Roger and Don. All of them were faced with the same problem. Lately, a fox had been seen at the edge of the forest not far from their chicken coop. The entire roost wondered what they should do to keep the fox at bay.

Each chicken had a different plan.

The coop first considered Pete's advice because he seemed to have the most energy. Pete called for proactive measures to be taken. *Proactive* is a word popular in books that your father probably reads if he is a businessman. It means that you need to anticipate what is going to happen and fix potential problems before they are real problems. While some might claim that *proactive* means clairvoyant or prophetic, it really just means what it looks like it means: you are *active* before (Latin *pro*) something happens.

Pete's plan involved building a higher fence around the chicken coop. He pushed for a lot of new taxes, a standing army and a certain strange contraption known as the egg launcher that was supposed to give the chickens what he called "a strategic advantage" over the fox.

While it is a good idea to always be prepared, it can go overboard. (One has only to be wanded endlessly by a turbaned Sikh at the security checkpoint at O'Hare Airport in Chicago—if I had only had a camera—to realize that sometimes proactivity can be overdone.) What's worse is that no one—besides God—can build a fool-proof system. Any system of defense or protection created by a human (or a rather bright chicken in this case) can be overcome simply by time, persistence and rationality on the part of an equally talented human (or a crafty fox).

The chickens also considered Roger's plan as well. His plan was reactive. Moms are usually reactive people—particularly if they have a few

young children. Reactive people see circumstances and react to them. A baby cries; mom feeds it. Jimmy scrapes his knee; mom puts on the bandage. Roger claimed that seeing the fox in the woods was no big problem and that having a standing army, drafting hens and having daily drills was "over the top." What the chickens needed to do was to be vigilant and keep watch to make sure that the fox did not come into the coop and they needed to sound the alarm if the fox did get in.

To be safe the chickens opted to combine the plans of Proactive Pete and Reactive Roger, but all did not go as planned. During one of Pete's "simulated fox invasions," a mass panic erupted when it was discovered that the fourteen-foot-high chicken wire fence could be tunneled under quite easily. Thus, massive depression set in. To add to that depression, Roger's reactive plan also showed signs of failure. This occurred when the fox made his first invasion. Unfortunately for Roger's plan, a rather dense young rooster named Eggbert was on the watch. He saw the fox coming but did not sound the alarm because he knew all of the trouble that Pete's proactive plan had caused and he knew that he was told not to sound the alarm unless the fox was *"in"* the chicken coop. So, he watched the fox dig under the coop and sounded the alarm only when the sly fiend had actually burrowed completely under the fence. In what must have seemed a mixture of ironic justice and sheer mercy, only Eggbert was eaten.

This, however, points up the problem in reactive systems. They demand vigilance and wisdom. Fools either over-react or react in a dim-witted manner and cause the system to fail. Thus it was in the case of Roger's defenses.

Finally, after Eggbert was eulogized, Don stepped to the center of the coop and clucked loudly, "Both plans have failed! Pete's proactive plan has failed to provide safety and wore us all out, and Roger's reactive plan failed and led to Eggbert's tragic demise." Many seemed to agree. "I have a new plan," he announced, "my plan is that we do nothing. We had no problem before we started making all these plans." He even argued that chickens release a strange scent when they were afraid that actually attracted foxes. So, Don counseled that they should do nothing, and they all agreed.

So, the foolish chickens planned to have no plan, hoping that utter ignorance would keep the fox at bay. Sadly, they did not realize that Don had made "an arrangement" with the wily fox that was bringing him the best feed that the fox could steal from the barn in exchange for his help. One by one the chickens disappeared. Don was the fattest and the last to go.

The moral of this story is that no defense provides all of the answers, but any defense is better than none (or, beware of the fat chicken who is ignored by the fox).

Over the centuries the church has faced many false teachers and teachings. In the past our wise forefathers have tried many different strategies to protect the church from what Paul called "savage wolves" (Acts 20:29) and what John called the spirit of antichrist (1 John 4:3). Some of them used proactive strategies by making baptismal vows that guarded the membership at the "front door" of the church. In other circumstances, when the first line of defense failed, courageous men like Athanasius manned the ramparts and *reacted* to heresy that was threatening to overwhelm the church. Their faithfulness protected and kept pure the gospel so that you and I could hear it and live. If they would have failed, we would have been lost in darkness. So, for the sake of Christ and for our great benefit they bore death, exile, removal from office and mockery.

Today, many church leaders have taken the plan of Do-Nothing Don and executed it almost flawlessly. The only thing that they will condemn is anyone who condemns anything, and so the fox is well fed, and we are unprotected.

GENERAL INFORMATION

Author and Context

The creeds that we will examine have no single author. The Apostles' Creed was attributed to the Twelve Apostles, but this is most likely not true. It was a baptismal creed that was in use in a basic form in the church at Rome by the year A.D. 150. When someone old enough to learn and recite the Creed was baptized in Rome, he would answer a few questions concerning what he believed. The answer to these questions was the Apostles' Creed. The Nicene Creed was penned at the famous Council of Nicea in A.D. 325. The Definition of Chalcedon was written by the Fourth Ecumenical Council in A.D. 451. (The term *ecumenical* means that representative bishops from the entire church attended the council.)

The author of these creeds in a holistic sense is the church, and they reflect her wisdom. The Apostles' Creed amazingly developed as the church hid in the catacombs and died in the Coliseum. It was proactive. The other two were reactive and became necessary as the false teachings of Arius almost overcame the church and as the heresies of Apollinarius, Nestorius and Eutyches divided the church (especially in the East).

Significance

The importance of the creeds is profound and has had a profound affect on all believers. These creeds outlined the faith for believers and helped Christians to systematically remember and articulate foundational matters about God and the gospel.

More than anything else the focus of the creeds is on the person of Christ. Not surprisingly, the Incarnation overwhelmed both the thoughts and imaginations of men, and as the gospel went out into the West many misunderstandings arose[1] Was Jesus God? Was He man? A robot? A ghost? A mix? There were many attempted explanations.

Many misunderstandings had their roots in Greek philosophy and were avoided in the Western part of the West (i.e., Latin Europe). The Greek-speaking church continually tried to use words that they had to borrow from Greek philosophy. It was difficult for the church to replace with more biblical concepts the meanings that the philosophers had given to words like *person, substance* and *being*. In the West, much of this controversy was avoided because of the insights of Tertullian, a brilliant early father who nailed many issues concerning the Trinity (he invented the word *Trinitas*[2]) and Christ (he coined the phrase "two Substances in one Person, united without confusion, and distinct in their operations"). While this might seem tedious or trivial, he saved everybody west of the Adriatic a lot of headaches.

Main Characters

The main character in the creeds is the Divine Trinity. The Apostles' and Nicene Creeds are structured after the pattern of the Trinity and have

The Trinity is shown in this detail from *Baptism of Christ* by sculptor and painter Andrea del Verrocchio (1435–1488).

three parts. The Definition of Chalcedon focuses on the person of Christ.

Most of the controversies in the early church had to do with wrong understandings of who Jesus was. For this reason, the paragraph in the Creeds that describes the Son is, by far, the longest, and the entire Definition of Chalcedon sets forth teaching about Jesus Christ. Against the heretics these creeds affirmed that Jesus was fully God, fully man and a historical figure. These creeds united believers and differentiated them from those who would not confess the truth about Jesus.

Setting

These creeds came into a world in which the gospel had overcome the persecuting empire of Rome. Emperor Constantine, who received baptism on his deathbed, ended the persecution of Christians by signing the Edict of Milan in A.D. 313. Suddenly, Christians, who had been meeting in catacombs, could come out and literally see the light of day.

As Christians saw the end of the persecution, however, they quickly found that Satan's new tactic to stop the spread of the gospel was even more sinister. Instead of persecuting the church from the outside, the devil raised up dissension and division among believers and introduced false teaching about Christ.

In order to deal with this new challenge the church met together and sought to see the truth in the Scriptures and end division where it could. When the church meets in a meeting with representative elders and bishops, this meeting is called an Ecumenical Council. There have been seven of these councils in the history of the church. The first and the last was in Nicea, three of the other five were in Constantinople and there was one in Ephesus and another in Chalcedon. Today, unfortunately, divisions in the church make Ecumenical Councils virtually impossible.

THE APOSTLES' CREED

I BELIEVE IN GOD THE FATHER ALMIGHTY, MAKER OF HEAVEN AND EARTH; AND IN JESUS CHRIST HIS ONLY SON OUR LORD; WHO WAS CONCEIVED BY THE HOLY GHOST, BORN OF THE VIRGIN MARY, SUFFERED UNDER PONTIUS PILATE, WAS CRUCIFIED, DEAD, AND BURIED; HE DESCENDED INTO HELL; THE THIRD DAY HE ROSE AGAIN FROM THE DEAD; HE ASCENDED INTO HEAVEN, AND SITTETH ON THE RIGHT HAND OF GOD THE FATHER ALMIGHTY; FROM THENCE HE SHALL COME TO JUDGE THE QUICK AND THE DEAD. I BELIEVE IN THE HOLY GHOST; THE HOLY CATHOLIC CHURCH; THE COMMUNION OF SAINTS; THE FORGIVENESS OF SINS; THE RESURRECTION OF THE BODY; AND THE LIFE EVERLASTING. AMEN.

Worldview

I once heard a speech given by a man who had had a very important job. His job involved doing nothing. He just walked around carried a briefcase and did nothing. He had his own professional security detail. If anyone approached him in a threatening manner, the bodyguards would have killed the person immediately. He was so important that no one could stay in a hotel room with him unless they had high level security clearance. Once he was staying in a hotel room with a man he did not like, and he found out that the man was a Canadian. He let the guards know, and they forced the hotel to separate them.

He must have been an important man, right?

Actually, he was not. He did, however, carry very important information. In that briefcase, which was handcuffed to his wrist every waking hour, were the launch codes for the nuclear arsenal of the United States. He traveled with the President just in case the codes were needed. Had someone gotten control of the briefcase, they would have been one step closer to launching missiles that could have destroyed millions of lives. So this man, an admiral, was intensely protected.

People guard whatever is precious to them. If you do not guard something, then it probably doesn't really mean a lot to you. Parents often carry large amounts of life insurance simply to protect their children. Money is kept in vaults. Briefcases are chained to the arms of men carrying launch codes because we protect what is important.

Long ago a treasure of inestimable value was delivered to our forefathers. It was called the gospel of Jesus Christ. Most of them came out of a hopeless way of life serving gods of wood and stone or knowing like the urbane, sophisticated Romans that all pagan religion was hopeless. Because they knew the futility of their way of life, they appreciated the gospel in a way that we can probably not even fathom. And so they protected it, because they wanted to give it to us. All of us who have received it owe them a debt that it would take an eternity to repay. Any cursory survey of church history should lead us to this conclusion: Creeds have been one of God's chief means of protecting the gospel.

The wise men who formulated the creeds protected the gospel proactively and reactively. First, they protected the membership of the church by forcing people to affirm truths about Jesus when they passed through the waters of baptism. The word creed comes from the Latin word *credo,* meaning "I believe." This was the first word that a person would have said as they affirmed their faith before the Roman Church. To get into the church the old baptismal creeds were hoops that one had to jump through. Many heretics were kept outside the church by words like "conceived by the Holy Ghost of the Virgin Mary, suffered under Pontius Pilate . . ." knowing that they could never affirm them.

Others protected the flock reactively. When heresy cropped up in the church, councils defined the faith in ways that clarified the truth and forced the ravenous wolves out of the church. The flock was spared and the gospel rolled down through the ages toward us.

We are going to consider the three most important creeds of the ancient church: the Apostles' Creed, the Nicene Creed and the Definition of Chalcedon. The Apostles' Creed was a baptismal creed of the Roman Church, which both precedes and comes after the Nicene Creed. How so? It was clearly in use before the Council of Nicea in A.D. 325, but it did not reach its final form until after the Nicene Creed was formulated. The Nicene Creed was the product of the great council that stemmed the tide of Arianism in the church. Finally, the Definition of Chalcedon further clarified church teaching on Jesus Christ.

Creeds were intimately connected to the errors of their day. A baptismal creed like the Apostles' Creed uses phrases to distinguish truth from error; let's examine a couple of the heresies that caused the church to pen these great statements of faith.

The Docetic Heresy: Jesus is a ghost

This was the belief of people called Docetic Gnostics.[3] They grasped half of the truth. They believed that Jesus was God, but denied that He was a real man. They said that He looked like a man, but that really He was a ghost. (In our day, many educated unbelievers are happy to admit that Jesus was a man, but they deny that He was God. Strikingly, the original heretics closest to Jesus' actual teaching were not foolish enough to make this mistake.) They said this because the Greek philosophers had convinced them that spirit was good and that flesh, or the material world, was evil. God, they reasoned, would never take on *real* flesh. For them, such a thought was blasphemy.

The apostle John dealt with these people and might have even started us on the way to a creed when he set up a test of orthodoxy to root out these Docetic heretics. In 1 John 4:2–3, he says:

> By this you know the Spirit of God: Every spirit that confesses that Jesus Christ has come in the flesh is of God, and every spirit that does not confess that Jesus Christ has come in the flesh is not of God. And this is the spirit of the Antichrist, which you have heard was coming, and is now already in the world.

It was not enough to claim that you loved Jesus. One had to affirm that Jesus came *in the flesh.*

This prevalent heresy was one of the factors that caused the Roman Church to make everyone it baptized affirm this creed, asking each one "Christian, what do you believe?" The person who was being baptized would answer using the words of the Apostles' Creed (see the text in the sidebar on the previous page).

THE NICENE CREED

WE BELIEVE IN ONE GOD THE FATHER ALMIGHTY, MAKER OF HEAVEN AND EARTH, AND OF ALL THINGS VISIBLE AND INVISIBLE; AND IN ONE LORD JESUS CHRIST, THE ONLY-BEGOTTEN SON OF GOD, BEGOTTEN OF HIS FATHER BEFORE ALL WORLDS, GOD OF GOD, LIGHT OF LIGHT, VERY GOD OF VERY GOD, BEGOTTEN, NOT MADE, BEING OF ONE SUBSTANCE WITH THE FATHER; BY WHOM ALL THINGS WERE MADE; WHO FOR US MEN, AND FOR OUR SALVATION, CAME DOWN FROM HEAVEN, AND WAS INCARNATE BY THE HOLY GHOST OF THE VIRGIN MARY, AND WAS MADE MAN; AND WAS CRUCIFIED ALSO FOR US UNDER PONTIUS PILATE; HE SUFFERED AND WAS BURIED, AND THE THIRD DAY HE ROSE AGAIN ACCORDING TO THE SCRIPTURES, AND ASCENDED INTO HEAVEN, AND SITTETH ON THE RIGHT HAND OF THE FATHER; AND HE SHALL COME AGAIN WITH GLORY TO JUDGE BOTH THE QUICK AND THE DEAD; WHOSE KINGDOM SHALL HAVE NO END. AND WE BELIEVE IN THE HOLY GHOST, THE LORD AND GIVER OF LIFE, WHO PROCEEDETH FROM THE FATHER AND THE SON, WHO WITH THE FATHER AND THE SON TOGETHER IS WORSHIPED AND GLORIFIED; WHO SPAKE BY THE PROPHETS. AND WE BELIEVE IN ONE HOLY CATHOLIC AND APOSTOLIC CHURCH; WE ACKNOWLEDGE ONE BAPTISM FOR THE REMISSION OF SINS; AND WE LOOK FOR THE RESURRECTION OF THE DEAD, AND THE LIFE OF THE WORLD TO COME. AMEN.

The text of the Apostles' Creed proclaims that Jesus was a real man who lived in a real place and died a real death. He was born of a real woman, and, in an odd turn of providence, the name of a pagan unbeliever, Pontius Pilate, is part of the great Christian confessions because early believers wanted to make the point utterly clear. Jesus was a man, not a ghost.

The Apostles' Creed also sets the basic form of a creed. In the ancient creeds Christians affirmed the Trinity. "I believe in God the Father Almighty... and in Jesus Christ, His only Son, our Lord...I believe in the Holy Ghost." This great mystery of a God in Whom dwelt both unity and diversity sat at the root and core of the faith that they confessed.

As the tide of Docetism waned, however, a new and more dangerous heresy arose.

The Arian Heresy: Jesus is the greatest creature, but is not God

Arius was a popular teacher in Alexandria. He taught that the Logos (the word used of Christ in John's Gospel) was the first and greatest created being. This Logos existed before anything else in the universe, except God—who is the only eternal being. While Arius and his followers revered Jesus Christ as the physical manifestation of this Logos, they did not believe that He was fully God.

What made it even worse was the Arius had a catchy jingle (always beware of theological jingles). It had one prominent lyric: *There was a time when he was not.* The *he* in this statement was Jesus. Arius taught that there was a time when the Son of God did not exist. He was the best and brightest creature, but not the equal of God the Father. Everyone loved his jingle and sang it as they paraded in support of Arius.

Because of the unrest caused by Arius's teaching, Emperor Constantine asked bishops from every part of the church to come to the town of Nicea and meet together to settle the theological controversy and bring peace back to the empire.

The bishops met, but initially they could not find language that would force the Arians out of the church. They tried Scripture verses, but as quickly as the orthodox would quote a Scripture, the Arians would re-interpret it to favor (or make room for) their teaching. Finally, led by Alexander, the bishop of Alexandria, and his able assistant Athanasius, in 325 the council settled on final language for the Nicene Creed (see the text in the sidebar on the previous page).

The section about Christ dominates this creed and is crafted so that Arians can not affirm it. It describes Christ as "God of God, Light of Light, very God of very God, begotten, not made, being of one substance with the Father." These phrases make it clear that Jesus is fully God.

As the council was crafting the Nicene Creed, all of the gospel hinged on one letter in one word of the creed. That word is the Greek word *homoousios,* which we translate as "being of one substance with the Father." The Arians were in favor of using the word *homoiousios* which means "being of similar substance with the Father." Can you even see the difference between the two words? It is only an *i.* In Greek it is the letter *iota.* If the council would have chosen to go along with the Arians, the creed would have ended up saying that Jesus was "similar to God"—similar to but not the same as and definitely not equal to the Father. When the Arians saw the word homoousios, however, they knew that they had lost. The church was affirming that Jesus was fully God.

As one might notice, the Nicene is very similar to the Apostles' Creed, but with some minor additions and what appear to be minor subtractions.[4] One difference is that the Nicene Creed is a creed made by a council not an individual baptismal vow, so the pronouns used are "we" instead of "I."

The Nicene Creed was a great step forward in protecting the gospel, but still other heresies arose.

The Apollinarian Heresy: Jesus is a divine robot

After Nicea, the church still struggled to explain what Jesus really was. A bishop of Laodicea named Apollinarius came up with his own answer. He affirmed that Jesus was fully God (just as the Nicene Creed stated). He also said that Jesus had a real human body, but, he claimed, Jesus' intellect was not like ours. It had been replaced by the divine nature. To put it simply, Jesus had a human body, but instead of a human soul He had the Spirit of God running His body. He was sort of like a robot or a cyborg (one that looks fully human but is a robot on the inside). Of course, Apollinarius was not saying that Jesus was full of circuits and wires. He was saying that Jesus' humanity was different from ours. We have both a body and a soul. He had only a human body.

While at first glance this might not seem objectionable, Gregory Nazianzus pointed out the flaw in Apollinarius's thinking:

> For that which He had not taken up, He has not saved. He saved that which He joined to His divinity. If only half of Adam had fallen, then it would be possible for Christ to take up and save only half. But if the entire human nature fell, all of it must be united to the Word in order to be saved as a whole.[5]

Gregory knew that Jesus only redeemed that which He Himself was. If Jesus was only a human body without a normal human soul, then only our bodies were redeemed by Him. But, Gregory reasoned, this is not the case, so we know that Apollinarius is wrong.

The Nestorian Heresy: Jesus is two persons; one human, the other divine

Nestorius, the Patriarch of Constantinople, was the next to lead a heretical movement. He moved away from the error of Apollinarius but went too far in the other direction, saying that Jesus was fully human (with both a body and soul) and fully divine, but that these two natures, the human and divine natures of Jesus, meant that really Jesus was two persons, a human person and a divine one.

He stumbled into this position as he sought to explain what Mary is. In the ancient church, Mary, the mother of Jesus, was given the title *theotokos*, or Mother of God. This title originally was connected not to the veneration and worship of Mary (as it seems to be today in some Catholic circles), but to questions about the nature of Jesus. What was born of Mary? Was it God or something else? The early church correctly answered that Mary's firstborn Son was, in fact, God; thus, Mary was the Mother of God. Nestorius claimed that Mary should not be called *theotokos*, but instead, *christotokos*, or the Mother of Christ. While this was certainly true, it meant a great deal that Nestorius would not affirm that Jesus was God, but instead just said that He was Christ. Drawing a distinction between Christ and God seemed wrongheaded and ill-advised.

This position immediately raised a number of questions. What was the connection between these two persons? Was the earthly Jesus God? Isn't the Christ also God? Eventually, Nestorianism was condemned. And to be entirely fair, it should be mentioned that some scholars believe that Nestorius himself was not really a Nestorian.

The Eutychian Heresy: Jesus is a mix of God and man

Eutyches, an unlearned monk in Constantinople, added the final heresy for our present consideration. His confused view read too much into that all-important phrase in the Nicene Creed *"being of one substance with the Father."* He claimed that this meant that Jesus was one substance with the Father, but not with us. He also claimed that Christ had two natures (human and divine) before the Incarnation and only one afterward. It was as if Christ's human nature was blended into the divine.

The Final Response: The Definition of Chalcedon

During this time, two schools of thought vied for theological dominance. These schools were named after the cities associated with them: Alexandria and Antioch. The *Alexandrine* school upheld Christ's divinity scrupulously, but at times this school was comfortable compromising his humanity. Those of the other school, the *Antiochenes*, upheld Christ's humanity, sometimes at the expense of His deity. Docetism and Eutychianism bothered the Antiochenes. Apollinarianism and Nestorianism angered the *Alexandrines.* Both sides battled for control. As these factions warred, the Western Church, usually represented by the Roman Pope, became more powerful, because they always seemed to be casting the deciding vote (Alexandria and Antioch always voted against each other).

Finally, a sly bishop of Alexandria named Dioscorus decided to put a political end to all of the debates. He engineered a "council" that would once and for all cement the Alexandrine position as the truly orthodox one. He so thoroughly controlled the council that only those who agreed with him were allowed to speak. When Flavian, the aged representative of the Pope, brought a letter to be read to the assembly, he was roughed up so badly that he died a few days later. The Antiochene school was condemned, and no one holding Antiochene positions could be ordained. Many appealed to Emperor Theodosius III because of Dioscorus's strong-armed tactics. The crafty bishop had already won the emperor's support by bribing him with a literal boatload of gold. People in Antioch were furious. The bishop of Rome was enraged and called the previous meeting "a robber's synod," but it seemed that Alexandria had triumphed once and for all.

But then something unexpected happened. Theodosius fell off his horse, broke his neck and died. His successor and sister Pulcheria was not satisfied with the outcome of the most recent council, and so she and her husband Marcian called a new one in the year A.D. 451. Nestorius and Dioscorus were condemned and a new creed was written. The Definition of Chalcedon sought to settle the disagreement about who Christ was (see the text in the sidebar on this page).

Finally, the church had spoken clearly and definitively: Christ is fully God and fully man—not a mix, a confusion or something that was different from God or man. Thus, Jesus is the equal of God the Father. In His divinity He is just like the Father. In His humanity, He is just like us, having both a human body and a human soul.

Although many controversies continued to rage,

THE DEFINITION OF CHALCEDON

THEREFORE, FOLLOWING THE HOLY FATHERS, WE ALL WITH ONE ACCORD TEACH MEN TO ACKNOWLEDGE ONE AND THE SAME SON, OUR LORD JESUS CHRIST, AT ONCE COMPLETE IN GODHEAD AND COMPLETE IN MANHOOD, TRULY GOD AND TRULY MAN, CONSISTING ALSO OF A REASONABLE SOUL AND BODY; OF ONE SUBSTANCE WITH THE FATHER AS REGARDS HIS GODHEAD, AND AT THE SAME TIME OF ONE SUBSTANCE WITH US AS REGARDS HIS MANHOOD; LIKE US IN ALL RESPECTS, APART FROM SIN; AS REGARDS HIS GODHEAD, BEGOTTEN OF THE FATHER BEFORE THE AGES, BUT YET AS REGARDS HIS MANHOOD BEGOTTEN, FOR US MEN AND FOR OUR SALVATION, OF MARY THE VIRGIN, THE GOD-BEARER; ONE AND THE SAME CHRIST, SON, LORD, ONLY-BEGOTTEN, RECOGNIZED IN TWO NATURES, WITHOUT CONFUSION, WITHOUT CHANGE, WITHOUT DIVISION, WITHOUT SEPARATION; THE DISTINCTION OF NATURES BEING IN NO WAY ANNULLED BY THE UNION, BUT RATHER THE CHARACTERISTICS OF EACH NATURE BEING PRESERVED AND COMING TOGETHER TO FORM ONE PERSON AND SUBSISTENCE, NOT AS PARTED OR SEPARATED INTO TWO PERSONS, BUT ONE AND THE SAME SON AND ONLY-BEGOTTEN GOD THE WORD, LORD JESUS CHRIST; EVEN AS THE PROPHETS FROM EARLIEST TIMES SPOKE OF HIM, AND OUR LORD JESUS CHRIST HIMSELF TAUGHT US, AND THE CREED OF THE FATHERS HAS HANDED DOWN TO US.

the early creedal work of the church did much to protect the gospel.

Still, many today want nothing to do with creeds. They blame doctrine and conviction for the sad divisions in the church and run from anything that smacks of making others sound wrong about anything. They have a myriad of objections, but I will deal with only a few:

The first, most prominent objection which lies at the root of the other objections is that creeds lead to division. On the surface this seems quite true, but in many ways it misses the point. Division is going to come. The question is from whom we as believers will be divided and with whom we will be united. Today, we have a promiscuous desire to join with everything and be divided from nothing. In some situations if someone says that an atheist lesbian should not be a pastor, they are castigated and condemned as being closed-minded. What a world we live in!

Today, the outcome of this fuzzy thinking can be clearly seen. We, as a church, are not divided from anything, and thus we stand for nothing. We have become salt that has lost its saltiness. We are like a body without an immune system. And we wonder why it seems that we are always sick.

Others (who are often brothers and sisters in Christ) reject the historic creeds for other reasons. Some do so because they want to have no man-made creeds. They say things like this: "No creed but Christ;" "No creed but the Bible;" or "No creed but the New Testament." While this initially might seem wise, all of these approaches run into the same problem: they are too vague to be meaningful. The problem today is not that people do not believe in Jesus, but that there are far too many Christs in which to believe and all of them except One are just vain imaginings. What happens if one of our Bible-believing brothers says that they have no creed but Christ and someone who does not believe the Bible comes up and says, "Me too! And I think that Jesus was a great moral teacher, but not God." Suddenly, the man who has no creed but Christ has some explaining to do. He does not agree with the other man, because they actually have *different* Christs. The man who has no creed but the Bible or the New Testament is immediately forced to use the words of man as soon as someone forces him to explain what he means by *Christ, Bible* or *New Testament.*

Many other churches that claim to have no creed actually are in the dangerous situation of actually having an unwritten creed. Unwritten creeds are dangerous because they do not clearly set limits on what is proper teaching in the church. This means that error can creep in more easily without being detected, to the destruction of many.

Finally, a more sophisticated group might say, I have no creed at all. While this might initially seem like a more defensible answer, it highlights one problem inherent or always present in all arguments against creeds, which is that creeds are unavoidable. Some groups admit that they have them; some groups claim not to have them, but simply have unspoken ones; other groups claim not to have them, and this very claim becomes their creed. Remember, a creed is just a list of the beliefs that you have and will not compromise. For some churches the only doctrine to which they are committed to not compromising is that they will have no creeds. While this might be unwise (having no creed is certainly not the most important point of Christian teaching from anyone's perspective), it is the only teaching that some groups say that they will defend. So, any group claiming to have no creed in reality has a creed which says: the only point of doctrine that we will defend is that we will have no creeds.

Thankfully, our forefathers in the faith, men like Athanasius and Gregory Nazianzus, knew that they played important roles in making sure that the gospel was preserved pure and uncorrupted. They knew that our eternal destinies rested on their faithfulness to this calling. They sacrificed much (as you read in the chapter on *On the Incarnation,* Athanasius was exiled a number of times and often ran for his life from murderers), and because of their *proactive* and *reactive* faithfulness, we know much truth about Christ. Even with all of this wisdom, however, they were not perpetually successful. Error and heresy still crept into the church at times despite the wise defenses of the creeds, but so much error has been avoided because of the creeds that we should carefully study them and thank God for them and for the great blessing they have been to the church.

Today, sadly, our churches are riddled with errors. Many pulpits are filled with pastors who deny the veracity or truthfulness of the Bible and encourage perversity. Unfortunately, the church today has failed to guard the gospel and has allowed false teaching to corrupt and overwhelm the truth. Like a human being without an immune system, the church is constantly falling ill due to viruses and germs, and we are unable to regain our health. We are like a country at a time of war that has no weapons. We have been unwilling to protect the truth, and now, without repentance, we are unable to effectively defend it. What will this mean for future generations? For your children and grandchildren? Will they know the gospel? Will you have the courage to protect it?

—*G. Tyler Fischer*

For Further Reading

Gonzalez, Justo. *The Story of Christianity. Vol. 1.* San Francisco: HarperCollins, 1984. 158-167; 251-265.

Spielvogel, Jackson J. *Western Civilization.* Seventh Edition. Belmont, Calif.: Thomson Wadsworth, 2009. 192.

Veritas Press History Cards: Middle Ages, Renaissance and Reformation. Lancaster, Pa.: Veritas Press. 4.

Veritas Press History Cards: New Testament, Greece and Rome. Lancaster, Pa.: Veritas Press. 31.

Session I: Prelude

A Question to Consider

How do you protect the things that you are willing to fight for, that is, how do you defend your "non-negotiables?"

From the General Information above answer the following questions:

1. How are creeds both a proactive and reactive defense?
2. What was the Docetic heresy and how does the Apostles' Creed and 1 John 4 address it?
3. What was the Arian heresy?
4. What Greek word (translated into a phrase in English) in the Nicene Creed caused the Arians to deny it?
5. What would have happened if Jesus had had a human body but a soul made up of the Holy Spirit (i.e., not a human soul or intellect)?
6. Why did the early church call Mary the *theotokos* or "Mother of God"?
7. Why is having a creed unavoidable?

Reading Assignment:
The Apostles' Creed

Session II: Discussion

The Apostles' Creed

A Question to Consider

What was Jesus doing during the three days when He was in the grave?

Discuss or list short answers to the following questions:

Text Analysis

1. How was Jesus born?
2. Is the description of Christ's life in the Apostles' Creed chronological or not (i.e., does it follow the order of how events occurred in time)? What does this imply about when the writers of the Apostles' Creed thought that Christ's descent into hell occurred?
3. How did Christ get to hell? (Don't make this too hard, I'm just asking about the direction He was going.)
4. What happened after three days?
5. What does Christ's future look like?

Cultural Analysis

1. What does our culture think about hell?
2. Would that view change if they thought that Jesus conquered hell?

Biblical Analysis

1. What Greek word did the New Testament use for "hell?" Did the authors of the New Testament deny or change the general Greek conception of the word, or did they just use it? What might this imply (Matt. 11:21–24, Luke 10:13–16)?
2. In the parable of the rich man and Lazarus, does the description that Christ gives fit with the understanding that the Old Testament saints were waiting in Hades (a holding place in hell) for Christ to come and rescue them (Luke 16:19–31)?
3. How might the phrase "the keys of Hades and of Death" be evidence that Christ sacked hell (Rev. 1:18)?
4. How might the words that Christ says from the cross, "it is finished" and "today you will be with me in Paradise," be used to prove that Christ was not in hell during the three days that His body was in the grave (Luke 23:43, John 19:30)?

Summa

Write an essay or discuss this question, integrating what you have learned from the material above.

What happened during the three days when Christ's body was in the grave?

Reading Assignment:
The Nicene Creed

Session III: Discussion

The Nicene Creed

A Question to Consider

If you were to make a "timeline" of the life of the Son of God, what would the major events be?

Discuss or list short answers to the following questions:

Text Analysis

1. Was Christ the Son of God before the incarnation? Did He exist before the world came into being?
2. What phrases does the Nicene Creed use to show us that Christ is fully God?
3. Why is it important that Christ is "of one substance with the Father" instead of "of similar substance with the Father?
4. What phrase from the Apostles' Creed is missing in the Nicene Creed? What does this tell us? (You might want to review the Worldview essay.)
5. Where is Christ now?

Cultural Analysis

1. What wrong ideas does our culture entertain today concerning Jesus?
2. Why is it difficult for our culture (and the ancient cultures) to believe that Jesus was and is God?

Biblical Analysis

1. How do the "I am" statements prove that Jesus thought that He was God (John 6:34–42, 10:7–21)?
2. What is the reaction of people when Jesus starts saying the "I am" statements?
3. How does Jesus' reaction to worship show that He was God (Luke 24:50–53, John 9:35–41)?

Summa

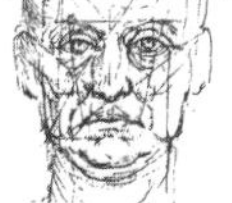

Write an essay or discuss this question, integrating what you have learned from the material above.

If someone challenged Christ's divinity, how would you argue for it?

Reading Assignment:
The Definition of Chalcedon

Session IV: Activity

The Definition of Chalcedon

The *Name that Heresy* Game

You will be given 15 statements about Christ. Many of them will be heretical, but we have mixed in a few true statements to keep you on your toes. You will be asked to tell if the statement is orthodox or heretical, and if it is heretical, to explain what is wrong with the statement and tell which heretic or group of heretics could have made the statement. (You might want to review the Worldview essay before playing the game.) You earn one point for each correct answer. So, it is possible to get 45 points. If you get more than 30 points, you may move on to the bonus round. (Both the statements and answers are provided in the teacher's edition.)

In this round you will be given statements from modern heretics along with a few orthodox statements to keep you honest. If you score 10 or above, you should get a dip of ice cream (defending the truth should have its rewards).

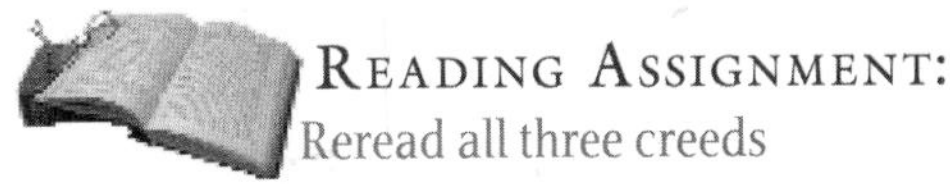

Reading Assignment:
Reread all three creeds

Session V: Writing

Writing Your Own Creed

With the great number of heresies and errors running loose in our culture today it might be wise for the church to meet together in council and revise the creeds or make a new doctrinal statement outlining orthodoxy. Today the church is so divided that this meeting seems unlikely, but who knows what the future holds? Maybe you will be part of a church council that sets out doctrinal standards to protect the church from falling into error. Listed below are a few summaries of weird and heretical teachings in our culture today. Note how a heresy contains elements of truth and common sense. This is always true of heresies, which is why they are not easily discarded.

Start with the Nicene Creed and make changes or additions to it to make clear that the church denies these wrong teachings. Remember that the job of creeds is to protect the

The Trinity by El Greco (Domenikos Theotocopoulos, 1541–1614) was the topmost painting in the high altarpiece of the church of S. Domingo el Antiguo. Looking at this piece today, in light of Openess Theology, a pandora's box of questions seem to rush upon us like, "Did God see the Crucifixion coming? Was he powerless to stop it?"

lambs by forcing the wolves out of the sheep pen. Be careful that your language is not ambiguous or unclear. If it is, the wolves will sneak back in.

The Heresy of Openness Theology

The following is a summary of Openness Theology given by Dr. John Sanders, who is an advocate of this type of theology. See the endnotes for explanations of some of the terms and doctrinal positions that Dr. Sanders mentions. As you read, see if you can discern differences between Openness Theology and the language of the creeds:

> According to openness theology, the triune God of love has, in almighty power, created all that is and is sovereign over all. In freedom God decided to create beings capable of experiencing his love. In creating us, the divine intention was that we would come to experience the triune love and respond to it with love of our own and freely come to collaborate with God towards the achievement of his goals. We believe love is the primary characteristic of God because the triune Godhead has eternally loved even prior to any creation. Divine holiness and justice are aspects of the divine love towards creatures, expressions of God's loving concern for us. Love takes many forms—it can even be experienced as wrath when the lover sees

the beloved destroying herself and others.

Second, God has, in sovereign freedom, decided to make some of his actions depend upon upon our requests and actions. God elicits our free collaboration in his plans. Hence, God can be influenced by what we do and God truly responds to what we do. God genuinely interacts and enters into dynamic give-and-take relationships with us. That God changes in some respects implies that God is temporal, working with us in time. God, at least since creation, experiences duration. God is everlasting through time rather than timelessly eternal.

Third, the only wise God has chosen to exercise general rather than meticulous providence, allowing space for us to operate and for God to be creative and resourceful in working with us. It was solely God's decision not to control every detail that happens in our lives. Moreover, God has flexible strategies. Though the divine nature does not change, God reacts to contingencies, even adjusting his plans, if necessary, to take into account the decisions of his free creatures. God is endlessly resourceful and wise in working towards the fulfillment of his ultimate goals. Sometimes God alone decides how to accomplish these goals. Usually, however, God elicits human cooperation such that it is both God and humanity who decide what the future shall be. God's plan is not a detailed script or blueprint, but a broad intention that allows for a variety of options regarding precisely how these goals may be reached. What God and people do in history matters. If the Hebrew midwives had feared Pharaoh rather than God and killed the baby boys, then God would have responded accordingly and a different story would have emerged. What people do and whether they come to trust God makes a difference concerning what God does—God does not fake the story of human history.

Fourth, God has granted us the type of freedom (libertarian) necessary for a truly personal relationship of love to develop. Again, this was God's decision, not ours. Despite the fact that we have abused our freedom by turning away from the divine love, God remains faithful to his intentions for creation and this faithful love was manifested most fully in the life and work of Jesus.

Finally, the omniscient God knows all that can be known given the sort of world he created. The content of divine omniscience has been debated in the Christian tradition; between Thomism and Molinism for example.[7] In the openness debate the focus is on the nature of the future: is it fully knowable, fully unknowable or partially knowable and partially unknowable? We believe that God could have known every event of the future had God decided to create a fully determined universe. However, in our view God decided to create beings with indeterministic freedom, which implies that God chose to create a universe in which the future is not entirely knowable, even for God. For many open theists the "future" is not a present reality—it does not exist—and God knows reality as it is.

This view may be called dynamic omniscience (it corresponds to the dynamic theory of time rather than the stasis theory[8]). According to this view God knows the past and present with exhaustive definite knowledge and knows the future as partly definite (closed) and partly indefinite (open). God's knowledge of the future contains knowledge of that which is determinate or settled as well as knowledge of possibilities (that which is indeterminate). The determined future includes the things that God has unilaterally decided to do and physically determined events (such as an asteroid hitting our moon). Hence, the future is partly open or indefinite and partly closed or definite and God knows it as such. God is not caught off-guard—he has foresight and anticipates what we will do.

Our rejection of divine timelessness and our affirmation of dynamic omniscience are the most controversial elements in our proposal and the view of foreknowledge receives the most attention. However, the watershed issue in the debate is not whether God has exhaustive definite foreknowledge but whether God is ever affected by and responds to what we do.

This is the same watershed that divides Calvinism from Arminianism.[9]

The Heresy of Mormonism

What follows are some distinctive Mormon teachings:

> The Savior promised that certain sacred acts performed in this life would be effective in the world to come. Consider His words to Peter: "And I will give you the keys of the kingdom of heaven, and whatever you bind on earth will be bound in heaven, and whatever you loose on earth will be loosed in heaven" (Matthew 16:19). When a marriage is performed by the proper authority in the holy temple, it can last through eternity rather than "till death do you part." Your marriage and family do not need to end at death. This promise can give you a sense of eternal belonging and eternal commitment.
>
> In the Old Testament God said, "Let us make man in our own image, after our likeness" (Genesis 1:26). Jacob declared that he had seen God "face to face" (Genesis 32:30). God spoke to Moses "face to face, as a man speaks to his friend" (Exodus 33:11). In the New Testament, when the Resurrected Christ appeared to His apostles, He told them, "handle me and see, for a spirit does not have

DESCENDED INTO HELL?

The clause "He descended into Hell" does not appear in older creeds of the church and was probably added after the fifth century, having been lifted from the Creed of Aquileia. The oldest form of the Apostles' Creed is called the Old Roman Form:

> I believe in God The Father Almighty.
> And in Jesus Christ, his only Son, our Lord;
> Who was born by the Holy Ghost of the Virgin Mary;
> Was crucified under Pontius Pilate and was buried;
> The third day he rose from the dead;
> He ascended into heaven; and sitteth
> on the right hand of the Father;
> From thence he shall come to judge
> the quick and the dead.
> And in the Holy Ghost;
> The Holy Church;
> The forgiveness of sins;
> The resurrection of the body.

Regardless of it's being inserted later, John Calvin maintained that the phrase ought not to be omitted because it sets forth what Christ suffered in the sight of men, and then appositely speaks of that invisible and incomprehensible judgment which he underwent in the sight of God in order that we might know not only that Christ's body was given as the price of our redemption, but that he paid a greater and more excellent price in suffering in his soul the terrible torments of a condemned and forsaken man.

flesh and bones as you see I have" (Luke 24:39). Later Stephen testified that he saw Jesus "standing on the right hand of God" (Acts 7:56). Modern-day revelation confirms these teachings from the Bible. God the Father and His son Jesus Christ, appeared to Joseph Smith in the spring of 1820. Joseph revealed that the Father and the Son each have a "body of flesh and bones as tangible as man's." God is our Heavenly Father, and we are created in his image.[10]

How would you augment or add to the Nicene Creed to address these more recent false teachings?

Optional Session: Discussion

The Insertion of the *Filioque* Clause

Before holding this discussion read the following introduction:

Change causes controversy and small changes (even ones that might appear insignificant initially) in creeds and confessions can have massive consequences over thousands of years.

In the Western Latin Church, a clause was added to the Nicene Creed. The original creed had said that the Holy Spirit "proceeded from the Father." The Western churches altered the creed by adding the words "and the Son" or in Latin *"filioque."* This small alteration deepened the divide between West and East which eventually led to the Great Schism of 1054. The East accused the West of altering the creed without a council and of shifting the Nicene understanding of the Trinity. The West thought that the East was failing to recognize something that was clear biblically and that was generally agreeable to the fathers of both the Eastern and Western tradition.

This change also shows a subtle difference between Western and Eastern Christianity. In the East, it seemed that power and dominance in the Trinity resided with the Father. The Son was begotten of Him. The Spirit proceeded from Him. Unity and power were at the roots of the Trinity. In the West, this change highlighted the Western view that emphasized the diversity of power within Trinity. "The Spirit proceeds from the Father *and the Son.*"

While this change might seem small over the centuries, it was at least a symptom of and probably contributed to very different views of authority in the East and West. In the East, power and dominance became the goal and power was increasingly unified. The emperor claimed power over the church, and the church became the servant of the emperor. In the West, the power of the church and the power of the government balanced each other. The West recognized greater diversity. Imperial power reigned in the East; a more shared view of power, although not without its own problems, resulted in the West, where both the king and the pope dominated from time to time.

Discuss or list short answers to the following questions:

Text Analysis

1. What does *filioque* mean? How did it get into the creed?
2. How does this clause change the view of authority within the Trinity?
3. To what subtle theological difference does the insertion of the *Filioque* clause point?
4. What is the result in history of these differing views of authority?

Cultural Analysis

1. Does our society today view authority as a unity or a diversity?
2. Where do you see unified, monolithic power in our society?
3. What sort of culture does a monolithic unitarian view of God create (think of Islam)?

Biblical Analysis

1. When the Bible speaks of the Holy Spirit, is the Spirit connected to the Father and the Son differently or similarly (Gal. 4:6, Rom. 8:9, Matt. 10:20, 1 Cor. 2:11)?
2. Did Jesus claim that the Spirit proceeded from Him (Luke, 24:49; John 15:26, 16:7, 20:22; Acts 2:33; Tit. 3:6)?
3. Should John 15:26 cause us to deny the procession of the Spirit from the Son?

SUMMA

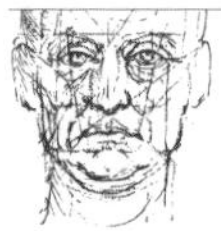

Write an essay or discuss this question, integrating what you have learned from the material above.

Should the Western church have added the Filioque clause?

ENDNOTES

1 Before we laugh too hard at the mistakes these people made, we should take care. We live in the day of liberal teaching that states, "Jesus was a great moral teacher not God" and of *The DaVinci Code.*

2 One has to wonder at the wisdom of simply making up a new word to avoid the baggage. What a smart move!

3 Docetic comes from the Greek word δοκεσις or "appearance" or "semblance."

4 The most notable "subtraction" would be the controversial phrase "He descended into hell." This phrase, however, was a late addition to the Apostles' Creed, so it was probably not subtracted out, but was simply not there.

5 Gregory Nazianzus, Epistle 101. Gregory was known as one of the three Great Cappadocians, along with Gregory of Nyssa and Basil the Great. With insights like this one it is understandable why he was included in such choice company.

6 *This endnote appears only in the teacher's edition.*

7 The debate between the followers of Thomas Aquinus' followers and Luis Molina, a sixteenth-century Catholic Jesuit theologian, centered on the reconciling God's grace with man's free will. Thomists usually start with the fact of God's effectual grace and try to fit man's free will with it. This leads Thomists to a more biblical view of God's omniscience. Molinists begin by saying that man has free will, and they try to create some sort of sovereignty and omniscience whereby God knows everything that anyone could possibly do, but God does not cause any of it to happen. They call this theory "middle knowledge." While Dr. Sanders claims that this debate is one that has been raging for a long time (so that he can push even further in an unbiblical direction), the logical problems of the Molinist system are evident. This information about Molinism can be found at Link 1 for this chapter at www.VeritasPress.com/OmniLinks.

8 This simply means that the Openness Theologian looks at his god with some sort of changing standards of perfection (dynamic) instead of an unchanging one (stasis—from which we get the word *static*).

9 This was taken from the Open Theism Information site that can be accessed at Link 2 for this chapter at www.VeritasPress.com/OmniLinks.

10 The source for this was the official website of the Church of Jesus Christ of Latter Day Saints in 2005.

Ecclesiastical History of the English People

Names matter. Adam called his wife *woman* because she was taken out of *man.* God changed Abram's name to *Abraham,* because he was going to be the father of many. His son was named *Isaac,* which means laughter, because both Abraham and his wife Sarah laughed at the thought of having a son in their old age. Jesus gave a new name, *Peter,* to a man who had been called Simon, because Simon stood on that same rock upon which Jesus was going to build His church. Names matter in the first place, and *renaming* matters also.

The Anglo-Saxons understood that names matter. They gave the name *Suffolk* to the place where folks in the south dwelt, and *Northumbria* is their name for the region north of the Humber River. They gave the name *Cambridge* to the place where a bridge spanned the river Cam, and *Oxford* is situated at a shallow stretch of the river Thames where oxen could ford across. About the year 672 an important monastery was founded near the place where the Wear River empties into the North Sea. So they called the place *Wearmouth.*

Bede entered this monastery at Wearmouth when he was only seven years old. He lived there (as well as at a companion monastery nearby, Jarrow) for the rest of his life. Bede is best known to us for writing the *Ecclesiastical History of the English People.* One of Bede's greatest legacies to us is found in this book, an unusual act of naming. Bede gave us a new way to name time.

A bearded god holding a stag in each hand from the side of the Gundestrup Cauldron, a twenty-pound silver bowl found in a peat bog at Gundestrup, Denmark. In the Celtic mind cauldrons were linked with fertility and the revival of the dead.

General Information

Author and Context

Many of us would not have wanted to live in Bede's era. Every growing season farmers hoped the seeds they planted would not wash away in the spring rains. If crops survived the rains, would they fall victim to an early frost? A farmer could not predict the weather. Sometimes a hostile army would trample or seize his crops. And if his wife became pregnant, would she survive the life-threatening rigors of carrying an unborn child to term and delivering a son or daughter? Many women died in childbirth, and a woman's death was as much a loss to household industry as it was a bitter sorrow. In Bede's day, childbearing killed about as many able women as warfare killed able men. And warfare was as common as childbearing. A safely delivered newborn was a rich blessing, but faced uncertain years ahead. Many children succumbed to disease and did not live to see age six or eight. By our standards, Bede lived in a brutal, hard, uncivilized age.

This savage landscape was interrupted by pockets of civilization. These were peaceful places where meals came regularly, singing was routine and the busy cares of the world were tended to in a way that left space in the schedule for art and scholarship to flourish. These pockets of civilization were the monasteries. A common misconception about early medieval monasteries is that they were places where monks went to escape from civilization. But the opposite is true: monks boldly went into untamed places and carved out fresh civilization by establishing

The opening page of the Gospel of Saint Luke showing the Evangelist and his symbol, the winged bull, with scenes from the life of Christ on either side. This particulary well-preserved illumination is from the sixth-century "Gospels of Saint Augustine." There is little doubt that this was among the books Bede mentions as having been sent to Saint Augustine by Pope Gregory the Great shortly after Augustine landed in England in A.D. 596.

monasteries. In doing so they carried literacy to places where people could not read, food to where people were underfed, medicine to the sick, and most importantly, they carried the Christian gospel to people who had not heard of Jesus. Of course, monks were far from perfect, but God raised them up to advance His kingdom in this important age of the church's immaturity. From the fifth through the eleventh centuries, the gospel filled Europe by way of monasteries. Bede lived in the middle of this era, born around 673 and dying in 735.

Bede spent his life in two of these monasteries, Wearmouth and Jarrow, which were near one another in both distance and organization. He seldom traveled outside these monasteries, and if he did, he did not go very far, and he liked it that way. He preferred to seek adventure by way of the scholarly life, surrounded by books and students, who read and sang and prayed together with him as part of a vigorous and diverse monastic community. Though Bede did not travel far, monks, scholars and dignitaries came from far away to visit Wearmouth and Jarrow. Bede's writings show that he was familiar with places and events that he had not witnessed, but which he had nonetheless learned a great deal about through books and through personal interaction with those who had firsthand knowledge.

Significance

The sometimes peaceful, sometimes turbulent story of the gospel's advance into Britain does indeed resemble the book of Acts in important ways. Sometimes good men raise unfaithful sons, like Eli in the Bible. Some church leaders cower in the face of persecution or difficulty, as Laurence, Mellitus and Justus did (book 2, chaps. 5–6). Others remain firm, even to the point of death, such as Alban (1.7). Sometimes heresies rise up, as with the false doctrines of Arius and Pelagius (1.8, 17). Sometimes faithful, conscientious church leaders disagree strongly with one another over matters of doctrine and liturgy, as with the Easter controversy.[1] But in the end, God grants victory to His people. Bede's record reminds us that the Church of Jesus Christ is messy and in need of sanctification, yet the gates of Hades will not prevail against her (Eph. 5:25–27, Matt. 16:18).

Bede's work became a standard for Christian historians to follow throughout the Middle Ages. Later historians looked back to Bede as their role model and learned his habit of discerning parallels between the events recorded in the Bible and other past events.

Main Characters

Bede's *Ecclesiastical History* covers a number of centuries and numerous kingdoms and churches. There are many important characters. More than any man, however, the gospel is the main character of his work. It is invading pagan kingdoms. It overthrows unbelief and establishes itself. It suffers setbacks and apostasy, only to reappear and move forward. It is truly the main character of this work.

The other most notable character is the church, for it is the church and its ministers that bear the gospel. Notably, there are two distinct churches in this work that are working to bring the pagan Britons, Angles, Saxons, Jutes, Celts and Picts to faith in Christ. One group is the Irish Church, founded by St. Patrick and led by inspiring leaders like St. Columba and Aidan of Iona. The Irish Church thrives on the edges of a continent that is reeling from massive barbarian invasion. Yet, the Irish are (as they so often are in history) undaunted, and they carry the gospel back to the pagans, risking life and limb.

The other church that is featured is the Roman/English Church. The visionary leadership of Gregory I, bishop of Rome, led him to send Augustine of Canterbury (this is not the Augustine of *Confessions* and *City of God* fame) to England to plant the gospel among the pagan kingdoms in places like Essex and Northumbria.

While these are some of the greatest names, this book lauds kings like Ethelbert (called Æthelberht in some versions) of Kent and Oswald of Northumbria, and it truly has a cast of hundreds.

Summary and Setting

Bede tells the story of the expansion of the gospel among the English. This expansion moves forward over time, but (like real history) is full of potholes, hills and obstacles. At some points it seems that paganism will push the gospel back into Ireland and back to mainland Europe, but in times of great need God raises up fearless men and women, and Christ's kingdom expands.

Ecclesiastical History of the English People also demonstrates how two churches with two traditions can try to work out their differences and work together. Some of the differences between the English and Irish churches might seem odd to us. Why should it matter how you cut your hair or when you celebrate Easter? These Christians, however, understood that differing practices would eventually lead to further disunity and division. Our divided modern-day churches could learn a lot from their commitment to Christian community in depth and fullness.

Worldview

Bede knew that kingdoms come and go, so he focused his attention on an institution that is truly lasting: the church. While he mentions many kings, his real heroes are churchmen. When he does describe kings, he is interested not so much in their political maneuvers as he is in how they affect the church. He also mentions war from time to time, but gives far more attention to the church's warfare against heresy, schism, false worship and apostasy.

Bede shows that the gospel achieved staying power in England through the missionary work of Augustine, who landed in Kent in 597. The pagan king of Kent, Ethelbert, received him well, likely due to the influence of his Christian wife (1.25). Ethelbert's conversion established Christianity in a lasting way (1.26), and Augustine became the first archbishop of Canterbury. Canterbury was the most prominent town in Ethelbert's realm, which at the time stretched as far north as the Humber River, and Augustine founded the church on land that Ethelbert gave him.

Bede devotes much attention to Augustine and also to the visionary who sent Augustine to England, Pope Gregory the Great. Don't be misled by the title "pope," for in Gregory's and Bede's day that title did not carry the meaning that it has with us today. In fact, today's notion of "pope" only began to emerge 500 years after Gregory. In Gregory's day, scores of bishops all over Europe were called "pope" (Latin *papa,* which simply means "father"), and the bishop of Rome was one bishop among many. Pope Gregory did not see himself as supreme over the other bishops or "popes," and he welcomed encouragement, correction and admonition from bishops in other cities. He condemned the idea that one bishop wielded authority over the whole church and stressed this point in several letters (Bede does not record these letters, but they are preserved elsewhere). Gregory even claimed that anyone who presumed to have such a lofty status in the church, or who calls himself a "universal" or "ecumenical" priest, is an *antichrist.* Why, then, did missionaries to England, such as Augustine, hold the popes of Rome in such high regard? Largely because Rome happened to be the place from where these missionaries were sent. When a missionary goes far off into the hinterlands, it's only natural that he will seek the advice and counsel of the church which sent him out. This is a key reason why it was so natural for the English missionaries to submit themselves to the bishops of Rome the way they did. Of course, widespread respect for the great city of Rome also had something to do with the influence of that city's bishop: the bishop of Rome was no ordinary bishop, because Rome was no ordinary place.

As the gospel advanced through England, Ethelbert of Kent was the first king to convert to Christianity. Ethelbert's daughter, Ethelberga (called Æthelburh in some editions) carried the gospel from Kent up to Northumbria when she was given in marriage to King Edwin, who in time turned to Christ (2.9–17). Beginning with Edwin, Bede's coverage of royalty focuses on kings of Northumbria. Edwin's immediate successors strayed from the gospel, but Oswald was faithful. Bede describes Oswald in language that reminds us of David and Solomon in the Bible.

Flowing out from Kent came many pastors and bishops. Paulinus, for example, accompanied Ethelbert's daughter to Northumbria and preached to Edwin. Paulinus set the stage for a church in that region. Other godly men went out from Kent or Northumbria to other areas, where they established churches and monasteries. These new foundations maintained contact with one another and with Rome. Some endured persecution and others won favor in the eyes of the kings who ruled over them.

Bede mentions other missionaries who came into Britain—not from Gaul or Rome, but from Ireland. The Irish had converted to Christianity in the wake of St. Patrick's missionary labors in the fifth century.

A celtic cross on the isle of Iona. In 563, St. Columcille and twelve companions crossed the Irish Sea and landed on a deserted isle that would eventually be known as Iona. This tiny island would go on to have a huge impact in converting the Picts, Scots and Northern English to Christianity.

They were the first peoples to embrace Christianity who had not previously been part of the Roman Empire. This was one reason why the customs of the Irish (or "Celtic") church differed from the customs of churchmen who came from Gaul or Rome. A minor difference was that the Irish monks shaved their heads differently than the European monks did (a monk's hairdo is called a *tonsure*). Another difference was their way of organizing monasteries. And by far the most important difference (to them) was how they determined the date of Easter, the most important Christian festival, which differed from the standard European way. Sometimes the Irish and European Easters fell on different Sundays!

Bede praised these Irish missionaries who came to England. First among them was Columba, who founded an Irish-type monastery on the island of Iona, on the west coast of what is now Scotland. When King Oswald of Northumbria requested a godly teacher, an Irishman named Aidan answered the call. Aidan came from Iona and established an important monastery and church on a beautiful island called Lindisfarne, which became a key place in the establishment of Christianity in that area (3.3–5 and 5.9). Like Wearmouth and Jarrow in Bede's day, Lindisfarne became a center of learning and the arts.

Bede records a clash between the European and Irish styles of Christianity, largely over the Easter question, and he explains how the matter was eventually settled in favor of the European scheme that had been adopted back in 325 at the Council of Nicea. Archbishop Theodore, who came to Canterbury from Tarsus, was instrumental in settling this controversy. By the end of his narrative, Bede surveys the England of his day and celebrates a once-pagan land now Christianized and a once-divided church now unified.

Besides the matters of controversy, Bede's work helps us to form a Christian view of history and time. Bede knew the common practice of naming time according to the reigns of kings, as in "the umpteenth year of the reign of so-and-so." Most ancient cultures, including the Israelites, named time this way. Assigning a king's name to time is a way of honoring that king. Bede explains this when he mentions the tragic reigns of Northumbrian kings who rejected the Christian faith and who thereby led the people of Northumbria into apostasy. Because these ungodly tyrants deserve no honor in our

The cathedral at Canterbury in the spring. Augustine of Canterbury was the first archbishop of Canterbury. Gregory the Great sent him as the leader of a group of missionaries to Anglo-Saxon England. Due to Bede's *Ecclesiastical History* we know a great deal about his life and career while in England.

historical memory, Bede says, we do not name time after them. He wrote, "So all those who compute the dates of kings have decided to abolish the memory of those perfidious kings and to assign this year to their successor, Oswald, a man beloved of God" (3.1). King Oswald reigned after these nasty kings and revived the Christian faith in Northumbria. Because we remember Oswald by honoring him, Bede explains that the years of his nasty predecessors were named "years before Oswald."

Bede wrote in Latin, and he knew that anyone who read Latin was familiar with the names that the Romans assigned to periods of time. Even we are familiar with how the Romans named their months. They named January in honor of Janus, god of doors; hence January opens the year. The Romans named February after their sacred season of purification called *februo.* March, named in honor of Mars, god of war, was originally the first month of their ten-month year. April comes from the Latin *aperire,* which means "to open;" thus April is named as the month when trees open their leaves. May is probably named after Maiesta, goddess of honor. June honors Juno, queen of Rome's gods. September comes from *septem,* or seven, and was originally the seventh month. October, November and December come from the words *octo, novem* and *decem,* the words for eight, nine and ten. Julius Caesar, a prideful man, renamed the fifth month after himself; what was once called *quintiles* (five) became July. Julius's successor liked this idea and renamed the sixth month after himself: *sextilis* (six) became August in honor of Augustus. Indeed, the names we give to time carry important meanings.

According to the Roman name for time, Bede finished his *Ecclesiastical History* in the year 1483—that is, 1,483 years from the founding of Rome. Some Romans might have said that he finished his work in the year of Augustus 759. To these different "names" for the year in which Bede completed his work, we can add the ancient Greek name: the Greeks would likely have said that it happened in 1506, because they named their years after the first Olympic games. Yet again, for thirteen years in the French Revolution, the French tried a different approach to naming time; their official calendar would have said that Bede finished his work 1,062 years before the French Republic. This strange French calendar did not last long; thankfully, Napoleon Bonaparte abolished it two hundred years ago.

Everyone agrees on *when* Bede finished writing his *Ecclesiastical History,* but there are different names we could give to that year. Which is correct—is it 731, 1483, 759, 1506, or 1060 B.F.R. (before the French Republic)? Why do *we* say that Bede finished his work in 731, when there are other ways to say it? We name the years the way we do because Bede taught us an excellent way to name time.

This painting depicts Saint Brendan the Navigator and many elements of his famous voyage, including the "mountains of floating glass" and the land to the west he is said to have discovered nearly one thousand years before Columbus. *National Geographic Magazine* covered the story of Tim Severin, who in the 1970s sailed a traditional Irish coracle made of wood and leather across the Atlantic, proving that Brendan could have made the historic journey. Bede wrote that Brendan was born near Tralee in County Kerry, founded many Celtic monasteries, sailed on several long voyages and died in Annaghdown in Ireland in A.D. 578.

In his *Ecclesiastical History,* Bede first mentions time in the second chapter: he gives the date for Julius Caesar's consulship as "the 693rd year from the building of Rome but the 60th before the incarnation of our Lord" (1.2). Bede's original audience was familiar with naming time according to years of Rome. But Bede also places the years of a king's rule alongside the years of Rome. He named time according to a great king, the King of Kings, Jesus Christ. This is what he meant by "the 60th *before the incarnation our Lord.*" He does something similar in the next chapter, saying that the emperor Claudius's expedition to Britain took place "in the 798th year after the founding of Rome," but several lines later he describes the close of the expedition this way: *"in the forty-sixth year after the birth of our Lord."* Bede's Latin expression is *annus ab incarnatione Domini,* which we now shorten to *anno Domini,* "the year of our Lord," and abbreviate as A.D. Likewise, we name the years before Christ by the abbreviation B.C. Because of Bede's influence, historians ever since have named years in honor of the reign of King Jesus. Everything belongs to Him, including every year.

Bede's *Ecclesiastical History* records the story of England's transition from a pagan land to a land saturated with the gospel. Bede himself played a role in this transformation, part of which was to honor Christ rather than pagan rulers in how years are named. But England's conversion to the gospel was not complete. Its incompleteness is symbolized by the tired old Saxon deities who are still remembered, however faintly, in our names for days in the week: after Tiea, Woden, Thor and Freya we have Tuesday, Wednesday, Thursday and Friday. Bede knew there was still work to be done, and that work still remains. On the other hand, it is a wonderful tribute to the gospel's converting power that these names for our days of the week are almost completely stripped of their pagan significance. Our idea of Wednesday has little to do with Woden, even as Woden has no part in true deity.

Still, in the resurrection of Christ the world began being definitively remade. This new life experienced by believers, however, did not undo all controversy between them. The resurrection of Christ is the central event of history. In this event God prevailed over death, and Adam's curse and its consequences were foiled. Christians remember Christ's resurrection at Easter, and it is fitting for Bede to make so much of Easter. Modern readers who approach Bede for the first time may wonder at all the fuss he makes of Easter. The fact that we wonder at it reveals as much about our own era as it reveals about Bede. Perhaps we should turn the question back upon ourselves: why do we not place as high an importance on the celebration of Easter as Bede does?

KING ALFRED ENACTS SWEEPING NEW LAW CODE BASED ON BIBLE

[WESSEX AP News: August 1, 884] The eagerly awaited new law code promised by King Alfred has become a reality. Yesterday the King conferred with his *Witum* (councillors) and finalized the *Code of Alfred.* The new code relies heavily on God's laws revealed in the Bible. King Alfred explained why, in establishing a good and fair legal code to guide the *Angle-cyn* (English people) it is necessary and wise to rely on God's laws rather than our own. "These are judgments which Almighty God Himself spoke to Moses and commanded him to keep. Now, since the Lord's only begotten Son our God and healing Christ has come to Middle Earth [Europe]—He said that He did not come to break nor to forbid these commandments but to approve them well, and to teach them with all mildheartedness and lowlymindedness." Thus the King's new code relies heavily on the Ten Commandments and Mosaic laws recorded in the Book of Exodus, Christ's Sermon on the Mount in the Gospel of Matthew and the apostolic teachings at the Synod of Jerusalem in the Book of Acts.

King Alfred has been working diligently on his code since his great victory over the pagan Danes and the subsequent conversion of the Danish king Guthrum, which has solidified and secured the Christian land of the *Angles* and removed for good the pagan Viking threat. Seeking to be faithful to Christ, the great King has emphasized that the code should protect and provide for not only the *Angles* but all foreigners alike, that all be treated equally before God.

In announcing the enactment of his code, Alfred made this concluding statement making the code effective immediately. "I, Alfred King of the West Saxons have then shewn these to all my *Witum*. And they have declared that it met with the approval of all—so that they should be observed."

*For more information on the amazing, faithful life of the only king in English history called "the Great," see Link 1 for this chapter at www.VeritasPress.com/OmniLinks.

Bede was deeply troubled, as were the saints he writes about, over the fact that godly people did not celebrate Easter on the same day. Bede was patient with Irish who had not yet been taught the proper way to reckon Easter; Columba and Aidan were among those he praised highly. But after the representatives of both Irish and European factions gathered at the Synod of Whitby (or Whidby) in 664 (3.25), where all agreed that the European custom was superior to the Irish, Bede lost patience with those who persisted in the Irish way. Now they knew better, and the best Irish theologians had admitted as much. It is important to see that, for Bede, an issue such as this was decided in a synod, a representative gathering of church leaders, rather than by simply seeking out the opinion of the bishop of Rome. A controversy was settled only when the whole church said so—as the English church settled the Easter controversy at the Synod of Whitby—and *not* when the pope of Rome said so. By the close of his narrative, Bede rejoiced to see that the last of the Irish holdouts had abandoned their divergent custom and joined the rest of the church in celebrating Easter (5.22). It is important that brethren dwell together in unity, even unity in their feasting.

Easter is not the only area of church life in which Bede honored the resurrection of Christ. He also saw resurrection power in the relics of the saints. Bede's many accounts of the miraculous power of relics strike us as odd, perhaps even bizarre and disturbing. For example, we read of Aidan, who died while leaning up against a post. Twice the post did not burn even though everything around it was destroyed by fire (3.17). We also read the strange account of Etheldreda (called Æthelthryth in some editions), whose coffin was opened years after her death, revealing that her body had not decomposed (4.19). In a similar story, Cuthbert's dead body did not decompose (4.28). In order to understand these stories, we must remember what the Bible teaches about what happens to God's people when they die. While our spirits go to be with God, this is not our final, glorious state. One day our dead bodies will rise from the grave, whole and without sin, disease or corruption—without any residue of death. Bede and other Christians who lived in his day believed firmly in the resurrection of the dead. They knew that the Bible teaches that every saint's body will one day emerge from the grave, just as Jesus' body once did. When a saint died, they believed that God would sometimes remind us of a future resurrection by bringing forth little touches of life—healings, miracles and unusual resistance to decomposition—from the dead bodies of saints.

This understanding of saint's bodies flourished in an immature age in the church, and many centuries after Bede's day it led to odd superstitions and dangerous heresies. But at the heart of this belief in Bede's time was the central event of history, which Easter commemorates: the resurrection of the dead. We may find it strange that God would bring about healings and miracles from the dead bodies of saints, but we all confess to something far stranger and far more wonderful: that God will one day bring forth each one of those bodies from the grave and restore it to life again, never again to taste death, just as He did with Jesus' body on that first Easter. Bede's fixation upon saints' bodies is closely tied to his fixation upon Easter, both of which are grounded in the resurrection.

Bede focuses on eternal priorities. Bede puzzles some readers today because they cannot figure out why he does not provide more information about the machinations of kings, warfare and trade. Of course, this tells us as much about these readers as it tells us about Bede: they don't have the same priorities. Bede understood that the church is an everlasting institution—the gates of Hades will not prevail against it—whereas kingdoms come and go. For this reason, Bede was the first (being inspired by Pope Gregory) to conceive of the English as one people. This may seem strange today, but the inhabitants of England used to think of themselves as Britons and Angles and Saxons and Jutes. Later they came to regard themselves as peoples of Sussex or Essex or Kent or Mercia or Northumbria, etc. In Bede's lifetime, these various kingdoms still had their own peculiar lands, customs and even languages. But they all had come to see themselves as one people—not according to their *national* citizenship, but according to their *church* membership. They all followed the same Savior and worshiped according to the same church order, which eventually included the same reckoning of Easter. This is what made them truly one people, English, even though they lived under different kings in separate realms.

As a monk, Bede kept up a daily regimen of prayers, Scripture reading and psalm singing at appointed times throughout the day. Together with his fellow monks he followed this routine over days, weeks, months and years. He was saturated in the Scriptures. Since books were scarce in his day (all books had to be copied by hand), individuals did not own personal Bibles. In monasteries, therefore, the Scriptures were read aloud and chanted throughout the day; Bible reading was public and liturgical rather than private and individualized. It had to be that way. Thus Bede came to understand that the Bible is a community document, divinely delivered to the people of God, rather than a personal possession.

Most of Bede's writings are commentaries on the Bible, many of which still survive today. We in our day are fascinated with his historical writing and easily forget that he saw himself primarily as a commentator on Scripture. In an important respect Bede thought of his *Ecclesiastical History* as a commentary on Scripture, for in it he narrated how the apostolic message spread after the age of the apostles—a sort of extension of the book of Acts. Therefore we should not be surprised when Bede describes people and events using biblical imagery. For example, when the evangelist Germanus sails the channel from Gaul (the ancient name for France), bringing sound teaching to England, we find him asleep in the ship tossed by stormy seas. After the sailors gave up, Germanus was awakened. He prayed, and the waters calmed (1.17). The story echoes the biblical account of Jesus calming the waters, and Bede writes in a way that underscores the similarities between these events, thereby reminding us that Christ continues to work in His people just

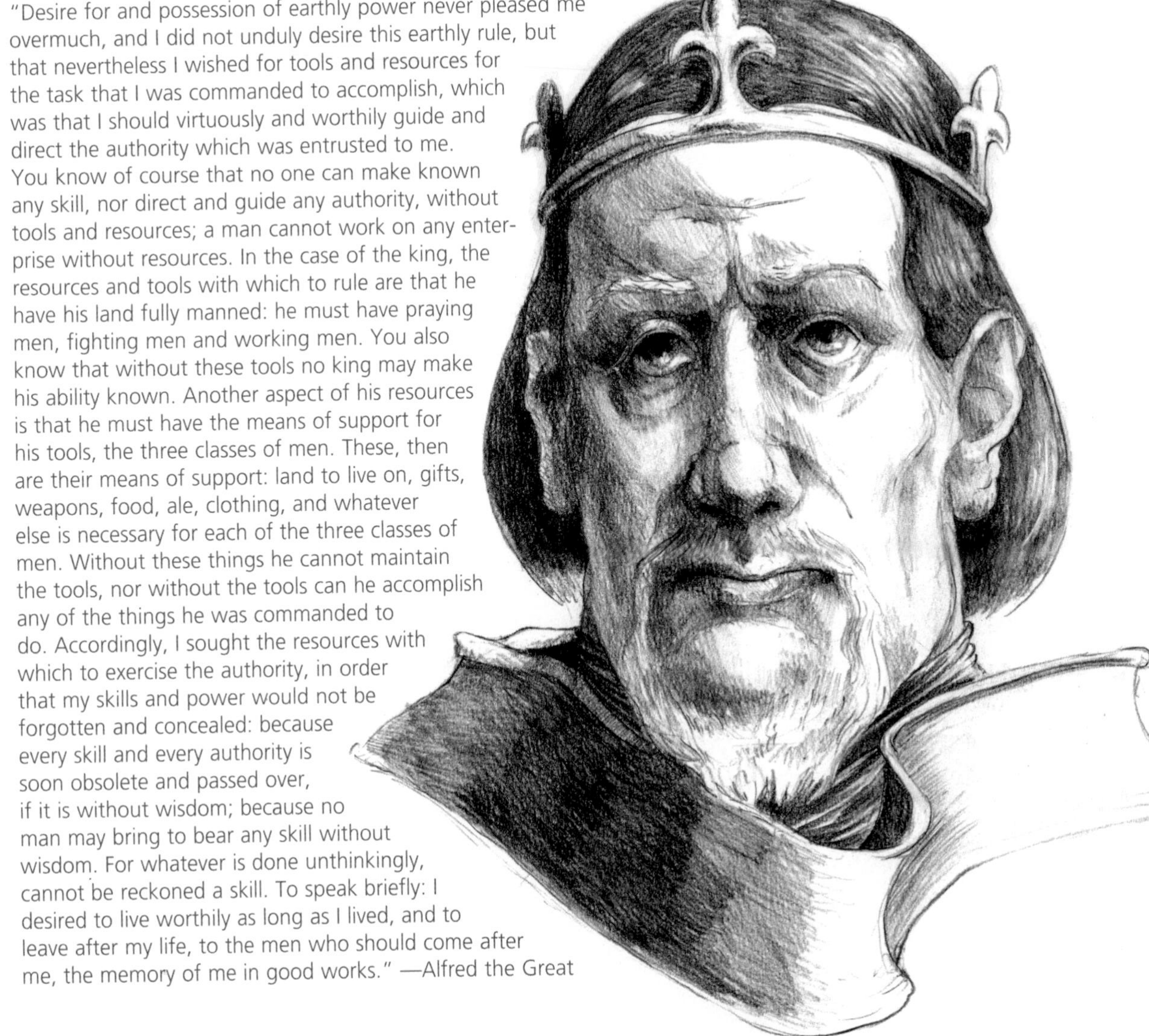

"Desire for and possession of earthly power never pleased me overmuch, and I did not unduly desire this earthly rule, but that nevertheless I wished for tools and resources for the task that I was commanded to accomplish, which was that I should virtuously and worthily guide and direct the authority which was entrusted to me. You know of course that no one can make known any skill, nor direct and guide any authority, without tools and resources; a man cannot work on any enterprise without resources. In the case of the king, the resources and tools with which to rule are that he have his land fully manned: he must have praying men, fighting men and working men. You also know that without these tools no king may make his ability known. Another aspect of his resources is that he must have the means of support for his tools, the three classes of men. These, then are their means of support: land to live on, gifts, weapons, food, ale, clothing, and whatever else is necessary for each of the three classes of men. Without these things he cannot maintain the tools, nor without the tools can he accomplish any of the things he was commanded to do. Accordingly, I sought the resources with which to exercise the authority, in order that my skills and power would not be forgotten and concealed: because every skill and every authority is soon obsolete and passed over, if it is without wisdom; because no man may bring to bear any skill without wisdom. For whatever is done unthinkingly, cannot be reckoned a skill. To speak briefly: I desired to live worthily as long as I lived, and to leave after my life, to the men who should come after me, the memory of me in good works." —Alfred the Great as He did when He dwelt among us. Similarly, when Bede writes about King Oswald of Northumbria, he wants to remind us of King David. Thus, by identifying biblical patterns in post-biblical events, Bede's history is a sort of commentary on Scripture. As a scholar who spent most of his life in a monastery, where the Scriptures were routinely read and chanted several times a day, Bede's historical outlook was shaped by events recorded in the Bible.

—*Christopher Schlect*

For Further Reading

Bede, *The Reckoning of Time.* Faith Wallis, trans. Liverpool University Press, 1999.

Blair, John. *The Church in Anglo-Saxon Society.* Oxford University Press, 2005.

Noble, Thomas F.X. and Head, Thomas, eds. *Soldiers of Christ: Saints and Saints' Lives from Late Antiquity and the Early Middle Ages.* Pennsylvania State University Press, 1995.

Spielvogel, Jackson J. *Western Civilization.* Seventh Edition. Belmont, Calif.: Thomson Wadsworth, 2009. 197–201.

Veritas Press History Cards: Middle Ages, Renaissance and Reformation. Lancaster, Pa.: Veritas Press. 2.

Webb, J.F. and Farmer, D.H., eds. *The Age of Bede.* Penguin, 1998.

Session I: Prelude

A Question to Consider

In what ways was the church of Bede's era *immature* by comparison to the church in your own age? In what ways do you think it was more *mature?*

From the General Information above, answer the following questions.

1. How did Bede influence the way we view time today?
2. What were Bede's sources of information for his *Ecclesiastical History?*
3. Why was the Bible a *public, community* document in Bede's day, in contrast to the private, personal document some see it as today?
4. What do the signs and wonders performed through relics have to do with the Easter controversy?
5. Bede wrote about the English *people.* Explain the difference between the terms English *nation* and English *people.*
6. How important is *church history* compared to *national history?*

Reading Assignment:
Book 1, chapters 1–16

Session II: Discussion

Book 1, chapters 1–16

A Question to Consider

Why should we study history?

Discuss or list short answers to the following questions:

Text Analysis

1. What has King Ceolwulf done recently that is so pleasing to Bede? Why is this pleasing to him (see the Author's Preface, "To the Most Glorious King Ceolwulf")?
2. In Bede's view, does it matter if history is recorded accurately? Couldn't moral anecdotes be told without reference to actual history?
3. How does Bede relate a feature of Britain to a feature of the Bible (1.1)?
4. What dating systems does Bede use (1.2 ff)?
5. How does Bede view the shrines of the martyrs set up after Diocletian's persecution of the church (1.8)?
6. In Bede's time the Britons were a nation distinct from the Picts, Irish and English. How does Bede view the Britons as a nation (1.8, 12, 14)?

Cultural Analysis

1. How does our culture view the study of history?
2. Then are professional historians a godly class of people, known for their gratitude to God?

Biblical Analysis

1. What importance is given to historical knowledge in Deuteronomy 6:20-25?
2. What importance is given to historical knowledge in Psalm 145:4-7?
3. How and why does Paul remind the Ephesians of their past in Ephesians 2:11-22?
4. How does Paul's instruction to Timothy bear on the study of history (1 Tim. 1:3-6)?

SUMMA

Write an essay or discuss this question, integrating what you have learned from the material above.

How can historical knowledge help us to live as Christians?

Optional Activity

Bede knew Eusebius's *History of the Church* in a Latin translation by Rufinus. Compare Bede's summary of his motives, goals and method in the Author's Preface, "To the Most Glorious King Ceolwulf," with those of Eusebius in his *History of the Church* (1.1). What similarities are there? What are the main differences?

READING ASSIGNMENT:
Book 1, chapters 17-31

SESSION III: RECITATION

Book 1, chapters 1-31

Comprehension Questions

Answer the following questions for factual recall:

1. What nation does Bede focus on in the early chapters of his *History* (see 1.1-22)? Why?
2. How does Bede portray the Britons (1.8-22)?
3. Who was Pelagius (1.10)?
4. When he first introduces the English, Bede calls them by their ancestral tribal names. Why did these tribes migrate to Britain (1.14-15)?
5. Who is sent to Britain to fight Pelagianism? How does he confront the heresy (1.17-21)?
6. Whom does Pope Gregory the Great send to evangelize the English? How does he encourage them (1.23)?
7. Describe the early stages of Augustine's career in Britain (1.25-27).
8. In Gregory's answer to Augustine's first question, what distinguishes Augustine's relationship to his clergy from the usual relationship of a bishop to his clergy (1.27)?
9. What else does Gregory send, and what further directions for church government does he give in 1.29?

READING ASSIGNMENT:
Book 1, chapters 32-34

SESSION IV: DISCUSSION

Book 1, chapters 32-34

A Question to Consider

Should Christians celebrate Halloween?

Discuss or list short answers to the following questions:

Text Analysis

1. In what ways do Bede and the characters in the *History* honor departed saints (refer to 1.7, 8, 18, 29, 30)?
2. What is Gregory's main concern in the letter in 1.30?
3. What does he say should be done (1.30)?
4. Why convert, and not destroy, them (1.30)?

Cultural Analysis

1. What are the main holidays in American culture, and in a few words, what do these mean?
2. Most unbelievers are happy to adopt Christian festivals, such as Christmas and Easter, into their unbelieving lifestyle. Is this inconsistent?
3. What meanings does Halloween have in our culture?

Biblical Analysis

1. What were the main festivals of Israel (Lev. 23)?
2. What do these all have in common?
3. Must all lawful feasts be commanded by God (Esther 9:18-32)?
4. So the church can legitimately establish a feast commemorating Jesus' work. But some people be-

lieve that Christmas was originally instituted to combat a pagan festival, borrowing some features of the pagan celebration in the process. If this were true, would it invalidate Christmas?

Summa

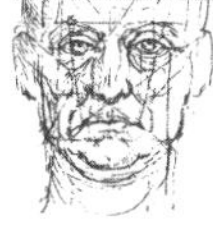

Write an essay or discuss this question, integrating what you have learned from the material above.

Based on the principles we have discussed, take a stance for or against Christian participation in the activities of Halloween.

Optional Activity

Read James Jordan's article, "Concerning Halloween."[2]

Reading Assignment:
Book 2, chapters 1–8

Session V: Discussion

Book 2, chapters 1–8

A Question to Consider

What is authority? Try thinking of your own definition, then choose one from a dictionary. Finally, think of some people who have authority over you.

Discuss or list short answers to the following questions:

Text Analysis

1. The medieval church made extensive use of symbolic objects. What object does Bede mention that attaches ecclesiastical authority to a person (1.29)? How does Gregory explain its rationale?
2. What title does Gregory use to identify himself to the missionaries, and what phrase does he address them with in his letter in 1.23?
3. With this in mind, what is Gregory's purpose in investing Augustine with ecclesiastical authority (1.23, 30)?
4. Another kind of authority given to Augustine, according to our text, is the power to perform miracles. What warnings does Gregory give regarding this authority (1.31)?
5. After King Ethelbert's conversion, what does Gregory tell him about his authority over his kingdom (1.32)?
6. How does Ethelbert's authority relate to Augustine's (1.32)?
7. How do the British bishops test Augustine's meekness and fitness to rule? Does he pass the test, and what is the result (2.2)?
8. What happens to the English church after Augustine's death (2.5)?

"Halloween" is simply a contraction for All Hallow's Eve (Hallow-Even—Hallow-E'n—Halloween). The word "hallow" means "saint," in that "hallow" is just an alternative form of the word "holy" ("hallowed be Thy name"). All Saints' Day is November 1. It is the celebration of the victory of the saints in union with Christ. The observance of various celebrations of All Saints arose in the late 300s, and these were united and fixed on November 1 in the late 700s. The origin of All Saints Day and All Saints Eve in Mediterranean Christianity had nothing to do with Celtic Druidism or the Church's fight against Druidism (assuming there ever was any such thing as Druidism, which is actually a myth concocted in the 19th century by neo-pagans). —James B. Jordan

Cultural Analysis

1. Why do men want authority?
2. Where can this be seen?

Biblical Analysis

1. Why does God place men in civil authority (Rom. 13)?
2. Why does God place men in authority in the church (Eph. 4:7–16)?
3. What does the mother of James and John ask Jesus to do? What does He answer? How do the other disciples react (Matt. 20:20–24)?
4. What two models of authority does Jesus describe? Which does He command His disciples to imitate (Matt. 20:25–28)?
5. How should we conduct ourselves with regard to those who rule over us (Ex. 20:12; Rom. 13:1–2; 1 Tim. 2:1–2)?

Summa

Write an essay or discuss this question, integrating what you have learned from the material above.

How does Gregory's model of Christian authority in the church and kingdom resemble the biblical model?

Reading Assignment:
Book 2, chapters 9–20

Session VI: Discussion

Book 2, chapters 9–20

A Question to Consider

Does prayer change the future?

Discuss or list short answers to the following questions:

Text Analysis

1. How does prayer figure in Bede's account of Augustine's mission to Kent (1.25, 26)?
2. What does Augustine pray for near the beginning of 2.2? Explain the circumstances and the outcome.
3. What are the monks praying for in 2.2? What happens to them? Why?
4. Who is Ethelberga? Why does Pope Boniface write to her? What does he tell her to do (2.11)?

Cultural Analysis

1. What are some ways that unbelievers talk about prayer?
2. Do Christians believe that God answers our prayers?

Biblical Analysis

1. What crisis leads Moses to pray for the people of Israel in Exodus 32? Does he change God's mind?
2. What condition does John say is sufficient for our prayer requests to be granted (1 John 5:14–15)?
3. What other condition does the New Testament associate with effective prayers (James 5:15–16; 1 John 3:22)?

Summa

Write an essay or discuss this question, integrating what you have learned from the material above.

How is prayer related to the advance of the gospel? Explain your answer with references to the Bible and to Anglo-Saxon history.

Reading Assignment:
Book 3, chapters 1–14

Session VII: Discussion

Book 3, chapters 1–14

A Question to Consider

Do miracles still occur?

Discuss or list short answers to the following questions:

Text Analysis

1. What miracles occur at the death of St. Alban, and with what results (1.7)?
2. What is Germanus's miracle in 1.18, and what is the result?
3. What is Augustine's miracle in 2.2, and what is the result?
4. Oswald's miracles occur after his death. What are some of them, and what is their purpose (3.9–13)?

Cultural Analysis

1. What are some of the attitudes that unbelievers frequently have toward miracles?
2. Is the absence (or near-absence) of miracles in the church today a stumbling block to unbelievers who might come to Christ?

Biblical Analysis

1. When John the Baptist sends messengers to Jesus to ask if He is the Messiah, how does He answer (Matt. 11:1–6)?
2. Explain how Jesus relates miracles and belief in Luke 10:13–16.
3. Why can't the disciples cast out the demon in Matthew 17:14–21?
4. Does Jesus say the disciples will lose the power to do great works after He leaves them (John 14:12–14)?

Summa

Write an essay or discuss this question, integrating what you have learned from the material above.

What can be said to an unbeliever who is familiar with Christian belief but wants to see a sign that the gospel is true?

Optional Activity

Ask your pastor if he has ever witnessed any miracles. If so, what happened? If not, ask why he thinks miracles are scarce.

Reading Assignment:

Book 3, chapters 15–30

Pelagius (c. 354–418) was a monk from Britain who did not believe in the doctrine of original sin. Instead, he taught that man was by nature innately good and that this nature was only modified by sin. R.C. Sproul writes, "The controversy began when the British monk, Pelagius, opposed at Rome Augustine's famous prayer: 'Grant what Thou commandest, and command what Thou dost desire.' Pelagius recoiled in horror at the idea that a divine gift (grace) is necessary to perform what God commands. For Pelagius and his followers responsibility always implies ability. If man has the moral responsibility to obey the law of God, he must also have the moral ability to do it. . . . Augustine did not deny that fallen man still has a will and that the will is capable of making choices. He argued that fallen man still has a free will (*liberium arbitrium*) but has lost his moral liberty (*libertas*). The state of original sin leaves us in the wretched condition of being unable to refrain from sinning. We still are able to choose what we desire, but our desires remain chained by our evil impulses. He argued that the freedom that remains in the will always leads to sin. Thus in the flesh we are free only to sin, a hollow freedom indeed. It is freedom without liberty, a real moral bondage. True liberty can only come from without, from the work of God on the soul. Therefore we are not only partly dependent upon grace for our conversion but totally dependent upon grace."

Chart 1: **SIX ELEMENTS OF WORLDVIEW**

ELEMENT	*ECCLESIASTICAL HISTORY*	BIBLE
Work: Is physical labor good? Is it really necessary?		
Division of labor in society: Are fundamentally different tasks given to different groups within society?		
Prayer and meditation: How much is too much?		
Pleasure vs. Asceticism: Should earthly pleasures be fled from or indulged in?		
Holiness: Is personal holiness attainable? By whom?		
Marriage and Virginity: How do they compare?		

Session VIII: Recitation

Book 3, chapters 15–30

Comprehension Questions

Answer the following questions for factual recall:

1. What story does Bede tell to explain the origin of Gregory's interest in the English (2.1)? Explain why you think, or do not think, Bede believes this story.
2. What power did the apostles have that Augustine lacks? The answer can be found comparing 1.25 with Acts 2.
3. How does Edwin's miraculous vision, related as a flashback in 2.12, figure in the long account of his conversion? Put the main events back into chronological order (2.9–14).
4. Who is Columba? Where does he found a monastery (3.4)?
5. What deeds, military and evangelical, did King Oswald do for his people (3.1–3)?
6. Who is Aidan? Where does he establish a bishopric (3.3)?
7. What reservations does Bede have about both Columba and Aidan (3.3, 3.4)?
8. Which king of the East Angles becomes a monk? How does he die (3.18)?
9. What is the basic problem at issue in the Synod of Whitby (called Streanaeshalch, 3.25)? Why does this matter, and what decision is arrived at?
10. Briefly summarize the Irish way of reckoning the date of Easter and the Roman one (3.25). How does each relate to the date for the Jewish Passover?

Reading Assignment:
Book 4, chapters 1–15

Session IX: Activity

Book 4, chapters 1–15

Biblical typology

In theology, *types* are people, things and events in the Old Testament that prefigure (i.e., come before and point to) people, things and events in the New Testament. For example, the ark which saved Noah and his family is a type of baptism (1 Pet. 3:21). Such relationships are typologies. The concept of *typology* can be extended beyond Scripture to other things. The purpose of this activity is to identify some typological connections between Bede's *History* and the Bible.

In the Worldview Essay and in Session II we saw how Bishop Germanus resembles Jesus when his followers have to wake him to calm the storm during their passage to Britain (1.17). Reread the following narratives and then read the biblical passages given. List the parallels. If no biblical passages are given, try to think of one on your own and list the parallels.

1. Crimes and judgment (1.14): Compare with Deuteronomy 28:47–59 and 2 Chronicles16:1–10.
2. Battle of Badon Hill (1.16): Compare with Judges 3:7–11.
3. Germanus gives sight to a blind girl (1.18, paragraph 1): Compare with 1 Kings 18:20–40.
4. The British bishops test Augustine, and he prophesies their doom (2.2, paragraphs 3 and 4).
5. Martyrdom of Alban (1.7): Compare with Matthew 26:57–66; 27:15–26; 27:32; Luke 23:39–43; John 19:28.
6. Wilfrid's ministry brings rain and fish (4.13).

READING ASSIGNMENT:
Book 4, chapters 16–32

SESSION X: WORLDVIEW ANALYSIS

Book 4, chapters 16–32

Bede and the Bible

You know by now that Bede's world was very different from ours. It differed in material terms—work was hard, transport and communication were slow, books were scarce and precious, life expectancy was short. It also differed in worldview. Chart 1 lists six elements of worldview. For each of these six elements list a couple of points describing how they are portrayed both in Bede's *History* and the Bible. Illustrate your points with specific references to the *History* and to the Bible.

SUMMA

Write an essay or discuss this question, integrating what you have learned from the material above.

What might be considered particular shortcomings of this early medieval worldview? What could the church learn today from this same worldview?

READING ASSIGNMENT:
Book 5, chapters 1–12.

SESSION XI: WRITING

Book 5, chapters 1–12

Progymnasmata

Classical training in rhetoric included preparatory writing exercises called the *progymnasmata.* These exercises in composition introduced the beginning student to basic forms and techniques that would be brought together when the student advanced to making speeches. One of these progymnasmata was called the *refutation.* In the refutation the student argued against the probability of a given event or mythical story. The opposite of this exercise was *confirmation,* in which the student argued for the probability of a given event or mythical story. Often the two were assigned together, so that the student would have to argue both sides of a question. In this session practice refutations and confirmations for two of Bede's miracle stories.

Refutation has three parts. First, the student undertakes to discredit the teller of the story. This could be done by attacking the source as misinformed or as dishonest. In the stories we will refute, it will be necessary to focus on Bede's descriptions of his sources—whether he saw the miracle himself, heard it from a reliable source or heard a "story that is told." The second part gives an exposition of the matter. This should be done briefly, but in such a way as to encourage doubt. The third and (usually) largest part brings out defects in the story under the following headings: a) A Lack of Clarity, e.g., "The account lacks supportive detail;" b) Implausibility, e.g., "Though God can work all things, no story like this has ever been told;" c) Impossibility, e.g., "This miracle is contrary to God's nature;" d) Inconsistency, e.g., "First we are told his thumb was broken, then we are told it was his skull;" e) Impropriety, e.g., "No holy man would have conducted himself in this way" and f) Inexpediency, e.g., "Saint Cuthbert desired to glorify God, but the flaunting behavior attributed to him in this story would on the contrary glorify the man."

Confirmation has three parts as well. First, the student praises the reliability of the speaker. Second, the student gives a narration of the matter in such a way that encourages belief. Third, the student underscores the strength of the story by addressing headings opposite to those in refutation: a) Clarity; b) Plausibility; c) Possibility; d) Consistency; e) Propriety and f) Expediency.

Reread the following miracle stories and then practice both refutation and confirmation for each. Use as many of the headings, a) through f), as you can. Other tactics can be used as well.

1. Baduthegn is cured through the intercession of Cuthbert (4.32).
2. Cuthbert's relics heal a monk's diseased eye (4.32).

READING ASSIGNMENT:
Book 5, chapters 13–19

SESSION XII: DISCUSSION

Book 5, chapters 13–19

A Question to Consider

Why is the church so divided today?

Discuss or list short answers to the following questions:.

Text Analysis

1. Who are Ronan and Finan? What is their conflict and what comes of it (3.25)?
2. What was King Oswy's opinion regarding Easter before the Synod of Whitby? Why does he change his mind (3.25)?
3. How does Bede portray Oswy in 4.5?
4. How does Bishop Colman respond to the decision of the Synod of Whitby? What does he go on to do (3.26, 4.4)?
5. Explain the circumstances in which Iona adopts the catholic dating of Easter. What persuades Adamnan to change (5.15)?

Cultural Analysis

1. Is the disunity of the church a stumbling block to unbelievers who might come to faith?
2. What do American Christians think about church unity?

Biblical Analysis

1. What does Paul urge in Ephesians 4:1-6, and what does he give as his reason?
2. In what ways does the Holy Spirit unite believers (1 Cor. 12)?

SUMMA

Write an essay or discuss this question, integrating what you have learned from the material above.

Do differences between church associations, denominations, etc., really matter, if we are one in the Holy Spirit?

READING ASSIGNMENT:
Book 5, chapters 20–24

SESSION XIII: RECITATION

Book 5, chapters 20–24

Comprehension Questions

Answer the following questions for factual recall:

1. Where does Archbishop Theodore come from, and what are some of his main accomplishments (4.1, 2, 5.8)?
2. What step does Archbishop Theodore take to protect future generations in Britain from heresy?
3. What virgin queen does Bede compose an acrostic hymn in honor of?
4. What is the story of Caedmon?
5. What draws God's wrath to Coldingham monastery (4.25)?
6. What does Egbert want to do, and what prevents him, in 5.9?
7. Who is Willibrord? What does he do upon arriving in Frisia (5.10–11)?

8. Who are Hewald the White and Hewald the Black? What are the circumstances of their deaths (5.10)?
9. What does Nechtan, king of the Picts, write to Ceolfrid for (5.21)?
10. What are the major occupations and events of Bede's life, as he describes them at the end of his History (see the "Autobiographical Note" at the end of Book 5)?

Session XIV: Activity

Review Game

If you are studying as a group, you can play this review game. One person will have to serve as judge, weighing the answers against those in the teacher's edition. Turns pass around the group clockwise. Address question 1 to the player whose name is alphabetically closest to *Caedmon.* Each missed question passes to the next player. Ask only one question of each player per turn. See who can acquire the most points! If you are studying by yourself, you can still keep track of your score out of the total 24 + 1!

1. What signs occur at the martyrdom of Alban?
2. What happens at the Battle of Badon Hill?
3. Who leads the campaign against British Pelagianism?
4. When he agrees to meet with the missionary Augustine, why does Ethelbert want the meeting to be outdoors?
5. Ethelbert knew of the Christian faith before Augustine's coming. How did he know?
6. What other king has a Christian wife who helps bring about her husband's conversion?
7. What is Gregory's advice to Augustine concerning pagan temples?
8. What is the *pallium?*
9. How does the study of history encourage virtue, according to Bede? (Recall the Preface, "To the Most Glorious King Ceolwulf.") For a bonus point: what Roman historian does Bede's thought resemble here?
10. Who was Pelagius?
11. What British king invites the ancestors of the English to Britain, and why?
12. What crime do the Britons commit against the English newcomers?
13. When other bishops are fleeing Britain, why does

The first record of the manuscript we call the Book of Kells occurred in A.D. 1006 in the annals of Ulster: "The great Gospel of Colmcille, the chief relic of the western world, was wickedly stolen during the night from the western sacristy of the great stone church of Cennanus on account of its wrought shrine. That Gospel was found after twenty nights and two months with its gold stolen from it, buried in the ground."

Laurence decide not to go?
14. Who is Penda?
15. How does a sparrow figure in the conversion of Northumbria?
16. What is the story of Coifi?
17. What saint's place of death becomes a holy site, and how is its holiness first discovered?
18. What happens at Lindisfarne?
19. Who is Theodore?
20. What king changes his mind at the Synod of Whitby?
21. Who refuses to change his views at the Synod of Whitby?
22. What hermit bishop harvests a large crop of barley from seed sown out of season?
23. What does Willibrord do?
24. What did Bede spend his life doing?

SESSION XV: EVALUATION

All tests and quizzes are to be given with an open book and a Bible available.

Grammar

Answer each of the following questions in complete sentences. Some answers may be longer than others (2 points per answer).

1. What are the nations of Britain? How, according to Bede, are they united through one language?
2. What faults are the Britons guilty of, according to Bede? Give specifics.
3. Who might justly be called the apostle to the English, according to Bede? Why does he deserve this title?
4. What is the story of Caedmon?
5. What is the story of Coifi?
6. Who refuses to change his views at the Synod of Whitby?
7. What does Willibrord do?

Logic

Answer two of the following three questions in complete sentences; your answers should be a paragraph or so. (10 points per answer)

1. How do the missionaries treat the kings and rulers whose people they seek to convert, and what role do these rulers play in the conversion of their peoples? Using specific instances, show that there is a general pattern.
2. Which side prevails at the Synod of Whitby and through what arguments?
3. What were the circumstances of Wilfrid's training? Why was this significant for the Synod of Whitby?

Lateral Thinking

Answer one of the following questions. These questions will require more substantial answers (16 points per answer).

1. In what ways is Bede's worldview more faithful to the Bible than is the worldview of modern evangelicals? In what ways, if any, is it less faithful?
2. What do we know of Bede's experiences as a monk—both from his autobiographical remarks and from his many descriptions of monasticism in general—and how does the *History* show the imprint of these experiences?

OPTIONAL SESSION A: ACTIVITY

Researching the Lindisfarne Gospels

Any good encyclopedia will have an article and description of the Lindisfarne Gospels. There are also many online resources.[3] Familiarize yourself with some of these resources and find out the answers to the questions below.

1. What are the Lindisfarne Gospels?
2. Where is the book now?
3. Who made the Lindisfarne Gospels, and how does this relate to Bede?
4. What are the names of the three ornamented pages at the beginning of each gospel?
5. What are the carpet pages?
6. What is an incipit page?
7. Study a picture of the incipit page to the Gospel of John (this may be viewed at Link 4 for this chapter at www.VeritasPress.com/OmniLinks). What words or parts of words can you make out? (Hint: the Gospel of John begins *In principio erat verbum et verbum erat apud deum et deus erat*

verbum—"In the beginning was the word and the word was with God and the word was God.")

8. What are the main symbols of the evangelists, and where do the Lindisfarne Gospels show these?

Like the Lindisfarne Gospels, the Book of Kells is a lavishly illuminated manuscript. It contains the four Gospels of the Bible in Latin and many beautiful illuminations like the one shown above.

Optional Session B: Activity

The Death of Bede

Read "Cuthbert's Letter on the Illness and Death of the Venerable Bede,"[4] then answer the following questions:

1. What good news has Cuthbert received in a letter from Cuthwin?
2. What has Cuthwin asked Cuthbert for?
3. What blessing did Bede receive, about two weeks before Easter and lasting till the day of the Lord's Ascension?
4. What does Cuthbert find so remarkable about Bede's last days?
5. In what ways does Bede's death shadow Jesus' death and ascension?
6. What do all who heard or saw Bede's death say about it?

Optional Session C: Writing

Historical Truth?

Bede, in his *Ecclesiastical History,* is interested not only in the historical truth of the stories he tells, but also in the power of stories to be morally instructive. Both of these are mentioned in the Preface, but they resurface throughout the *History* itself. Here are some examples of how these interests may be seen.

History as actual events

- In the Preface, Bede describes in some detail the contacts that he used as his sources, apparently with the purpose of showing that his sources and their stories are reliable.
- Bede often takes pains to establish the credibility of specific stories by vouching for the integrity of his source (e.g., 3.16; 4.3, 7, 14, 19, 31; 5.1, 2 etc.).

History as moral instruction

- Bede sometimes remarks that a given story is *said* to have happened, as if to admit that it might be less reliable (e.g., 1.1; 2.1; 3.5, 6).

- In the Preface, Bede says the "true law of history" requires that he record, not just what he is sure really happened, but all those things which reached him by common report and that might be instructive.
- Sometimes Bede observes about one of his stories that it is morally instructive, or a helpful source of motivation (e.g., 4.7, 14; 5.12, 13, 14).

Is Bede more interested in historical truth or moral instructiveness? Or, for Bede, are historical truth and moral instructiveness really different aspects of the same thing? Reread the visions of the afterlife reported in 5.12–14 and decide whether you think Bede believed these stories really happened. Explain your position in a short essay, supporting your claims with specific references to the text. Also discuss Bede's view of history as event and of history as moral instruction.

Endnotes

1. The Easter Controversy concerned the formula that was applied by the Irish and Roman churches to calculate the date on which Easter was to be celebrated. The formulas were similar, but sometimes resulted in the Roman and Irish churches celebrating Easter on different Sundays. This diversity upset the unity of the two churches.
2. This article can be found at Link 2 for this chapter at www.VeritasPress.com/OmniLinks.
3. Images and descriptions are available at Link 3 for this chapter at www.VeritasPress.com/OmniLinks.
4. The letter can be found many places online, including through Link 5 for this chapter at www.VeritasPress.com/OmniLinks.

The Rule of St. Benedict

The sun peeked above the horizon showing a bright countryside. A man worked at plowing, sweat already forming in beads on his forehead. Behind him arose a sandstone monastery. It was just beginning to buzz with activity. One monk milking the cows, another carrying dung from stalls. The monk in the field looked up when a stranger called with fiery eyes, "Brother Monk, at sundown the Lord will return. Follow me, Jesus is coming. The end of the world is at hand. Put down your plow."

This traveling stranger, also a kind of monk, was not part of the abbot's charge. He traveled from place to place, shouting a shocking message of doom. "The black death is God's wrath. The end is near!" The stranger pleaded with the man in the field to stop this worldly work and to embark upon a more spiritual work of warning souls. The end was near.

At first the plowing monk replied, "Brother, if I do not finish the plowing and planting, my brothers in the monastery will have no grain at harvest."

The stranger reasoned, "The barley will be burned up in the judgment. So will you, if you do not obey God's call to escape from this world."

"But this barley is for ale," argued the monk.

"Even so," said the stranger, "We must soberly await the end. We must be ready for the rapture."

The monk pondered this for a moment. "Brother, I have obeyed the call of God to do this work before me."

The stranger urged, "This work will perish. Prepare for the end!"

"But this work is to serve my brothers. It will disappoint them not to have ale. My calling is to work heartily as unto the Lord in this field."

The stranger, seeing the hard-heartedness of this monk, rode away in search of other souls to warn.

General Information

Author and Context

St. Benedict of Nursia (c. 480–543) changed the world. Though monks and their communities existed for centuries before Benedict, *The Catholic Encyclopedia* calls him the "founder of western monasticism."[1] What is known of St. Benedict's life comes from the second book of the *Dialogues* of Gregory I. It is more of a character sketch than a biography and contains some interesting stories of miracles. The book is entitled *Containing the Life and Miracles of St. Benedict (Bennet) of Nursia.* St. Gregory writes that the *Rule* is his real biography. Gregory records of "Benedictus" or "Bennet" that even from his youth he "carried always the mind of an old man; for his age was inferior to his virtue."[2] We learn that he was born in the province of Nursia of devout and wealthy parents. An accepted tradition is that Benedict had a twin sister, Scholastica. Nursia is a village high in the mountains northeast of Rome. He received a "classical education" at Rome. Because he saw the city as depraved and those who were trained this way as dissolute and lewd, he turned away from his books and his father's house and wealth. He heard the monastic call. He became a hermit for three years and stayed in a cave alone. He was fed by bread lowered on a rope by another monk named Romanus. While Benedict was a hermit, he was discovered by a group of monks and asked to become their leader. In a bad turn of events, those monks later tried to kill him with poison wine. But as Gregory tells it, when Benedict blessed the pitcher of poisoned wine, it shattered.

Benedict went on to establish twelve monasteries south of Rome. His first miracle was to restore by prayer a broken clay wheat-sifter (*capisterium*) which had been accidentally shattered. By about 529, he moved to Monte Cassino, southeast of Rome. It was there that he wrote the Rule.

Significance

When you are patron saint of a continent, you know that you are at the top of the game of sainthood. At the dedication of the rebuilt monastery of Monte Cassino in 1964, Pope Paul VI proclaimed St. Benedict to be "the principal, heavenly patron of the whole of Europe." This exaggerates the place of Benedict, but it is due to St. Benedict's stabilizing influence in monastic life that many of the great manuscripts were preserved, even the Scriptures. St. Benedict did not establish the monastery of Monte Cassino in order to preserve the learning of the ages. But in fact, that is what happened. Civilization was preserved by the hard work and discipline of Benedictine monks. The influence of the *Rule* and the Benedictine monastic tradition was not continuous from his day forward. In 577, within a few decades of Benedict's death, Monte Cassino was destroyed by Germanic invaders. Monte Cassino was not rebuilt until 730. Some of the scattered monks went to Rome and had contact with Gregory I. Benedict's work began to be forgotten. It did not appear in official church circles until around 720. Gregory's *Dialogues* became an important work a few hundred years later, as those in Northern Europe wanted Roman books. Under Charlemagne (c. 800), Benedict's *Rule* was preferred to other, harsher monastic teachings. It spread throughout Western Europe.

In this piece, artist Tanja Butler depicts Benedict and the Benedictine motto *Ora et Labora,* that is, "Pray and Work." It is through living out this idea that the monks introduced into Western culture the idea of the dignity of work—they could glorify God by both being scholars and working in the fields to bring in the harvest.

Setting

The significance of Benedict's work arises as we contrast monastic life as practiced in accordance to his *Rule* with monks before his time. There had been those who wished to escape the corruption of the world and practice holiness in solitude. We can see this from Benedict's own biography. He was a hermit for a few years but finally became part of a monastic community. He moved from being a hermit to being a *cenobite* (a monk in a monastic community, from the Greek word *koinonia,* meaning "community"). Hermits, also called anchorites, left society to dwell alone. Sometimes they took a disciple with them. Since the early examples are the "desert fathers," they are also known as *eremites,* "inhabitants of a desert," from the Greek *eremos.* Jerome, translator of the Latin Bible (Vulgate), writes about some of the first hermits, living around A.D. 250. Athanasius, the great defender of the deity of Christ, writes about them in his life of St. Anthony. It was St. Anthony who made this kind of life popular at the beginning of the fourth century. Especially after persecutions arose in the empire, hermits sought this life apart from a corrupt society. They lived all over the ancient Christian world, in Egypt, Palestine, the Sinai peninsula, Mesopotamia, Syria and Asia Minor. The Syrian hermits subjected their bodies to hardship. They stayed for years on the top of pillars (*stylites*). They condemned themselves to remain standing, in open air (*stationaries*). Others locked themselves in cells so they could not come out (*recluses*). Many doctors of the church, like St. Basil, St. Gregory of Nazianzus, St. John Chrysostom and St. Jerome, belonged to their number. Monasteries sometimes arose from a band of disciples around a hermit. This we also see in the life of Benedict. As a result of Benedict's *Rule* many communities throughout Europe were stabilized with an ethic of work and worship. The preservation and transmission of much of Western civilization was the result.

Worldview

What would you do if you knew that Jesus would return at sundown? Many would respond that they would go evangelize their neighbors, or read the Bible for the rest of the day or pray until then. The Benedictine monk's response in the story above helps us see something very important. The monk would answer this question, "If I knew Jesus would return at sundown, I would finish plowing the field." The monk saw his work in the field as fulfilling God's good purpose. This was just as spiritual as evangelism, reading the Bible or praying, since this was his duty.

The story above illustrates for us the value in medieval monasticism in one sense. There are also inconsistencies in monasticism that we must explore. In our day, especially in America, it cuts against the grain to imagine a young person pursuing a monastic life. Monastic callings do not get much air-time on reality TV shows, MTV or VH1. They are hardly ever featured on prime time.

We may have a stereotype of monks which sees them as dreary, dark-clad, chanting religious freaks. But not all monks were the same. St. Benedict actually reformed the monastic movement by writing his *Rule.* In the final chapter he makes clear that the *Rule* is not offered as an ideal of perfection, but as a means towards godliness. It was for beginners to grow in the life of disciplined spirituality. Like training for the Marines, discipline produces fidelity. It was not to be harsh, though some of it may sound that way to us.

In the first chapter he speaks of four principle kinds of monks: Cenobites, those living in a monastery under an abbot, which is what he advocates; Anchorites, or hermits, living a solitary life after long probation in the monastery; Sarabites (also spelled *sarabaites*), living by twos and threes together, without any fixed rule or lawfully constituted superior; and Gyrovagi (also spelled *gyrovagues*), monastic vagrants, who wander from one monastery to another, like the one in the story above. The Gyrovagi discredit the monastic profession, according to Benedict. It is for the Cenobites that the *Rule* is written. This gives us a sense of the landscape in Benedict's day. There were many religious, weird people, just as there are today. But Benedict wants to help those who are pursuing a holy calling to serve God. He does so by stabilizing the monastic life into a community of the faithful, where reasonable discipline is embraced.

However reasonable Benedict's *Rule* is in comparison to harsher approaches, today we have a disdain for monastic life. What assumptions in our time must we unpack to appreciate the monastic movement for what it was? Our ideas of spirituality and work will need to be adjusted. As a culture we are becoming less and less consistent with the "Protestant Work Ethic." This is the value that all callings or "vocations" (from the Latin, *vocatio*) can be done to the glory of God and that hard work is a productive virtue.[3]

In this way, St. Benedict's *Rule* is remarkable. Manual labor for monks was essential for growth in spiritual maturity. Work produced Christian disciples. Work was not, as the civilization of the time taught, the condition peculiar to slaves; it is the creational mandate and is universal for mankind. Work is necessary for our well-being and essentially part of being Christian. Jesus labored as a carpenter before His kingdom was to come.

The work of Bendictine-like monasticism was thoroughly productive—so much so that he is considered the "patron of Europe," as mentioned above. Such work produced many of the architectural triumphs which are the glory of the Christian world. Cathedrals, abbeys and churches all over Western Europe were the result of Benedictine builders. Labor in the soil made for a harvest of agricultural prosperity in Europe. Careful husbandry was studied, and it produced valuable crops and gardens for growing healthy seed stock. Also, the calling of study and writing led to great scholarship and the preservation of the ancient texts of Scripture and the pre-Christian classics. The regulations regarding the education of children directly contributed to famous monastic schools and universities which flourished in medieval times. Monasteries housed hospitals, orphanages, schools, places of charity and social services.

All of this is striking in contrast to our very secularized approach to work and our very Gnostic or anti-material approach to spirituality. Our culture represents work as something to totally avoid if you can. If you must work, it is only for money or pleasures (which idea is often thought to be sinful as well). On the other hand, our super-spirituality would have us leave ordinary life and enter a kind of evangelical cloister, instead of seeing work as a central aspect of taking dominion to the end of serving God. This view would say that we should become missionaries or ministers if we are really spiritual.

We find it difficult in contemporary society to see all of life as spiritual. The monastic movement had a very earthy, mulch-like spirituality. You could smell the spirituality of hard-working monks. A monk knew he

Monks are shown praying in this illustration from the *Tres Belles Heures*. Aside from the order's founder, perhaps the most famous Benedictine monk is the fictional Brother Cadfael. Ellis Peters (Edith Pargeter) created the character to serve as the detective hero of her excellent medieval murder mysteries, *The Cadfael Chronicles*.

was serving God by planting, plowing or brewing. And yet, the cloistered nature of monastery life suggested that outside the walls was the "world." In fact, Benedict wished for monasteries to be self-sufficient and self-sustaining so that monks would not need to leave and be dependent on the world outside at all. They were little cities.

The most important work of the monk was the "work of God," the *opus Dei*—the liturgy of worship. Worship and devotion through prayers, readings and the Eucharist or Lord's Supper formed the daily core of monastic life. We do not value liturgy or believe in the reality of the *opus Dei* unless we experience an emotional high in it. And, as a culture, we tend to think that rock music does that better than chanting the Psalms in Latin. In the monastic patterns suggested by St. Benedict we find the tension of an earthly spirituality and a kind of cloistered spirituality and yet a high view of worship which was at the center of a life of hard work.

The *Rule* aimed to create communities of faith. The *Rule* oriented the monasteries toward a self-sufficient community, like an island of charity and benevolence in a hostile and uncivilized world. Monasteries aimed at spiritual discipline woven into a community of worship. Life was molded into patterns of regular prayer, reading, Eucharist, litanies and manual labor. This meant that for much of the Middle Ages, with Rome in ruins and no centralized governmental power, monasteries were very basic to the social fabric. This only began to change with the development of cities.

We have a saying that a person may be "so heavenly-minded they are no earthly good." This could not be said of all monks, as the above story illustrates. In the best light they had an earthly spirituality. But a great distortion present from the earliest days of the Christian faith blossomed by late medieval times. This distortion was a kind of anti-creational, anti-world spirituality, sacred versus secular spirituality, that hated the world made up of matter and sought to simply sit, think about God and escape the prison of this material existence (this might sound familiar if you paid attention to Plato in *Omnibus I*). In this twisted form of Christian thinking, the highest calling was monastic and everything else was a lower calling. To get married and raise a family was not as spiritual as joining a convent or "monking-out."

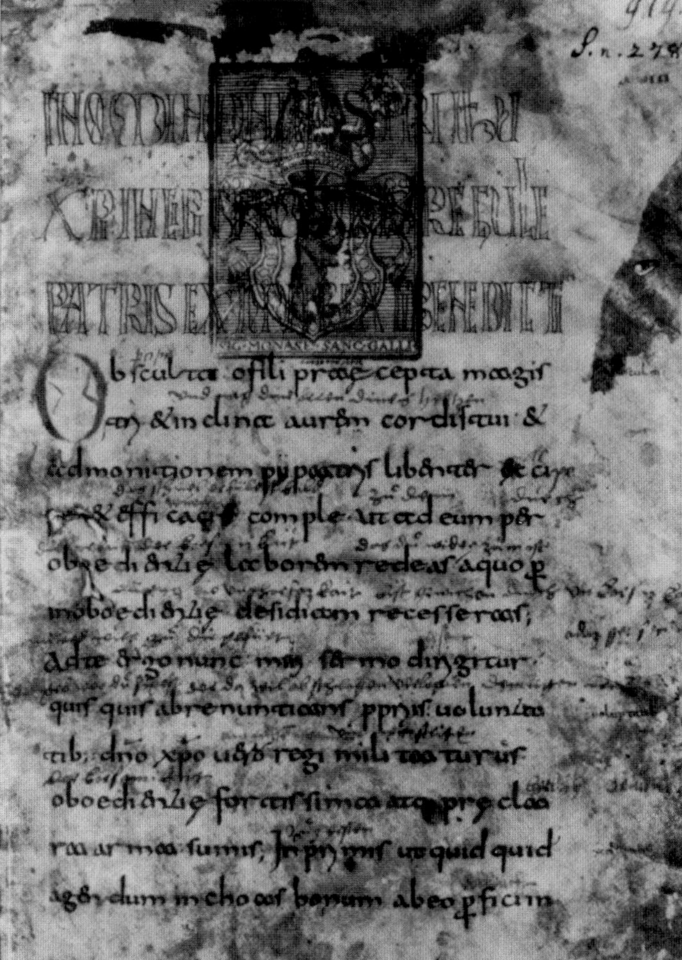

The first page of the St. Gallen manuscript of the *Rule of St. Benedict* begins, "Listen my son to the master's commands . . ."

This type of monk has been rightly criticized by people, like the sharp-tongued Ambrose Bierce, who said, "a monk of St. Benedict, croaking a text. Black friars in this world, fried black in the next."[4]

In this we see the tension that has been tugging at the faith all along. *Christians must either renounce the world or reconstruct the world according to God's will.* Much of medieval piety, following from Greek philosophy's love of "spirit" and hatred of the ever-changing material world, sought righteousness by renouncing the world. This thread of spirituality runs back to the earliest days of Christians in the Roman Empire, which was infested with Greek thinking. Otherworldly contemplation perfected the spiritual flame of the righteous. This world's stuff only dragged one down. Instead of having a robust view of creation

"In the dead of night he suddenly beheld a flood of light shining down from above more brilliant than the sun, and . . . the whole world was gathered up before his eyes in what appeared to be a single ray of light."—*The Life and Miracles of Saint Benedict* by Pope Gregory the Great.

and the incarnation, abstaining from creational delights became the means to a deeper life in Christ—never mind that Jesus sinlessly came down to earth as a flesh-and-blood man who laughed, got mad, made wine, drank it, fished and beat up corrupt temple officials. The strain of other-worldly spirituality wanted "the things of earth to grow strangely dim."

Over the centuries, there were many excesses of monkish, ascetic (anti-physical) behavior. There have been many attempts at X-game, X-treme spirituality, like self-mutilation, castration, wearing of hairshirts to irritate the skin, austere fasts, self-denial of all creational delights and, of course, celibacy. This upper-story spirituality has never really left the church. It still exists in some Roman Catholic settings where mortification of the flesh comes through acts of penance using whips or hard beds.

Throughout history wayward attempts and X-treme spirituality required church councils and bishops to step in to rebuke the absurdity of these attempts. For example, we know very well of the council of Nicea's (A.D. 325) teachings on the divinity of Jesus, but many of the decrees of the council dealt with practical matters, like whether those who had been castrated should be clergymen. The very first Canon of Nicea addresses this:

> If any one in sickness has been subjected by physicians to a surgical operation, or if he has been castrated by barbarians, let him remain among the clergy; but, if any one in sound health has castrated himself, it behooves that such an one, if already enrolled among the clergy, should cease [from his ministry] . . ."[5]

So, medieval Christianity, like the early seed of upper-story Christian spirituality, was against the world. To live as a butcher, baker or candle-stick maker was to choose a second-rate spirituality. Real spirituality meant vows of poverty, the complete renunciation of all worldly possessions and avoiding physical indulgences.

The Reformation caused such thinking to be overturned. A huge shift took place in the minds of Christians who were no longer on the road to Rome. They were world-affirming. The ordinary callings of people were valued. The monastic distinction of sacred versus secular was rejected. All of life should be spiritual, since we could serve God in every facet of His creation. The Reformation put Christians intentionally on the road to remaking the world according to the biblical blueprint.

Martin Luther attacked the false spirituality of monasticism. He argued against monastic vows in a book called, *The Judgment of Martin Luther on Monastic Vows.* It represented his final blow against what he saw as a corrupt Roman Catholic Church. Luther did not absolutely reject the possibility of monastic vows, but he did reject the idea that such vows should be a permanent or eternally binding vow.[6] Not only did he take a wife (a former nun at that), but he would argue that "household chores are more to be valued that all the works of monks and nuns." And, "God pays no attention to the insignificance of the work being done, but looks at the heart which is serving him in the work. This is true even of such everyday tasks as washing dishes or milking cows."[7]

The Reformation restored the best of medieval views of an earthly spirituality and extended that beyond the walls of the monasteries to the whole of the city and countryside. Godliness can be just as true for the minister as for the milk-maid. God-approved service is for all callings, not just those doing supposed "spiritual" things.

We have seen an erosion of the high watermark of the Reformation. Like the above story, we sometimes deny that work in this world is spiritual. We would stop mowing the yard and give out gospel tracts if we thought that Jesus was about to return.

We live in a time in which the church or church institutions are on the fringes of our society. We have reverted to a sacred/secular split. Today, unfortunately, the secular absorbs most of life. The major institutions which at one time were monastic and godly are now totally secularized and devoid of a God-centeredness. There are no new cathedrals that rise at the town center. There are no hospitals actually run by the church. There are no universities which are the scholarly preservation of biblical texts and learning. They are "multiversities," without the unity of the Trinitarian Christian faith at the center.

The institutions which were the foundations of much of our civilization were once the result of the labor of monastic communities. More generally, the church provided the scholarly, social and scientific achievements for a great civilization. Our culture has climbed up the ladder the church provided. But now we have kicked away that very ladder.

—*Gregg Strawbridge*

For Further Reading

Gonzalez, Justo. *The Story of Christianity. Vol. 1.* San Francisco: HarperCollins, 1984. 206–216.

Schaff, Philip. *History of the Christian Church, vol. 4, Mediaeval Christianity.* Peabody, Mass.: Hendrickson, 1996 [1885].

Spielvogel, Jackson J. *Western Civilization.* Seventh Edition. Belmont, Calif.: Thomson Wadsworth, 2009. 195–197.

Veritas Press History Cards: Middle Ages, Renaissance and Reformation. Lancaster, Pa.: Veritas Press. 5.

SESSION I: PRELUDE

A Question to Consider

What is holiness like? How do you recognize a holy person?

From the General Information above answer the following questions:

1. How did St. Benedict change the world?
2. Did St. Benedict's life experience affect his monastic views?
3. What kinds of monks existed at the time of St. Benedict, and why did they live as they did?
4. In what ways do Benedict's views on work conflict with our culture's views today?
5. Did St. Benedict understand spiritual maturity in the same way as Christians do today?
7. In what ways is the tradition of monasticism influenced by bad philosophy?
8. How did the Reformation affect views about monasticism and spirituality?

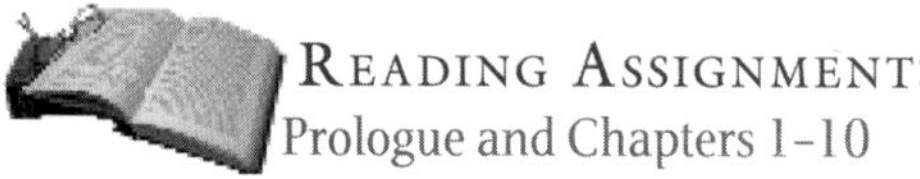

READING ASSIGNMENT:
Prologue and Chapters 1–10

SESSION II: DISCUSSION

Prologue and Chapters 1–10.

A Question to Consider

How disciplined should you be in your attempts to be holy?

Discuss or list short answers to the following questions:

Text Analysis

1. What type of monk does Benedict think is the best? Why (chap. 1)?
2. Which is the worst (chap. 1)?
3. How does living in a community prepare a monk for further, more intense service (chap. 1)?
4. What is an abbot to be like (chap. 2)?
5. What is the main goal of disciple (chaps. 5–7)?
6. What are the steps that a monk is to take to reach this goal (chaps. 5–7)?

Cultural Analysis

1. What is our culture's attitude toward discipline?
2. What would most people in our culture think about the goal suggested by Benedict and the means of reaching it?

Biblical Analysis

1. How do we know that joy and self-disciple are not mutually exclusive? (Gal. 5:22–26)
2. Christ was called a "wine bibber and a glutton," but did He fast? Why or why not? (Matt. 4:1–11)

SUMMA

Write an essay or discuss this question, integrating what you have learned from the material above.
What is the purpose of discipline?

READING ASSIGNMENT:
Chapters 11–20

SESSION III: DISCUSSION

Chapters 11–20

A Question to Consider

Should we have monks and monasteries today?

Discuss or list short answers to the following questions:

Text Analysis

1. What affected the order of worship (chaps. 10, 15)?
2. How often are the monks at worship (chap. 16)?
3. How familiar are the monks supposed to be with the Scriptures (chap. 18)?
4. How does Benedict describe a monk who did not

read all of the Psalms each week (chap. 18)?

5. What is the monks' attitude to be in prayer (chap. 20)?
6. What is life in the monastery like (chaps. 11–20)?

Cultural Analysis

1. What would our culture think of someone who went to worship seven times a day?
2. What varies according to seasons in our culture?

Biblical Analysis

1. Are the Nazirites examples of Old Testament monks (Num. 6)?
2. Was John the Baptist a monk (Luke 1:13–17; Matt. 3:1–12)?

Summa

Write an essay or discuss this question, integrating what you have learned from the material above.

Should we have monasteries and monks today?

Reading Assignment:
Chapters 21–46

Session IV: Recitation

Chapters 1–46

Comprehension Questions

Answer the following questions for factual recall:

1. What were the four kinds of monks? What differentiated the four types?
2. What is the goal of living in community in the monastery?
3. How many worship services are the monks who are obeying the *Rule* supposed to have?
4. How are the monks to sleep, and with what are they not to sleep?
5. What are the degrees of excommunication?
6. How are disobedient monks to be punished?
7. How many personal possessions are the monks allowed to have?
8. What arrangements are to be made for the monks for meals?
9. When are monks given more food and drink?
10. What do the monks to talk about at night?

Reading Assignment:
Chapters 47–73

Session V: Discussion

Chapters 47–73

A Question to Consider

What part does physical labor play in the Christian life?

Discuss or list short answers to the following questions:

Text Analysis

1. What does Benedict call "the enemy of the soul (chap. 48)?
2. Do monks do the harvesting themselves (chap. 48)?
3. Who does Benedict say are "really monks" (chap. 48)?
4. How hard are the monks supposed to work (chap. 48)?
5. How does the daily schedule change between October and Lent and then after Easter through October (chap. 48)?

Cultural Analysis

1. What is our culture's attitude toward hard, physically demanding labor?
2. Does technology (which makes physical labor easier) make us into softer, weaker and lesser people?

Biblical Analysis

1. Was David a sensitive, spiritual man or a rough and tumble physical man? (1 Sam. 17:34–37, 2 Sam. 1:17–27)
2. In light of Jesus' job while growing up, which of the paintings on the left is a truer representation

of His body? (The artist that painted the first one is Peter Paul Rubens; the second is attributed to Bernardo Daddi.)[10]

3. How does God describe labor or the lack thereof (Prov. 6:6, 9; 13:11)?
4. How does life in the Garden show us God's view of labor (Gen. 2:8–17)?
5. How does the Sabbath Commandment show us God's view of work (Ex. 20:8–11)?

SUMMA

Write an essay or discuss this question, integrating what you have learned from the material above.

Should Christians involved in physical labor feel themselves somehow lesser in their calling, or should the opposite be true?

OPTIONAL SESSION: ACTIVITY

Monk for a Day

See what it is like to be a monk. You may discover that worshiping God this much is more than most of us are ready for. We will shorten all of the services, but it will still be a challenge. If possible, try to do it in a community, either with your family, fellow students or both. (For the brave, perhaps you could try to convince your pastor to have the entire church hold a "Monk Weekend"—if you do, do not tell him that I told you to suggest this.) Here is the basic schedule from Chapter 16:

LAUDS (before sunrise—5 am).
PRIME (during the first hour of the day—7 am)
TERCE (during the third hour of the day—9 am)
SEXT (during the sixth hour of the day—12 am, or preceding lunch)
NONE (during the ninth hour—3 pm, or at the end of the school day)
VESPERS (usually prayed before dinner)
COMPLINE (after meal and sunset, or just before bed)

For each service a leader and a reader should be chosen. Here is a suggested liturgy to follow (this one is fitted to Advent).

LAUDS

LEADER: God said, Let there be Light and there was light.
PEOPLE: And the light shines in the darkness and the darkness did not comprehend it.
SONG: O Come, O Come Emmanuel
READING: Isa. 7:13–16; 9:1–7
BENEDICTION: Rom. 16:25–27

PRIME

PEOPLE: God, come to my assistance, Lord, make haste to help me. Glory be to the Father, and to the Son, and to the Holy Spirit; as it was in the beginning, is now, and will be for ever. Amen.
LEADER: The Lord looks tenderly on those who are poor.
SONG: Of the Father's Love Begotten (*it will sound more monastic if you sing it to the tune of Divinum Mysterium*)
READING: Matt. 1:18–21
BENEDICTION: Jude 24–25

TERCE

LEADER: The Lord is in His holy temple.
PEOPLE: The Lord's throne is in heaven; His eyes behold, His eyelids test the sons of men.
SONG: Once in Royal David's City
READING: Luke 1:26–38
BENEDICTION: Rom. 15:5–6

SEXT

LEADER: Come let us worship and bow down; let us kneel before the Lord, our God, our Maker.
PEOPLE: For He is our God, and we are the people of His pasture and the sheep of His hand.
SONG: Let All Mortal Flesh Keep Silence
READING: Luke 1:39–56 (the Magnificat)
BENEDICTION: 1 Thess. 5:23

NONE

PEOPLE: Lord, open my lips and my mouth will proclaim your praise.
LEADER: Let us approach the Lord with praise

and thanksgiving.
SONG: Joy to the World
READING: Luke 1:67–79 (the Benedictus)
BENEDICTION: 2 Thess. 3:16

VESPERS
LEADER: I will extol You, O Lord, for You have lifted me up, and have not let my foes rejoice over me.
PEOPLE: O Lord my God, I cried out to You, and You healed me. O Lord, You brought my soul up from the grave; You have kept me alive, that I should not go down to the pit. Sing praise to the Lord, You saints of His, and give thanks at the remembrance of His holy name.
SONG: O, Come All Ye Faithful
READING: Luke 2:1–14
BENEDICTION: Heb. 13:20–21

COMPLINE
LEADER: Unless the Lord builds the house, they labor in vain who build it; unless the Lord guards the city, the watchman stays awake in vain.
PEOPLE: It is vain for you to rise up early, to sit up late, to eat the bread of sorrows; for so He gives His beloved sleep.
SONG: Silent Night
READING: Luke 2:25–33 (Nunc Dimittis)
BENEDICTION: Num. 6:24–26

All of the hymns may be found online at Link 5 for this chapter at www.VeritasPress.com/OmniLinks.

Optional Activities

Monking Out

Here are some optional choices that could help you really get at home with being a monk.

Option 1: Weekend Option

Instead of trying only a day, give the life of a monk a little longer to grow on you. Spend the entire weekend at a church or at local camp grounds with your classmates and family, practicing the daily life of a monk. Let your teacher or one of the fathers be the abbot. He will plan out the worship and the daily tasks, such as kitchen labor and hoeing the weeds.

A fresco from the eighth or ninth century showing Benedict carrying a model of his monastery at Monte Cassino.

OPTION 2: PHYSICAL LABOR

The monks were not just sitting around all day in contemplation. The contemplative life was active as well. Find a project that you can spend the weekend working on. Go to your minister and ask him if there is anything that needs to be done around the church. After he realizes that you are serious, ask if you and your friends can go down to the sanctuary seven times a day (with proper adult supervision) during the Friday and Saturday workday. Work and worship all Friday night and Saturday and stop at sundown on Saturday for the beginning of the Sabbath. You may be more thankful for the Sabbath than normal!

OPTION 3: NO, IT'S NOT A DIET—WE ALWAYS EAT LIKE THIS!

You will probably need some help from Mom on this one. She will have to read Chapters 34–41 (it is only seven or eight pages). Have her plan out the first annual "Eat Like a Monk" Weekend. You will not be having too much meat—unless you are sick. Have her plan out the menu according to these chapters. Dad can get into the act too. Remember, the harder you work, the more food you need—you might want to remind him of this while you are carrying a couple tons of rocks for his landscaping plans.

OPTION 4: THE ULTIMATE MONK WEEKEND

Maybe you have gone past normal communal living. You are ready for the ultimate challenge: living as a hermit. No let up in the worship, and you have to do all of the work yourself. Perhaps you and some friends and family could go out to a state park and set up tents close enough to each other so there is help in a time of emergency, but far enough apart so that you can feel alone. After you spend the weekend worshiping and eking out an existence, take some time to compare notes with your friends and family. What where the most difficult aspects of the weekend? What was unexpectedly easy or likable? What did this teach you about being a monk?

ENDNOTES

1 *The Catholic Encyclopedia* is available online at Link 1 for this chapter at www.VeritasPress.com/OmniLinks.
2 *The Dialogues* is available online at Link 2 for this chapter at www.VeritasPress.com/OmniLinks.
3 McGrath, Alister. *Reformation Thought.* Grand Rapids, Mich.: Baker, 1993. 222.
4 This is from Bierce's famous *Devil's Dictionary.* While Bierce, a writer of supernatural stories such as *An Occurrence at Owl Creek Bridge,* was an odd duck and an unbeliever, he remains eminently quotable and hilarious.
5 Schaff, Philip, ed. *Nicene and Post-Nicene Fathers, Vol. 19: The Seven Ecumenical Councils of the Undivided Church.* Peabody, Mass.: Hendrickson, 1995 [1900]. 8.
6 Lohse, Bernard. *Martin Luther: An Introduction to His Life and Work.* Philadelphia: Fortress, 1986. 49.
7 McGrath, 222.
8 *This endnote appears only in the teacher's edition.*
9 *This endnote appears only in the teacher's edition.*
10 The Rubens painting may be found at Link 3 for this chapter at www.VeritasPress.com/OmniLinks. The work attributed to Daddi is at Link 4.

Beowulf

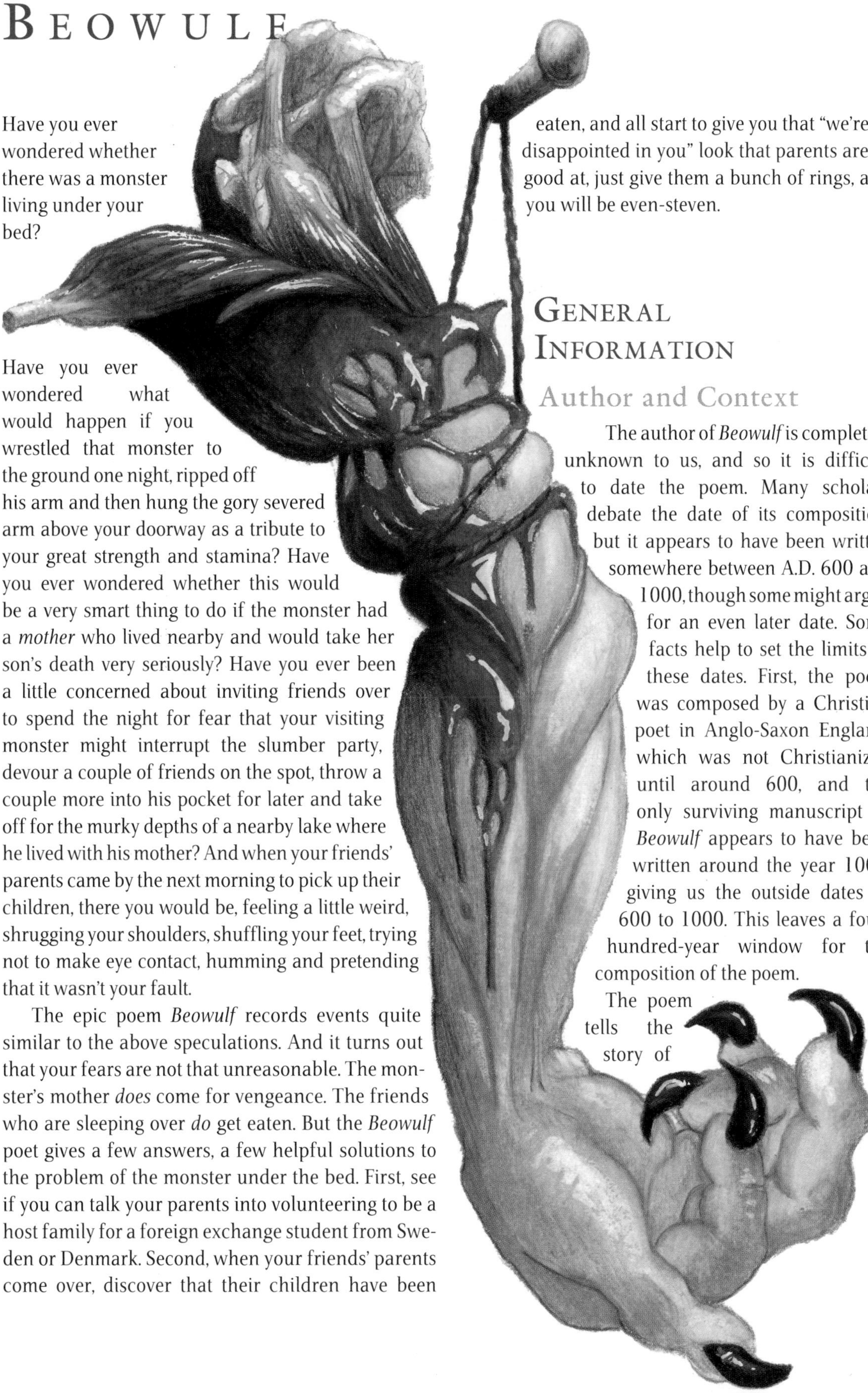

Have you ever wondered whether there was a monster living under your bed?

Have you ever wondered what would happen if you wrestled that monster to the ground one night, ripped off his arm and then hung the gory severed arm above your doorway as a tribute to your great strength and stamina? Have you ever wondered whether this would be a very smart thing to do if the monster had a *mother* who lived nearby and would take her son's death very seriously? Have you ever been a little concerned about inviting friends over to spend the night for fear that your visiting monster might interrupt the slumber party, devour a couple of friends on the spot, throw a couple more into his pocket for later and take off for the murky depths of a nearby lake where he lived with his mother? And when your friends' parents came by the next morning to pick up their children, there you would be, feeling a little weird, shrugging your shoulders, shuffling your feet, trying not to make eye contact, humming and pretending that it wasn't your fault.

The epic poem *Beowulf* records events quite similar to the above speculations. And it turns out that your fears are not that unreasonable. The monster's mother *does* come for vengeance. The friends who are sleeping over *do* get eaten. But the *Beowulf* poet gives a few answers, a few helpful solutions to the problem of the monster under the bed. First, see if you can talk your parents into volunteering to be a host family for a foreign exchange student from Sweden or Denmark. Second, when your friends' parents come over, discover that their children have been eaten, and all start to give you that "we're so disappointed in you" look that parents are so good at, just give them a bunch of rings, and you will be even-steven.

General Information

Author and Context

The author of *Beowulf* is completely unknown to us, and so it is difficult to date the poem. Many scholars debate the date of its composition, but it appears to have been written somewhere between A.D. 600 and 1000, though some might argue for an even later date. Some facts help to set the limits of these dates. First, the poem was composed by a Christian poet in Anglo-Saxon England, which was not Christianized until around 600, and the only surviving manuscript of *Beowulf* appears to have been written around the year 1000, giving us the outside dates of 600 to 1000. This leaves a four-hundred-year window for the composition of the poem.

The poem tells the story of

Beowulf is a mighty warrior with the strength of thirty in his hand grip. This artist's depiction of him shows him as the rugged outdoorsmen we expect him to be. While he is depicted here as middle-aged, the Old English poem follows Beowulf from his youth to his heroic old age.

a famous Geat warrior named Beowulf. The G in "Geat" is actually pronounced more like a Y, and so the name "Geat" is actually pronounced more like how we would say the word "yacht." The Geats lived in the south of modern Sweden. From there Beowulf visits the famous mead-hall Heorot, the pride of the Danes, found in northern Denmark. Both the Danes and the Geats are forefathers of what would become the Vikings, who would later raid England, and it is difficult to think of why an Anglo-Saxon poet would want to write a poem glorifying the heroes of these tribes.

In order to understand this, we need to know a little something about the history of early England. As early as the ministry of the apostle Paul, the Roman Empire included the island of Britain. But centuries later, as Germanic tribes began to sack the city of Rome, the legions who had once protected Britain were called back to Rome to defend that important city. This left Britain and her inhabitants very vulnerable to the surrounding barbarian tribes. The British people then began to hire mercenaries from some of the Germanic tribes on the European continent to come and help defend the British. This worked well at first, but the various mercenaries began to wonder why they should work for something that they could just take by force. Thus, the Germanic tribes of the Angles, the Saxons and the Jutes began migrating to what we now know as England, conquering it for themselves and driving the Brits into the far reaches of places like Wales. It is from two of these invading tribes that we get the name for their language: Anglo-Saxon.

Shortly after their arrival, a missionary, Augustine of Canterbury, began to preach the gospel to these pagans. By the year 598, Pope Gregory announced that Augustine had baptized ten thousand of the Anglo-Saxons. And so by the year 600 it would be possible for a Christian poet to be writing in Anglo-Saxon, on the island that we now call England. But conversion to Christianity was not always easy. Only a generation before, the Anglo-Saxons had been Germanic Vikings themselves. They still remembered their previous pagan ways, listened to tales of the great warriors of previous generations and even traded with their Norse pagan neighbors.

This sets the stage for a very curious sort of poem: a poem full of Christian allusions, written by a Christian about a pagan culture and a pagan hero, which sometimes pretends that they are worshipers of God and sometimes admits that they are all pagans.

Significance

At 3,182 lines, *Beowulf* is the longest Anglo-Saxon poem known to the modern world. Frequently, the poet will reference another poem or legend in a knowing sort of way, expecting his readers to already be familiar with a number of other legends. But most of these have been lost to us, making the poem *Beowulf* a rare glimpse into a world which has become almost completely inaccessible to us.

More important than that is the greatness of the work itself. *Beowulf* has long been recognized as one of the great and influential stories of antiquity. It was one of J.R.R. Tolkien's favorite works. Many elements of Tolkien's stories can be found all the way back in *Beowulf.* Orcs, Ents, runic letters, the Riders of Rohan and the sleeping Dragon angered by the stealing of one small goblet are all found in *Beowulf,* long before they appear in Tolkien's works.

Main Characters

Hrothgar is the builder of Heorot, the king of the Danes and the son of Healfdene. He was once a great warrior, but he is now old and can no longer fight. His great mead-hall, Heorot, is known throughout the land as one of the most magnificent halls around, and Hrothgar is well known for his generosity. Men from all over gather together at Heorot, because of its fame. But this crowd provokes the evil beast Grendel, who is angered when he hears all of the rejoicing in Heorot. Ask yourself several things about Hrothgar as you read. First, is Hrothgar a pagan, or does he believe in God? This is not an easy question to answer. Second, we are told that Hrothgar has ruled for fifty winters when Beowulf shows up. The exact same thing is said of Beowulf when he faces the dragon. If Beowulf was still willing to fight at this age, is Hrothgar's reluctance to fight a flaw in his character?

Wealhtheow is Hrothgar's wife, queen of the Danes. When the men are drinking in the mead-hall, Wealhtheow appears, pouring each man's drink and even giving out treasure to the men as a reward. It would be easy (but foolish) to underestimate Wealhtheow's importance. She is Hrothgar's wisest counselor and tries to enlist Beowulf's aid to avert future disaster. Notice how she subtly seeks Beowulf's support for her sons (Hrethric and Hrothmund). You'll have to pay very close attention throughout the poem to figure out what danger she correctly suspects.

Hrothulf is Hrothgar's nephew. The Danish throne would be his if it weren't for Hrethric and Hrothmund.

Unferth is one of Hrothgar's warriors. That's funny, didn't all the brave men die fighting Grendel? Don't you wonder why Unferth is still alive? Unferth is bothered by Beowulf's presence and begins to taunt him. This is a common practice with the Vikings, referred to as "flyting." Usually the taunts center around the other person's mother. However, Unferth's taunts are a bit cleaner than usual. Beowulf counters by pointing out that Unferth is well known for killing his own family. Does this make you suspect anything when Unferth is found sitting between Hrothgar and Hrothulf?

Grendel, a monster who lives out in the moors, is descended from Cain. He still has the shape of a man, but is grossly deformed. He can't stand to hear Heorot's poet sing about God and his creation, and so he begins sneaking in at night and devouring anyone in the hall. It would appear that Grendel comes to hold Heorot every night, but abandons it to Hrothgar during the day. And if this wasn't all bad enough, he still lives with his mother.

Grendel's mother appears to be a lot like Grendel, but female. She lives at the bottom of a fog-covered lake. Interestingly, early Anglo-Saxon sermons describe hell with very similar imagery. Beowulf must swim underwater to get to her cave. But once he is there he finds that the cave is full of air. Grendel and his mother are often connected to a rebellion prior to Noah's flood. (Look for passages that might make this connection.)

Beowulf, a Geat, was known early on as a lazy boy, and no one thought he would amount to much. However, he soon earned a name for himself as a great warrior of incredible strength. His father, Ecgtheow, had once killed a man named Heatholaf. This started a great feud, and Ecgtheow had to run away. Hrothgar, the Danish king, took him in, protected him, and even paid the wergild (a payment that settled the debt from murdering someone). Ecgtheow was eventually able to return to the Geats, and he married the king's daughter, who bore him Beowulf. This meant that Beowulf was within the kingly line and was later the king's nephew. The Anglo-Saxons held the relationship between a man and his sister's son as a very important bond, sometimes even more binding than the relationship between a father and his son. This was the relationship between Beowulf and his uncle, the king, Hygelac.

Beowulf goes to Heorot to fight Grendel, probably because of the debt owed to Hrothgar's kindness to his father. When he returns, he serves Hygelac, the Geatish king, faithfully. He is even there fighting alongside him when the king is killed by the Franks. A startling fact demonstrates that the author of *Beowulf* was working with real historical events when he wrote his poem. Gregory of Tours records the battle in which Hygelac dies in his *Historia Francorum* (History of the Franks). How much of this do you think really happened? The poet tells us that Beowulf was actually at the battle where Hygelac died, the same battle that Gregory of Tours records. Was Beowulf a historical character? We can also learn from Gregory of Tours that Hygelac died in A.D. 520. This helps us to date the events of the poem. Beowulf refuses to take the throne after Hygelac's death and supports Hygelac's son as king. After the death of Hygelac's son, Beowulf finally takes the Geatish throne and rules for fifty years. We are told that these are years of peace and prosperity for the Geats, and no one dares to attack until after Beowulf's death.

Wiglaf is a young kinsman of Beowulf's. He follows him to his final battle with the dragon. Of all the men that follow Beowulf to his battle, only Wiglaf refuses to run away. His help allows Beowulf to slay the dragon, but it is not enough to keep the Geatish king alive. After Beowulf's death, Wiglaf gives a speech with grim predictions. As you read, ask yourself why *Beowulf* ends on such a grim and hopeless note.

Summary and Setting

The poem opens describing a hopeless situation. The great mead-hall of the Danes, Heorot, is visited nightly by the monster Grendel, who devours anyone he finds. In all the Danish kingdom, there is no one strong enough to fight Grendel. But a great warrior in the Geatish kingdom hears of the Danes' distress. Beowulf gathers thirteen warriors and sails to Heorot. Beowulf is so mighty that the guard charged with watching the coast recognizes immediately that this is a formidable man.

Beowulf makes good his boasts the very first night of his visit. Without even using weapons, he is able to rip Grendel's arm off at the shoulder. Though Grendel gets away, it is obvious that the wound is severe enough to guarantee Grendel's death. The Danes throw quite the party in Heorot that night to celebrate their deliverance, not knowing that Grendel has a mother who takes the death of her son rather badly. She makes a visit to Heorot to avenge her son, and the next morning Beowulf has another job to do. This time Beowulf must swim to the bottom of a lake to fight the monster and, again, all goes well and another party is thrown.

Beowulf returns home to the Geats and eventually finds himself as king of the tribe. All goes well for fifty years, until a dragon is awakened by a runaway slave who has stolen a goblet from the dragon's hoard. The dragon goes on a rampage throughout the Geatish kingdom, seeking revenge. King Beowulf must go and fight again in order to defend his people. He takes a band of eleven men with him to fight the dragon. The fire of the dragon proves too much for Beowulf, and the aged king begins to falter. Of the eleven men, only one, Wiglaf, actually stays to aid Beowulf in his fight. With Wiglaf's help the dragon is eventually defeated, but not before the dragon is able to sink his poisonous fangs into Beowulf's neck. The Geatish king is dying fast, and Wiglaf barely has time to show him the treasure he has won before he breathes his last.

The poem ends with Wiglaf scolding the cowardice of the other ten warriors and then pronouncing a doom on the Geatish kingdom. Without a king like Beowulf, what hope do the Geats have? Beowulf is buried in a barrow on the coastline, visible for miles around.

Worldview

Christianity in Beowulf

One of the most intriguing questions that comes to mind when discussing the worldview of *Beowulf* is the question of its Christianity. That the poet was a Christian, writing for a Christian audience, is obvious. The poet refers to God throughout, constantly alludes to biblical stories like Creation, the story of Cain and Abel, and the Flood. But what are we to make of the faith of the characters *within* the poem? The poet seems a bit inconsistent. At one moment the walls of Heorot echo with the song of the bard who tells of God's creative power, giving glory to the Almighty Creator God of the Bible (lines 86–98). The next moment the folly of the Danes' paganism is highlighted (lines 175–188). Sorting out this tension between paganism and Christianity in *Beowulf* is not very easy, but we should notice that throughout the poem, success is always brought by the mercy and grace of God. It would seem that the poet wanted to be honest about the paganism of his ancestors and therefore included the fact that they were prone to pagan practices. And yet he saw a virtue in their strength and courage, which he greatly admired. As a Christian, the poet credited this strength to the only thing that made sense to him—the grace and mercy of God.

Another possibility is that the *Beowulf* author wanted to show these pagan ancestors as noble, while at the same time demonstrating that such nobility apart from Christ is still inadequate to save. Taken this way, the poem can be read as an evangelistic effort, preparing pagans who were tired of their blood vengeance code for the preaching of Christ.

Throughout the work, the triune nature of God is never really clearly expressed, and the work of Christ on the cross is never really mentioned. Because of this, some have suggested that the *Beowulf* poet pictured his characters as Old Testament saints—that is, men who knew and worshiped the one true Creator God, but who had not yet received the fullness of revelation that came through the Son and the New Testament. The reader can probably picture the character of *Beowulf* very similar to the way one might picture King David. Another argument for reading Beowulf this way is the fact that, though the poem includes a wealth of references to events in Scripture, the poem never makes reference to any event in the New Testament. The *Beowulf* poet constantly portrays the faith of his characters as an Old Testament faith.

As you read *Beowulf*, be sure to avoid the mistake, so common in our day, of picturing the entire story in various shades of a dreary gray. This notion, that the early medievals spent their time living in burlap sacks, caked in mud, and always smelling like something you might have stepped in, is wrong-headed and clearly betrays an inability to read carefully. It shouldn't take long to realize (if you are paying attention as you read) that our Anglo-Saxon fathers considered beauty one of the greatest gifts that God has given mankind.

The Anglo-Saxon understanding of beauty begins with God's work at Creation. The word most commonly used in *Beowulf* to describe God's creative action is the verb *scop* (pronounced SHOPE), which literally means to shape. God is the Great Shaper, and all the natural beauty that the Anglo-Saxon's eye saw all around him was the fruit of this great Artist's imagination. Since God was an artist, the Anglo-Saxons understood that, as Christians, it was their job to be artists as well. Therefore, a helmet wasn't just great because of its strength, but also because of its beauty. Frequently the helmets were ornamented to look like boar's heads, as was the prow of Beowulf's ship. Swords were also crafted with appearance in mind. One common way to add beauty to a sword was the process of "pattern-welding." The craftsman would take several bars of differently shaded iron, twist the bars together, and then hammer the twisted bars out into a sword. The result would be a sword with various serpentine patterns worked into the blade. As you work through *Beowulf,* carefully read the various descriptions of armor, weapons, ships, treasure and the famous hall of Heorot, and ask yourself whether "gray, dark and dreary" really describes the Anglo-Saxon world.

However, there was also another meaning to the word *scop,* a meaning that would be terrible for us to miss at this point. *Scop* was also the word for a poet. The Anglo-Saxons understood that in using beautiful words and imagery to craft a poem, the poet imitated God's own creative work in making this middle-earth. An example of this tendency towards ornamentation in Anglo-Saxon poetry might be the poetic work of the kenning. A *kenning* is a compound of two words creating a third with a new meaning. For instance, rather than saying something boring, like, "Beowulf crossed the sea," an Anglo-Saxon poet might say, "Beowulf crossed the whale-road." Throne becomes "treasure-seat." A dragon is a "sky-plague." And a body is a "bone-house." These kennings are just a few examples of how the poet, the scop, sought to beautify his poem and glorify God by imitating God's creativity.

Another important element we need to understand is the question of fate. Prior to the coming of the gospel, the Germanic and Norse tribes had a deep belief in fate, an impersonal determinism that controlled one's future regardless of a man's personal decisions. The word for fate was *wyrd* (pronounced like the word *weird*) and literally meant "that which will be." The Beowulf poet often lists *wyrd* as the ultimate cause determining the outcome of events. Although *wyrd* was once a pagan fatalism, the *wyrd* of Beowulf is a bit different. Although it still sovereignly determines what the future will bring ("fate goes ever as fate must," line 455), it is no longer the impersonal force that must be dreaded and feared. As the Geats fall asleep for the first night in Heorot, the poet tells us that God had already determined a future victory for Beowulf and that "the truth is clear: Almighty God rules over mankind and always has" (lines 700–702). Another Anglo-Saxon poem, *The Fortunes of Destiny,* concludes that God has determined the destiny of every single man and then exhorts the listeners to give thanks to God for this. This is the difference between an impersonal determinism and a covenanting God who determines all that will come to pass. God can be thanked for his sovereign plans, because we have been promised that he will cause all things to work out for our good. A pagan understanding of *wyrd* gives no such promise.

That Beowulf is the hero of the poem is rather easy to notice. But what is it about Beowulf that makes him heroic? The author obviously considered Beowulf's virtues worthy for a Christian to emulate, but what were those virtues, and why were they important for an Anglo-Saxon society to emulate?

In order to answer these questions, we must begin by discussing some of the basic elements of Anglo-Saxon society. One of the most fundamental relationships that existed in this culture was the relationship between the lord and his warriors. The lord was the ring-giver, the man who would

The mead-hall represented a safe haven for warriors as they returned from battle. In *Beowulf* there are two examples of mead-halls, Hrothgar's great hall of Heorot and Hygelac's hall. The hall was also a place for the community to gather and hear stories that carried their traditions to the next generations.

generously reward all who served him, welcoming them into his hall, lavishing gifts upon them, but expecting loyalty from them the day that an enemy intruded. The warriors were referred to as "thanes." These were men who usually lived in the hall of their lord, swearing loyalty to him in exchange for his generosity. A generous ring-giver and loyal thanes, then, formed the foundation of a stable Anglo-Saxon society. But when either of these two parties failed to fulfill their obligations, the society crumbled. To illustrate the expectations that the Anglo-Saxons had of both the ring-giver and his thanes, consider two important speeches.

The first speech (almost a sermon) is given by Hrothgar after Beowulf has defeated Grendel's mother and is about to return to the Geats (lines 1687–1784). In this speech, Hrothgar gives Beowulf advice on what kind of lord he ought to be. Bad kings are the ones who grow obsessed with their power and forget that it was a gift, which can also be taken away. They stop giving rings, grow suspicious of even their own kin, begin murdering them and are full of pride and jealousy. Heremod is an example of this kind of king and is referred to several times in other places throughout the poem as a wicked king. Hrothgar urges Beowulf to avoid this folly, to be a generous king and to remember that, even after a king has ruled peacefully for fifty winters, a "sudden reversal" can come and, therefore, a king must not grow complacent.

The second speech is a rebuke delivered by Wiglaf to the ten thanes who ran away from the fight with the dragon. "Anyone ready to admit the truth will surely realize that the lord of men who showered you with gifts and gave you the armour you are standing in—when he would distribute helmets and mail-shirts to men on the mead-benches, a prince treating his thanes in the hall to the best he could find, far or near—was throwing weapons uselessly away. It would be a sad waste when the war broke out" (lines 2864–2872). Wiglaf goes on to predict that the Geatish society is now done for. The Franks and the Frisians will soon be coming to wipe out the last of the Geats. When the thanes lack the courage to fulfill the oaths made at the mead-bench, the society is doomed.

Beowulf's success and failure is then measured according to these standards. Was he a loyal oath-keeping thane? Was he a generous ring-giving lord, who was wise, cautious and prepared to the end? Both of these questions have to be answered with a resounding "yes." Beowulf's willingness to travel to Heorot to free the hall of Grendel made him the most faithful thane a ring-giver could ever have. And, during his reign the Geats experienced unparalleled peace due to wisdom and generosity. Lastly, his death while fighting the dragon proves that he had not grown complacent in his success. But if Beowulf is such a success, then why does the poem end with such a dark foreboding? If Beowulf is such a hero, why does the poem read as such a tragedy?

When Beowulf returns to Hygelac, after his visit to Heorot, he begins to relate to the Geatish king his encounters with the Danes. He tells Hygelac that the Danish princess, Freawaru, will probably be married off to Ingeld of the Heathobards, to end a feud with the Heathobards. The practice of marrying a daughter to an enemy was common, and the bride was referred to as a "peace-weaver" (another kenning—see above). The idea was that by joining the two families in marriage, the feud could be ended. Beowulf predicts a bad end for this match (lines 2026–2069). They will all stand at the wedding feast, the Danes all dressed up in their best armor and jewelry (which happens to have been pillaged from dead Heathobards). Two Heathobards will stand next to one another at the feast, an old man and a young man. The old man will direct the young man's attention to one of the Danes and the decorative sword that he is proudly wearing. "Don't you recognize that sword?" he will say. "That was your father's sword, who wore that into battle. That man must be the son of the man who killed your father. Look how proud he is of his heirloom." Of course, the wedding will be interrupted by a slaughter, and the sought-after peace will evaporate.

This illustrates something about the hopelessness of the culture that Beowulf lives in. Though he may always succeed as an individual, according to the standard of virtue that the poem uses, he will never be able to bring about any sort of lasting peaceful resolution. This is because the characters in the poem can only imagine that resolution to their problems will come by means of vengeance, rather than forgiveness.

The day after Beowulf kills Grendel, the hall of Heorot fills with thanes to celebrate their deliverance. The poet, the *scop,* begins to tell a tale to entertain the guests (lines 1070–1158). He tells the story of the

"Many a serpent, mere-dragons wondrous . . . Go on the sea-deeps their sorrowful journey." In spite of an arduous swim, Beowulf is still able to kill the mighty sea monster.

tragedy of Hildeburh, a Dane who married the Frisian prince Finn. Her brother Hnaef and around sixty other Danish men were visiting the Frisians when, for reasons not given, the Frisians turned on the Danes and began slaughtering them. During this battle both Hnaef and Hildeburh's son were killed. It would appear that her son fought on the side of her brother, rather than on the side of his father. Remember that the relationship between a boy and his mother's brother was frequently stronger than that of a son and his father. A truce was reached as winter approachds, and the Danes spent the winter plotting revenge. Finally, when spring came and a voyage home was possible, the Danes ambushed the Frisians, killing Finn, seizing Hildeburh and then returning home.

The story is a depressing tale of vengeance and loss. No one really won anything other than revenge. And given the nature of the culture, it is likely that the story is not over yet. Surely a young Frisian boy had been left behind somewhere, plotting a future revenge on the Danes. So why would the Danes, full of joy over the destruction of Grendel, pick this depressing tale to celebrate their victory? This question gets even more interesting when we consider that this story is being told *as Grendel's mother approaches.* And why is Grendel's mother approaching? To avenge the death of her son. "Then it became clear, obvious to everyone once the fight was over, that an avenger lurked and was still alive, grimly biding time" (lines 1255–1258). Hrothgar announces that Grendel's mother has "taken up the feud" (line 1233) that she is "driven to avenge her kinsman's death" (line 1340).

Beowulf eventually fails because the entire culture is failing. The crime of Grendel, coming and raiding the mead-hall, is the very thing that Hrothgar's ancestor, Shield Sheafson, became famous for doing (lines 4–6), but we are told that he was "one good king" (line 11). The entire society, though notable for its virtues of courage and strength in adversity, was a culture doomed to failure. It was a society where the line between hero and villain was often fairly blurry. The *Beowulf* poet, though obviously deeply moved by the nobility of his ancestors, accurately portrays the ultimate hopelessness of this pagan world.

The closing scene is an appropriately morbid image: Beowulf's body lies atop a tall funeral pyre; the pyre is burning and the flames begin to lick Beowulf's lifeless body, as an Anglo-Saxon woman (some speculate that this could be Hygd, Hygelac's widow) sings her funeral dirge, "a wild litany of nightmare and lament: her nation invaded, enemies on the rampage, bodies in piles, slavery and abasement" (lines 3152–3156).

But for our poet, this is not quite the last word. Remember that Gregory of Tours tells us that Hygelac died raiding the Franks in 520. But by 598 Augustine of Canterbury had baptized ten thousand Anglo-Saxons. Giving a few years for the reign of Hygelac's son and then another fifty years for the reign of Beowulf, the poem closes only moments before the barbarian Anglo-Saxons would first receive the gospel. Our poet wrote at enough of a distance from his pagan ancestors that he was able to recognize and praise their virtues, and yet he also recognized the hopelessness of the world that they lived in. The *Beowulf* poet does a masterful job of leaving us with these pagan people on the very doorstep of the church. What seems like an ending of despair is actually filled with hope. And in doing this, he gives us a tremendous amount of wisdom, teaching us how to understand pagan literature in a way that glorifies and honors God.

—*Ben Merkle*

For Further Reading

Crossley-Holland, Kevin, ed. *The Anglo-Saxon World: An Anthology.* Oxford: Oxford University Press, 1999.[1]

Campbell, James, ed. *The Anglo-Saxons.* New York: Penguin, 1991.[2]

Session I: Prelude

A Question to Consider

Think of several characters in non-Christian stories whom you admire. How would you explain the gospel to them in a way that they might find appealing? Does your answer compromise the gospel? Does your answer reveal something admirable about the gospel that you did not ever notice before?

From the General Information above answer the following questions:

1. Where does *Beowulf* take place?
2. When was the poem written?
3. Are the characters in the poem Christians?
4. Which characters prove to be

Though not as powerful as her son, Grendel's mother is a formidable foe to all that fight against her. She lives with her son in a swampy lake.

faithful thanes (warriors), and which characters prove to be unfaithful?

5. In what ways does *Beowulf* destroy some of the stereotypes of the early medieval era as being a drab, dark and dreary time to live?
6. What is the difference between the pagan Norse *wyrd*, or fate, and the Christian understanding of fate exemplified in *Beowulf?*
7. In what way is the ending of *Beowulf* a tragic ending, and in what way is it not?

READING ASSIGNMENT:
Lines 1–257

SESSION II: RECITATION

Lines 1–257

Answer the following questions for factual recall:

Comprehension Questions

1. Who was the founder of the "Spear-Dane's" royal dynasty, and what was he like?
2. Why does the poet say that the Lord makes Beow (not the hero of the poem), son of Shield, renowned throughout the north?
3. What did the Danes do when Shield the "ring-giver" (lord and king) died?
4. What is the name of the famous mead-hall which Hrothgar built?
5. What does the poet say will be unleashed in time that will destroy the great mead-hall?
6. What was it that irritates the demon Grendel so much and makes him cranky about Heorot?

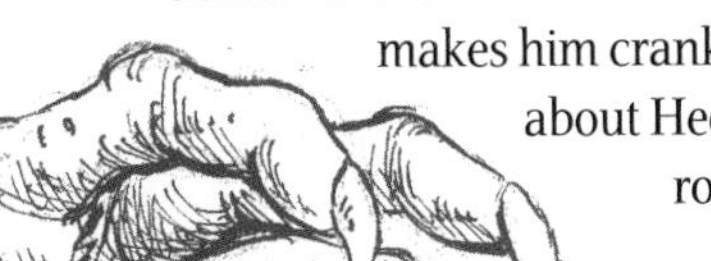

7. Where does Grendel come from?
8. What does the poet say is Grendel's nature?
9. How does the poet describe the destructive twelve-year reign of Grendel over Heorot, whereby the Danes' "pleasant time" is brought to an end by the murderous rampaging of Grendel? Why doesn't Grendel haunt the throne itself in Heorot even though he takes over the great hall?
10. Who do the Danes turn to for help in this bitter time of distress?
11. Who takes on the challenge to do something about the Danes' serious plight?

READING ASSIGNMENT:
Lines 258–498

SESSION III: DISCUSSION

Lines 258–498

A Question to Consider

Does Grendel have any "good" in him; does he have any redeeming qualities?

Discuss or write answers to the following questions:

Text Analysis

1. How does the poet of *Beowulf* describe evil?
2. What is the cultural evil inherent in Hrothgar's story about how he "healed the feud" started by Beowulf's father?

Cultural Analysis

1. How does our culture look at evil?
2. What are some examples of this in our culture?

Biblical Analysis

1. What does the Bible say about evil?
2. What is at the root of all evil (Gen. 3 & 4)?

SUMMA

Write an essay or discuss this question, integrating what you have learned from the material above.

Is the *Beowulf* poet's view of good and evil more or less biblical than our culture's view of good and evil?

READING ASSIGNMENT:
Lines 499–709

SESSION IV: ACTIVITY

Lines 499–709

Anglo-Saxon Poetry

This session introduces aspects of Anglo-Saxon (also called Old English) poetry which can be learned and incorporated in modern poetry. There are many different types of poetic devices in literature, and different peoples at different times have stressed some devices more than others. For example, the Hebrews stressed the poetic device of parallelism, as found in the Psalms and other Old Testament poetry. Much European and English poetry of the past stressed rhyming and formal meter. Chaucer made iambic pentameter a favorite of English poets for several centuries.

Ancient Anglo-Saxon poetry followed old Germanic verse. The meter goes by stress-count (stressed syllables) rather than syllable count as we are used to in, say, iambic pentameter (five pairs of syllables, second syllable stressed). Anglo-Saxon verse balances two main stresses in each half of a line.

Alliteration (the repetition of sounds) is often used in contemporary poetry, but the Anglo-Saxons used it even more. *Beowulf* uses alliteration in almost every line, with at least one alliterating word in each half-line, but often more. For example, line 4 in the original Old English reads:

Oft ***Sc***yld ***Sc***efing   *s*ceathena ***th***eatum

More importantly for the following exercise is the kenning, a combination of two words that forms a new expression signifying a person or thing. Kennings can be very expressive and add great beauty and force to the poem. Sometimes the poet uses two or three different kennings to refer to one thing or person.

Exercise One

The following is a list of some of the many kennings in *Beowulf*, as literally translated into modern English. Name the thing or person that each of the kennings signifies.

1. battle-dress, mail-shirt, war-mask
2. battle-sweat
3. bone-house
4. earth-hall
5. folk-right
6. flashing-light
7. gold-giver, ring-giver
8. helm-bearer, shield-warrior
9. hoard-guard, life-evil, war-flier
10. mead-hall
11. peace-weaver
12. ringed-prow, sea-wood
13. swan-road, whale-road
14. war-steam
15. word-hoard

Exercise Two

Create at least five of your own kennings that represent persons or things.

READING ASSIGNMENT:
Lines 710–1061

SESSION V: RECITATION

Lines 258–1061

Comprehension Questions

Answer the following questions for factual recall:

1. After the Danish coastal guards let Beowulf and his thanes go to see Hrothgar, why does the Danish king recognize Beowulf's name?
2. What was Beowulf's one request to King Hrothgar?
3. The Geats and Danes feast together in the great hall, all acknowledging the great feats of Beowulf, except Unferth. Why is Unferth skeptical?
4. What is Beowulf's response?
   What is Beowulf's formal boast at the end of the feast?
6. What does Hrothgar promise to Beowulf if he beats Grendel, and in what does Beowulf place his trust for this battle?
7. What weapon does Beowulf refuse to use against Grendel, and why?
8. As the Geats await Grendel's attack, what does the poet forecast about the battle, and who does he say controls the outcome?
9. How does Grendel approach Beowulf to attack him?
10. What does Beowulf display to show his victory

against Grendel?

11. At the victory feast held in honor of Beowulf's victory, what story does the king's poet sing about first?
12. Whom does Beowulf thank for his victory, and to whom does the poet attribute Beowulf's victory?

Reading Assignment:
Lines 1062–1278

Session VI: Discussion
Lines 1062–1278

A Question to Consider

Have you ever participated in a feud or desired to take revenge on anybody? What motivated you to desire revenge?

Discuss or write answers to the following questions:

Text Analysis

1. In the so-called "Finnsburg episode," the story of the feud between the Danes and the Frisians under King Finn is recalled by the court poet at the celebration feast after Beowulf's victory over Grendel. What motivated the Danes to break the truce with the Frisians, kill Finn, loot his stronghold and take Hildeburh, his wife, back to Daneland?
2. After the Finnsburg episode, what does the *Beowulf* poet tells us of the future fate of the Geat king Hygelac?

"Monster" is the term that comes to mind when one thinks of Grendel. A descendant of Cain, he is also referred to as an enormous ogre or a giant troll. Scholars argue about what kind of creature he was, but they do not argue over the fact that he was a hideous one.

Warfare was a regular part of Anglo-Saxon life. Here we see a re-enactor's "tools of the trade" for living as Beowulf might have. Swords were often heirlooms passed down from father to son, and many have runes or decorations on them which tell a story. Beowulf retrieves from Grendel's lair a sword wrought by giants that is engraved with an ancient tale about how the God of creation washed away the earth-giants with a great flood.

3. What do these stories foreshadow in the poem?
4. Read lines 2020–2068, where Beowulf later foresees the grim consequences of a proposed marriage re-igniting a feud between the Danes and the Heathobards. What does he foresee happening?
5. Read lines 2911–2927. What does the messenger who tells the Geats of Beowulf's death predict?
6. What do the above episodes, as well as other relationships throughout the poem, tell us about the pagan Germanic culture of death before the conversion to Christianity?
7. Was Beowulf's desire to take on Grendel motivated by revenge or vengeance?

Cultural Analysis

1. How did the influence of Christianity overcome the pagan warrior culture?
2. How has weakness and apostasy in the church in the last hundred years manifested itself in a return of the influence of the pagan culture of death in our society?
3. What global conflicts in our current world are reminiscent of the ancient pagan warrior conceptions of honor, revenge and blood feuds?

Biblical Analysis

1. Why are all peoples and cultures so prone to feuding and blood feuds, and why did such feuds dominate ancient pagan cultures (Rom. 3:11–18)?
2. What episode in the life of David shows God's redemption of the ancient pagan concept of revenge for dishonor (1 Sam. 25:2–39)?
3. Who was the first man recorded to have taken blood vengeance for an injury to him, who also bragged about his policy of vengeance (Gen. 4:16–24)?
4. What is the biblical view of vengeance? Is the ancient practice of blood vengeance biblical (Lev. 19:18; Deut. 24:16; 1 Sam. 25:2–39; 2 Kings 14:5–6; Matt. 5:38–48; 18:21–35; 12:19–20; and Heb. 10:30)?

Summa

Write an essay or discuss this question, integrating what you have learned from the material above.

What was unbiblical about Hengest's desires prior to the ambush of Finn, and what assumptions about reality did Hengest have to make to fuel those desires?

Reading Assignment:
Lines 1279–1491

Session VII: Activity

Lines 1279–1491

Know Your Pagan Gods

Today we are going to learn a little about some of the key gods that are never mentioned by name in *Beowulf*, but are always lurking about in the shadows of the pagan Germanic warrior culture represented in the story. (Briefly review lines 175–188 where the Christian Anglo-Saxon poet notes that his pagan ancestors made offerings and swore oaths to pagan idols.) All the Germanic and Scandinavian tribes mentioned in *Beowulf* worshiped a pantheon of similar pagan gods before their conversion to Christianity.

As you create your analysis of the Norse gods, you should craft it so that you can eventually present it to others—preferably younger students or siblings. So, it needs to be interesting to hold your listeners' attention. One of the ways to make your report interesting is by presenting the Norse gods in a metaphor that students—or adults—can understand. A metaphor represents one thing as if it were another. Shakespeare uses a metaphor when he says "All the world is a stage." We use metaphors all the time

COOL KENNINGS

One of the wonderful aspects of Anglo-Saxon poetry is the creative use of "kennings" as a poetic device. Kennings are compound words or phrases that identify persons, places or things in expressive imagery. Kennings usually use colorful figures of speech that substitute for the common name of the thing an attribute of it or something closely related to it. They produce evocative images which delight and stick in the mind of the reader. They are also used to assist in remembering important things or persons and to avoid excessive repetition of names in the story. The following chart is a list of some of the kennings in *Beowulf,* showing the Anglo-Saxon original, a line in *Beowulf* where it can be found, a modern English translation, and the person, place or thing represented by the kenning.

KENNING	LINE #	ENGLISH TRANSLATION	THING OR PERSON
Hron-rade	10	Whale-road	Sea
Swan-rade	200	Swan-road	Sea
Ban-locan	818	Bone-lappings	Ligaments
Helm Scyldinga	1321	Scylding's helm	Hrothgar
Heath-stapa	1368	Heath-stepper	Deer
Beado-leoma	1523	Battle-torch	Unferth's sword
Rodores-candel	1572	Sky-candle	Sun
Wael-rapas	1610	Water-ropes	Icicles
Heofones wynne	1801	Heaven's joy	Dawn
Ganotes baeth	1862	Seahawk (gannet) bath	Sea
Hring-naca	1863	Whorled prows	Ship
Woruld-candel	1965	World-candle	Sun
Heofones gim	2072	Heaven's gem	Sun
Eald uht-sceatha	2271	Old night-ravager	Dragon
Banhus	2508	Bone-house	Body
Wil-geofa Wedra leoda	2900	Wish-granter *of the* Western people	King Beowulf
Isern-scure	3116	Iron-shower	battle
Straela storm	3117	Arrow storm	battle

because they help us to understand difficult things by linking them to items that we better understand. God could have said that He was omnipotent, but He usually says that He has a "strong arm" (Ps. 89:13) because we understand what a strong arm is like.

So, first, choose a metaphor for your presentation. It could be the acting troupe of the Norse gods, or the dinner party of the Norse gods. Do some research[3] and craft a short report that could be presented to others that uses your metaphor to help them understand the different roles of the gods.

READING ASSIGNMENT:
Lines 1492–1812

SESSION VIII: DISCUSSION

Lines 1279–1812

A Question to Consider

What is the perfect hero like?

Discuss or write answers to the following questions:

Text Analysis

1. What makes Beowulf a hero?
2. What are the required qualities for a hero in the Germanic warrior culture represented in *Beowulf*?
3. Grendel is strong and subdues the Danes. Is he a hero?
4. Regarding literary and popular stories in general, what are the basic traits of heroes?

Cultural Analysis

1. What types of people are heroes in our current culture?
2. What seem to be required traits for modern heroes?
3. What is the hero attribute that remains constant between the ancient Germanic heroic code and modern versions of the hero?

Biblical Analysis

1. Whom does the Bible portray as heroes (Heb. 11)?
2. What are the key qualities of biblical heroes, and what is the most significant difference between man's natural view of heroes and the biblical view of heroes (God's view) (Heb. 11)?

SUMMA

Write an essay or discuss this question, integrating what you have learned from the material above.

Why is biblical heroism the only heroism that, in principle, all Christians qualify for?

READING ASSIGNMENT:
Lines 1813–2069

SESSION IX: RECITATION

Lines 1061–2069

Comprehension Questions

Answer the following questions for factual recall:

1. The king's poet tells a long story at the victory feast about what?
2. Whom did Hildeburh lose in the battle between the Frisians and Danes, started by Jute mercenaries working for King Finn?
3. Why did Finn call a truce with the Danes?
4. What spurred the Danes to renew the feud after the winter?
5. What did the Danes do?
6. When Grendel's mother attacks in revenge, what does she escape with?
7. What does Beowulf tell Hrothgar, who is grieving over Grendel's mother's attack and the death of his counselor Aeschere? What is the heroic code he proclaims?
8. How does Beowulf slay Grendel's mother?
9. What happens to the sword, and what spoils does Beowulf return from her lair with?
10. At the celebration feast, what does Hrothgar tell Beowulf?
11. When Beowulf returns home to Geatland, he tells what happened in the land of the Danes and foresees grim consequences of a proposed marriage involving the Danes and the Heathobards. Why is he pessimistic about the proposed marriage?

READING ASSIGNMENT:
Lines 2070–2323

Session X: Writing

Lines 2070–2323

A Riddling Contest

Describe any person, place, thing, situation or event in a poem at least 10 lines long, imitating Anglo-Saxon poetic style. If you like, you may write the poem as a riddle, a favorite exercise of Anglo-Saxon poets. Remember to keep the lines compact (ideally lines should be four to ten syllables long, with each half-line having two or three stressed syllables), and use alliteration and kennings. Rhymes are not necessary (though you can use them), since they weren't stressed in Anglo-Saxon poetry. Feel free to use the kennings you created in Session IV. Read your riddle to others and reward those who can figure out the answer. If a number of you are writing riddles, read them aloud and reward the writer who creates the best riddle.

Reading Assignment:
Lines 2324–2537

Session XI: Discussion

Lines 2070–2537

A Question to Consider

What makes a monster a monster?

Discuss or write answers to the following questions:

Text Analysis

1. What is the purpose of the four monster scenes in *Beowulf?*
2. What do the sea monsters, Grendel, and Grendel's mother represent in the story?
3. What does the dragon in the story represent?
4. The final monster in *Beowulf,* the dragon, is a hoarder of treasure. What is the significance of gold and treasure in the story?

Cultural Analysis

1. How does our modern culture view monsters?
2. The pagan Germanic warrior culture feared the chaos and destruction caused by the "monsters"

Chart 1: **PAGAN AND BIBLICAL WORLDVIEWS**

TOPIC	PAGAN WORLDVIEW	BIBLICAL WORLDVIEW
God	There are many gods who cannot always be trusted, must often be appeased and sometimes are evil. They fight among themselves and, like men, are ultimately at the mercy of impersonal fate.	The God of Scripture is sovereign creator and sustainer of the universe, always faithful to His word and His covenant with men. God is good. God is love. Nothing happens that God does not decree and control.
Man		
Man's Highest Good		
Man's Problem		
Salvation		
Neighbor and Enemy		
Afterlife		

of blood-feuds, tribalism and rapacious, power-hungry greed cloaked under cover of an offended or exaggerated sense of honor. What "monsters" does our modern culture fear?

Biblical Analysis

1. Are there monsters in the Bible (Isa. 27:1, 51:9; Job 26:12–13; Job 40–41; Rev. 12:9, 21:1ff)?
2. What are the similarities between the monsters in *Beowulf* and those of the Bible?

SUMMA

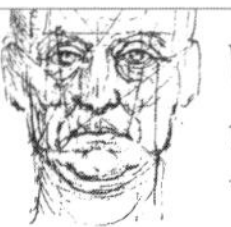

Write an essay or discuss this question, integrating what you have learned from the material above.

What is the only solution to our fear of "monsters?"

READING ASSIGNMENT:
Lines 2538-2846

SESSION XII: ANALYSIS

Lines 2538-2846

Pagan Worldviews

Using your knowledge of the northern pagan gods and the pagan culture represented in *Beowulf*, compare and contrast the worldview of the pagan warrior tribes in *Beowulf* with the biblical worldview by completing Chart 1. For our purposes here, we are constructing a chart with seven categories (God, man, man's highest goal, man's problem, salvation, neighbor and enemy, after death). There could be other areas in which to compare their views.

READING ASSIGNMENT:
Lines 2847-3182

SESSION XIII: ANALYSIS

Lines 2847-3182

Pagan Worldviews II

Discuss or write answers to the following questions:

1. How does a story (any story) reflect a biblical worldview?
2. How does *Beowulf* reflect a biblical view of the world?
3. Sometimes the poet of *Beowulf* seems to be saying that his ancestors were helpless creatures of fate who had no knowledge of God. Is this a realistic or biblical view of Beowulf's ancestors (Rom. 1)?

SESSION XIV: RECITATION

Lines 2070-3182

Comprehension Questions

Answer the following questions for factual recall:

1. After Beowulf tells the Geat king Hygelac about his battles with the monsters and the rewards he received from King Hrothgar, what does he do with his treasure haul?
2. How is Beowulf's status changed as a result of his adventure to Daneland?
3. What happens for the next fifty years?
4. Why does the dragon attack the Geats and burn Beowulf's own home?
5. Why didn't Beowulf gather

a large army to fight the dragon?

6. Why was Beowulf's bid for a complete and glorious victory foiled?
7. After his sword failed and Beowulf had to retreat, what did his band of comrades do?
8. Who was the one faithful comrade who continued to stand by Beowulf and rebuked the comrades who fled?
9. How did Wiglaf and Beowulf respond to being left alone to fight the dragon?
10. Before Beowulf dies of his mortal wound, what does he do?
11. Why are the Geats afraid of the future after the death of Beowulf?
12. What was the Geat woman's dreadful lament at Beowulf's funeral?

Session XV: Evaluation

Grammar

Answer each of the following questions in complete sentences. Some answers may be longer than others (2 points per answer).

1. When was *Beowulf* written and who wrote it?
2. Who is Beowulf, and what time period is the setting of the poem?
3. What is the significance of Heorot in the story?
4. How does Beowulf vanquish Grendel?
5. How does Beowulf subdue Grendel's mother (i.e., "monstrous hell-bride")?
6. What is the main attribute of Beowulf's fifty-year rule as king of the Geats?
7. What did the lamenting Geat woman at Beowulf's funeral sing out in grief?

Logic

Answer the following questions in complete sentences; your answers should be a paragraph or so. Answer two of the three questions (10 points per answer).

1. What makes Beowulf a literary "Christ figure?"
2. Why can't the hero and Christ figure Beowulf permanently solve the problems of the Geats' warrior culture? How is this literary situation similar to King David's historical situation in the Old Testament?
3. What is the difference in how Beowulf is portrayed in the two halves of the poem?

Lateral Thinking

Answer one of the following questions. These questions will require more substantial answers (16 points per answer).

1. What are the similarities between Grendel and the progenitor, or founder, of his line, Cain?
2. God tells us that the only way men can be happy is to be totally committed to Him, totally loyal to their Lord. The ancient Germanic warrior code also stressed the undivided loyalty of thanes to their lord or ring-giver. Why was this ultimately unsuccessful in the Germanic warrior culture?

The *Beowulf* poet describes the last monster to be destroyed by Beowulf as a fifty-foot, fire-breathing dragon that lives near the sea at Hronesness.

Optional Session A: Writing

More Anglo-Saxon Riddles

Read four or five selections of Anglo-Saxon riddles from *The Old English Riddles of the Exeter Book* or other translations of Anglo-Saxon riddles.[7] Write your own riddle, in Anglo-Saxon-type poetry, at least ten lines long. Read it aloud to other students or your instructor and have them guess the answer to the riddle.

Optional Session B: Activity

Seeing and Hearing

Research the basics of the Anglo-Saxon (Old English) alphabet and phonetics. (An excellent site can be found at Link 5 for this chapter at www.Veritas-Press.com/OmniLinks.) Listen to passages of *Beowulf* in the original Anglo-Saxon,[9] then practice reading a page of the original *Beowulf* text on your own.

Chart 2: **INFLUENCE OF ANGLO-SAXON WORDS**

Lord of the Rings author and creator of Middle-earth, J.R.R. Tolkien, was an Anglo-Saxon scholar. He translated *Beowulf* and wrote the most important article ever written on the first great heroic poem in English, entitled *Beowulf: The Monsters and the Critics.* Tolkien said that *Beowulf* was among his most valued sources in the creation of his mythical world in *The Lord of the Rings.* Tolkien used many Anglo-Saxon names and phrases from *Beowulf* to engender a sense of antiquity and believability for his mythical world, integrating fragments of real history with his invented history. The following chart lists some of the Anglo-Saxon words and names used in pure or modified form in works by Tolkien.

OLD ENGLISH WORD	BEOWULF REFERENCE	MODERN ENGLISH EQUIVALENT	TOLKIEN'S USAGE
Beorn	line 1299		
Eotenas	line 112		
Fródan/fróda	lines 2025, 2928		
Máthmas	line 1867		
Medu-seld	line 3065		
Middan-geard	line 75		
Myrcan	line 1405		
Orc-néas	line 112		
Searo	line 406		
Thenga	line 2033		
Ylfe	line 112		

Answer the following questions about the Anglo-Saxon alphabet:

1. What modern English letters were not in the Anglo-Saxon alphabet?
2. Which modern English letters were rarely used in Anglo-Saxon?
3. Write the entire Anglo-Saxon Alphabet.
4. What sounds do the last three letters of the Anglo-Saxon alphabet represent?

Optional Session C: Activity

Anglo-Saxon Influence

Research J.R.R. Tolkien's use of ideas and words from *Beowulf* in *The Hobbit* and *The Lord of the Rings.* (An excellent resource can be found online at Link 7 for this chapter at www.VeritasPress.com/OmniLinks.) Use your research and the original lines in *Beowulf* to identify the basic definition of the Anglo-Saxon words in Chart 2. Then fill in the Modern English equivalents in the third column of the chart and Tolkien's equivalent in the fourth column.

Endnotes

1 This book has a collection of Anglo-Saxon poetry that is excellent for getting a sense of context for *Beowulf.*
2 This book gives a fantastic summary of Anglo-Saxon culture, with some of the best pictures available.
3 Some good information on the Norse gods is available at Link 1 for this chapter at www.VeritasPress.com/OmniLinks.
4 *This endnote appears only in the teacher's edition.*
5 Ibid., 381. *This endnote appears only in the teacher's edition.*
6 *This endnote appears only in the teacher's edition.*
7 You can find them at Links 2 and 3 for this chapter at www.VeritasPress.com/OmniLinks.
8 *This endnote appears only in the teacher's edition.*
9 These audio clips can be found at numerous places online, but there are some good ones at Link 6 for this chapter at www.VeritasPress.com/OmniLinks.

The Song of Roland

All werthy men that luffes to hear
Of chevallry that byfore us were
That doughty weren of dede
Of Charlles Magne de Fraunce,
  the heghe Kynge of alle
That oft sythes made hethyn men for-to falle,
That styffely satte one stede;
This geste es soothe; witnes the buke,
The ryghte lele trouthe, whoso will luke,
In cronekill for-to rede.[1]

The greatest conflict of the past century has not been between Communism and Democracy. It has not been between Liberalism and Conservatism. It has not been between Socialism and Capitalism. It has not been between Rich and Poor, Proletariat and Bourgeoisie, Industrialism and Agrarianism, Nationalism and Colonialism, Management and Labor, First World and Third World, East and West, North and South, Allied and Axis or NATO and Soviet. All of these conflicts have been important, of course. All of them helped to define the modern era significantly. None of them should be in

Oliver's fair sister, Aude, is betrothed to Roland. Upon hearing of Roland's death, Aude is stricken with grief. Charlemagne proposes that she may marry his own son, Louis, heir to his kingdom. She replies, "God and His saints and angels now forfend I should live on when Roland's life is spent!" and falls dead at the king's feet.

any way underestimated.

But while every one of these conflicts has pitted ardent foes against one another and as a result, has actually altered the course and character of recent history, none of them could be characterized as the most convulsive conflict of the past century. The most convulsive conflict of past century—and indeed, the most convulsive conflict of the past millennium—has undoubtedly been between Islam and Civilization; it has been between Islam and Freedom; it has been between Islam and Order; it has been between Islam and Progress; it has been between Islam and Hope; it has been between Islam and the Gospel—and the fruits of the Gospel. While every other conflict pitting men and nations against one another has inevitably waxed and waned, this furious struggle has remained all too constant. The tension between Islam and every aspiration and yearning of man intrudes on nearly every issue, every discipline, every epoch and every locale—a fact that is more evident today than perhaps ever before.

To be sure, in the grand scheme of things, "that pesky Meccan heresy," as one writer has characterized Islam, is just one component part of the whole world-system of unbelief wrought by the Fall and is thus simply one among many revolutionary attempts to counter the gospel. Or, perhaps better, Islam is just a single aspect of the one great error of revolt against God. So for instance, radical Islamicists from the House of Saud, the Hashemite kingdoms, Hamas, or the PLO have through the years lent support to revolutionary and/or terrorist organizations around the world like the IRA, the Red Brigade, the Shining Path and the Khmer Rouge, to say nothing of their complicity with the Kaiser, il Duce and the Fuehrer—thus, revealing their essential, innate revolutionary character. They are, were and ever will be kith and kin, fellow-travelers and birds of a feather—part of the same revolt against the truth and the Truth.

But during the past one thousand years, the most persistent, plaguing and noxious of the many and varied pretenders to truth in this chaotic but unified revolution has undoubtedly been Islam. It should probably not surprise us to learn then that the literature of the West has reflected this great conflict in a myriad of ways that we might not have noticed before if our own troubles with Islam had not come to dominate the headlines, define our foreign policy and give new urgency to the day-to-day mission of our churches.

Themes revolving around the persistent conflict with Islam crop up in the oddest places, it seems. They intrude on William Shakespeare's plays and Walter Scott's novels. They make prominent appearances in the great poetic works of Dante, Milton, Chaucer. They form the backdrop for the stories of Robin Hood, Richard the Lionheart, Wallace and Bruce, Don Quixote, St. Francis, St. Louis, El Cid, Marco Polo, Henry the Navigator, Columbus, Magellan, King Arthur and the Knights of the Round Table. They even make appearances in *Pilgrim's Progress, The Charge of the Light Brigade, Huckleberry Finn, Moby Dick, The Talisman, Greenmantle* and *Ivanhoe.*

Some have gone so far as to argue that the very idea of the Western-style novel emerged from songs of chivalry, stories of knights in shining armor and legends of the crusaders. One of the very earliest—and one of the best—of these tales describing the great conflict between Islam and the West is *The Song of Roland.* It is one of those strange works of literature that is almost entirely fictional but which nevertheless is more truthful than most history books that are filled with carefully verified facts. Indeed, its "true lies" tell us much about ourselves, our world and the shaping of Western Civilization that we might not otherwise know.

General Information

Author and Context

La Chanson de Roland, or *The Song of Roland,* is one of the oldest and best-known examples of the medieval French chivalric ballads known as the *chansons de geste*—or literally, "songs of deeds." Traditional folk musicians, minstrels and jongleurs, would often travel from town to town, market to market and castle to castle singing about the epic adventures of great heroes from the distant past. The best stories were, over long periods of time, standardized into a single form. About a hundred of these popular epic poems survive, dating from around the eleventh to the fifteenth century.

Thus, we do not actually know who the various composers of *The Song of Roland* were or even when the poem took its present form. All indications are that there was a single, very gifted, final editor who took various strands of the popular oral tradition and wove them together into a creative masterpiece sometime between A.D. 1098–1100. This would mean that the poem was written during the time of the First Crusade—indeed, most scholars believe that the story was intended to encourage Christians to fully comprehend the danger that Islam posed to Christian civilization.

The poem actually describes events that had occurred several centuries earlier, during the reign of the Frankish warrior-king Charlemagne. Though almost none of the details of the poem are historically accurate, they became an essential part of what Europeans remembered about the past. History can be, after all, not so much what actually happened, as it is what we *think* happened. As a result, fictionalized legends like this one can often have more influence than careful historiography can.

The composer got nearly all the facts terribly wrong: Charlemagne was not yet the emperor; the bandits who slaughtered the rear-guard of the army were Basques not Saracens; the invasion of the Spanish Moors was but a brief expedition, not a seven-year-long campaign; revenge for the ambush was never undertaken; and the rivalry between Roland and Ganelon never happened, so far as we know—in fact, there is good reason to suspect that the two men were not even alive at the same time.

Here is what we do know with some certainty: during the afternoon of August 15, 778, the rearguard of Charlemagne's Frankish army was ambushed and slaughtered in the Roncevaux of the Pyrenees Mountains while returning from a raid on Moorish garrisons in northern Navarre and Leon. Accounts from this distant age are usually very sketchy, but the most reliable account of the event comes from Einhard, who was Charlemagne's court historian and biographer:

> At a moment when Charlemagne's army was stretched out in a long column of march, as the nature of the local defiles forced it to be, these Basques, who had set their ambush on the very top of one of the mountains, came rushing down on the last part of the baggage train and the troops who were marching in support of the rearguard and so protecting the army which had gone on ahead. The Basques forced them down into the valley beneath, joined battle with them and killed them to the last man. They then snatched up the baggage, and, protected as they were by the cover of darkness, which was just beginning to fall, scattered in all directions without losing a moment. In this feat the Basques were helped by the lightness of their arms and by the nature of the terrain in which the battle was fought. On the other hand, the heavy nature of their own equipment and the unevenness of the ground completely hampered the Franks in their resistance to the Basques. In this battle died Eggihard, who was in charge of the King's table, Anshelm, the Count of the palace, and Roland, Lord of the Breton Marches, along with a great number of others. What is more, this assault could not be avenged there and then, for, once it was over, the enemy dispersed in such a way that no one knew where or among which people they could be found.[2]

From this slight and fragmentary account, romantic balladeers began to piece together a tale of courage, honor, passion, betrayal, adventure, enmity and revenge that eventually became not only a great work of literature but also the essential historical reference point for the whole system of noble Christian chivalry.

Significance

Mention chivalry and most of us are apt to think of knights in shining armor, damsels in distress, crusaders embarking on a great challenge or pilgrims intent on a great quest. It is a rather romantic notion that brings to mind Arthur and his Round Table, Ivanhoe and his lost honor, Guinevere and her threatened virtue, and Rapunsel and her dire straits. It evokes images of the long ago and the far away. It is, for us, rather passé. It is a positively medieval concept—a long forgotten relic of the sentimental past. But chivalry is a code of honorable conduct that need not necessarily be tied to any particular time or place or cultural context. As wise men and women through out all time have known, it is a standard of virtuous behavior that has inspired great men and women through all the ages—causing them to long for a kinder, gentler society that abides by the conditions of genuine civilization.

Nevertheless, chivalry as a coherent code of conduct did have its origins in the early days of the medieval civilization in Europe when Christian men struggled to understand how they were to ethically respond to the threats posed against them by their unbelieving neighbors. Drawing equally from the church's established teaching on virtue, from the examples of godly heroes of the faith and from the emerging ideas of a "just war theory," a kind of moral philosophy about society, manners and justice gradually emerged.

The Song of Roland both established and illustrated the notion that chivalry is the ideal code of ethical behavior—ultimately based on Scripture—that defines the limits of proper action toward friend and foe alike. For several generations of European Christians it was one of the most powerful means by which such cultural standards were woven into the hearts and lives of the people. That might be a little difficult for us to understand, since we have only the written version of the poem with which to interact—in fact, we probably ought to admit right from the start that as it appears on the page, the poem is a little dry, repetitive and overbearing. Actually, the *chansons de geste* were not intended to be read. They were written to be performed.

So today, we are actually at something of a disadvantage: *The Song of Roland* was meant to be seen and heard, accompanied by music, perhaps actors and certainly in the context of feasting and celebration. In addition, the poem probably would not have been performed at a single sitting. Instead, the *jongleur* might only perform a few scenes from the poem, merely summarizing the essential preceding parts and for the sake of context. Several features of the poem made such performances easier: it consists of roughly 4,000 lines of verse, divided into 298 poetic units, each of which is called a *laisse* [LAZE]; these *laisses* are irregular in length, averaging just under fourteen lines; the lines are mostly decasyllabic, having ten syllables, and are connected by either assonance, which is something like a very weak rhyming scheme; the laisses are regularly punctuated with a kind of echo effect so that slightly different versions of the same event recur consecutively in order to slow the pace of the story—kind of like slow motion in a movie; the *laisses* are filled with formulaic phrases which helped the performer remember the tale and provided easy "visual" clues for the listener—a technique commonly employed in epics since the time of Homer. All in all, the style, structure and literary composition of the poem would have made it a kind of operatic drama.

The tremendous popularity of *The Song of Roland* made it an iconic symbol of chivalry and heroism while establishing a clear distinction between the ruthless barbarism of Islam and the charitable virtue of Christianity. It provided a sense of the ideal Christian warrior and held up a vision of principled righteousness in the midst of this poor, fallen world. In other words, this epic poem actually became a kind of societal manifesto. Even after the

Charlemagne (Charles the Great) was king of the Franks from 771 to 814. His name in Latin is *Carolus Magnus,* for which is named the "Carolingian" dynasty. By greatly expanding his empire, Charlemagne largely unified western Europe. By the time *The Song of Roland* was written, Charlemagne had become the legendary ideal king of Christendom, a continental counterpart to King Arthur in medieval chivalric stories.

passion for the Crusades died down and prophets of Modernity and Enlightenment began to recite the funeral sermon of the Christian West, *The Song of Roland* helped to define the medieval age and its men of valor.

There is never a doubt about who the good guys and the bad guys are. Good and evil are easy to pick out. There is no moral ambivalence about war and its hazards here, as in the *Iliad* or the *Aeneid.* Virtue and vice are set in plain opposition to one another. God's good providence and the machinations of greedy, foolish and unscrupulous men are exposed for what they actually are.

Main Characters

The Song of Roland, like virtually all the *chansons de geste,* has a veritable cast of thousands. Often a character is introduced only moments before he is killed off in a battle scene—and there are battle scenes galore in the poem. But the main characters are fairly easy to identify:

CHARLEMAGNE Charles the Great (742–814) was the king of the Franks and the future emperor of the Holy Roman Empire. In the poem he is presented as the ideal Christian king, a mighty warrior and a servant of justice. He is also portrayed as Roland's uncle and kinsman redeemer.

ROLAND Though mentioned only in passing by historians as the ill-fated prefect of the Breton Marches who was among those who fell at Roncevaux, in *The Song of Roland* he is the principal hero-martyr. He is one of the twelve Christian peers of France pitted against the twelve Saracen lords—notice that the cast of characters deliberately brings to mind the twelve sons of Isaac and the twelve sons of Ishmael. He is also Charlemagne's favorite, an ideal Christian knight and an ardent foe of the heathen Saracens.

OLIVER Another of the twelve peers of France, Oliver is Roland's best friend. Where Roland is brash and bold, Oliver is wise and prudent. Their conversations—and their disagreements—provide the principle didactic sections of the poem.

TURPIN A courageous archbishop, Turpin fights to the death at the side of Roland and Oliver. He understands the danger posed by the Islamic hoard and provides the theological justification for the war against their tyranny and barbarism.

GANELON The jealous stepfather of Roland, Ganelon is a well-respected Frankish baron who treacherously betrays the rearguard of Charlemagne's army, knowing full well the slaughter that would result. In the end, he gets his just desserts, but not before great suffering is inflicted.

PINABEL Ganelon's dear friend and a well-respected Frankish baron himself, Pinabel defends Ganelon at his trial. He is ultimately killed in trial-by-combat, thus revealing his complicity in Ganelon's treachery.

AUDE The paragon of chastity, beauty and virtue, Aude is Oliver's sister and Roland's faithful fiancée. She is stricken with grief and dies the moment she hears of Roland's death.

MARSILION The Saracen king of the last Islamic stronghold to withstand the Franks against the Frankish army, Marsilion is the quintessential villain. He gave permission for the ambush at Roncevaux and the death of Roland.

BRAMIMONDE The Saracen queen, who ultimately loses faith in Islam following the defeat of the Saracen armies. When the Franks take Saragossa, Charlemagne decides to bring her back to Aix, where she converts to the Christian faith. At her baptism, she takes the name Juliana.

BALIGANT The emir of Babylon, Baligant is the great hero of Islam. Years after he had been summoned to aid the Spanish Saracens, he arrives with an enormous army to do battle with Charlemagne.

BLANCANDRIN Marsilion's shrewd advisor, who plots a deceitful ruse to distract Charlemagne. The ruse is that Marsilion will come to Aix and convert to Christianity to save their honor and lands from the great Frankish army. Marsilion picks him to deliver the peace offer to the Franks. He and the Frank Ganelon then plot together the ambush at Roncevaux and the death of Roland.

AELROTH Marsilion's nephew, Aelroth, is a brash Saracen warrior—a kind of evil twin to Roland. He leads the twelve Saracen lords in the ambush of the Frankish rear guard. Ultimately though, Roland kills him in the battle that ensues.

Summary

The storyline of *The Song of Roland* is full of blood and thunder, valor and betrayal, faithfulness and vain-glorying, romance and adventure—in other words, it is full of all the things that make for a great yarn.

For seven long years, Charlemagne has made war against the Spanish Saracens who had occupied the once-Christian lands south of the Pyrenees for a full generation. Only one Muslim stronghold remains, Marsilion's Saragossa. Certain that his capitulation is probably inevitable, the king and his advisors plot a ruse to distract Charlemagne. He promises to convert to Christianity and serve as Charlemagne's vassal if the Franks will end their siege. Of course, the promise is altogether empty, but the Franks, weary of the long and difficult war, accept Marsilion's offer.

The Franks convene a council in order to choose an envoy to negotiate in the court of the Saracens. Roland nominates his stepfather, Ganelon. But, thinking that Roland is simply attempting to send him away on a hopelessly dangerous mission, Ganelon is enraged. In truth, he has long harbored a bitter jealousy of Roland. Thus, while he is in the court of the Saracens he betrays his stepson, devising for the enemy an ambush of the Frankish rearguard while Charlemagne leads the armies across the mountains back into France. He knows that Roland will lead the rearguard. With Roland dead, Ganelon promises the pagans that Charlemagne will surely lose the will to fight.

After Ganelon returns from his diplomatic mission with assurances of the Saracen's good intentions, the Franks prepare to return home. Roland, as expected, takes up the rearguard. The twelve peers, the pride of chivalry and Charlemagne's most beloved knights, go with him. They set out with Oliver, Roland's prudent friend, and Archbishop Turpin, a fiery, warrior-clergymen. At the pass of Roncevaux, a vastly superior force ambushes the Christians. Oliver admonishes Roland to call for help—to blow his horn in alarm. Roland refuses, vowing to fight valiantly to the end. Alas, the end comes quickly and disastrously. Roland finally sounds the trumpet, but he already realizes that it is too late for anything except revenge.

Hearing the desperate alarm, Charlemagne and

"While Charlemagne and his peers gazed in rapt delight upon this vision, there came down from the mountain crags a beautiful creature such as none of them had ever before seen. It was a noble stag, white as the drifted snow, his head crowned with wide-branching antlers, from every point of which bright sunbeams seemed to flash . . . the wondrous white stag . . . filled their minds with a new-born hope . . . The white stag went first, steadily following a narrow pathway, which led upward by many steep ascents, seemingly to the very clouds; and behind him rode Charlemagne, keeping ever in view his radiant, hopeful guide, and followed by the long line of knights and warriors, who, cheered by his earnest faith, never once feared the end." —James Baldwin, *Story of Roland*

the Franks return only to be overwhelmed with grief at the sight of the massacre. He immediately pursues the Islamic horde's force and is aided by a providential exposure of the enemy. Only a tiny remnant of the vast Saracen army is able to seek refuge behind the walls of Saragossa—among them, Marsilion.

Just as the Saracens began to despair of any hope, Baligant, the powerful emir of Babylon, arrives to save the day. The emir engages the Frankish army back at Roncevaux where Charlemagne has returned to care for the wounded and to honor the fallen. A terrible battle ensues, marked by a host of one-on-one duels between the Christian and the Saracen champions. Finally, Charlemagne and Baligant themselves meet. Under the grace of God, Charlemagne prevails and the Saracen host melts away. The Franks then march back to Saragossa, and the city quickly falls into their hands.

The traitor Ganelon is put on trial, and he is nearly acquitted. But once again, God's hand intervenes, and Ganelon's guilt is exposed. Once justice has been served, Charlemagne announces to all that Bramimonde has decided of her own accord to become a Christian. Her baptism is cause for great joy, and all seems right with the world at last.

But all's not well that ends well. In this world of woe, wickedness presses in at every turn. Thus, that very night, the angel Gabriel comes to Charlemagne in a dream and tells him that he must depart for a new war against the minions of wickedness. Reluctant, weary and tearful, Charlemagne submits himself to God's will. Thus, he once again prepares himself and his men for the travails of war.

Worldview

Edward Stratemeyer was arguably among the most prolific and influential American authors. Indeed, he wrote more and sold more than almost any other writer who has ever lived anywhere at any time—some 1,300 novels selling in excess of 500 million copies. He created more than 125 different series—many of them familiar and beloved American cultural icons.

You say you've never heard of him? Well maybe you know him by one of his many pseudonyms: Franklin W. Dixon, Victor Appleton, Carolyn Keene, Roy Rockwood, Laura Lee Hope, or Ralph Bonehill. Still doesn't ring a bell? Surely you're familiar with his famous characters: the Hardy Boys, Nancy Drew, Tom Swift, the Rover Boys, Jack Ranger, Bomba the Jungle Boy, the Dana Girls, the Bobsey Twins, Dave Dashaway and Don Sturdy. All were invented by this lone writer: Edward Stratemeyer.

At the height of his career in the 1920s, he employed an entire syndicate of editors, copy writers, stenographers, co-authors and secretaries just to keep up with his prodigious creativity. With their assistance he was able to produce an astonishing literary legacy, practically inventing an entirely new genre of juvenile fiction.

According to Stratemeyer, all of his books had a single uniting theme: the vital importance of moral character. He attributed all his success and the enduring popularity of the series he created to the fact that he never wavered in this regard. "The history of the world, the outcome of great events, and the establishment of true heroism will always entirely depend upon this," he said.[3]

"Every story worth retelling," he asserted, "is the fruit of internal uprightness at work in the external world. Whenever any mystery appears, its solution will depend upon the exercise of ethics, first and foremost. Whenever any adventure arises, its resolution will depend upon the exertion of morals. Whenever any question emerges, its outcome will depend upon the establishment of standards. In every circumstance, character is the issue. It is the issue which underlies all other issues."[4]

That was why all his books were attempts to modernize and update the old *chansons de geste* like *The Song of Roland.* "Chivalry is at the heart of character. Thus, it must be at the heart of every good tale, well told."[5]

When the destiny of men and nations hangs in the balance, it is not the Dow Jones Industrial Average that matters most. It is not the International Balance of Trade that matters the most. It is not the Gross National Product that matters the most. It is not the State of the Union that matters most. When push comes to shove, what matters most is not so much what we do, as who we are. Character is the fundamental issue. Whether we are writing a story for boys and girls, giving direction to a family or a community or establishing standards for an entire nation, character is always the issue that supercedes

Of course, real fans of Frank and Joe's exploits know that book #77 is not Mystery of the Sword of Marsilion, *but they also know that if the villain's blade were to turn up in Barmet Bay, the famous high school detectives would leave no part of Bayport unsearched to solve the mystery of it.*

all other issues.

Leadership expert John C. Maxwell has said, "Crisis doesn't make character, but it certainly reveals it. Adversity is a crossroad that makes a person choose one of two paths: character or compromise. Every time he chooses character, he becomes stronger, even if that choice brings negative consequences."[6] Substantive character will always make us. The lack of it will just as surely break us.

In the Apostle Paul's letter to the Philippians, he concludes his discussion of the joyous and mature life in Christ with a list of moral attributes that were to be studied by the believers ever afterward:

> "Whatever things are true, whatever things are noble, whatever things are just, whatever things are pure, whatever things are lovely, whatever things are of good report, if there is any virtue and if there is anything praiseworthy—meditate on these things." (Philippians 4:8)

This list was a kind of curriculum of righteousness. The Apostle Paul made it plain that the moral attributes were in fact a part of the inheritance the believers had received because of their position in Christ—notice how often the phrase "in Christ" recurs in the little epistle, and particularly in the fourth chapter. In some ways paralleling the list of the fruit of the Spirit in Galatians 5 and the list of the Beatitudes of Matthew 5, this curriculum of righteousness provided a distinctive glimpse into the substantive character of the dynamic Christian life. The idea is simply that Christian men and societies are to be very different. They are to give evidence that believers are "being transformed into glory," that they are "citizens of heaven," that the "good work" begun in them would be "brought to completion" (Phil. 3:20, 21; 1:6).

The Song of Roland assumes that such things are not only true, but that they are also good and beautiful. At the heart of the chivalrous code of the medieval world—at the heart of Roland, Oliver, Turpin and Charlemagne's valor—is this notion that Christian character is to beautifully manifest the mind and spirit of Christ. There is such a thing as living for the honor of Christ—even in the midst of this poor, fallen world.

These days the very idea of living with such principled character for the sake of honor seems strangely absurd. It seems to us to be such a lost cause. We tend to be terribly practical—so much so that we are willing to swallow all manner of indignity so as not to create a furor. Compromise is our immediate response to the slings and arrows of injustice. Honor is a veritable lost cause. But history is filled to overflowing with examples of stalwart men and women who followed in the chivalrous footsteps of Roland, believing that honor was the one thing that men and nations must never be willing exchange—not at any price; not for peace or prosperity; not for comfort or contentment; not for appearance or affluence. As Samuel Johnson quipped, "Nothing is ended with honor which does not conclude better than it began."

There is something very attractive about the bravery, loyalty and noble bearing of Roland's lost cause that continues to attract the affections of men and nations. As at no other time in recent memory, men and nations are yearning for the kind of glory Western civilization offered in days gone by—a glory whose stewardship was entrusted to guardians of chivalry like Roland.

The reality is that such a medieval legacy has forever been an alluring paradox. It has been a romantic riddle. On the one hand, it was marked by the greatest virtues of morality, charity and selflessness; on the other hand, it was marred by the flaming vices of perversity, betrayal and avarice. It was often timid, monkish and isolated; oftener still, it was bold, ostentatious and adventurous. It was mystical; it was worldly. It was tender-hearted; it was cruel. It was ascetic; it was sensual. It was miserly; it was pretentious. It gripped men with a morbid superstition; it set them free with an untamed inquisitiveness. It exulted in pomp, circumstance and ceremony; it cowered in poverty, tyranny and injustice. It united men with faith, hope and love; it divided them with war, pestilence and prejudice. It was so unstable it could hardly have been expected to last a week; it was so stable that it actually lasted a millennium.

The contrast with modern culture is stark. The contrast is stark precisely because men like Roland actually lived out—however imperfectly—the implications of the worldview of Christendom. Now, whenever the subject of worldview comes up, we moderns typically think of philosophy. And that is really too bad. We think of intellectual niggling. We think of theological lint-picking. We think of the brief and blinding oblivion of ivory tower speculation, of thickly obscure tomes and of inscrutable logical complexities. In fact, a worldview is as practical as garden arbors, public manners, whistling at work, dinnertime rituals and architectural angels. It is less metaphysical than understanding marginal market buying at the stock exchange or legislative initiatives in congress. It is less esoteric than typing a chapter for this book into a laptop computer or sending an instant text message across the continent with a mobile phone. It is instead, as down to earth as inculcating a culture-wide appetite for beauty, truth and goodness.

That is precisely what Roland was fighting for when he faced the Muslim horde at Roncevaux. And as a result, his was anything but a lost cause.

—*George Grant*

For Further Reading

Keen, Maurice. *Chivalry.* New Haven, Conn.: Yale University Press, 1984.

Shepherd, Stephen A. *Middle English Romances.* New York: W.W. Norton, 1995.

Spielvogel, Jackson J. *Western Civilization.* Seventh Edition. Belmont, Calif.: Thomson Wadsworth, 2009. 224–228.

Veritas Press History Cards: Middle Ages. Lancaster, Pa.: Veritas Press. 7-8.

York, Byron and Nolan, William. *Chansons de Geste.* London: Belvedere Press, 2001.

Session I: Prelude

A Question to Consider

How do Trinitarian beliefs produce better civilizations than Unitarian ones? (Compare Christian cultures with Islamic ones.)

From the General Information above answer the following questions:

1. What has been the most important struggle of the last millennium?
2. What is a *chansons de geste* or a "song of deeds"?
3. What mistakes did the writer of *The Song of Roland* make concerning the actual historical events?
4. Why is it unimportant that the writer of *The Song of Roland* got the facts of the actual battle so wrong?
5. In *The Song of Roland*, what is the character Roland like?

Reading Assignment:
Laisses 1–31

Session II: Discussion

Laisses 1–31

A Question to Consider

Is terrorism a result of Islam?

Discuss or list short answers to the following questions:

Text Analysis

1. How is Marsilion first described? What does this tell us about his place in the tale?
2. Describe Blancandrin's plan. What kind of sin is he suggesting?
3. Why doesn't Roland trust Marsilion?
4. Eventually, Charlemagne decides to trust Marsilion. Why does he do this?

According to Muslim tradition, Allah gradually revealed the Koran (or Qur'an) to Mohammed over many years. It is the sacred text of Islam and was completed in the decades following Mohammed's death in 632. The battle depicted in *The Song of Roland* occurred in 778, not even 150 years later. Dorothy Sayers speculates that the poet of *The Song* may not have been aware that the Koran even existed.

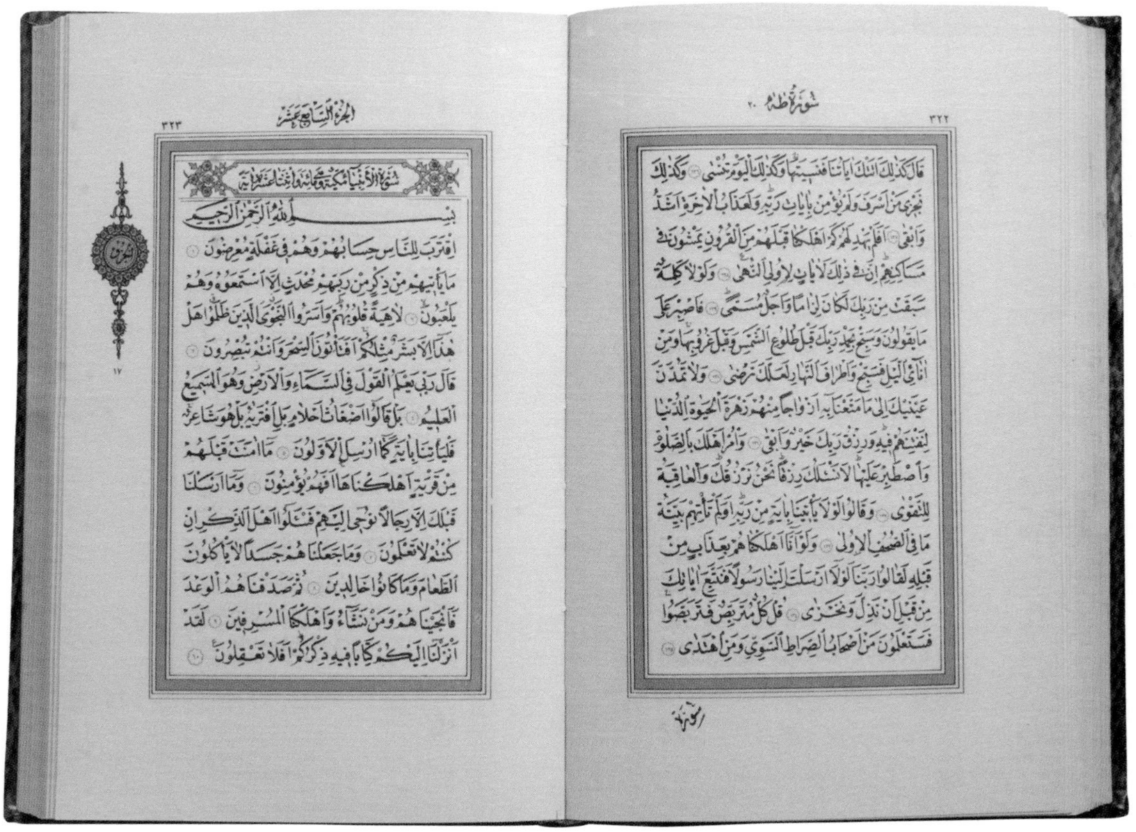

5. What sort of sin do Ganelon and Blancandrin conspire to bring about? Is Ganelon behaving more like a Frank or a Saracen?

Cultural Analysis

1. How does our culture say we ought to treat Muslims? Is that right?
2. What is the "war on terrorism"? Is it a war on Islam?
3. Does our culture believe that there is any link between terrorism and Islam?

Biblical Analysis

1. In the Bible, what is war for (Ex. 17:16; Deut. 7:1,2)?
2. In the Great War seen in the Bible, what is the first attack of the serpent (Gen. 3)? Is this similar to what the Muslims do in *The Song of Roland?*
3. What does Psalm 2 say about the wicked and war? How does this relate to Islam?

SUMMA

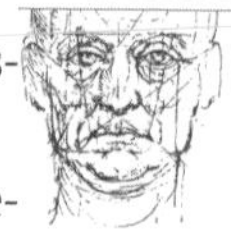

Write an essay or discuss this question, integrating what you have learned from the material above.

Are all unbelievers deceitful?

READING ASSIGNMENT:

Laisses 32–68

SESSION III: WRITING

Laisses 32–68

Write an essay explaining the difference in honor between the Franks and the Saracens. In particular, look at the differences between the way that Roland behaves and the way that Ganelon, in league with the Saracens, behaves. Do the Saracens have any honor? Does Roland?

READING ASSIGNMENT:

Laisses 69–103

Oliver demonstrates prudence, sagacity and loyalty in advising Roland and staying by his side even when he disagrees with Roland's decisions. Roland's closest friend and confidant, Oliver counters Roland's reckless courage with poise and wisdom in combat.

Session IV: Discussion

Laisses 69–103

A Question to Consider

What if someone you trusted let you down and did not live up to the trust that you placed in them? Would you trust them again? Why or why not?

Discuss or list short answers to the following questions:

Text Analysis

1. Are the Saracens in *The Song of Roland* trustworthy? Why or why not?
2. Are the Franks trustworthy?
3. Was Charlemagne right to trust Marsilion?
4. Charlemagne has dreams that scare him. Why do they scare him? Does he trust them?
5. When Roland refuses to blow his horn, what is he placing his trust in? What is he refusing to place his trust in?
6. Is Roland someone we should trust?

Cultural Analysis

1. What does our culture mean when it says things like "it might be true for you, but not for me" or "truth is relative"?
2. Does our culture trust the right things? What does it trust?
3. Who does our culture look to as authorities? Are they trustworthy?

Biblical Analysis

1. What sort of people should we avoid as our friends (Ps. 1:1)?
2. Psalm 55 is about the betrayal of friends. How does Psalm 55:20–21 apply to Ganelon?
3. Proverbs 6:16–19 describes the seven things the Lord hates. How many of these involve deception? What does that tell you about God?
4. What does Jesus call Himself in John 14:6? What is His relationship to lies?
5. Whom should we trust in all things (Ps. 11:1; 31:14; Eph. 3:11–12)?

Summa

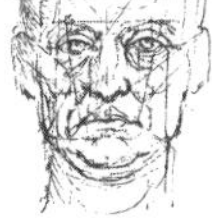

Write an essay or discuss this question, integrating what you have learned from the material above.

In what sort of people ought we to place our trust?

Reading Assignment:

Laisses 104–139

Session V: Recitation

Laisses 104–139

Comprehension Questions

Answer the following questions for factual recall:

1. Why does Roland at first refuse to blow his horn?
2. How is Ganelon's death foreshadowed?
3. Who wins the initial battle?
4. What happens to change the situation?
5. Which three warriors band together as the Saracens turn the tide?
6. What is the name of Roland's horn?
7. When does Roland finally decide to blow his horn?
8. Why does Oliver become angry with Roland?
9. Does Roland think that Charlemagne will get to them in time to help?
10. Does Charlemagne come right away when he hears the horn? Why or why not?
11. While Charlemagne goes to Roland's rescue, what does he do with Ganelon?

Reading Assignment:

Laisses 140–176

Session VI: Discussion

Laisses 140–176

A Question to Consider

What sort of actions can you think of that are brave? Are any of those actions things that you would consider foolish? What is the difference?

Discuss or list short answers to the following questions:

Text Analysis

1. Why doesn't Roland blow his horn when Oliver first asks him to?
2. What does Roland do when Oliver dies? Is it the action of a brave man?
3. The Franks lose many men because the Saracens are too many. According to the poem, whose fault is this?
4. Is the death of Roland a good thing? Whose fault is it?
5. Does Roland think that his action was foolish?
6. Is Roland wise? Is he brave?

Cultural Analysis

1. What if Roland were a modern-day American soldier, and he and his men had been surrounded by the enemy in a surprise attack? Let's imagine that he had had the opportunity to call for reinforcements, but he decided not to do so, and all of the soldiers were killed. He had not called for help because he did not want to shame his country. What do you think the response of our culture would be?
2. What sort of bravery is praised in our culture?
3. What sort of foolhardiness is praised in our culture?

Biblical Analysis

1. Was David being brave or foolish when he confronted Goliath (1 Sam. 17)?
2. Read Numbers 14. After Moses explains the Israelites' punishment, they decide to invade the land after all. Was this bravery or foolhardiness?
3. How were Peter and John brave in Acts 4:1-31? Why do you think they were brave?
4. According to the Bible, what does it mean to be brave (Ps. 118:6-7)?

SUMMA

Write an essay or discuss this question, integrating what you have learned from the material above.

When have you crossed the line between bravery and foolhardiness?

Optional Activity

Perhaps you or someone you know plays a horn of some sort. Ask them to show you how it works. If you get a chance, take it outside and blow on it (make sure that you won't bother anyone). With a partner's help, figure out how far away Charlemagne could be and still be able to hear it.

READING ASSIGNMENT:
Laisses 177-202

SESSION VII: RECITATION

Laisses 177-202

Comprehension Questions

Answer the following questions for factual recall:

1. Where does Roland go after he dies?
2. How do the Franks react after they reach the battlefield?
3. What does Charlemagne ask God for as he seeks the Franks' vengeance? Does God grant his request?
4. What do the Franks do when they catch up to the fleeing Saracens?
5. What is special about Charlemagne's sword?
6. Who guards Charlemagne while he sleeps?
7. Where does Marsilion escape? What wound did he receive in the battle?
8. Who is Baligant? Why does he arrive so suddenly?
9. Why is Queen Bramimonde unhappy with her pagan gods?
10. Why does Baligant head out with his army right away?

READING ASSIGNMENT:
Laisses 203-238

Session VIII: Discussion

Laisses 203–238

A Question to Consider

Is our current president a good one?

Discuss or list short answers to the following questions:

Text Analysis

1. How does Charlemagne make important decisions, such as the decision to show mercy to Marsilion?
2. What does Charlemagne do after he hears Roland's horn? How does this show him to be a good leader?
3. What does the emperor do when he sees Roland dead on the ground? What does this show about his character?
4. Before he enters the battle against the new forces, what does Charlemagne do?
5. Does Charlemagne participate in the battle? How do his actions in the battle show his leadership?
6. In the poem, is Charlemagne shown to be a good leader?

Cultural Analysis

1. Who does our culture look to for help in times of need?
2. What does our culture believe makes a leader?
3. What qualities does our culture look for in a president? Are all of these qualities praiseworthy?

Biblical Analysis

1. How was Gideon a good leader (Judg. 6–8)?
2. Why was Saul a poor king (1 Sam. 13; 15)?
3. Is Jesus a leader (Ps. 2:6; Luke 1:33; Eph. 5:23)? How?

Summa

Write an essay or discuss this question, integrating what you have learned from the material above.

What makes someone a good leader?

Reading Assignment:

Laisses 239–267

Session IX: Debate

Laisses 239–267

Question to Debate

Was Roland right not to call for help?

Split into two teams of roughly equal size. Amend the following rules for the debate as suits your needs:

Rules for Debate

Turn the students' chairs so that each team is facing the other.

Each side will speak for no more than two minutes before letting the other side speak.

The teacher will make sure that everyone speaks, which may involve calling on quieter students.

The teacher will give one point to every helpful comment that is given; two points will be given if what the student says is particularly insightful or if the student points out a fallacy the other team has committed.

One point will be taken away if any of the students speak out of turn.

Though the students must remain quiet, they will be permitted to communicate through written notes to help them consult during the debate.

Remember that reasons are required. A statement without a reason is an opinion and does not contribute to your side.

If you intend to have a formal debate (with opening statements, closing statements, rebuttals, etc.), then you will need to determine who will speak when. After each side is prepared, determine which side goes first. Then proceed! For individual students with no debating opponents, write out what you would say as a "position paper" for each phase of the debate.

Reading Assignment:

Laisses 268–291

SESSION X: WRITING

Progymnasmata

Classical training in rhetoric included preparatory writing exercises called the progymnasmata. These exercises in composition introduced the beginning student to basic forms and techniques that would then be used and combined when practicing more advanced exercises and speeches. One of these progymnasmata was called a *chreia,* or "saying exercise," and was simply a concise exposition of some memorable saying or deed.

A chreia has eight paragraphs. The first is the *Panegyric* which is a paragraph in which you praise the person who uttered the wise saying. The second is called the *Paraphrastic*. In this short paragraph you put the saying into your own words. This paragraph often begins with something like: "When Saint Augustine said that evil was the deprivation of good he meant that..." In the third paragraph, called *From the Cause,* you explain the motivation of the person. The fourth paragraph is called *From the Contrary,* and in it you explain what would have happened if the opposite of the saying or action had occurred. For example, "If Diogenes had not struck the inept teacher, bad education would have continued." In the fifth paragraph, called the *Analogy,* you liken the saying or action to something else, usually something more concrete and easier to understand. The sixth paragraph is similar to the fifth. It is called *Example,* and in it you show the wisdom of the saying or deed by pointing your reader to a specific instance in which this wisdom was demonstrated. The *Analogy* is dif-

A knight's life depended on his armor, his sword and his horse. Naming a horse is a common practice today, but cherished swords also had names: Charlemagne's sword was called Joyeuse; Roland named his sword Durendal and Oliver's was named Hauteclaire.

ferent from the *Example* in that it is about a general practice (e.g., "Education is like a harvest: you work hard and reap great reward.") whereas the *Example* is about a specific person, place or thing (e.g., "Erasmus studied many things and became a learned man."). The seventh paragraph is called the *Testimony* of the Ancients. Here you quote a sage person from the past who testifies to the truth of the saying. Finally, in the eighth paragraph called the *Epilogue*, you sum up the *Chreia*.

Write a chreia on Duke Naimon's statement that "Now that he comes on your mercy to call, foul sin it were to vex him any more" (laisse 16, l. 239–240).

I. Panegyric
- Praise the person(s) who uttered the wise saying(s)

II. Paraphrastic
- Put the saying into your own words

III. From the Cause
- Explain the motivation of the speaker

IV. From the Contrary
- Explain the consequences if the opposite of the saying or action had occurred

V. Analogy
- Liken the saying to something else

VI. Example
- Point the reader to a specific instance in which the wisdom of the situation was demonstrated

VII. Testimony of the Ancients
- Quote a sage person from the past who testifies to the truth of the saying

VIII. Epilogue
- Summarize your previous paragraphs

Optional Session A: Discussion

A Question to Consider

What is treason?

Discuss or list short answers to the following questions:

Text Analysis

1. Why does Ganelon betray Roland?
2. How does Ganelon limit his betrayal to Roland?
3. After his plot is exposed, Ganelon is put on trial. How does he defend himself?
4. What end does Ganelon meet? Does he deserve it?
5. Is Ganelon as evil as the Saracens? Why or why not?

Cultural Analysis

1. In our culture, is betraying another person ever acceptable? Explain.
2. According to our culture, what is treason?

Biblical Analysis

1. What does Proverbs say about betrayal (11:13; 25:9)?
2. Ahithophel was a traitor to David (2 Sam. 16:15–17:23). He betrayed his king and worked for his usurping son, Absalom. What was his end? Do you think this was just?
3. Judas is the most famous traitor in history. He betrayed our Lord and Savior. What was his end? Was his betrayal of Christ a good thing?

Summa

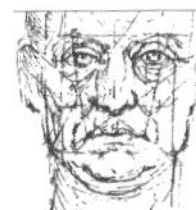

Write an essay or discuss this question, integrating what you have learned from the material above.

Should treason be a capital crime? Why or why not?

Optional Session B: Evaluation

All tests and quizzes are to be given with an open book and a Bible available.

Grammar

Answer each of the following questions in complete sentences. Some answers may be longer than others. (2 points per answer)

1. Who is Charlemagne?
2. Who are the Franks fighting?
3. Why does Ganelon betray Roland?
4. Who tries to convince Roland to call for help when he realizes they have been ambushed?
5. Why does Roland refuse to call for help?
6. Do the Franks win the war?
7. How is Ganelon punished?

Logic

Answer the following questions in complete sentences; your answer should be a paragraph or so. Answer two of the three questions. (10 points per answer)

1. What does *The Song of Roland* teach us about loyalty?
2. What does *The Song of Roland* teach us about betrayal?
3. What does *The Song of Roland* teach us about God?

Lateral Thinking

Answer one of the following questions. These questions will require more substantial answers. (16 points per answer)

1. Laisses 245 and 246 contrast Charlemagne's charge to his troops before the final battle with that of the Babylonian emir, Baligant. What differences can you see between the two speeches? What similarities are there? Do they use different things to motivate their men? What does this show about the different sides?
2. The book of Joshua is about the conquering of a new land. Is the war that is fought in the book of Joshua similar to the war that Charlemagne fights in Spain? If so, how? How is it different?

Endnotes

1 From the Middle English romance, *The Siege of Melayne:* "All worthy men who love to hear/of past chivalry/of those valiant deeds/of Charlemagne of France, the exalted king of all/that oft times made the heathen fall/that proudly sat upon war-steed/this song is true; here is the sourcebook/whoever will investigate will discover the truth/herein is the chronicle for all to read."

2 From Einhard's *Vita Karoli Magni.*

3 Dockery, Herman. *The Era of Juvenile Fiction.* New York: Laramie and Sons, 1956. 23.

4 Ibid.

5 Ibid.

6 Maxwell, John C. *The 21 Indispensable Qualities of a Leader.* Nashville, Tenn.: Thomas Nelson, 1999. 3–4.

7 *This endnote appears only in the teacher's edition.*

PRIMARY BOOKS

Second Semester

The History of the Kings of Britain

If you were not getting along with the Germans, seeing how they were poisoning your leaders, lighting your bedroom on fire and stomping on all your stuff, would you ever trust them? Would you agree to meet with them peacefully to discuss a treaty? And what would you do when you and all your men went to meet with them unarmed and they all pulled knives out of their boots and killed four hundred of you (though one of your friends found a wooden stake and killed seventy of them)? How would you commemorate the dead? What sort of structure would you set up in your backyard so that you and your people would always remember what to think of Saxon-Germans?

It's a difficult question, and British engineers and workmen were unable to come up with a suitable answer, especially since the structure needed to last forever. But Merlin can be a useful friend, and he knew exactly what to do: steal Stonehenge. It's big, it's noticeable, and it's hard to forget. It's even harder to steal. Stonehenge has been moved twice, according to Geoffrey of Monmouth. The first time, giants brought it to Ireland from Africa to use as a bathing circle (each stone has a special property). The second time, Merlin helped steal it from the Irish to mark the graves of those betrayed and murdered by the Germans.

Stonehenge is pretty well watched, and caution is particularly necessary, as a number of King Arthur's family members are now buried beneath it. But above all, if the Germans are being pesky enough that you'd like to steal Stonehenge, you'll need a big backyard.

General Information

Author and Context

Gaufridus Monemutensis, as Geoffrey of Monmouth refers to himself, is a somewhat elusive historical character. He was not concerned with relating to us the details of his own life and seems to assume that any of his readers would be familiar with him. But he did not anticipate us, his readers some nine hundred years after he apparently completed his text of *The History of the Kings of Britain.* Our knowledge of him is sparser than that which we have of his friends. It appears to many experts that he spent at least twenty years at Oxford (from roughly 1130–1150) and that he probably held a position at the College of St. George's. It was during that period that he wrote his *History.* He tells us that he was working from a text, merely as a translator, though that is not something that modern "experts" are necessarily willing to accept. According to Geoffrey he was given a "certain very ancient book written in the British language" by Walter the Archdeacon of Oxford who asked him to translate it into Latin. This book sets out the history of the Briton kings from their coming to their going, from Brutus to Cadwallo, spanning some nineteen hundred years. At another request, Geoffrey translated *The Prophecies of Merlin* into Latin and included them in his book which was completed in 1136.

Geoffrey himself went on to be made Bishop of Asaph in Wales. According to Welsh histories, he died in 1155, and according to Geoffrey, the Welsh were the last of the true British while the rest of the island was populated by German Saxons.

Significance

If Britain is at all significant, then so is the work of Geoffrey of Monmouth. If the British people and the people now called British who live on that small, wet and foggy island have affected and modified the story of mankind on this mostly blue planet, then the story of the island's origins is itself significant. God saw fit to include genealogies in the Old Testament while impatient moderns are not sure why. But Christians should have no trouble understanding why genealogies and histories are important. They are important because bloodlines matter; origins matter. Christ came from Abraham, from a barren Sarah, from Rebekah, from Rachel, from Rahab the harlot, from King David the adulterer and from Boaz. The story begins long before the climax and long before the present. Britain's family tree should be important to us because God has been telling the story of a particular island for a long time, and He has used that island in wild and various ways. Its story is not yet over, and like any story, reading the beginning makes reading the middle more enjoyable and occasionally profoundly more understandable.

Of course many people sniff and look embarrassed when someone wants to believe that *The His-*

Shortly after 1155 a translation into the Anglo-Saxon tongue appeared from the pen of a writer named Layamon. He added vivid details about the inception of the Round Table: "Afterwards it saith in the tale, that the king went to Cornwall; there came to him anon one that was a crafty workman, and met the king, and fair him greeted: 'Hail be thou, Arthur, noblest of kings! I am thine own man; through many land I have gone; I know of treeworks, wondrous crafts. I heard say beyond the sea new tidings, that thy knights gan to fight at thy board; on a midwinter's day many there fell; for their mickle mood brought murderous play, and for their high lineage each would be within. But I will thee work a board exceeding fair, that thereat may sit sixteen hundred and more, all turn about, so that none be without; without and within, man against man. And when thou wilt ride, with thee thou mightest it carry, and set it where thou wilt, after thy will; and then thou needest never fear, to the world's end, that ever any moody knight at thy board may fight, for there shall the high be even with the low.' Timber was caused to be brought, and the board to be begun; in four weeks' time the work was completed." This page shows William Morris's tapestry of the Round Table and on the oppsite page knights of the Round Table discovering the Grail.

tory of the Kings of Britain is actually, well, some sort of recognizable history. How could we believe an author who obviously believed in a powerful wizard named Merlin and a king named Arthur? How can we keep straight faces when Geoffrey tells us that the British and the Romans were related and that British kings occasionally sacked Rome?

Even without disputing the attacks on Geoffrey's historicity, or attempting to defend him in some of his wilder claims, his work remains significant. In many ways it is foundational to all the stories of King Arthur and his Knights of the Round Table that have ever been told. This book brings us the most mythic king of the western world and begins, though not single-handedly, a literary tradition that exists even to this day. Go to Britain. Find yourself a pub in the true back country, where the dirt in the knuckles of the customers is in their souls as well. Stand and raise your glass and loudly deny that Arthur will ever return and see what happens. The results should be interesting.

Main Characters

There are approximately ninety kings in Geoffrey's *History* with whom you should be familiar, to say nothing of their mothers, uncles, cousins, concubines and loyal knights. The cast of characters is long and star-studded, ranging from Vortigern to Julius Caesar, Claudius to Merlin, King Cole of merry-old-soul fame to King Lear of Shakespearean *King Lear* fame. And of course, there are the core Arthurian characters, as well as Aeneas and the first Trojan founders of Rome. It is quite a collection, and some are more important than others: the founder, Brutus the Trojan; Belinus, who sacked Rome; Utherpendragon, the father of Arthur; Arthur himself, with his queen Guinevere and his knights Cadon, Gawain, Bedevere and Kay. There are also the essential villains: Vortigern, the fool who first brought the lying Saxons over from Germany, and Mordred, the ultimate destroyer of Arthurian greatness and of old Britain itself.

Summary and Setting

Geoffrey concerns himself solely with the British, and particularly the British kings. His usage of the term Briton is different than our own might be. To us, the British consist of whoever happens to be living in Britain. We work with a modern conception of the nation-state as simply boundaries and borders and people who live within them. Geoffrey still lived in a time when blood was more important than borders. The British were those who came from Troy by way of Rome. The British were not the Scots, nor the Irish, nor the Picts.[1] The British were not the Saxons nor the later-coming Normans. The British were one people, one large extended family sprouting off from the household of Aeneas the Trojan and including King Arthur.

The History begins with the coming of the British and the story of their first king, Brutus, and they recount the various highs and lows of British rule until Arthur was betrayed and the last of the British kings were driven from the island, some returning to Rome, and the Saxons finally and completely inhabited England. Over the course of nearly two thousand years the Britons came, their rule, strength and wealth ebbed and flowed, and then they finally retreated from the island, pushed by the hand of God, who used plague and famine to accomplish what no invader could.

Worldview

According to Ambrose Bierce, the word *mythology* should be defined as, "The body of a primitive people's beliefs concerning its origin, early history, heroes, deities and so forth, as distinguished from the true accounts which it invents later."

Ambrose Bierce was as cynical as any man, and in this case, his cynicism touches the truth. A distrust in the "omniscient" extrapolations of modern historians is a healthy thing. From our perch some millennia later, we believe that we can arrive at a sufficiently established position on the history of Britain, and it has very little to do with the history Geoffrey lays out for us. Geoffrey, in our modern wisdom, is written off, dismissed and ignored. He knew nothing. We know more. He didn't footnote correctly.

The arrogance of contemporary man will, hopefully, someday have its own little exhibit dedicated to its ludicrousness in a museum of Folly Through the Ages. In the modern era, men chose to believe in spontaneous generation (the belief that meat simply turned into flies and that rags turned into mice, etc.), and they called it science. Now, having rejected that idea, they have chosen to embrace evolution (the belief that hydrogen is a colorless odorless gas that when given billions of years gradually turns into cows, grasshoppers, apple blossoms, the Pacific Ocean and New York City). The irony of all this is that this very same modern man claims to have embraced *doubt* as a worldview and believes that everything must be firmly established, well-footnoted and proven thoroughly before he will accept it. Modern man claims that *he* doubts everything, but then falls for any strange and silly story (like evolution) that he can think of, so long as he is the one who thought of it. What modern man will never do is believe a strange and silly story told by a non-modern man.

One of the things that gives us our firmly held view that "we know best" is our materialism. We assume that there is no spiritual realm (because it cannot be demonstrated in a laboratory), and we notice that throughout the entire history of man, every other nation, people, or historian has taken the spiritual realm for granted. Not only did the ancients take the spiritual world for granted, they believed that the activities of gods/demons/angels drastically impacted what happened here in the lives of men. No man who believes that history was actually influenced this way will be taken seriously by modern scholarship. As it turns out, most every man who lived prior to our own modern age believed that history was influenced this way, and so not one of them is taken seriously by modern scholarship, especially when he undertakes an explanation of *The History of the Kings of Britain.*

The modern doubt of Geoffrey of Monmouth's honesty begins immediately, in Geoffrey's dedication of his book. He is dedicating the book to Robert, Earl of Gloucester (the bastard son of King Henry I), and to Waleran, Count of Mellent. Neither of these names are essential to an understanding of Geoffrey, but in his dedication to them, he provides his sources. He tells us (and them) that this history is not written from his own private knowledge, nor is it collected broadly from multiple accounts (as Herodotus's *Histories* were). Geoffrey is working as a translator. He tells us that he will be working with his own homely turns of phrase, but that his source is an ancient book of history written in British and given to him by the Archdeacon of Oxford. Geoffrey is writing in the 1130s, and this book is ancient even to him.

Well, where is this alleged ancient book, if he wants us to believe it ever existed? How can we be expected to trust the writing of an historian if he doesn't provide his sources? Those are the sort of objections raised against Geoffrey's history. Some current experts claim that Geoffrey simply integrated some well-known history with a bunch of fiction from his own mind. Some think he just wrote down whatever Walter, the Archdeacon of Oxford, told him to and then called his friend Walter an "ancient book written in the British language." Some of the more wild free-living historians suggest that Geoffrey may have been telling the truth, that there might have been an old manuscript that he was translating. Of course, it's only a suggestion; it can't be proven.

MERLIN AMBROSIUS

Geoffrey of Monmouth introduced Merlin into the mythos of King Arthur from a traditional Welsh tale of a bard and prophet named Myrddin. Rather than use *Merdinus,* the Latin version of *Myrddin,* Geoffrey gave his character the name *Merlinus* to avoid his Anglo-Norman audience associating the character with a rude French word. Geoffrey first mentions Merlin in his account about the mid-fifth-century British king Vortigern trying to build a fortress, which keeps collapsing. The king's wizards tell him that the only way for the foundations of his fortress to be made secure is to sprinkle the blood of a fatherless youth onto the stones. Since Merlin's mother maintained that he had been conceived without her having relations with a man, Vortigern had Merlin brought before him. But rather than become a sacrificial victim, Merlin amazed the king by prophesying about the true nature of the problem with the fortress's foundations. Thus, Merlin became known as one possessing supernatural powers.

During the reign of Ambrosius, Merlin was asked by the king to erect a memorial to 460 British nobles who had been massacred. So Merlin went to Ireland and, by the use of his extraordinary powers, brought the stones of the Giant's Ring back to a site just west of Amesbury—a place we now call Stonehenge.

When Uther became king, he persuaded Merlin to transform him into the likeness of one of his enemies so that he could deceive this enemy's wife. With her, Uther fathered Arthur. Beyond this, Merlin has little to do with Arthur in Geoffrey's *History.* Later tradition has Merlin as Arthur's advisor, and Sir Thomas Malory presents him as such in *L'Morte d'Arthur.* Merlin comes to be known as Arthur's tutor and is presented as the one who sets up the sword-in-the-stone contest, persuades the mystic Lady of the Lake to present the king with the magical sword, Excalibur, creates the Round Table, aids and directs the events of the kingdom of Camelot and accompanies Arthur to the Isle of Avalon for the healing of his wounds.

The character of Merlin has appeared in a myriad of other novels, poems, plays and films. For example, Mark Twain made Merlin a villain in his novel *A Connecticut Yankee in King Arthur's Court;* The television show *Star Trek* has Merlin in an episode as Flint, an immortal man born in 3834 B.C.; the BBC's *Doctor Who* identifies Merlin as a future version of himself in the episode called "Battlefield;" Nikolai Tolstoy wrote a non-fiction trilogy of Merlin the Wild; in both the comic book universes of Marvel and DC, Merlin is a legendary wizard who has created many superheroes and even returns with Arthur to save the planet from alien attack in *Camelot 3000;* and in Stephen R. Lawhead's excellent *Pendragon* series, Merlin is the son of a druid bard and a princess of lost Atlantis who prepares the way for Arthur Pendragon, Lord of the Kingdom of Summer.

But why would Geoffrey lie? Should we, students of history, assume that every claim made by a past historian is false until we can establish it as true for ourselves? We may well decide to assume that an historian was mistaken, but in this case, current historians do not simply assume that Geoffrey was mistaken, they assume that he was a liar trying to pass off some of his own romantic fiction as history.

If we decide to doubt Geoffrey, we should have good cause. We should have other conflicting sources, or see some sort of motivation for falsehood. As Christians, we should never dismiss someone out of hand for the same sort of reason that would get a good portion of Scripture dismissed out of hand.

Lewis Thorpe, in the introduction to his own translation of Geoffrey (Penguin Classics), says, "The first half of Geoffrey's book is a well-ordered chronicle of what might well appear to be remote but nevertheless historical events, were it not for their very strangeness, the imaginative treatment given to some of them and their factual extravagance in certain fields of history where we are too well informed from other sources to allow ourselves to be misled." But this changes when "we read of the discovery by Vortigern's messengers of the boy Merlin, the soothsayer son of an incubus, or a fallen angel who fell because of the sin of lust, and a princess who had entered a nunnery, a discovery to be followed a little later by the long interpolation devoted to Merlin's prophecies. If we have been deceived before, and Merlin is the first really otherworldly element in the book, then we now at once realize how far away we are from anything which can ever approach real history," which is to say that the supernatural has no place in "real history." Demonic influence in history is immediately out of the question, and so Geoffrey finds himself generally discredited simply for believing that Merlin the magician truly existed and had true powers.

Other experts have gone so far as to say that it is difficult to determine how much we can assume that Geoffrey was embellishing because his primary goal had nothing to do with the truth. Thorpe quotes Acton Griscom in his introduction as saying, "[F]irst and foremost, Geoffrey was bent on turning chronicle history into literature." It is the sound of an historian almost bitter at Geoffrey for taking the sacred calling of historian so lightly.

At the very least, Geoffrey is given credit for his literary contribution. Merlin the wizard passes into the treasure trove of story characters thanks to Geoffrey. The

Thou art here, the Lord's Anointed,
King of men and knight of heaven,
To the trust thou art appointed,
Unto thee the sword is given;
As a sign for thee, a token
That the light again is breaking
Thro' the gloom of time unspoken
To the dawn and to the waking.
—an excerpt from the poem "Excalibur" by John Grosvenor Wilson

In Welsh legends the sword is called *Caledfwlch,* and Geoffrey of Monmouth calls the blade *Caliburn*, but the famous blade is now known as Excalibur. Merlin, who brings Arthur to the Lady of the Lake to receive Excalibur, informs the king that the scabbard is worth far more than the sword itself, for the former will protect its bearer from injury. This magical sword is from Avalon and should not be confused with the sword pulled from the stone. That sword was broken in Arthur's fight against King Pellinore.

ironic thing is that some now claim that he doesn't deserve the credit, as earlier Welsh manuscripts apparently reference Merlin in the same light. The irony is that Geoffrey wouldn't expect the credit, and discovering an earlier manuscript should be no surprise to us. Geoffrey already told us that there was one and that he was translating it.

A great deal of what he says does overlap with two other chronicles: *De excidio Britanniae* written by Gildas and *Historia Brittonum* by Nennius. Nennius is thought by many to have provided the essential seed that became Geoffrey's Arthur.

Christian readers should be more sensitive to falsehood than others, but they should be sensitive for the correct reasons. Believing that a wizard named Merlin walked this planet with real power is no more difficult than believing that the sun stopped in the sky, that the whole world was flooded, that Adam was made from dust and Eve from a rib, that Christ fed the five thousand and walked on water which He could have just as easily turned into wine, that He was killed and ultimately rose from the dead and sits at the right hand of God the Father where He will judge the whole earth. If we had been deceived into believing the Scriptures related real historical events, surely these things show us "how far away we are from anything which can ever approach real history."

Christians should never find themselves embracing the arrogant doubt of materialistic moderns. So what might we learn if we try to take Geoffrey at *face value?* What is the single most important political event of the ancient world? To be fair, it was an event that had been long dismissed as ahistorical, and it took place in a city long thought to be fictitious. Homer was a poet, so he obviously was making things up. Virgil was a poet, so we can't trust him. Geoffrey was trying to turn his history into literature, so he isn't helpful. Herodotus is hardly trustworthy because he says that he once saw the bones of flying snakes.

King Arthur's wife, Guinevere, is the daughter of Leodegrance. She spends her final days in a monastery after her affair with Lancelot destroys the kingdom. She was originally seen in the legends as the Flower Bride, a representation of an ancient goddess whose function was to be fought over by summer and winter. The characters of Arthur and Lancelot represented the seasons.

L'Morte d'Arthur (1860), James Archer's richly colored painting of Arthur's death by the shores of Avalon with three queens in attendance. After Bedevere throws Excalibur into the lake, Morgan le Fay arrives with three other women—the Queen of Northgales, the Queen of the Waste Lands and the Lady of the Lake.

There is no more certain fact about the ancient world, than that there was a great city called Troy and that a syndicate of Greek kings sacked it. It may not have taken ten years. Herodotus may be right, and Helen might have been in Egypt the whole time. But it happened. A great Trojan race was shattered and scattered. Troy was destroyed, and its people traveled the world as refugees seeking new places.

Heinrich Schliemann was much maligned by many who dislike the untrained archeological techniques he used, but he took Homer, Virgil and the other ancients seriously. Laughed at around the world, he traveled to Turkey with nothing but Homer as a guide, and he found Troy. There it was, big and spectacular, buried beneath a hill. Who would have thought that, when the ancients told the stories of their origins, they actually meant what they said?

Virgil is dismissed. He was simply flattering the Romans with an alleged history. But why would they want to believe they were descended from a people who lost the big war? Is that flattery? Why do all these peoples claim that they were descended from the

Trojan losers and not from the Greek winners? Well, maybe it's because they were.

Geoffrey gives us another Trojan, Brutus, coming from the Romans after the accidental slaying of his father. He comes to Britain following the advice of an oracle and establishes his kingdom after killing the necessary giants. The Britons, at least up to the time of Geoffrey, all considered themselves cousins to the Romans, descended from the same defeated people. There is no fundamental reason to disbelieve them. They had to come from somewhere and they might have had a better sense of where that somewhere was than we do. The Trojan War is reported to us as essential to the political formation of the ancient world, and we still withhold judgment as to whether or not it even actually happened.

But if we begin by believing Geoffrey and move beyond the treatment of Brutus as the "supposed" founder and accept that he landed, killed the giants and peopled the island, then where are we left? Must we follow Geoffrey through every account with wide-eyed credulity? No, but neither should we assume him to be a liar. We should disbelieve him when disbelief is justified, not simply when belief makes modernism uncomfortable. Both fortunately and unfortunately, Geoffrey is all too believable.

Many ancient histories, like what is relayed to us through Homer or Herodotus, reveal the complete darkness of men and peoples left to themselves in the sin of Adam. Geoffrey tells a nineteen-hundred-year-long story that straddles the darkest portions of early paganism in Britain right up through the conversion of the entire island, back into darkness, occasionally nominal faith and occasionally total apostasy. Geoffrey shows a great deal of darkness, but one of the most depressing aspects of his storytelling is that the darkness that existed *before* the conversion of Britain seems to be of nearly an identical shade as the darkness of the Christian kings themselves (though this is somewhat misleading, since he is emphasizing political shifts not cultural ones).

We should not be surprised when we see peoples imitating the behavior of their gods. When a god is worshiped simply because of its size, its strength, its ability to inflict pain, then there is never a relationship of love or affection. Do pagans who offer up their young to mix human blood with mortar and make their brickwork blessed love the gods that demand such sacrifices? Do they ever believe that such a god loves them? There is nothing irrational about the servants of such gods invading and slaughtering the inhabitants of a land that they want. In Adam, that behavior is expected. Cain murdered Abel, and so a train of bloodshed began that will run to the end of the world.

But there is very little light in Geoffrey. Contrary to the claims of secular historians, he does not give us a shiny, glossed hero. There are men who accomplish great things, and respect shows through in many of the passages, but he does not give us anything like the literary heroes that we get in other stories of Arthur. These men still had beards and weren't yet waxing their chests.

Utherpendragon, a great general and king, a Christian man, lusts so heartily and publicly for the wife of one of his knights that a civil war breaks out. The war has one goal and one goal only, that the king Utherpendragon would be able to sleep with this woman. Thousands of men die, and Uther sits in his tent and bemoans the painfulness of his desire. He just has to have satisfaction. So Merlin provides him with a potion that will make him look like the woman's husband, he sneaks into the fortress where the husband has attempted to protect her from the king's lust, and he sleeps with her. The husband is then killed in battle and Uther is able to take the woman as his wife.

King Arthur is conceived by Uther in that act of adultery. This is not the birth of a literary hero and Christ figure. While we may not believe that Merlin had some herbs that could make a man take on the form of another (which we shouldn't), this account feels historical because there is no motivation to lie. Geoffrey obviously honors Arthur as a great Christian king, and making up a conception story like this would conflict with that. It should at least be obvious that Geoffrey believes what he says, and that makes the story even more unfortunate. The only apparent difference between the Christian and pagan kings seems to be that the Christians pray to God to help them sate their lust for the blood or the wife of their neighbor, while the pagans simply shed it or take her. The converted Britons seem to have borne little fruit, at least from the distant perspective that Geoffrey gives us. Arthur himself is a pious man, with the Virgin Mary on his shield so that he can think of her all the time. But he hasn't the slightest hesitation when it comes to conquering and slaughtering the inhabitants of the islands surrounding Britain or doing the same to the nations and peoples on the continent. And neither he nor Geoffrey seem to see any contradiction between this behavior and his faith.

If a king grew strong, then it was expected that he would flex himself, proclaim his strength and demand that everyone around him pay tribute. If they said yes, then great. If they said *no*, then you had to invade. Otherwise they might think you were weak. If you were strong then there was no wickedness in taking lands, so long as you kept treaties, became friends with those beneath you whom you may have just conquered and were generous with the wealth and protection that your strength provided. Arthur may have conquered countries, but kings once conquered became allies two days after. There was a strange political system that we cannot understand from where we sit, with more than an additional millennium of the fruit of the gospel to influence us. In Geoffrey's world, betrayal, oath-breaking and lying were all problems, but good honest conquest was not. We can be grateful that the world has changed for the better through the influence of Christ, and we can see the inconsistencies between bloody conquest for conquest's sake and Christianity. But in a world where such behavior was expected, it is more difficult to condemn Arthur's actions than to condemn the actions of a man who tries to do the same today. Arthur may have sinned, and Geoffrey may have been unable to see it, but he sinned against lesser light.

But then Geoffrey may not have been as blind to it as we might think. The three central heroes that seem to dominate the whole of Geoffrey are conquerors: Brutus himself, who slaughtered his way from coastline to coastline until he settled in Britain; Belinus, one of the more successful kings, who managed to conquer his way all the way to the gates of Rome and then to sack the city itself; and Arthur, who was legendary for his strength and the enormity of his conquests. He too would have sacked Rome if Mordred's betrayal and adultery with Guinevere hadn't brought him hurrying back to fight yet another civil war on the island. Mordred was killed, and Arthur was mortally wounded and taken to Avalon to heal. C.S. Lewis (and some traditions) would like us to believe that Arthur, like Enoch, was caught up into heaven where he waits for the prophecies of Merlin to be fulfilled, when he shall return (like Aslan) and make all wrongs right.

Geoffrey tells a different story. Arthur may have been the pinnacle of goodness when it came to the kings of Britain, but he was not the pinnacle of strength. He was on the downward slope. The Saxons had already infested Britain more than once and were howling at the gates when he died. Britain never truly recovered and the last barrage of British kings and tyrants could not stay out of the folly of bloodthirst and greed. Geoffrey tells us of the final judgment of God upon these sins: the British are driven off their island by plague and famine, and some of their royalty travel to Rome to do penance for their sins. Some Britons survive and become the persecuted Welsh. The Saxons come once and for all and rule more wisely than the British. King David may have been faithful in many ways, but he was not fit to build the House of the Lord. King Arthur may have been noble, but he and his people were not fit to rule in their own houses. His family was torn apart and his posterity destroyed and pushed out from their own nation.

Brutus arrived a refugee, and the British left refugees. Geoffrey sees this clearly, and while his heart is obviously with the British (the Welsh, where he would eventually become a bishop), he also sees the sin and the justice of God just as clearly.

However, the irony of the British Isles continued, and by the time of Geoffrey the Saxons were already complaining of the heavy Norman hand. Saxons quickly saw themselves as the true British and had to grapple with a new invader. Robin Hood was a Saxon beneath Norman rulers, and he is said to have died less than a century after Geoffrey.

Where are the British now? Like the Trojans, they were scattered, but where they settled is harder to say. Once again, contrary to our own modern confidence, thanks to Geoffrey, we have a better sense of where they were fifteen hundred years ago than where they are now.

—N.D. Wilson

For Further Reading

Spielvogel, Jackson J. *Western Civilization.* Seventh Edition. Belmont, Calif.: ThomsonWadsworth, 2009. 190.

Veritas Press History Cards: Middle Ages, Renaissance and Reformation. Lancaster, Pa.: Veritas Press. 2.

Session I: Prelude

A Question to Consider

Are modern historians more trustworthy than the ancient, untrained chroniclers?

From the General Information above answer the following questions:

1. What historical event brought about the founding of both Rome and Britain?
2. What made a king in ancient Britain? Once made, how would he retain his crown?
3. Should Christians be uncomfortable with Geoffrey's views on conquest?
4. Where did Stonehenge come from? Should we assume that Geoffrey is lying, telling the truth, or neither?
5. What character, more than any other, discredits Geoffrey in the eyes of secularist moderns? How should Christians react to the same character?
6. What is the moral of the story? What happens in the end?

Reading Assignment:

Part I, chapters 1–11

The wedding of Arthur and Guinevere, painted by Arthur Rackham. Rackham was born in 1867 and studied at the City of London School. His first book with illustrations done specifically on commission was printed in 1896.

Session II: Discussion

Part I, chapters 1–11

A Question to Consider

Where do you come from? Does it matter?

Discuss or list short answers to the following questions:

Text Analysis

1. Where did the Britons come from?
2. How does Brutus rise to power?
3. How does Brutus liberate the descendants of the Trojans from the Greeks?
4. Why does Brutus decide to leave Greece?
5. What does Diana prophesy to Brutus?

The earliest mention of Guinevere is in the Welsh tale *Culhwch ap Olwen,* where she is just Arthur's queen. Geoffrey transforms Guinevere (whom he calls Ganhumara, and the Welsh referred to as Gwenhwyfar) into a beautiful lady with a Roman heritage, raised in the house of Duke Cador of Cornwall, who betrays the king and helps the usurper Mordred. Other writers would later clear her of that charge, but the famous queen never is able to escape scandal. Chrétien de Troyes invents Lancelot and introduces him to the Round Table with the idea that Arthur's queen breaks her wedding vows with Arthur's "first knight." Later Sir Thomas Malory suggests that Arthur knew about his wife's betrayal and ignored it, but then in the end sentenced her to be burned at the stake for treason. Tennyson points to Guinevere's infidelity as the principal flaw in Arthur's court, keeping Lancelot from the Holy Grail and driving Balin and Pelleas mad. Many tales end with Guinevere as a contrite abbess in a nunnery.

6. How do you think Brutus's Trojan origin will affect his descendants and the history of his nation?

Cultural Analysis

1. What does our contemporary secular culture have to say about individuals and their choices?
2. Where does it place the blame when "evils" (such as crime, disease, famine) occur?

Biblical Analysis

1. What does the Bible say about the effect of one generation upon the next (Deut. 5:9-10, 7:9-10, 24:16)? Can you think of any examples?
2. How can we be held responsible for sin when we are born sinners?

SUMMA

Write an essay or discuss this question, integrating what you have learned from the material above.

Does a person's beginning determine or limit his end? Feel free to use examples from the Bible, your own life or the story of Brutus.

READING ASSIGNMENT:
Part I, chapters 12–18

SESSION III: WRITING

Part I, chapters 12–18

Family History Project

First, interview your parents and relatives about your family history: how, when and why they came to America; what countries they hail from; whether there are any exciting stories involving famous historical events or people. Write a brief summary of your findings, analyze and discuss them, asking yourself questions such as these: How has my Scandinavian heritage affected me and my family? How did my father's side of the family come to a knowledge of Christ, and did successive generations remain faithful or fall away? Does our family still follow Japanese customs in how we celebrate our birthdays? Why or why not?

READING ASSIGNMENT:
Part II, chapters 1–17

Session IV: Discussion
Part II, chapters 1–17

A Question to Consider
Have you ever betrayed anyone?

Discuss or list short answers to the following questions:

Text Analysis
1. What sort of king is Locrinus, son of Brutus?
2. What happens after King Maddan dies?
3. Who is King Leir?
4. What is the story of Ferrex and Porrex?
5. What sort of king is Dunvallo Molmutius?

Cultural Analysis
1. In books and movies of our day, is betrayal seen as good or bad?
2. What would Americans consider to be the worst type of betrayal?

Biblical Analysis
1. Is betrayal ever justifiable for a Christian (Ps. 15:4, James 5:12)?
2. What biblical response should you have when someone betrays you (2 Sam. 15–18)?

Summa

Write an essay or discuss this question, integrating what you have learned from the material above.

Look up the words *betray* and *treachery* in the dictionary. How does the origin of these words deepen your understanding of what they mean?[2]

Reading Assignment:
Part III, chapters 1–20

Session V: Recitation
Parts I–III

Comprehension Questions
Answer the following questions for factual recall:
1. What sort of island is Britain, according to Geoffrey?
2. Is Diana's prophecy to Brutus fulfilled?
3. What role does Corineus have in the founding of Britain?
4. What role do giants have in the founding of Britain?
5. How does Britain get its name? What about Cornwall?
6. How is London founded?
7. What does Bladud accomplish during his reign?
8. Is Rome founded before or after Britain?
9. Who is Belinus?
10. Why is Lud important?

Reading Assignment:
Part IV, chapters 1–20

Session VI: Discussion
Part IV, chapters 1–20

A Question to Consider
If you were one of Caesar's advisors, would you counsel him to invade the island of Britain? Why or why not?

Discuss or list short answers to the following questions:

Text Analysis
1. What are Caesar's reasons for invading Britain?
2. What is Cassivelaunus's reply?
3. What is the outcome of Caesar's first invasion?
4. How do the Gauls respond to this?
5. What is the outcome of Caesar's second invasion?

Cultural Analysis
1. According to our culture, how will world peace be accomplished?
2. How do Americans view invading other countries?

Biblical Analysis
1. According to the Bible, how will world peace be accomplished (Is. 2:4, 9:6–7, 11:1–10)?
2. Why did the Israelites invade Canaan (Gen. 15:16 and Josh. 1)?

SUMMA

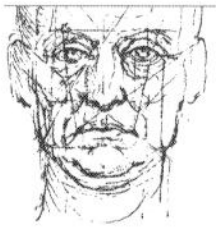

Write an essay or discuss this question, integrating what you have learned from the material above.

What are some justifiable reasons to invade a nation?

READING ASSIGNMENT:
Part V, chapters 1–11

SESSION VII: DISCUSSION

Part V, chapters 1–11

A Question to Consider

What is a martyr?

Discuss or list short answers to the following questions:

Text Analysis

1. When does the Christian faith first suffer significant persecution in Britain?
2. Does Geoffrey view this persecution as a good thing?
3. Which martyrs does Geoffrey mention?
4. What does Bede add in his account of this same persecution (*Ecclesiastical History of the English People*, I.6–7)?

Cultural Analysis

1. Does our culture honor martyrs?
2. What are some of the ways in which our culture shows this honor? Are these ways appropriate?
3. Do Christians today honor martyrs?

Biblical Analysis

1. What does the Bible have to say about martyrs (Matt. 23:35; Acts 6, 7, 22:30; Rev. 2:12–13, 17:5–6)?

SUMMA

Write an essay or discuss this question, integrating what you have learned from the material above.

How should believers honor Christian martyrs?

READING ASSIGNMENT:
Part V, chapter 12–Part VI, chapter 9

SESSION VIII: ANALYSIS

Part V, chapter 12–Part VI, chapter 9

Geoffrey's Christianity
His view of God, man and the world.

Geoffrey does not always agree with the actions of some of his characters, and with others he sometimes verbalizes approval of them. Find examples of such metanarratives (where Geoffrey steps outside of his story and offers commentary on it) to help answer the following questions:

1. Does Geoffrey believe in the God of the Bible?
2. What is Geoffrey's view of man and sin?
3. What is his view of the church?
4. How does he view the supernatural?
5. Why is Geoffrey writing his history?

READING ASSIGNMENT:
Part VI, chapters 10–19

SESSION IX: RECITATION

Parts IV–VI

Comprehension Questions

Answer the following questions for factual recall:

1. What is Yellow Death?
2. What happens between Cassivelaunus and Androgeus?
3. What happens during the reign of Guiderius?
4. What role does the Roman emperor Severus play in British history?
5. How does Emperor Diocletian affect Britain?
6. Where does the custom of *wassail* come from?
7. What treachery does Hengist perpetrate?
8. Who is Eldol?
9. How is Merlin involved in Geoffrey's narrative?

READING ASSIGNMENT:
The material for Session X (to prepare for a debate)

Chart 1: COMPARISON OF PROPHECIES

PROPHECY	PROPHECY REFERENCE	MERLIN	BIBLE REFERENCE	PROPHETS IN THE BIBLE
Animals (what/whom do they represent?)	VII.3		Rev. 12:9, 20:2	
	VII.3		Dan. 8:20	
Political events that they prophesied	VII.4		Dan. 2:36–45	
	VII.3		Josh. 6:26, 1 Kings 16:34	
			Rev. 13	
	VII.3			
			Gen. 3:15	
Religious events that they prophesied	VII.3			
			Matt. 24:1–2	
	VII.3			
			Isa. 40:3	
	VII.3			

Session X: Activity

Debate on Magic

Is there such a thing as "good" magic?

In a classroom setting, divide the class up into affirmative and negative and structure the debate as time allows. Usually a formal debate consists of opening statements, cross-examinations, rebuttals and concluding arguments. For those not in a classroom situation, individual students should write arguments for each side.

Reading Assignment:
Part VII, chapters 1–4

Session XI: Discussion

Part VII, chapters 1–4

A Question to Consider

If you were Moses, would you stone Merlin?

Discuss or list short answers to the following questions:

Cultural Analysis

1. What sort of prophecies are made by our secular culture?
2. What sort of prophecies are made by Christians?

Text and Biblical Analysis

Complete Chart 1, by referring to the listed sections of *The History of the Kings of Britain* and the Bible to compare how biblical prophecies and Merlin's prophecies were both similar and dissimilar.

Now analyze your findings. What similarities are there between the two sets of prophecy? Where do they differ? Why?

Summa

Write an essay or discuss this question, integrating what you have learned from the material above.

Do you think any of Merlin's prophecies were fulfilled?

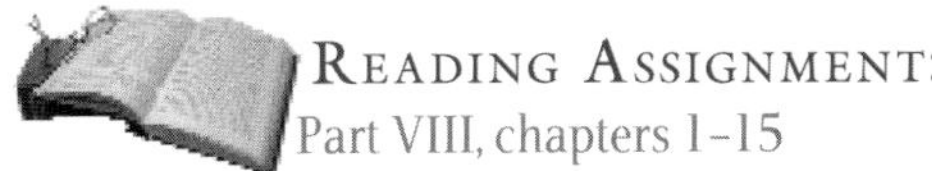

Reading Assignment:
Part VIII, chapters 1–15

SESSION XII: ACTIVITY

Part VIII, chapters 1–15

Debate

Debate: Is deceit in war ever lawful? In other words, is there any difference between Ehud (Judg. 3) and Eopa (VIII.14)?

You have already discussed the issue of betrayal. Apply what you learned there to these issues. How is deceit in war similar to or different from betrayal?

If you have already had a more formal debate (Session X), this can be made into more of an informal dialoguing debate, with the teacher as moderator. Make sure you define your terms! Individual students can write arguments for both sides, or else a more thorough defense of one side or the other.

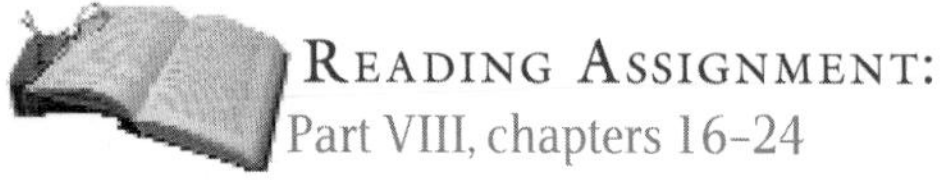

READING ASSIGNMENT:
Part VIII, chapters 16–24

SESSION XIII: WRITING

Part VIII, chapters 16–24

Stonehenge Story

Write a short story about the origin or theft of Stonehenge. Get creative and write it from the perspective of the giants or the Irish, since Geoffrey has already given it to us from the British perspective.

READING ASSIGNMENT:
Part IX, chapters 1–14

SESSION XIV: DISCUSSION

Part IX, chapters 1–14

A Question to Consider

What makes a great king?

Discuss or list short answers to the following questions:

Text Analysis

1. What qualities does the young Arthur possess?
2. Who is King Hoel?
3. What happens at the Siege of Bath?
4. What is the outcome of the Battle of Loch Lomond?
5. Describe Arthur's court.

Cultural Analysis

1. Which historical figures are admired by Americans today? Why?

Biblical Analysis

1. What does a godly king look like? Look at passages such as Ex. 18:18–23, Prov. 16:10–15, 20:8 and 26–28 and 1 Sam. 8:9–19, and give some examples.
2. Is every Christian called to be a leader?

SUMMA

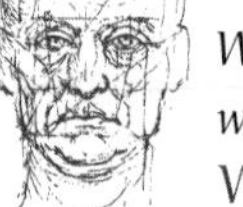

Write an essay or discuss this question, integrating what you have learned from the material above.

Would you gladly follow King Arthur? Explain and defend your answer.

READING ASSIGNMENT:
None

SESSION XV: RECITATION

Part VIII, chapters 1–24

Comprehension Questions

Answer the following questions for factual recall:

1. What is the fate of Vortigern?
2. How does Hengist meet his end?
3. What is the history of the Giants' Ring?
4. Why does Aurelius decide to take it?
5. How do the Britons bring it over?
6. How does Aurelius Ambrosius die?
7. What sort of king is Uther?
8. How does Uther die?

READING ASSIGNMENT:
Part IX, chapter 15–Part X, chapter 5

Session XVI: Discussion

Part IX, chapter 15–Part X, chapter 5

A Question to Consider

Would you have sided with the Romans or the Britons when the Roman Senate challenged Arthur?

Discuss or list short answers to the following questions:

Text Analysis

1. What are the Roman arguments in favor of the Britons to paying tribute?
2. What are Arthur's arguments that it is actually Rome who should be paying tribute to Britain and not the other way around?
3. How do the other Britons react to Arthur's stand against the Romans?
4. What happens when Arthur sends Gawain and two other leaders to challenge Lucius?

Cultural Analysis

1. How would the UN react to this war between Rome and Britain?
2. Would our culture agree with Arthur's statement in IX.16 that "nothing that is acquired by force and violence can ever be held legally by anyone"?

Biblical Analysis

1. Is the system of taking hostages and tribute a biblical one (2 Sam. 8:1-4)?

It is legend that King Arthur will one day return to save England, but Merlin Ambrosius already has—in C.S. Lewis's 1946 novel *That Hideous Strength.* In that book Merlin has slept for centuries and is awakened for a battle against the materialistic agents of the Devil. In this story Merlin mentions "Numinor" as the True West—a tip of the hat to J.R.R. Tolkien's *The Silmarillion.* That Númenor was misspelled, and the mistake that Valinor—not Númenor—is the True West, can be attributed to the fact that *The Silmarillon* had not yet been published, so Lewis would only have heard it read aloud when it was shared with the Inklings.

SUMMA

Write an essay or discuss this question, integrating what you have learned from the material above.

Would you rather take tribute or pay it?

READING ASSIGNMENT:
Part X, chapter 6–Part XI, chapter 9

SESSION XVII: WRITING

Part X, chapter 6–Part XI, chapter 9

A Giant Fable

Write a fable on Arthur's battle either with the giant of Mont-St.-Michel or with the giant Retho (X.3). A fable takes narrative and amplifies it with dialogue. Geoffrey's account of the giant of Mont-St.-Michel is rather extended, but the only speech is given by the nurse. If you choose this story, amplify with speeches by the giant, Arthur or his companions Kay and Bedevere. The story of his fight with Retho is much more condensed and is told by Arthur as a sort of flashback. With this one, take Geoffrey's indirect discourse and expand it into fiery speeches by Retho or Arthur.

READING ASSIGNMENT:
Part XI, chapter 10–Part XII, chapter 19

SESSION XVIII: DISCUSSION

Part XI, chapter 10–Part XII, chapter 19

A Question to Consider

Will our nation exist in 500 years?

Discuss or list short answers to the following questions:

Text Analysis

1. Read the following selections from Geoffrey and summarize his view of why nations come to an end: VI.3, XI.9, and XII.6.

Cultural Analysis

1. Would our culture agree with Geoffrey's analysis?
2. How would our culture "fix" the problems plaguing Britain at the end of the book?

Biblical Analysis

1. Why did Jerusalem fall (2 Chron. 36:13–17)?
2. Read Deuteronomy 8. How does this apply to the Britons?

SUMMA

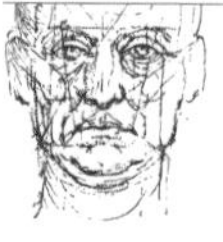

Write an essay or discuss this question, integrating what you have learned from the material above.

Do you agree with Geoffrey's assessment of the reasons for Britain's downfall? Defend your answer.

SESSION XIX: EVALUATION

Grammar

Answer each of the following questions in complete sentences. Some answers may be longer than others. (2 points per answer)

1. Why is Brutus's "Trojan-ness" important?
2. What is Belinus's greatest military accomplishment?
3. Who brings Merlin into the story and why?
4. Why does Arthur abandon his attack on Rome?
5. How does King Arthur die?
6. Who is Brian?
7. How does Geoffrey's *History* end?

Logic

Answer the following question in complete sentences; your answer should be a paragraph or so. Answer two of the three questions. (10 points per answer)

1. What is Geoffrey's view of conquest?
2. How do the Britons view treachery?
3. How do the Britons view the family?

Lateral Thinking

Answer one of the following questions. These questions will require more substantial answers. (16 points per answer)

1. Bring out the similarities between Bilbo and King Arthur, keeping in mind the importance of origin and family.

2. Compare the role of woman as peace-weaver in Geoffrey's *History* (III.7), Livy's *History* (I.913, II.40—"the Sabine women") and *Beowulf* (lines 2021–2038—Beowulf's fear of the resumption of the feud at the wedding).

King Arthur and Charlemagne by Giacomo Jaquerio

Session XX: Activity

Medieval Feast and Knightly Revelry

You've read the book. You've seen pictures. Now is the time to suit up in armor or silk. Follow the example of Arthur and his court in IX.12–14 and have a procession with all manner of regalia. Then, if you know any medieval tunes (or Renaissance tunes, if you must), sing them (Arthur and his knights heard choirs after their procession). Now that appetites are sufficiently aroused, proceed further to the feast. If you wish to observe the ancient custom of Troy, as the Britons did, the men and women will feast separately. You may wish to try fresh game, followed by an herb-and-flower salad, finishing up with a spinach tart.3 Or perhaps the sweet-tooths among you may desire to try only the crispels or the pokerounce.4 Invigorated by the food and drink you have consumed, commence any sort of knightly contests for which you have the time and resources. The gentlemen may wish to have a sword fighting tournament (swords made prosaically of PVC pipe and duct tape work well and are safer than their metallic cousins). Or for the sedentary, let there be rounds of chess or dice or knucklebones.5 Let prizes be awarded to the valiant, and let the climax of the games be a grand ball, in which medieval dances are danced. And in all things let courteousness abound. Arthur would wish it.

Optional Session A: Worldview Analysis

Bede vs. Geoffrey

What do Bede and Geoffrey have in common as historians? How do they differ?

Review the accounts of Augustine's coming to Britain in Bede (I.23ff) and in Geoffrey (XI.12ff), then discuss or list short answers to the following questions:

1. How do the goals of these men affect their account of Augustine's coming?
2. Are there any discrepancies in their accounts?
3. What stylistic similarities and differences are there?
4. Which historian do you prefer? Why?

OPTIONAL SESSION B: WRITING

Progymnasmata

Classical training in rhetoric included preparatory writing exercises called the *progymnasmata*. These exercises in composition introduced the beginning student to basic forms and techniques that would then be used and combined when practicing more advanced exercises and speeches. One of these *progymnasmata* was called the *encomium*, a composition written to praise an individual. Its opposite exercise (which condemns an individual) is called a *vituperation* (or an invective). This writing exercise expounds the virtues or condemns the vices of a specific person (e.g., Joe is a strong warrior), but does not talk about virtue in a general sense (e.g., strength in war is admirable).

The encomium and the vituperation each have six parts. The *Prologue* comes first. It introduces the topic and, at the end of the paragraph, states or implies the opinion of the writer. The second part of this exercise is a paragraph called *Description of Heritage*. In this paragraph the writer looks for ways to praise or condemn the person on account of his family history. For instance, if a person comes from righteous parents, then highlight the fact that he learned his righteous habits at home and added to the glory of the family name. A vituperation would emphasize that he comes from a family or nation that taught him wrong beliefs or bad habits. Next comes a paragraph called *Description of Upbringing*. The point is to show how the person profited from a good education or overcame a bad one (this is for the encomium). For the vituperation you should attempt to show how he failed to profit from a good education or learned well the lessons of a bad education. The most powerful part of the en-

The earliest record of a cup from the Last Supper was from a seventh-century Anglo-Saxon pilgrim who said it was a two-handled silver chalice kept in a chapel near Jerusalem. In literature, the earliest record of the Holy Grail is in Chrétien's unfinished poem *Perceval, or the Story of the Grail:* "A girl came in, fair and comely and beautifully adorned, and between her hands she held a grail. And when she carried the grail in, the hall was suffused by a light so brilliant that the candles lost their brightness as do the moon or stars when the sun rises."

Chart 2: **DEBATE**

CONSIDERATION	ARTHUR WOULD MAKE A BETTER KING	BEOWULF WOULD MAKE A BETTER KING
His Christianity		
His conquests		
His justice/mercy		
His humility		
His men's view of him		

comium comes next: *the Description of Deeds.* In this section the writer praises the excellencies of the mind, body and fortune of the subject. For example, the writer praises the practice of philosophical virtue, the way the person looked and his wealth, influence or social stature. Since Christianity has transformed our society it seems out of place to dwell on physical appearance or possessions (i.e., he was evil because he was quite homely, or it is obvious that he was a good man because he was fabulously rich), so instead the paragraph should concentrate on the actions and motives of the subject. This can be especially powerful if his life demonstrates a pattern. Next is a *Comparison* of the subject to someone else to portray him in a favorable light (if it is an encomium). An unfavorable comparison is best for vituperation. The final paragraph is an *Exhortation or Prayer* in which others are called on to imitate this person's example or a proclamation to everyone telling them not to go down the wicked path that this person did.

Write a vituperation of King Arthur. Above all you must be persuasive—almost every audience will be hostile.

I. Prologue
   - Introduce the topic
   - State your opinion

II. Description of Heritage
   - Praise or condemn the person on account of his family history

III. Description of Upbringing
   - Show how the person profited or failed to profit from his education

IV. Description of Deeds
   - Praise or condemn the excellencies or deficiencies of his actions and motives

V. Comparison
   - Portray the person favorably or unfavorably in comparison to someone else

VI. Exhortation or Prayer
   - Call upon others to either imitate or shun this person's example

Optional Session C: Activity

Debate

Debate (in either a formal or informal setting) the following proposition: Affirmed: Arthur makes a better king than Beowulf.

Students should incorporate what they discussed in Session XIV, about the qualities of a good leader. Complete Chart 2 to organize your ideas. You can also make it personal: would you rather serve Beowulf or Arthur?

Optional Session D: Activity

"On second thought, let's not go to Camelot. It is a silly place."

Watch a parent-approved movie about Arthur and compare its portrayal of him with Geoffrey's (either in discussion or in a short essay). Possible choices: *The Sword in the Stone, King Arthur, First Knight, Monty Python and the Holy Grail* or *Excalibur.* More obscure films, cartoons and shorts can be found by doing an internet search.

"The Lady of the Lake, her arm clad in the purest shimmering samite, held aloft Excalibur from the bosom of the water, signifying by divine providence that I, Arthur, was to carry Excalibur. That is why I am your king!"

Endnotes

1 The Picts were a tribe that inhabited Scotland and often tattooed themselves and painted themselves blue.

2 You can also look online at a good etymology dictionary. One may be found at Link 1 for this chapter at www.VeritasPress.com/OmniLinks.

3 There are several websites with medieval recipes. One site which has the original medieval text, along with adaptations for the modern cook can be found at Link 2 for this chapter at www.VeritasPress.com/OmniLinks.

4 Recipes for these desserts, as well as other, more savory dishes can be found at Link 3 for this chapter at www.VeritasPress.com/OmniLinks.

5 The rules for many medieval card and board games can be found at Link 4 for this chapter at www.VeritasPress.com/OmniLinks.

MACBETH

Macbeth Meeting with the Witches (c. 1780) by George Romney (1734–1802).

When you were little, did you ever stare at a stranger at the mall, or at another customer at a restaurant, because you didn't know if they were a man or a woman? I hope your mother told you to stop staring—perhaps she whispered to you that you could ask about it in the car.

We live in an age of profound sexual confusion. We no longer know how men are supposed to look and behave and how women are supposed to look and behave. On the one hand, women are depicted as mannish, aggressive and violent. In movies, on television, in video games and in all other forms of popular entertainment, we are surrounded by images of women warriors with pumped-up muscles and a bad attitude. On the other hand, in many movies and television shows, men, especially fathers, are weak and foolish. The "sensitive guy" (and he's always a "guy," not a man) became a popular cultural figure in the late twentieth century. He was in touch with his feelings. He was warm and cozy. He was one of the girls.

On the other hand (there are always three hands), many films and video games depict men as brutes—violent, murderous sexual predators. Real men get their way, and if they don't they break your knees. In reaction to the laughable sensitive guys of the late twentieth century, the early twenty-first century has seen a resurgence of militant maleness. There is now a "Men's Channel" featuring sports and outdoor activities, and television is full of programs showing men behaving like overgrown teenagers.

All this is not even to mention the attacks against traditional sexual roles coming, often loudly, from the homosexual community.

We have lost any idea that women can be strong without using brass knuckles or knowing kick-boxing moves. We have lost any idea that men can be compassionate without becoming women.

What's responsible for this confusion? Much of the confusion is attributable to a movement known as feminism. Feminism has its origins in nineteenth-century movements to give women the privilege of voting, but the movement really took off during the twentieth century. Feminism has been one of the most successful political and intellectual movements of the last century. It is a very diverse movement, but there are several common features. It was a political movement, attempting to change the laws and structures of society, politics and business, to open opportunities for women in areas of life traditionally reserved for men. Feminism is also an intellectual movement that frequently challenges traditional understandings of masculinity and femininity.

One of the ironies of the feminist movement is that the results of it have often been anti-woman. Feminists have often attempted to win greater freedom and opportunity for women by attacking feminine roles and callings (like motherhood and home-making). Feminists who claim to be speaking on behalf of women's uniqueness end up telling women to become more like men. That, to put it mildly, is not a way to advance femininity.

The widespread impact of the feminist movement, especially in its more radical forms, is a sign of a widespread cultural blindness. It has become controversial to point out that men and women have different desires, different ways of approaching and experiencing life, different roles in family and society. Women carry infants within their bodies and have breasts to feed newborns. Men don't. How could God have made it more obvious that women are designed for the care of young children? Despite repeated failures, our culture is always ready to try, with one last valiant effort, to milk the bull.

From a Christian perspective, feminism must be seen as a reaction to the sins and abdication of men. If men were genuinely devoted to Christ-like masculinity, if they truly gave themselves for their wives and daughters as Jesus did for His bride, if men honored women as their glory and crown, the feminist movement would have had very little impact. Feminism is a movement about women, but it is just as importantly a movement that poses questions to men. What does it mean to be a man? Christian men are not supposed to be brutal, but Christian men are not supposed to be stuffed teddy bears either. Where is the balance?

Macbeth provides a good platform for discussing these questions. Macbeth is a great warrior, yet his wife considers him too full of breast milk to carry out his plans. For her, to be a man is to be a murderer; every man is a bloody man. During the play, Macbeth conforms to his wife's conception of manhood, but that only leads to tyranny and personal disaster. By depicting the consequences of Macbeth's pursuit of a particular version of manhood, the play addresses crucial issues for our time. And as we work on sorting this out, it is all right to stare.

GENERAL INFORMATION

Author and Context

Though his plays were frequently based in fact, Shakespeare took liberties with chronology and historical detail in order to highlight moral and dramatic issues. This is true of *Macbeth*. Though the story is based on the life of the Macbeth who ruled Scotland during the eleventh century, Shakespeare's Macbeth differs from the historical Macbeth in several ways. Shakespeare departed from his principal source, Raphael Holinshed's *Chronicle of Scottish History*, in several respects. In Shakespeare's play, King Duncan is not the incompetent king depicted by Holinshed but a model Christian king. He is said to be "gracious" and without fault. Moreover, in the play, Banquo is not part of the conspiracy against Duncan, as he is in Holinshed. Shakespeare's Macbeth acts without aid from the other thanes of Scotland but with the knowledge and encouragement only of his wife. Finally, in the play Macduff kills Macbeth at the battle of Dunsinane, and Malcolm immediately takes the throne. In fact, neither of these events followed so closely after the battle of Dunsinane.

The first two changes are especially important to Shakespeare's purposes. Far from seeking the good of his nation, Macbeth himself admits that "I have no spur to prick the sides of my intent, but only vaulting ambition, which o'erleaps itself and falls on the other." The play directs its primary attention to the consequences of Macbeth's vaulting ambition and the deeds it inspires. There are, of course, times and places where the existing order of things has become so unjust and evil that it must be resisted to the point of overthrowing it. But Scotland under Duncan is not a totalitarian state, and Macbeth is not resisting injustice.

Macbeth opened as a play during the reign of James I, a Scottish king supposedly descended from Duncan. James was probably in the audience when the play was first produced. Marjorie Garber points out that James would have been particularly intrigued by the witches, since he "was a scholar of witches and witchcraft, the author of a book called *Daemonologie* (1597)."[1] Macbeth also makes some veiled references to the "Gunpowder Plot" of 1605, an effort by radical Catholics to blow up Parliament with the king, queen and prince present. When the Catholics were later put on trial, they gave "equivocal" or ambiguous answers to questions, bringing the issue of "equivocation" to public attention. Shakespeare's use of the word in Act 5 scene 5 would evoke memories of the recently foiled plot.

Significance

According to Marjorie Garber, *Macbeth* has an uncanny history on stage: "It has always been considered by actors to be an unlucky play. Many will refuse to wear costumes that have appeared in productions of it; most, once they are acclimated to the mores of the theater world, will not mention the play's title or the names of any of its characters, onstage or in the wings or dressing rooms . . .. Accidents have befallen many casts and productions around the world since the play was first performed: *real* murders committed onstage, fires, falling scenery. One actress playing Lady Macbeth decided that the sleepwalking scene would be more realistic if she closed her eyes; she walked straight off the stage and fell into the orchestra

pit, seriously injuring herself."[2] A mystery novel by Ngaio Marsh, *Light Thickens,* takes these superstitions as its premise.

Despite the risks, the play is performed and read enough to be one of the best-known of Shakespeare's plays, and many of its scenes and lines have become proverbial. Macbeth's lament that life is "full of sound and fury, signifying nothing" gave to William Faulkner inspiration for a famous modern stream-of-consciousness novel. Lady Macbeth's sleepwalking and mantra of "out, out damned spot" sells cleaning products and has become a symbol of unatoned guilt.

Main Characters

The main characters in the play are Macbeth himself and Lady Macbeth. Macbeth is a *thane*, or nobleman, of Scotland, a vassal to the good king Duncan. Together, Macbeth and his wife scheme to murder Duncan and to set Macbeth on the throne. Once that deed is done, Duncan's son, Malcolm, flees from Scotland to England, seeking safety from the dangerous new king. Other thanes include Banquo, Macduff and Ross. The ones that Macbeth does not murder escape to join Malcolm, who works to overthrow Macbeth and restore himself as the rightful king of Scotland. Macduff fulfills the witches' prophecy by killing Macbeth.

Summary and Setting

Significantly, the play begins with witches on stage, making plans to meet Macbeth and deliver prophecies to him concerning his future inheritance of the crown of Scotland. Returning from a battle in which he has been the hero, Macbeth meets the witches and is struck by the prediction, since it matches his own ambitions, and he begins to ponder whether he should speed things on a bit by killing the reigning king, Duncan. Banquo, another Scottish thane, also hears the prophecy, but wonders, reasonably enough, if witches with beards are trustworthy. Macbeth returns home, and he and his wife discuss the prophecies. Lady Macbeth is keen on becoming queen and seduces, cajoles and bullies Macbeth to agreeing.

Duncan stays the night at Macbeth's castle at Dunsinane, and during the night Macbeth sneaks into his room to kill him. The next morning, Duncan's body

Out, damned spot! out, I say!

is discovered, and Macbeth soon becomes king. Remembering that the witches predicted that Banquo's children would inherit the throne, Macbeth sends two assassins to kill Banquo and his son. They kill Banquo, but his son, Fleance, escapes, leaving Macbeth with continuing fears of losing the throne. At a state banquet, Macbeth sees Banquo's ghost sitting in the king's chair, and his manic response takes much of the joy out of the meal. Meanwhile, Duncan's son Malcolm is in England preparing to take an army to Scotland to recover the throne, and Macduff, another thane, goes to join him there.

In an effort to clarify his direction, Macbeth returns to the witches, and they give him a series of ambiguous prophesies. They tell him that he will not be killed by any man of woman born and that he will reign over Scotland until Birnam Woods come to Dunsinane. Macbeth continues his reign with renewed confidence, thinking that he is invulnerable. He dispatches more murderers to kill Macduff because of his betrayal. Macduff has already left Scotland, but the murderers kill his family.

Act 5 begins with Lady Macbeth sleepwalking, frantically attempting to wash the stain of blood from her hands. Malcolm's army enters Scotland and marches toward Dunsinane, and as they march, two of the witches' prophecies are fulfilled. Malcolm instructs his men to cut branches from the trees of Birnam Wood to use as camouflage as they approach the castle; thus Birnam Wood comes to Dunsinane. And Macduff, while fighting with Macbeth, reveals that he was born by Caesarean section and thus is not "a man of woman born." He kills Macbeth. Malcolm is proclaimed as king, promising to renew Scotland by the "grace of Grace."

Worldview

What does it mean to be a man? Two answers to this question are presented by the play, and Macbeth is forced to choose between them. When Lady Macbeth urges him to kill Duncan, he protests, "I dare do all that may become a man; who dares do more is none" (1.7). On this view, one cannot be a man without recognizing limitations on desires and actions. Whoever tries to do more than "becomes a man" becomes less than a man. Lady Macbeth, by contrast, operates on the view that you are not a man unless you act on every single desire. Any effort to control desire or to place any limits whatever on action—all these for Lady Macbeth amount to nothing but cowardice. To be a man is to ignore all moral constraints. In the final analysis, for Lady Macbeth to be a true man is to be a murderer. Only the bloody man is truly a man. (Note the frequent use of the word "blood" throughout this play.)

After hesitations and doubts, Macbeth acts on the latter view, and his choice is personally devastating. On this level, the play is about the collapse of a man's soul, about a man sliding, due to his own unrepented sins, into hell. Macbeth begins as a hero of Scotland and a somewhat admirable character. He seems loyal to his king, and his wife's description suggests that he has moral scruples as well. His assault on the order of the world turns him into a beast. By the end of play, Macbeth is being seen, and even sees himself, as a subhuman creature: a baited bear, a hell-hound, a devil. He has dared do more than becomes a man, and at the last he is none.

In pursuing this path toward manhood, Macbeth is, ironically, led by women. *Macbeth* begins with witches or "wyrd sisters," the fates and instruments of hell. Throughout the play, they are never far from the action or from Macbeth's mind. By opening the play with witches, Shakespeare pointed to the ultimate origins of Macbeth's actions, the sparks of whose ambition are brought to full flame by the temptations of the witches. By falling under the witches' spell, Macbeth repeats Satan's original sin, for in Shakespeare's day, it was common belief that Satan had fallen from heaven because he exalted himself above his station.

Macbeth's wife becomes an instrument for hellish powers, guiding her husband toward murder as the witches have done. When Lady Macbeth first appears in the play, she is fearful that Macbeth lacks the courage to take the "nearest way" to the throne. She recognizes his ambition, but also knows that he does not like to get his hands dirty. He is too full of "the milk of human kindness" (1.5), which suggests that, in her opinion, Macbeth is rather feminine. Lady Macbeth's evaluation of her husband is based on her view of manhood. She is contemptuous of Macbeth's wish to achieve his ambitions "without the illness should attend it"; she thinks him womanish for wanting to act "holily." To spur his ambition, she will have to "pour my spirits in thine ear" and "chastise with the valor of my tongue." In *Hamlet,* temptation is linked to pouring poison in the ear, and this is precisely what Lady Macbeth plans. She is a temptress, an aggressive Eve to Macbeth's reluctant Adam. (In Genesis, it should be noted, Adam is primarily responsible for the sin, since he was present with Eve when she was tempted; see Gen. 3:6.)

In fulfilling her role as temptress, Lady Macbeth appeals for help to the "spirits that tend on mortal thoughts" whom she calls "murdering ministers." From this point on, Lady Macbeth becomes a demonic instrument who browbeats Macbeth into taking Duncan's life. She asks the instruments of evil to

> Unsex me here,
> And fill me, from the crown to the toe, top-full
> Of direst cruelty! Make thick my blood,
> Stop up th' access and passage to remorse,
> That no compunctious visitings of nature
> Shake my fell purpose, nor keep peace between
> Th'effect and it! Come to my woman's breasts,
> And take my milk for gall, you murd'ring
> ministers (1.5.).

"Unsex me here" means "make me a man," and for Lady Macbeth, as we saw above, being manly means putting aside all moral restrictions, all boundaries and limits on desire and action, all natural feelings of sympathy and tenderness. Specifically, being manly means being willing to kill to achieve one's desires. Macbeth is too full of the milk of kindness, but Lady Macbeth asks that her milk be exchanged for gall, a bitter liquid that poisons rather than nourishes. Gall is also daring (think of the common expression, "he had the gall to . . ."); Lady Macbeth wants to replace the milk of kindness and moral restraint with the gall to dare do all she can imagine doing.

The exchange between Macbeth and his wife is crucial for the whole play (1.7) and for the themes of manhood and ambition. This scene takes place while Duncan and the rest of the people are feasting. Macbeth withdraws from the feast to consider what he should do. Even before the decisive act, his isolation is beginning. The feast is a symbol of social harmony, peace, fellowship, but Macbeth is not at the feast. Instead, he removes himself to contemplate an act that will destroy all feasting, fellowship and order in Scotland. Macbeth's soliloquy begins with these lines:

> If it were done when 'tis done, then 'twere well
> It were done quickly. If th' assassination
> Could trammel up the consequence, and catch,
> With its surcease, success; that but this blow
> Might be the be-all and the end-all here,
> But here, upon this bank and shoal of time,
> We'd jump the life to come (1.7)

Throughout the play, "done," "do," and "act" are key words. *Macbeth* is about the risks that attend all human action. By tracing the consequences of Macbeth's act, the play shows insistently that human doing always has results. Macbeth, however, wishes for a world where this is not true. In the opening lines of his speech, Macbeth is using "done" in two senses. In the first use ("If it were done"), the word means "finished" or "completed." The second use ("when 'tis done") refers to doing the act of murder. Thus, we could paraphrase Macbeth this way: "If all my ambitions could be completely satisfied by this one act of murder, then I should act quickly to kill Duncan." He wants, as he says, his one act to be the "be-all and end-all" and to "jump the life to come." In short, he wants his killing of Duncan to stop the historical process of cause and effect, of sin and judgment, and bring an end to time. This throws some light on Lady Macbeth's instructions about how to "beguile the time" (1.5). Both Macbeth and his wife want to fool time, to act murderously without suffering the temporal effects of the action. They hope that darkness will not only hide them from light's exposure but from time itself. Macbeth's ambiguous use of language also highlights that he is under the control of the witches, who always speak with "double" meanings.

As Macbeth's soliloquy moves on, however, it is clear that he knows he cannot beguile time or escape the temporal results of what he does. He knows that there is a justice operating in the world and that this justice "commends th' ingredients of our poison'd chalice to our own lips." God punishes by causing the wicked to fall into their own traps, to drink the poison they intend for others. By the end of the soliloquy, he has concluded, "We will proceed no further in this business." He is operating on an understanding of manhood that is completely different from his wife's; his soliloquy is based on the principle that he "dare do all that may become a man; who dares do more is none." Being a man as opposed to a beast

Cawdor Castle is famous for its associations with *MacBeth*. The Thanedom of Cawdor was promised to MacBeth by the witches, and people like to imagine that the castle was the setting for the murder of King Duncan. But this is impossible, since Cawdor Castle was not built until the late fourteenth century. Although the murder of Duncan takes place at Inverness Castle and Duncan could not have lost any blood or Lady Macbeth any sleep in this house, Cawdor still has its own creepy charm: two ghosts are said to haunt the premises—one is a lady in a blue velvet dress; the other is thought to be the first Lord Cawdor.

means accepting limitations and acting according to moral laws. Macbeth's hesitations are based not only on fear but on a sense of the moral obligations that go along with his roles as Duncan's subject, host and kinsman.

If Macbeth's soliloquy shows that he is open to grace, Lady Macbeth, the tempting instrument of hell, works to close it off, with ultimate success. The fact that Macbeth follows his wife into what he knows to be sin is a sign of the disorder that is already beginning. She shames Macbeth by saying, in effect, that she is more daring than he, and her violent language employs again the imagery of mother's milk:

I have given suck, and know
How tender 'tis to love the babe that milks me.
I would, while it was smiling in my face,
Have pluck'd my nipple from his boneless gums
And dash'd the brains out, had I so sworn as you
Have done to this (1.7).

Lady Macbeth's milk of human kindness has been turned, as she hoped, to gall. By her own definition, she has become more the man than her husband. We feel that she has not only been "unsexed," but that

she has entirely left off her humanity. And we know that Macbeth has been won over by her demonic will when, instead of being horrified by his wife's willingness to kill her own children, he says admiringly, "bring forth men-children only." At this very moment Macbeth exchanges his own view of manhood for his wife's: Henceforth, morality will no longer make the man; murder will.

Their conversation after Macbeth has murdered the king also reveals their different conceptions of manhood, this time focusing on the question of guilt. Macbeth notices the blood on his hands, and in the exchange that follows we see how Macbeth's view of the murder differs (at this point) from his wife's. Macbeth is the bloody man. Earlier, he was stained with the blood of Duncan's enemies, now with Duncan's own; before, he was bloody in the king's service, now in treason. His hands are so bloody, so defiled by his murder of an innocent and helpless king, that if he tried to wash them, they would defile the seas and yet not be cleansed. Nature itself, far from removing his defilement, is itself defiled by his crime. When Macduff later discovers Duncan's body, Macbeth makes a speech in which it is evident that he already feels the weight of his act. From now on, life seems pointless: "all is but toys" (2.3). These words have a triple meaning: to the audience in the theater Macbeth is putting on a show, play-acting his grief, and his equivocal words hide his meaning rather than revealing it; to the thanes, his words indicate the depth of Macbeth's grief and his love for the dead king; at the deepest level, he is revealing his own sense

Hecate is a pre-Olympian earth goddess, sometimes thought to be a Titaness, who was not banned into the underworld realms after their defeat by the Olympians, because she was the only Titan who aided Zeus. She is a goddess of sorcery and is called the "Queen of Ghosts." In Act 3, scene 5, she appears to the witches to find out why she hasn't been included in their meetings with Macbeth. She says of Macbeth: "He shall spurn fate, scorn death, and bear / His hopes 'bove wisdom, grace, and fear: / And you all know security / Is mortals' chiefest enemy."

of the meaninglessness and futility of life. Seeking to become a man by "o'erleaping" time and morality, he has become "none."

Lady Macbeth does not believe in guilt. She wants to return to Duncan's room and "gild" the faces of the guards so that it seems their "guilt." By putting a "gilt" of blood on them, she will clothe them with "guilt." Guilt is for her purely an external, public matter; so long as no one knows we are guilty, she says, we are fine. Where Macbeth believes that even the ocean could not cleanse his hands, Lady Macbeth believes that the job can be done with a little water. Her hands, she says, are bloody too: but her heart is not lily white (milky) like her husband's. Lady Macbeth is still playing the man, or, perhaps we should say, the beast.

Lady Macbeth's skepticism about guilt doesn't last to the end of the play. At the opening of Acts 5, she cannot sleep, for Macbeth has murdered sleep for her as well as for himself. She had told Macbeth to forget his crimes, but now she cannot clear her conscience of her share in Duncan's murder, or the killing of Banquo and the family of Macduff, the "thane of Fife." She has learned that guilt is not "gilt." She no longer believes a little water can remove the stain from her hands; in fact, even all the perfume of Arabia cannot sweeten the smell of her defiled hand, no more than Neptune's ocean could cleanse Macbeth's. Before, she had said, "What's done is done." Now, she says, "what's done cannot be undone." These may sound the same, but they are exactly opposite. The first statement means, "Duncan is dead, and we cannot bring him back to life. There is no reason to make a fuss. So let's just forget about it and get on." The second statement is despairing: Now she wishes she could undo what has been done and lives in anguish because she cannot. Before, she had wanted to be cloaked in the "dunnest smoke of hell;" now she finds herself in "murky" hell and is horrified.

Much of the play depicts the results of Macbeth's pursuit of murderous manhood. First, there are important consequences for Macbeth himself. One of the chief consequences is that Macbeth has to keep murdering. Once you have acted on the principle that power is the only good, one murder will not be enough. There will always be people who threaten your power—because they have too much power, or because they know how you got power—and you will have to find ways to get rid of them. You will begin to see daggers in every smile. An ambitious murder is like a pebble dropped into a pool, which produces ripples of violence that, unchecked, spread to the furthest edges.

Macbeth wants to drop the pebble without making ripples. In one sense, obviously, his wish does not and cannot come to pass. Murder has effects, some of them immediate. In another, more subtle sense, Macbeth gets precisely what he wished for. He wants his act to bring an end to time, with its ceaseless flow of actions and consequences, of sins and judgments, and for Macbeth, time does end. Macbeth no longer marks his life by a rhythm of waking and sleeping; instead, he exists in a sleepless present. Time does not have meaning and direction; it becomes a tale told by an idiot, meandering here and there with no pattern. Life does not move, as it should, toward an old age surrounded by troops of friends but toward utter isolation. Sleep is not Macbeth's only unintended victim. The thane of Glamis has also murdered time.

Primarily, however, time ends because, though Macbeth has become king, he has no future, and he has no future because Banquo has an assured future. The wyrd sisters told Banquo that his children would be kings. Since the prophecies of the sisters have come true for Macbeth, he concludes they will come true for Banquo as well. Macbeth, moreover, killed to make the prophecies come true, and perhaps he fears Banquo will also kill. Though Macbeth is now king, so long as Banquo and his sons live, Macbeth knows that his is a "fruitless crown" and a "barren scepter" (3.1), since his children will not succeed him. He realizes bitterly that he has given his "eternal jewel" to the "common enemy of man"—he has sold his soul to the devil—to make the seed of Banquo kings. Macbeth concludes that being king is not enough: "To be thus is nothing, but to be safely thus." To be safely thus, Macbeth hires three murderers to kill Banquo and Fleance, Banquo's son. He wants to make sure that no seed of Banquo lives to see the last prophecy fulfilled.

Once a murderer has killed and killed again, he has a conscience to deal with. Macbeth works hard to overcome his conscience. Despite his efforts, Macbeth is haunted by his crimes, a fact brought out clearly in the banquet scene. As he repeatedly promised, Banquo attends the feast, not letting a little thing like death keep him away. Banquo's ghost not only appears but usurps Macbeth's place at the table, a sign of Macbeth's future. Though he murdered Duncan and had Banquo killed, Macbeth is still not safely thus. He will lose his seat of honor to the descendants of the dead Banquo.

People are very hard to kill in Shakespeare's plays. Well might Macbeth long for the good old days

> when the brains were out the man would die,
> And there an end; but now they rise again,
> With twenty mortal murders on their crowns,
> And push us from our stools (3.4).

Caesar, Hamlet's father, Banquo—all return from the dead to haunt the living. The point is not that Shakespeare was superstitious. The point is that crimes will not go away. Sinners cannot avoid judgment for our actions. The blood of innocent Abel will cry out from the ground against Cain. Nothing is ever entirely done when 'tis done.

Macbeth commits several murders and suffers the consequences of debilitating guilt. Further, he becomes isolated from his subjects and even his wife. Shakespeare shares the opinion, reflected in different ways in both ancient paganism and in Christianity, that one can lead a good life only in a community, only as he shares that life with others. Christianity teaches that God is One and Three, both a Person and a society of Persons. Man, made in God's image, reflects that image fully only when he lives in close communion with his fellows, for it is not good for man to be alone. Because of sin, men and women are not only separated from God but from each other. One of the first effects of sin was a rupture in Adam's relationship with Eve, as he changed from her protector to her accuser (Gen. 3:12). Persistence in sin breaks the bonds that hold people together as families, neighborhoods, churches, nations.

Macbeth powerfully depicts this process. As Macbeth pursues his ambitions, he becomes increasingly isolated. This is why Shakespeare did not include Banquo in Macbeth's original conspiracy: In order to murder Duncan, Macbeth removes himself from the company of the other thanes of Scotland, lest they discover his plans. Though Lady Macbeth encourages his plot to murder Duncan, even his bond with her is eventually broken as she follows her own pathetic pathway to hell and insanity, finally committing suicide.

The people of Scotland turn against their king; though their curses are not "loud," they are "deep" (5.3). In a despairing mood, Macbeth reflects that old age should be accompanied by "honor, love, obedience, troops of friends," but as he grows older he is more and more alone. Deprived of fellowship, and with his own reason dethroned, Macbeth's life becomes meaningless. Informed of Lady Macbeth's death, he muses on the uselessness and vanity of it all. Unrepented evil can only lead to despair and nothingness: no friends, no companions, no love, no sleep.

Macbeth's sins lead the whole nation into destruction. Man cannot live outside of society, and he cannot live happily and well in a disordered political community. The political consequences of Macbeth's ambition are equally profound. Overthrowing the established order turns the world to chaos. "Boundless intemperance," Macduff observes, "is a tyranny" (4.3). Driven by the logic of his ambition and his view of manhood, Macbeth becomes willing to do whatever it takes to maintain his power. Sinful human beings are capable of using power for good ends. Even the aspiration to have and use power is not evil; Paul says it is a good thing for a man to aspire to the office of overseer in the church (1 Tim. 3:1), and no doubt the same thing could be said of those who aspire to political office (Rom. 13:1–7). But power is not an end in itself. When power is the only good, anything that secures power is, by definition, good. This is Macbeth's situation after he kills Duncan. As one crime leads to another, Macbeth comes to see the blood of his victims as a river, into which he has "stepp'd so far" that he thinks he cannot turn back. Ruled by Macbeth, Scotland plunges into a dark age.

The social and political chaos of Scotland is highlighted especially by the use of "equivocal" language, words with deceptively double meanings. We have all been reminded to "Say what you mean and mean what you say." No one follows this advice in *Macbeth,* where communication is cloaked under ambiguous and misleading words. Macbeth trusts the witches, but their words prove unreliable. Macbeth, having entrusted himself to the "juggling fiends," becomes like them, using words to hide his real intentions and feelings. One of Satan's main lines of attack is the corruption of language (Gen. 3:1–6), for he knows as well as anyone that "in the beginning was the Word" (John 1:1). Again, this is part of the breakdown of Scottish society that results from Macbeth's ambition, as well as a cause of further unraveling of social ties. There is no possibility for orderly communal life if we cannot trust that people mean what they say. If no wife can trust her husband's "I do"; if no buyer can trust the merchant's sale's pitch; if rulers cannot trust their advisors to speak honestly, society collapses.

The witch scene at the opening of the play not only highlights the demonic influence behind Macbeth's sins, it also shows the demonic origin behind the confusion of language. The witches use words demonically, changing and shifting meanings, saying one thing but meaning another, reversing, twisting and tangling the meanings of words. The devil is a liar, Jesus said; more than that, the devil lies by saying things that sound true. Satan twists words to make them sound good, but what he says is a lie. The meaning of the witches' haunting chant, "fair is foul and foul is fair," is difficult to explain, but at least it signals the over-turning of all values. Witches are agents of chaos, intent on creating a world in which good will be called evil and evil good. They find in Macbeth an all too willing accomplice.

Macbeth has been duly warned. When the witches' first prediction comes true, Macbeth halts between two courses of action (1.3). On the one hand, he reasons, "I became Cawdor without doing anything, so maybe I can just wait and become king in the same way." But his soliloquy shows that he is already contemplating a more active course. Banquo's reaction to the announcement that Macbeth is thane of Cawdor is more fundamental: "What, can the devil speak true?" Banquo does not think in political terms, as Macbeth does; he gets to the heart of the question: can the devil (the witches) be trusted? The fulfillment of the witches' prophecy to Macbeth seems to provide evidence that they can. Banquo, however, does not believe witches can be trusted, and his skepticism becomes even clearer when, after a few moments of silence, he warns,

Exulting in the prophecy of the apparition, Macbeth says, "That will never be. / Who can move the forest, bid the tree / To walk away from his earth-bound root? / Sweet predictions, good! / Rebellion's head will never rise until the wood / Of Birnam rise, and our high-placed Macbeth / Shall live until his dying day, the death of / His own time and mortal custom."

> But 'tis strange,
> And oftentimes, to win us to our harm
> The instruments of darkness tell us truths,
> Win us with honest trifles, to betray's
> In deepest consequence (1.3).

Satan does not come initially with an outright lie. That would be too obvious. Instead, he tells us trivial truths so that, when we see his words confirmed, we begin to place our confidence in him. Once we are hooked, he betrays us in matters that are far from trivial. Banquo's words precisely predict Macbeth's future, but Macbeth ignores the warning.

Even nature reflects the disorder of Scotland. Lennox, who accompanies Macduff, reports on the strange occurrences of the preceding night (2.3; 2.4). Winds blew so hard that a chimney was toppled, and the air—the filthy, demon-filled air—was filled with strange noises. As in *Julius Caesar,* the death of a ruler is reflected in natural omens; the disorder of nature reflects the disorder of the nation. Later, an anonymous old man tells Ross of a similar omen: a falcon towering in the sky was attacked and killed by a "mousing hawk." This is even more pointedly a natural sign of the murder of Duncan; a low bird (the mousing hawk—Macbeth) killed a higher (the falcon—Duncan). As the old man comments, "tis unnatural"—as unnatural as a thane killing his king. The blood on Macbeth's hands has, as he realized it would, defiled the world. The darkness that Macbeth called upon has not covered his deed, but it has enveloped the nation.

Leo Salinger has written that there is a "faith" behind Shakespeare's comedies: Human beings are capable of destroying themselves and everything around them, but are entirely incapable of repairing the damage once it's done. Though *Macbeth* is a tragedy, this is a note struck resoundingly at the end of the play. At the beginning of Act 5, a Doctor speaks about Lady Macbeth's madness, suggesting to her husband that she needs God's forgiveness: "More needs she the divine than the physician. God, God forgive us all" (5.1). No medical technique can heal a wounded conscience; only Divine mercy is sufficient medicine for such an illness. The Doctor's diagnosis is taken up by Malcolm at the very end of the play. Malcolm proves himself an ideal king when, after his victory over Macbeth, he shares his plans to return exiles to Scotland, to purge out whoever remains of Macbeth's supporters (which cannot be very numerous), all with reliance on the "grace of Grace" (5.9). Like the Doctor, Malcolm recognizes that healing and redemption from sin and its effects comes only by God's mercy. From the Doctor's opening words to Malcolm's last speech, the whole point of Act 5 is to emphasize that Scotland can only be healed and restored with God's intervention.

Allied with Malcolm, who is in turn allied with Edward, full of grace, Macduff is triumphant. When Macbeth consulted the witches in Act 4, they showed him a vision of a "bloody child," and now that "bloody child" takes vengeance against Macbeth, the bloody man. The product of a miracle birth, Macduff slays the "serpent" who under the cover of the "innocent flower" has poisoned Scotland. Like another great Hero, Macduff crushes this serpent's head, and Malcolm proceeds to take the throne and begins the restoration of Scotland relying on the "grace of Grace."

—Peter J. Leithart

For Further Reading

Bloom, Harold, ed. *William Shakespeare's Macbeth.* New York: Chelsea House, 1987.

Garber, Marjorie. *Shakespeare After All.* New York: Pantheon, 2004. 695–723.

Goddard, Harold. *The Meaning of Shakespeare.* Chicago: University of Chicago Press, 1951. Vol. 2, 107–135.

Leithart, Peter. *Brightest Heaven of Invention.* Moscow, Idaho: Canon Press, 1996. 163–203.

Session I: Prelude

A Question to Consider

What is manhood? What does it mean to be a man?

From the General Information above, answer the following questions:

1. What was Shakespeare's chief source for *Macbeth*? How did he change it?
2. Why would James I be particularly interested in the witches of the play?
3. What was the Gunpowder Plot?
4. Summarize the storyline of *Macbeth.*
5. What kind of character is Lady Macbeth?
6. What kind of character is Macbeth?

Reading Assignment:
Acts 1–2

Session II: Discussion

Acts 1–2

A Question to Consider

What is manhood? What does it mean to be a man? What different conceptions of manhood does *Macbeth* depict?

Discuss or list short answers to the following questions:

Text Analysis

1. What has Macbeth been doing when the play opens?
2. What do the witches look like? Why is that important?
3. What does Duncan think about Dunsinane? Why is that important?
4. How does Lady Macbeth attempt to convince her husband to kill the king?
5. What view of masculinity is implied by Macbeth's statement, "I dare do all that may become a man; who dares do more is none" (1.7)?
6. What is Macbeth's state of mind when he goes off to kill Duncan?

Cultural Analysis

1. A study of depictions of masculinity in the media claims that "In most media portrayals, male characters are rewarded for self-control and the control of others, aggression and violence, financial independence, and physical desirability." It concludes, "The portrayal and acceptance of men by the media as socially powerful and physically violent serve to reinforce assumptions about how men and boys should act in society, how they should treat each other, as well as how they should treat women and children." What does that statement mean? What is being said about popular conceptions of manhood? Do you agree or disagree? Give examples.
2. Anne Fausto-Sterling writes that "labeling someone a man or a woman is a social decision. We may use scientific knowledge to help us make the decision, but only our beliefs about gender—not science—can define our sex." What does she mean by this? Is this a biblical perspective?
3. In a 1999 article in the *Weekly Standard,* David Skinner noted that "only 20 percent or so of adult white males are totally without what's technically referred to as 'terminal pigmented chest hair.' And yet, in the last few years, practically every Hollywood male sex symbol, when standing half-dressed for his more intimate scenes, looks as if he has absolutely no chest hair. Tom Cruise. Matt Damon. Keanu Reeves. Brad Pitt. All of them look like boys. One even sees older actors depilated to look like the boy-man stars who now capture every significant romantic role. The traditional Hollywood aesthetic in which old was never sexy has been carried to a new extreme: Now only the immature is sexy." What is Skinner's point?

Biblical Analysis

1. Jesus is "true man" as well as "true God." List three ways that Jesus shows true masculinity. (Matt. 23:1–38, John 8:1–11, Eph. 5:22–33)
2. Genesis 2 describes the origins of sexual difference. How does Genesis 2 define masculinity and femininity?

Summa

Write an essay or discuss this question, integrating what you have learned from the material above.

What is manhood according to Scripture? How does *Macbeth* depict false versions of manhood?

Session III: Discussion

Acts 1–2

A Question to Consider

What is ambition? Is it good or bad? How is ambition related to manhood? How does ambition work itself out in *Macbeth?*

Discuss or list short answers to the following questions:

Text Analysis

1. What are Macbeth's first lines in the play? Why is that important?
2. Compare and contrast Macbeth's and Banquo's reactions to the witches' prophecies.
3. Explain the imagery of "borrowed robes" in 1.3. Remember that kings and noblemen often wore robes that symbolized their office and place in society.
4. What is the Porter talking about in 2.3? Why is that important?
5. What does Macbeth do to Duncan's guards? Why?

Cultural Analysis

1. In his *Chronicles*, Holinshed compares Macbeth and Duncan:

"Malcolme had two daughters, the one which was this Beatrice, being giuen in marriage vnto one Abbanath Crinen, a man of great nobilitie, and thane of the Iles and west parts of Scotland, bare of that mariage the foresaid Duncane; the other called Doada, was maried vnto Sincell the thane of Glammis, by whom she had issue one Makbeth a valiant gentleman, and one that if he had not béen somewhat cruel of nature, might haue been thought most worthie the gouernment of the realme. On the other part, Duncane was so soft and gentle of nature, that the people wished the inclinations and maners of these two cousins to haue been so tempered and interchangeablie bestowed betwixt them, that where the one had too

To know my deed, 'twere best not know myself.
Wake Duncan with thy knocking!
I would thou couldst!

much of clemencie, and the other of crueltie, the meane vertue betwixt these two extremities might haue reigned by indifferent partition in them both, so should Duncane haue proued a worthy king, and Makbeth an excellent capteine."

What is being said?

2. Give three examples of how advertising encourages false ambitions.

Biblical Analysis

1. Examine 1 Corinthians 7:17–24. What does it teach about ambition?
2. The Bible urges us to be content (Phil. 4:11). Is this compatible with ambition? Is ambition a form of covetousness?

Summa

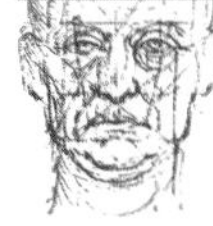

Write an essay or discuss this question, integrating what you have learned from the material above.

What kind of ambitions should Christian men pursue?

Reading Assignment:
Acts 3–4

Session IV: Recitation

Acts 3–4

Comprehension Questions

Answer the following questions for factual recall:

1. Why is Macbeth hostile to Banquo?
2. What does Macbeth do to Banquo?
3. What happens during the banquet?
4. How does Lady Macbeth behave before and after the banquet?
5. What are Lennox and the lord speaking about in 3.6?
6. What apparitions do the witches show Macbeth?
7. What do the apparitions in Act 4 mean?
8. What are Malcolm and Macduff talking about in 4.3?

Session V: Activity

*Macbeth*FX

1. Draw a cartoon version of either the whole play of *Macbeth* or some crucial scene or sequence of scenes. Imagine that the cartoons will be used as storyboards for a film.
2. *Macbeth* is full of "special effects." The witches vanish into the air (after 1.3), Macbeth sees a dagger hanging before him as he goes to murder Duncan (2.1), and the witches show Macbeth a series of visions or apparitions when he returns to visit them (4.1). Either 1) research how these effects were achieved on the Elizabethan stage or 2) come up with plans for achieving these effects themselves.

Reading Assignment:
Act 5

Session VI: Discussion

Act 5

A Question to Consider

What are the effects of sin on the sinner? How does *Macbeth* depict these effects?

Discuss or list short answers to the following questions:

Text Analysis

1. What effect does Macbeth's crime have on his ability to sleep?
2. What does the banquet scene tell you about Macbeth's state of mind?
3. What is Macbeth saying in the closing speech of 3.4?
4. Describe the changes in the relationship of Macbeth to his wife through the second half of the play.
5. How does Lady Macbeth's state of mind change during the play?

Cultural Analysis

1. Ian Johnston has written of Sigmund Freud's view of guilt: "fundamental to Freud's view of civilization is the idea that human beings are essentially biological creatures with strong instincts, among which is aggression, which Freud calls 'an original self-subsisting instinctual disposition in man . . . the greatest impediment to civilization.' The question then obviously arises: How does civilization channel, cope with, control, or suppress this anti-social instinct? In Chapter VII [*of Civilization and Its Discontents*] Freud develops the theory of the superego, the internalization of aggressiveness and redirecting of it back onto the ego and the consequent creation in human beings of guilt, which expresses itself as a 'need for punishment.' And this primal guilt is, according to Freud, the origin of civilization." What is Freud saying about the origins of guilt? Is this true?
2. Is it true that all sinners are miserable? Explain.

Biblical Analysis

1. According to Psalm 115, what effect does idolatry have on idol-worshipers?
2. What do the following Bible passages have to say about sleep: Psalm 4:8, 121:4, 127:2?

SUMMA

Write an essay or discuss this question, integrating what you have learned from the material above.

How does sin affect the sinner? What psychological effects does guilt produce?

SESSION VII: DISCUSSION

Acts 2-5

A Question to Consider

What are the effects of sin on political and social life? How does *Macbeth* depict these effects?

Discuss or list short answers to the following questions:

Text Analysis

1. What is being discussed in 2.4? What does this have to do with the play?
2. What kind of king is Macbeth?
3. What is the point of the discussion between Malcolm and Macduff in 4.3?
4. Why does Macbeth keep calling for Seyton in 5.3? What does that say about his kingdom?

Cultural Analysis

1. Sharon Hayes wrote an analysis of President Clinton's scandal with Monica Lewinsky, concluding: "The president has been humiliated a hundred times over through this case, and his lack of discretion has shamed him around the globe. But are humiliation and personal indiscretion unethical acts? I suggest that they are not. What Clinton did with Lewinsky did nothing to harm or adversely influence the carrying out of his duties as president, nor did his liaison interfere with his public duties and responsibilities. It was a stupid act, but not an unethical or illegal one." What do you think of this? Is this a biblical position?
2. Pennsylvania Senator Rick Santorum[5] has said, "If the Supreme Court says that you have the right to consensual (gay) sex within your home, then you have the right to bigamy, you have the right to polygamy, you have the right to incest, you have the right to adultery. You have the right to anything. All of those things are antithetical to a healthy, stable, traditional family. And that's sort of where we are in today's world, unfortunately. It all comes from, I would argue, this right to privacy that doesn't exist, in my opinion, in the United States Constitution." Evaluate Senator Santorum's argument.

Biblical Analysis

1. What effects do David's sins have on his ability to rule? Solomon's?
2. What are the qualifications for rulers according to Exodus 18:13–26? How does Macbeth match up?

SUMMA

Write an essay or discuss this question, integrating what you have learned from the material above.

How does the sin of a ruler affect social and political life?

Session VIII: Activity

Performance

Memorize a speech from the play to deliver in front of your class or to your family.

Prepare a scene from the play to present to your audience.

Session IX: Writing

Rewriting Macbeth

Option 1: Theme paper

Write a paper of between 500 and 1,000 words on one of the topics below, or on some topic of your own choosing. Make sure you state your thesis clearly and provide evidence from the play to support your conclusions.

Option 2: Creative Writing

Put the story of Macbeth into a different setting and rewrite the play, or scenes of the play, accordingly. It would be interesting, for instance, to send an investigator from Scotland Yard to Dunsinane to begin an investigation.

Session X: Evaluation

Grammar

Answer each of the following questions with complete sentences. Some answers may be longer than others. (2 points per answer)

1. Where did Shakespeare get the story of Macbeth? How did he change it?
2. What does Macbeth do to become king of Scotland?
3. What role does Lady Macbeth have in Macbeth's plot?
4. What misleading prophecies do the witches give Macbeth?
5. What does the doctor say about Lady Macbeth?
6. Who kills Macbeth, and who succeeds him as king?

Logic

Answer the follow questions in complete sentences. Your answer should be a paragraph or so. Answer two of the three questions. (10 points per answer)

1. Compare Lady Macbeth's conception of manhood with a biblical idea of manhood.
2. What effects do Macbeth's sins have on him personally?
3. Explain the social and political effects of Macbeth's sins. Cite specific passages in the text.

Lateral Thinking

Answer one of the following questions. These questions will require more substantial answers. (16 points per answer)

1. Ian Johnston has written that the warrior society of Homer's *Iliad* functions "without any apparent sense of guilt. People in the *Iliad* function without this internalized authority, without a sense of sin, without everything that Freud tells us is necessary for civilization. The warriors do not weigh the perils of sin in their mental activity (which appears very different from our own), nor do they suffer internalized punishment when they make a mistake (e.g., Agamemnon's folly)."[6] With this in mind, compare Achilles' psychological reaction to his situation to Macbeth's.
2. Choose one of the Twelve Caesars of Suetonius, and compare and contrast his reign with that of Macbeth.

Optional Session A: Activity

Celluloid *Macbeth*

Watch a film version of *Macbeth* and review how the filmmaker captures the characters and atmosphere of the play.

OPTIONAL SESSION B: ART ANALYSIS.

But How Do You Know She's a Witch?

Examine the two paintings, which can be found by clicking Links 3 and 4 for this chapter at www.Veritas-Press.com/OmniLinks. The first was painted in 1750 by John Wootton, the second in 1793-1794 by Henry Fuseli.

Answer the following questions:

1. What scene from the play do the two paintings depict?
2. How are the paintings different in their depiction of scenery and landscape?
3. How do the two paintings differ in their depiction of the human characters?
4. Which of the two paintings better captures the atmosphere of Shakespeare's play? Which painting *feels* like the play?

ENDNOTES

1 Garber, Marjorie. *Shakespeare After All.* New York: Pantheon, 2004. 697.
2 Ibid., 695-696.
3 *This endnote appears only in the teacher's edition.*
4 *This endnote appears only in the teacher's edition.*
5 He is a United States Senator at the time of this printing.
6 Johnston, Ian. "On Freud's *Civilization and Its Discontents,*" 1993 lecture available at Link 1 for this chapter at www.VeritasPress.com/OmniLinks.
7 *This endnote appears only in the teacher's edition.*

Sir Gawain and the Green Knight

You should know you are in a battle as you read these words. Spilled blood is not scarce even though you probably can't see any at the present moment. Men have died in the battle of which you are a part—women, too. You have friends that someday will die in an ignoble way; they will not die with honor or on the side for which they should have been fighting. And more importantly, there is no way for you to opt out of the fight.

But now I would like to draw your attention to a certain weapon,

"Is the Green Knight in the *Sir Gawain* poem some kind of divine/Christ figure? Holly (green and red) is an emblem of Christ's life-giving shedding of blood, and the Green Knight carries holly into Arthur's court at the beginning. In fact, he becomes "holly" when he's beheaded (blood on his green self), not to mention that he receives a death blow and lives."
—Peter Leithart

with which you need to be familiar. If you are able, get up from your desk, walk over to the nearest bookshelf and pull off one of the best yarns gathering dust. You are now holding a potent weapon, a story. In fact, the people who have had the most impact throughout history knew how to use what you are now holding in your hand, and you will need to learn how to pull its trigger. Look at how Jesus used stories by telling parables, for example.

Have you ever thought about pulling the trigger of a story? Did you ever think that stories were like bullets? It's true. Stories are weapons that will be used by the leaders of your culture and society. But this is not because stories convince like a letter to your congressman might convince; this is because stories draw people into them through attraction and beauty. This is not a bad thing; it's impossible to avoid. You just need to be sure that your stories are attracting people to the truth and not to a lie. If you will allow a mixed metaphor, you need to make sure that when you pull the trigger, the gun is pointing where it should be. And as you read this work and others, pay attention to the craft of story and poetry; this is a type of boot camp. Don't leave without knowing how to fight joyfully and skillfully with your weapons.

General Information

Author and Context

Sir Gawain and the Green Knight is one of the jewels of medieval literature. Unfortunately for us, its author is unknown. We do not know the reason for this. In the Middle Ages, they were not very fussy about making sure that authors necessarily became famous and well-known. In fact, most of the time the purpose of poetry was to make the hero or the characters in the story live on in the memory of the world. They focused on the characters in the story more than the author. In some cases we do know who the authors were (e.g., Chaucer, who wrote *The Canterbury Tales*), but medieval authors were much more likely to be unknown than authors today. Frankly, however, we do not know if the author is unnamed because of humility or because his name was accidentally lost.

Sir Gawain and the Green Knight was written sometime in the mid to late fourteenth century. Around this time there was a revival in a style of poetry known as *alliterative poetry.* To put it simply, we normally think of poetry as lines of verse that have a regular metrical pattern and that rhyme, like *spot/shot.* Alliterative poetry is based on accented consonants that "rhyme" (consonants are used more frequently, but vowels are not completely excluded from the operating principle of alliterative poetry). Tongue-twisters capture some of this idea: *Sally sells seashells down by the seashore.* Listen to all the s sounds. Tongue-twisters are an extreme of the principle that is being used in alliterative poetry and therefore are not good examples to follow when writing this kind of poetry. But they do sort of give you an idea. And the translation of *Sir Gawain* by J.R.R. Tolkien does a very good job of bringing the alliteration into the modern English language. But in the two hundred years before the time of this poem, the predominant kind of poetry was not alliterative, but metrical and rhyming (e.g., Chaucer again). And really, *Sir Gawain and the Green Knight* did not cause alliterative poetry to catch on as the more popular form. Even to this day, Geoffrey Chaucer is known as "the father of English poetry."

Sir Gawain as imagined by Howard Pyle.

Significance

Chaucer and the Gawain poet were contemporaries, but their poetry had different fates. Fortunately for Chaucer, his work never disappeared and has been read continuously from his day to ours. But the Gawain poet's work went into a hibernation of sorts and was not rediscovered until 1839. Chaucer and the Gawain poet were both English but used different styles of the language. Chaucer's dialect is more in line with what we use today, and even a modern reader can follow *The Canterbury Tales* without too much trouble. But *Sir Gawain and the Green Knight* is much harder to read because the dialect is far more foreign and strange to us than Chaucer's. This difference is reasonable, because Chaucer was from the big city of London, while, from what we can gather, the Gawain poet was from the Northwest Midland area of England. It is helpful to remember that there were no quick and easy methods of communication during the time of these poets; therefore people who lived relatively close together (according to our modern standards) still might differ in their manners of speech in a marked way because they did not often hear each other's variations of the English language.[1]

Despite the differences between Chaucer and the Gawain poet, the skill of both is very impressive. In fact, many people think that the Gawain poet was more talented than Chaucer. This makes the rediscovery of *Sir Gawain and the Green Knight* even more exciting. And it is very obvious when one reads the poem that its author was very gifted in imaginative ability and poetic technique.

Sir Gawain and the Green Knight is contained in the same manuscript with three other works. They are known as *Pearl, Purity* and *Patience.* As far as we know, the poems appear to be written by the same author. *Pearl* appears to be an elegy, which is a poem lamenting someone who has died, in this case most likely the poet's daughter. *Purity* and *Patience* are both didactic poems teaching the virtues of their respective titles. If you want to see the *Sir Gawain* manuscript you will have to make a trip to the British Museum (maybe this is something you could talk your dad into making part of a family vacation).

SIR GAWAIN AND THE PENTANGLE

Sir Gawain was the nephew of King Arthur, a knight and member of Arthur's roundtable. Gawain adopted the pentangle as his personal symbol and placed it on his shield, in gold on a red background.

A pentangle is a five-pointed star that has been a symbol for many things since ancient times (usually symbolic of excellence, power or a defense against evil). Even today it is often used as a commercial, political or military icon (such as the Department of Defense's Pentagon building, five-star generals, the stars on many flags, including the United States' flag, and modern corporate symbols such as Texaco, Converse and DC Comics).

For Gawain as a Christian knight, one of the five points of the pentangle represented the five virtues of generosity, courtesy, chastity, chivalry and piety. In the Arthurian romances, such as *Sir Gawain and the Green Knight* and *Le Morte D'Arthur,* the knightly virtues are the ideals which are tested in some manner in the knight's quest and adventures. Interestingly, in *Sir Gawain and the Green Knight,* Sir Gawain believes he has failed his chivalric tests, yet both the Green Knight and Arthur's court recognize Gawain as a hero. What do you think is the significance of Gawain's trading the pentangle for the protection of the green girdle?

Main Characters

The title of the poem gives us the names of the two most important characters. Sir Gawain is the hero of the story and has a long track record in the Arthurian legends outside of this poem. He is the nephew of King Arthur and a knight at his Round Table. His reputation is stellar, and he is known as a faithful and brave soldier. Under the name Gwalchmei, he appears in some of the Welsh mythologies, specifically the *Mabinogion.* In the *Mabinogion,* Gwalchmei (Sir Gawain) is renowned not only for his ability to fight, but also for his eloquence. He purportedly can accomplish more with his skilled speech than other knights can with their weapons. In other words, Sir Gawain is a talented poet and rhetorician. Sir Gawain also shows up in Geoffrey of Monmouth's work under several different names: Gualguinus, Gualgwinus and Walwanius. You will also notice different spellings of Sir Gawain's name in the present poem. In addition to these examples and many others of Sir Gawain's presence in medieval literature, it is very important to note his appearance in one of the most famous works of English history written by William of Malmesbury, entitled *A History of the Norman Kings.* In that work a small section is dedicated to the discovery of Sir Gawain's grave in what is now known as Pembrokeshire, Wales. Of the more interesting details given to us, one is the description of Sir Gawain's tomb being 14 feet in length. This is not altogether uncommon, because Arthur and his knights were frequently described as giants. We cannot be absolutely sure about how big Sir Gawain was, but we should remember that he was a real person in history as reported by William of Malmesbury.

The Green Knight is Bertilak, the lord of the castle at which Sir Gawain stays during his journey to the Green Chapel. The Green Knight challenges Sir Gawain to a game at Arthur's castle and then to another game at his own castle. Lady Bertilak is the wife of Lord Bertilak and three times attempts to seduce Sir Gawain into adultery.

Summary and Setting

The setting and tone of the poem are festive and full of vibrant colors. The story starts on Christmas day at a feast in Camelot. King Arthur and his nobles, knights and ladies of the court are celebrating the holy day with great merriment and lightheartedness. The poet tells us that they feasted upon the finest food, they danced till their hearts were dizzy, they sang Christmas carols and chimed noels, they gave heaps of gifts (*handsels*) to each other, they played games laced with laughter and gratitude, and they filled the cathedral with praises to God for the Incarnation. It is hard for us to imagine a people happier than they were. And the only way anyone can be as happy as they were is by putting Christ at the center of the celebration. Near the end of their multiday festival they gather for a feast on New Year's Day. But before King Arthur can taste the meat and drink the wine, he, like a good Christian host, must wait until everyone else is served and must have a great story or adventure told, or even a physical challenge brought to the court. Finally, just as the first course has been served, a noise is heard and the Green Knight appears to Arthur and his friends. The Green Knight proposes a contest, explaining that he has not come to fight, but to engage in a little sport. He challenges anyone to come and give him a blow with his axe. Whoever accepts the challenge wins the axe, but must also meet the Green Knight exactly one year later and receive the same stroke from the Green Knight. Eventually, Sir Gawain accepts the challenge and takes a swing. We had better stop here or we'll be giving away too much.

Worldview

Today is a normal day. There has been a light drizzle, and every time you walk outside water glances off your eyeglasses and blurs the scenery. You walk into math class, wipe your glasses off with a cloth and pull out your notebook. The teacher begins talking, but you can tell that something is different. He is no longer saying normal things about numbers. He is telling you that the fear of the Lord is the square root of four. He continues on and declares that Christ's example can be learned from algebraic formulas (let he who has wisdom understand). Finally, the teacher explains that wisdom can be attained by practicing a weird form of addition that was just invented. You are confused, not by what he is saying, but by why he is saying it. You know that the Bible was given to teach us how to obey God and put our trust in Him. And you know that Moses did not come down from Mt. Sinai with multiplica-

tion tablets. You read the Psalms and notice how God says that each generation of believers must not forget to tell the next generation the stories of God's faithfulness and the adventures of his people. You cannot remember any biblical example of what the teacher is saying, and you are pretty sure that your memory is correct. Later that evening, your dad confirms what you had been thinking and says that there is a reason why the Bible was not given to us in the form of numbers and math equations.

The red blood burst bright from the green body,
yet the fellow neither faltered nor fell
but stepped strongly out on sturdy thighs,
reached roughly right through their legs,
grabbed his graceful head
and lifted it from the ground,
ran to his horse, caught hold of the reins,
stepped in the stirrup, strode into the saddle,
the head dangling by the hair from his hand,
and seated himself as firmly in the saddle
as if he were unhurt, though he sat
on his horse without a head.

As creatures of God, we tend to learn best from stories. Stories stay in our memories and demonstrate for us what we should be doing in our own lives. They give us something to imitate and follow. It's hard to imagine what the world would be like if there were no stories or no examples. If there even *were* such a world, it would not be anything close to the wonderful creation that we are a part of today. You and I would not be the same people, if we were people at all. Numbers are a part of the story, and in one sense people do tell stories with numbers (Euclid, for example, and parts of the book of Numbers). But those numbers are not the building blocks of narratives and plots. And narrative is *what* God created the world to be and *how* he brought it to be.

First, we need to consider the importance of virtue. *Sir Gawain and the Green Knight* is clearly a Christian poem. This does not mean there are no errors or unbiblical teachings in the story, but it does mean that a fellow Christian, whom we will probably see in heaven someday, composed this poem. During the period in which *Sir Gawain and the Green Knight* was written, there were a whole cluster of stories and poetry called *romances* which were designed to teach a knight how to fulfill his calling to the best of his ability according to the code of chivalry. The word *romance* meant something different for people in the fourteenth century than it does for us today. Frequently, it did include an aspect of love, but romance then had more to do with adventure motivated by love and honor than what we would call a romantic love story today. And the old romantic stories were of knights going out into adventures of peril and risk, claiming victory for the kingdom from which they were sent. But the code of chivalry and the romantic notions of virtue were not always identical with Christian virtue. And the Gawain poet had this in mind as he wrote the poem. He wanted to show the difference between the cliché virtues of chivalry and the Bible's teaching on virtue. But the chivalric code was not completely impure, and therefore we also see the Gawain poet blend some of those ideas with the biblical virtues. The goal of the poet was to provide an example that could be imitated. And this particular story of Sir Gawain is on the subject of what it means to be a Christian knight.

Whenever we deal with a particular worldview or a piece of literature we must always examine the source of virtue. This is important because, as James points out when talking about sins of the tongue, fresh water and bitter water cannot both flow from the same spring. When someone suggests that you should question authority, you ought to immediately identify the source of that command and question whether they have the authority to say so. If the source is not God, the source should be questioned and disobeyed. It is important to note that God establishes authorities that must be obeyed, such as parents and governments; their source of authority is God.

The Greeks are an example of this point in literature. The Greek gods were selfish, petty, vindictive—nearly human. They were not really gods; they were just bigger versions of sinful men. And because they were the source of power and virtue, men like Achilles and the other Greek warriors fought purely for selfish and prideful reasons. The source was bitter and so was the water.

Christian heroes cannot be like pagan heroes and therefore must have a different source of virtue. The source of virtue in *Sir Gawain and the Green Knight* is the Triune God of Scripture. Where do we see this in the poem? One of the key places where we discover the source of virtue is in the scene where Sir Gawain puts on his armor as he leaves Camelot to go find the Green Knight. Most importantly, he is given a shield with a symbol on it called the Endless Knot or the Pentangle, which is basically a star. The poet explains the imagery of the five-pointed object: "So it suits well this knight and his unsullied arms; / for ever faithful in five points, and five times under each . . .." Basically each point symbolizes five more points: the five senses, the five fingers, the five wounds of Christ, the five joys of Mary for her Son and the five virtues. The poet tells us that King Solomon shaped this star (a pentangle within a circle is a symbol used in many Jewish synagogues today), and therefore we can deduce that this is a Christian symbol. We should also remember that all Christians are required to put on the shield of faith, which is able to protect us from the fiery arrows of the wicked (Eph. 6:16). Shields in themselves are very Christian symbols, and Sir Gawain's shield points to the fact that the knight obtains his strength and protection from the God of all creation. It is in the context of Sir Gawain going to battle that we see the shield emphasized by the poet more than any other weapon or piece of armor. And as we will find out later, the main battle that Sir Gawain will engage in is one more of virtue than of physical combat. We must remember that the Triune God is the source of Sir Gawain's strength in maintaining his purity; and it is Sir Gawain's shield that points to this fact.

But we also find one of the unbiblical notions in the poem on this same subject, as the poet tells us there is a picture of Mary on the inside of Sir Gawain's shield. Now there is nothing wrong with a picture of Mary in and of itself, and there is nothing wrong with looking at pictures of Mary. But the way in which Sir Gawain uses the picture of Mary is a problem. After he has been on his journey for some time, he prays to Mary that she might provide a place for him to stay, and this indicates for us that the Protestant Reformation was yet to happen. The poet, of course, sees nothing wrong with Sir Gawain doing this and in fact presents it as a virtue; but really it is a Roman Catholic virtue, not a biblical virtue. Jesus taught us how to pray, and He did not teach us to pray to his mother, blessed though she was.

Another central point in *Sir Gawain and the Green Knight* is the rejection of adulterous love and marital infidelity. This ends up being one of Sir Gawain's greatest challenges. He spends three days at Bertilak's castle being tempted by Bertilak's wife. Each morning Bertilak is up early and out hunting, but Sir Gawain sleeps in and lollygags the day away. This sets him up for the attempted seduction by Lady Bertilak. Lady Bertilak, we are told, is a beautiful woman. And she uses methods that are very revealing and important to notice. In many ways, she is like the seductress in Proverbs 7: she goes out of her way to catch Sir Gawain (Prov. 7:11–12); she uses flattery (Prov. 7:21); she also explains that no one will catch them (Prov. 19–20); she deceitfully invokes her "Christianity" (Prov. 7:14). All these things add up to make Lady Bertilak a classic example of the *strange* woman. She does not offer virtue to the faithful knight of Camelot, and he ultimately rejects all of her attempts to seduce him. Sir Gawain remains holy and innocent of sin.

During the period in which *Sir Gawain and the Green Knight* was written, there was a tradition of literature and an accompanying philosophy, known as the courtly love genre. It is very important to read *Sir Gawain and the Green Knight* in this context or one will miss important aspects of the poem. Andrew the Chaplain, who lived later in the twelfth century, wrote a popular handbook for his time called *The Art of Courtly Love.* One of the twelve chief rules of love requires a knight to be obedient in all things to the commands of ladies and to strive to join himself to the service of love. Along with this there is a detailed code of chivalry that must be strictly followed. Some of this code is good and teaches virtues like honor, honesty and faithfulness; but generally speaking, the courtly love movement was built on a foundation that was not completely biblical, especially in its openness to relationships outside of marriage that could lead some husband to love another woman with more fervor than his own wife. And the literature of courtly love aimed at teaching this code to its readers. But in contrast to this, Sir Gawain provides an example of a knight who rejects any kind of love that is not virtuous. He demonstrates that a knight is ultimately in submission to God and not to the whims of noble ladies. And this is virtue, to love God above all else and to hate sin at whatever the cost. The example for Sir Gawain is the example of Christ (Heb. 1:9); or to put it another way, Jesus Christ is the ultimate Knight.

This leads us to a discussion of what it means to be a man. Understanding what it means to be a man cannot be separated from what it means to be virtuous. The two go together. But too often in our day, we like to make men conform to a definition of virtue that is not biblical. To illustrate using the story of Sir Gawain, we want modern men to sit at the Round Table but not get up to fight the Green Knight. We want dainty nobles. But God does not want this and neither did the Gawain poet. If you want to understand this more, ask your dad (boys only) for permission to fight another good Christian friend (his dad will have to give permission, too) and ask that both dads be referees so that any anger or whining will be called and penalized. And you must use boxing gloves. But as we look at Sir Gawain and the Green Knight, what characteristics do we see concerning what it means to be a man?

Sir Gawain and the Green Knight is a joy-driven fairy tale. This cannot be emphasized enough. The colors, the feasting, the laughing, the happiness even in the face of danger, the joy of the Lord, all give the poem its momentum. And this joy factor is one of the most striking and essential components of a fairy tale. Have you ever noticed that the classic ending of a fairy tale frequently says something like, "And they lived happily ever after"? Joy is also the mark of a wise man. The joy of the Lord is a man's strength (Neh. 8:10). In Ecclesiastes, Solomon repeatedly commands us to take joy in our food, our jobs, our wives and our lives. And if a man cannot rejoice, as Paul exhorts (Phil. 4:4), then he is not acting like a Christian man. In the story we do not always see Sir Gawain rejoicing. Sometimes this is justified, specifically when he is convicted of sin. But overall, Sir Gawain knows the importance of joy, from being one of the best knights in the culture of cheer that was Camelot, to his celebration of the Christian calendar throughout the poem. In fact, the poem really is a celebration which takes us through the liturgy of the Christian year.[2] We move through the Christmas season, New Year's included (also known as the Day of Circumcision), through Lent, summer, to Michaelmas (which is the feast of St. Michael the archangel on September 29) and All Saints' Day (also known as All Hallows, which takes place on November 1) when Sir Gawain leaves for his meeting with the Green Knight. Then, of course, we celebrate one more Christmas and another New Year's when Sir Gawain fulfills his vow.

A Christian man is a churchman. He loves the church, because he is with the people of God, worshiping the God of the Bible. We can see that the church was important to Sir Gawain because it was always on his mind, even when he was all alone on his journey. Out of all the things he could ask for, and admittedly he did ask for lodging, he prayed that he could go to church on Christmas. How many men plan their lives, their vacations, their business trips and their families around a faithful and exuberant church? How many of us even know when Ascension Sunday and Pentecost are? Even when Sir Gawain was fighting giants, he went to church. Worship on the Lord's Day is the center of his world and should be the center of ours.

A Christian man is courageous. Another way to put this would be that cowardice is a sin. Cowards do not grow in sanctification, because they are scared of being uncomfortable. Here Sir Gawain is a model of courage. First, he is the only knight to step forward and offer to take the place of King Arthur in the challenge with the Green Knight. Secondly, he keeps his vow with the Green Knight and travels for a long time by himself, fighting all kinds of wild creatures until he accomplishes his mission to meet the Green Knight. Sir Gawain is also courageous in the fact that he does not succumb to the wiles of Lady Bertilak. Looking through the lens of courtly love, Sir Gawain was rude and impolite to Bertilak's wife. But he was less concerned about his reputation with the lady than he was with God. Because he feared God, he didn't fear Lady Bertilak. The fear of the Lord is an antidote to all other fears. And successful knights can't have those. There is also the question of humor and beauty. For the Gawain poet, there is no relativism when it comes to beauty. One obvious example of this is the contrast that he gives between Lady Bertilak, her maidens, Guinevere and the older lady of the court. Lady Bertilak is superior in beauty. Specifically, the poet gives us a very stark contrast between Bertilak's wife and the older lady of the court. Lady Bertilak is very beautiful and attractive, while the older lady is quite ugly. The fact that she was willing to commit adultery did not change the fact that she was objectively and externally beautiful. The loss of that would come later. The Gawain poet and the nobles of Camelot are also concerned with beauty in celebration. And because their celebrations flow out of the liturgy of the church, they recognize the joy and beauty of the Christian Sabbath. If we go by Camelot's standards, the Lord's Day should be the most beautiful day of the week.

The Gawain poet also revels in the blessings of comedy. We cannot read *Sir Gawain and the Green Knight* and miss the humor of the poem without missing an important part of the meaning. The poet makes it hard to miss the fact that most of the characters in the poem delight in laughter and frivolity. They don't appear to be as somber and serious as many modern textbooks make the medievals out to be. In fact, the poem intends to deliver a blow to the self-seriousness and pettiness of the chivalric code. This is made especially clear at the end of the poem when Sir Gawain, although a mostly faithful knight, cannot seem to get over his dishonest acquiring of the green belt. Everyone takes the situation lightly except for Sir Gawain. The Green Knight forgives him, and he was the one with whom Sir Gawain had made the vow, and King Arthur actually makes the green belt required attire for all of Camelot.

As you take a step back from this poem, you can see that the poet was very concerned with the truth of poetry.[3] And the truth he was after is the goal of creating a world like the one God created. The Gawain poet sees that God has given us his law to obey so that we can be successful, according to the biblical definition, in His world. Why else was the poet trying to paint a picture of a Christian knight? He wanted to instruct his readers. But he also knew that God likes to laugh. Have you ever realized that God expects laughter of you? When you think about imitating Christ, do you ever try to imitate the holiness of his laughter? In his great book *Orthodoxy,* G.K. Chesterton says that Jesus Christ successfully kept a gigantic secret while he was here on this earth. He kept the secret because it was too big to share. And that secret was his

The beautiful wife of Lord Bertilak de Hautdesert, who is left with Gawain to entertain him as his host goes out hunting. The fair lady flirts ardently with the good knight but is only able to get him to kiss her. In the end she gives him a silk belt as a token of her love.

anvil-heavy gladness; if he had revealed all of it to us, we would have been crushed. And it appears that the poet of *Sir Gawain and the Green Knight* felt the same way as Chesterton and tried to give us a taste of that pure green joy.

—*Aaron Rench*

One Christmas in Camelot King Arthur sat
at ease with his lords and loyal liegemen
arranged as brothers round the Round Table.
Their reckless jokes rang about that rich hall
till they turned from the table to the tournament field
and jousted like gentlemen with lances and laughs,
then trooped to court in a carolling crowd.

For Further Reading

Cowan, Louise and Guinness, Os. *Invitation to the Classics.* Grand Rapids, Mich.: Baker Books, 1998. 103–106.

Spielvogel, Jackson J. *Western Civilization.* Seventh Edition. Belmont, Calif.: Thomson Wadsworth, 2009. 247–250, 271–284.

Veritas Press History Cards: Middle Ages, Renaissance and Reformation. Lancaster, Pa.: Veritas Press. 12.

SESSION I: PRELUDE

A Question to Consider

How important is poetry and symbolism to our lives?

From the General Information above answer the following questions:

1. What is one way in which you will need to use poetry in your life?
2. How do stories and poetry persuade?
3. What was Sir Gawain's (Gwalchmei's) reputation in the Welsh book of stories known as the *Mabinogion?*
4. For what pre-feast events does King Arthur wait before eating?

5. What is Lady Bertilak's most important weapon as she tries to seduce Sir Gawain?
6. Can one refuse to be a poet, or is poetry inevitable?

Reading Assignment:
Stanzas 1–6

Session II: Discussion

Stanzas 1–6

A Question to Consider

We must be literary critics of some sort to know the ingredients of a good story. How do we learn to be discerning literary critics?

Discuss or list short answers to the following questions:

Text Analysis

1. How did the Gawain poet learn the story of Sir Gawain? What can we deduce from this about the origin of stories in general?
2. How does the setting of this story explain the joy and feasting that is taking place in Camelot?
3. How does the term "Dark Ages" seem to be an inaccurate description of the time when King Arthur reigned?
4. What does King Arthur think about storytelling in general?

Cultural Analysis

1. What is the difference between the Christian and the sentimentalist views of evil?
2. Is it sinful to watch movies or read books that have evil things in them? To whom should you go for direction regarding your entertainment standards?

Biblical Analysis

1. Pretend that you are a literary critic who believes that God cannot use evil to bring about his purposes. Because of this belief, you also believe that the best works of art do not represent any kind of "evil" at all. You might look at one of Thomas Kinkade's paintings for an idea of this kind of approach. Now, with this in mind, how would you rewrite Ecclesiastes 3:1–11 so that it matches this unbiblical worldview? (Keep in mind that the reason for doing this is to find out what is wrong with sentimentalism, not what is wrong with Ecclesiastes 3:1–11.) In other words, what might you leave out of this passage?

Summa

Write an essay or discuss this question, integrating what you have learned from the material above.

How is Jesus an example to us of the perfect literary critic?

Reading Assignment:
Stanzas 7–21

Session III: Recitation

Stanzas 1–21

Comprehension Questions

Answer the following questions for factual recall:

1. According to the Gawain poet, who was the founder of Britain?
2. Who is the most honored British king of whom the Gawain poet has ever heard, and where did the Gawain poet find this out?
3. In what location and what time of year does the story begin?
4. What did the men and women of Camelot do on New Year's Day?
5. What two items does the Green Knight have in his hands when he enters the court of Camelot?
6. What is the Green Knight's purpose in coming to Camelot, and what do the holly and the axe mean?
7. Why does Sir Gawain want to take King Arthur's place in the challenge with the Green Knight? How does Sir Gawain view himself?

8. What is the name of the place where Sir Gawain must meet the Green Knight?

READING ASSIGNMENT:
Stanzas 22–45

SESSION IV: WRITING

Stanzas 22–45

Alliterative Meter

As mentioned earlier, *Sir Gawain and the Green Knight* was written in *alliterative meter*. This is a very interesting form of verse and more common in Old English poetry than in Greek or Latin poetry. *Beowulf* is another great example of some wonderful poetry composed in alliterative meter. Generally speaking, alliteration (also known as initial rhyme) is an echoing of the beginning consonants in words closely spaced and occurs regularly even in poetry not written in alliterative meter. Alliterative meter takes this principle and applies it in a more uniform fashion, turning it into the driving rhythmic force of a poem. As with all poetry, the principle is not without exceptions, and in fact good alliterative poetry will have plenty of those; but it still comprises the backbone of this type of verse. It is very important for any poet working in the English language today that he have a rudimentary, if not fluid, grasp of the mechanics of alliterative verse. First, look at a few examples of basic alliteration, as opposed to poetry composed in alliterative meter.

Gerard Manley Hopkins (1844–1889) wrote some wonderful poems and is a good example of a more modern poet employing alliteration with great skill. He was heavily influenced by the Old English rhythms and the alliterative metrical system. Read out loud the following lines from some of his poems:

The world is charged with the grandeur of God.
It will flame out, like **sh**ining from **sh**ook foil;

Fresh-**f**irecoal chestnut-**f**alls; **f**inches' wings;

With **s**wift, **s**low; **s**weet, **s**our; a**d**azzle, **d**im;

Listen to the *sh, f, s* and *d* sounds in these lines. When clustered together the consonants chime with each other.

It's actually difficult to find a poet who doesn't use alliteration at some point in his poems, and here is another example from Robert Herrick (1591-1674):

I sing of **b**rooks, of **b**lossoms, **b**irds and **b**owers

And yet another example from John Donne (1572–1631):

Your force, to **b**reak, **b**low, **b**urn, and make me new.

Now, let's turn to a short explanation and some examples of poetry written in alliterative meter. Typically, a line in this style is broken up into four main stresses or accents. In the middle of these four stresses is a space known as a caesura. The caesura is sort of like a comma, in that it can be used to indicate a pause. But many times this pause is not noticeable to the ear, or on the page when translated. Frequently it is the first three accents in a line that will alliterate, leaving the last accent out of the consonant rhyme. This means that there will be two accents that alliterate before the caesura, and the first accent after the caesura will alliterate back with the first two. If this sounds confusing, look at these examples from *Beowulf:*

greedy and **gr**im, he **gr**abbed thirty men

now **s**ettled that **s**core: he **s**aw the monster

In both examples you can see some sort of pause (caesura) in the middle of the line (at the punctuation), and you can also observe that the last accent in each line (*men* in the first and *monster* in the second) does not echo back to the previous three accents in the line. Now let's look specifically at *Sir Gawain and the Green Knight.* In Tolkien's translation, it is easy to find examples. Here are a few:

> on a **l**ow mound above a **l**awn, **l**aced under the branches
>
> Then he **g**oaded **G**ringolet with his **g**ilded heels
>
> all of **h**ard **h**ewn stone to the **h**igh cornice
>
> **t**all **t**owers set in **t**urns, and as **t**ines clustering
>
> and on the **c**old earth on their knees in **c**ourtesy knelt

Now that you have noticed this pattern, it will probably be difficult to read the rest of the poem without seeing and hearing it on every page. The last example above shows that, while there is a basic pattern, there are many variations. One final feature to notice about alliterative meter are the four short lines that appear at the end of each stanza. This is known as the bob and wheel. We will also not go into an explanation of this mechanism here, but notice that end rhyme is a key aspect of the bob and wheel.

Space will not permit a deeper exploration of the manifestations that alliterative meter can take, but from even this short sketch of alliterative meter, you should begin to see the talent and skill involved in writing a poem like *Sir Gawain and the Green Knight.* Therefore, this is the perfect time to jump into the writing assignment itself.

Referring to the instructions above, write 15–25 lines of alliterative meter. As a subject, choose between a battle, a feast or a hunt. This is a good opportunity to look at other stories, whether from the Bible, history or literature, and adapt them to your poem. For example, if you write a poem about a battle scene, write about the battle in which David sends Uriah onto the front lines to be killed. If you write about a feast, write specifically about a Christmas feast in Narnia. If you write about a hunt, you could write about David being hunted by Saul

While Gawain and the green lady play a game of testing the knight's virtues of courtesy and chastity, his host is out hunting. The host's dangerous sport succeeds in bringing back several quarry. First there is a noble "beast of venery," a deer, then the boar's head impaled on a pike, and finally, from the lowest class of the beasts of the chase, a pelt from the deceitful fox—an animal despised as vermin.

and use some of the Psalms; or you could even write an alliterative poem about a hunting trip or fishing trip that you went on with your dad.

As you write the poem, think about writing in such a way so that certain lines get stuck in the heads of yourself, family members or friends. Do this by using images and sounds that are memorable, that catch people off guard but still make sense. Here is an example that might come from a battle scene:

> In the metal-storm, blood and soldiers sparked;
> while only lunar mist lit the blue lamps of night.

It needs to be stressed that because alliterative meter is probably a new concept to you, and because it already has so many variations, you need not follow the basic principle rigidly. In other words, don't write every line with the first three accents alliterating. Mix it up. Occasionally, make the last three accents alliterate or just the middle two. No matter what you try, it's probably been done before. If you aren't sure where the accents are in every line, just do your best. With practice you will get better; without practice, you won't. Alliterative poems that do the same thing every line can get a little boring. But remember to make the normal pattern conform to what we discussed earlier (the first three accents alliterate).

Writing a poem like this will help you see not only what the Gawain poet is saying, but also how he is saying it. This exercise will help you get inside of the poem, not just as a reader, but also as a poet. You will experience a small taste of what the Gawain poet went through as he composed this fantastic poem. When you have finished composing your poem, read it out loud after dinner with your family (remember, this is part of your assignment). This is a great way not only to get feedback and criticism of your poem, but also a great way to enjoy poetry and stories in general. Plan on writing more poems like this in the future and read them aloud also. You could even prepare a special poem about a feast and read it at your Christmas or Thanksgiving dinner.

READING ASSIGNMENT:
Stanzas 46–62

SESSION V: DISCUSSION

Stanzas 46–62

A Question to Consider

What is virtue?

Discuss or list short answers to the following questions:

Text Analysis

1. What is Sir Gawain's first response when he wakes up to see Lady Bertilak beside his bed?
2. What is the difference between the speech of Lady Bertilak and that of Sir Gawain when she comes into his bedroom for the first time?
3. In their second bedroom encounter, what code of virtue does Lady Bertilak try to hold Sir Gawain accountable to? What two systems of virtue are in conflict?
4. Is Sir Gawain's time well spent with Lady Bertilak and her friends?

Cultural Analysis

1. How do various cultures use words and labels to define what is virtuous?
2. How is adultery viewed by our modern culture?

Biblical Analysis

1. In the Bible, what is adultery (Matt. 5:27–28; Ex. 20:14; Gen. 39:7–9; Hosea 5:3–4)?
2. In the typical action movie, the hero is usually not a model of virtue. He pursues fornicating relationships with many women, he breaks all the rules, has family problems and cannot submit to those in authority over him. Virtue and strength are not presented as friends. In contrast to Hollywood, how does the Bible describe a true hero (Judg. 15; Prov. 7:24–27; Mark 3:27)?

SUMMA

Write an essay or discuss this question, integrating what you have learned from the material above.

Does biblical virtue interfere with heroic actions?

READING ASSIGNMENT:
Stanzas 63–79

Session VI: Recitation

Stanzas 46–79

Comprehension Questions

Answer the following questions for factual recall:

1. What does Lord Bertilak do in the morning before he leaves for his first hunt?
2. What is Gawain the bold doing while Lord Bertilak is out on his hunt?
3. What is Sir Gawain's first defense against the wiles of Lady Bertilak?
4. What does Lady Bertilak say about her husband in her attempt to seduce Sir Gawain?
5. In contrast to Lord Bertilak, what does Sir Gawain do after the lady leaves his bedroom?
6. What do Lord Bertilak and Sir Gawain exchange after the first day, and what does Lord Bertilak ask Sir Gawain at that meeting?
7. What do Bertilak and Gawain exchange after the second day?
8. What does Gawain do after his third encounter with Lady Bertilak?
9. What do Bertilak and Gawain exchange after the third day?

Reading Assignment:

Stanzas 80–99

Morgan le Fay lives in the castle with the Green Knight, and it is she who sent the jade giant to Camelot to test the truth of the fame of Gawain—and to frighten Guinevere. Her enmity towards Guinevere has its origin in the *Vulgate Lancelot*, where Morgan le Fay is having an affair with Guinevere's cousin and Guinevere puts an end to it. Morgan le Fay is Arthur's half-sister and his mortal enemy because Arthur's father, Uther, killed her father in battle over her mother. Yet in spite of this hostility, Morgan le Fay is one of the women at the end of the Arthur saga who takes the king in a barge to Avalon to be healed.

SESSION VII: DISCUSSION

Stanzas 80–99

A Question to Consider

What makes a man unmanly?

Discuss or list short answers to the following questions:

Text Analysis

1. What does the quality of Sir Gawain's sleep tell us about his condition the night before he goes to meet the Green Knight?
2. Do Sir Gawain's emotions impact his decision to go and meet the Green Knight?
3. Does Gawain's wearing the green belt remove every basis for fear?
4. What is Gawain's ultimate concern?
5. Is Gawain's conviction completely accurate and on target?

Cultural Analysis

1. What should we learn from professional athletes who turn sporting events into barroom brawls?
2. Is it usually wrong for a thirteen-year-old boy to cry?

Biblical Analysis

1. How does the Bible view an emotionally undisciplined man (Prov. 25:28)?
2. Is every kind of fear wrong (Prov. 1:7)?
3. What kind of impact does the fear of the Lord have on other fears (Ps. 34:4–10)?

SUMMA

Write an essay or discuss this question, integrating what you have learned from the material above.

Are emotions antithetical to being a man?

READING ASSIGNMENT:

Stanzas 100–101

SESSION VIII: DISCUSSION

Stanzas 96–101

A Question to Consider

What is comedy?

Discuss or list short answers to the following questions:

Text Analysis

1. Do the Green Knight and Sir Gawain have what might be considered normal interaction between a soldier and a giant after a conflict?
2. What has kept Gawain alive up to the end of the story?
3. When Gawain leaves the Green Chapel and the Green Knight, is his journey almost finished?
4. What is Camelot's response after hearing the story of Sir Gawain's encounter with the Green Knight?

Cultural Analysis

1. If you were to categorize the story of evolution, what literary genre would it belong to?
2. How does secularism gut humor and laughter?

Biblical Analysis

1. How do we know that the biblical vision provides the lightness needed to make comedy work (Matt. 11:28–30)?
2. Can comedy be used as a weapon against sin (Prov. 26:14; Matt. 19:24)?

SUMMA

Write an essay or discuss this question, integrating what you have learned from the material above.

What is the basis for comedy?

SESSION IX: ANALYSIS

Sir Gawain and Proverbs 7

Does the Gawain poet give an accurate and biblical description of an adulteress? Complete Chart 1.

Chart 1: COMPARISON OF ADULTERY IN SIR GAWAIN AND PROVERBS 7

	LADY BERTILAK	THE PROVERBS 7 ADULTERESS
Who initiates the situation?	Lady Bertilak initiates by entering Gawain's bedroom three days in a row.	Verse 13 says that she caught him, and that she left her house to get him (vs. 11 & 12)
Where does the seduction take place?		
What role does religion play?		
Does love come up in the conversation?		
Where is the adulteress's husband? Why is this significant?		
What is her most potent weapon?		
Does she prey on strong or weak men?		

Session X: Writing

Writing a Comedy

Write a short comedy, employing some of the basic elements of humorous storytelling. Choose if you will write a short play or just a short story; a satire (irony or caustic wit used to attack or expose folly, vice or stupidity); or a farce (a light dramatic work in which highly improbable plot situations, exaggerated characters and often slapstick elements are used for humorous effect). The length must be a minimum of 500 words and a maximum of 1,200.

There are many elements that can be employed in a humorous story, but make sure that you use at least some of the following basic elements:

ELEMENT 1: Exaggeration

- Represent something as greater than is actually the case, or overstate it.

ELEMENT 2: Surprise

- Cause your reader to feel wonder, astonishment or amazement, as at something unanticipated.

ELEMENT 3: Interaction between characters of contrast

- This is particularly funny when the characters react to each other in unexpected ways.

ELEMENT 4: Happy ending

- End your story with goodness on the triumphant side.

In the example below, a short satire, you will find examples of these elements indicated in bold. There are many more (and better) examples of humorous writing everywhere. When you read these kinds of stories, note how the author makes you laugh. What devices does he use? What kinds of characters are funny? One of the greatest comic writers of all time is P.G. Wodehouse, who wrote over ninety novels in his lifetime. Read them.

Jared: A Satire

Jared was your typical, easily annoyed person. When he had nothing better to do, he found that it wasn't difficult to spend the entire day running the over-population formula again and again (**ELEMENT #1, Exaggeration**) until he was so nervous that he had to either call his mom back in San Diego or make a visit to the university librarian, whose name was Mrs. Sfitz. Usually, one of these ladies was able to calm Jared's nerves by urging him to make a run to the local organic food store and down a gingko relaxation drink.

Jared had lots of problems with lots of things. Specifically, he had a problem with an exuberant young lady named Abby. His problem with Abby was not that she treated him rudely or unkindly; because she didn't. His problem was that Abby didn't seem to be worried about the big problems facing the world today and that she was never convinced by Jared's explanations of why people should be. In fact, these explanations tended to produce laughter in Abby—the exact opposite reaction that Jared sought.

Because Jared was so easily frustrated, his ability to see things clearly and entirely was impaired. He drove a new Jeep that ran on fuel made from garbanzo beans (**ELEMENT #2, Surprise**) and with a bumper sticker that said: "Don't Talk On Your Cell and Drive." It wasn't a very catchy bumper sticker, but then again, Jared wasn't a very memorable guy (only his emotional reactions were ever remembered, if anything). Somehow Jared didn't see that his habit of driving around town while reading the newspaper was in contradiction with the important message that was stuck to the plastic bumper of his very underpowered Jeep.

After Jared felt that he had come up with this very original bumper sticker, he tried to get the campus police force to endorse his new idea, but he cried during his sales pitch to the cops, and they recommended that Jared take the bumper sticker to the campus psychiatrist and pursue further help that way. Jared didn't like the fact that the police, the very people who should be concerned about safety, told him that he needed help. Jared knew better. He knew that people needed his help; he didn't need theirs.

Jared was now angry. He had already been to see Shirley, the campus psychiatrist, although he didn't mention it to the police, and she had given him several forms of anxiety medication. By this time he had taken five of the eight pills that he was supposed to take that day, and he could now feel the need to take the other three. This also upset him, because he had told Shirley that it was high time she doubled the recommended dosage. He explained that he had more responsibility than the average student activist, and this meant that he needed more than the average amount of meds to cope with his high calling. Shirley assured Jared of the highness of his calling, but his prescription still read the same after that visit.

As Jared drove home he opened up the paper to an article documenting the story of how whales needed help. Jared wept. He had witnessed enough evil for the day. His tears dripped onto the letters, and the letters poured their ink onto his hands. Jared cried some more. Suddenly Jared's garbanzo-powered car slammed to a stop. He had rear-ended a compact car, and the driver had already gotten out and was walking back towards him. Fortunately, Jared had been going only about 15 miles per hour, and it appeared that no one was hurt. As the driver of the compact car came closer, Jared could see that it was Abby. She looked relieved. When Jared observed that everything was all right, he continued his light sobbing. Abby walked up to his window and asked if he was OK. Jared could feel his anxiety meds wearing off and in a calmer moment blew his nose on a picture of a beached whale (**ELEMENT #3, Interaction between contrasting characters**).

Next fall, when school started, Jared transferred to a university in Vermont. But when all the incoming students went to orientation at Jared's old school, the campus police instructed them on safe driving in a college town. And at the end of the four-minute safety video was a picture of a red-eyed Jared holding a newspaper in a smashed Jeep. Attached to this picture was a warning to pay attention while driving. Abby's sister, a new freshman, laughed and walked out (**ELEMENT #4, Happy Ending**).

Optional Session A: Activity

A Feast at Camelot

As we have noted already, *Sir Gawain and the Green Knight* is a joy-driven poem with an emphasis on feasting and enjoying life. Now it is time for you to imitate this culture by throwing your own feast. Your primary goal in this activity is to make it as enjoyable an experience as possible for everyone involved. Feel free to be creative, but one idea is to specifically schedule the banquet as a Sabbath feast on a Saturday night in preparation for church the next morning. This gives you all Saturday to work on preparing the meal and the table decorations. You will probably need to begin preparing before Saturday, especially in terms of researching the historical foods that you will be cooking. Depending on where you are in the school year, another idea might be to host a Christmas or Epiphany feast. These are applicable, because the feasting in the poem usually takes place during the advent season. There are many medieval recipes centered around these holidays, so there should be no lack of ideas. But you may need to do some significant research to make your menu selections.[4]

As part of the feast you will also need to think about the non-food activities. If you are planning a Sabbath feast, you may want to sing a Psalm or two. Obviously, if you are planning a Christmas dinner, you may want to make sure that everyone has access to particular hymns and carols that you have chosen before hand. You will also want to carefully select recorded music to play during the meal (or hire a live string quartet). You may also want to have a reading at some point in the meal. Choose someone to read it, and make sure that it doesn't drag. Comedy can be good, or some alliterative poetry would also be very appropriate. You might want to look at *Robin Hood* and find the scene where a barmaid sings the story of Sir Gawain. This is probably an accurate representation of how poems like *Beowulf* and *Sir Gawain* were actually rehearsed. Think how impressive it would be to actually memorize a section out of one of those poems and recite it at the dinner. Also, don't forget that you have already composed your own poem; this would be a good time to read or recite that. Remember that King Arthur did not eat until someone either told a story or brought a challenge. You don't have to follow this particular order, but you should follow it somehow.

Protocol must also be followed. All the ladies should be seated before any of the men are. Ladies should also be first in any line that may form (it would be great if you didn't have to serve the meal buffet style, but if you do, ladies first).

What kind of entertainment will you have? Does someone in the class play baroque guitar? That person needs to perform. There is also some great medieval music for recorder. Another great option is to put together a small choral group to sing some medieval carols or songs. Dance may also be integrated; specifically, dance in which everyone participates.

Finally, make sure that someone is organizing the event as a whole. You will want to have a schedule planned beforehand so you'll know how the entire evening is going to go. You will also want to send out invitations in advance, requesting that the guests reply in advance to confirm their attendance. Be very thoughtful in the planning process, consciously making sure that what you plan will enhance the enjoyment of everyone. God is glorified by the faithful feasting of his people.

Additional Activity

In addition to the feast, it would not hurt to do a study and write a paper on God's view of the table. How is it to be celebrated? What impact does the Lord's Supper have on our daily dinners and our special celebrations? What does the Lord's Prayer teach us about food?

Optional Session B: Activity

Play the Bard

Oral performances were a popular way for stories to be presented during the middle ages. Sir Gawain was a popular character in many of these stories, and we can see this just by observing a scene taken from *The Merry Adventures of Robin Hood.* In one of Robin Hood's first adventures, he meets up with a Tinker-minstrel in a tavern called *The Blue Boar Inn:* "Then he sang an ancient ballad of the time of good King Arthur, called the Marriage of Sir Gawaine, which you may some time read, yourself, in stout English of early times; and as he sang, all listened to that noble tale of noble knight and his sacrifice to his king."[5]

Your assignment is to recite a section of *Sir Gawain and the Green Knight,* or even another portion of a ballad like T*he Courtship of Miles Standish,* by Henry Wadsworth Longfellow, or an entire shorter ballad like *The Cremation of Sam McGee,* by Robert W. Service. Depending on the setting, it would be great to add things to your performance, like costumes, mugs of cold root beer or apple cider and even a quality accent (important, only a *quality* accent will suffice).

ENDNOTES

1 Savage, Henry Lyttleton. *The Gawain-Poet: Studies in His Personality and Background.* Chapel Hill: University of North Carolina Press, 1956. 9.

2 Christians in the ancient and medieval church developed something that came to be known as the church calendar or the Christian calendar. In the Christian calendar the important events of redemption were the high points or holy days (holidays) of the year. The year really began with Advent and Christmas and followed through Lent, Easter, Ascension and Pentecost. The church celebrated these and other great redemptive events. Strikingly, in the northern hemisphere—where the calendar developed—these events are intricately linked to the natural world—particularly to light and darkness. Christmas occurs just as we pass the Winter Solstice—the darkest day of the year. So Christmas is celebrated when the light begins to overcome the darkness. Easter is celebrated around the time when the light starts to dominate the darkness by taking up more than twelve hours. This happens as we pass the Spring Equinox. Thankfully, our Christian forefathers put an amazing amount of thought and wisdom into their integration of Christianity into the fabric of life. Sadly, modern believers have turned a blind eye to their father's wisdom and what the natural world seems to be screaming at us. For more information, see Phelan, Walter S, *The Christmas Hero and Yuletide Tradition in Sir Gawain and the Green Knight.* Lewiston/Queenston/Lampeter: The Edwin Mellen Press, 1992, 23.

3 Phelan, 277.

4 Medieval recipes and games can be found at Links 1-5 for this chapter at www.VeritasPress.com/OmniLinks.

5 Pyle, Howard. *The Merry Adventures of Robin Hood.* New York: Dover, 1968

The Divine Comedy: Inferno

> "From each hole's mouth stuck out a sinner's feet
> And legs up to the calf; but all the main
> Part of the body was hid within the pit.
>
> "The soles of them were all on fire, whence pain
> Made their joints quiver and thrash with such
> strong throes,
> They'd have snapped withies and hempen
> ropes in twain.
>
> "And as on oily matter the flame flows
> On the outer surface only, in lambent flashes,
> So did it here, flickering from heels to toes."
> XIX.22–30

Sound familiar? It should. If not, perhaps recently you have seen the fellow who "with his hands wrenched open his own breast" (XXVIII.29)? He is the same fellow who was split in two from the head down so that his pluck, spleen, liver and intestines gaped. You should remember him because you have met him—probably recently, too.

You have been to Hell. Believe it or not, and even if you have not read *Inferno* yet, you already have experienced the first third of *The Divine Comedy*. Yes, even if you have been living in a cave and have just now for the first time heard of Dante, you are already familiar with what is about to come. You are not just about to read of something entirely new, for you have already been there. *You have been to Hell.*

General Information

Author and Context

Let us meet Italy's famed poet, the eminent son of Florence, Dante Alighieri (1261–1321). Dante is best known for the glorious epic poem, *The Divine Comedy*. The *Comedy* is one complete poem with three parts: *Inferno, Purgatorio* and *Paradiso.*[1] Dante wrote the *Comedy* in the common Italian language of his day, not Latin, so that the common man of Florence and all Italy could read it.

Dante's home was the wealthy city of Florence, where, in the years leading up to the Renaissance, magnificent architecture abounded. Good art and fine music were appreciated then much more than today, and Florence went on to become arguably the most important Renaissance city during the fifteenth and sixteenth centuries. Dante loved Florence, and his love for his city is an important part of the *Comedy.*

Dante's age was a time of complicated politics, and he put to use every one of his skills as a poet, philosopher, theologian, lawyer, politician, diplomat and experienced soldier. These politics were quite complicated, but in a nutshell, Florence was split between two main political groups called the Guelfs and the Ghibellines. Politically, Dante fell into the Guelf party, which usually held more power than the Ghibellines during his life. But (believe it or not), because politics was messier in thirteenth century Florence than even today, Dante was still not safe. Dante's own Guelf party split into the Black Guelfs and White Guelfs. This time Dante, a White, was not on the winning side and was exiled from Florence for the last twenty or so years of his life.

Politics, though, is not the only thing to know about Dante. Dante was not yet twenty when his parents died, and around 1285 Dante married Gemma Donati. In that day marriages were usually arranged for political or financial reasons. Dante and Gemma married and had four children, but we should not expect that Dante "romantically loved" Gemma—at least not as we think of "romantic love." In fact, Dante never mentions his wife in his writings. This may sound odd, but we cannot say it is wrong that Dante did not "romantically love" his wife so long as he was biblically faithful to her (and we have many reasons to believe he was), which is a biblical love.

Dante and Beatrice by Pre-Raphaelite painter Henry Holiday (1839–1927). Dante sees in Beatrice a proof of God's existence, power and love.

Significance

It is quite difficult to ever measure the vast significance of an epic poem—especially if we are trying to measure the impact of Homer's *Iliad* and *Odyssey*, Virgil's *Aeneid*, Milton's *Paradise Lost* and *The Divine Comedy*. These are usually considered the main epic poems in Western Civilization. If you recall from the *Odyssey* and *Aeneid* readings in *Omnibus I*, Douglas Wilson wrote there that epic poems are "carriers" of culture. In other words, an epic poem is a significant reflection of the culture it came from, as well as a significant influence on future cultures. All epics deserve our attention, and the same goes for Dante.

But as important as it is to extend the "genealogical line" of classical epic poetry, Dante did more. Dante is the greatest epic poet to write an allegory about the way to God.

Dante writes in the classical tradition, but his story is the Christian story. A man is lost, and he is redeemed by the Son of God. This simple story line is vastly different from the other classical epics. Christians may rightly rejoice over Dante's genius, just as the folks in Florence still revere Dante—for he writes about our city, the City of God.[2]

Main Characters

Dante is the author of this epic poem, and he is the epic hero. No other epic poet has made himself the hero in his poem. This means that while the *Comedy* is a narrative story with universal themes, this story is Dante's testimony. It is universal *and* personal. Of all the epic poems, Dante's is arguably the most personal. He does not just talk about human desires and longings, he talks about his longing for God.

In the *Comedy*, Virgil, the writer of the *Aeneid*, is not quite all there. In fact, he is a shade. Virgil guides Dante through Hell and to the top of Purgatory. Now the *Comedy* is a complex allegory, and Virgil provides a good example of this. Virgil represents the best of human wisdom, philosophy and, of course, poetry. So in other words, to read allegorically, when we see Virgil literally guiding Dante by the hand, we ought to think of how human wisdom, philosophy and poetry guide Dante—and as we put ourselves in Dante's shoes, we see how "Virgil" may guide us. We should think of Virgil as a representation of common grace, the grace which is available to Christians and non-Christians alike.

Beatrice is Dante's love, but we cannot explain that fully yet. Read on, though, for she is a remarkable lady. Dante was nine (a very significant number) when he first saw Beatrice in Florence, and even though he scarcely knew her, he loved her. Again, this may seem strange, but think of Beatrice as a powerful experience, an experience of God in some way. This experience of seeing Beatrice helped Dante see, understand and know God—almost like a sacrament. Because of how that experience deeply affected Dante, Beatrice represents God's special grace, and she is his guide from the top of Purgatory into Paradise. Not incidentally, Beatrice's name means "blessed" or "salvation." She is a beautiful and complex image, and because she is an image dealing with issues of Christ, salvation, the church, the sacraments and the whole realm of special grace, we must be discerning to grasp such a complex image.

Even though Beatrice does not really appear in *Inferno*, she is a main character in the whole poem. Throughout, her name is evoked, and she always spurs Dante forward on his journey.

Summary and Setting

Have you ever thought about what happens when you look into a mirror? What your eyes see is actually different from what you really are. You see an image, but the image is not you. The image and "you" are not literally the same thing, but both exist, and both are real.

An allegory is something like a mirror. Dorothy Sayers said an allegory is the depiction of real life through images. So when Dante the poet from Florence (real life) writes about (or "looks into") Dante the epic hero of the *Comedy* (the image), we have an allegory. It is very important to understand the allegory as you read the *Comedy*.

Because the *Comedy* is an allegory, it is both easy and incredibly challenging to summarize. On one moral level, we can quickly summarize the whole *Comedy* as a story of a lost man who finds God. On another political level, Dante compares the "lost man" to the "lost city." Dante believes that the only way Florence will find peace is through a sole emperor who redeems the city, just as Christ redeems His bride. To understand these levels of the allegory, we have to decipher all of the images. Some are difficult, some are easy, but when you understand the images, it will help you understand the real thing Dante is talking about—just as looking in the mirror at your *image* probably helps *you* (the real thing) comb your hair.

Dante is lost in a *dark wood.* When he tries to escape he is sorely afflicted by a leopard, a lion and a wolf (all symbolic), until a wise guide, Virgil, leads Dante from one side of the earth, through Hell and out the other side of earth. Together they spiral up the Mountain of Purgatory until Beatrice (special grace) comes to be Dante's guide when Virgil can go no farther. Lady Beatrice guides Dante beyond the moon, past the sun, the planets, and even the stars, to a miraculous place called the Empyrean, where Dante beholds God.

The whole of Dante's journey through Hell, up Purgatory and into Paradise covers the span of about a week. In particular, *Inferno* covers three special liturgical days: Dante and Virgil descend into Hell on Maundy Thursday only to rise from Hell the morning of Easter Sunday.

Worldview

A Creative Christian Epic

Imagine a stick figure world. Imagine that this world was created like our world, but that the god of this world was not a skilled creator. In fact, his creativity was so limited that he only had the skill to create two dimensions of reality. Whereas in our three-dimensional world you can see form and depth, all you can see in this dull world are stick figures. Your parents are stick figures, your friends are stick figures, and your dogs, Mackenzie and Grace, are stick figures. But it gets worse. This god might as well be color-blind, for in his limited creativity he can create only in black and white. No more deep blue skies; just a black line. No more magnificent sunsets; just a black circle with wavy lines for sun-rays. These stick figures are reality in this world, and this reality is very, very *dull.* There is no creativity.

Thankfully, we do not live in such a dull world. Quite the opposite: God is the greatest creative Being. He is the supreme Creator. God created out of nothing, *ex nihilo,* and it all was good. Knowing God is the first step towards

A detail of Auguste Rodin's *Gates of Hell,* shown in its entirety on the opposite page. On August 16, 1880, Rodin received a commission from the Directorate of Fine Arts for a door covered with relief sculpture inspired by Dante's *The Divine Comedy.* The subject may have been Rodin's idea since he was known to keep a copy of the book in his pocket. The work is 21 feet tall, thirteen wide and three deep and contains 180 figures that measure from six inches up to four feet. Some of his most popular works, such as *The Thinker* and *The Kiss,* were originally conceived as part of the *Gates.*

understanding creativity, and imitating God's beauty is the first step towards being creative. When we gaze upon God's nature and His works of creation, we should be driven to creativity. We long for it, and as God's image-bearers, we are made to create. We were made to be artists, architects, musicians and poets. The creation must create.

Dante's *Divine Comedy* exemplifies this creativity, and he has created beautiful poetry that speaks to the most important issues of the Trinity, fallen man and redeemed man. The *Comedy* is no bore, and Dante is no stick figure poet. In *Inferno,* Dante's subject matter is gloomy and ominous, and yet he creatively interacts with sin and fallen man. This epic poem is creative on many levels. Dante's images of the way to God are some of the most vivid the Western tradition has ever seen. Dante's verse also bears a unique creative mark. The rhyme scheme of the *Comedy* is called *terza rima,* which we shall explore later.

The form of this poem is creative, too. The *Comedy* is an epic, which is a complicated form of poetry. An epic usually has nine elements: narrative story; *in media res* (begins in the middle of the story); appeal to the muses; epic hero; grand journey; interaction with divinities; universal themes; epic catalogue; and traditional verse or meter. The *Comedy* contains all these elements, and yet Dante's creativity shines through most of all in a tenth element that his Christian faith "added" to the epic form. This element is so important, it is the title. This element is *comedy.*

On this point of comedy in epic literature, it is helpful to remember back to the chapter on the *Odyssey* in *Omnibus I*[3] where it is noted that the point of a classical comedy was to ridicule vice, whereas Dante's *Comedy* reflects the happy ending that Christianity brings to the world. While Dante acknowledges his poet-forefathers and writes in the classical epic tradition of Homer and Virgil, his poem does not come from the same worldview as Homer and Virgil. Dante's poem revolves around redemption, which is a distinctive of Christianity. There are redemptive elements to Homer's and Virgil's poems, but the central characters of the *Iliad, Odyssey* and *Aeneid* are not redeemed by sacrificial love as Dante is. Hence, those poems do not have the same happy ending as the *Comedy.* For example, when Odysseus vanquishes the suitors and reclaims his home, he is triumphant, but that is the end of the story—triumph, not redemption. We cannot really say it is a happy ending; in a way, the poem just stops. Athena commands Odysseus to cease fire, and that is it. This point is even stronger with *Gilgamesh.* At the end of that epic, the hero is downright un-happy. Now it is not quite right to say that Homer's and Virgil's poems or the *Epic of Gilgamesh* are *flawed,* but they are "incomplete stories" because they lack the best sort of ending. A happy ending comes only with redemption, something Odysseus and Gilgamesh never find on their own, nor from multiple false gods. When we think we "live happily ever after," we fail to consider the thought that at some point we die. However, Christ conquered death! Christ alone brings eternal peace and happiness.

Christ alone brings redemption, and that gives Dante a creative advantage as a storyteller. His story is the comedy of Christ coming to redeem a lost world. Dante begins his journey lost in the dark wood, but before the first canto—which are divisions in a poem, like a chapter in a book—ends, he is on the redemptive path towards the Sun. Dante's happy ending is foreshadowed from the beginning, just as Christ is foreshadowed in the Garden of Eden (Gen. 3:15), and Dante is redeemed, just as the Bride is redeemed by Christ at the "end" of the human story (or, more precisely, the eternal beginning—meaning the beginning of our eternal existence with God).

Thus, the *Comedy* is an imitation of the greatest gospel story. It is a journey, so all men may enjoy the *Comedy,* but Christians especially should revel in the redemptive worldview of the *Comedy.* If you have ever wearied of reading about other worldviews, or if you have ever felt that reading classical Western literature is like exploring foreign cities (beautiful, but still foreign), you will enjoy this trinitarian comedy.

Because we are talking about a trinitarian poet, our questions for Dante may be much more specific than the questions we ask pagan authors. We may debate over passages of Scripture with Dante and know that he also understands Scripture is the Word of God. Dante is also no weak theologian. We must not forget that the *Comedy* is poetry, and we should first let the beauty of Dante's images go to work on us. But that said, Dante is not one to shy away from good debate. In the *Comedy,* we have an epic from the Western canon that will spark what C.S. Lewis called "in-house debates." In-house debates were arguments Lewis thought should be held among Christians and not flaunted in a way that might distract the watching world. The point is not to hide these debates, but to be discerning about how these issues are viewed—just as wise parents usually differ behind closed doors, out of earshot of young children.

Given its subject matter, the *Comedy* will spark quite more than its share of in-house debates—especially *Inferno.* Imagine the angst and ire in today's evangelical world if a contemporary poet began to place Hollywood celebrities and Washington politicians in Hell (which Dante does with his contemporaries). How would today's church react to seeing Bill Clinton listed amongst the lustful who are perpetually blown about in a howling wind, or equally, in the brotherhood of falsifiers, those stricken with diseased bodies that rot away over and over for eternity? The reaction would not be pretty. Then there are other more serious in-house questions we must ask Dante, questions about Mary, the papal authority, the sacramental theology of the Roman Catholic church, and so forth. These are real questions, and we must hold Dante accountable to Scripture. Dante was a Christian living in medieval times, and so the *Comedy* reflects the good and the bad issues of the church in those days. The Roman Catholic Church (and Dante) erred. The idolatry of Mary was one of the most visible errors of the church then, and faithfulChristians must absolutely reject idolatry. At the same time, evangelicals must not overreact and deny the truth and beauty of the poem because of such grave errors. We must read carefully and critically, always weighing the poem through the lens of Scripture. Dante was a fallen man and shows the errors of his day just as we will show the errors of our day to future generations of Christians. We must be faithful to identify these errors in Dante, just as we seek to do so in ourselves.

But enough on that for now. The *Comedy* is an epic poem with many layers. It is not solely theological. Dante always presents many opportunities to debate all areas of life, from theology, politics, history, and so forth, but the *Comedy* is primarily about seeking the light in a dark world and discovering the way of life out of death. For now, it is most important to recognize Dante's creative poetry. Dante has modeled the Christian principle of creativity, and his classical epic tells the story of redemption through the comedy of Christ.

Our Own Personal Hell

Do you know the story of Socrates and the slave boy from Plato's *Meno* dialogue? In this story, the great philosopher Socrates proves that you do not need to have studied geometry to talk about it. To prove his point, he grabs the nearest unlearned slave boy and asks him questions about shapes and figures that the boy can quickly figure out in his head. Socrates uses this example to show that the slave boy has knowledge "in himself," and Socrates would say that you, too, have geometry and knowledge "in you."

Something similar happens with Dante's *Inferno,* though the thing that is in you is not nearly so nice a thing as geometry. This takes

As Dante enters the gates of Hell, he comes to a region known as the Vestibule of the Futile. In the ultimate example of brand loyalty, the souls here eternally chase a banner while being stung by wasps and horseflies.

us back to the claim we made at the beginning—*you have been to Hell.* It is a rather bold claim, yet it is true in a way, because the sin that Dante will show us in Hell is the sin we see everywhere in this fallen world. Worst of all, it is the sin that is *in you* and *in all mankind.* Socrates shows the slave boy that geometry is "in him," and though Dante is not asking Socratic questions to show us sin in the *Inferno,* his images go to work, showing us what is in us. Because it is in us, we are more than prepared to study sin in Dante's Hell. We know sin all too well, because we are all fallen in the first Adam.

Now to be precise, the claim *you have been to Hell* is not true in the sense that you have literally been there. One must be dead and apart from Christ to *literally* go to Hell (though Christ is the only man to return from Hell, according to Dante). But in another way, because *Inferno* is about imagining sin, we have already *been* there. Even if you are not aware of your experience with sin, it is still there, because we are born in sin. Both redeemed and unredeemed mankind live with sin every single nanosecond, and if you do not see it, this is because you are not looking. In this sense, if we had perfect minds that could quickly identify our own sin, we would not need to look into the allegorical mirror of Inferno. We would not need to look into Dante's images of sin, because we would be seeing them in our own hearts. We have already done these things.

This is not to say that we have committed every sin that Dante will describe for us, but we must admit that we are capable of committing all sins. Indeed, on one level, we already have committed the worst sins.

> You have heard that it was said to those of old, "You shall not murder, and whoever murders will be in danger of the judgment." But I say to you that whoever is angry with his brother without a cause shall be in danger of the judgment. And whoever says to his brother, "Raca!" shall be in danger of the council. But whoever says, "You fool!" shall be in danger of hell fire (Matt. 5:21–22).

That said, we must prepare to read *Inferno* by admitting our own familiarity with our own sin. It may sound odd to think that our familiarity with sin makes

Charon, surly boatman of the river Acheron, always treated spirits roughly on their way to Hell. You can only imagine his shock when he finds a living person trying to cross into the realms of the damned.

us familiar with *Inferno,* but read on and see if Dante's imagination of Hell does not seem familiar. Once you understand what Dante is talking about in his images, you may find that he is talking about things all too familiar to us—frighteningly familiar. Remember too, that Dante's characters being judged in Hell are his contemporaries. Talk about familiarity for Dante. If we imagine knowing the people as Dante knew them, the *Comedy* comes to life.

So, our own sin is the first reason we are well prepared to experience Dante's Hell. Some will agree with that, but find Dante's Hell grotesque. Dante certainly does have a wild imagination—that is, a wild trinitarian imagination. To read Dante, you must be patient and gird your loins. This journey is for the adventurous, not the timid. Dante faces horrid scenes and, while he is most polite, he will not spare the gruesome, bloody images of sin. On one level, *Inferno* is this way because Dante was not one to mince words. If you are uncomfortable with "sticky, polite company"—like those euphemistic folks who say something "smells peculiar" when really it straight up *reeks* like a chicken farm in July—Dante is your friend. Dante pulls no punches.

The other reason to be courageous with Dante's wild imagination goes back to sin. Sin is not pretty. It never has been and never will be, no matter how enticing the serpent may be. Imagine meeting a man who pulls open his own ribcage. You have at least seen him on the news. He is Osama Bin Laden, who carries on the discord of Mohammed, the prophet of Islam. When Dante describes a ripped-open ribcage, dripping with blood and spilling out the internal organs, he is thinking of the sin of discord, or perhaps we might say the *advanced* Christian heresy of Islam. Heresy for Dante is no unintentional theological error; it is the intentional distortion of Truth. Mohammed took this heresy and sowed discord by exchanging the City of God for a black rock in Mecca. Think of September 11. The sin we see in Dante's Hell rages around us today. We know these men, these images in Hell. *Inferno* is not a soft poem, but neither is the biblical view of sin soft or pleasant. When Scripture tells us of the mothers that ate their children during Ben-hadad's siege of Samaria (2 Kings 6), the image of sinners spending eternity stuffed like candles, head down in holes while flames feed off their feet is not inappropriate.

Most of all, when we think of the greatest act of love—the bloody, gruesome, crucifixion of God's Son—we cannot hesitate to gaze fully on sin. Dante's images help us see sin as sin. Dante's clear poetic vision and brutal honesty with the sin we so like to ignore ought to expand our view and appreciation of the Cross.

Remember, we know these things because these things are within us. Sin is in us.

Dante's Theology of Sin

What is the imagination? What is the imagination that Dante invokes to educate his readers so eloquently about sin? Dante's poetry is all about the imagination. The imagination is one of those unique things that you recognize best when you do not think about it. So forget about trying to define the imagination for a moment, and just imagine . . . imagine an enormously deep crater deep within the earth—this crater is exactly six-million and sixty-six feet deep! Fire lives in this jagged crater, morphing light in glowing tones of garnet red, bleeding blackness without hope. Demons, demons and more hideous demons are everywhere, surfing the crashing tongues of flames. They are like the rotting claws of Satan, and of course they are red with pointy horns. Their whips love to tear the poor, pitiful lost souls that are thrown down from the roof above, clawing the air like hail refusing to fall into fire. If only the sinners had known! They feel cheated and wish they had had more time on earth to make better decisions and be good people. All the sinners disagree with their cruel punishment. Who would choose this place? Woe of woes! The demons gaze upwards, eyes dripping poison, watching the poor people fall. And the demons are chanting, always chanting, "Out, out, damned soul!" And they are whipping . . . whipping . . . always whipping. Always chanting, "Out, out damned soul!" And sometimes through the screams one will say—"Welcome. This is Hell."

But it is not. Nor is Heaven a place with puffy clouds, golden harps and pudgy Pillsbury dough angels. The Triune God in Heaven did not create a feeble cosmos that we inhabit, so then we should not imagine a feeble Heaven or Hell. Sadly, we do imagine horribly all the time—like the above image

Virgil and Dante crossing the river Acheron in an engraving by Gustave Doré.

of Hell. There have even been movies made where Satan pops up onto earth out of an elevator. To go even lower, we can ask for some Hollywood actor or director's imagination of Satan. It is easy to imagine poorly, and too often we live in a world that thinks stick figure art is imaginative beauty.

So what is the imagination? The imagination at work with poetry means picturing with the mind's eye *real* things. Hell is a very real thing, and Dante's imagination of it is without comparison. So why do we imagine so poorly so often? As is the case with most problems, poor theology is the big issue. Poor theology is exactly the problem with most images and conceptions of sin and Hell.

What is sin, and what is Hell? These primary theological questions form the core of *Inferno.* Dante, the epic hero, must learn these things so that he can progress on his journey. The *Comedy* as a whole parallels the gospel, and so man's sinful inadequacy is the starting point. Dante's theology of sin revolves around the will. Adam's willful "want of conformity to God" is the occasion for all the sins that follow in all mankind. Sin occurs every time man's will goes against God's will, which is revealed to man in God's word. Adam willed to be a god unto himself by contradicting the will of God. That was the first sin, and sin continues because all men are Adam's children, hence receiving his fallen will. This theology of sin is the assumption of Dante's Hell, not a poorly imagined red demon with a barbed tail on his left shoulder.

A poor theology of sin leads us to think of Hell as a camp that wars against the rival camp of righteousness and Heaven. Dante's Hell does not war against Heaven as we often think of war. Dante's Hell wars against Heaven through hatred, but Dante's Hell is without power to strike Heaven. We often use words such as "war" and "rival" to speak of those in Hell being against Heaven, but because of Christ, the war is over. Heaven and Hell are not two camps that balance each other out like equal scales (or as though there were two kings from the beginning, rather than one King only). This "scales thinking" often suggests that Christ is opposite Satan. Not true. If we want a "balancing opposite," we had best say the angel Michael is opposite the fallen angel Satan. Christ is not opposite Satan, for Christ is one with God, and there is no legitimate opposition to God. There are only those who willfully move away from Him, hating

Him and screaming at Him as they fall into oblivion. God *is,* and He did not create His world while Satan simultaneously created his own. Hell is not *that sort* of rival camp to Heaven. God instructed Moses to tell Pharaoh the name, "I am." God is, and sin is "not." Sin is not really *opposed* to righteousness as we think of opposition, like two teams meeting on a field. When Christ was on the cross, His battle was not with Satan, but was instead the great punishment of being separated from the Father and punished for our sins. We must understand this to understand sin in *Inferno.* Christ does not war against Satan on a level plain, nor is Dante's Hell a place of genuine opposition to Heaven. Heaven rules over Dante's Hell. Sin for Dante is the movement away from righteousness. Note the words we use to describe sin. Sin is the "*want* of conformity" to God. Sin can never be *for* anything; it must always be *away* from, or *against* God.

We can think of it this way. God made Adam, and imagine that God placed him on a platform suspended above an infinite gulf. Let us call the platform "God's will." Adam was perfectly free to stay on the platform, but he did not. He was tempted to see if he could float on his own. He tried, and he left God's will. He went from something (the platform) to nothing (very thin cold air). Now to complete this simple image, imagine that Christ reaches down to redeem His chosen ones from the infinite freefall into nothingness, but in a mysterious way, some do not wish to be redeemed.

That said, Hell is a place for unregenerate sinners who

Judas, Brutus and Cassius get their just desserts for being traitors to both Lord and empire. Judas is head first as the worst sinner, Cassius the Epicurean screams in his torments forever and Brutus the Stoic suffers but utters no sound. He has a stiff upper lip for all eternity.

cannot be at home in Heaven. Hell is the place for those who will to jump into nothingness. Odd as it may seem, those in Dante's Hell do not *want* to be in Heaven. Remember the poorly imagined image of Hell where those lost forever felt cheated and desperately wanted more time to make a wiser choice? This is not the Hell of the Bible, nor is this Dante's Hell. Biblically, all men are dead in sin. God told Adam that if he ate the forbidden fruit, "you shall surely die" (Gen. 2:17). Paul writes to the saints in Ephesus: "And you were dead in trespasses and sins . . ." (Eph. 2:1) Dead is *dead*, and all men who are not claimed by Christ are dead and remain dead. This means that those who hate God will always hate God. If the heathen nations rage on earth,[4] how much more do they rage in Hell? Dante's Hell is not a place of repentance; it is a place of increased rage and hate. Dante's images in Hell hate Heaven, and while they of course loathe the consequences (or the realization of their sin), they necessarily continue in willful sin and hate in Hell.

Dante's Hell is an actualization of sin. This means that the sins in Hell are the same as on earth, just magnified. In a way, we can say they are finally given the appropriate setting for what they yearn for—the void away from God. God gave man a will, and man's will chose Hell. Man's will chose to turn from God (pure being) to sin (nothingness). *Inferno* beautifully illustrates these definitions of sin and Hell. Perhaps the most vivid illustration is Vanni Fucci, the thief of the Eighth Circle who answers Dante's question at Heaven's behest and then blasphemes God with an obscene gesture. Vanni Fucci is not repenting of his sins, begging for forgiveness. He is exactly where he wants to be—hating God, yet away from God.

These definitions of sin and Hell greatly affect our view of judgment too. For Dante, the judgment that sinners face is self-inflicted. Minos, the judge in Dante's Hell, gives sinners the life in Hell that they chose on earth. Think back to the platform illustration—if you jump from the platform, *you* willed to jump, and falling is your judgment. This is how Dante sees the inhabitants of Hell. They are in Hell what they were on earth. Each image you will see in *Inferno* matches the way the individual lived and who he is. For instance, Dante sees in the Vestibule of Hell those who did not choose to serve God or hated God while living. Now, while dead, their choice is their punishment. In the Vestibule, they are not as dead, or as deep, in Hell as they desire, but neither are they alive. They are damned, but just within the gate of Hell. They "live" the life of indecision that they led on earth. Their sin is their Hell. The punishment does not just *fit* the crime. The punishment is living the crime forever.

Love in Hell

Now before we end, we must remember that Hell is a place for the dead, but *Inferno* is a poem for the living. In other words, we must remember that Dante is imagining what Hell looks like in order that we who are living may better know what sin is. Dante is not literally mapping out Hell. Dante has no idea what Hell literally looks like. Dante was alive as he wrote, and we the readers must connect the dots between Dante's imagination and the real truths about God and man that Dante's images bring to mind.

Inferno is not about soft truths. Dante writes truthfully and so puts the hard truths of damnation alongside the beautiful truths of redemption. This is how Christ prayed in His High Priestly Prayer:

> "I pray for them. I do not pray for the world but for those whom You have given Me, for they are Yours" (John 17:9).

Inferno shows the first step of the way to God—repentance of sin. Repentance is the way of life, and we must know what sin is in order to really mean what we say when we repent of sin. *Inferno* is, above all, an education in sin and a lesson in repentance.

So finally, we must remember the bright side of *Inferno.* Without Christ's work in Dante's life, Dante cannot experience the vision of God that culminates this epic journey—which he does in *Paradiso.* For all the horrors Dante sees in *Hell, Inferno,* like the whole *Comedy,* is about love. Even in Hell, this creative epic poem is about love. Dante does not remain in Hell, but passes through Hell because he has been loved. Dante does not journey on his own strength or any false

"Turn thee about, and shut thine eyelids tight; / If Gorgon show her face and thou thereon / Look once, there's no returning to the light." The Gorgons in the City of Dis guard the gates to enter nether Hell and refuse to let Virgil and Dante pass. Only the angels of God can let the travelers through. In Greek mythology a Gorgon is a vicious feminine creature whose appearance turns anyone who lays eyes upon it to stone.

strength, or else this would be an epic like the others. Dante is acted upon by love, and he responds in love. This love leads Dante out of Hell "to look once more upon the stars."

—*Matthew S. Vest*

For Further Reading

Leithart, Peter. *Ascent to Love.* Moscow, Idaho: Canon Press, 2001.

Williams, Charles. *The Figure of Beatrice.* Boydell & Brewer, 1994.

Session I: Prelude

A Question to Consider

Is Hell a necessary part of fallen creation? Why?

From the General Information above, answer the following questions:

1. List the highlights of Dante's life that are important for understanding the *Comedy.*
2. What are the main epic poems in the Western canon? Why are epics important?
3. What is the significance of Virgil being Dante's guide?
4. How is an allegory similar to looking in a mirror?
5. How is *The Divine Comedy* a more complete story than the *Epic of Gilgamesh,* the *Odyssey* or the *Aeneid?*
6. In what way is it true that even those who have not read *Inferno* have already been to Hell?

Reading Assignment:
Canto I

Session II: Activity and Recitation

Canto I

Prologue to the *Comedy*

Canto I works as a prologue to the whole *Divine Comedy* for several reasons. First, the *Comedy* has one hundred cantos: thirty-four in *Inferno* and thirty-three each in *Purgatorio* and *Paradiso.* Dante loves significant numbers and number patterns, so it makes sense numerically that the extra canto in *Inferno* deserves special attention. Another reason to see Canto I as the prologue is that the appeal to the muses does not occur until Canto II. Lastly, the whole *Comedy* allegorically appears in Canto I. Hence, the images in Canto I are very important, and they allude to the story of the whole comedic journey right in the beginning. This also makes Canto I the ideal place to begin reading for both the story and the allegory that we discussed in the General Information section above. The translator, Dorothy Sayers, has nifty little notes on both the story and the allegorical images for each canto.

You should usually read the canto first for the story, and then do your best to figure out what the key characters, or images, in the story represent. For example, think of *Pilgrim's Progress:* a man named *Christian* walks into a city named *Vanity Fair,* and you know immediately the developing story line (the hero is walking into a city) as well as the allegory (the sin of vanity tempts Christians, and we willingly walk into this sin). Bunyan made this allegory easy by *naming* his characters in the story with the allegorical meanings he wanted to convey. As you may already have noticed, it will not be that easy with the *Comedy,* but if you pay attention to the details, the challenge to interpret the characters in the story will be a good game.

Having read Canto I once, you may already have an idea what the key images represent, especially if you referenced Miss Sayers' notes on the images. For this session read through Canto I again aloud and then discuss or answer the following questions:[5]

1. Why is the dark wood a good image for sin or error (I.2)?
2. Why is the mountain a good image for the *road of repentance* and the *way to God* (I.13–15)?
3. Why is the leopard a good image for lust and youth? Why the lion for pride and manhood? Why the wolf for avarice and age (I.31–59)?
4. Dante says the greyhound will be a "savior to Italy." Find the other descriptions of the greyhound. Based on these details, what type of savior might the greyhound be? Political? Spiritual (I.100–111)?
5. In canto I, lines 16–18, Dante writes:
   "Then I looked up, and saw the morning rays
   Mantel its shoulder from that planet bright
   Which guides men's feet aright on all their ways;"
   How do these lines allude to Christ and Heaven?

Reading Assignment:
Cantos II–IV

Session III: Discussion

Cantos II–IV

A Question to Consider

Why does sin cause death?

Discuss or list short answers to the following questions.

Text Analysis

1. According to the inscription on the gate of Hell, why did God make Hell?
2. What do these words from the inscription on the gate of Hell mean?

   "Nothing ere I was made was made to be
   Save things eterne, and I eterne abide;
   Lay down all hope, you that go in by me."
   (III.8–10)

3. What does Dante fear after he reads the inscription on the gate?
4. Why do the damned in the Vestibule desire to cross the Acheron?
5. What is Dante's initial impression of Limbo? How is this impression different from his impression of the Vestibule?
6. According to Virgil, why are the noble pagans in Hell?

Cultural Analysis

1. What does today's culture believe sin is?
2. How does today's culture view death?

Biblical Analysis

1. Think about the story of Adam's sin of eating the forbidden fruit. According to this important biblical episode, what is the essence of sin (Gen. 3)?
2. Read Genesis 2:17 and Ephesians 2:1. In light of these verses, what does the Bible say about sin and death? How are sin and death related?
3. According to Romans 9:22–24, how does even sin bring God glory?

SUMMA

Write an essay or discuss this question, integrating what you have learned from the material above.

Why do all men without Christ deserve death?

READING ASSIGNMENT:
Cantos V–VII

SESSION IV: ACTIVITY

Cantos V–VII

Terza Rima

Dante loved number symbolism. You may have already noticed that each stanza has three lines, each line having eleven syllables (hendecasyllabic lines). So, each stanza has thirty-three syllables—which is the exact same number of cantos in *Purgatorio* and *Paradiso.* Thirty-three syllables per stanza, thirty-three cantos per book of the *Comedy,* and three times three is nine, a very important number for the *Comedy.*

But all that aside, one of the most distinctive features of *The Divine Comedy* is the rhyme scheme. It is called *terza rima* and has this pattern: ABA, BCB, CDC ... XYX, ZYZ, Z. The opening lines look like this:

Midway this way of life we're bound upon, **A**
I woke to find myself in a dark wood, **B**
Where the right road was wholly
lost and gone. **A**
Ay me! how hard to speak of it–that rude **B**
And rough and stubborn forest!
the mere breath **C**
Of memory stirs the old fear in the blood; **B**

This pattern runs nonstop through each canto, and it is not easy to replicate in English—in part because Italian has many more words that end in vowels (especially "a" and "o") than English does. This rhyme scheme, though, is loaded with symbolism. First, we have three, the number of the Trinity, that pervades every part of the poem. Secondly, the rhyme scheme makes each stanza connect to the stanza before and the stanza after. In this way, the terza rima scheme takes the "past" into the "now" and yet always looks "forward." This is symbolic of the Christian philosophy of how to live in time. We always look to our past history to better understand the now, yet we look forward so that every part of the now will advance Christ's kingdom.

So it is time to try your hand at writing stanzas in terza rima. For now, do not worry too much about the meter or the number of syllables in each line. Aim for ten or eleven syllables, but the important thing is the rhyme scheme. It will be a challenge to find enough rhymes in English, but be creative. Look to any section of *Inferno* as your example. It is fine to imitate Dante closely.

Write four stanzas, for a total of twelve lines. You need not write about Hell, but do write on the theme of sin.

Optional Exercise

Memorize the opening eighteen lines of *Inferno.* As you learned in Session I, allusion to Hell, Purgatory and Heaven are all in Canto I. The dark wood corresponds to Hell; the hill corresponds to Purgatory; the sun alludes to Heaven. Memorizing these lines gives you a key to the whole *Comedy.*

READING ASSIGNMENT:
Cantos VIII–X

SESSION V: RECITATION

Cantos I–X

Comprehension Questions

Answer the following questions for factual recall:

1. What are the three beasts in Canto I, and what do they represent?

2. Dante doubts his worth to journey on this "great enterprise," and he specifically says he is "not Aeneas . . . not Paul." What does Virgil tell Dante that motivates him to press on?
3. Who are in the Vestibule? What is their punishment?
4. What is the river that Dante and Virgil cross over from the Vestibule to Limbo? Who is the ferryman?
5. Which fellow Italians does Dante speak to in the second circle of lust? What is their story?
6. What sinners are in the Third Circle? What is their punishment?
7. Why are the spendthrifts and hoarders faceless in the Fourth Circle?
8. How does Dante react to Filippo Argenti's attack while crossing the river Styx in Phlegyas's boat? How does Virgil react to Dante's reaction?
9. Why can the heavenly messenger easily open the gates to the City of Dis when Virgil cannot?
10. According to Farinata, what can the damned in Hell know about events on earth?

READING ASSIGNMENT:
Cantos XI–XIV

Session VI: Activity

Cantos XI–XIV

Diagram of Hell

In Canto XI, Virgil explains the layout of Hell to Dante while they are acclimating to the horrid stench that arises from below in the Seventh Circle. The layout of Hell is important because it maps out Dante's journey, and it shows Dante's hierarchy of sin. Sin naturally progresses (or rather *digresses*) and spreads throughout the world (Gen. 6:5–6), and Dante sees this progression as he descends into Hell.

Draw, sketch, or even paint a cross-diagram of Hell as Virgil describes it. If possible, draw on quality paper (or paint on the appropriate material) so that you can keep your artwork. Do your best to take into account the details you have read about each part of Hell so far and include that in your drawing. Be as detailed and artistic as you can. Since you have not yet read about the lower regions of Hell, you will have to work solely from Virgil's description.

Dante's arrangement of sins in Hell has fascinated readers for hundreds of years. As you create your layout of Hell, discuss with your classmates or write down your thoughts on Dante's arrangement of sins in Hell. Do you agree with Dante's arrangement of sins in Hell? Why or why not?

Optional Activity

If time allows, take the above assignment to a whole new artistic level. Paint a cross section of Dante's Hell on an empty wall in a classroom or hallway. Of course, if your artistic skills are undeveloped, you may want to find a wall in someone's barn or basement. If you have the skills, though, paint a large mural. You could arrange this project so

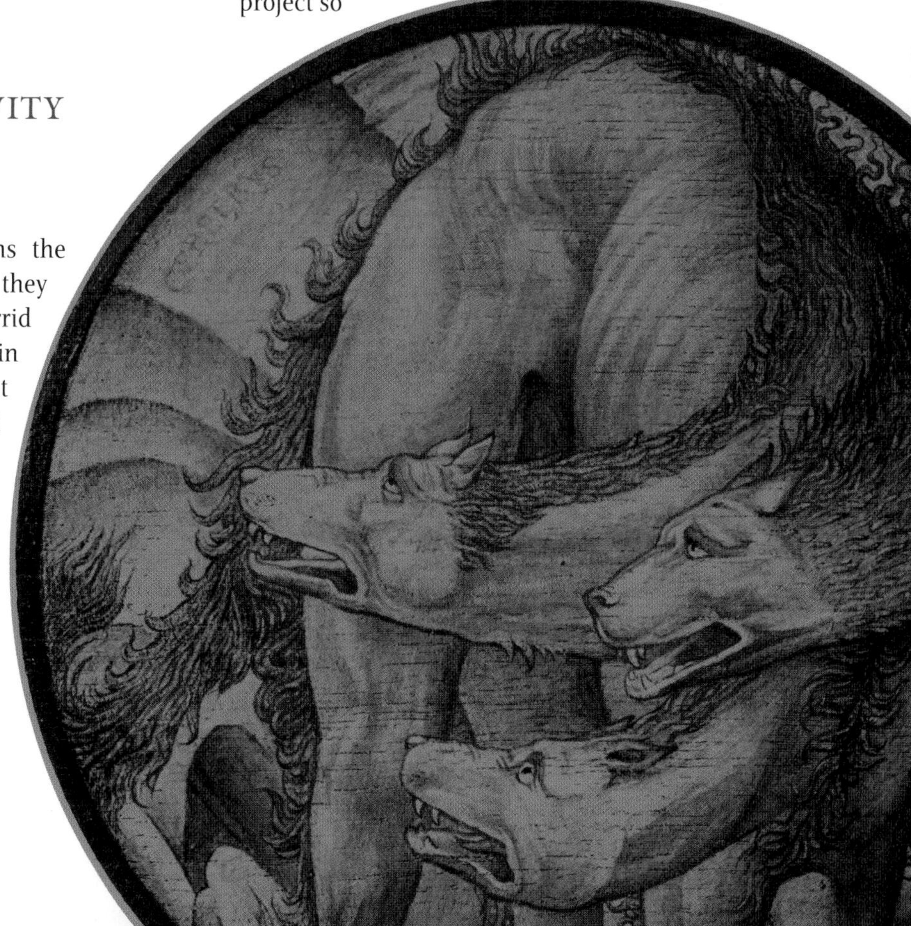

Cerebus, the three-headed dog, feasts on the gluttonous in the second circle of Hell.

that over time you continue filling in detail. If you do this, be sure to have fun with Dante's wild images and medieval love of numbers imagery.

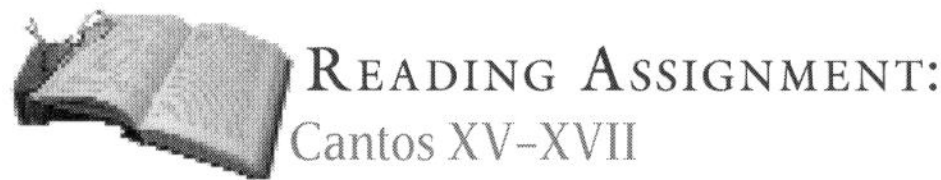

READING ASSIGNMENT:
Cantos XV–XVII

SUMMA

Write an essay or discuss this question, integrating what you have learned from the material above.
What is violence?

READING ASSIGNMENT:
Cantos XVIII–XIX

SESSION VII: DISCUSSION

Cantos XII–XVII

A Question to Consider

What is violence?

Discuss or list short answers to the following questions:

Text Analysis

1. How does the image of the Minotaur help us understand violence? The centaurs?
2. How does Dante define or explain the sins of those boiling in the river of blood?
3. In Canto XIII, Dante talks to the withered tree, Pier delle Vigne, who tells him why he is punished as a tree. What does Dante learn about the sin of suicide from Pier?
4. In the desert of burning sand where fire falls from above, Dante sees blasphemers, sodomites and usurers. What do these sins have in common that makes them sins of violence?

Cultural Analysis

1. How would today's culture define violence?
2. What are some examples of violence as our culture defines it?
3. How does our culture combat violence?

Biblical Analysis

1. What does Scripture teach about violence (Gen. 4)?
2. In 1 Timothy 3:1-7, Paul presents the qualifications for an overseer, or elder. What does this passage say about violence?

Dante gives us a preview of the three major divisions of Hell in the figures of the leopard (the sins of youth), the lion (the sins of adulthood), and the she-wolf (the sins of old age). Dante probably was inspired to choose these three beasts from Jeremiah 5:6, where the prophet preaches to those who refuse to repent for their sins: "Therefore a lion from the forest shall slay them, / A wolf of the deserts shall destroy them; / A leopard will watch over their cities. / Everyone who goes out from there shall be torn in pieces, / Because their transgressions are many; / Their backslidings have increased."

Session VIII: Discussion

Cantos XVIII–XIX

A Question to Consider

What constitutes deception?

Discuss or list short answers to the following questions:

Text Analysis

1. Look back to what Dante says of fraud in Canto XI. What is fraud?
2. Venedico prostituted his sister. How is this fraud?
3. Why is Jason in the pit of fraud?
4. What can we learn about deception from panderers and seducers?
5. Dante assigns flattery to the first bowge. How is flattery deception?
6. How can we deduce from Dante that simony is a worse form of fraud than flattery or pandering and seducing?

Cultural Analysis

1. John Q. wants a "no-fault divorce." His wife does not. What does our culture think about this?
2. What are some examples of deception in today's culture?
3. In light of these examples, how does today's culture define deception?

Biblical Analysis

1. Biblically, how is all sin connected to deception (consider Gen. 3:13)?
2. How does the serpent's deception in Genesis 3 distort the image of God? Of man?
3. How does Dante's view of pandering and seduction, flattery and simony fit with Ephesians 5:6?

Summa

Write an essay or discuss this question, integrating what you have learned from the material above.

How is deception related to fraud?

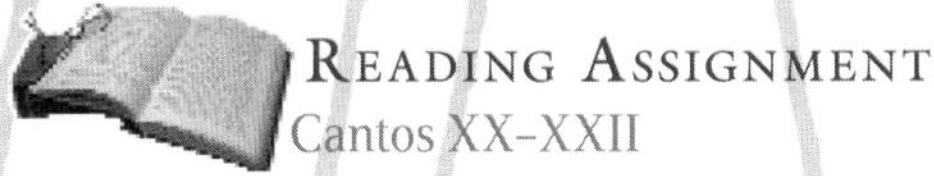

Reading Assignment:

Cantos XX–XXII

Session IX: Recitation

Cantos XI–XXII

Comprehension Questions

Answer the following questions for factual recall:

1. What are the three main divisions of Hell according to Dante's classification of sin?
2. What are the nine circles in Dante's Hell?
3. What river must Dante and Virgil cross to reach the Seventh Circle of Hell? Who carries Dante across?
4. What is the punishment for those who are violent against self, violent against God and violent against nature?
5. Who carries Dante and Virgil down the Great Barrier? How is he summoned?
6. Which sinners are assigned to the first five bowges of the Eighth Circle?
7. Why are the simoniacs head-down in the many holes aligning their bowge?
8. Why does Virgil rebuke Dante for weeping at the sight of the sorcerers?
9. In the bowge of the barrators, the demon Belzecue tells Dante and Virgil how the bridges over the bowges were made. How were they made?
10. How does the Navarrese barrator best the demons in "sport"?

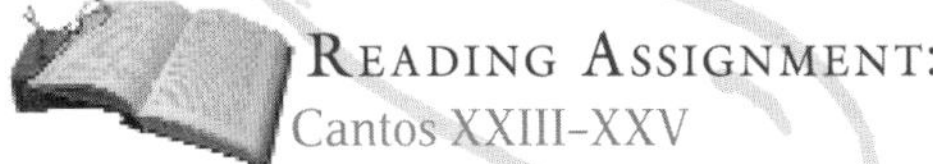

Reading Assignment:

Cantos XXIII–XXV

Session X: Discussion

Cantos XXIII–XXV

A Question to Consider

Is hatred a part of every sin?

Discuss or list short answers to the following questions:

Text Analysis

1. How does Vanni Fucci show his rage and hatred for God?
2. What separates Vanni Fucci's attitude and persona from the other sinners we have seen so far in Hell? What is similar?

3. How is the thieves' punishment in Cantos XXIV and XXV well suited to their sin?
4. What does the metamorphosis of the thief and the snake say about the sin of theft? About all sin?

Cultural Analysis

1. How does today's culture view hate?
2. Does today's culture see any connection between hate and sin? What about today's churches?

Biblical Analysis

1. Read Leviticus 19:17. How can we define hate in accord with this verse?
2. Now read John 15:18–27. What does this passage say about sin and hate?

SUMMA

Write an essay or discuss this question, integrating what you have learned from the material above.

Does hate have an opposite? If so, what is it? Why?

SESSION XI: WRITING

Progymnasmata

If you take the word *progymnasmata* apart, it means "before exercises." That is, these writing and speaking exercises come *before* you find yourself in a situation that requires you to speak or to write quickly, usually on the spot. If you have done your exercises, you are equipped for that moment. In this session you will prepare for that moment by practicing with the *chreia*, or "saying exercise."

If you remember, the chreia is a concise exposition of some memorable saying or deed. The chreia has eight elements, or paragraphs. The first is the *Panegyric*, which is a paragraph in which you praise the person who uttered the wise saying. The second paragraph is the *Paraphrastic*. In this paragraph you must sum up in your own words the wise saying. For example, you might say, "When Virgil rebuked Dante for showing pity over the sorcerers, he was teaching Dante that . . ." The third paragraph explains the motivation of the person; it is called *From the Cause*. The next element is *From the Contrary*. Here you must explain what would happen if the opposite of the saying or deed had occurred. For example: "If Virgil had not swept up Dante and carried him away from the death-minded demons, the *Comedy* would not be a comedy." The fifth paragraph is the *Analogy*, where you liken this saying or action to something else in a way that makes the statement you are praising easier to understand. You may even want to develop a general metaphor for your Analogy. The sixth paragraph is similar to the fifth, but is more specific. It is called the *Example*. For the Example, list a specific instance in which the wisdom of the deed or saying is demonstrated. For instance, if you are talking about Virgil's exceptional teaching that guides Dante, list a specific teaching moment that greatly helped Dante on his way. The seventh paragraph is the *Testimony* to the Ancients. This is the time to quote a wise sage from the past who testifies to the truth of the saying. Finally, in the eighth paragraph, the *Epilogue*, sum up the whole chreia.

Write a chreia about the creation of Hell. You may want to refer to these words from the inscription on the lintel of the gate of Hell: Justice moved my great maker; God eternal / Wrought me: the power and the unsearchably / High wisdom, and the primal love supernal (III.4–6).

I. Panegyric
   - Praise the person(s) who uttered the wise saying(s) or did the great deed

II. Paraphrase
   - Put the saying into your own words

III. From the Cause
   - Explain the motivation of the speaker

IV. From the Contrary
   - Explain the consequences if the opposite of the saying or action had occurred

V. Analogy
   - Liken the saying or action to something else

VI. Example
   - Point the reader to a specific instance in which the wisdom of the saying was demonstrated

VII. Testimony of the Ancients
   - Quote a sage person from the past who testifies to the truth of the saying

VIII. Epilogue
   - Summarize your previous paragraphs

READING ASSIGNMENT: Cantos XXVI–XXVIII

Session XII: Discussion

Cantos XXVI–XXVIII

A Question to Consider

Which is worse—to commit sin yourself or to lead another person into sin?

Discuss or list short answers to the following questions:

Text Analysis

1. According to Dante, how was Ulysses guilty of false counsel in the incident of the Trojan horse?
2. Considering the sins Ulysses confesses against Troy, why is he listed in the eighth bowge and not in the Seventh Circle with the violent, or elsewhere?
3. Ulysses tells a story of the great journey he took after he returned to Ithaka. How did Ulysses give false counsel to his men on this journey?
4. How is Guido's false counsel like Ulysses'? Which counsel was worse?

Cultural Analysis

1. Would most Americans think Ulysses guilty of sin because of the Trojan horse?
2. Do most people in today's culture think it is worse to sin or to lead another into sin?

Biblical Analysis

1. Which commandment would false counsel violate (Ex. 20)? How?
2. Read 1 Timothy 6:3–10. What does this passage say about false teachers?

Summa

Write an essay or discuss this question, integrating what you have learned from the material above.

Which is worse: to commit sin yourself or to lead another person into sin?

Reading Assignment:

Cantos XXIX–XXXI

Session XIII: Discussion

Cantos XXIX–XXXI

A Question to Consider

How is sin a distortion of God's will?

Discuss or list short answers to the following questions:

Text Analysis

1. How are the sins of the falsifiers distortions of God's will? How are they punished?
2. What types of falsifying did Gianni Schicchi and Myrrha commit?
3. Looking at the first twenty-seven lines of Canto XXIX, what is the similarity between the images of Juno, Athamas and Hecuba?
4. Why is Dante so interested in the quarrel between Adam of Brescia and Sinon of Troy?
5. Why does Virgil rebuke Dante for his interest in the quarrel?

Cultural Analysis

1. What are some outward, visible signs of sin in today's culture?
2. How might Dante assess today's cultural sins? Is there one particular Circle in Hell where Dante might place America?

Biblical Analysis

1. What can we learn about Christ's will from His prayers in the Garden of Gethsemane (Matt. 26:36-46)?
2. Is man's will always bound to distort God's will (2 Cor. 5:17–21)?

Summa

Write an essay or discuss this question, integrating what you have learned from the material above.

How does God react to man's sin?

Reading Assignment:

Cantos XXXII–XXXIV

SESSION XIV: REVIEW

Cantos I–XXXIV

Comprehension Questions

Answer these questions for factual recall:

1. What are the three beasts that Dante faces in Canto I? What do they represent?
2. Briefly describe the arrangement of the first five circles of Hell (include the Vestibule in your description as well).
3. Who are the two main images of heresy? How are the tombs in the Sixth Circle fitting images of heresy?
4. Describe the three divisions of Violence.
5. Write out a chart connecting the sins with the punishments in the Eighth Circle.
6. Describe the Ninth Circle, the realm of complex fraud.

SESSION XV: EVALUATION

Grammar

Briefly identify the following characters, things, or people with one or two sentences. Answer each of the following questions in complete sentences. (2 points per answer)

1. St. Lucy

Dante and the Three Kingdoms by Domenico di Michelino (1417–1491). Oil on canvas, Museo dell'Opera del Duomo, Florence.

2. Beatrice
3. Paolo and Francesca
4. City of Dis
5. Brunetto Latini
6. Geryon
7. Vanni Fucci di Pistoia

Logic

Answer the following questions in complete sentences; your answer should be a paragraph or so. Answer two of the three questions. (10 points per answer)

1. How does Canto I serve as a prologue to the whole *Divine Comedy?* In other words, how does Canto I tell the story of the whole *Comedy?*
2. Why do "those who die beneath God's righteous ire" desire to die?
3. Why is Virgil rebuffed at the city gates of Dis?

Lateral Thinking

Answer one of the following questions. These questions will require more substantial answers. (16 points per answer)

1. What is the theological significance of the message on the gate of Hell?
2. Genesis 2:17 tells us that all sin causes death. Does this mean that all sins are equal? Why or why not?

Optional Session A: Activity

Sculpting Hell

Build a cross section model of Hell out of clay or some other fitting material. Use the diagram of Hell from Session VI as your guide. To maximize that gravity problem, it may work best first to build a mountain similar to the very unoriginal volcano science experiment (the one with baking-soda and vinegar). Once the volcano has set enough to handle it, work in pairs if possible and cut the volcano in half. Use the halves as cross section models of Hell. Once it has really set, paint scenes from the Inferno in each level. Be creative. Perhaps even a piece of glass placed over drawings of frozen traitors can be your chilly Lake of Cocytus.

Optional Session B: Activity

The Three Beasts Game

For Groups

From the nearest available chest of toys, borrow a leopard (or member of the feline family), a lion and a wolf. Arrange the seats or classroom desks in a circle. The goal of this game is to align the sins with their corresponding circles of Hell and the punishments these sins fall under. For instance, if the sin "heresy" is called out, the first student to raise his hand and answer "Sixth Circle" gets to claim the violent lion. The lion trophy is safely his until another question on a sin of violence comes up. If he correctly answers that one too, the lion remains his. He can keep the lion until someone beats him to the answer about a sin of violence. Keep score so that each time you get one of the beasts, you get a point. First one to get 10 points wins.

Play the game in three levels. Level one is to align the sin with the circle, level two is to align the sin with its punishment. (To keep things from getting too complicated, the teacher should always call out the sin and let the students call out the circle or punishment.)

For the Individual

Write out all the sins in *Inferno* on index cards and shuffle them. Pull a card out at random and identify the circle in which that sin belongs. Identifying the sin with the circle is level one. Level two of this game is to identify the sin with the punishment. See how many you can match in a row, up to ten. You can miss one, but if you miss two in a row, you have to start counting over with one.

Optional Session C: Analyze the Art

Dante and the Three Kingdoms

Look at the painting by Domenico di Michelino *Dante and the Three Kingdoms* on the previous page and then answer the following questions:

1. What are the main images in this painting?

2. How do these images tell the story of the *Comedy?*
3. Compare and contrast the postures of those descending into Hell and those in Purgatory.
4. What is significant about Dante's crown and the color of his robe?
5. Why is Dante gazing upon Florence? What emotion does Domenico paint into Dante's gaze?
6. In the painting, do you suppose it is better for Dante to gaze upon Florence or Paradise? Why?

ENDNOTES

1 The recommended, three-volume translation of the *Comedy* by Dorothy Sayers bears the English titles *Hell, Purgatory* and *Paradise* on the book covers. However, in her introduction and notes, Sayers uses the Italian titles *Inferno, Purgatorio* and *Paradiso* to refer to the parts of the poem and the names Hell, Purgatory and Paradise to refer to the actual places. *Ascent to Love,* Peter Leithart's guide to the *Comedy,* follows the same pattern. We follow their pattern in this chapter.

2 Given the significance of the *Comedy,* it is nearly tragic to read only a third of the *Comedy* for *Omnibus II.* But lest this "tragedy" interfere with this reading of *Inferno,* take courage and know that *Purgatorio* and *Paradiso* are coming soon in *Omnibus V.* The other option is to read ahead. It is a myth that good students do not read ahead.

3 *Omnibus I,* p. 103.

4 See Psalm 2.

5 This is the same Dorothy Sayers whose essay called *The Lost Tools of Learning* sparked a resurgence of classical Christian education, so the translator of the version of Dante that many of you are using is partially responsible for the schools, homeschools and curriculum that you are using.

The Canterbury Tales

Just imagine what it would be like to be one of a group of thirty people to go on a five-day bus trip to Washington, D.C., or the Grand Canyon. Now also imagine that you have never met any of your co-travelers before. They are all of different ages and have varied occupations; among them is a doctor, a lawyer, a chef, a farmer, several pastors, a college student, an older woman, a couple of nuns and a military officer. Since no one has an iPod, a cell phone, or a hand-held video game, some sort of amusement is called for. So the host of this unusual group (who is the tour guide and the proprietor of a bed & breakfast) suggests that each person should tell two stories on the way and two more on the return trip. Not only would it make the trip more interesting, but the stories would be as different from one another as the people were. Some of

The rooster Chanticleer, king of his farmland kingdom, quotes intellectuals, dreams great dreams and is very elegant (as roosters go). He has every characteristic of a person belonging to the upper class. Chaucer's tale is one of mocking the clueless.

the stories would be funny or romantic, some might be serious or tragic, some would teach good things and some might be downright tacky and vulgar, especially if the storyteller were drunk. The one thing you would not have would be boredom. That's what you would get if you gathered up such a wild assortment of bus travelers, and that's what we have in Chaucer's *Canterbury Tales*. Chaucer's travelers are going to Canterbury Cathedral on a pilgrimage, they are on horseback, and they are chatty. So when we read his *Canterbury Tales*, we get quite a lively description of life in the Middle Ages in England.

General Information

Author and Context

If you ever have the chance to travel to London and the good fortune of visiting Westminster Abbey, be sure to go to "Poets' Corner," where many of England's greatest writers and poets are buried. There you will find the tomb of Geoffrey Chaucer, the man who is called the Father of English poetry.

Born in London sometime between 1340 and 1343 during the reign of King Edward III, Geoffrey Chaucer was born into a middle-class family. He was a learned man with broad experience. In his early years he served as a page, as a soldier in the army, and he was even captured in France and ransomed. He later worked as a diplomat, traveled abroad and was promoted to various positions at court during the reigns of King Edward III and King Richard II. Chaucer's life-long benefactor was the powerful John of Gaunt, Duke of Lancaster. (John of Gaunt was also a strong supporter of John Wycliffe, and there is good reason as well for suspecting that Chaucer himself may have been sympathetic to the Lollards,[1] which is what followers of Wycliffe were called.)

These varied experiences and connections gave Chaucer a broad acquaintance with English life which he readily incorporated into his tales, for his pilgrims range from those in the upper, educated class, to the working class and the clergy. The tales themselves Chaucer brought from many sources, and he retells them with his own fresh twists and insights, often satirizing different aspects of life. Many years later his literary descendent John Dryden would say of *The Canterbury Tales*, "Here is God's plenty."

Chaucer probably began writing his tales in 1385 (or 1386) and continued until his death on October 25, 1400. Though his initial plan of 120 stories was far from complete, we have a wonderful description of medieval England and portraits of a wide range of early English characters.

Significance

Chaucer lived during the period in English history when our language was still in transition. The earliest writers had used the Anglo-Saxon dialects brought in by those warring tribes, but by the time of Chaucer the language had changed to what we now call Middle English, the language used from about 1100–1485. Two major dialects (as well as several minor ones) were in use during Chaucer's time. Because Chaucer wrote his *Canterbury Tales* in the East Midland dialect of London, this influenced the way our language developed, which was to favor Chaucer's choice. If you read *The Canterbury Tales* in Chaucer's English, you will see how much our language has changed. Although you will recognize many words, it really looks (and sounds) like a foreign tongue. (To hear the opening lines of the *Prologue* recited in Middle English, click Link 1 for this chapter at www.VeritasPress.com/OmniLinks.) When you hear parts of *The Canterbury Tales* read in Middle English, you will agree that it sounds delightfully musical to our modern ear.

All but two of Chaucer's tales are written in poetry. He was the first English poet to write in what is called heroic couplets (two lines of rhymed iambic pentameter). *The Canterbury Tales* include about 17,000 lines of such poetry and are found in ten fragments, each containing different tales. The earliest copy of the tales is the Hengwrt manuscript which is kept in the National Library of Wales. But perhaps the best known copy of *The Canterbury Tales* (called the Ellesmere manuscript) is in the Huntington Library in San Marino, California. This copy is illustrated beautifully and is thought to have been copied by the same scribe as the Hengwrt manuscript. *The Canterbury Tales* were first printed by William Caxton in 1478.

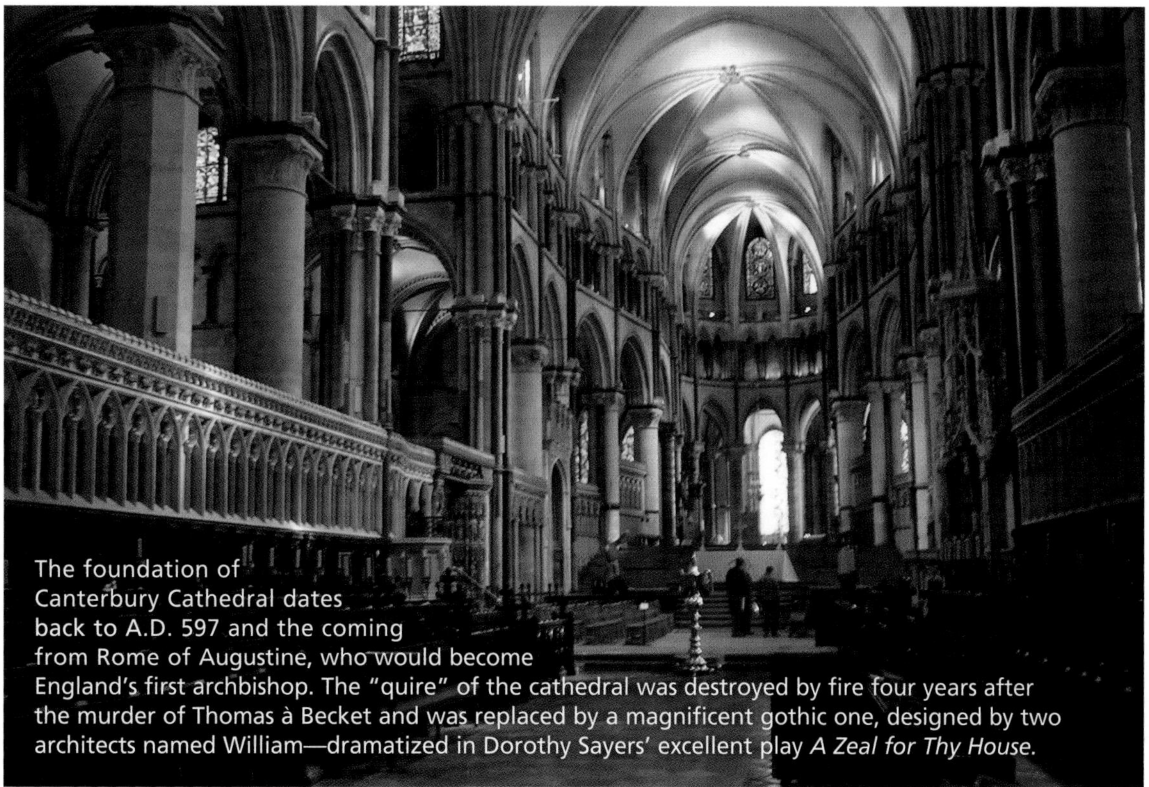

The foundation of Canterbury Cathedral dates back to A.D. 597 and the coming from Rome of Augustine, who would become England's first archbishop. The "quire" of the cathedral was destroyed by fire four years after the murder of Thomas à Becket and was replaced by a magnificent gothic one, designed by two architects named William—dramatized in Dorothy Sayers' excellent play *A Zeal for Thy House*.

Summary and Setting

The Canterbury Tales is constructed as though it is a careful report of stories told by travelers making a pilgrimage to Canterbury Cathedral. Though many faithful pilgrims would do penance (or ask for healing) at St. Thomas à Becket's shrine, others simply went as tourists. Chaucer's plan for his collection of stories was to have each of the 29 pilgrims tell two stories on each way of the journey. Including himself as one of the pilgrims, this would have meant a total of 120 tales. Whether he really ever intended to include so many tales is uncertain, but he finished only 24 before his death. The host, who is the innkeeper where the pilgrimage begins, has suggested a contest: the one whom he judges to tell the best tale will get supper paid for by the other travelers when they return from Canterbury back to the inn. The travelers all agree with the plan and draw lots to see who will be first. The noble knight is chosen, and so the tales begin with his.

Given this format, Chaucer had tremendous freedom to include all kinds of stories, stories as varied as his group of pilgrims. *The Knight's Tale* is a *courtly romance* (a tale with the ideals of medieval chivalry) set in classical Greece; *The Wife of Bath's Tale* is a story with a moral point (called an *exemplum*) set in King Arthur's day; *The Nun's Priest's Tale* is a charming beast fable (using animals to convey a moral tale) and *The Clerk's Tale* is a story about patience and humility, attributed to Petrarch. Chaucer himself went on a pilgrimage to Canterbury in April of 1388.

Worldview

Whenever we sit down to read anything, we need to be thinking about a couple of things: What is this author saying or assuming about the ultimate questions of life? Is the author right? If you really were part of a group of travelers who were telling stories, you would not only be listening to each story for enjoyment, you should also be analyzing the content of the story. You probably already do this unconsciously, but it is even better to be deliberately thinking about such things.

The first thing you would wonder about is the story teller. Is this person reliable? Is he or she a Christian, telling this story with a biblical mindset? Or, is this person not to be trusted? Is this storyteller a thief? A liar? Is he filled with bitterness or resentment? These things can be pretty obvious. In *The Canterbury Tales* we have both kinds of storytellers: some are admirable characters, and some are not.

C.S. Lewis once said that literature should teach what is useful, honor the honorable and appreciate the delightful. *The Canterbury Tales* fulfill these standards in varying degrees. We will look at a few of them with this background in mind.

The other important thing we must bear in mind is the historical context. When were these tales written, and what was going on during that time? Chaucer wrote his tales at the end of the fourteenth century. This is, of course, before the great Reformation, and the powerful English church was being pulled from two directions: the pope and the king both wanted control over the church, and the troubles that resulted are what fill most of the history books dealing with this period. It was also an age of superstition, with people thinking that they could earn their salvation through "good works" or by making pilgrimages and doing penance. Canterbury was the "religious capital" of England and thus a popular destination for such pilgrimages.

In his *Prologue* Chaucer introduces the various characters making this trip to Canterbury Cathedral, describing their appearance as well as their personality. Among the travelers are a noble knight, a squire, a yeoman, a prioress traveling with a nun and three priests, a monk, a wanton friar, a not-so-honest merchant, a virtuous clerk, the wife of Bath, a pious parish priest, an honest ploughman, an obnoxious miller and the host who will be the guide of the journey as well as the judge of the best story. (Chaucer will himself turn up later as a character in the story.)

Just from reading the *Prologue* we can easily see which characters are the godly ones (not very many) and which of them we cannot trust. Chaucer has done us a favor in giving us the short character sketch of each person, and he freely criticizes and satirizes as he goes. He obviously knows the difference between the hypocrite and the sincere Christian, for both the parish priest and the ploughman are extolled for being consistent Christians. Between each tale is a short prologue which includes comments from the host as well as interaction between some of the characters. In the final section of Chaucer's *Prologue,* he claims that he will faithfully record each tale using the same words

The Knight's Tale is about two knights, Arcite and Palamon, who are imprisoned by Theseus, duke of Athens. In prison they see and fall in love with the sister of Hippolyta, Emily. They variously get out of prison and end up in a tournament over Emily arranged by Theseus. The story is a loose translation and condensed version of *Teseida delle nozze di Emilia* by Giovanni Boccaccio, and in it the knight introduces many typical aspects of knighthood, such as courtly love.

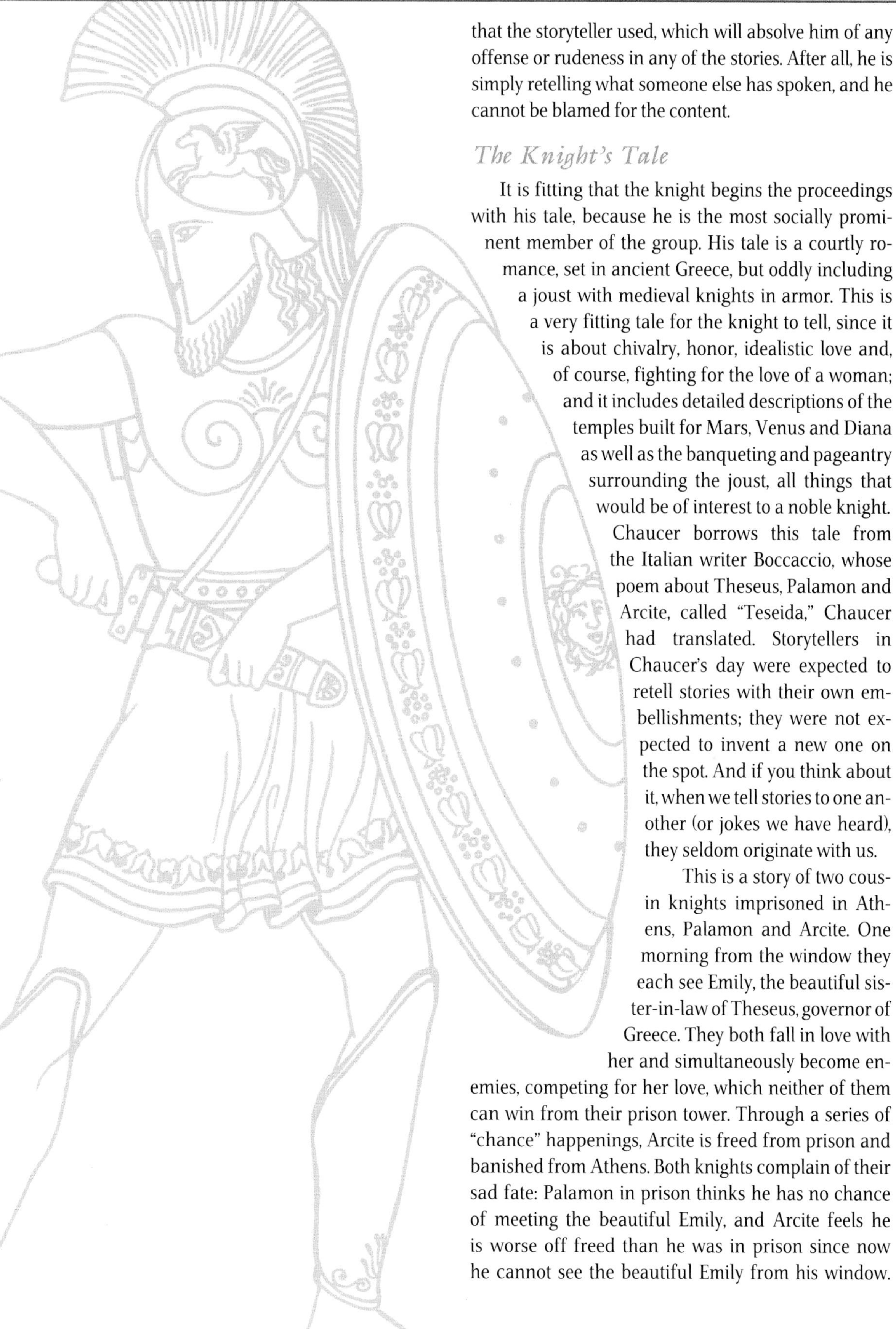

that the storyteller used, which will absolve him of any offense or rudeness in any of the stories. After all, he is simply retelling what someone else has spoken, and he cannot be blamed for the content.

The Knight's Tale

It is fitting that the knight begins the proceedings with his tale, because he is the most socially prominent member of the group. His tale is a courtly romance, set in ancient Greece, but oddly including a joust with medieval knights in armor. This is a very fitting tale for the knight to tell, since it is about chivalry, honor, idealistic love and, of course, fighting for the love of a woman; and it includes detailed descriptions of the temples built for Mars, Venus and Diana as well as the banqueting and pageantry surrounding the joust, all things that would be of interest to a noble knight. Chaucer borrows this tale from the Italian writer Boccaccio, whose poem about Theseus, Palamon and Arcite, called "Teseida," Chaucer had translated. Storytellers in Chaucer's day were expected to retell stories with their own embellishments; they were not expected to invent a new one on the spot. And if you think about it, when we tell stories to one another (or jokes we have heard), they seldom originate with us.

This is a story of two cousin knights imprisoned in Athens, Palamon and Arcite. One morning from the window they each see Emily, the beautiful sister-in-law of Theseus, governor of Greece. They both fall in love with her and simultaneously become enemies, competing for her love, which neither of them can win from their prison tower. Through a series of "chance" happenings, Arcite is freed from prison and banished from Athens. Both knights complain of their sad fate: Palamon in prison thinks he has no chance of meeting the beautiful Emily, and Arcite feels he is worse off freed than he was in prison since now he cannot see the beautiful Emily from his window.

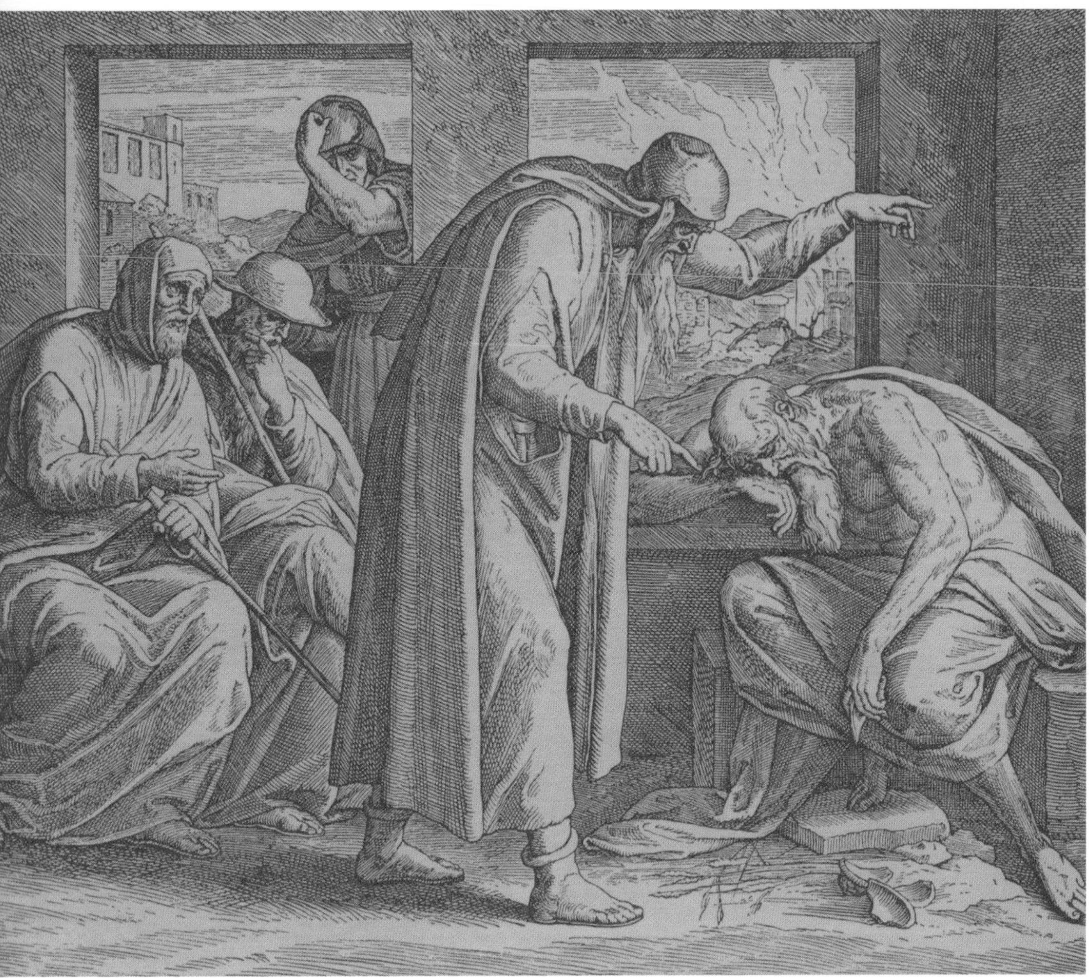

The Clerk's Tale tells of a young woman whose husband tests her loyalty in a series of unimaginable tortures that recall the trials of Job. The tale applauds the virtues of patience and noble suffering in women, though the Clerk says that it would be impossible for any woman to endure the suffering that she faces. The Clerk suggests that women should strive toward the woman's example but not follow her to such an extreme end.

Through another series of "chance" happenings, Palamon escapes from prison, and Arcite returns to Athens disguised, and the two former friends and now determined enemies meet accidentally in a field. They begin fighting over Emily but are discovered by Theseus, who intervenes. He decides that they should both return in a year with a hundred knights for a joust, and the winner will be given Emily's hand in marriage.

Chaucer is making fun of chivalry and courtly love in this story where chance seems to rule everything. Before the great joust, both men appeal to the gods: Palamon seeks out Venus in her temple and asks for the love of Emily; Arcite appeals to Mars for victory in war and is granted it; and poor Emily beseeches the goddess Diana to give her the one who loves her more, if she must marry one of them. There is some discord in heaven over these requests, since each god has made conflicting promises. But Jupiter decides how it will all turn out.

The theme or moral of the tale is "Alas, why is it people so dispraise God's providence or Fortune and her ways, that oft and variously in their scheme includes far better things than they could dream?" Both men were so miserable with their plight, envying the position of the other, they let their so-called love for Emily destroy their love for one another and make their lives useless and pitiful. "What is so foolish as a man in love?" the Knight asks in his tale.

As in classical literature, the gods cause havoc in the lives of these men. Fate is unpredictable, cold and based on the whims of the gods. But in telling the tale, Chaucer implies that it is really "God's providence" that is lovingly designing the outcome, not a mindless fate.

After the Knight finishes his tale, the obnoxious and drunk Miller insists on telling his, which turns out to be coarse, just like Chaucer warned the readers that it might be. His vulgar (but jolly) story offends the Reeve, so the Reeve returns the favor. His tale is another bawdy tale (called a *fabliau*), this time about a Miller. But we press on to higher ground and will next consider *The Wife of Bath's Tale.*

The Wife of Bath's Tale

This tale is called an *exemplum* (meaning "example" in Latin), or a story with a point. The Wife of Bath has a long prologue preceding her tale in which she very frankly tells her own life story of her five marriages and how she gained the mastery over each husband. Then she finally turns to her tale which, not surprisingly, is about what women really want in marriage.

First the story background: A traveling knight raped a lone maiden in the countryside, is tried in King Arthur's court and is sentenced to death. The queen seeks to save his life and proposes a deal: his life will be spared if he can find out within a year "What is the thing that women most desire?" He spends the year searching for the answer but no two women agree. Finally, as he is returning to court to face his punishment, he meets an old hag who offers to help him. They make a bargain: he will do whatever she requires if her answer saves his life. Then she tells him that what women really want is to rule over their husbands. When he supplies the answer at court, he is granted his life, but the old hag then calls on him before the court to honor his pledge to her for saving his life. She asks him to marry her!

Though very dejected at the prospect of marrying the old hag, he follows through. On their wedding night he is repulsed at the thought of sharing the bed with her. She chastises him for looking down on her poverty and old age and for his lack of gentle manners. She reminds him that gentility and virtue have more to do with deeds than with birth or lineage. "Vice and bad manners are what make a churl," she says. Part of the humor in her long lecture to him is all the classical as well as biblical allusions she uses, indicating that she is well educated and genteel herself. The old hag then lectures her young husband on the reasons why it is preferable to have an ugly, but faithful wife, rather than a beautiful wife who will be sought after by all his friends. She asks him which he would prefer. In the end, he says he will let her decide what is best.

This idea that women want to rule their husbands is supported by the Bible. In fact, it is part of the curse in Genesis 3:16, "thy desire shall be to thy husband, and he shall rule over thee." Fallen woman does not want to submit to her husband's authority, and it doesn't much matter if it is in our modern age or in the Middle Ages.

After the tale concludes, the Friar, who has been glowering at the Summoner, says he will tell a tale about a Summoner since there is nothing good about them. The Summoner says to go ahead, he will get even when it is his turn, and the good Host breaks up the squabble. But the two tales that follow expose the conflict that exists between the two vocations. But then the host turns to the Clerk and asks for a lively tale that is not too academic.

The Clerk's Tale

The Clerk is the most respected person next to the knight. His tale is a direct response to the Wife of Bath's tale. She has shown that women want to rule their husbands, so the clerk tells a tale about a humble and obedient woman who was extremely submissive to her cruel and heartless husband. The Clerk credits Petrarch, an Italian poet of the fourteenth century, as the source of this tale.

Griselda and Walter are the main characters of this story that is set in Italy, where Walter is a bachelor king. In response to the pleading of his lords, he agrees to marry, and he selects the beautiful daughter of a poor man for his bride. The king makes Griselda promise that she will always obey him cheerfully without a word, no matter how difficult or painful the request. The first trial comes after the birth of their first child, a baby girl. Walter has the child taken away from her mother, and Griselda thinks the child will be murdered, yet she quietly submits. Later when she bears a son, the same thing happens. Years later Walter tells her he has been granted a divorce and is going to remarry. Never flinching, Griselda quietly submits and returns to her father's home after helping to prepare the house for the young and beautiful bride.

The Clerk admits at the end of the tale that women should not imitate Griselda in going too far to submit to tyrannical and cruel husbands like Walter. But he connects her behavior to how Christians should submit to God patiently in all He does in their lives. Of course, God is not cruel like Walter, but the Clerk quotes the book of James, saying that God tests His saints for their good, but never beyond what they are able to endure.

Chaucer added an "envoy" to the story (which he probably added years after he had first written the tale) in which he is playfully ironic, telling wives not to imitate Griselda, but to return evil for evil, to never revere their husbands, to insult them and take the lead.

The Clerk's Tale is followed by several more of various kinds: some about marriage and love, *The Prioress's Tale* which is a saint's legend of a murdered child, and *The Tale of Sir Topas* and *The Tale of Melibee,* both told by Chaucer himself as a fellow traveler. But we must turn to *The Nun's Priest's Tale.*

The Nun's Priest's Tale

In the sixth century B.C. Aesop wrote his fables about talking beasts, instructing his readers with a moral point to the story. Chaucer's *Nun's Priest's Tale* is very similar: it is an absurd story about barnyard chickens written in a *mock heroic* tone. This term refers to a piece of writing that elevates some trivial subject (in this case, a fox chasing a rooster) as though it is a great epic. The chickens are discussing dreams, theological subjects (divine foreknowledge), using classical allusions, lofty language and quoting Latin (incorrectly). Of course this is intended to be funny and to poke fun, not at chickens, but at man. When these discussions take place in the hen house, it is meant to be ironic and comic, making fun of man's misplaced self-importance and dignity by having the rooster act like a human male.

The gist of the story is this: Chanticleer the rooster has had a troubling dream of being chased by a fox. When he pours out his fears to his fair hen Pertelote, she chides him for being a coward and says he has lost her love for not being more manly (which is an odd adjective for a chicken). She then attributes his dream to bad digestion and prescribes a purge (or laxative) for his cure. Chanticleer corrects Pertelote's view of his dream with examples from ancient books and says that God uses dreams to warn and reveal the future. "One never should be careless about dreams," he says and claims they are a sign of "trouble breeding." He continues his long lecture citing many ancient sources and ends with a mistaken translation of a Latin verse that really means "Woman is the downfall of man" by saying that "Woman is man's delight and all his bliss." A month or so later, Chanticleer and his seven wives are enjoying the sunny barnyard when he spies a sly fox "lying low." Before the rooster can run away, the fox engages him in a conversation, flattering Chanticleer by telling him that he has really come to the barnyard just to hear him sing. He claims that he had heard Chanticleer's father, who was also a great singer. The rooster is so full of pride over this that he is not cautious, and he closes his eyes and begins "to sing with all his might." Predictably, the fox makes his move, grabs the rooster by the gorge and runs away. The hens began making such a racket that the men, the women, the dogs and the rest of the farm animals are roused, and they begin to chase the fox.

Chaucer ends the tale with his moral point: "Be on your guard against the flatterers of the world." He then follows this with a prayer to God that He will "make us all good men, and bring us to his heavenly bliss. Amen."

Now we must pass over many more tales and turn to the end of Chaucer's work.

When the humans begin to chase the fox, and the whole barnyard adds their noises to the fray the narrator gives the reader the only contemporary reference in *The Canterbury Tales: Certes, he Jakke Straw and his meynee / Ne made nevere shoutes half so shrille / Whan that they wolden any Flemyng kille, /As thilke day was maad upon the fox.* Jack Straw was the leader of the English Peasants' Rebellion in 1381, placing the completion of the story of Chanticleer to the 1380s.

Chaucer's Retractions: The Maker of this Book here takes his Leave

We have looked at only four of the tales in this collection, which is admittedly a very small sampling of Geoffrey Chaucer. It is much like falling asleep on your bus trip and missing out on fifty of the sixty stories. So you'll have to go back sometime when you have time and read them all. Chaucer's stories have been left to us in ten fragments, and no one knows for sure what order he would have arranged them in a final edition. But he closes the tales with his retraction that is important for us to note. In his closing comments he says that if there is anything worthy in the book, then thank the Lord Jesus Christ for it because He is the source of all that is good. And if there is anything displeasing, he says "to impute it to the fault of my want of ability, and not to my will, who would very gladly have said better if I had had the power." But he then goes on to ask the reader to pray for him that Christ would forgive him for "my translations and enditings of worldly vanities, which I revoke in my retractions," and he lists among these works "*The Tales of Canterbury,* those that tend towards sin." He thanks God for his translation of Boethius and other devotional works and concludes with prayers for grace, penitence and confession, so that he will be among those saved. "Here ends the book of the *Tales of Canterbury* compiled by Geoffrey Chaucer, on whose soul Jesu Christ have mercy. Amen."

It is indeed rare today to have an author give glory to God for the good work he has done and to publicly repent of any sinful writings. We must appreciate this aspect of Chaucer's work, even though we do not know what led to this retraction and which specific tales he thought sinful (though we can guess). Nevertheless, we can see that as he sought to produce a collection of tales that were believable, tales that an assortment of medieval English men and women might really tell on a pilgrimage, he succeeded in far more. He has painted for us a picture in miniature of English life, and he has done it in delightful poetry. He has preserved for us a vivid and unvarnished description of the character of everyday people and everyday life in England seven hundred years ago. And for this we can add our hearty *amen.*

But we must also admire Chaucer for writing with a Christian perspective on life, even though some of the stories may include unbiblical material. He praises what is good, he laughs at what is funny, and he satirizes and criticizes what is bad. He is obviously very familiar with the Bible, and he quotes Scripture in Middle English and not from the Latin Vulgate, which was quite a radical thing to do in his day. He is openly critical of the excesses and abuses in the church throughout his tales. He clearly sees man as a sinner, and he knows salvation is found only in Christ, not in doing religious works. Overall, I believe that we can truly say that Geoffrey Chaucer in his *Tales of Canterbury* honors what is honorable, teaches what is good and useful, and delights us all the while.

—*Nancy Wilson*

For Further Reading

Benson, Larry, ed. *The Riverside Chaucer.* Boston: Houghton Mifflin, 1990.

Boitani, Piere and Mann, Jill, eds. *The Cambridge Companion to Chaucer.* Second Edition. Cambridge: Cambridge University Press, 2004.

Cowan, Louise and Guinness, Os. *Invitation to the Classics.* Grand Rapids, Mich.: Baker Books, 1998. 107-112.

Tuchman, Barbara. *A Distant Mirror: The Calamitous 14th Century.* New York: Random House, 1979.

Session I: Prelude

A Question to Consider

What makes a story a Christian story? Does the author? The plot? The themes? Something else?

From the General Information above answer the following questions:

1. What was Chaucer's original plan for *The Canterbury Tales?* Did he complete it?
2. What is the significance of the title of the book?
3. Explain Chaucer's use of satire in The Nun's Priest's Tale.
4. Explain the meaning of Dryden's comment, "Here is God's plenty."
5. Why would *The Canterbury Tales* be of importance to the historian?
6. Which tale deals with the theme of chance? Do you think that Chaucer is saying that fate or chance really governs the universe?
7. What meter did Chaucer use to write his *Canterbury Tales?*

Reading Assignment:
General Prologue

Session II: Recitation

General Prologue

Answer the following questions for factual recall:

Comprehension Questions

1. What time of the year, and from where (including the name of the inn) does the pilgrimage to Canterbury begin?
2. What is the "bearing" of the Knight, which is somewhat of a surprise given his extensive success on many foreign battlefields?
3. Who is the pilgrim of whom Chaucer says he "could make songs and poems and recite, / Knew how to joust and dance, to draw and write"?
4. What are the main characteristics of the Nun or Prioress?
5. What does the Monk think of *The Rule of St. Benedict* and why?
6. What is the key trait of the Friar by which he obtains the money and girls he desires?
7. How does the Merchant cover up the fact he is in debt?
8. What examples does Chaucer give of the Skipper ignoring the "nicer rules of conscience"?
9. Why does Chaucer say that the Wife of Bath "knew the remedies for love's mischances"?
10. How does Chaucer say he is going to "give account" of all the pilgrim's stories?
11. Who will be the judge of the best tale, and what will the teller of the best tale win, according to the Host? What is the standard that the judge will judge by?

Reading Assignment:
The Knight's Tale, Parts I and II

The Wife of Bath's Tale begins with a scene that could well be illustrated by this painting *The Knight, the Young Girl, and Death* by Hans Baldung Grien. Her tale utilizes the "loathly lady" motif found in other stories like *Sir Gawain and the Green Knight.* But Chaucer departs from the common path of these stories with the initial rape and emphasis on the redemption of the knight through his decision to be faithful. This is a Northern Renaissance treatment of the traditional theme of "Death and the Maiden," which itself is a variation of the "Dance of Death." The *Dans Macabre* has a history going back to at least early medieval times; it usually shows skeletal figures in varying degrees of decomposition dancing with (or sometimes killing) members of every level of human society. This *memento mori* (reminder of death) calls the viewer to a more devout engagement with his Christianity. This particular picture shows Death engaging a beautiful and fashionably dressed young girl; fortunately for her she is rescued by a dashing young man. However, Death grips the hem of her dress in his teeth, leading us to believe that her rescue, timely as it is, is only a temporary one. Death will eventually have her. The idea is to show the viewer that neither youth, wealth nor bravery are adequate guards against the inevitability of death.

Session III: Discussion

Prologue and *The Knight's Tale*, Parts I and II

A Question to Consider

How can you tell that someone is a hypocrite?

Discuss or write short answers to the following questions:

Text Analysis

1. How does Chaucer's *Prologue* show hypocrisy in some of the Canterbury pilgrims?
2. Which characters in the *Prologue* are the most hypocritical?
3. What are some examples of hypocritical characters from the *Prologue?*

Cultural Analysis

1. How does our culture view hypocrisy?
2. Why isn't our culture concerned about the hypocrisy of "spin"?

Biblical Analysis

1. How does the Bible define a hypocrite (Ps. 26:4; Mark 7:6; Matt. 6:2, 5, 16; 23:25–30)?
2. What does Jesus say about such hypocrisy in the religious leaders (Matt. 23:29–36)?

SUMMA

Write an essay or discuss this question, integrating what you have learned from the material above.

How is Chaucer's view of hypocrisy in the *Tales* more biblical than our culture's view of hypocrisy?

READING ASSIGNMENT:
The Knight's Tale, Parts III and IV

SESSION IV: DISCUSSION

The Knight's Tale, Parts III and IV

A Question to Consider

Near the end of *The Hobbit* the wizard Gandalf says to Bilbo Baggins, "Surely you don't disbelieve the prophecies because you had a hand in bringing them about yourself? You don't really suppose, do you, that all your adventures and escapes were managed by mere luck, just for your sole benefit? You are a very fine person, Mr. Baggins, and I am very fond of you; but you are only quite a little fellow in a wide world after all!" Is there such a thing as "luck" or "chance"?

Discuss or write short answers to the following questions:

Text Analysis

1. What is the *Knight's Tale* about?
2. How does Chaucer utilize "chance" in the *Knight's Tale?*
3. How does the story end up making fun of courtly love and chivalry?
4. What is the theme or moral of the *Knight's Tale?*
5. What is the tale's view of "chance" or fate?

Cultural Analysis

1. Does our culture have an "ideal" view of love like the courtly love of late medieval times?
2. What is our culture's view of "chance" and fate?

Biblical Analysis

1. What is the Bible's view of love (Eph. 5:21–33, 1 John 4:8)?
2. How is this view similar to or different from the courtly love ideal or our own culture's vision of love between a man and a woman?
3. What is the Bible's view of "chance" and fate (Eph. 1:11; Prov. 16:1, 9, 33; Eccles. 9:11; 1 Kings 22:13–40)?
4. What is the "destiny" of all God's people, and what has God promised about all their experiences, good and bad, in this life (Eph. 1:15–2:10)?

SUMMA

Write an essay or discuss this question, integrating what you have learned from the material above.

Does *The Knight's Tale* imply a biblical view of providence rather than a view of fate like ancient Greece or our modern culture?

READING ASSIGNMENT:
The Wife of Bath's Prologue

SESSION V: WRITING

da DUM/DUM DUM

Chaucer is the father of classic English poetry. He was the first English poet to write what came to be known as "rhyming couplets" (two lines of rhymed iambic pentameter). All Chaucer's tales except two (the prose *Tale of Melibeus* and *Parson's Tale*) are poetic (written in verse). All the verse narratives except *The Monk's Tale* are written in rhyming couplets or in stanzas of seven lines of iambic pentameter.

Poetic meter (language sound patterns in the verse) varies among languages and poetic traditions. Remember *Beowulf's* Old English (Anglo-Saxon) poetry was written in "alliterative verse," **four strongly stressed syllables that often alliterate** (repeat the same sounds) with no particular number of unstressed syllables. Here, for example, is line 188 from Heaney's translation of *Beowulf* with the four stressed syllables highlighted:

And **find friend**ship in the **fa**ther's em**brace**

Because of changes in the English language due to the influx of French- and Latin-based words after the Norman invasion of 1066, Middle and Modern English verse is based on the rhythm created by patterns of stressed and unstressed syllables. Each unit in a pattern is called a "foot." The meter made popular by Chaucer is called iambic pentameter: five (hence pentameter) iambs, which are feet with one unstressed syllable followed by one stressed syllable. Here, for example is the line in Chaucer's *Prologue* that introduces his description of the Knight with the five feet highlighted and the rhythm underneath (Coghill's translation):

There **was** a **Knight**, a **most** dis **tin** guished **man**,
(da **DUM**) (da **DUM**) (da **DUM**) (da **DUM**) (da **DUM**)

Technically, iambic pentameter refers to five iambs in a row, like the line above. However, in practice most poets, including Chaucer, vary some lines from a strict iambic pentameter in order to highlight important words or shifts in the poem and to create more interest in the overall rhythm of the poem. Chaucer often inverts the first iamb (to *DUM da*) and ends lines with *da DUM da*.

An excellent and beautiful example of varied iambic pentameter to emphasize meaning by changing rhythm is provided by the first four lines of a famous sonnet by seventeenth-century English poet John Donne:

Batter my **heart** three-**per**soned **God**, for **you**
As **yet** but **knock, breathe, shine** and **seek** to **mend**.
That **I** may **rise** and **stand o'erthrow** me and
bend
Your **force** to **break, blow, burn** and **make** me
new.

The rhythm here is:

DUM da/da **DUM**/da **DUM**/da **DUM**/da **DUM**
Da **DUM**/da **DUM/DUM DUM**/da **DUM**/da **DUM**
Da **DUM**/da **DUM**/da **DUM/DUM DUM**/dada **DUM**
Da **DUM**/da **DUM/DUM DUM**/da **DUM**/da
DUM

Notice how the poet stresses the key verb "batter" in the opening line with inversion—the first syllable is the stressed syllable in "batter." He then slows down the rhythm of the iambic pentameter in lines 2 and 4 with parallel rhythms that highlight what God does to the poet ("knock, breathe, shine and seek to mend") and what the poet asks God to do ("break, blow, burn and make me new"). Notice too how the last line is first slowed by the "break, blow, burn" (DUM / DUM DUM) rhythm, then speeds up to emphasize the conclusion "and make me new" (da DUM / da

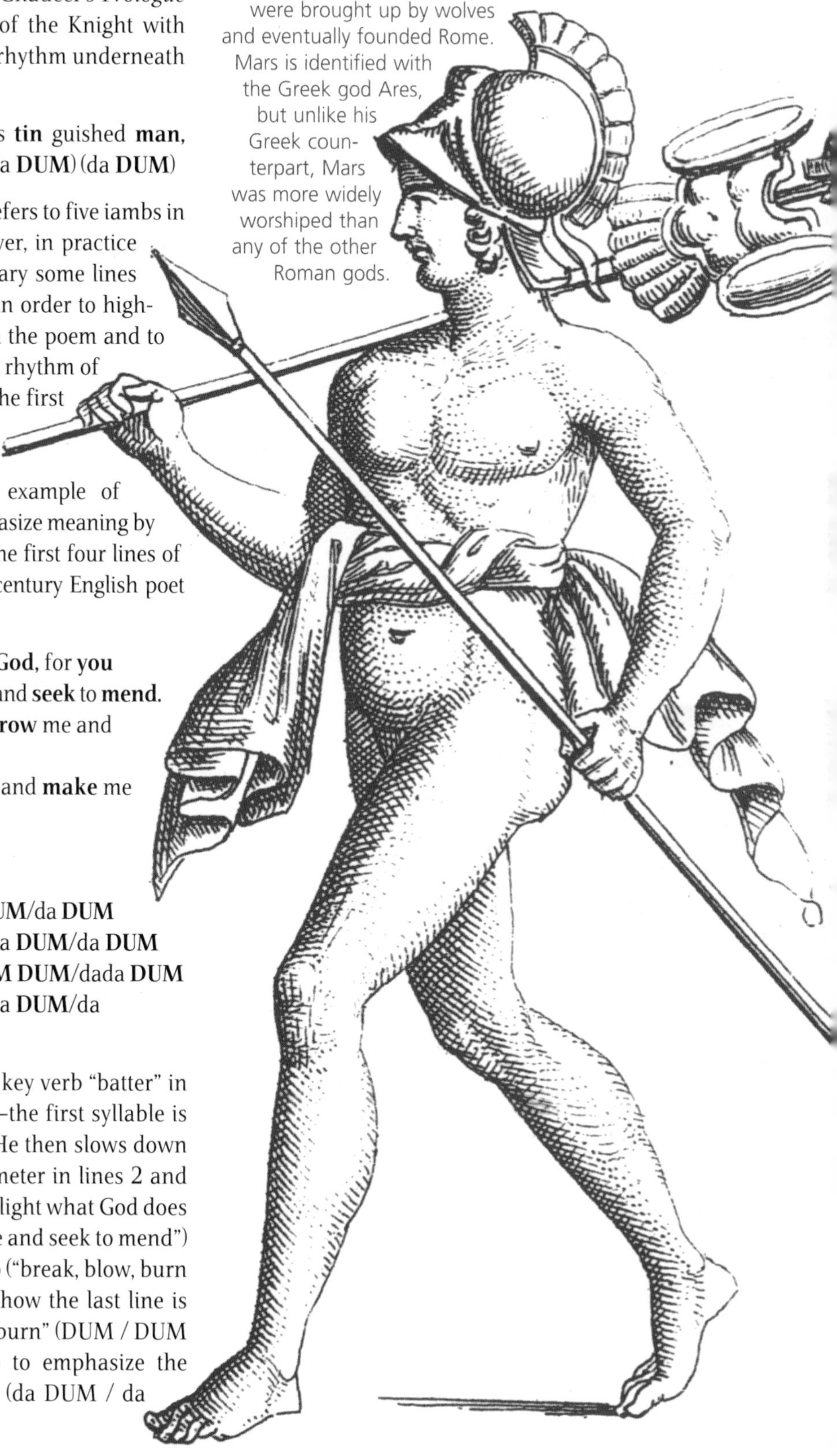

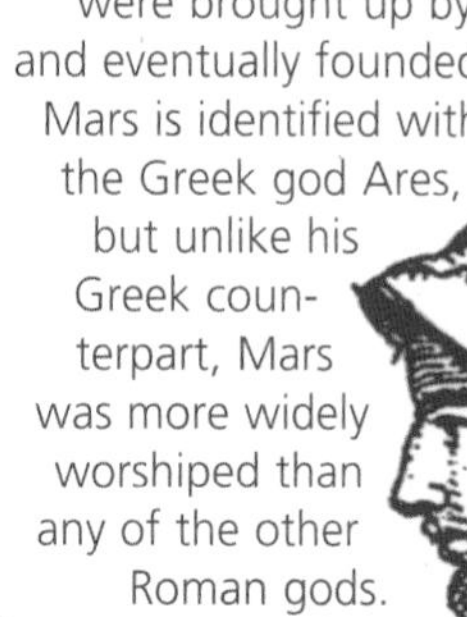

Mars, the Roman god of war and agriculture, raped the vestal virgin Rhea Silvia while she slept, and she gave birth to the twins Romulus and Remus. The boys were brought up by wolves and eventually founded Rome. Mars is identified with the Greek god Ares, but unlike his Greek counterpart, Mars was more widely worshiped than any of the other Roman gods.

DUM). Be sure to read the lines out loud to see for yourself how the rhythm in lines 2 and 4 first slows, then speeds up at the end.

Write at least seven lines of iambic pentameter vividly describing something about a person or thing in the manner Chaucer does in his Prologue. Vary the rhythm slightly for appropriate emphasis. You may choose the rhyme scheme. Suggestions include ababbcc, abababa, abcabca, abbcdda, abcdcba, aabbcca.

READING ASSIGNMENT:
The Wife of Bath's Tale

The Wife of Bath's prologue is twice as long as her tale. Alyson or Alys (she calls herself both) is a terrible old harridan, has had five husbands—defending her many marriages with biblical misquotes—and there are hints in the text that she may have murdered her fourth husband. A self-professed authority on men and women, she tells a story of a knight sent on a quest to find out what women want.

SESSION VI: RECITATION

The Wife of Bath's Prologue and *Tale*

Answer the following questions for factual recall:

1. Why does the Wife of Bath consider herself an authority on marriage?
2. Despite saying at the outset that "experience" will be her guide, how does the Wife of Bath then attempt to justify her "authority"?
3. How does she rate her five husbands?
4. How does the Wife of Bath say she manipulated her husbands?
5. Which of her husbands was the only one she ever loved, and why did she have trouble with him?
6. In *The Wife of Bath's Tale,* what is the crime that begins the story, and when (historical time period) does it occur?
7. How does the knight avoid the immediate penalty of beheading for his ghastly crime?
8. How successful is he in obtaining the answer by roaming throughout the country and posing the question to every woman he meets?
9. What happens when the knight heads home dejectedly without an answer as the day of judgment draws near?
10. How does the old woman save the knight's life?
11. After the knight's life is saved what does the old ugly woman do?
12. What does the old woman tell the knight when he admits he can hardly bear the shame of having such an ugly, lowborn wife?
13. What happens at the end of the tale?

READING ASSIGNMENT:
The Clerk's Tale, Prologue and Parts I-III

SESSION VII: ACTIVITY

Comedy

The word "comedy" means two different things in literature or stories. We usually think of comedy as something funny or humorous or satirical. That's one definition. The other is actually older, and it means the basic plot structure of all stories with a happy (rather than tragic) ending. That plot structure is built into all such stories because this is God's world. His story, which includes all the other stories in the world, has this same comedy plot structure, which is a U-shaped plot: the story begins in a good state, changes when bad or difficult things happen and ends in a better state because the difficulties are overcome and the good overcomes the bad.

We, of course, are in the midst of God's story in real life right now. After being in paradise, man rebelled against God. God, through the incarnation of Jesus Christ and the work of His Spirit, is now in the midst of redeeming the world to bring it to the eventual state of purity and goodness that we all long for. *The Canterbury Tales* as a whole is a comedy in this second sense of the word, because Chaucer sees God's good end and trusts in His ways, as he expresses it in the prose of *The Parson's Tale.* But the *Prologue* and many of the tales also are or contain much comedic writing in the first sense—funny or humorous or satiric.

There are many types of comedic writing, and most of these types can also be found in the Bible. Here are a few of the most important types.

Situation Comedy—humor "rooted in the external events of a story's plot . . .. It consists of embarrassing or inopportune occurrences, physical mishaps that strike us as funny ('slapstick comedy'), mistaken identity, misunderstanding, personality clashes and (at the lower end of the comic scale) comedy arising from sex . . . or other bodily functions."[2] Two favorite subsets of Situation Comedy include Slapstick and Personality Clashes.

Slapstick Comedy—physical mishaps (like the proverbial slipping on a banana peel). The Three Stooges are probably the classic example of slapstick comedy.

Comedy of Personality Clashes—conflicts or strained relations caused by personality clashes and gender or professional prejudices or rivalries.

Comedy of Human Nature (in Character Sketches and Portraits)—humor caused by the incongruities and foibles of universal, fallen, human nature.

Satiric Comedy—ridicule, rebuke or sarcasm which exposes vice or folly in human behavior, including inconsistencies between ideal and actual behavior.

Comic Irony—saying or doing one thing while meaning the opposite. Claiming something clearly contrary to fact or pretending a clear impossibility is possible.

Comic Verbal Wit—the most subtle form of humor "consists not in *what* the author portrays but in *how* he . . . portrays it. Here the humor arises from the cleverness with which the writer expresses things. Key ingredients are irony or incongruity, understatement, pun or wordplay, euphemism (a roundabout way of naming something) and parody (imitating a literary genre or work but with comic effect)."[3]

Below are several references to and descriptions of passages from The Canterbury Tales. *For each passage, identify which of the above comedic types applies. Please note that a passage may reflect more than one comedic type.*

1. Reread the *Prologue's* description of the Friar. Notice how depraved the Friar is, yet Chaucer the narrator says he is "a noble pillar to his [monastic] order."
2. In the *Prologue's* description of the Cook, Chaucer first expounds on all the different ways the Cook is skillful at his calling and then says in the last three lines about the Cook, in the original Middle English, "But greet harm was it, as it thoughte me, / That on his shine a mormal hadde he. / For blankmanger, that made he with the beste." A "mormal" was a festering, open sore that was hard not to scratch. "Blankmanger" was an elaborate "white" stew made of minced chicken, cream, rice, almonds and lots of spices that took much "hands on" preparation. So you can guess the grossness of what Chaucer is hinting at.
3. Reread the *Prologue's* description of the Monk. Notice how his life is governed by his passion for hunting, a "worldly" pursuit which monastic rules did not permit monks to undertake.
4. Reread the *Prologue* where it describes the Prioress. She has supposedly renounced worldliness in her position, "yet she is preoccupied with being fashionable in appearance and manners. The narrator claims that she is all conscience and tender heart, yet she caters to the dainty appetites of her dogs in a day of poverty."[4]

5. Think about what made the Wife of Bath's prologue and her tale humorous. One reason was herself, her life and character. She is a combination of character "types:" the domineering woman, shrewish wife and oversexed female.
6. The so-called "marriage group" of stories in *The Canterbury Tales* focus on, among other things, the nature of authority in marriage. These include *The Wife of Bath's Tale* and *The Clerk's Tale.* Most of the stories center on *extreme* examples pitted against one another. Some of the comedy of the *Tales* stems from this "battle of the sexes."
7. *The Nun's Priest's Tale* is the first and greatest mock epic in the English language, telling the story of Chanticleer and Pertelote. It treats a realistic farmyard event in the style of an ancient epic.

READING ASSIGNMENT:
The Clerk's Tale, Parts IV–VI

SESSION VIII: RECITATION

The Clerk's Tale

1. Who implores King Walter to get married and why?
2. When King Walter asks the poor but beautiful Griselda to marry him, what are the conditions she must agree to?
3. What wonderful personal qualities has Griselda always possessed that help to spread her fame to lands far and wide after her marriage to Walter?
4. After Griselda has their first child, a girl, what does the king decide to do to resolve any doubt about his wife's steadfastness?
5. Four years later Griselda bears her husband a son, and the people are happy that now there is an heir to the throne. When the son reaches the age of two, how does Walter again test the patience and fidelity of Griselda?
6. When the daughter reaches twelve years of age, Walter puts Griselda to one final test. What is it?
7. How does Griselda respond?
8. What does Walter do next and why?
9. How does their relationship end up?
10. At the end of the tale, what is the Clerk's commentary on women?
11. What does the Clerk then say to the wife of Bath and why?

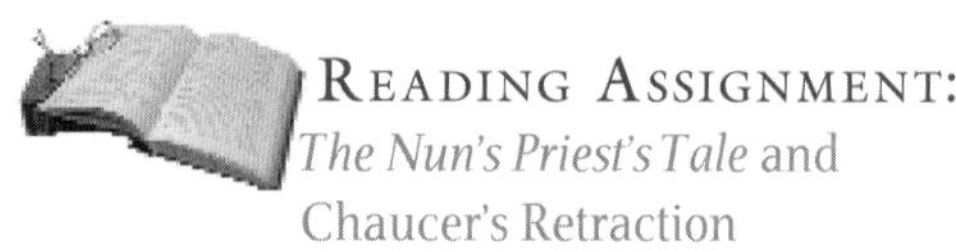

READING ASSIGNMENT:
The Nun's Priest's Tale and Chaucer's Retraction

SESSION IX: DISCUSSION

The Nun's Priest's Tale and Chaucer's Retraction

A Question to Consider

What makes a story funny?

Discuss or write short answers to the following questions:

Text Analysis

1. What kind of story is The Nun's Priest's Tale? (You might want to look up the word fableaux.)
2. Why is it funny that the main characters are a rooster and a hen?
3. What makes the characters of Chanticleer and Pertelote so funny?
4. What is funny about how the main action of the story is set up by Chaucer?
5. How does Chaucer use the translation of the Latin phrase by Chanticleer for comic effect?
6. How does Chaucer show the humor and danger of vanity in this story?

Cultural Analysis

1. What modern popular story medium largely began, and continues to be based loosely on, the idea and comedy of "beast fables"? (Hint: this medium started when "moving pictures" began in the early 1900s.)
2. How does our culture view the "battle of the sexes" and husband/wife relations? How does that view affect popular humor regarding the "battle of the sexes"?

Biblical Analysis

1. One of the amazing things about the Bible is how its historical narratives contain practically every type of story there is, including humorous stories and situations. This is not surprising when we think about it, however, since all stories man creates follow the patterns set by God's "Big Story" of

real life. Give an example of a "beast fable" type of narrative in the Bible that really happened (Num. 22-24).

2. Jacob and Boaz of the Old Testament are unexpectedly confronted with situations involving women in Genesis 29 and Ruth 3 respectively. What makes these situations humorous?
3. How does the Bible view the "battle of the sexes" (Eph. 5; 1 Pet. 3; Deut. 22:5; 1 Cor. 11:7; Matt. 5:28; 1 Tim. 2)?

Summa

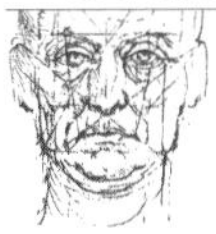

Write an essay or discuss this question, integrating what you have learned from the material above.

Why should we be thankful for the gift of humor in our fallen world?

Session X: Review

Grammar

1. What time of the year, and from where (including the name of the inn), does the pilgrimage to Canterbury begin?
2. What is the "bearing" of the knight, which is somewhat of a surprise given his extensive success on many foreign battlefields?
3. Why does Chaucer say that the Wife of Bath "knew the remedies for love's mischances"?
4. Given all of Chaucer's descriptions, which two pilgrims are most biblical or sanctified as evidenced in their actions, behavior and attitudes?
5. How does Chaucer say he is going to "give account" of all the pilgrim's stories?
6. In *The Wife of Bath's Tale*, how does the knight who raped a young maiden avoid the immediate penalty of beheading for his ghastly crime?
7. In *The Wife of Bath's Tale*, how does the ugly old woman save the knight's life?

Logic

Comparison of Tales

Fill in Chart 1.

Lateral Thinking

1. Argue whether the view of husband/wife relations in either *The Wife of Bath's Tale*, or *The Clerk's Tale*, or neither, is the biblical view of marital relationships.
2. Assuming the fictional Wife of Bath was never regenerated and never came to serve the Lord Jesus before she died, argue what circle of Dante's Hell she belongs in and why.

Chart 1: COMPARISON OF TALES

TALES	TYPE OF STORY	MORAL OF THE TALE	WHAT'S BIBLICAL ABOUT THE TALE	WHAT'S UNBIBLICAL ABOUT THE TALE
Knight's Tale	Courtly Romance	Man's foolish complaints and attempts to manipulate "fate"	The Providence of God is in control of all things and is good.	Confusion of Jupiter with the Triune God of Scripture
Wife of Bath's Tale	Exemplum (story with a moral point) Exemplum			
Clerk's Tale	Beast Fable			
Nun's Priest's Tale	(Comic Fable, Fableaux)			

Optional Session A: Activity

Humor in the Bible

Although God's Word is serious, it also has much humor in it. "Either to underemphasize its humor or overemphasize it distorts the Bible .... The humor of the Bible is not [usually] of the rollicking type but the subtle and intellectual type for which the term *wit* is often an accurate designation."[6] The Bible contains a wide array of literary types of humor, including Situation Comedy, Character Type Comedy, Satiric Humor and Ironic Humor.

Situation Comedy

1. Read Judges 3:12–30 and describe what makes the story about the Moabite king Eglon and Ehud the Israelite humorous.
2. Read the story about how Jacob meets Rachel in Genesis 29:1–12 and explain the humor in the story.

Character Type Humor

1. What makes the character of Jesus' disciple Peter humorous (Matt. 16:17–23, 26:34)?

Satire and Irony

1. Read Proverbs 19:13; 19:24; 22:13; 27:14; Ecclesiastes 10. Describe the humorous satire in these passages.
2. What is so funny in the story of Elijah's confrontation with the prophets of Baal on Mount Carmel in 1 Kings 18:20–40?
3. What does Aaron say that is so funny when Moses confronts him with his offense in carving the golden calf "with an engraving tool" in Exodus 32?

Optional Session B: Activity

A Mildly Medieval Movie

Watch the movie *A Knight's Tale*[10] and answer the following questions:

1. How does the movie mimic Chaucer's *Canterbury Tales?*
2. How does the movie emulate the style of Chaucer's *Knight's Tale?*
3. What other comedic devices similar to those used by Chaucer does the movie use?
4. What is Chaucer's role in the movie?
5. What two characters in the movie does Chaucer pledge to make infamous in his future story writing?
6. In what scene does the movie clearly portray the hero William as a Christ figure?
7. In what way, besides the happy ending for the hero, does the movie evidence a biblical worldview?

Endnotes

1 The Lollards were preachers who followed the pre-Reformation church reformer and Oxford professor John Wycliffe.
2 Ryken, Leland. *Realms of Gold.* Shaw: Wheaton, Ill., 1991. 47. Much of the information in this section is derived from Chapter 2 dealing with *The Canterbury Tales.*
3 Ryken, 55.
4 Ryken, 51–52.
5 *This endnote appears only in the teacher's edition.*
6 Ryken, Leland, et al., ed. *Dictionary of Biblical Imagery.* Downers Grove, Ill.: InterVarsity Press, 1998. 411. The material in this session is largely drawn from the entry for "Humor."
7 *This endnote appears only in the teacher's edition.*
8 *This endnote appears only in the teacher's edition.*
9 *This endnote appears only in the teacher's edition.*
10 Parents please note: this movie is rated PG-13. It has a couple of curse words (none using the Lord's name). There is no sexually suggestive nudity. There is a small amount of nudity from behind—Chaucer is naked when they meet him because he has lost everything, including his clothes. There is no frontal nudity. The average eighth grader might not be able to filter this material and discern all of the historical anachronisms—i.e., the modern elements that have been injected into the story. The teacher should carefully walk the students through it and analyze it or you should consider omitting it.

A woodcut depicting Martin Luther as an Augustinian monk.

Bondage of the Will

You're a soldier. But you weren't always one. You don't remember your parents; you had no brothers or sisters. You were found. You were an infant left to die on the side of the road, but an old, rich man found you. He took you to his castle and washed you. He fed you, he clothed you, and as you grew strong, he trained you. He taught you how to swing a sword. You trained for many years, working day and night. The old man taught you footwork, riding skills and how to wear your armor—a brilliant, shimmering silver and gold. But there were others. The lord had rescued many children, all left for dead, and he trained them all for battle. A great war had spread through all the lands, and as you trained you spent more time outside the castle, keeping the territory clear of the enemy.

One day when you and many others had left the castle, you came upon a skirmish. There across the plain, waving dark against the sky was the black mark of the enemy. Lines drew close, hands were poised, and the horses whinnied and snorted, anxious for the fray. Just when the first lunges of your forces pushed forward into their ranks, a great cry was heard down your line and the battle paused momentarily. An older soldier, with faded and damaged armor rode out in front of the knights of the lord.

"Halt!" he cried. "These are indeed the enemy, but there is a better way than fighting. If we are patient and discuss matters civilly, we shall soon find that they will come over to our side peacefully." But when he had said this, a young, brash knight rode out to meet him crying as he came,

"Fool! Idiot! We have nothing in common with these! The lord does indeed happily take refugees, and an offer of surrender should be made first. But if they will not, it is folly to debate. We have been trained to fight! All that we have is from the lord! It is good and right that we should show forth his kindness to us by obeying him here." But the older knight replied,

"Silence, young Turk! You have not yet learned to respect your elders! You have not been out on many expeditions, but for many years now, this has been our practice. All the great knights you've heard of have all followed this way. Stop your insolence and get back

A woodcut by Wittenberg's famous painter and printmaker Lucas Cranach (1472–1553) showing Luther in 1546.

into ranks! Certainly, the lord has given us many things, but that is a trifling matter. We are here now, and we must act in accordance to our situation now."

"No, you stupid mule! I have always respected my elders, and I have even respected you, but I refuse to let this drivel that you're spouting go unchecked. It is not a trifling matter whether or not we obey the lord. It is not a trifling matter to recognize that he has made us who we are. For if he has made us, then we owe him all that we are. And if you do not get out of my way now, I will be forced to strike you down first before I attack and finish off the enemy."

What do you do? Whose side do you take? Are you confident of your way? Do you follow the old, confident knight or the young, brash knight? You are about to find yourself in the middle of a similar conflict. So get ready to join the battle.

General Information

Author and Context

Martin Luther was born November 10, 1483, in Eisleben, Saxony. The second of what would eventually be four sons and four daughters, Martin was baptized the day after his birth in the Church of Saints Peter and Paul by Pastor Bartholomy Rennebecher. Luther began his formal education at a very early age as attested by the fact that, for at least the first few years, he was carried to school in Mansfield. He attended the Latin Grammar School for probably around ten years, studying the *trivium:* grammar, logic and rhetoric. Luther was able to read, write and speak Latin fluently before he was twelve years old. In addition to the academic training, wound through the curriculum was a thorough Christian education. Psalms and creeds were memorized; prayers were recited before and after meals, and he would have learned prayers of confession, the Lord's Prayer, as well as the Hail Mary. Luther spent several more years studying in various schools until he enrolled in Erfurt University when he was eighteen. He completed both a bachelor's degree and a master's degree in four years. And while at the university, Luther saw the Bible for the very first time in his life, "I was twenty years old before I had ever seen the Bible."[1]

Although he was qualified to begin teaching, he followed his father's advice and registered for the School of Law at Erfurt in the spring of 1505. However, his law career was to be short lived. While there may have been other causes, a lightning storm on

July 16 terrified Luther to such a degree that the next day he entered the Black Cloister of the Reformed Congregation of Augustinian Hermits in Erfurt. It is somewhat unclear if the lightening actually struck Luther or (as in some accounts) it struck a friend next to him, but however it happened, Luther later told a friend that when the thunderbolt struck he cried out, "Help, Saint Anna, I will become a monk!" And the next day he did.

He was formally accepted into Holy Orders in the fall, and by 1507 he performed his first Mass. While at the monastery he tirelessly studied Scripture and the church fathers and Saint Augustine in particular. Within a few years he was transferred to Wittenberg, Germany, where he lectured in philosophy and theology at the new university there. Luther, even during these early years, was recognized as a gifted man. He spoke confidently and with feeling. He, unlike many of the instructors of his day, aroused hope and faith and imagination in the hearts and minds of his hearers. In 1512 he was created a Doctor of Divinity, although he only reluctantly accepted the appointment. But it was on October 31, 1517, when Luther nailed his 95 theses on the church door that Luther's name began to become international. Although Luther was interested only in correcting what he originally saw only as a mistaken explanation concerning indulgences, it was like he kicked at a small clump of grass and unearthed an entire hornet's nest.

On the Babylonian Captivity of the Church, The Freedom of the Christian Man and numerous other letters, commentaries and devotionals came from the pen of Martin Luther. These thousands of pages are filled with energetic and pastoral exhortations, as well as serving as a written record of the growing fracture between himself and the Church of Rome. As the debates and trials heated to a boil, it became increasingly clear that he was dealing not merely with a sick appendage but a diseased and mortally ill body. Child bishops, immoral indulgence salesmen, obese cardinals, and stubborn blindness throughout the hierarchy of the church were increasingly repugnant to Luther. His works are consequently full of pope bashing and abuse mocking, two of Luther's most prized pastimes. He repudiated his monastic life in 1524, and the following year on June 13, he married Katharina von Bora, a runaway nun, whom he called "my Kate." His marriage was rather sudden, and he was ridiculed by many and even some fellow evangelicals. But his marriage to Kate appears to have been a great joy to him as he later said to a friend that he would not give up his wife for the whole kingdom of France or all the riches of the Venetians. His German Bible was published in 1534, and in his lifetime he saw the proliferation of the gospel in Germany.

As you will soon find out for yourself, Luther was a bold and tenacious man. He never had any use for beating around the bush, and he was not afraid to stand up to anyone even if it was the most powerful and influential man in the world. If Luther thought you were a cad, he would tell you straight out without blinking once. Luther was also a fighter, and he had no use for striking bargains with enemies. But Luther was not just an armed man with too much time on his hands. Luther was a man who loved the Triune God with all that he was, and perhaps the highest proof of that was his love for God's Word. He was not content to go about his business and see other churchmen blatantly disregarding the clear teaching of Scripture. Love is not love unless it defends the beloved against any hostile threat. Luther fought so fiercely, because he loved God and His Word so strongly.

Significance

The Bondage of the Will was a direct response to a shorter treatise by the eminent classical scholar Erasmus of Rotterdam. This treatise or "our friend the diatribe" as Luther mockingly refers to it, was entitled *On Freewill* and served as the kindling for Luther's bonfire. Erasmus was born sometime in the late 1460s in Rotterdam (as his name suggests). He, like Luther, joined the monastic life for a few years, but his interests were far more academic, and after seven years, he received permission to take a leave of absence, from which he never returned. In terms of immediate effect, Erasmus's treatise published in 1524 heralds the official breach between Erasmus and Luther. While Luther's teachings were condemned and denounced much earlier by many officials throughout the Church of Rome, including the pope himself, Erasmus was sympathetic to calls for reforming the church. Erasmus, like Luther, was very critical of the abuses in the church. He had made his own jabs at the increasingly rampant folly throughout the church, and he taught quite publicly in defense of returning to a simpler, catholic faith. But when Luther, in Erasmus's mind, began pushing past the major abuses, pursuing an open and flamboyant break with the Church of Rome, Erasmus could no longer hold back. There were also immense political pressures throughout the church for Erasmus to confront Luther. Many went so far as to accuse Erasmus of being a closet Lutheran because Erasmus had openly defended Luther in the first few years of the Reformation.

When Luther finally replied with *The Bondage of the Will* in December, 1525, it was nothing short of explosive. The energy and urgency with which he writes colors every page, and whereas Erasmus sought to critique something which he saw as peripheral and relatively unimportant, Luther lambastes Erasmus throughout, contradicting his ignorance and vacillating stances on the issue. For Luther, the debate over free will was nothing short of the gospel itself. Today, many regard *The Bondage of the Will* as Luther's finest work, both for its rhetorical diversity and its theological acumen or shrewdness. Luther is loud and punchy throughout the book, and he attacks at every angle with an ingenuity rarely equaled.

Summary and Setting

Surely one of the greatest historical events of Luther's era was the invention of the moveable type printing press. As early as 1460, the invention was being used to mass print Bibles, pamphlets and theological treatises. But this was nothing compared to what the Reformation would produce. In fact, it is quite likely that, apart from the printing press, you or I might never have even known the name Martin Luther. Moreover, many of the early theses, treatises and tracts that Luther wrote were published without Luther's knowledge or consent. Their printings poured throughout Germany, and the country was ablaze with the help of a few blocks of wood and some ink and paper.

Also significant to the historical setting is what modern historians have called the Renaissance. The term has been applied to the late Middle Ages because in some places there seems to have been some renewed interest in the literature and languages of antiquity. The cultures of Greece and Rome were revived by some, including Erasmus, and these students of the classics became known as humanists, lovers of the humanities: art, history, languages, literature, philosophy and theology. Whether or not there really was a "re-birth" of these studies, the academies of Luther's day were certainly filled with various influences that in one way or another were connected with the studies of these humanists. Some reacted against their teachings, and others sought to harmonize them with medieval theory and Scripture.

One late medieval example of this kind of study was *nominalism*, a theory propounded by a number of philosophers, but by William of Ockham in particular. Nominalism was a radical break and reaction away from the classical philosophy of Aristotle and Plato. Where Aristotle and Plato had taught that the world coheres or holds together because of "forms" (they differed as to where the forms were located), Ockham replied that there were no forms, only names. Rather than trying to locate common traits in some kind of spiritual or transcendent reality, Ockham said it was merely a function of language. Related to this was a very stark distinction between nature and grace, faith and reason. Nominalism, attempting to repudiate the "forms" of Hellenistic thought, divided the natural world from the supernatural world. In the natural world it was fitting and right to use reason and logic to study and describe its movement and attributes. When it came to heaven or God however, faith was necessary, and it was imperative that one not misapply these distinct tools or regions. This was a philosophy with growing adherence during the late 1400s and early 1500s, and we know that it was particularly popular at Erfurt University when Luther attended.

Luther was a medieval man. But when we say he was medieval, we're not just referring to his dates, the years that appear on his tomb. We're referring to the world he lived in. The medieval universe was not really any different from the one we live in today, but it was *looked at* differently. The assumptions and beliefs that were commonly held then were somewhat different from what you and I may be used to today. One significant difference was in the realm of authority and power. To medieval men and women, the grandest, all encompassing institution was the church. From birth to death, marriage, festivals, schools, laws and many courts, the church was at the center. Today if you were asked what the biggest, most important or powerful thing was, you might say, "The government," "the United States," "the United Nations" or some other court or civil authority. That is a significant difference between then and now. Very much related to the fact that medieval society was so centered on the life of the church, is also the fact that the world was seen in the light of the Christian faith. Not everything that was believed was true certainly, but the assumption that God runs and orders everything was widespread. But if God runs and orders everything then that means the world is a very personal place. Things happen because God or His messengers make them happen. Plagues and sickness, sin and wickedness, blessings and harvest and everything else might rightly be attributed to God and His messengers in the form of angels or demons (Ps. 78:49; 103:20-21; 104:4). The stars and planets which spin through the heavens are God's rulers of life (Gen. 1:16-18). One's destiny, gifts and talents might all be read in the stars, because the heavens declare the glory of God and their words go out through all the earth (Ps. 8:1-4). While we might think some of the ways these truths were applied seem silly, at its heart there was a true and lively faith in the God of the Bible. Related to this kind of faith was also a deep anxiety and fear. In the several centuries just prior to Martin Luther in particular, great evil had emerged in the Church of Rome, particularly in the pope and many of the other high church officials. These men not only waxed fat in their laziness and immoral indulgence, but they also used their positions in order to pilfer and steal from the very people they were supposed to be caring for and shepherding. Imagine if the position of pastor went to whoever could pay the highest price!

Adam and Eve by Peter Paul Rubens. In this painting Rubens captures the apostle Paul's teaching in 1 Timothy 2:14 that Eve was deceived but not Adam: "And Adam was not deceived, but the woman being deceived, fell into transgression." Adam reaches to stop his wife from sinning but the fox in the background, a symbol in Christian art for cunning and deception, tells us that the serpent's lie has already taken root in Eve's mind. After seeing his wife break the covenant with God, Adam also took the fruit and ate it, sinning on behalf of himself and all of mankind descending from him.

What if sometimes rich metropolitans purchased the pastorate for their twelve-year-old sons? You might laugh, but that's the kind of thing that was happening in Europe at this time. All manner of schemes and plots were hatched in the minds of these despicable churchmen, and holding the prize of salvation over the heads of their people, they enslaved many of them with the fear of damnation. This was the late medieval world of Luther, a world swirling with faith and fear, where in some ways they saw the world more clearly and in others were held down beneath the heavy burdens of tyranny.

Worldview

We are at war. Right now, we are on a battle field. What are you doing? Are you fighting? Maybe you're watching the fight from the sidelines. Maybe you're running away from the fray. Or perhaps you didn't even know there was a fight taking place. So you're sitting out in the middle of the field somewhere, dismembering daisies. But as Christians, we are at war. St. Paul says this when he writes to Timothy and exhorts him to fight the good fight of faith and to lay hold of eternal life (1 Tim. 6:12). That means to have faith is to be in a fight; to be faithful is to be a fighter. In another place Paul urges all Christians to put on the full armor of God (Eph. 6:11ff). Is Paul only joking? Does he mean for us only to wear the armor around the house, occasionally flexing and making witty remarks to the mirror? What good is a sword if it doesn't cut? What good is a shield if it does not fend? The Christian life is a life at war, and if we are to be faithful, we must join in the fray.

Luther's wife Katharina von Bora was a nun who had escaped from her convent by hiding in a barrel that had once held pickled fish. These are engravings of Luther and his wife based on paintings by one of the greatest German painters of the day, Lucas Cranach. Cranach and his son happened to live only a few doors away from the famous Reformer.

Perhaps one of the most striking things about *The Bondage of the Will* at the outset is Luther's tone and delivery, his rhetoric. Luther is at war. Luther swings his words around like a mace, and fires his language like arrows into a sea of roaring enemies. Luther does not write as though Erasmus is over for an afternoon tea. He writes as though Erasmus is a great enemy, and he charges into the fight with a battle cry piercing the air. This begins even in the introduction where Luther says that he hasn't responded to Erasmus's treatise sooner because "it struck me as so worthless and poor that my heart went out to you for having defiled your lovely, brilliant flow of language with such vile stuff" (I). Thus we have met Luther: brash and unrestrained in his disdain for what Erasmus has written. But he goes on, "I thought it outrageous to convey material of so low a quality in the trappings of such rare eloquence; it is like using gold or silver dishes to carry garden rubbish or dung." Luther cannot mock the treatise's value any more completely: It ought to be bagged several times and tossed into the "round file." Luther is at war. And closely related to Luther's bellicose berating is his confidence: "For though what you think and write about 'free-will' is wrong, I owe you no small debt of thanks for making me far surer of my own view . . .." Luther runs at Erasmus like David to Goliath, sure of his position and sure of his victory, yelling up at the intellectual giant, describing how he will cut off his head when he is finished (1 Sam. 17:45–47). Luther finishes his introduction assuring Erasmus of defeat: free will "is in a worse state than before [you wrote] . . .. It is like the woman in the Gospel; the more the doctors treat the case, the worse it gets . . .. But may I ask you, my dear Erasmus, to bear with my want of eloquence, as I in these matters bear with your want of knowledge." Erasmus has not only failed to defend his case, he has now actually worsened it. Luther knows that he stands on the truth, and he has not the slightest intention of doubting. He will see Erasmus dead on the field with his head lopped off, and whatever philosophical armies were arrayed to defend him will be made food for carrion-eaters.

Luther begins in this way and hardly lets up through the entire book. Why is Luther so riled up? What it so dangerous, so deadly, so appalling, that Luther is on the warpath against Erasmus? Erasmus has sought to play nice with the idol of free will. He, a Christian scholar and teacher, has been playing footsy with a demon under the table. Idols are for breaking and burning. Idols are for destruction. Idols are never friends, allies, living room decorations or lawn ornaments. Being nice, polite or even just indifferent to idols is absolutely forbidden by God (Ex. 20:4–6, Judg. 2:1–2, 1 John 5:21). Luther has found himself in contact with idolatry. He can do nothing but fight.

"Free will" is a buzzword. It's a big, shiny, *impotent* missile, an ice sculpture of a nuclear warhead. In certain dim lighting with snatches of a Hitchcock soundtrack whining in the background, it might seem a touch threatening, but out in the light of day it's nothing. I'd even say it's safe around children. The fact is that the Christian Church throughout the ages has always believed in the sovereignty of God. We have always believed that Jesus Christ is Lord, and we have always insisted that He is Lord of everything. From the deepest canyons at the bottom of the sea to the farthest reaches of the galaxies, Jesus Christ is the King of it all. Furthermore, we have always believed that God made everything and that it is His sheer pleasure and grace that keeps everything existing. The writer of Hebrews says that Jesus upholds all things by the word of His power. Remember how God made the world: He spoke. He spoke His Word which, as it turns out, is His Son! That's what John says: "[a] ll things were made through Him" (John 1:1–3). But how, we might wonder, does the Father speaking the Son make a brilliant world with starfish and zebras? The Bible says that this happens through the power of the Holy Spirit. The Holy Spirit is what makes things live (Gen. 2:7). The Holy Spirit is the One Who makes everything move and have colors and beauty (Ex. 31:3–5). We know that the Spirit was involved in Creation because He was there when it happened (Gen. 1:2, Job 33:4). And furthermore, we know that it is the Spirit Who makes us alive in Christ (1 Pet. 3:18). So what does this have to do with free will? Well, the question has to do with thank you cards. It has to do with whether you need to give thanks for anything. Given creation and given the fact that Jesus is King over everything, do we have any need to give thanks? The answer is obvious: We must be thankful for everything! We should be bursting with gratitude for everything. Take skin, for instance. We should be thankful for skin. Look at your skin. There it is. You're covered in it. Yep. And . . . it's waterproof. It's true. And what about dandelions? From unwanted weeds to fuzzy-headed flowers, how do they do that? And the list could go on and on forever: stars, rain, fingernails, the color blue, ice cream, sand, electricity, peanut butter and everything else that makes this world what it is. In the history of theology and philosophy, free will has been the ridiculous heading for all manner of ingratitude. Men, grasping and seizing after honor and glory, have refused to be thankful and have looked for ways to claim something for their very own selves.

But someone will say, "Sure, you listed all the good things, but what about the bad things?" Well, the Bible says God does those too. "I form the light and create darkness, I make peace and create calamity; I, the LORD, do all these things" (Isa. 45:7). It doesn't have to get more explicit than that, but the fact that there are calamities, the fact that there are "bad things" should make us pause and wonder for a moment *why* there are bad things. Our minds should immediately be drawn to the Fall. Adam and Eve sinned, and from that point on, we have all been under the curse of death and plagued by sin. So if you think about it, things could actually be a whole lot worse. In fact, they *should* be a whole lot worse. Life is a gift, and even hard lives and difficult providences are far better than we deserve. Evil and wickedness don't pose any threat to God's providence. Rather, they are still abundant blessings because God still "upholds" us by the Word of His power. That's what thankfulness means: we don't deserve it. Seen from this light, there really is no "problem of evil" as some fuzzy-headed philosophers have called it. Rather, the real problem, the real discrepancy is the good. How can a just God give wicked men anything good? How can a good God save evil men? Well, the name we usually give this is grace. It's the grace of God, the undeserved favor of God that gives us far better than we deserve day after day, every minute of our lives.

But what about freedom? How does the Spirit enliven the world, guiding every last, scattered detail to the perfect plan and counsel of God? We need to say several things here. First, the Spirit is not a puppeteer that He might force us to bend to His ends. God is not violent or coercive. This is the danger Luther sees in using the term "necessity." He does go on to use the term, but he recognizes its weakness first: "I could wish, indeed, that a better term was available for our discussion than the accepted one, *necessity,* which cannot accurately be used of either man's will or God's. Its meaning is too harsh, and foreign to the subject; for it suggests some sort of compulsion, and something that is against one's will, which is no part of the view under debate" (II.iv). We do not act and live and breathe out of *necessity* in the sense of compulsion or coercion. The Spirit working out the will of God in our lives does not make us schizophrenic. Rather, the will of God is like a waterfall, spilling out of the Triune fellowship. And we must remember that God is love. It is love that moves the world. It's the love of God overflowing in the Trinity that spills out, creating, upholding and guiding a world to perfection. So "necessity" really is a bad term; it sounds like something is being forced. But God is like a lover who woos his love to Himself. And God is the perfect Lover and woos not only us but every atom and molecule of creation. God works His will in the world by the power of His Spirit, winning and wooing the world with true love.

Secondly, we must assert that freedom is first and foremost an attribute of God. The Triune God is freedom and liberty *par excellence.* This means that anything keeping us from fellowship with God is keeping us from freedom. For our bodies to be free, for our minds and wills and affections to be free, we must be in communion with the Trinity. Sin and all of its effects are stocks and chains that bind us in our darkness. So we might speak of three kinds of freedom: There is freedom not to sin, freedom to sin or not, and freedom only to sin. Or we could put it another way: Adam had the option to die or not die (depending on his obedience or disobedience), we have only the option of dying, but when we are raised from the dead we will have only the option of living. We always have the ability to be what we are. We are always free within the confines of our nature, but if God is our standard of freedom, we simply are not there yet. Furthermore, as Luther points out, the freedom to only sin is not really any kind of freedom at all. It's a twisting of words to tell someone that they are free to be in jail. Therefore, there are really only two kinds of freedom: imper-

fect freedom that God gives His people in this life and perfected freedom in the resurrection. Apart from the saving grace of God all men are in bondage to sin and death.

Lastly, we must determine not to be cranky or meddlesome neighbors. We've all read stories and perhaps even had the opportunity to live next door to a crank who delights to hear juicy tidbits of information from your home, and from these scraps they concoct all manner of ridiculous and half-baked stories. Of course, no one in his right mind wants to do that. The problem is that sin is not operating out of a right mind. Sin is not exactly clear thinking or healthy living. Too many people, Christian and non-Christian alike, have spent far too long peering into the physics of freedom and sovereignty. We must not be like the Nominalists, dividing faith from reason as though they apply to different worlds. Faith is true reason in heaven and earth, and all godless reason is folly. And in faith, we have very clear things like creation and the Lordship of Jesus. We also have His covenant with us, which means that we are God's people and that He always fights for us. We need to have faith in what we have been given and not pry into the secret counsels of God. We must not be meddlesome. We know that God has secret counsels; He does not tell us everything. "Remember the former things of old, For I am God, and there is no other; I am God, and there is none like Me, Declaring the end from the beginning, And from ancient times things that are not yet done, Saying, 'My counsel shall stand, And I will do all My pleasure'" (Isa. 46:9–10). But God doesn't just keep us in the dark. He doesn't tell us to seek Him in vain, as though He were telling us one thing while His will was working out a different plan behind the scenes. God doesn't tell us to step forward and then laugh after he has pushed us down the stairs. God is not a deceitful parent. God is a faithful father who has adopted us and claimed us as His people in His covenant with us. "The secret things belong to the LORD our God, but those things which are revealed belong to us and to our children forever, that we may do all the words of this law" (Deut. 29:29). God has given us His law. He has given us His Word which we know to be trustworthy, and thus we have no reason to fear if we believe. It is only the ungodly, the wicked and the rebellious who have to fear. To them God is terrible. God will mock their follies, and He will wait for them in secret and destroy them in their evil ways. But He delights to save and to have mercy, as He has shown Himself to us. How and who and when He saves are His own secret counsels, but we know that He has shown Himself to us, and we will never be put to shame.

A woodcut attacking the Roman Church by showing Luther's preaching as pointing to Christ but Roman teaching being that of the Antichrist. Martin Luther knew that only a small fraction of the public could read his writings, so he collaborated with Lucas Cranach. Their work together helped establish a deep friendship, with Luther being named godfather to Cranach's daughter Anna.

We began by talking about fighting. *The Bondage of the Will* is Luther's great assault on Erasmus and many of the philosophers of his day whom he refers to as Sophists. And Luther never backed away. In his *Table Talk*, a collection of devotionals and commentary, he says, "Erasmus of Rotterdam is the vilest miscreant that ever disgraced the earth."

And later, "Whenever I pray, I pray for a curse upon Erasmus." And finally, "I hold Erasmus of Rotterdam to be Christ's most bitter enemy." These are scathing words for the most celebrated teacher of his day. How can Luther—the great reformer—write these things? Isn't it unloving? Isn't it unkind? Obviously, we know that Martin Luther was a man, and as such he erred and sinned like the rest of the descendants of Adam. And it's certainly possible that he may have overstepped some line of Christian charity somewhere in his discourse with Erasmus. But at least in what we have read here and what you will read in *The Bondage of the Will,* it does not seem likely that Luther has overstepped. Luther is defending nothing less than the Lordship of Jesus Christ. But someone might say, it's all well and good for Jesus to be Lord, but that doesn't mean that God makes everything happen. But it does. Because if there is *any* area that is somehow outside of God's will, then it does not have to bow the knee to Christ. And furthermore it must not have been created by God. But both of these statements are contrary to the Scriptures (Phil. 2:10; Ps. 145:10; 148; John 1:3). As we noted earlier, all attempts to find some thing, some place or some situation that is somehow outside of God's providence are attempts to find something for which we do not have to be thankful. But not only is this incredibly arrogant, it's also quite rude. God made everything, us included, and we should not be looking for ways to get out of saying "thank you." Quite the contrary, we ought to be looking for ways to be more thankful. We ought to be looking for more areas in our lives that are gifts from God, because all of it is.

Philip Melanchthon, a close friend of Martin Luther and a professor of New Testament at Wittenberg University, drafted the *Augsburg Confession* for the Lutheran Lords and Free Territories. Albrecht Dürer's engraved portrait of Luther's fellow-reformer, Melanchthon, was made in 1526.

This is Luther's fight. This is the point of the scathing remarks and review. Luther loves God, and wants to give Him thanks. He's not just calling names to make himself feel big. And we, no less than Luther, need to strive for this kind of love, a love that defends and fights for the right and privilege to give thanks to God. Too often we believe that being a Christian simply means "being nice." But the fact of the matter is that being a Christian means being Christ-like. Read the gospels. Christ wasn't exactly the most peaceful fellow. Everywhere he went he was starting controversies, offending people and calling names. Christ was at war. And if Christ was at war, that means we are in a war. We are in the same war, the same that Christ was in, the same that Luther was in. Since the fall of Adam and Eve, and especially since the life, death and resurrection of Jesus, the history of mankind can be divided into two: the kingdom of God and the kingdom of man. St. Augustine described these in terms of two cities. These two cities are at continual war, and the central reason for war is who all praise and glory ought to go to. The City of God is insistent that the Triune God is the rightful object of all praise and glory, but the City of Man in various and sundry ways wants to give bits and pieces (and some times large chunks) of praise to men and creatures. This is the battle that you are in, and you are charged by God to fight (1 Tim. 6:12, Eph. 6:11-18). You do not have the option of not fighting. When Christians lay down their arms, they are like Erasmus or the old knight, hoping for peace, considering the truth a trivial thing. But not only is this cowardly, it is also treacherous. We have our orders, and disobedience is treason to the crown. We must fight like Luther. We must fight like the young knight. We must fight by loving God's law and obeying His commands. We must fight by denouncing all attempts at ingratitude and pettiness in ourselves and others. And we must fight by determining ourselves to worship the Triune God with His people on the Lord's Day, and from there, to be full of thanksgiving for all things in every moment of our lives: in our thoughts, in our words, in our actions and way down into our bones.

—Toby Sumpter

For Further Reading

Gritsch, Eric W. *Martin—God's Court Jester: Luther in Retrospect.* Philadelphia: Fortress Press, 1983.

Hazlitt, William, ed. *Table Talk of Martin Luther.* London: George Bell & Sons, 1909.

Spielvogel, Jackson J. *Western Civilization.* Seventh Edition. Belmont, Calif.: Thomson Wadsworth, 2009. 373-383.

Veritas Press History Cards: Middle Ages, Renaissance and Reformation. Lancaster, Pa.: Veritas Press. 27.

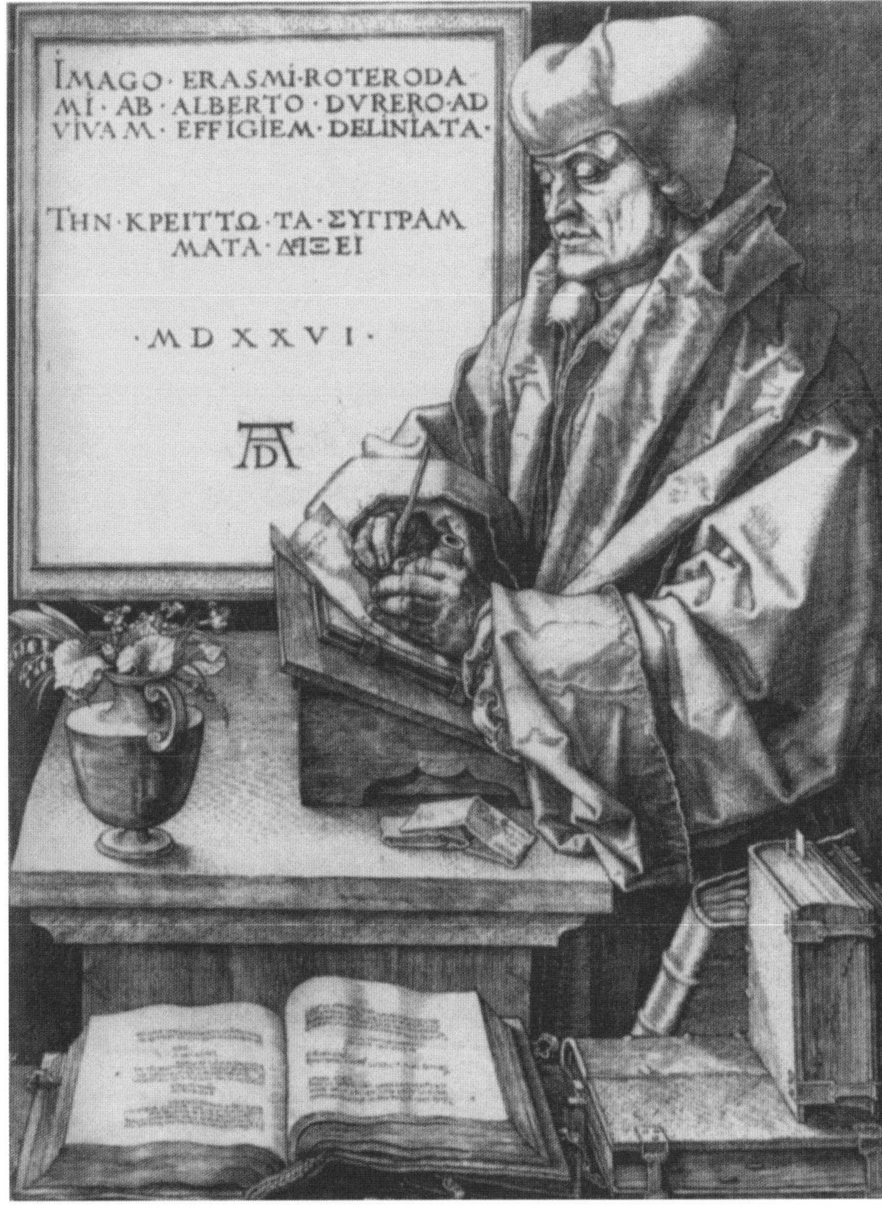

Albrecht Dürer met Erasmus several times and sketched him on his travels but did not make this engraving until many years later, and only then because a close friend urged him. Yet Erasmus had a great admiration for Dürer, whom he praised as the greatest of graphic artists. *Erasmus of Rotterdam* was Dürer's last engraving.

SESSION I: PRELUDE

A Question to Consider

What is the difference between freedom and slavery? How are they related?

From the General Information above answer the following questions:

1. What does it mean to be "medieval?"
2. What sort of man was Martin Luther?
3. How might the Renaissance have affected the debate between Erasmus and Luther?
4. How are Creation and Kingship related to thank you cards?
5. What does it mean to act like a Christian? How has this been misunderstood?
6. How should Christians fight ingratitude?

READING ASSIGNMENT:
Chapters I–II.iii

SESSION II: DISCUSSION

Chapters I–II.iii

A Question to Consider

Are free will and the sovereignty of God peripheral (unimportant) issues for living a faithful Christian life?

Discuss or list short answers to the following questions:

Text Analysis

1. What is Luther's general opinion of Erasmus's treatise *On Freewill* (I)?
2. Why is Luther writing a response to Erasmus (I)?
3. Why are "assertions" important (I)?
4. What is the perspicuity of Scripture? How many kinds are there (II.ii)?
5. How important does Luther think a true understanding of free will is (II.iii)?

Cultural Analysis

1. How does our modern culture view truth and assertions?
2. How are modern assumptions about the perspicuity of the world revealed in their assertions about truth?
3. What does our modern culture believe freedom or free will is?
4. While there is a lot less actual enslavement (men owned by other men as property) in our world today, what are some modern forms of slavery in our culture?

Biblical Analysis

1. Read 1 John 3:14–24. Can Christians be sure of anything?
2. The writer of Hebrews exhorts us to be "established by grace" (Heb. 13:9). How does grace make us confident?
3. According to the Bible are people automatically born free? Where does freedom come from?
4. What's the connection between the slavery of sin and the bondage of physical enslavement? Give examples from Scripture. (Ex. 1, 2 Kings 21, 23)

SUMMA

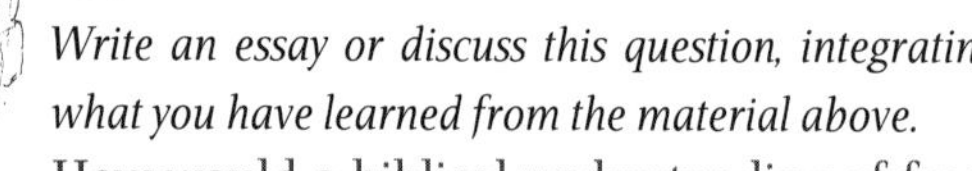

Write an essay or discuss this question, integrating what you have learned from the material above.

How would a biblical understanding of freedom effect political and social concerns (e.g. socialism, poverty, abuse) in our modern culture?

READING ASSIGNMENT:
Chapter II.iv–x

SESSION III: DISCUSSION

Chapter II.iv–x

A Question to Consider

What is "necessity?"

Discuss or list short answers to the following questions:

Text Analysis

1. What is Luther's opinion of the term "necessity" (II.iv)?
2. What two kinds of necessity do the "Sophists" distinguish, and what does Luther think of the distinction (II.iv)?
3. Why, according to Luther, is the foreknowledge of God so important (II.iv, vi)?

4. What disadvantages does Erasmus see in proclaiming the foreknowledge of God (II.vi)?
5. What are the two reasons Luther gives in defense of proclaiming the foreknowledge of God (II.vii)?
6. What do most people think free will is, according to Luther (II.ix)?

Cultural Analysis

1. Why do some moderns have difficulty with the foreknowledge of God?
2. According to modern culture, are people basically good or evil? How might that influence their reactions to the doctrine of foreknowledge?
3. Historically, there has been a lot more continuity between generations, sons following in the general steps of their fathers. What does modernity think of that? How could that have correlation to a lack of any doctrine of foreknowledge?

Biblical Analysis

1. Read Ecclesiastes 3. From beginning to end, how much of history does God know and do? How should we respond to this?
2. Given the fact that many moderns don't like the doctrine of foreknowledge due to their "high" view of the nature of man (being basically good), how might God's foreknowledge of the murder of Jesus persuade them that God can be trusted (Acts 2:22–36)?

Summa

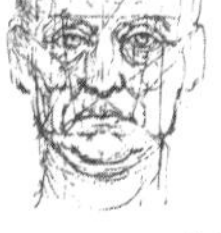

Write an essay or discuss this question, integrating what you have learned from the material above.

Why are necessity and the foreknowledge of God wonderful truths?

Reading Assignment:

Chapter III.i–iii

Session IV: Writing

Chapter III.i–iii

Limericks on Erasmus

Write a limerick (or several) making fun of Erasmus of Rotterdam. One rhetorical device (among many) that Luther employs is satire. You ought to have some fuel by now from Luther, who hardly writes a page without taking a jab at the foolishness or inconsistencies of Erasmus. A limerick is a short poem of five lines which roughly follows an anapestic meter (having a metric foot characterized by two short syl-

A woodcut by Cranach from a book by Luther, called *Passional of Christ and Antichrist,* showing a hypocritical and corrupt papacy.

lables followed by a long one) and a rhyme scheme of AABBA. You should pick one or two specific things that Erasmus says that are worthy of satire. Here are two examples below to get you thinking.

Erasmus was a brainy phantasm
Who echoed like a towering chasm
Though many would follow
His words would ring hollow
As he spewed them out with a spasm

Now you try. Have fun!

READING ASSIGNMENT:
Chapter III.iv–vi

SESSION V: ACTIVITY

Chapter III.iv–vi

Debate

Divide the class into two teams. One side will argue for an Erasmian stance on free will and necessity while the other side will argue for a Lutheran stance. Each team should assign each student to contribute to at least one of the phases of the debate as follows:

Opening remarks (stating central position and defense)
Attack (based on history)
Defense (based on history)
Attack (based on reputation and outcome)
Defense (based on reputation and outcome)
Open questions and argumentation
Concluding remarks and exhortation

Each portion of the debate should be timed, and speakers should not be allowed to go over two minutes (though they may stop short if they wish). A coin may be tossed to see which team opens, but both teams send their representative up for each section of the debate. Remarks may be scripted, but the best orators will be able to make a coherent presentation and respond to anything already mentioned in the opposition's argumentation.

If class size is smaller or you are in a homeschool setting, one student may take more than one portion (or all) of the parts of the debate. Or if class size is fairly large, a third or fourth team might be created and assigned one of the sides of the debate as well. A moderator might also be chosen or other students might play the part of an active audience that cheers and boos at appropriate places. If time is watched carefully, the debate should last only 30–40 minutes.

After the closing remarks a judgment should be made (by either the teacher or a vote of the class) to decide which team argued most persuasively. After the judgment is rendered, take time to explore the content of the arguments as well.

READING ASSIGNMENT:
Chapter IV.i–vi

SESSION VI: DISCUSSION

Chapter IV.i–vi

A Question to Consider

What is the meaning of a word? What determines its meaning?

Discuss or list short answers to the following questions:

Text Analysis

1. What is Luther's objection to Erasmus's definition of free will (IV.i)?
2. How has Erasmus contradicted himself in setting forth his definition of free will (IV.i)?
3. What are the three types of free will that Erasmus outlines? What does Luther make of these three options (IV.iii)?
4. How does Ecclesiasticus fail to defend free will according to Luther (IV.vi)?

Cultural Analysis

1. How does our culture use words?
2. What are some ways that our culture abuses words?
3. Words sometimes vary in meaning (e.g., draw, space, state). But how can this truth be abused?

Biblical Analysis

1. How sure is God's word to us? (Isa. 40:8, Ps. 119:89, 1 Pet. 1:23–25)
2. If Jesus is the Word of God (John 1:1), what does that teach us about language in general?
3. How is linguistic relativism an attack on creation?

Summa

Write an essay or discuss this question, integrating what you have learned from the material above.

How might a biblical view of words and their meanings equip Christians to be more effective when interacting with the unbelieving culture?

Reading Assignment:
Chapter IV.vii–xii

Session VII: Analysis

Chapter IV.vii–xii

Compare and contrast the views of Pelagius and Luther on various topics by completing Chart 1. Throughout *The Bondage of the Will,* Luther compares Erasmus to Pelagius and at times accuses him of being worse! Now see for yourself. After you have filled in Luther's side of the chart, discuss where you think Erasmus would fall on these issues.

Reading Assignment:
Chapters IV.xiii–V.iii

Session VIII: Recitation

Chapters I–IV

Comprehension Questions

Answer the following questions for factual recall:

1. What does Luther think of Erasmus's treatise *On Freewill?*
2. Why must Christians delight in assertions?
3. What is the perspicuity of Scripture?
4. What are the two kinds of perspicuity that Luther describes?
5. Why is believing in the foreknowledge of God necessary for salvation?
6. What does Erasmus believe the disadvantages are to teaching people about the foreknowledge of God?
7. Why, according to Luther, is a will without grace not free?
8. What does Luther make of Erasmus's argument from antiquity?
9. What is Erasmus's first definition of free will?
10. How does Erasmus contradict his own definition of free will?

Reading Assignment:
Chapter V.iv–x

Session IX: Writing

Chapter V.iv–x

Creative Writing

In this section, Luther tangles with Erasmus on some of the inter-workings of free will and foreknowledge. He particularly covers how men can do evil without God being guilty of their sins, the discontinuity of free will and foreknowledge, and God's supreme rule and right to do as He pleases. Paul covers many of the same themes in the book of Romans, and he finishes his discourse on the subject with a doxology of praise to God (Rom. 11:33–36) and exhorts his readers to humbly serve God and their neighbors (Rom. 12). This means that our response to the doctrines of predestination and foreknowledge needs to always begin with rejoicing and praise, and it should always be followed by humble obedience.

Write a short story (1,000–1,500 words) in which thankfulness and gratitude are the hinge upon which the resolution rides. The conflict or problem can be of your own choosing, but let thanksgiving be the power of resolution. Do your best not to let the story seem tacky or gooey. A well-crafted story ought to be a pleasure to read, and the theme of gratitude should be woven into the plot carefully. Nevertheless, make it clear that thankfulness is the hero.

Reading Assignment:
Chapter V.xi–xiv

Chart I: **COMPARING AND CONTRASTING PELAGIUS AND LUTHER**

TOPIC	PELAGIUS	LUTHER
Adam and his sin	Adam was created innocent, and when he sinned he became a bad example to the human race. But Adam's sin was not passed down through the generations. Natural man at birth is just like Adam was	
Natural man	created, wholly innocent and without sin. Christ came to inaugurate a good example to counteract the	
Christ	"bad influence" of Adam's sin. Christ shows men how they too can seek God and please Him by imitating Christ. The Cross is a great example of love and self sacrifice. The Resurrection does not affect anyone other than Jesus, but it	
The Cross and Resurrection	is a picture of how goodness overcomes evil. Grace is creation. God does aid and help us, but He does this through natural revelation and common grace. He gives us food and blessings, and these help us to turn ourselves to	
Grace	God. Justification is by faith alone, but justification only means to have any sins you may have committed forgiven. It doesn't change a person's nature; it just gives you that clean slate	
Faith alone	again. Good works are the ladder by which any man may pursue God and attain eternal salvation. A life of poverty and asceticism is a particularly good way to	
Good works	encourage the good works that are necessary for salvation. The law teaches us how to please God so that we may be saved. The law of Moses can save someone just as ably as the gospel of Jesus. Both show men the way to please God	
The Law	and follow Him. Death is a natural part of creation. Adam would have died whether or not he sinned.	
Death		

Session X: Discussion

Chapter V.xi–xiv

A Question to Consider

How do we know that what we believe about Jesus is true?

Discuss or list short answers to the following questions:

Text Analysis

1. Why does Luther accuse Erasmus of making Paul into a laughing-stock (V.xi)?
2. What does Luther think of Jerome's use of the Scriptures (V.xi)?

3. How do the New Testament writers use Old Testament passages? What should this teach us about interpreting Scripture (V.xi)?
4. What is the difference between what we "ought" to do and what we "can" do? Why is this distinction important in Luther's discussion (V.xi)?
5. How does a simile "halt" (V.xii)?
6. What is Luther's central complaint with Erasmus's use of the Bible (V.xiv)?

Cultural Analysis

1. What does our contemporary culture think of the Bible?
2. In the Roman Catholic Church and in the Eastern Orthodox Church, tradition is held to be just as important as Scripture and often even more important. As a result, doctrines like the veneration of icons (praying and bowing to pictures of saints), the absolute authority and infallibility of the pope, purgatory and distorted views of the Lord's Supper are embraced. How do Protestants view tradition with regard to the authority of Scripture?
3. The doctrine of the supremacy and sufficiency of Scripture is often referred to as the doctrine of *sola scriptura,* which means "Scripture alone." How might a hearty embrace of this teaching effect our modern culture? In what ways does the authority and sufficiency of Scripture affect art, music, entertainment and politics?

Biblical Analysis

1. Read Matthew 15:1–9. What is Jesus' complaint with the scribes and Pharisees?
2. Read 2 Thessalonians 3:6–15. How can we be sure we're not missing any vital information (traditions) concerning the Christian faith that is not in Scripture?
3. In 2 Thessalonians 2:15, Paul exhorts his readers to keep all the traditions that he delivered to them whether in word or epistle. How is this yet another assurance that Scripture is sufficient?
4. What is Scripture promised to be capable of doing (2 Tim. 3:14–17)?

Summa

Write an essay or discuss this question, integrating what you have learned from the material above.

What is *sola scriptura,* and how does Luther display it in his confrontation of Erasmus?

Reading Assignment:
Chapter VI.i–iv

Session XI: Discussion

Chapter VI.i–iv

A Question to Consider

What is sin?

Discuss or list short answers to the following questions:

Text Analysis

1. What does Jerome say that "flesh" means in Scripture (VI.i, iv)?
2. Why does Luther say that good works are incapable of preparing someone for the grace of God (VI.iii)?
3. What does Luther say that "flesh" and "spirit" refer to (VI.iv)?
4. What does Erasmus insist that the "spirit" is (VI.iv)?
5. Why is Erasmus's view of "spirit" absurd (VI.iv)?

Cultural Analysis

1. In what ways does our culture pretend that it's doing fine without God?
2. What is the difference between trendy outcasts (the kid at the mall dressed in clothes meant to make them look fashionably grungy) and the real outcasts (whose clothes are tattered because they can't afford new ones)? Why should it matter to Christians?

Biblical Analysis

1. Jesus says that He did not come for the righteous (Matt. 9: 12–13), but in Romans, Paul says that there are none righteous (Rom. 3:10–11). Is there anyone that Jesus did not come for?

2. Why is it necessary that Christians insist upon pointing out the sinfulness of man? (Rom. 5:20–21)
3. What is the biblical doctrine of Original Sin? (Rom. 3:9, 23; 5:12; 1 John 1:8; Gal. 3:22)

Summa

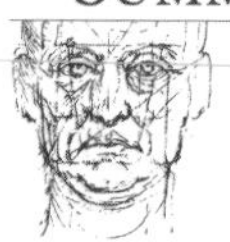

Write an essay or discuss this question, integrating what you have learned from the material above.

Why is the doctrine of man's fallen nature (or Original Sin) so important for the world?

Reading Assignment:
Chapter VI.v–ix

Session XII: Recitation

Chapters V–VI

Comprehension Questions

Answer the following questions for factual recall:

1. How does the Diatribe evade the force of the clearest passages from Scripture concerning free will and God's sovereignty?
2. What, according to Luther, is Erasmus' "prettiest thought"?
3. What is Luther's response to Erasmus's charge that Luther's God is "absurd"?
4. How does Luther say God hardens man?
5. What is the "sound sense" that the Diatribe finally suggests?
6. What are the two kinds of necessity that Luther delineates? Which is he trying to defend?
7. How does Erasmus show "little reverence for the majesty of the Holy Ghost"?
8. Are men able to prepare themselves for the grace of God?
9. Why should we try to do anything at all if God is in control of everything?
10. How does Erasmus interpret John 15:5? What does Luther think?

Reading Assignment:
Chapter VII.i–iv

Session XIII: Writing

Chapter VII.i–iv

Poetry

Here is the poem "The Hound of Heaven" by Francis Thompson. Read the poem aloud and discuss it, beginning with the questions that follow:

The Hound of Heaven

I fled Him, down the nights and down the days;
I fled Him, down the arches of the years;
I fled Him, down the labyrinthine ways
Of my own mind; and in the mist of tears
I hid from Him, and under running laughter.
Up vistaed hopes I sped;
And shot, precipitated,
Adown Titanic glooms of chasmèd fears,
From those strong Feet that followed,
followed after.
But with unhurrying chase,
And unperturbèd pace,
Deliberate speed, majestic instancy,
They beat—and a voice beat
More instant than the Feet—
"All things betray thee, who betrayest Me."
I pleaded, outlaw-wise,
By many a hearted casement, curtained red,
Trellised with intertwining charities;
(For, though I knew His love Who followèd,
Yet was I sore adread
Lest, having Him, I must have naught beside.)
But, if one little casement parted wide,
The gust of his approach would clash it to:
Fear wist not to evade, as Love wist to pursue.
Across the margent of the world I fled,
And troubled the gold gateways of the stars,
Smiting for shelter on their clangèd bars;
Fretted to dulcet jars
And silvern chatter the pale ports o' the moon.
I said to Dawn : Be sudden—to Eve: Be soon;
With thy young skiey blossoms heap me over
From this tremendous Lover—
Float thy vague veil about me, lest He see!
I tempted all His servitors, but to find
My own betrayal in their constancy,
In faith to Him their fickleness to me,
Their traitorous trueness, and their loyal deceit.

To all swift things for swiftness did I sue;
Clung to the whistling mane of every wind.
But whether they swept, smoothly fleet,
The long savannahs of the blue;
Or whether, Thunder-driven,
They clanged his chariot 'thwart a heaven,
Plashy with flying lightnings round the spurn
o' their feet:—
Fear wist not to evade as Love wist to pursue.
Still with unhurrying chase,
And unperturbèd pace,
Deliberate speed, majestic instancy,
Came on the following Feet,
And a Voice above their beat—
"Naught shelters thee, who wilt not shelter Me."
I sought no more that after which I strayed,
In face of man or maid;
But still within the little children's eyes
Seems something, something that replies,
They at least are for me, surely for me!
I turned me to them very wistfully;
But just as their young eyes grew sudden fair
With dawning answers there,
Their angel plucked them from me by the hair.
"Come then, ye other children, Nature's—share
With me" (said I) "your delicate fellowship;
Let me greet you lip to lip,
Let me twine with you caresses,
Wantoning
With our Lady-Mother's vagrant tresses,
Banqueting
With her in her wind-walled palace,
Underneath her azured daïs,
Quaffing, as your taintless way is,
From a chalice
Lucent-weeping out of the dayspring."
So it was done:
I in their delicate fellowship was one—
Drew the bolt of Nature's secrecies.
I knew all the swift importings
On the wilful face of skies;
I knew how the clouds arise
Spumèd of the wild sea-snortings;
All that's born or dies
Rose and drooped with; made them shapers
Of mine own moods, or wailful or divine;
With them joyed and was bereaven.
I was heavy with the even,
When she lit her glimmering tapers
Round the day's dead sanctities.

A linocut by Edward Knippers that seems to illustrate well Martin Luther's declaration: ". . . '[F]ree-will' without God's grace is not free at all, but is the permanent prisoner and bondslave of evil, since it cannot turn itself to good."

I laughed in the morning's eyes.
I triumphed and I saddened with all weather,
Heaven and I wept together,
And its sweet tears were salt with mortal mine;
Against the red throb of its sunset-heart
I laid my own to beat,
And share commingling heat;
But not by that, by that, was eased my
human smart.
In vain my tears were wet on Heaven's
grey cheek.
For ah! we know not what each other says,
These things and I; in sound I speak—
Their sound is but their stir, they speak
by silences.
Nature, poor stepdame, cannot slake my drouth;
Let her, if she would owe me,
Drop yon blue bosom-veil of sky, and show me
The breasts o' her tenderness;
Never did any milk of hers once bless
My thirsting mouth.
Nigh and nigh draws the chase,
With unperturbèd pace,
Deliberate speed, majestic instancy;
And past those noisèd Feet
A Voice comes yet more fleet—
"Lo ! naught contents thee, who content'st
not Me."
Naked I wait thy Love's uplifted stroke!
My harness piece by piece Thou hast hewn
from me,
And smitten me to my knee;
I am defenceless utterly.
I slept, methinks, and woke,
And, slowly gazing, find me stripped in sleep.
In the rash lustihead of my young powers,
I shook the pillaring hours
And pulled my life upon me; grimed with smears,
I stand amid the dust o' the mounded years—
My mangled youth lies dead beneath the heap.
My days have crackled and gone up in smoke,
Have puffed and burst as sun-starts on a stream.
Yea, faileth now even dream
The dreamer, and the lute the lutanist;
Even the linked fantasies, in whose blossomy
twist
I swung the earth a trinket at my wrist,
Are yielding; cords of all too weak account
For earth with heavy griefs so overplussed.
Ah! is Thy love indeed
A weed, albeit an amaranthine weed,
Suffering no flowers except its own to mount?
Ah! must—
Designer infinite!—
Ah! must Thou char the wood ere Thou canst
limn with it?
My freshness spent its wavering shower i'
the dust;
And now my heart is as a broken fount,
Wherein tear-drippings stagnate, spilt down ever
From the dank thoughts that shiver
Upon the sighful branches of my mind.
Such is; what is to be?
The pulp so bitter, how shall taste the rind?
I dimly guess what Time in mists confounds;
Yet ever and anon a trumpet sounds
From the hid battlements of Eternity;
Those shaken mists a space unsettle, then
Round the half-glimpsed turrets slowly
wash again.
But not ere him who summoneth
I first have seen, enwound
With glooming robes purpureal,
cypress-crowned;
His name I know, and what his trumpet saith.
Whether man's heart or life it be which yields
Thee harvest, must Thy harvest-fields
Be dunged with rotten death?
Now of that long pursuit
Comes on at hand the bruit;
That Voice is round me like a bursting sea:
"And is thy earth so marred,
Shattered in shard on shard?
Lo, all things fly thee, for thou fliest me!
"Strange, piteous, futile thing!
Wherefore should any set thee love apart?
Seeing none but I makes much of naught"
(He said),
"And human love needs human meriting:
How hast thou merited—
Of all man's clotted clay the dingiest clot?
Alack, thou knowest not
How little worthy of any love thou art!
Whom wilt thou find to love ignoble thee,
Save Me, save only Me?
All which I took from thee I did but take,

Not for thy harms,
But just that thou might'st seek it in My arms.
All which thy child's mistake
Fancies as lost, I have stored for thee at home:
Rise, clasp My hand, and come!"
Halts by me that footfall:
Is my gloom, after all,
Shade of His hand, outstretched caressingly?
"Ah, fondest, blindest, weakest,
I am He Whom thou seekest!
Thou dravest love from thee, who dravest me."[2]

1. Who is the narrator fleeing from?
2. To what or whom does he flee?
3. Why doesn't anything shelter him or give him contentment? Why does everything run from him?
4. At the end why does God say that He took everything?
5. What is this poem a picture of?
6. Does God pursue every man in the whole world in the same way (John 6:39–40; 10:1–29)?

Reading Assignment:
Chapters VII.v–VIII

Session XIV: Recitation

Chapters V–VIII

Comprehension Questions

Answer the following questions for factual recall:

1. How can men do evil things within the providence and will of God and God still remain guiltless of their evil?
2. How did God harden the heart of Pharaoh?
3. How does Luther answer the question, "Why did God let Adam fall?"
4. Why is Erasmus's use of the Scriptures (especially Paul) so distressing to Luther?
5. Why is Erasmus's view of "spirit" so repugnant?
6. What does Erasmus think it means when John quotes Jesus saying, "Without me you can do nothing"?
7. Do men cooperate with God? Why or why not?
8. What, according to Luther, is free will at its best?

Session XV: Evaluation

All tests and quizzes are to be given with an open book and a Bible available.

Grammar

Answer each of the following questions in complete sentences. Some answers may be longer than others. (2 points per answer)

1. What is free will according to Erasmus?
2. What is free will according to Luther?
3. Do Erasmus and Luther agree about what free will is?
4. Why is sin perhaps the best argument against free will?
5. What is foreknowledge? Why does it destroy free will?
6. Why can't there be anything good in man before he is saved?
7. How does Luther argue against Erasmus's "argument from antiquity"?

Logic

Answer the following questions in complete sentences; your answer should be a paragraph or so. Answer two of the three questions. (10 points per answer)

1. How does Jesus, being the Word of God, make Christians more confident in arguing with nonbelievers?
2. What is Erasmus's view of the whole free will/foreknowledge controversy? What does Luther think?
3. What was Pelagius's view of man? What does the Bible teach?

Lateral Thinking

Answer one of the following questions. These questions will require more substantial answers. (16 points per answer)

1. How would a Christian view of Original Sin and Freedom benefit our modern culture?
2. How would a robust doctrine of the Foreknowledge of God and *sola scriptura* transform a culture?

Optional Session A: Activity

Drama

Imagine the following situation: You are aboard an airplane over the Pacific Ocean. During the flight, it is announced that there is not enough fuel to reach Hawaii (your intended destination). Nor is there enough fuel to get back to the mainland or any other known island (just play along). The plane will be able to stay airborne for only another 30 minutes before it attempts a water landing.

Among the crew and passengers are none other than Martin Luther and Erasmus of Rotterdam. Take turns playing passengers and these two theologians. There is obviously a bit of concern and surely a touch of apprehension regarding the proposed water landing. It's likely that many (if not all) of the passengers and crew will perish in the crash. Use the suggested script below as a jumping off spot (no pun intended!) for more impromptu discussion. Have fun!

An Airborne Dialogue

(The captain has just announced that the plane will be making an unexpected water landing in 30 minutes.)

Passenger 1: Why is this happening to me?!

Erasmus: The world is a mysterious place, and we cannot really know answers to difficult questions like that. Sit down and say your prayers!

Luther: Actually this is happening for our good and God's glory. Have you put your trust in God? If not then this is God's way of calling you to repentance. If you already have, then this is God's way of testing your faith. Do you believe that He will take care of you in life and death?

Passenger 2: Did God know that this was going to happen and still let it happen anyway?

Erasmus: God "*kind* of" knew about it. But God does not want to interfere with the free will of men, especially the pilot and whoever else is the cause of this unfortunate event.

Luther: Free will? Bosh! What about my free will? What about his free will (referring to Passenger 2)? How come God valued the pilot's free will over ours?

Erasmus: I, well, er . . . that is to say: Perhaps he did more good works than you. Maybe if you hadn't been so divisive (looking at Luther) and inquisitive (looking at Passenger 1 and 2) He would have valued you more.

Passenger 3: Dr. Erasmus, you said that God "kind of knew" this was going to happen. What does that mean?

Erasmus: It means that God foresees the future with His eyes kind of squinted like this (Erasmus squints his eyes), but in order to give us freedom He doesn't fully decide what will happen.

Everyone: Huh? (everyone looks confused)

Passenger 3: So are you saying that the history of the world is in the hands of men?

Erasmus: Now you've got it! Isn't it beautiful?

Passenger 3: But I thought you said that God values some people over others and allows their free will to overrule other people's free will sometimes.

Erasmus: Ah yes, well you see, this whole area really isn't all that important actually. I'm really a firm believer in just living peacefully and believing in God.

Luther: But that's the question: which god?

Erasmus: The Christian God, of course.

Luther: And where might we learn about this Christian God?

Erasmus: Now you're being a little childish, aren't you? But I will humor you. We learn about the Christian God in the Holy Scriptures, in the church fathers, the creeds, the councils and, of course, from the pope himself.

Passenger 4: Now I'm no theologian, but I think sometimes all those things don't agree. Sometimes church fathers have disagreed and sometimes popes have disagreed. How do you know who is right?

Erasmus: I, er . . . umm . . . you see, again, I think this is all being very nit-picky. Why don't we just all sit down and relax and sing a round of "Kum Ba Ya."

All Passengers: What?!

Passenger 1: You call that comfort?! I'm about to plunge some 30,000 feet into the ocean, and you want to sing a camp fire song?! I want to know what's going on! You're supposed to be some kind of scholar-genius. Give me some answers!

Luther: Calm down friends. I agree that this Dr. Erasmus is full of fluff. The truth is that the Christian God is in charge of everything. And that means that He actually planned this plane crash. He saw it coming, and He planned it that way. He didn't squint at all. He wants this to happen. So that leaves us with making sure that we respond rightly.

Passenger 5: What a stupid god! I can't believe in a god that just willy-nilly sends a few hundred people to their grave. I have a young son and a wife at home!

Luther: Actually Erasmus serves the stupid god. He's the god that sees "sort of." He's the god that needs glasses, and he shrugs his shoulders when you pray to him and lets forgetful pilots send you to your grave. The Christian God sees everything and rules everything so that there are no accidents.

Finish the dialogue, incorporating the following lines:

Passenger 2: But we don't deserve this!

Passenger 3: So you said that since God does all things, the only thing left for us to make sure of is our response. But how can we respond? Why does it matter how we respond if God does everything? Aren't we just puppets doing whatever He makes us do?

Passenger 4: So how should we respond to this Christian God?

Optional Activity

Watch *Luther,* the movie. While this show is not about the debate between Luther and Erasmus directly, it is a glimpse into Luther's life, his concerns and the struggle he faced with the Church of Rome. Write a brief review of the movie, and in particular discuss any aspects of Luther's life or the broader controversy that he had with the Church of Rome that may have influenced his argumentation with Erasmus.

OPTIONAL SESSION B: WRITING

Examining An Examination

Read Erasmus's dialogue *An Examination Concerning the Faith,* which can be found in a collection entitled *The Colloquies of Erasmus.*[3] The principle characters are a Lutheran and a Roman Catholic who are discussing the basic tenants of the Christian faith through the words of the Apostles' Creed. Erasmus's purpose is obviously to try reconciling members of the Church of Rome and Protestants. After reading the Examination, do you have the same view of Erasmus as you did after reading *The Bondage of the Will?* Why or why not? Discuss the concerns of both Luther and Erasmus, writing one paragraph for Luther and another for Erasmus.

OPTIONAL SESSION C: ACTIVITY

Public Speaking

Prepare a five minute speech in which a particular view of something is critiqued. The topic may be cultural, political, theological or something else with approval from the teacher. Your speech should include critiques of faulty logic or reasoning, as well as a positive suggestion or demonstration of a better alternative. Follow this outline:

I. Introduction (30 sec.)
   - Introduce the topic and explain why it is important to consider. Introduce an alternative to what is sometimes thought.

II. Critiques of Faulty Reasoning (1 min. 20 sec.)
   - Expose where the opposing view has gone wrong. This may include informal logical fallacies (such as affirming the consequent). Especially highlight any faulty assumptions (such as assuming a greater value for something because it is newer or older) and weaknesses in the evidence of the opponents.

III. Suggested Alternative (1 min. 20 sec.)
   - Present your own view on the subject. Define and defend your thesis carefully. Explain why it is the preferable view, and appeal to various kinds of authorities: authorities of antiquity, biblical authority, or the authority of someone who is known for his wisdom or insight.

IV. Defense of Alternative against attack (1 min. 20 sec.)
   - Imagine what kinds of attacks might be leveled against your position. Will someone disagree with your definition of something? Defend your definition from this attack. Will you be accused of using a weak authority? Defend your use of this authority and explain why it can sustain the attack.

V. Conclusion and Exhortation (30 sec.)
   - Re-summarize the entirety of your speech, defending the importance of the subject matter, the weakness of opposing views and finally reaffirming your own thesis. Finally, your speech should end with an exhortation to your listeners to accept and implement your view.

ENDNOTES

1 This quote and other biographical data were taken from Gritsch, Eric W. *Martin—God's Court Jester: Luther in Retrospect.* Philadelphia: Fortress Press, 1983 and from Hazlitt, William, ed. *Table Talk of Martin Luther.* London: George Bell & Sons, 1909.

2 This poem can be found at Link 1 for this chapter at www.VeritasPress.com/OmniLinks.

3 *The Colloquies of Erasmus* can be found at Link 2 for this chapter at www.VeritasPress.com/OmniLinks.

Secondary Books

First Semester

The Hobbit

Have you ever been in an airport that had moving sidewalks? Now suppose the road in front of your house were constantly *moving* just like that, like a thick asphalt river. And suppose you always had to be *really* careful whenever you went outside—because if you missed your step you might be swept away by the road and carried off into adventures. Men like C.S. Lewis, G.K. Chesterton, and J.R.R. Tolkien all had something in common—besides the fact that their first names were initials—and this was that they told wonderful fairy tales. And fairy tales are the best way of illustrating just how adventurous your front yard actually is, especially when you get close to the road. You can't be too careful when you step out the front door.

Now you may have stepped out *your* front door many times and never gotten swept away. Does this mean that these tales are all a lie? Not at all—but it *does* indicate that something is wrong. If the road in front of your house is not moving constantly, threatening or promising to take you off to fantastic places, then you have not been reading enough of the right kind of book. Perhaps you have not even read *one* book of the right kind. And if that is so, then it is time to read *The Hobbit,* a book about a road in front of a house that carried a hobbit into fantastic adventures.

Gandalf produces a map from the folds of his robe that will lead the eager dwarves and one rather unwilling hobbit on a tremendous adventure. Later in their journey they learn that a portion of the map is written in moon runes. Elrond explains to the travelers that such runes "can only be seen when the moon shines behind them . . ."

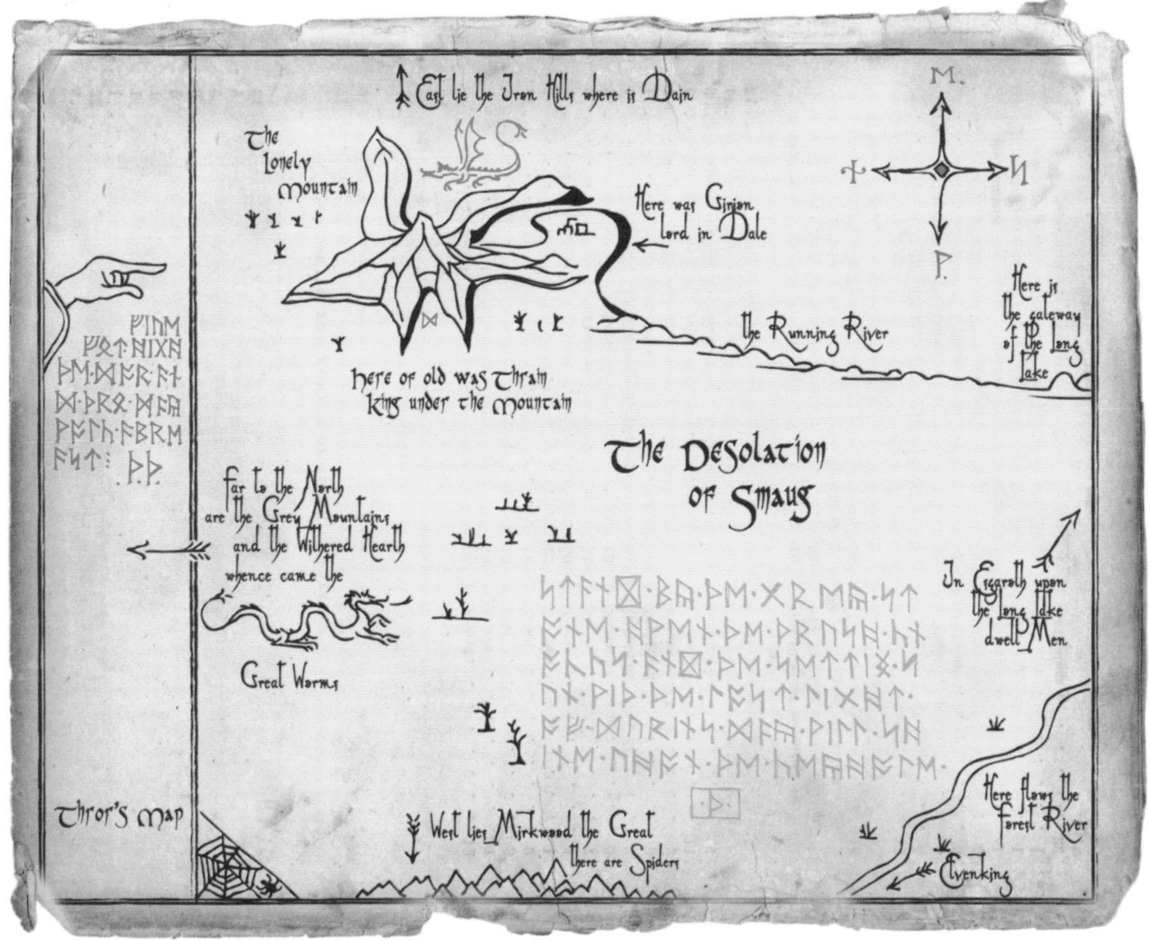

General Information

Author and Context

J.R.R. Tolkien (1892–1973) was a professor of English at Oxford University in England and a great scholar. He was good friends with C.S. Lewis, another great Oxford scholar. Both Tolkien and Lewis—while contributing in important ways to their respective fields of scholarship at the university— became famous for another reason entirely. In Tolkien's case, his fame began with the book you are about to read—*The Hobbit.* The story began when Prof. Tolkien was grading exams and found that a student had left a blank page. So Prof. Tolkien jotted this line on that exam paper: "In a hole in the ground there lived a hobbit." He later said, "Eventually I thought I'd better find out what hobbits were like. But that's only the beginning."[1]

J.R.R. Tolkien was an Anglo-Saxon scholar, and he was devoted to the study of languages. He was an expert in numerous languages, and his love for them comes out in his stories about Middle-earth. Drawing on his expertise in Anglo-Saxon, he even *invented* a language for the elves in his stories. Throughout these stories, Tolkien's love for languages and his love for growing things come out in many ways.

Significance

Many books that are best-sellers in their day are virtually unknown a generation later. This is true even of books that can be described as runaway best-sellers. They sell millions of copies when they are first published but usually end up in yard sales twenty years later. Sheer volume of sales in a book's early years do not necessarily guarantee longevity. But when a book is a best-seller and continues to sell well over the course of many decades, it potentially shapes the way many people think, and then how generations think. When this happens, a book passes the first test of becoming a classic. Not every book that lasts is a classic, but every classic lasts. And while some believe it is too early to determine, many will likely read and enjoy and have their thinking affected by *The Hobbit* and The *Lord of the Rings* for centuries. Some of C.S. Lewis's books, like his friend Tolkien's, will likely become classics, too.

This is significant because much of the literature of the twentieth century was characterized by rebellion against God and against the world as He created it. And yet most of these rebellious books will end up (along with other rubbish from the twentieth century) in the "dust bin of history." At the same time, significant Christian literature from the century past, while perhaps fewer in number than the rebellious books of that era, will likely endure for subsequent generations. In short, this book (and the others that follow) is likely to be very significant in the history of literature—leaving behind a number of secular books that pretended for a time to have literary weight and merit. These books are being studied in classical Christian schools and in homeschools across the nation, playing an important role in establishing what constitutes classical literature.

Main Characters

The central character in this book is Bilbo Baggins, a clever and pleasant hobbit, who discovers in the course of his adventures that he is far *tougher* and *important* than he ever thought he was. He is prodded into his adventures by Gandalf the Grey, a wizard and protector of the hobbits who comes to visit them periodically. Bilbo goes off on his adventure with some dwarves whose leader is Thorin Oakenshield. We are also introduced in this book to

Trolls are evil creatures that were made by Melkor in mockery of the Ents. There are different varieties of trolls found in Middle-earth, and the kind Bilbo meets are likely Stone-trolls, since Appendix F1 of *The Lord of the Rings* mentions that ". . . in the Westlands the Stone-trolls spoke a debased form of the Common Speech." This description certainly matches Bert, Bill and Tom quite well.

Gollum, a pitiful creature who used to be something like a hobbit before he was wasted away by the terrible power of a ring he had found. Waiting at the end of the book is the terrible character of Smaug the dragon.

Along with certain key individuals in this book, we are also introduced to the races of Middle-earth. The races include the elves, who live in the midst of a melancholy beauty until the time when they will depart into the West. Orcs, or goblins, are twisted elves. Dwarves are miners, jewelers and craftsmen. Hobbits live in a tucked away place called the Shire, minding their own business for the most part. And there are men in Middle-earth whose time, or age, is approaching. Tolkien is telling the story of how our world grew into the age of men.

Summary and Setting

J.R.R. Tolkien was an Englishman who was saddened by the fact that England had no mythology. The peoples who lived around the Mediterranean had their gods, mythologies, and heroes— Jupiter and Juno, Venus and Mars, Aeneas and Ulysses, and many others. The people of Scandinavia had their gods and myths also—Thor and Odin and the rest. But the people of England did not have any ancient tales like this at all. So J.R.R. Tolkien decided the best thing to do would be to write a mythology for England. And that is what he did. This story began as a tiny tale about a hobbit named Bilbo and eventually it grew into a detailed history of Middle-earth, complete with a creation story, a story of the fall and the tale of the transition between Middle-earth and the world we live in today. That larger story is told in the sequel, *The Lord of the Rings*, and in the prequel, *The Silmarillion.*

The myth, set in Middle-earth, has no connection to recorded history in these stories. Tolkien loved antiquity, and in order to satisfy him a story had to be *very* remote in time. At the same time, it *is* intended to bring us tales from the times before we have a recorded history for the people of England.

Worldview

As we seek to understand *The Hobbit,* this material will apply to a student's understanding of the subsequent trilogy, *The Lord of the Rings.* The essays for each of these books will necessarily be inter-dependent and some of what is said in each applies to all of them. Some of the discussion in each essay, however, focuses on the events of that book only.

In order to understand this book from a biblical worldview, we must realize that J.R.R. Tolkien was a devout Catholic. He was one of the men who was used by God to bring C.S. Lewis back to the Christian faith of his childhood. However, one of the things that *divided* Tolkien and Lewis was the fact that Lewis was a Protestant and Tolkien was a Roman Catholic. Tolkien's

Tolkien wrote in a letter that "Though a skin-changer and no doubt a bit of a magician, Beorn was a Man." In Old English *beorn* originally meant "bear," but it eventually changed to mean "warrior." Therefore, Beorn's power to transform from a bear to a man reflects the linguistic development of his name. Beorn's son, Grimbeorn the Old, can also take on the shape of a bear. Both skin-changers live in the Vales of Anduin near Mirkwood.

"commitment to Christianity and in particular to the Catholic Church was total."[2]

But how is this relevant? The differences between Protestants and Roman Catholics are not part of the history of Middle-earth. Further, the stories told in *The Hobbit* and in subsequent books are not autobiographical. The relevance of Tolkien's religious commitment, however, can be seen in this way: He attributed the formation of these stories to a particular mental process.

> "One writes such a story not out of the leaves of trees still to be observed, not by means of botany and soil-science; but it grows like a seed in the dark out of the leaf-mould of the mind: out of all that has been seen or thought or read, that has long ago been forgotten, descending into the deeps."[3]

What we need to do here is simply understand that Tolkien's faith, which was extremely important to him, was a crucial part of "the leaf-mould" of his mind and helped to determine what grew there. When we compare the works of Lewis and Tolkien together, and see how similar they are, we can clearly see the basic Trinitarian faith that they both shared. At the same time, some peculiar Protestant emphases are far more prominent in Lewis than they are in Tolkien—a good example of this would be the importance assigned to *grace* in Lewis's fantasies.

Nevertheless, Middle-earth is still a profoundly Christian place, despite the fact that all the stories occur outside the history of the prophets in the Old Testament or of Christ and the apostles in the New. This must be emphasized because when the works of Tolkien became popular to a large reading audience in England and America, Tolkien's uniquely Christian vision was taken over by those who wanted to use it to promote a neo-pagan vision of the world. Many of the "Dungeons & Dragons" types who really like Tolkien's world are not really aware of how Christian it is. And sadly, some Christians have been fooled in the same way—put off, for example, by the importance of Gandalf the wizard in the story. Doesn't the Bible say we are not supposed to listen to *wizards?*

On the subject of magic, we will have more to say later, but for now we may be content with a simpler answer. Our acquaintance with Middle-earth begins with *The Hobbit* and continues with *The Lord of the Rings,* where the story set in motion by Bilbo comes to a glorious climax. But Tolkien also wrote a mythology for the world of Middle-earth, a book called *The Silmarillion.* In that book he explains how the world was created, we learn the name of the God who created it (Iluvatar), and we get a good grasp of where everything came from. In *The Silmarillion,* Tolkien explains the role of various angels called the *valar.* And among the lesser valar we find Gandalf and the other "wizards." This is just another way of saying that Gandalf is not a wizard in *our* sense at all (a man trying to get illicit power through spells and other evil means), but is rather an angelic minister sent to protect the inhabitants of Middle-earth.

The Hobbit is a much "homier" book than *The Lord of the Rings.* It begins in a small place with a small hobbit, and even though Bilbo goes out into the great wide world and has adventures there, the adventures are on a much smaller scale than what we find in *The Lord of the Rings.* Bilbo is hired by the dwarves as a burglar to help them get their treasure back from a dragon, and it is not until we get to the very end of the book that we begin to suspect that much larger forces are involved in this world.

The Shire fits us like an old slipper, and though the adventures range far and wide, Tolkien does not let us forget that the justification for all the epic conflict is the defense and protection of places like the Shire. This means that *The Hobbit* is the place where we first get acquainted with the center of the world, which is a table covered with food, in front of every fat hobbit's fireplace. And pipes afterwards.

We are also introduced in this book to the elf Elrond, who lives in Rivendell at the "Last Homely House" (chap. 3). This is an image of what is truly important throughout Middle-earth—there is a center in this world worth defending, a lovely place. But this is not a world for sentimentalists because evil does threaten that which is good and really might destroy it. Through this moral center, threatened by evil, we can see that Tolkien is giving us a true picture of the world.

Another way his Christian vision comes through is the ambiguity in how he draws the lines of good and evil. There are, of course, creatures that are entirely given over to evil, like the goblins. We don't meet any reformed goblins throughout the length and breadth of Middle-earth. There are also beings that are out of the reach of temptation (in the West). The ambiguity is found in the fact that *all* the noble characters in this book are susceptible to temptation. Tolkien paints a picture of true nobility for us, but it is not a nobility that cannot be tempted.

Tolkien sets this up for us in Bilbo's accidental discovery of the ring of power in a dark corridor under the mountain. "He guessed as well as he could, and crawled along for a good way, till suddenly his hand met what felt like a tiny ring of cold metal lying on the floor of the tunnel. It was a turning point in his career, but he did not know it" (chap. 5). Shortly after this, he meets the ring's most recent owner, a pitiful character named Gollum. They get into a riddling match, which Bilbo (kind of) wins.

This is very important and shows what Tolkien is teaching us about this ring of power and all other things like it. Many years before, when Gollum and his companion had chanced upon the ring, Gollum murdered that companion for the sake of the ring. As soon as someone comes in contact with it, the power of the ring begins to turn and stretch the person in the wrong directions. This happens to Bilbo as well.

> "He knew of course, that the riddle-game was sacred and of immense antiquity, and even wicked creatures were afraid to cheat when they played at it. But he felt he could not trust this slimy thing to keep any promise at a pinch. Any excuse would do for him to slide out of it. *And after all that last question had not been a genuine riddle according to the ancient laws"* (chap. 5, emphasis mine).

Now we sympathize with Bilbo, because he was in a tight spot, but the riddle game had ancient laws, and Bilbo was not *quite* within the rules. His title to the ring was not completely, totally and entirely honest. Given the nature of the ring, this is how it had to be. Nevertheless, though Bilbo was affected by the ring, he was never turned by it, the way Gollum had been. But he was vulnerable. Tolkien is teaching us that here in Middle-earth, in all our conflicts, many of them very necessary, while there may be some true black hats in the conflict, the white hats are always capable of getting dirty and becoming black themselves.

Another Christian theme of Tolkien's that runs throughout these works is his loathing of machines and contraptions that are used to wield power over living and growing things. "Now goblins are cruel, wicked, and bad-hearted. They make no beautiful things, but they make many clever ones" (chap. 4). Tolkien does not object to craftsmanship, because the elves make many beautiful things. But the desire to make beautiful things can be turned, along with the makers, and clever things can be used to destroy.

Bilbo grows in his abilities throughout the book, and he does so in a manner that greatly impresses the dwarves. He gets away from the goblins in the cave, and he rescues the dwarves from the spiders in the forest. He also rescues them from the wood-elves there. As Bilbo is being transformed, we are fascinated by this because as Christians we understand the importance of sanctification, at least in Christian stories, where there is evil on the outside to be overcome, as well as fears on the inside. Think of a story where the lead character was exactly the same on the last page as he had been on the first page. How boring would that be? But we rejoice as the humble hobbit grows into his true identity, especially as he rescues the dwarves from the spiders.

> "Old fat spider spinning in a tree!
> Old fat spider can't see me!
> Attercop! Attercop!
> Won't you stop,
> Stop your spinning and look for me?" (chap. 8).

Incidentally, this is one place where we can see Tolkien's love of the Anglo-Saxon language coming out. *Attercop* is not just a nonsense word put into Bilbo's poem to make it more insulting. It was not the Middle-earth equivalent of *neener neener. Attercop* is actually the Anglo-Saxon word for *spider.* And the language from which Anglo-Saxon descended was the ancient mythological language of Middle-earth.

There is one more important Christian theme that is worth noting—and it is the great theme of the danger of greed. Men come into the book right near the end. The men of Lake-town are not as great as they used to be, although some remember their former authority. The Master of Lake-town had been "giving his mind to trade and tolls, to cargoes and gold, to which habit he owed his position" (chap.10). This is another element in Tolkien's books—greed is one of the great enemies.

Why are men included in the book? Up to this point, it has all been hobbits, a wizard, orcs, dwarves

Bilbo comes upon Isildur's Bane deep in the Misty Mountains. Its previous owner obtained it through murder, and though Bilbo does not kill for it, he does break the rules of the time-honored Riddle-game in his attempt to escape Gollum and the goblin tunnels.

and elves. The reason is, I believe, that Tolkien is a master writer of the fairy tale. And one of the fundamental lessons of the fairy tale, going back to the promise given to Adam and Eve and their descendents in the Garden, is that a descendant of Eve, called the seed of the woman, will crush the head of the serpent in the Garden. And it is important for us to note that the serpent in the Garden of Eden was not a big garden snake, but was rather a *dragon.* The Bible says this explicitly (Rev. 12:9), and so when the serpent in the Garden is named, we ought to think of him as a dragon or *worm* in the older sense of that last word. Smaug truly fits the description of such a beast (mainly because he was more subtle than all the other creatures). "No dragon can resist the fascination of riddling talk and of wasting time trying to understand it" (chap. 12). Tolkien has understood our great adversary well and has painted him in colors true to Scripture. Satan is the father of lies, and the dragon is always of that same brood.

It is therefore not an accident that in many popular movies and stories today we have examples of what can be called metaphor-morphing, or *metamorphing* for short. In many recent works of fiction, dragons are portrayed as misunderstood or mistreated. They are portrayed this way because the dragon is still lying to us.

The Bible promises us that Christ, as *man,* will slay the dragon. And this is why all knights in the Christian tradition, from Beowulf to St. George, always slay the dragon. When the apostle Paul says that the God of peace will crush Satan beneath the believers' feet (Rom. 16: 20), he is referring to a promise of dragon-slaying (Gen. 3:15). It is important that Smaug be killed not by an elf, or a dwarf or a hobbit. True to the fairy tale, and true to Scripture, the dragon is slain by a man.

> "No one had dared to give battle to him for many an age; nor would they have dared now, if it had not been for the grim-voiced man (Bard was his name), who ran to and fro cheering on the archers and urging the Master to order them to

fight to the last arrow" (chap. 14).

And it is that man, Bard, who shoots the fatal arrow.

In the main themes of his work, J.R.R. Tolkien has given us an enthralling and very Christian view of the world—even though he is showing us our world by showing it to us before it really became our world. Some things change, but the fundamental issues, the permanent things, do not.

—*Douglas Wilson*

For Further Reading

Carpenter, Humphrey, ed. *The Letters of J.R.R. Tolkien.* New York: Houghton Mifflin, 1981.

Carpenter, Humphrey. *Tolkien.* New York: Ballantine Books, 1977.

Newsom, William Chad. *Talking of Dragons.* Ross-shire, Scotland: Christian Focus Publications, 2005.

Peters, Thomas. *The Christian Imagination.* San Franciso, Ignatius Press, 2000.

Tolkien, J.R.R. *The Silmarillion.* New York: Houghton Mifflin, 1977.

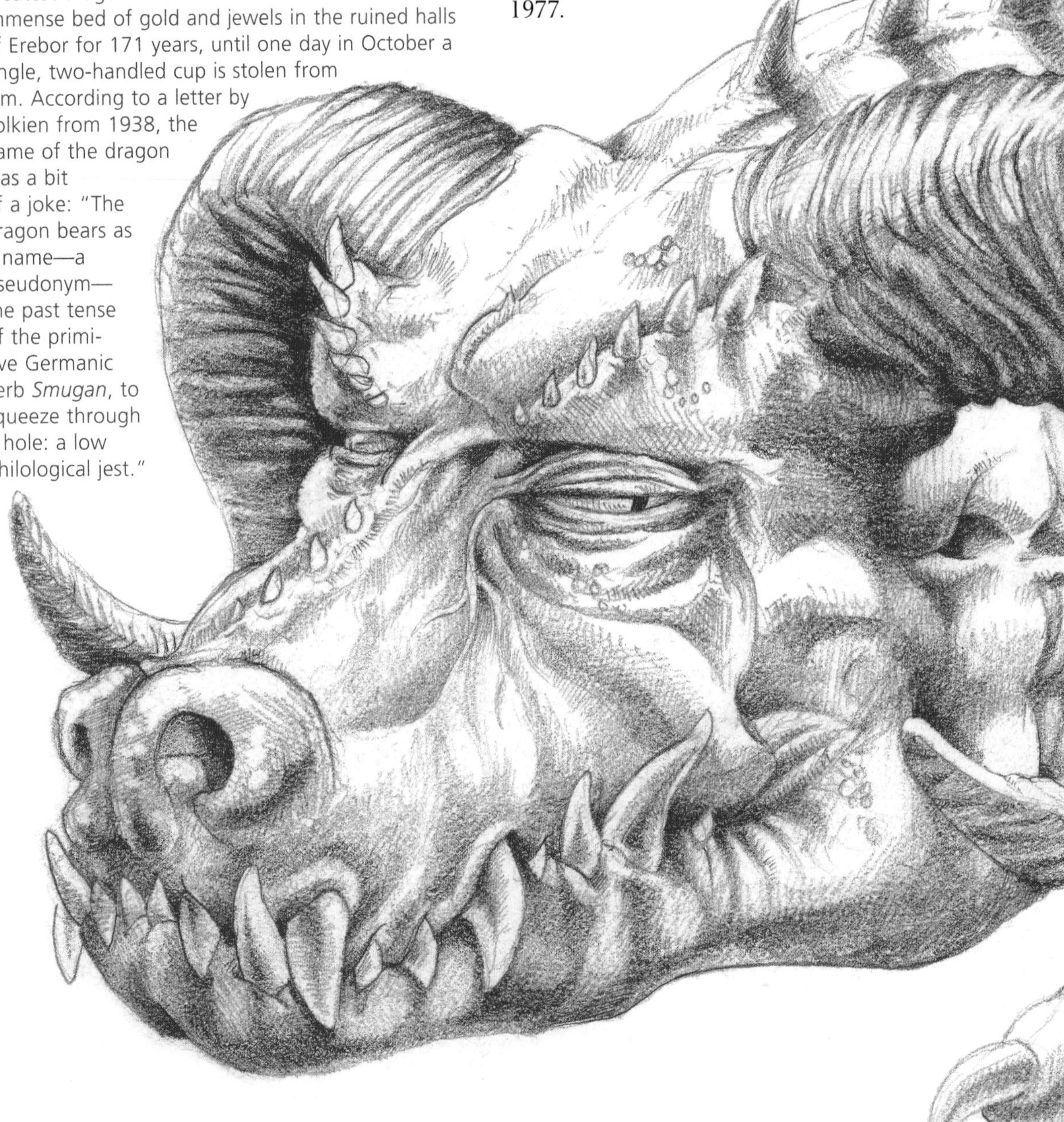

Smaug is the last of the great fire-drakes and the greatest dragon of his time. He has lain on an immense bed of gold and jewels in the ruined halls of Erebor for 171 years, until one day in October a single, two-handled cup is stolen from him. According to a letter by Tolkien from 1938, the name of the dragon was a bit of a joke: "The dragon bears as a name—a pseudonym—the past tense of the primitive Germanic verb *Smugan*, to squeeze through a hole: a low philological jest."

Session I: Prelude

A Question to Consider

What religious differences did C.S. Lewis have with his friend J.R.R. Tolkien? How do these differences show up in the different worlds that they each created?

From the General Information above answer the following questions:

1. How does Bilbo come to possess the ring? Does he come by it honestly?
2. What kind of wizard is Gandalf?
3. What is the difference in these books between the good guys and bad guys?
4. Why do men come into the tale near the end?
5. How is Smaug true to form?

Optional Activity A

Pick three scenes from *The Hobbit*, and write a stage play or screenplay for those scenes. Make sure that the script follows the standard form, with stage directions and everything. You might want to check on the internet for some help on the form to follow. When you have a script, round up your brothers and sisters, friends, neighbors or classmates and act out the scenes.

Optional Activity B

Look at the form and meter of Bilbo's Attercop poem and write two more verses of it.

Reading Assignment:
Chapters 1–4

Session II: Discussion

Chapters 1–4

A Question to Consider

What are the key ingredients to living in "community?"

Discuss or list short answers to the following questions:

Text Analysis

1. Why is Bilbo Baggins so opposed to the offer of an adventure from Gandalf?
2. Describe the hospitality that Bilbo finds himself providing to the dwarves.
3. What causes Bilbo to change his mind about going on the adventure?
4. Another ingredient to developing community can be having a "common cause." Is this important to the community of the adventurers?
5. What typifies the "community" of the trolls?

Cultural Analysis

1. Around what does community develop in our culture?
2. How well do we know (and care for) our neighbors?

Biblical Analysis

1. In 1 Timothy 3:2 we see that among the qualifications for bishop (or elder) that he should be *hospitable*. Why is being hospitable so important to be mentioned here?
2. Hebrews 13:2 says, "Do not forget to entertain strangers, for by so doing some have unwittingly entertained angels." Is this still true today?
3. We find the value of a friend in Ecclesiastes 4:9-12. What does this Scripture teach about community?

Summa

Write an essay or discuss this question, integrating what you have learned from the material above.

What is it about "community" that we find appealing?

Reading Assignment:
Chapters 5–7

SESSION III: RECITATION

Chapters 1–7

1. Name the three most important characters in the story so far.
2. How many dwarves go on the adventure? Name as many as you can.
3. What happens to trolls when they are exposed to daylight?
4. Why does Bilbo sulk when Gandalf rushes him off to the Green Dragon Inn?
5. What is Rivendell like?
6. After sleeping in a cave, Bilbo awakens with a start to find several problems. What are they?
7. How does Bilbo discover the ring?
8. Describe Gollum.
9. What strange power does Bilbo find the ring has?
10. Why do Gandalf, Bilbo and the dwarves quickly climb trees? What further predicament results? How are they finally rescued?
11. After the eagles rescue them , who provides for the needs of the travelers?

READING ASSIGNMENT:
Chapters 8–10

SESSION IV: DISCUSSION

Chapters 8–10

A Question to Consider

What events happen in our lives that make us feel like we are becoming adults?

Discuss or list short answers to the following questions:

Text Analysis

1. What event causes Bilbo to become a different person?
2. What does Bilbo name his sword?
3. How do the dwarves get free from the spiders?
4. Who is discovered to be missing? What difficulty is he experiencing?

Cultural Analysis

1. What are some unfortunate *rites of passage* that our culture seems to recognize?
2. Why might our culture have informally recognized such events (discussed above) as signs of children becoming adults?

Biblical Analysis

1. What book of the Bible stands out as the most important book to help a child become an adult? How does it do that?
2. How do we see Jesus going from being a boy to being a man in Luke 2?
3. In Genesis 39 we see Joseph as a slave in Egypt. In Genesis 37 we see him as a brother and son who dreams (and tells) of having his older brothers and parents be in subjection to him. What event occurs that causes Joseph to grow up quickly?

SUMMA

Write an essay or discuss this question, integrating what you have learned from the material above.

What might we look forward to (or have experienced already) to help us transition from being a child to being an adult?

READING ASSIGNMENT:
Chapters 11–14

Session V: Activity

Chapters 1–14

Who Am I?

As you read through *The Hobbit* and later *The Lord of the Rings*, it is important that you are able to keep the different characters straight. It is also helpful to understand their characters traits, in order to better understand what Tolkien was trying to communicate. Below you will find statements about individual characters or races. It is up to you to provide the answer to "Who am I?"

1. We are little people, roughly half the size of humans, with thick hair on our feet, round bellies and a love of good food, comfort, and security. Who are we?
2. I live at Bag End. Who am I?
3. I appear as an old man wearing a long cloak and carrying a staff. You might also know me for my fireworks display. Who am I?
4. I am the head dwarf. Who am I?
5. I am the great dragon who lives in and guards Lonely Mountain. Who am I?
6. We are short-tempered, dull witted and will eat just about anything. Who are we?
7. My father was from the well-to-do, conventional Baggins family, but my mother was from the Tooks, a wealthy eccentric family. Who am I?
8. We turn to stone when exposed to daylight? Who are we?
9. I always speak to myself because I never have anyone else to speak to. Who am I?
10. I am a man who can turn into a bear. Who am I?
11. I am Thorin's grandfather. Who am I?
12. We were the first creatures in Middle-Earth. We are immortal unless killed in battle. Who are we?
13. I'm a small, strange, slimy creature who lives deep in the caves beneath the Misty Mountains. Who am I?
14. I am the master of Rivendell, as strong as a warrior and as wise as a wizard. Who am I?

"So began a battle that none had expected; and it was called the Battle of Five Armies, and it was very terrible. Upon one side were the Goblins and the wild Wolves, and upon the other were Elves and Men and Dwarves." The goblins have hated the dwarves since the dwarves' victory over them at the Battle of Nanduhirion. When the dwarves that Bilbo is traveling with kill the Great Goblin, it rekindles the memories of the goblins' war with the dwarves. So Bolg, whose father Azog was killed at Nanduhirion, leads the goblins and their allies out of the Misty Mountains against the dwarves, men and elves.

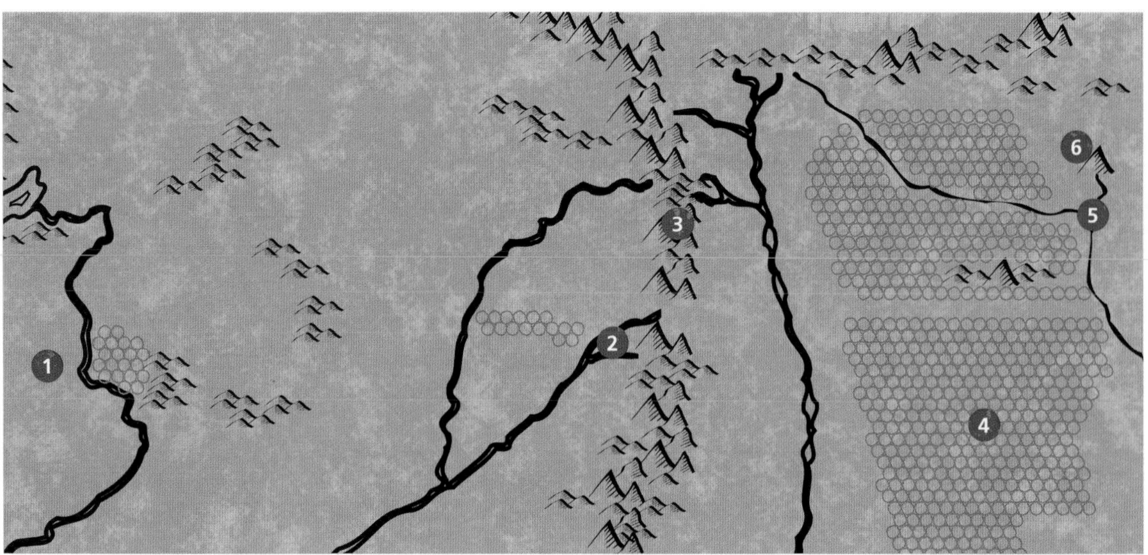

15. We are fair-faced, have beautiful voices and are wonderful craftsmen. Who are we?
16. We are evil creatures whom Bilbo encounters. We are famous for our ability to make cruel weapons and devices for torture. Who are we?

READING ASSIGNMENT:
Chapters 15–19

SESSION VI: RECITATION

Chapters 8–19

1. Beorn warns the travelers not to touch a stream that they will cross in the bleak forest of Mirkwood. Who touches it? What happens?
2. How does the party get separated in Mirkwood?
3. What happens to Bilbo while he sleeps? How does he escape?
4. Why does Bilbo not get caught (like the others) by the wood elves?
5. How does he free the dwarves?
6. Why do the people of Lake Town (a.k.a. Esgaraoth) treat Thorin like a king and the others like royalty?
7. How many entrances are there to Smaug's lair in the mountain? Which one do they seek to use? Why?
8. What does Bilbo find when he explores the inside of the mountain? What does he leave with?
9. What proves to be the dragon's weakness?
10. After Smaug causes much damage to the buildings of Lake-town by breathing fire on them, who finally shoots an arrow that kills Smaug? How does he know where to shoot?
11. Why is Thorin unwilling to share the treasure with the surviving people of Lake-town? How does the standoff finally get resolved?
12. What is the Battle of the Five Armies?
13. What does Bilbo find upon returning to Bag End?

OPTIONAL SESSION: ACTIVITY

Making a Map

Draw a map like the one shown on this page. Fill in the names of the places that relate to Bilbo's journey. Identify all the numbered locations, then add some of your own.

ENDNOTES

1 Humphrey Carpenter, *Tolkien* (New York, Ballantine Books, 1977), p. 193.
2 Ibid., p. 143.
3 Ibid., pp. 140-141.

The Fellowship of the Ring

When you were little, did you ever lie on a couch or bed and hang your head over the edge to look at the room upside down? All of a sudden, things that were very familiar to you looked strange and odd—that piano hanging from the ceiling, for instance.

Similar to this, good writers make you look at ordinary things differently. And once you learn this trick, you can just keep going. This doesn't mean that you are constantly confused about your living room, but rather that you have looked at it so many different ways that you now understand it in its ordinary setting. If you excel at this, you will come to be amazed that a right side up piano sticks to the *floor.*

We necessarily see things first in their first appearance, but through reading and meditating on books like this, we should learn to get past that. For example, when the hobbits first meet Strider, they have been fleeing from the Nazgûl, and so they are understandably suspicious. But they are reassured, and decide that Strider is a good man. As Frodo put it, if Strider had been evil, he would "seem fairer and feel fouler, if you understand" (book 1, chap. 10). But even when they decide that he is not evil and that he might be a help to them, they have no idea what kind of man he is. He is going to be revealed much later as a very different kind of good character than how he first appears.

If we learn to think past superficial appearances (Strider), and at the same time to take appearances realistically into account (Gollum), we are learning to look at the world from different angles, but in such a way as to keep the constant things constant.

Another good example of this involves Strider (again). Perhaps some of you have seen the bumper sticker that says "Not all those who wander are lost" (book 1, chap. 10). What other bumper stickers do you frequently see? I don't know about you, but I see stickers about freeing Tibet, the Grateful Dead and a sticker for the Green Party presidential candidate, whoever that was. And yet, the quote comes from one of the noblest characters in a Christian novel. See, appearances can be tricky—although the chances are good that the fellow who put it on his car did not really understand what he was saying.

Let's look at it from different angles, hanging our head off the couch. Some people who wander *are* lost—like Gollum. Some who are lost don't wander at all—like the malicious tree in Bombadil's wood—"filled with a hatred of things that go free upon the earth" (book 1, chap. 7). Some people who don't wander aren't lost—like old Farmer Maggot. But not all who wander are lost—like Strider. A lot depends.

In order to see things "upside down" without getting confused, it is important to be looking at concrete things, like the furniture in your living room, or characters in a story, such as the story we are now about to read. It is crucial that we not try this with *abstractions*—if we only have the bumper sticker, we don't know if the person has read Tolkien with wisdom, or if he has read Tolkien and completely missed the

"Three Rings for the
Elven-kings under the sky,
Seven for the Dwarf-lords
in their halls of stone,
Nine for the Mortal Men
doomed to die,
One for the Dark Lord
on his dark throne
In the Land of Mordor
where the Shadows lie.
One Ring to rule them all,
One Ring to find them,
One Ring to bring them all
and in the darkness bind them,
In the Land of Mordor
where the Shadows lie."

point, or if he has never read Tolkien and just picked the bumper sticker up somewhere. Maybe it is his mother's car.

Our task is different. We want to enjoy *The Fellowship of the Ring* and learn wisdom through very different characters. We are safe doing this in this story, for we are in the hands of a very great writer.

The elves call Tom "Iarwain Ben-adar" (Oldest and Fatherless). He lives in a valley east of the Shire where he displays extraordinary powers and sings nonsensical songs. Tolkien is equally mysterious as to who or what Tom is in a letter he wrote: "And even in a mythical age there must be some enigmas, as there always are. Tom Bombadil is one (intentionally)." Goldberry is mysterious as well. She seems to be a river-spirit, though some have suggested that both she and Tom are Maiar, a lesser angelic being. In another letter Tolkien wrote: "We are . . . in real river-lands in autumn. Goldberry represents the actual seasonal changes in such lands." Whatever they are in Tolkien's imagination, Tom and Goldberry are beautiful literary delights that teach us what "good" looks like, as they mirror, to some degree, Adam and Eve in their unfallen state.

General Information

Main Characters

The Fellowship of the Ring introduces us to Bilbo's heir and successor, Frodo. His most important inheritance is the ring that Bilbo obtained from Gollum, but that odd ring has now been discovered to be the one Ring of Power. Frodo is accompanied on his adventure by his loyal attendant, Samwise Gamgee. Filling out the entourage of hobbits, we find Merry and Pippin. Gandalf the Grey is a central character in this book, and we start to discover how important he is to all of Middle-earth. The hobbits travel first to the house of Elrond, one of the great elves, at Rivendell. There, a council is held that determines that the ring must be destroyed. This mission is entrusted to a fellowship of representatives from all the noble races of Middle-earth. The fellowship of the ring includes Gandalf the wizard, Frodo and his three hobbit companions, Legolas the elf, Gimli the dwarf, and two men, Boromir and Aragorn. The fellowship eventually meets the elven queen Galadriel in the forest of Lothlorien.

Worldview

As we consider *The Fellowship of the Ring*, we will review some of the basic principles discussed in the essay on *The Hobbit* and point out how those principles are reinforced by themes and events in this book. Then we will move on to any worldview issues that we have not yet discussed.

On the subject of magic, the *fundamental* issue for Christians in this book is the magician's desire for power and control. A magician seeks to manipulate the matter around him in such a way as to wield power over it, and through it, over others. As such, depending on motives, there might be very little spiritual difference between an alchemist and a chemist. Magic should therefore not be defined as doing something remarkable. When Jesus walked on water, was He doing "magic?" Rather, magic is trying to wrest power from the created order in order to exercise that power over others. This is to be distinguished from exercising dominion, which works *with* the created order in order to serve God and others.

Tolkien certainly regarded the magic of Sauron and Saruman as evil and wicked, but he also did not really distinguish it from what many moderns would call the advance of science. Tolkien, like his friend C.S. Lewis, had fought in the First World War. In fact, his foundational image for Mordor was the great, industrial war machine set up in France in World War I to destroy hundreds of thousands of young men there. Tolkien hated things that clanked and smoked and believed they would always bite and devour. He saw modernization as just another manifestation of man's temptation to manipulate matter in order to get this kind of mastery or control. This, for Tolkien, was the heart of magic, and it was to be decisively rejected.

This helps us make sense of the decision reached at the Council of Elrond. The *Lord of the Rings* is not a book promoting magic, with a little "good guy magic" or "white magic" thrown in to make it palatable for Christians. The *Lord of the Rings* is actually one of the most profoundly anti-magic books available. Why is this?

If magic is about acquiring the power to wield power over others, and then doing so, what does the Council of Elrond decide to do? Through an odd circumstance, they came to possess the Ring of Power, and this Ring (wielded by someone like Gandalf, or Elrond) *would* overthrow Sauron and all their enemies completely. They would be able to wield power decisively. But when they had overthrown Sauron, they would discover that they had done so by *becoming* Sauron.

This is why they decide to destroy the Ring. When Frodo, at the fateful moment, says, "I will take the Ring" (book 2, chap. 2), he is saying not just that he will undertake a very dangerous mission. It is indeed dangerous, but fundamentally, it is a mission of repudiation. The good guys have the ultimate weapon, the ultimate power, and they *refuse* to use it. Think for a moment how strange this is as a story line. Most wartime adventure stories are about trying to acquire a great weapon, or destroy one in the enemy's possession. This story is about trying to destroy the enemy's great weapon that is in *your* possession the entire time.

So this is the great test Gandalf passes early on. "'No!' cried Gandalf, springing to his feet. 'With that power I should have power too great and terrible. And over me the Ring would gain a power still greater and more deadly'" (book 1, chap. 2). Elrond passes the test at the Council. "'I fear to take the Ring to hide it. I will not take the Ring to wield it'" (book 2, chap. 2). Late in the book, Galadriel passes the test, and speaks of it explicitly in those terms: "'I pass the test,' she said. 'I will diminish, and go into the West, and remain Galadriel'" (book 2, chap. 7).

At the end of this book, in the breaking of the fellowship of the ring, Boromir fails the test, although he does redeem himself in his valiant death. But the reason he failed the test is that he never understood the underlying principle. (And one of the great blessings for students in reading this book is that of learning this principle.) At the Council of Elrond, Boromir deferred to the judgment of others, but the reason they had for attempting to destroy the Ring *did not make deep spiritual sense to him.* "'I do not understand all this,' he said. 'Why do you speak ever of hiding and destroying?'" (book 2, chap. 2). And because of this lack of wisdom, he faltered when he was tempted. He did not lack courage, but he did not have the right kind of wisdom.

All this reveals the basic difference between magicians and those who are not magicians. Gandalf says that what they have decided to do is an option that would never even occur to Sauron. He could not conceive of doing something like this himself, and therefore cannot imagine if his enemies came to possess the Ring, that they would attempt to destroy it, because "the only measure that he knows is desire, desire for power; and so he judges all hearts" (book 2, chap. 2).

Related to this is the reason why Saruman fell. As Elrond put it, "It is perilous to study too deeply the arts of the Enemy, for good or for ill" (book 2, chap. 2). When good confronts evil, there is always a temptation to "fight fire with fire." But those who fight evil must constantly beware of the temptation of becoming what they are fighting.

We see the same kind of issue (though on a smaller scale) when we see the effect that the Ring has had on Bilbo, and we come to expect similar things with Frodo the Ring-bearer. When Gandalf is explaining how he became suspicious about the Ring, the effect that it had had on Bilbo was one of his concerns. In the essay on *The Hobbit,* it was explained that Bilbo obtained the Ring through means that were not *strictly* speaking honest. This is made explicit in *The Fellowship of the Ring.*

> "When I at last got the truth out of him, I saw at once that he had been trying to put his claim to the ring beyond doubt. Much like Gollum with his 'birthday present'. The lies were too much alike for my comfort" (book 1, chap. 2).

But the resilience and toughness of hobbits is nevertheless seen in this, far more than in their latent abilities in adventuring. Bilbo is affected by the Ring, but he possessed it for many years without becoming possessed by it. "'For he gave it up in the end of his own accord: an important point'" (book 1, chap. 2). Frodo shows the same tough resilience, almost to the end. In the background material on *The Hobbit,* we learned that elves (and orcs) and hobbits were representative of various aspects of man. In the First World War, Tolkien acquired a high respect for the nobility of ordinary foot soldiers from non-aristocratic backgrounds. In Tolkien's mind, hobbits were representative of the common, sturdy individual of this type, and his depiction of hobbits in this way shows his high respect for "ordinary people." And a central part of Tolkien's admiration is seen in the hobbits' resistance to what might be called the "high" temptations.

While Tolkien honors the ordinariness of the hobbits in their Shire, he also shows that they (ungratefully) had taken far too much for granted. "They were in fact sheltered, but they had ceased to remember it." Among the noble races of Middle-earth, Tolkien realistically shows us that all is not universal peace and harmony. There are differences between them, and there are tensions. Tolkien paints the dwarves in such a way as to make us sympathize with them in their differences with the elves. And he paints the elves in such a way as to make us sympathize with *them* as well. This is one of the reasons why time in Middle-earth helps a thoughtful reader to think more like a charitable Christian—a common temptation for many is to view the world as though one's own perspective is the only perspective possible. Reading stories like this helps us to both sympathize with dwarves and be exasperated with dwarves. We love the Shire, and yet can be exasperated with the hobbits. We see that men are the cause of much turmoil in the world, and yet we find that men are found selflessly (and thanklessly) protecting the Shire.

Tom Bombadil tells the hobbits of "sons of forgotten kings walking in loneliness" (book 1, chap. 8). Shortly after this, we meet Strider the Ranger who is part of a band of men protecting the hobbits, who blissfully take everything for granted. Hobbits spent their time in a particular way and consistently took things for granted: "Growing food and eating it occupied most their time." And the hobbits are cautioned by the elf Gildor early in their adventures, "The wide world is all about you: you can fence yourselves in, but you cannot forever fence it out" (book 1, chap. 3). But although hobbits are capable of taking things for granted, and growing very fat as they do so, there is much more to them than this.

> "There is a seed of courage hidden (often deeply, it is true) in the heart of the fattest and most timid hobbit, waiting for some final and desperate danger to make it grow" (book 1, chap. 8).

J.R.R. Tolkien "cordially disliked allegory" in all its manifestations, and I am afraid we would annoy him terribly if we tried to read *The Lord of the Rings* in an allegorical way. We therefore ought not to try to piece together "a meaning" for the books that is tied to general truths or abstractions, or to events in our own world. The Ring did not stand for the atomic bomb, for example, although some have tried to read it in that way. As C.S. Lewis pointed out, the chronology of this is impossible because Tolkien had been working on this story about the Ring of Power long before the atom bomb was invented. And the story of Middle-earth should not be read as a Christian allegory either, with various characters representing certain traits or characteristics (as in *Pilgrim's Progress*), or even anything as indirect as C.S. Lewis's "supposal"

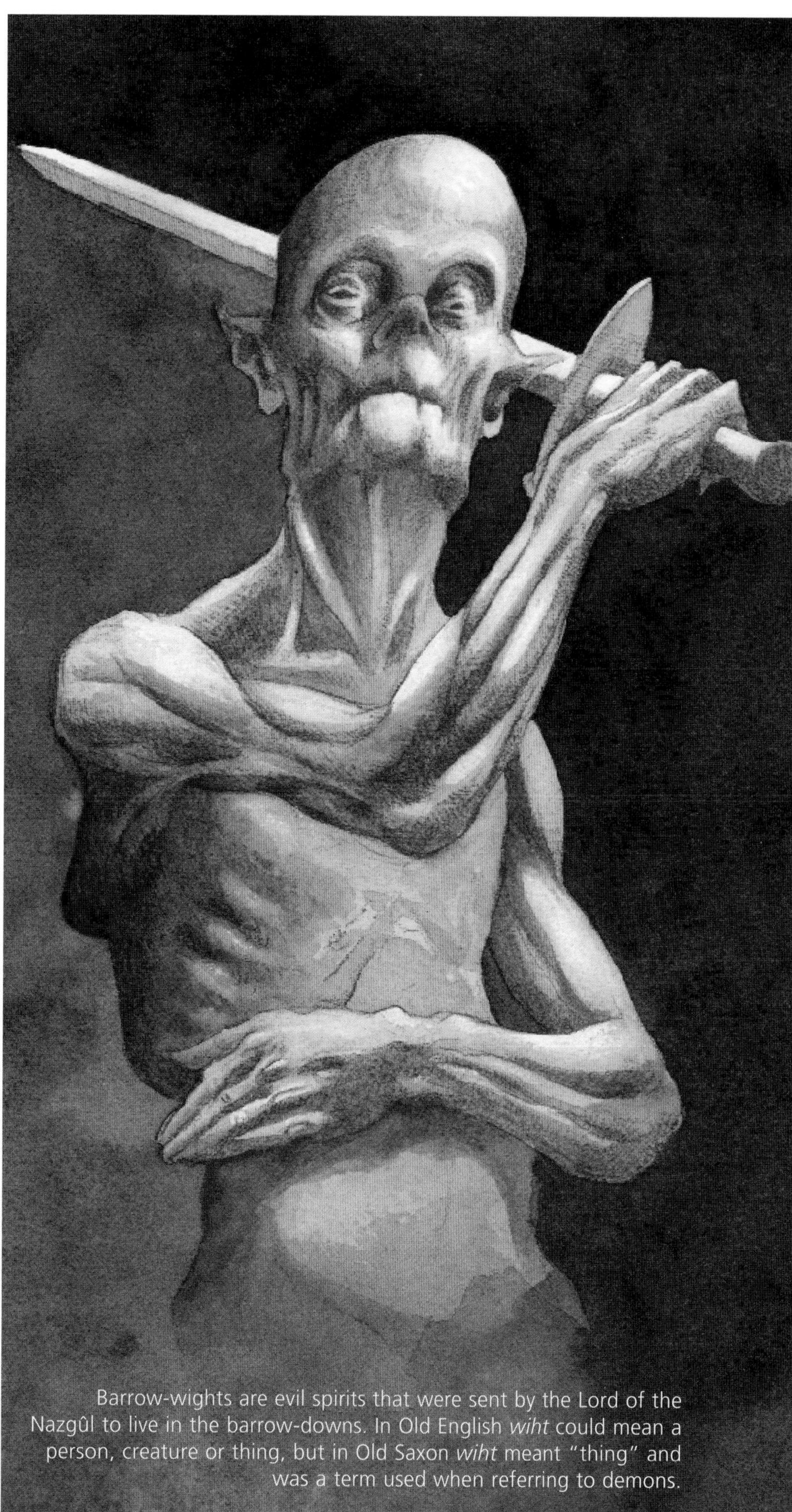

Barrow-wights are evil spirits that were sent by the Lord of the Nazgûl to live in the barrow-downs. In Old English *wiht* could mean a person, creature or thing, but in Old Saxon *wiht* meant "thing" and was a term used when referring to demons.

about a character like Aslan.

Having said this, and emphasized it, we still have to qualify it. This is because Tolkien was self-consciously writing mythology, and this meant that he was appealing to the great themes of human existence. And this means that characters like Gandalf and Aragorn have to be understood as *Christ figures.* This is different from saying that they represent Christ in an allegorical way. Aragorn is not Christ in that world, and neither is Gandalf. But because of how God made the world, the pattern of death and resurrection is inescapable, and fictional characters who go through that process are to that extent a Christ figure.

We see the first part of this with Gandalf in *The Fellowship of the Ring* (we will discuss Aragorn later). He stands between the rest of the fellowship and the Balrog in the Mines of Moria, and he falls into the depths as a result of his fight with that monster. His last words were, "Fly, you fools!" (book 2, chap. 5). In his death for others, Gandalf is very much a Christ figure.

As we saw in *The Hobbit,* Bilbo grew in his abilities throughout that book, and he became a much worthier hobbit. This is a theme that runs throughout these works. Frodo shrinks from the responsibility that has been handed to him, but Gandalf admonishes him. "... But that is not for them to decide. All we have to decide is what to do with the time that is given us" (book 1, chap. 2). Throughout Middle-earth, reality is never "optional." "But you have been chosen, and you must therefore use such strength and heart and wits as you have" (book 1, chap. 2).

Another point is this. Christians differ among themselves about the course of history, and whether it will have what we call a "happy ending." All Christians are ultimately optimistic, because all Christians believe in heaven, but Christians do differ among themselves about whether history *prior* to the end of the world will end well. Tolkien very definitely belonged to the group that thought of history as containing tales of great nobility, surrounded by sadness. Before Strider sings a particular lay, he says, "it is sad, *as are all the tales of Middle-earth*" (book 1, chap. 11, emphasis mine). And Galadriel speaks of it in this way—"through the ages of the world we have fought *the long defeat*" (book 2, chap. 7). This was very much Tolkien's frame of mind and fit his personality well. This lines up with the Norse mythology that he loved so well, where the Norse eschatology has the gods and the monsters fight it out at the very end of the world, and the gods *lose.* In the Norse and Anglo-Saxon world, defeat was no refutation at all. The whole universe is just one gigantic Alamo. This makes for tales of great courage, but is also something of a downer. One of the problems that the Anglo-Saxons had to solve was how to incorporate the ultimately optimistic Christian vision with their own pessimistic way of looking at everything.

One last comment needs to be made about the very eccentric character of Tom Bombadil—a sort of Middle-earth Melchizedek. He combines a robust sunniness and goodness with an (*almost* culpable) carelessness about the great issues that are afflicting Middle-earth. If he were given the Ring, he would not be seduced by it, but it is also true that he would probably lose it. He is a very entertaining character, and for various reasons, he doesn't quite fit in the books, any more than he fits in the world events that are swirling around him. "Eldest, that's what I am" (book 1, chap. 7). Speaking of himself, Tom says, "Tom remembers the first raindrop and the first acorn" (book 1, chap. 7). Unlike Gandalf and Aragorn, Tom Bombadil does not really constitute a Christ figure—he is too detached, too impervious. The speculation offered by Robert Foster is probably the best. "A being, lord and master of the Old Forest. His race is unknown, although it is possible that he was a Maia 'gone native.'"[1] The Maiar were lesser Ainur (angelic beings), and other examples of them would include Sauron and the Balrogs.

But we will not talk about the Balrogs too much, because you do have to get to sleep tonight.

—Douglas Wilson

The inscription on the One Ring says: "Ash nazg durbatulûk, ash nazg gimbatul, ash nazg thrakatulûk, agh burzum-ishi krimpatul," which Gandalf says is Elvish of an ancient mode.

For Further Reading

Carpenter, Humphrey, ed. *The Letters of J.R.R. Tolkien.* New York: Houghton Mifflin, 1981.

Carpenter, Humphrey. *Tolkien.* New York: Ballantine Books, 1977.

Newsom, William Chad. *Talking of Dragons.* Ross-shire, Scotland: Christian Focus Publications, 2005.

Peters, Thomas. *The Christian Imagination.* San Francisco: Ignatius Press, 2000.

Tolkien, J.R.R. *The Silmarillion.* New York: Houghton Mifflin, 1977.

Session I: Prelude

A Question to Consider

What is magic? Is magic bad? Does Tolkien encourage magic?

From the General Information above answer the following questions:

1. What is the difference between technology and magic?
2. Why does the Council of Elrond decide to try to destroy the Ring?
3. What is the great test in this book?
4. Is *The Lord of the Rings* an allegory?
5. Who is Tom Bombadil?

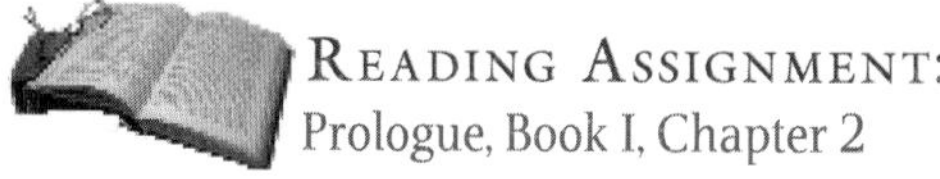

Reading Assignment:
Prologue, Book I, Chapter 2

Session II: Discussion

Prologue, Book I, Chapter 2

A Question to Consider

Have you ever "stuck your foot in your mouth" by speaking before having all the facts?

Discuss or list short answers to the following questions:

Text Analysis

1. What did the Hobbits think about Frodo and about where he came from?
2. After reading the Prologue, how would you describe the inhabitants of the Shire?
3. While Gandalf is talking to Frodo about wanting to save the Shire, he says that Hobbits really are amazing creatures. What does he say about how easy it is to understand Hobbits?

Cultural Analysis

1. Name two or three instances from world history where there have been great consequences because conclusions were reached prematurely.
2. How should we deal with cultural differences that we might have trouble appreciating or understanding?
3. Have you ever been to a friend's home where their house rules were different from yours? What should you do?

Biblical Analysis

1. What does Proverbs say about the humility we should have in these situations (Prov. 3:34; 11:2; 15:33; 29:23; 16:5; 22:4)?
2. What does Proverbs say that might aid us in being slow to open our mouths in this area (10:19; 13:3; 17:27; 18:13; 29:11)?

Summa

Write an essay or discuss this question, integrating what you have learned from the material above.

How can we show love to our neighbor by avoiding jumping to conclusions about them?

Reading Assignment:
Book I, Chapters 3–5

SESSION III: RECITATION

Book I, Chapters 1–4

Comprehension Questions

Answer the following questions for factual recall:

1. What birthday is Mr. Bilbo Baggin's celebrating at the beginning of the story?
2. What was the local legend about the Hill at Bag End?
3. How are Bilbo and Frodo related?
4. What caused Bilbo to be able to vanish before people's eyes at the end his birthday party?
5. What item does Bilbo leave in an envelope for Frodo when he departs?
6. What occurs when Gandalf throws the Ring into the middle of a glowing corner of the fire?
7. What is the one thing keeping the Dark Lord Sauron from covering all the land in darkness?
8. Who comes to question Sam's father about the whereabouts of Mr. Baggins?
9. Whom do the hobbits visit as they take a short-cut across the fields between Woody end and the Brandywine River ferry? What does he do for them?

READING ASSIGNMENT:
Book I, Chapters 6–8

SESSION IV: ACTIVITY

Book I, Chapters 6-8

Character Chart

There are a number of characters in *The Fellowship of the Ring*. It seems as if every time you turn another page you encounter another name. The characters in Chart 1 have been divided into the races that populate Middle-earth. As you encounter the different characters along the way, fill in the chart. You also may want to consult other resources on *The Lord of the Rings*.

We will revisit this chart at the end of the study when you may fill in more information, or you can fill in information as you come to it in the story. Today, fill in what you know for the blue items. Today's work will focus mainly on the Hobbits, because they have dominated our reading to this point. There are some characters that you might know from *The Hobbit*. If you have not yet met a character, you do not need to fill out information on them today, but as you read through *The Fellowship*, make sure you look for the characters and races that are listed.

Chart 1: **RACES AND CHARACTERS**

RACES	DESCRIPTION
Hobbits	
Elves	
Men	
Dwarves	
Orcs	
Uruk-hai	
Black Riders/ Nazgul/Ringwraiths	

CHARACTERS	
Bilbo Baggins	
Frodo Baggins	
Lobelia Sackville-Baggins	
Ham Gamgee (the Gaffer)	
Meriadoc (Merry) Brandybuck	
Peregrin (Pippin) Took	
Samwise (Sam) Gamgee	
Aragorn (Strider)	
Boromir	
Arwen	
Elrond Halfelven	
Galadriel	
Gimli	
Legolas	
Tom Bombadil	
Gandalf the Grey	
Gollum	
Saruman the White	
Sauron	
The Balrog of Moriah	

READING ASSIGNMENT:
Book I, Chapters 9–11

Session V: Recitation

Book I, Chapters 5–11

Comprehension Questions

Answer the following questions for factual recall:

1. Why does Frodo buy a house in Crickhollow?
2. What does Frodo dream that gives a glimpse into the future?
3. How do the hobbits escape from Old Man Willow in the Old Forest?
4. What does Frodo dream while spending the night in the house of Tom Bombadil?
5. What is unique about Tom Bombadil's age?
6. What does not happen to Tom Bombadil when he puts the Ring on?
7. What two groups live in Bree?
8. Whom do the hobbits meet at the inn? What is his real name? How do they know this?
9. What special ability does Frodo have concerning the Black Riders when he puts on the Ring?

Reading Assignment:
Book I, Chapter 12–Book II, Chapter 1

Session VI: Discussion

Book I, Chapters 1–12

A Question to Consider

Does power always corrupt?

Discuss or list short answers to the following questions:

Text Analysis

1. What special powers does Frodo have by possessing the Ring?
2. Why does Sauron want the Ring?
3. How does Frodo use the Ring in Book I, chapter 11?
4. What sense does the reader get concerning how Frodo feels and thinks about using the Ring?

Cultural Analysis

1. What happens to many individuals who win the lottery?
2. What might explain this phenomenon?
3. What is the culture's general view concerning what defines corruption?

Biblical Analysis

1. What advice did Moses' father-in-law give him concerning the power he exerted over the people (Exod. 18)?
2. Are there examples in Scripture of individuals who had power but were not corrupt?
3. What must we conclude then concerning power and corruption (Matt. 13:33–37 and Rom. 8:8; then see the story of Saul in 1 Sam. 8–9; 13:8–23;14:24–46; 15; 28; 31)?

Summa

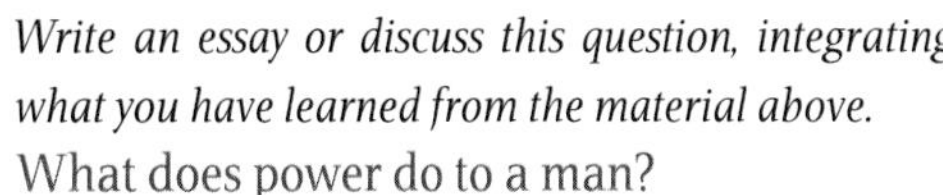

Write an essay or discuss this question, integrating what you have learned from the material above. What does power do to a man?

Optional Activity

Write a paragraph or two in the style of *The Screwtape Letters*. You are an elder demon (Screwtape) writing to a younger demon (Wormwood), giving him advice on how to corrupt his "subject." Your subject is Frodo. He is at the stage where you now find him in the book. He is struggling with what to do with the Ring. Be sure to include in your advice to Wormwood the kinds of things that would aid in the corruption of Frodo.

Reading Assignment:
Book II, Chapters 2–3

Session VII: Discussion

Book II, Chapter 2-3

A Question to Consider

Can people who are extremely different be brought into a community? How?

Text Analysis

1. What is discussed at the Council of Elrond?
2. What differences are there among the group?
3. What do the different groups have in common?
4. What is Elrond's final decision?

Cultural Analysis

1. What is multiculturalism?
2. What is the unifying force of multiculturalism?
3. What does the culture have to offer in terms of creating true community from diversity? Where is the problem with this view?

Biblical Analysis

1. What implication concerning the formation of true community from diversity is there in the Great Commission (Matt. 28:18–20)?
2. In Jesus' High Priestly prayer in John 17 what is the unifying factor?
3. What do we learn about the unity of the body from Ephesians 4?
4. What do we learn from Revelation 5:9 about the creation of community from diverse groups?

SUMMA

Write an essay or discuss this question, integrating what you have learned from the material above.

What is the only hope for man having community when there is so much diversity among us?

READING ASSIGNMENT:
Book II, Chapter 4–5

SESSION VIII: RECITATION

Book I, Chapter 12–Book II, Chapter 4

Comprehension Questions

Answer the following questions for factual recall:

1. What does Strider tell Sam about Frodo's wound?
2. How does he heal him?
3. What would have happened if the splinter from the Black Rider's knife had reached his heart?
4. What are the Ringwraiths?
5. What is the point of the Council of Elrond?
6. What is revealed about Strider in Boromir's dream?
7. Who are the nine that make up the fellowship?
8. What parting gift does Bilbo give to Frodo?
9. Why is Gimli so eager to go to Moria?

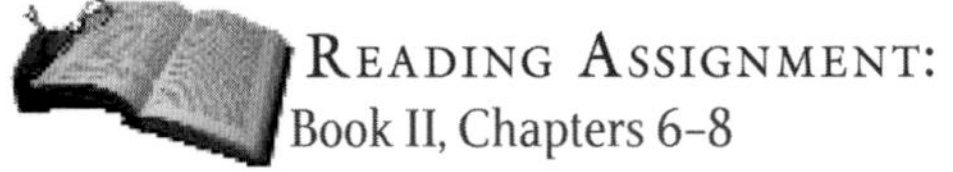

READING ASSIGNMENT:
Book II, Chapters 6–8

SESSION IX: WRITING

Book II, Chapters 6-8

Prophecy in *The Lord of the Rings*

Answer the following questions about the use of prophecy in Book II, Chapters 1-8.

1. What prophecy does Aragorn give concerning Gandalf in book II, chapter four?
2. Does the prophecy come true? How does this shape our view of Aragorn?
3. Tolkien uses prophecies throughout this story, and often they come in the form of songs or verses. What effect does the use of the prophetic word have?
4. How does Tolkien's use of prophecy compare to the purpose for prophecy in Scripture?

Activity A

Write your own prophecy into the novel. Be sure not to jump ahead of what we have read up to this point. Place the prophecy somewhere between the beginning of Book I and Book II, chapter 8. Be sure to follow Tolkien's practice of making it vague enough so that the exact future event is not given away and specific enough to keep the reader interested and looking for the upcoming event in light of the prophecy.

Activity B

Up to this point Tolkien has been giving the reader hints concerning Boromir's obsession with the Ring. Write a series of events that include a prophecy about what you think will transpire with Boromir.

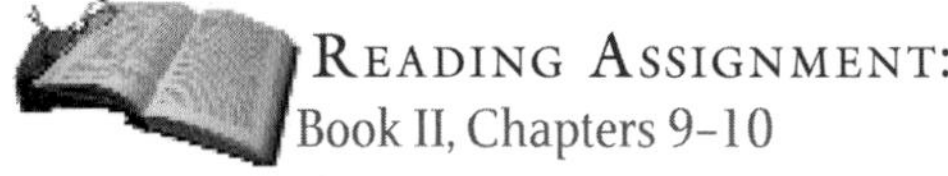

READING ASSIGNMENT:
Book II, Chapters 9–10

SESSION X: DISCUSSION

Book II, Chapters 7-10

A Question to Consider

How does sin gain power over us?

Text Analysis

1. What is Galadriel's response when Frodo offers her the Ring to keep?

2. How is Boromir handling his desire for the Ring?
3. By the end of the book, does Frodo succeed in resisting the lure of the Ring?

Cultural Analysis

1. What is our culture's idea of sin?
2. Even though the biblical idea of sin is lacking from our culture, what is the general understanding of how an individual falls into "sin?"

Biblical Analysis

1. What does James 1:14-15 say about how an individual falls under the power of sin?
2. What principles do we learn from Psalm 1 concerning how we succumb to sin?
3. What do we learn from Romans 1:18-32 about the individual who continues in sin?

Summa

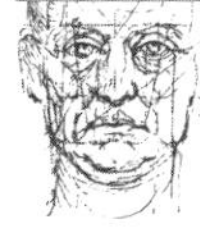

Write an essay or discuss this question, integrating what you have learned from the material above.

Combine the three passages above and map out the process an individual goes through in coming under the power and penalty of sin. How does Tolkien illustrate this process?

CAN BALROGS FLY?

Balrogs are spirits of fire that appear man-like, carry whips of flame and shroud themselves in shadow. They began, like Sauron, as Maiar. They were allies in ancient times with Melkor. Most of the Balrogs were destroyed in the War of Wrath, but some escaped into Middle-earth.

Truly, balrogs are fearsome creatures, but what is truly terrifying is the battles they stir among Tolkien aficionados. The debate centers on *The Fellowship of the Ring* and comes down to the question of whether or not balrogs have *wings.* It says that the balrog "halted again, facing him, and the shadow about it reached out like two vast wings." Does this mean the balrog has wings, or is it just a simile? Two paragraphs later it says, ". . . suddenly it drew itself up to a great height, and its wings were spread from wall to wall . . . "

To one group of readers, this passage describes literal wings and to the other they are metaphorical. The pro-wing faction points to this scene, as well as a description found in some of Tolkien's other writings, where it says that "[s]wiftly they arose, and they passed with winged speed . . .." The wingless balrog party points out that, in situations when it would be helpful to be able to fly, the balrogs do not. The prime example held up at this point is Gandalf's confrontation in *The Fellowship* with the balrog.

Session XI: Recitation

Book II, Chapters 5–10

Comprehension Questions

Answer the following questions for factual recall:

1. What does Gandalf find inside the chamber containing Balin's tomb?
2. What does Frodo do to the cave-troll?
3. What happens to Gandalf in his encounter with the Balrog? What are his last words?
4. Who assumes command after Gandalf is gone?
5. What is Aragorn amazed to find as he tends to Frodo's wound?
6. What is Galadriel's response when Frodo tries to give her the Ring? Why does she respond in this way?
7. When the group is trying to decide where to go next, what is Boromir's suggestion?
8. What does it mean when Sting, Frodo's sword, glows?
9. What does Boromir do when Frodo refuses to take the Ring to Minas Tirith?
10. At the end of the book the Fellowship is divided. Who ends up being the only one to accompany Frodo?

Session XII: Activity

Character Chart

Now, we are going to return to the character chart that we began in Session IV and fill in the rest of the information. Many of these characters will continue to be important as we venture into the rest of the Trilogy. You should be able to fill in all of the information now. You may also enter additional information to the sections that we filled in earlier.

Optional Activities

Once you have read *The Lord of the Rings* (preferably several times), it may be safe to watch Peter Jackson's rendition of it in film. You don't want your basic idea of the story to be shaped by the movie. When you are watching the movie, keep a note pad handy to jot down any places where the movie and the book diverge. When you are done, go back through your list and see how many of your discrepancies you can prove and how many are perhaps just interpretive questions.

Optional Session A: Evaluation

Grammar

Answer each of the following questions in complete sentences. Some answers may be longer than others (2 points per answer).

1. What is the English translation of the writing on the Ring?
2. At the beginning of the book why did Frodo buy a house in Crickhollow?
3. What is unique about Tom Bombadil's age? What does not happen to Tom Bombadil when he puts on the Ring?
4. What special ability does Frodo have concerning the Black Riders when he puts on the Ring?
5. How does Aragorn heal Frodo?
6. What is the purpose of the Council of Elrond?
7. What is Galadriel's response when Frodo tries to give her the Ring? Why does she respond in this way?

Logic

Answer the following questions in complete sentences; your answer should be a paragraph or so. Answer two of the three questions. (10 points per answer)

1. Compare how the following individuals deal with the Ring's power: Galadriel, Frodo, Boromir.
2. There is much debate about whether or not Tolkien intends certain characters to be viewed as "Christ figures." Make a case for Aragorn being understood as a type of Christ.
3. Explain what effect prophecy has in a story. What would be missing without it? How does the specific prophecy concerning Gandalf's death function in *The Fellowship of the Ring?*

Lateral Thinking

Answer one of the following questions. These questions will require more substantial answers. (16 points per answer)

1. Relate the biblical principles concerning sin in James 1:14–15, Psalm 1 and Romans 1:18–32 to

Boromir, the heir of the Steward of Gondor, High Warden of the White Tower, eldest son of Steward Denethor II of Gondor and brother to Faramir, was a valiant and courageous man. When confronted with the Ring of Power, he said, "True-hearted Men, they will not be corrupted. We of Minas Tirith have been staunch through long years of trial. We do not desire the power of wizard-lords, only strength to defend ourselves, strength in a just cause. And behold! in our need chance brings to light the Ring of Power. It is a gift, I say; a gift to the foes of Mordor. It is mad not to use it, to use the power of the Enemy against him."

the manner in which the following individuals deal with the Ring's power: Frodo, Galadriel and Boromir.

2. What is the modern understanding of the word "multicultural?" Can multiculturalism be good? How is it possible for individuals from different ethnic, economic and cultural backgrounds to come together to form true community as we see in the formation of the Fellowship? What was the glue that held them together? Why does our culture's "community" fall apart?

Optional Session B: Creative Writing

The Fellowship of the Ring

Dialogue between characters in a good story always has a purpose. It is not there just to create a feeling of realism or pass time. Dialogue has a job to do. Bad dialogue just sits there with no goal. Good dialogue pulls the reader further into the story and, generally, does two things: (a) reveals more about the characters and (b) moves the story's action toward a goal. Dialogue that fails to accomplish these goals will tend to bore the reader.

Certainly, both of these requirements can be met without using dialogue. A writer could simply tell us that a character is generous or silly. But readers like to figure out puzzles; we like to get involved in a story without being told everything. Dialogue is a great means for involving the reader indirectly, that is, without giving everything away in a flat, obvious way. It's as if we are listening in on a conversation without people explaining every little word.

Readers get even more interested in reading dialogue when a subtext is at work. A subtext is a deeper or a background meaning or message at work behind what people say on the surface. For example, imagine some scene in a modern story where one friend, Janet, while alone yesterday, broke some family antique belonging to her friend Erica, an antique Erica begged her not to touch. Erica suspects Janet, but Janet hasn't confessed yet. A few days later they meet to cook breakfast at Erica's house. On the surface, they talk about the best ways to cook eggs, and neither of them says anything specifically about the broken antique. They just talk about eggs, about cracking eggs, about breaking egg yolks. Can you sense how tense such a scene might be? Have you ever been part of a conversation where some bigger concern looms in the background but no one is willing to talk about it? That's subtext creating tension. And that's what hooks readers into reading more. Good writers are masters of subtext and use it regularly.

We can spot subtext at work in many parts of Tolkien's work. As just one example, consider the end of chapter IV, "A Shortcut to Mushrooms." There we find

Frodo, Pippin and Sam cutting through farmer Maggot's land, and the farmer starts to sick his dogs on the hobbits. The farmer finally welcomes them, but he wants to know why the strange, Black Riders have been looking for Frodo. Sam is suspicious; "he had a natural mistrust of the inhabitants of other parts of the Shire." We have multiple suspicions at work, and yet the surface talk is genuinely friendly. Frodo can't tell this simple farmer all about his mission, and yet he can't say he doesn't trust him. The farmer knows Frodo faces some trouble, but he doesn't force him to say what it is. The dialogue throughout this scene is indirect, full of subtext and reveals more to us about the character of the hobbits, as well as showing us how dangerously close the Black Riders are. It's a minor but important bit of dialogue that does everything good dialogue is supposed to do.

Try writing some similar dialogue for a scene very much like this one. Think of it as a scene Tolkien wrote for this story but lost.

1. Plan on writing about a page or two of dialogue, without any other descriptions or narration. It will look more like a play script than a typical Tolkien chapter.
2. Use just Frodo, Sam and one new character they meet on the same road as the farmer.
3. Make this new character much less friendly to Frodo and Sam. Make him or her more afraid of the strange things going on. Make him or her suspicious that Frodo is the bad one and the Black Rider is some good agent of the law.
4. Pick a new setting, not a farm. Have Frodo and Sam, perhaps, sneak through a small town and meet up with some shopkeeper.
5. Have Frodo and Sam ask for some help and have them pretend not to know the shopkeeper, though they've met in the past over some embarrassing incident.
6. Have the shopkeeper keep asking odd, suspicious questions of Frodo. Let the reader see that the shopkeeper remembers some "bad" incident involving Frodo.
7. Don't let any of the three characters make direct reference to this "bad" incident or misunderstanding in the past. Have them talk about innocent, surface things.
8. As the dialogue moves on, use it to show us something good about the character of Frodo. Let us see in Frodo's answers that he is honest, courageous or something similar. Maybe let us see him protect his friend Sam. Show us something good about Sam's character, too, like loyalty. Let him see the shopkeeper's suspicion and try to indirectly protect his friend.

Your biggest goal as a writer is to keep your reader hooked. Once you've finished your brief dialogue, go back through and edit it. Cut out everything that is too direct, too obvious or not tense. Cut out any flat small talk like greetings. Make the first line hook your reader with tension. Test it out on someone and ask them if it held their attention at every point. Be teachable. Good dialogue writing takes years to perfect; have fun with this brief exercise.

ENDNOTES

1 Foster, Robert. *The Complete Guide to Middle-earth.* New York: Ballantine Books, 1971. 491.

The Nine Tailors

It's a lovely day. The sun is smiling, and the trees are overhead laughing as they sway to the rhythm of the breeze. The rehearsal is also going splendidly. Apart from being a little nervous and mispronouncing a few words, you know your lines, and the world is your audience. And the king! Yes, the king will love it. You're pausing back stage, waiting for your cue. Oops! There it was! The director has reprimanded you. You take a deep breath and shake your head to clear your mind. Something odd waggles in your hair on your head, but no time to think: you're on! You begin the lines, but something is all wrong. Everyone is looking at you and pointing, but they are not looking with admiration or expectation or anything close to it. Rather, the stage is clearing. No one is in the right place; you can't finish your line; people are yelling and running. Props are falling as your friends flee, faces like ash, eyes bursting with terror. Shouts and mad scrambles, and you're alone. The forest is all around you, and the voices of your friends die away in the distance.

Perhaps you recognize this story from Shakespeare's *A Midsummer Night's Dream.* Of course, the play actor was Bottom the Weaver, who was given an ass's head by the playful fairy henchman, Puck. But what if something like this were really true? What if you woke one morning and, glancing into the mirror, you noticed that you were growing whiskers? Not just the kind you young men *think* you're growing, mind you. But what if big, long, cat-like whiskers had sprouted out your nose? Or even worse: what if you also had tusks, enormous ivory tubas, curling out from beneath your upper lip, hanging down to your shoulders? You might laugh, you might cry, you might do any number of things. You might think: "This can't be happening!" Or maybe you think this is all silly to begin with because, you say, such things can't happen. But that is the question: What is possible, anyway? What kind of world do we live in?

Geoffrey of Monmouth believed that the city of York's foundation dated from the time that "king David ruled in Judea." The cathedral as it stands today dates primarily from the thirteenth and fourteenth centuries.

General Information

Author and Context

Dorothy Leigh Sayers was born at Oxford, England, on June 13, 1893. Her father was a minister in the Church of England, and thus she grew up in the church and was well acquainted with its teachings, forms and cultural life. She attended boarding school for several years growing up and went to Somerville College at Oxford University. She graduated with First Class Honors for her Master of Arts in Modern Languages, although she did not actually receive the degree until 1920, when she was among the first class of women ever to receive their degrees from the University. She enjoyed acting, and as a young girl she spent many hours pretending to be one of the musketeers from the novel by Dumas. Her first writing to be published was a small collection of poems in 1916. Her first novel, *Whose Body?,* was published in 1923. She wrote many other essays, novels and plays, including a detective novel entitled *The Floating Admiral,* which was collaboratively written by the Detection Club and included such august members as Agatha Christie and G. K. Chesterton. Sayers' book, *The Nine Tailors,* was published in 1934, a continuation of the Lord Peter Wimsey series of detective and mystery novels. The final installment came in 1937 with *Busman's Honeymoon.* As she got older, her writing moved in a more scholarly direction. From detective novels she moved on to plays and direct apologies for the Christian faith, her faith becoming more and more explicit in her writing. One of her forays in Christian theology, and one of her most celebrated works of non-fiction, is *The Mind of the Maker,* a Trinitarian analysis of the imago Dei, exploring creativity and imagination. In 1954 Sayers began producing her earliest work on Dante. A translation of *The Divine Comedy* was her last project, and she died on December 17, 1957, with a number of cantos remaining in her translation of *Paradiso.* Her translation and notes were finished by a friend and published posthumously in 1962.

In 1923 Dorothy Leigh Sayers published her first novel, *Whose Body*, which introduced Lord Peter Wimsey. She once said "The only Christian work is good work, well done."

Sayers, in addition to these academic and professional achievements, had a household with a number of cats. She is said to have regularly worn a rather outlandish style of dress, which unfortunately proved to be an unsightly purple more often than not. One friend remarked that these dresses also tended to come with a rather overindulgence of lace in all the wrong places. She was often seen walking through town in fur coats. Her hair, thin as it was, seldom showed signs of care. And as far as physical appearance is concerned, she was simply not the most beautiful of women. She is described as being rather plain with large, deep blue eyes and glasses, somewhat awkward and with hardly a neck to speak of. But it was this woman who, despite these apparent flaws, was hardly plain in her speech or lacking in loveliness in her writings. She knew her art, and she stuck to it.

Dorothy Sayers was also good friends with a number of other famous and influential characters of her time period, G.K. Chesterton, Charles Williams, C.S. Lewis and T.S. Eliot among them. But Sayers adds her own significance to the literary and theological world of the first half of the twentieth century. Sayers was energetic and passionate about everything she did. She was playful and witty, and she always seemed up for a game or a good joke. Sometimes letters were written with pseudonyms between herself and Charles Williams. Using titles of nobility and referring to fellow dukes and knights, simple salutations and recognitions were exchanged. But Sayers played seriously. She clung to her Christian convictions with tenacity, and while she sometimes questioned the direct approach of her contemporaries, her faith permeated everything she wrote.

Significance

The Nine Tailors is considered by many to be her finest work of fiction. Coming towards the end of her famed Lord Peter Wimsey detective series, it is among a select few where her attention turned away from the ordinary English murder mystery. That is to say, in many ways, the great significance of *The Nine Tailors* is seen by what it is not. Of course there are stolen jewels and a mysterious and disfigured body is unearthed in an English churchyard, but in many ways what one might expect of the great detective tale is all backward and wrong. Please understand, *The Nine Tailors* is suspenseful, humorous and quite rewarding, but Sayers has taken the usual detective form and transfigured it into something far more stupendous.

If you have ever read any Sir Arthur Conan Doyle, you know what the usual detective form is. Sharp, snappy detective with slightly slower and bumbling sidekick are met by someone in need, usually a young woman. Someone has been murdered or robbed, the case is accepted and the detectives follow the young woman to the scene of the crime. A short investigation takes place, Sherlock sums the evidence, deduces the when, why, how and who with startling brilliance and punctilious rigidity, and the world is shown once again to be a logical and coherent place to live. But *The Nine Tailors* opens with our hero, that great, formidable English gentleman, Lord Peter Wimsey, getting into a car accident. This is startling; this is funny; this is absurd. This is like James Bond tripping on a banana peel, or Jeeves falling into a lake. The book opens with the hero making a blunder. And even though we might justify it by the fact that he was driving in hazardous winter conditions, and (we are later informed) that particular spot in the road is notoriously perilous, nevertheless we must begin with the fact that our hero

Sherlock Holmes was a detective famous for his razor-sharp powers of observation, which he applied to solving baffling mysteries. He lived in a flat at 221B Baker Street in London and was accompanied on his cases by his friend Dr. Watson, who would record his investigations and publish them for the public to read. Holmes's most famous cases are *The Hound of the Baskervilles* and *A Study in Scarlet*. The cool, calculating and decidedly *un*Wimsey-esque detective has been portrayed in radio, television and movies, most notably by actor Basil Rathbone from 1939–46 and in the 80's and 90's by Jeremy Brett.

has miffed his swing and hence the rest of the story peers out at us somewhat cock-eyed. In this way, Sayers makes a unique contribution to the mystery novel genre in general, but *The Nine Tailors* is also a fine novel in its own right. The details of change-ringing, the geological descriptions of the Fens and a party of colorful characters are all woven together masterfully to form a splendid piece of literature.

Main Characters

Lord Peter Wimsey is the hero of our story. He is an English gentleman with an interest in detection and justice, having been involved in a number of other cases. Wimsey is not only keen, witty and likeable but also human, as revealed by occasions where he is stumped or has an accident. Next to Bunter, Wimsey's careful but hardly insignificant footman, we meet Mr. Venables, the "gentle and scholarly" clergyman. Mr. Venables is the rector (pastor) of the parish of Fenchurch St. Paul in the Fens of East Anglia, England. He is a faithful shepherd of his flock, proven as we meet him, by his visiting and encouraging a sick man and his wife. Mr. Venables is not only faithful in his visitation and concern for the "three hundred and forty souls" in his parish but also has an insatiable love for his church building, its famously tall tower and, in particular, its bells. Mrs. Venables is a kindly woman who is the mind of her forgetful husband. For all his care, he's absent minded, as evidenced by his losing his keys from time to time. Mrs. Venables is hospitable and loving. At times she speaks her mind on a subject, and she isn't afraid to say what or who she doesn't trust. The list of characters goes on: Superintendent Blundell, Will Thoday, Mary Thoday, Deacon, Cranton, Hilary Thorpe, Potty Peake and a number of other townspeople. This, too, is rather uncharacteristic of the detective novel. Why should Sayers's readers care about the parishioners of Fenchurch St. Paul? What do all those different chaps and women have to do with the mystery? But this is precisely Sayers's point. She said one time that if the mystery genre was to survive the sifting of time it would have to grow up and become beautiful. And that is just what has happened here. Without growing up into literature, the mystery story is just a complicated crossword puzzle.

But this story has more than a simple Dickens' overload of colorful characters. Rather, when you really get down to it, it's the bells. Woven throughout the mysterious tale is the terminology and technique of campanology, the study of change-ringing. You see, as one writer has remarked, *The Nine Tailors* is a book about bells. But don't roll your eyes or drift off just yet. Sayers is doing something with the bells. Again, it is worth pausing momentarily to ask ourselves what a detective novel has to do with the study of ringing bells. Is there really that much to know? Well, actually *yes.* The bells are as complex as a person, and in many ways, the bells are the central character(s) of the story. They have names and voices, adding to their personification: Gaude, Sabaoth, John, Jericho, Jubilee, Dimity and Tailor Paul. Another, by the name of Batty Thomas, once saved the church and on other occasions killed two men. The bells also bear to the countryside the tidings of baptisms, marriages and death. In the event of a death, nine tailors for a man and six for a woman are rung, and the age of the deceased is rung out after that.

Summary and Setting

Lord Peter Wimsey meets the bells when he shelters at the rectory of St. Paul's while his car is being repaired. St. Paul's is located somewhere in the Fens of East Anglia. East Anglia is in the southeast corner of England, just east and a touch north of London. The Fens is a region of lowlands, and thus they tend to be a bit wet. Intricate systems of drainage using canals and dikes clear the land for agricultural uses. There, when one of the change-ringers falls ill, Wimsey fills in, ringing in New Year's Day. During his stay, Wimsey is introduced to the mystery of the Wilbraham emeralds, a necklace that was stolen but never recovered. Even though those believed to be the thieves, Mr. Deacon and Mr. Cranton, had been caught and imprisoned, the jewels themselves had never been found. Following Wimsey's departure from St. Paul's, a corpse is found in a grave in the churchyard. Of course that's where corpses are supposed to be found, but in this case a body has been added to a grave that was not its own. Mr. Venables contacts Wimsey to aid in solving the mystery, and Wimsey takes the case. The obvious questions: Whose body has been found? Who killed the man, and why? From the beginning we suspect that this murder is in some way connected to the missing Wilbraham jewels. Potty Peake, the community half-wit, occasionally shows his face and relays with very little coherence various esoteric descriptions of murders and hangings. Hilary Thorpe, the daughter of the husband and wife in whose grave was found the mysterious corpse, finds a queer poem at the base of the bell chamber while helping Mr. Godfrey oil the bells. And in one of Bunter's rare moments in the spotlight, he feigns to be a gentleman named Paul Tailor, a pseudonym for someone surely connected to the whole affair, and intercepts an interesting letter in the mail. These clues lead the detective and Superintendent Blundell to France and back, and finally, with the help of Will and Jim Thoday, the trail leads right back into St. Paul's.

Lord Peter ends up helping to ring in the New Year on the eight tower bells of the parish church. Each bell was rung about 15,000 times—nine hours of continuous ringing!

Worldview

So much of modern conflict and argument is over the nature of the world. If the universe is just a cosmic burp which accidentally spewed the galaxies into being, planets into orbits and touched off the several-billion-year process of making people out of plankton, then we're all dominoes in a huge, meaningless nothingness. Sometimes even when the world is admitted to have been created by a god, this god is imagined as a very large and distant brain. And this brain functions a lot like the fastest computer in the world. Billions of numbers and letters, beeping and humming methodically somewhere up there in the sky. Both visions of the world, however, fall considerably short of the glories we see every day. Hot air balloons, zebras and chocolate are each in their own way proofs against the nihilism of evolution and the tedium of rationalism. If the world were only an accident, it would have no meaning; if the world were merely a complex set of equations and symbols, it would be utterly boring.

Most lies are half truths. And so are rationalism and evolutionism. It is true that numbers and symbols, equations and logic, deduction and rational analysis are useful descriptions. Whenever we drive over large suspension bridges or fly in an airplane, we ought to be thankful for all the honest and hard-working engineers and mathematicians. Likewise, it is true that strange things happen in the world we live in. Sometimes the sea parts to reveal dry ground. Sometimes an ass will talk to its overbearing master. Sometimes the sun stays in the sky for longer than can be reasonably explained. Stars are known to come down out of the sky and fight the enemies of Israel, and at another time they form a chorus announcing the birth of the Savior. Men call fire down from heaven, diseases are healed and young men walk through flames unharmed. A corpse comes to life after touching the bones of a prophet, an ax head floats and men walk on water. Evolution is right, in that the world is often an unreasonable place. It doesn't cooperate with what we understand as normal. It doesn't follow the rules all the time. Rationalism is the overemphasis on reason with a good bit of disdain for the material world; evolutionism is the overemphasis of the unreasonable with a good bit of angst or worry for the supernatural, which all seems rather odd. But you see, in many ways they're just two extremes.

But what they both have in common are their attempts to pull a fabulous, mind-blowing world out of the hat they stole from us. It *is* a miraculous event, making something out of nothing, turning emptiness into star-spangled galaxies and worlds of color and life, but the Triune God created the heavens and the earth, and all other substitutes for this vision are folly. So which is it? Is the world reasonable or not, orderly or not, predictable or not, logical or not? To such questions we must simply laugh. It's a bit like asking if a judge is skinny or fat. It all depends, we might say. Our real concern ought to be whether or not the judge is *good*. If the judge is just, if the judge is good, then we know he can be trusted. The same is true with the Triune God. It's tempting to want a simple answer, a straightforward *yes* or *no*. But God refuses to be placed into our categories. God is not an accidental force, nor is He a distant computer brain on the outskirts of the universe. He is one God in three persons, intimately involved in every detail of the world.

The Nine Tailors begins, as we've already noted, with the dignified detective getting mud on his face. But the rest of the mystery is a winding road with incidents and accidents, vague hints and slow-going progress. At some points in the book, clear reasoning and careful deduction reveal a lead and point to a conclusion. At other points, mix-ups and goofs prove to be the revealers of the truth. At one point Blundell says, "Just where we were before." "Yes," replies Wimsey, "It's like Looking-Glass Country. Takes all the running we can do to stay in the same place." Potty Peake, the village idiot, is another example of this. He babbles incessantly but nevertheless clearly indicates that he saw two men in the church late one night. What does this mean, and what can be done? In this case, nothing. "He was not good at remembering dates, and his conversation, while full of strange hints and prophecies had a way of escaping from the restraints of logic and playing gruesomely among the dangling bell-ropes." While this is meant as a description of Potty Peake, it sums up nicely the rest of the evidence.

Another incident is the deciphering of the meaning of Hilary's poem. In a standard detective novel, the masterful detective has been secretly studying up on some eccentric hobby that ties directly into his ability to solve the mystery. Wimsey, if he were Sherlock Holmes, would glanced at the poem, scribble down a few words or numbers, turn around and announce the results after only a couple of minutes. But here Wimsey is stumped, and it's an old clergyman with failing eyes who accidentally sees the solution to the riddle.

In other ways Wimsey makes great headway with careful reasoning and thinking. He finds the rope used to tie the victim at the bottom of a well next to the cemetery. The letter addressed to 'Paul Tailor' is intercepted by Wimsey and Bunter and is traced to France, and the woman who wrote it is located and questioned. Cranton is also hunted down and questioned, and Wimsey and Blundell know they are dealing with the mystery of the Wilbraham jewels all over again. But what are we to do with all these leads, all these clues, all these premises—and no conclusion? Wimsey says it best himself:

> "I think I have been the most unmitigated and unconscionable ass that ever brayed in a sleuth-hound's skin. Now, however, I have solved the entire problem, with one trivial exception. Probably you have done so too."

"I'll buy it," said Mr. Blundell. "I'm like you, my lord, I'm doing no more guessing. What's the bit you haven't solved, by the way?"

"Well, the murder," said his lordship, with an embarrassed cough. "I can't quite make out who did that, or how. But that, as I say, is a trifle . . ."

Wimsey goes on to list everything that he has deduced, which is quite a bit of the surrounding details, including who the dead man is. But still mocking him all along are the central questions. And this is not what a hero detective is supposed to say! He's supposed to say that he's figured it all out and tell the whole story Everyone is shocked, delighted and happy for the solution, and then everyone goes home elated. Wimsey simply can't break through it. He's reached a ceiling in his reasoning. As Mrs. Venables says, "There are always wheels within wheels."

A village idiot, a blind clergyman and a depressed detective—in the end these are more important in solving the mystery than all the standard routines of sleuthing, questioning and pondering. But what does Sayers mean by all this? We began by discussing our world and the extremes of evolutionism and rationalism. It appears that Sayers is presenting a picture of the world that in many ways combats both errors. The world does have many reasonable and predictable elements: men can be traced and tracked down; many questions can be asked and answered. But the world is also a strange and mystical place, and it doesn't always follow our rules or plans. Dams burst, idiots speak the truth, cars run off the road and bellowing bells deal out the justice of God. This world is the playground of the Triune God, and all our efforts to understand and decipher are merely drops in the ocean of His wisdom.

Fenchurch St. Paul is a microcosm of the universe, but this is no Edgar Allen Poe story. Sayers is not merely pretending that bells do creepy things on their own sometimes. The bells are the mouths of God. They are the booming voice of the church, the exhilarating and terrifying force of the Triune fellowship working in and through history. Towering high above the fens, they rumble out the great decrees of God: baptism, marriage and death, holding time and eternity in one firm grasp.

But *The Nine Tailors* ends with a flood. Spring rains overflow dams and sluices, racing madly down their courses, covering fields and plains, destroying homes and property. Men, women, children and animals clamber into St. Paul's while the fens are overrun with some eight feet of water for fourteen days and nights. But the church is not a chaotic pile of tattered lives. The pigs, cattle, birds and hamsters go down below, beds and cots are organized into groups, school lessons resume, stoves are lit, food and drink are plenty, a nursing sta-

CHANGE RINGING

Ben Johnson once wrote "Bell ringing is the poetry of steeples." Many of us have heard church bells ringing on Sunday mornings or at weddings. These may ring out a tune or a hymn, and bells of this sort are called carillons or chimes. The bells do not swing, and the tune is "played" by one person.

The bell ringing that is such a major part of *The Nine Tailors* is a different kind, called *change ringing.* Each bell is swung by someone, called a ringer, pulling on a rope. With each pull the bell swings from the "mouth up" position, through a full 360 degrees, stopping in the same position and causing the clapper to sound a single note. There is usually one ringer for each bell. Since each bell is tuned to a different note on the scale, the order in which the bells are rung controls the melody. Changing the order changes the tune, and that is why the technique is called change ringing.

tion is erected and church services continue. Cows are milked, meals are shared, committees meet, games are held; there's a baptism and a wedding celebration and our very own Lord Peter Wimsey goes swimming down the village street.

St. Paul's is of course a new Noah's Ark. The world of Fenchurch St. Paul is being remade much like God did in the early chapters of Genesis. And it's all being remade in the church. Living, real living, laughter, food and fellowship are found in the community of believers. The church is literally (as a building) the place of God's salvation, but Sayers means more than that. The flood is also a giant baptism of sorts, cleansing the land from its crimes (1 Pet. 3:20–21).

"Nine Tailors make a man in Christ" is a recurring line throughout the story, and of course it's also in the title of the book. The book is about bells, but these are not merely bells, they are the mouthpiece and hand of God in Fenchurch St. Paul's. But the bells are also the Nine Tailors; they are death. And strangely they are also life. At one point Hezekiah and Wimsey have this interchange:

> "Ringing Tailor Paul seems to be a healthy occupation," said Wimsey. "His servants live to a ripe old age, what?"
>
> "Ah!" said Hezekiah. "So they du, young man, so they du, if so be they're faithful tu 'un an' don't go a-angerin' 'un. They bells du know well who's a-haulin' of 'un. Wunnerful understandin' they is. They can't abide a wicked man. They lays in wait to overthrow 'un. An' she allus done well by me. Make righteousness your course bell, my lord, an' keep a-follerin' on her an' she'll see you through your changes till Death calls you to stand. Yew ain't no call to be afeard o' the bells if so be as yew follows righteousness."

The bells are death, but if righteousness is our course, then even in Death they become our defense. Ringing Tailor Paul is a healthy occupation, and we have no need to fear.

Life is not just atoms and chemicals acting and reacting in a chaotic symphony of accidents. Nor is life an algebra problem, where all you have to do is plug and chug. That is the meaning of our beginning illustration when we asked what kind of world we actually live in. We don't live in a boring, predictable world like the rationalist believes. But neither do we live in a random world of anarchy. When Bottom turned into a donkey, it happened for good reason. But only a certain kind of God could rule a world like the one we live in.

The Father, Son and Spirit who created, love and indwell this universe are persons. The Triune God gives all the purpose and meaning and levity to the world that He wants. It is a temptation to want easy answers. It is a temptation to always want the yes or no,

In *The City of God*, Augustine points to Noah's ark as a symbol of Christ's church on pilgrimage through the wicked world, symbolized by the flood. He wrote that the size of the ark symbolized the human body in whose form Christ was to come. The door represented the wound in Christ's side when he was pierced with the spear since from the wound flowed the blood and water of the sacraments of baptism and communion by which believers are initiated.

logic or not, reasonable or not sorts of things made plain. But the Trinity is a holy, creative and imaginative God Who visits His people with words and numbers, sunsets and strawberries, and in the end He is far too brilliant and amazing to begin to comprehend. As Mr. Venables says, "God speaks through those mouths of inarticulate metal. He is a righteous judge, strong and patient, and is provoked every day." We live in His world, we live in His universe. He makes the rules because he designed the game. Nine tailors make a man because the way to life is by dying, following Christ and taking up His cross every day. And facing any problem, we ought to remember the Rector's words: "My dear boy, it does not do for us to take too much thought for the morrow. It is better to follow the truth and leave the result in the hand of God. He can foresee where we cannot, because He knows all the facts."

—*Toby Sumpter*

For Further Reading

Durkin, Mary Brian O.P. *Dorothy L. Sayers.* Boston, Mass.: Twayne Publishers, 1980.

Hannay, Margaret P. ed. *As Her Wimsey Took Her.* Kent, Ohio: Kent State University Press, 1979.

Sayers, Dorothy L. *The Mind of the Maker.* New York, N.Y.: Harper Collins, 1987.

Session I: Prelude

A Question to Consider

What is the world like? (How would you describe it to someone who had never been here?)

From the General Information above answer the following questions:

1. What is Evolutionism?
2. What is Rationalism?
3. How is the Triune God different from Rationalism and Evolutionism?
4. What are the Nine Tailors? How do they picture the Trinity?
5. How is Lord Peter Wimsey not a normal English detective?
6. How do the accidents in the story reveal Sayer's view of the world?
7. What aspects of Sayer's life might also prove she had this view of the world?

Reading Assignment:
Kent Treble Bob Major: The First and Second Courses[1]

Session II: Discussion

Kent Treble Bob Major: The First and Second Courses

A Question to Consider

Why is death difficult?

Discuss or list short answers to the following questions:

Text Analysis

1. What is the feat that the Rector is attempting to accomplish on New Year's Day?
2. What is rung first before the "big ring" begins?
3. Who is the lady who dies while Wimsey is waiting for his car to be repaired?
4. Summarize the mystery of the Wilbraham jewels as told by Joe Hinkins.

Cultural Analysis

1. How do Americans view death and dying?
2. How should Christians view death and dying?
3. How does our society view the elderly or disabled?
4. How should Christians care for the elderly and disabled?

Biblical Analysis

1. What does the Bible require of us in regard to our treatment of widows, orphans, the poor and strangers in our society (Deut. 16, 24, 26)?
2. In light of those passages or others, why does God require us to be so generous and caring for outcasts and strangers?
3. In our own society, who would the "strangers" be?
4. What does the resurrection mean for believing widows, orphans, the poor and other outcasts?

SUMMA

Write an essay or discuss this question, integrating what you have learned from the material above.

How does a Christian view of death lead to loving the outcasts of society?

Optional Activity

Visit a nursing home or the home of an elderly neighbor. Introduce yourself and try to converse with several different people. Ask them about their lives, families and interests. Ask them if they have any needs and (as you are able) try to find an area in which you can help them.

READING ASSIGNMENT:
Grandsire Triples: The First and Second Parts

SESSION III: DISCUSSION

Grandsire Triples: The First and Second Parts

A Question to Consider

When is mathematics useful? When is it not?

Discuss or list short answers to the following questions:

Text Analysis

1. How does math relate to change-ringing?
2. How many bells are rung when someone dies?
3. How many bells are rung for the corpse found in Mrs. Thorpe's grave?
4. How does math relate to investigation in general and to Lord Peter Wimsey's investigation in particular?

Cultural Analysis

1. What does our culture think about the value of mathematics? Compare it to literature or poetry.
2. Is our culture's view of math and science healthy?

Biblical Analysis

1. What does God think about math? Cite specific examples as proof (Why are numbers like three, seven, twelve and forty meaningful biblically?)

SUMMA

Write an essay or discuss this question, integrating what you have learned from the material above.

What is a Christian view of mathematics?

Optional Activity

Pick a Bible story with numbers in it (e.g., Gen. 6, 11, Num. 2, 7, 2 Chron. 26–27, Mark 5:21–43, Rev. 21:9–27). Memorize the numbers, think about them and the story they are in. Attempt to draw conclusions about the way God told the story, the numbers he used and the significance of math to what it means.

READING ASSIGNMENT:
Grandsire Triples: The Third, Fourth and Fifth Parts

SESSION IV: DISCUSSION

Grandsire Triples: The Third, Fourth and Fifth Parts

A Question to Consider

Is it ever right for a Christian to lie?

Discuss or list short answers to the following questions:

Text Analysis

1. How do Deacon's and Cranton's stories differ?
2. How is the Superintendent sure that Deacon was a lying?
3. What does it mean on when Blundell says, "I don't like witnesses to be so damned particular about the exact truth...?"
4. How does Bunter lie?

Cultural Analysis

1. How does our culture view lying and deception?
2. What are examples of acceptable lies in our modern culture?

Biblical Analysis

1. Compare the stories of Abraham (Gen. 12:10–13:2; Gen. 20), Isaac (Gen. 26:1–14), Gideon (Judg. 6:11), and Rahab (Josh. 2). Is the deception and lying in these stories godly or not? Defend your answer from Scripture.

2. When God promises the destruction of Nineveh and then relents (Jon. 3:4–10) or declares Hezekiah's death and relents (2 Kings 20:1–11) or sends a lying spirit to King Ahab in order to bring him down (1 Kings 22:20–23), is God lying? Why or why not?
3. What does John 14:6 mean when it says that Jesus is the Truth?
4. How is the Cross an act of deception on the part of God? What about the gospel? (1 Cor. 2:7–8)

Summa

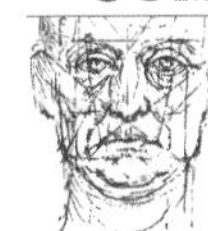

Write an essay or discuss this question, integrating what you have learned from the material above.

How is truth personal?

Reading Assignment:

Grandsire Triples: The Sixth and Seventh Parts

Now the Angel of the LORD came and sat under the terebinth tree which was in Ophrah, which belonged to Joash the Abiezrite, while his son Gideon threshed wheat in the winepress, in order to hide it from the Midianites. And the Angel of the LORD appeared to him, and said to him, "The LORD is with you, you mighty man of valor!"

Session V: Discussion

Grandsire Triples: The Sixth and Seventh Parts

A Question to Consider

When is logic useful? When is it not?

Discuss or list short answers to the following questions:

Text Analysis

1. What are some of the logical deductions made after Suzanne Legros has been questioned?

2. When Potty Peake is interviewed, he says he saw Number Nine. Who is that?
3. Why doesn't Wimsey think Jim Thoday buried the corpse?
4. Why does Wimsey conclude that the scrap of paper Hilary found was not written by Potty?
5. Why does Wimsey suspect that "Hilary's poem" was written by someone involved in the Wilbraham jewels mystery?

Cultural Analysis

1. What does our modern culture think about logic?
2. What are some examples of how little moderns care for logic?

Biblical Analysis

1. What does the Bible say about logic (John 1:1–11; word = logos in Greek, which can also be rendered logic)?
2. Read Job 38–42:6. What is God's argument against Job? What does God's argument teach us about argumentation and logic in general?

SUMMA

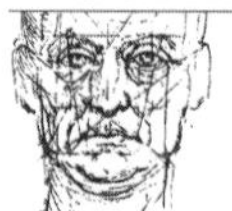

Write an essay or discuss this question, integrating what you have learned from the material above.

How is logic related to Jesus Christ? (How is sin then related to logic?)

READING ASSIGNMENT:
Grandsire Triples: The Eighth and Ninth Parts

SESSION VI: ACTIVITY

Grandsire Triples: The Eighth and Ninth Parts

The Bells

Read *The Bells* by Edgar Allen Poe out loud, or in a group setting divide the reading up among the students:

I
Hear the sledges with the bells—
Silver bells!
What a world of merriment their melody
foretells!
How they tinkle, tinkle, tinkle,
In the icy air of night!
While the stars that oversprinkle
All the heavens, seem to twinkle
With a crystalline delight;
Keeping time, time, time,
In a sort of Runic rhyme,
To the tintinnabulation that so
musically wells
From the bells, bells, bells, bells,
Bells, bells, bells—
From the jingling and the tinkling of the bells.

II
Hear the mellow wedding bells—
Golden bells!
What a world of happiness their harmony
foretells!
Through the balmy air of night
How they ring out their delight!—
From the molten-golden notes,
And all in tune,
What a liquid ditty floats
To the turtle-dove that listens,
while she gloats
On the moon!
Oh, from out the sounding cells,
What a gush of euphony voluminously wells!
How it swells!
How it dwells
On the Future!—how it tells
Of the rapture that impels
To the swinging and the ringing
Of the bells, bells, bells—
Of the bells, bells, bells, bells,
Bells, bells, bells—
To the rhyming and the chiming of the bells!

III
Hear the loud alarum bells—
Brazen bells!
What a tale of terror, now, their
turbulency tells!
In the startled ear of night
How they scream out their affright!
Too much horrified to speak,
They can only shriek, shriek,
Out of tune,

In a clamorous appealing to the mercy
of the fire,
In a mad expostulation with the deaf
and frantic fire,
Leaping higher, higher, higher,
With a desperate desire,
And a resolute endeavor
Now—now to sit, or never,
By the side of the pale-faced moon.
Oh, the bells, bells, bells!
What a tale their terror tells
Of Despair!
How they clang, and clash and roar!
What a horror they outpour
On the bosom of the palpitating air!
Yet the ear, it fully knows,
By the twanging,
And the clanging,
How the danger ebbs and flows;
Yet the ear distinctly tells,
In the jangling,
And the wrangling,
How the danger sinks and swells,
By the sinking or the swelling in the
anger of the bells—
Of the bells—
Of the bells, bells, bells, bells,
Bells, bells, bells—
In the clamor and the clanging of the bells!

IV
Hear the tolling of the bells—
Iron bells!
What a world of solemn thought
their monody compels!
In the silence of the night,
How we shiver with affright
At the melancholy menace of their tone!
For every sound that floats
From the rust within their throats
Is a groan.
And the people—ah, the people—
They that dwell up in the steeple,
All alone,
And who, tolling, tolling, tolling,
In that muffled monotone,
Feel a glory in so rolling
On the human heart a stone—
They are neither man nor woman—
They are neither brute nor human—
They are Ghouls: —
And their king it is who tolls:—
And he rolls, rolls, rolls,
Rolls
A paean from the bells!
And his merry bosom swells
With the paean of the bells!
And he dances, and he yells;
Keeping time, time, time,
In a sort of Runic rhyme,
To the paean of the bells:—
Of the bells:
Keeping time, time, time
In a sort of Runic rhyme,
To the throbbing of the bells—
Of the bells, bells, bells:—
To the sobbing of the bells:—
Keeping time, time, time,
As he knells, knells, knells,
In a happy Runic rhyme,
To the rolling of the bells—
Of the bells, bells, bells—
To the tolling of the bells—
Of the bells, bells, bells, bells,
Bells, bells, bells,—
To the moaning and the groaning of the bells.

Try to "hear" as you read the sound of the bells that Poe is describing. Talk about the sorts of things you imagine. How would the ringing of the bells sound different at a funeral than the ringing at a baptism or a wedding? Discuss how different sorts of bells and different sorts of rings affect you. Discuss what different kinds of bells and rings mean and why. Perhaps after an initial read through, work on certain sections or memorize parts (or the entirety) of the poem and plan a recital. Give drama and life to your reading or reciting, bellowing out the low, rolling bells and clanging and dinging the smaller, tinkling bells.

Stedman's Triples: The First Part

Just as the architecture of an ancient church prominently displays the bell tower, Dorothy Sayers gives the bells of Fenchurch St. Paul a dominant role in this mystery novel. The critic and mystery writer H.R.F. Keating included *The Nine Tailors* in his list of the one hundred best crime and mystery books ever published.

Session VII: Writing

Grandsire Triples: The Tenth Part and Stedman's Triples: The First Part

Poetry Code

Write a poem using some kind of code. It may be a simple code or something rather difficult, but be consistent throughout. Be as creative as possible, trying to make the poem seem as real or authentic as possible while still communicating something if the poem were to be deciphered. Trade poems with members of your class or family and try to break each others' codes. Perhaps after a bit, you might think of certain hints to give one another (if they are stumped) without giving the whole thing away. Here's an example:

In northern tales, handsome elegance
Bestows exceptional grace in near nostalgia

I never guessed: when a sacred thought
Has emerged, Wielded over river dreams.

Can you decipher the code? The first letter of every word is the key. Taking all the first letters of every word in order, you should form the words: "In the beginning was the Word."

Reading Assignment:
Stedman's Triples: The Second, Third, Fourth and Fifth Parts

Session VIII: Activity

Stedman's Triples: The Second, Third, Fourth and Fifth Parts

Interrogation

Dramatize an interrogation. Take turns playing Deacon, Cranton, Will Thoday, Mary Thoday and perhaps other characters. Turn the lights out and point a bright light on the suspect. Try to stay in character as long as possible, asking questions concerning the events about which you have read to this point. As a guide, begin by making a list of what you know about every character. Describe their dispositions, their involvement and how you view them. Use these lists as informal scripts for your dramatizations. Improvise within the characters' possibilities and have fun with it.

Use the following questions as a starting point for your interrogation. Students should be evaluated by how well they are able to answer questions. Roles may also be reversed, with the student asking questions of a teacher. A student may then be judged on his/her ability to discern good answers.

TO ASK DEACON:

1. Where were you the night of the Wilbraham jewel robbery?
2. Where have you been since your hearing and trial?
3. How did you convince Cranton to help you? Didn't he suspect that you might double cross him again?

TO ASK CRANTON:

1. Where were you the night of the Wilbraham jewel robbery?
2. Why were you in Fenchurch St. Paul's right before New Year's Day? Why did you suddenly disappear a few days later?
3. How did Deacon die? And if you didn't kill Deacon, who did?

TO ASK WILL THODAY:

1. Who did you first think the dead man was who was found in Mrs. Thorpe's grave?
2. When did you know that the corpse was Deacon's? How did you find out?
3. What were all your dealings with Deacon?

TO ASK MARY THODAY:

1. Did you suspect that the corpse in Mrs. Thorpe's grave was your ex-husband?
2. When did you suspect or realize that the corpse was Deacon's?
3. Why did you and your husband skip church and suddenly leave town after you realized it was Deacon's corpse?

Use these characters and questions as a starting point. Develop your own questions for other characters (e.g., Jim Thoday or Potty Peake) and question them about different aspects of the mystery. You might even suppose Wimsey, Venables, Parker or Blundell in different spots throughout the story. See if you can remember what they know at different points.

Reading Assignment:
Kent Treble Bob Major: The First, Second and Third Parts

Session IX: Evaluation

The Nine Tailors

Test may be taken with an open Bible and an open book.

Grammar

Answer the following questions in complete sentences. Some answers may be longer than others. (2 points per answer)

1. How did Lord Peter Wimsey become acquainted with Fenchurch St. Paul?
2. How was the mysterious corpse found?
3. Summarize the mystery of the Wilbraham emeralds at the beginning of the story.
4. How is the dead man traced to France?
5. Who is Potty Peake?

Logic

Choose two out of the following three questions to answer in a paragraph or two. (10 points per answer)

1. How is Mr. Venables like Noah?
2. How is Wimsey not like other popular detectives? How does this evidence Sayers's worldview?
3. What is the significance of the bells having names?

Lateral

Answer one of the following questions. These questions will require more substantial answers. (16 points per answer)

1. What is the meaning of the title of the book, *The Nine Tailors?*
2. What is Dorothy Sayers's view of logic? What is the Christian view of logic? Is Sayers right? Explain.

Optional Session A: Activity

Campanology

Visit the National Cathedral or another famous cathedral in England or America. Try to find one with bells. Take a tour, read about its history and learn about what makes it unique and distinctive.

Alternatively, research the science of campanology. Check out books from the library, do an internet search or ask friends or family who may know. Answer the following questions: How are peals organized? What does the musical notation look like? How is the technique of ringing related to the size and setting of the bells? Write a short essay recording your findings. Sometimes change-ringers practice using hand bells. Locate a set of hand bells and learn a short peal. Plan a performance and give a presentation of your findings before your class or another audience.[2]

Optional Session B: Activity

Poetry Code

Try to decipher the following, more difficult, poem. Hint: Pay special attention to any numeric patterns.

Hymn

Thee we praise unto endless ages and forever
Galaxies resound your ring
And we (and I in you)
Sing (with countless millions gathered in
    your name).
In everlasting brilliance, You,
    beyond our wildest hopes
With triumphant risen Son
Reign as (with You upholding everything)

Endnotes

1 Since there are no chapter numbers, chapters will be referenced by title. This provides the additional benefit of acquainting the reader with change ringing terminology.

2 Websites with information about change ringing, including audio samples of actual peals, can be found at Links 1and 2 for this chapter at www.VeritasPress.com/OmniLinks.

The Dragon and the Raven

You and I have been very blessed. Never in our lifetimes has our country[1] been invaded. We have never had another country come and try to take ours away from us. We have never had to muster arms and defend ourselves because there were enemy troops on our own soil. The last time that enemy troops landed in this country was the nineteenth century and John Adams was president. That was almost two hundred years ago.

But what if it did happen? What if you heard on the news that a hostile army was landing on the Oregon coast? What if they told you that the army had decided that it didn't want our land? The soldiers claimed they weren't there to take over. They only wanted to take everything we owned: our valuables, our weapons, our food and our mothers and sisters. What would you do?

This is very similar to the situation that the hero of *The Dragon and the Raven* finds himself in. Edmund is a boy of only fourteen when the Danes invade England. They are not primarily there for conquest, but rather for plunder and spoils. They don't really want to live in the land. They want to kill all the inhabitants and take their stuff.

Would you fight back?

An early Viking period "picture-stone," showing a Viking warship and a Viking raid on horseback. These stones emphasized the importance of mobile Viking forces using boats and horses.

Kings College Chapel, Cambridge, is an example of the Perpendicular Gothic style, seen only in England. G.A. Henty attended college at Cambridge University in what was at the time of our story called East Anglia, north of Kent.

GENERAL INFORMATION

Author and Context

He is rightly nicknamed "The Prince of Storytellers." G.A. Henty began to express his love of storytelling when he would tell exciting stories to his own children after dinner. There were times when one story would stretch into weeks. A friend who was impressed by Henty's ability to captivate his own children recommended that he write out the stories, and today we have approximately 144 stories to enjoy.

George Alfred Henty (1832–1902) was an English war correspondent and author. While engaging in a rigorous course of study at Westminster School and Cambridge University he participated in boxing, wrestling and rowing. He went on to have extensive experience with war, starting with his entry in the Crimean War, and then later as a war correspondent in Europe and Africa. He covered the Garibaldi revolution in Italy, the Franco-Prussian War, Austro-Italian War, Turkish-Serbian War and the Spanish conflict with the Carlists. During the Italian skirmishes, troops from that country took Henty prisoner, thinking him an Austrian spy. They sentenced him to death, but his convincing argument to a commanding general won him release.

Henty was a prolific writer as he pioneered both adventure and historical fiction. Most of his novels involve a young hero who finds himself in the midst of the world events of his day. Henty's books entertain while at the same time educating the reader about the particular historical event which forms the backdrop of the book.

G.A. Henty has inspired many generations to a study of history. He has entertained millions and fathered a literary genre that features adventure and history combined into a historic novel. He lived the adventurous life and danger that gave him license to speak of war and action.

Significance

Through her history, Great Britain has suffered numerous invasions. Julius Caesar landed before Jesus Christ was born and claimed the island for Rome, paying little attention to the Britons who were already present. The Angles, the Saxons and the Jutes invaded in the mid-400s, and the Vikings began making trips in the 800s and continued for almost two hundred years. The Normans, under William the Conqueror, famously invaded in 1066. No one has succeeded since, but Britain remained a tantalizing prize for many kings for centuries.

The Dragon and the Raven gives us some of the context for just one of these invasions—that of the Vikings. It covers the critical early period when the fate of England rested on whether or not the Saxons could fight off the invaders. If the Norsemen had succeeded in overwhelming the entire island, our own history would be very different today. Instead of the Christian heritage that we as Americans have inherited from Great Britain, the pagan Norse gods would be in our intellectual bloodstream. Alfred the Great was the king at that time, and he is credited with saving England from the barbarians.

Main Characters

Edmund is our hero. He is a Saxon, a member of one of the Germanic tribes who invaded Britain and resettled it. Edmund begins the book as a youth of fourteen. As events unfold, he grows from a boy into a man. He and his companion Egbert spend the book fighting the Danes, who have traveled across the North Sea from Scandinavia to plunder England. The Danes are also frequently called Northmen. Alfred the Great, the king of England, leads the Saxons against the invaders. He works with Edmund to help keep England safe. Siegbert is a Danish jarl (or chieftain) whose life Edmund spares, and Freda is his beautiful daughter who befriends Edmund. Sweyn is the name of the chief villain, an unscrupulous Dane who kidnaps Freda from her father.

Summary and Setting

By the middle of the 800s, the Viking invasions of England were in full swing. They had realized that the monasteries and fertile lands of England offered easy targets. England was not united at this point in history—in fact, the word "England" did not even exist. It was made up of several smaller kingdoms, such as Mercia, East Anglia and Wessex. The Vikings took advantage of this disunity. They could pick off the British kingdoms one by one, and they did. When Alfred came to the throne of Wessex in 871, it looked as though he would be next.

When *The Dragon and the Raven* begins, East Anglia is about to be conquered and Alfred is a prince. As Edmund grows and matures into a warrior, he watches as the Danes take over most of England and drive out the inhabitants. After Alfred ascends to the throne, Edmund works with him to fight back against the invasions. Edmund puts together an elite band of Saxon warriors and builds a ship, the *Dragon,* to harass the Vikings. He spares the life of a Danish jarl, Siegbert, who returns the favor when Edmund is captured and enslaved by the Danes. After returning home, Edmund helps King Alfred to win the decisive Battle of Edington, and the Vikings are pushed back. He also aids in the defense of Paris against a Viking army that threatens to overrun France. In France, he gets a call for help from Siegbert, whose beautiful daughter has been kidnapped by Edmund's former enemy, Sweyn.

Worldview

Put yourself in Edmund's shoes. Your family's property has been taken away. Your father has just died in a battle, trying to defend the country he loves. The Vikings are coming. They do not particularly want to take you as a slave or have you join their side. They simply want to kill you, take your gold and then move on to someone else a bit richer. They are not really conquerors. They are plunderers. Put yourself in

Edmund's shoes. He fought back.

When a country is under direct attack, its citizens fight to defend themselves. When the Normans invaded England in 1066, the Anglo-Saxons fought back. When the Nazis invaded France in the 1940s, the French people fought back against the invaders. It is a universal human impulse to defend what we think ought to be ours. We fight to keep our stuff ours.

But is it right for a Christian to fight? After all, didn't Jesus tell us to turn the other cheek (Matt. 5:39)? Some Christians believe that it is never right to fight someone else, even in self-defense. They would rather die than physically harm someone else. Is this a biblical attitude?

At its heart, our faith is a faith of love, mercy and peace. God extends love and mercy to us in salvation. He gives us peace with Him. We should strive to imitate God in all we do. This means we ought to imitate God in His peace, His mercy and His love. We are to follow God in all things.

But God is not just a God of peace and love. God is also a God of war. He fights and destroys His enemies. There are many places in the Bible where God tells His people to destroy another nation (Ex. 17:14; Josh. 6:17). God always wins His battles.

If we are imitating God, then we must also fight and destroy His enemies. Sometimes, it is difficult to tell who God's enemies are. But we are at war with them nonetheless, and we are to fight. But we are to be of good cheer, for Christ has overcome the world (John 16:33). The story in the book of Revelation also gives us a glimpse of the great story of victory that is being told in history. Although it sometimes seems as though His enemies are powerful and unconquerable, God is always in control of the situation. God's enemies are destroyed and vanquished. They will no longer be a threat to Jesus Christ and His church.

Sometimes the ways that God uses to destroy His enemies are not violent, and this is a lesson we ought to keep in mind as well. Think of the apostle Paul, who was converted after trying to exterminate the Christian church. In a sense, this enemy of God was destroyed. Sometimes the best way to fight back against our enemies is to tell them the gospel. We see that Edmund does this when he meets Freda and her father. At first, he is intending to kill them, like the other Vikings he has defeated. But Edmund instead shows them compassion and mercy. Because he lets them go, a friendship is forged. At the end of the book, this friendship has become a brotherhood in Christ as Siegbert and Freda are baptized. Edmund did not kill his enemy, but he did destroy him just as certainly when he made his enemy his friend.

At the same time that Freda is baptized, she is also married to Edmund. It is clear that Edmund has loved her for a long time, but he does not marry her. He realizes that he cannot until she is a Christian. Does this really matter? Is it really that important to marry a Christian? God thinks so—He tells us so many times in His word. The Bible tells us that marrying unbelievers is wrong (1 Cor. 7:39; 2 Cor. 6:14). We see the consequences of this sort of action with King Solomon. Solomon is the wisest man in the world, but he is led astray because of his marriages to pagan women (1 Kings 11:1–13).[2]

Edmund even sends his wife to a convent for a short time after her rescue so that she can learn the basic doctrines of Christianity. He wants her to understand what she believes. Edmund is wiser than Solomon in this area. He does not let emotions or attraction blind him to his need to have a godly Christian wife. It is easy for a young man to assume that because he is "in love" this feeling will cover any differences of religion or upbringing. This is false—the Bible is full of examples of men who are led astray by deceitful women (Judg. 16). Edmund wisely does not let this happen to him.

When he doesn't let his emotions get the better of him, Edmund is displaying a Christian sense of discipline. He is showing self-control. This is a trait that he shows throughout his adventures. He disciplines his band of soldiers so that they become the most trained force in the Saxon army. They obey every one of his commands as soon as he gives them. They are well disciplined.

Discipline is a character trait that we should seek after. Edmund and his men are excellent examples of the kind of discipline that a young Christian man should seek to have. A young man should think before he speaks; this is discipline of the tongue. A young man should think about what is right before he acts; this is discipline of his actions. Discipline often involves patience, waiting for the right time. The reason parents discipline their children is so that they will discipline themselves later on. Edmund himself is an example of what we should strive for.

Edmund is also an example of many other traits that we ought to imitate. Through the course of the book, Edmund is shown to be a godly Christian hero. At one point in the book, Freda asks Edmund how Christians can be heroes, if they do not fight. She thinks that a hero must be someone who fights valiantly. Edmund tells her that, in Christianity, courage is not the highest virtue. He explains that love and unselfishness are the highest virtues.

Ultimately, a Christian hero is one who imitates Jesus Christ. Christ is the ultimate hero. He humbled Himself that He might save His people (Phil. 2:5–11), and this is something that we ought to imitate. The closer that a man's life imitates the life of Jesus, the closer he is to being like the ultimate Hero.

What attributes does Edmund share with his Savior? We have already spoken of the discipline that Edmund shows in the book. Jesus was also disciplined in His time here on earth. He did not speak except when He knew what He was going to say. He did not act except when the time was right (John 12:23). Edmund also waits for the right time when he waits for the right moment to attack Sweyn's ship. He is patient to wait for the chance to marry Freda as well.

King Alfred the Great bestows a royal cape and sword on his grandson and future Anglo-Saxon king, Athelstan. After the death of Alfred the Great, his son Edward the Elder ruled England from 899 to 925. Edward's son Athelstan subsequently ruled England from 925 to 940, the first of three of Alfred's grandsons to rule in succession.

Another Christ-like attribute of our young hero is that he is wise. After King Alfred offers Edmund land, Edmund rules it well. During the lulls of the war, as the Danes regroup before sending another wave of attacks, Edmund returns home and helps his countrymen with their affairs. When Edmund makes decisions where he is going to send his ship, the Dragon, he does so carefully and cautiously. He does not take unnecessary risks.

Edmund is also a merciful hero. He does not fight for fighting's sake. His purpose in fighting against the invaders is simply to protect his homeland. He does not attack the helpless, as shown when he spares Siegbert's life. When he is fighting Sweyn in single combat, Edmund does not attack when his opponent has stopped to take a breath. He allows Sweyn the time to recuperate and does not attack him when he is down. Just as God shows us mercy that we might come to know Him better, Edmund shows mercy to his enemies.

But Edmund is not the only character in the story who is praiseworthy. Edmund's servant Egbert is a wonderful example of loyalty. Eldred, Edmund's father, instructs Egbert to leave the battle if it is going poorly and join Edmund so that the two of them can escape. Egbert obeys even though he does not wish to. He stays by Edmund's side for the rest of the book, staying loyal to Edmund and Eldred's command. Another example of loyalty lies in the character of Freda, who keeps her promise to wait for Edmund to return.

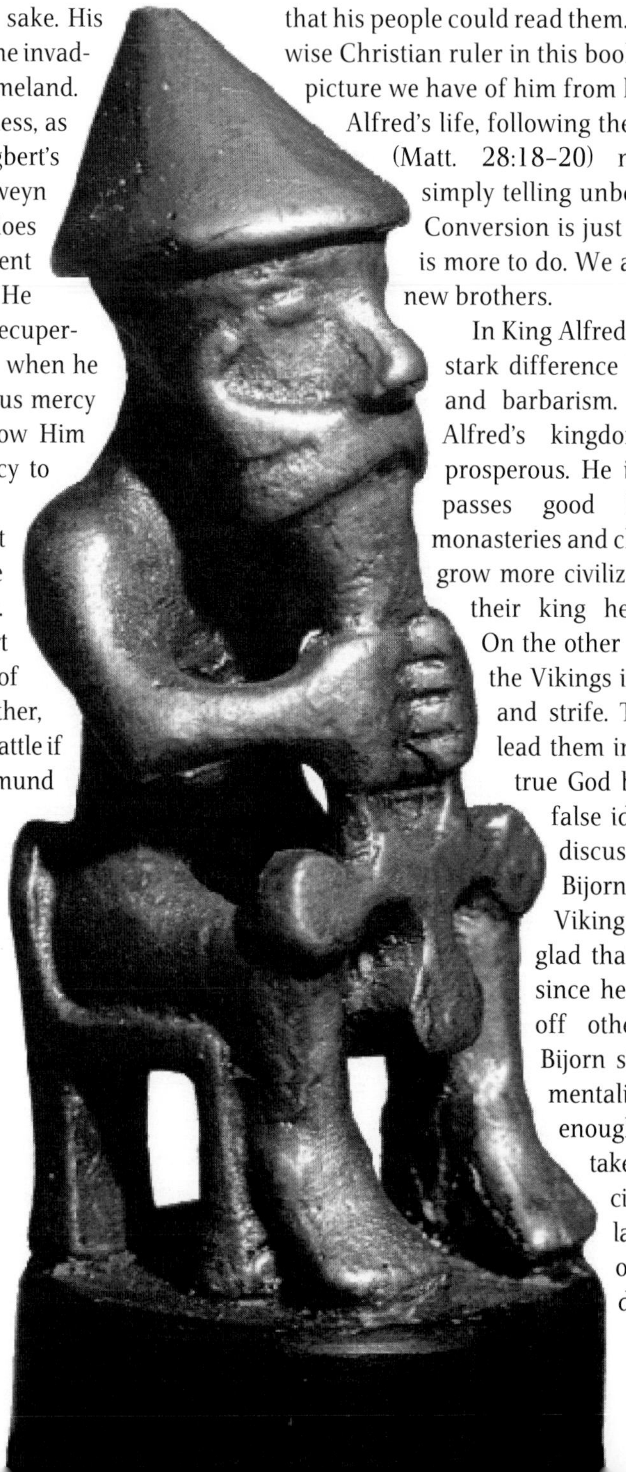

An ancient figurine of Thor, the mighty Norse god of thunder. Thor was famed for his powerful hammer, called *Mjollnir*—one blow from the hammer meant certain death, and the hammer would always return to Thor of its own will.

King Alfred also embodies many good Christian traits. He leads his people in battle against their enemy, as a Christian king does. He helps them rebuild when their churches and homes are in ruins after the attacks of the Vikings. He improves their learning by building schools and promoting education. Alfred also translated many books so that his people could read them. He is presented as a wise Christian ruler in this book, which is the same picture we have of him from history. As we see in Alfred's life, following the Great Commission (Matt. 28:18–20) means more than simply telling unbelievers about Jesus. Conversion is just the first step. There is more to do. We are also to teach our new brothers.

In King Alfred's actions, we see the stark difference between civilization and barbarism. On the one hand, Alfred's kingdom is happy and prosperous. He improves education, passes good laws and builds monasteries and churches. The Saxons grow more civilized and Christian as their king helps improve them. On the other hand, the culture of the Vikings is full of lawlessness and strife. Their priests do not lead them in the worship of the true God but instead promote false idols. When Edmund discusses with the jarl Bijorn the idea of laws, the Viking declares that he is glad that there are no laws, since he would rather carry off other people's things. Bijorn shows us the Viking mentality: if I am strong enough, I am allowed to take your stuff. The civilization that Alfred lays the foundation of is based on a different assumption, the assumption that we can keep our own stuff.

All of these men are righteous examples because they have rightly imitated their God, who is righteous. But the Vikings are also imitating their gods. Their gods are warlike and barbaric. Edmund is the hero for the Christian Saxons because he is merciful, brave and righteous. He is imitating his God. The Viking standards for heroes are different. For them, a hero is whoever takes home the most plunder. Whoever conquers the most cities or captures the most gold is the hero. This is because the Vikings are imitating their petty gods, who deal in stuff and great acts of valor. For the Christian, however, there is more to being a hero than simply fighting all the battles in the front line.

Like Christians, the Vikings believe they are going to a blessed place in the afterlife. Unlike Christians, though, they do not believe that the way has been prepared for them by their God and Savior. Bijorn tells Edmund that he also believes in an afterlife: "No Northman fears death, for he knows that a joyous time awaits him." The jarl does not say how he knows, or who gets to go. We are left with a vague heaven quite unlike the glorious home that Christ has prepared for us.

Though there are many examples of righteousness, Sweyn, the villain, shows us how not to behave. He is the opposite of Edmund, and because of this they run into many conflicts. Sweyn is arrogant and presumptuous, while Edmund is wise and does not provoke a fight. Edmund is unwilling to fight the hot-headed Dane, even though if he wins he will be freed. Unlike Edmund, who risks his life to save Freda's, Sweyn is concerned with getting his own way. He kidnaps Freda in order to force her to become his wife. This is not the selfless act of love that a husband is required to perform daily. It is a seizure of forbidden fruit. Sweyn, like Adam, is punished for his theft.

Just like in the great story that the Bible gives us, the true hero wins out in the end. He rescues his love and brings peace to his kingdom. Edmund ends the book as a wise ruler who encourages peace. Like Christ, he is a warrior not because he loves war but because he loves peace.

The Dragon and the Raven is a story of great deeds in desperate times. The lessons that we learn from Edmund's life are things that we can use in our own. But perhaps the greatest lesson is what happened afterwards. Because of the hard work of King Alfred and his men, England was transformed from a nation besieged by Danish raiders and full of pagan ignorance into a land where the name of Christ was proclaimed and preached. For hundreds of years afterwards, the name of Christ was rightly proclaimed in Britain. Because the Christians fought back and defended themselves, they not only saved the Christian faith in their land, they also strengthened it. May God give us grace to do the same when we are under attack.

—*O. Woelke Leithart*

For Further Reading

Blair, John. *The Anglo-Saxon Age: A Very Short Introduction.* Oxford: Oxford University Press, 2002.

Spielvogel, Jackson J. *Western Civilization.* Seventh Edition. Belmont, Calif.: Thomson Wadsworth, 2009. 231, 247, 248.

Veritas Press History Cards: Middle Ages, Renaissance and Reformation. Lancaster, Pa.: Veritas Press. 2 & 9.

Session I: Prelude

A Question to Consider

How can we learn from past wars?

From the General Information above answer the following questions:

1. What in G.A. Henty's life helped him prepare for writing the kinds of books he did?
2. Why is it important to learn about the Viking invasions of England?
3. What nationality is Edmund?
4. How does Edmund help King Alfred fight the Danish invaders?
5. Are Christians allowed to fight back in self-defense? Explain.
6. Does God always fight against His enemies using violence? What else does He use?
7. What does Edmund want Freda to do before he marries her? Why?

Reading Assignment:
Chapters 1–4

Fancy, carved dragon figureheads, like the one shown here, were often found on the prows of feared Viking raiding ships. The Vikings used long, streamlined "long-ships" for making land raids from rivers and estuaries. The fronts of the ships were usually decorated with fearsome dragon or snake heads. The Vikings would use these decorations only when raiding land sites, removing them on the open sea so they would not be damaged by the rough waters.

Session II: Discussion

Chapters 1–4

A Question to Consider

Pretend for a moment that you are a king. What could provoke you to go to war?

Discuss or list short answers to the following questions:

Text Analysis

1. Why are the Vikings invading Britain?
2. To whom does Edmund's father, Eldred, turn for help?
3. Do the Saxons decide to fight? Why?
4. Are the Saxons easy to defeat? Why is or isn't this the case?
5. Why doesn't the Abbot of Croyland flee?
6. How do the Saxons respond when Wessex is invaded? Do they win? Why or why not?

Cultural Analysis

1. According to our culture, how should we behave in wars?
2. How does our culture justify war?
3. Does our culture want Christians to fight in defense of their faith? Should we defend our faith?

Biblical Analysis

1. Does the Bible ever say it is right to fight in a war (Joshua; 1 Sam. 15; Ps. 144)?
2. How do believers in the Bible respond when enemies attack them (Ex. 17; Esther)?
3. One reason the Saxons are defeated is because they are not united (chap. 3). Do you think this lesson could be applied to the church today? How?
4. How does Christ respond when His church is under attack (Ps. 2; Rev. 19:11–16)?
5. When the church is under spiritual attack, how should we respond?

Summa

Write an essay or discuss this question, integrating what you have learned from the material above.

How should we behave in war?

Reading Assignment:

Chapters 5–8

Session III: Discussion

Chapters 5–8

A Question to Consider

Why is it good for parents to discipline their children?

Discuss or list short answers to the following questions:

Textual Analysis

1. Why do the Danes win most of the battles in the first part of the book?
2. What is different about Edmund's band of men that he puts together?
3. How does Edmund's band succeed?
4. Do the Danes show that they are disciplined? What is their main strength?
5. How does the training the men received help them when they start fighting from the *Dragon?*

Cultural Analysis

1. In the modern world, which is more prized, patience or impatience? Give an example.
2. What does discipline mean in our culture? Is this what discipline means from a biblical worldview?
3. In our culture, are parents supposed to discipline their children?
4. Though our culture does not praise the process of discipline, does it praise its effects?

Biblical Analysis

1. What does the Bible teach about discipline (Prov. 13:24; 19:18; 22:6; 22:15; 29:17)?
2. Think back to the story of Eli that you read last year[5] (1 Sam. 23). Why does God judge Eli?
3. Does the Bible teach that it is important for parents to discipline children?
4. How does the idea of disciplining children relate to the discipline that Edmund puts together when he forms his warrior band?
5. Does God discipline us (Heb. 12:5–11)? Why? Is He forming us into a well-trained warrior band?

Summa

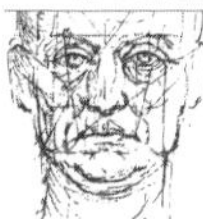

Write an essay or discuss this question, integrating what you have learned from the material above.

Why is discipline important?

Reading Assignment:

Chapters 9–12

Session IV: Recitation

Chapters 9–12

Comprehension Questions

Answer the following questions for factual recall:

1. To whom is Edmund led after his capture?
2. What makes the jarl decide to keep Edmund as a slave?
3. Whom does Sweyn have his heart set on marrying? Does his father believe that his suit is likely to be successful?
4. Why doesn't Siegbert believe that the Danes need laws?
5. How does Edmund explain to Freda that he can, as a Christian, still fight wars?
6. Why does Siegbert's agreement to redeem Edmund from slavery fail?
7. Whom does Edmund have to fight? Why? How does Edmund win the combat?
8. What promise does Edmund make to Freda before he leaves?
9. Why has King Alfred been hiding on the Isle of Athelney?
10. Why does Alfred place Edmund's band of men in the middle of the army?
11. Why do the Danes surrender? What does their king, Guthorn, ask for after they surrender?
12. How does Alfred treat Guthorn after the battle is over?
13. In the short years of peace that follow, what do Alfred and Edmund spend their time doing?

Reading Assignment:

Chapters 13–16

SESSION V: ACTIVITY

Chapters 13–16

Cartography

Throughout his adventures, Edmund travels all over Europe. Print out the map provided in the teacher's edition. Record the route of Edmund's travels either by drawing a line or numbering the places in the order that he visits them. After you are done, you can color your map if you like.

The map provides some of the locations Edmund visits, although the more you add beyond this list, the better. The map includes locations Edmund will visit in the remaining chapters that have not yet been assigned. You may complete the route after finishing the book.

READING ASSIGNMENT:
Chapters 17–19

SESSION VI: DISCUSSION

Chapters 17–19

A Question to Consider

What is a hero?

Discuss or list short answers to the following questions:

Textual Analysis

1. What is Edmund's reaction to hearing Freda has been kidnapped?
2. When he finds Sweyn's camp, what does Edmund do?
3. Does Edmund allow himself to be frustrated by missing the ship in the fog?
4. How long does Edmund pursue Sweyn? What does this tell us about the young Saxon?
5. How does Edmund show himself to be like Jesus Christ in his rescue of Freda?

Freda, the heroine of our story and beautiful daughter of Danish jarl, Siegbert. While the villain, Sweyn, kidnaps Freda and tries to force her to become his wife, Edmund risks his life to save hers.

Cultural Analysis

1. Does our culture have heroes? Give some examples.
2. Where do the heroes of our culture get their strength?
3. What values are most prized in our culture?

Biblical Analysis

1. Was Abraham heroic? How (Gen. 15; Rom. 4; Heb. 11:8–10)?
2. David is a hero in the Bible. How do we see this in his life?
3. How is Jesus the greatest Hero in the Bible?
4. What sort of love ought a true hero to have (John 15:13)?

Summa

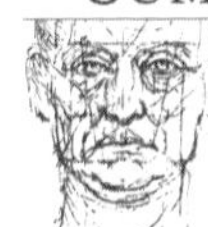

Write an essay or discuss this question, integrating what you have learned from the material above.

How can we be Christian heroes?

Optional Session: Writing

Progymnasmata

Classical training in rhetoric included preparatory writing exercises called the progymnasmata. These exercises in composition introduced the beginning student to basic forms and techniques that would then be used and combined when practicing more advanced exercises and speeches. One of these progymnasmata was called a chreia, or "saying exercise," and was simply a concise exposition of some memorable saying or deed.

A chreia has eight paragraphs. The first is the *Panegyric* which is a paragraph in which you praise the person who uttered the wise saying. The second is called the *Paraphrastic.* In this short paragraph you put the saying into your own words. This paragraph often begins with something like: "When Saint Augustine said that evil was the deprivation of good, he meant that . . . ." In the third paragraph, called *From the Cause,* you explain the motivation of the person. The fourth paragraph is called *From the Contrary,* and in it you explain what would have happened if the opposite of the saying or action had occurred. For example, "If Diogenes had not struck the inept teacher, bad education would have continued." In the fifth paragraph, called the *Analogy,* you liken the saying or action to something else, usually something more concrete and easier to understand. The sixth paragraph is similar to the fifth. It is called *Example,* and in it you show the wisdom of the saying or deed by pointing your reader to a specific instance in which this wisdom was demonstrated. *The Analogy* is different from the *Example* in that it is about a general practice (e.g., "Education is like a harvest: you work hard and reap great reward."), whereas the *Example* is about a specific person, place or thing (e.g., "Erasmus studied many things and became a learned man."). The seventh paragraph is called the *Testimony of the Ancients.* Here you quote a sage person from the past who testifies to the truth of the saying. Finally, in the eighth paragraph, called the *Epilogue,* you sum up the *Chreia.*

Write a chreia on Edmund's statement in chapter 10 that "Christianity does not forbid men to defend themselves; for, did it do so, a band of pagans might ravage all the Christian nations in the world."

I. Panegyric
- Praise the person(s) who uttered the wise saying(s)

II. Paraphrastic
- Put the saying into your own words

III. From the Cause
- Explain the motivation of the speaker

IV. From the Contrary
- Explain the consequences if the opposite of the saying or action had occurred

V. Analogy
- Liken the saying to something else

VI. Example
- Point the reader to a specific instance in which the wisdom of the situation was demonstrated

VII. Testimony of the Ancients
- Quote a sage person from the past who testifies to the truth of the saying

VIII. Epilogue
- Summarize your previous paragraphs

ENDNOTES

1 Assuming that you live in the United States.
2 Of course, Solomon also married 1,000 women, which would be the downfall of anyone.
3 *This endnote appears only in the teacher's edition.*
4 *This endnote appears only in the teacher's edition.*
5 Assuming you used *Omnibus I.*

Gospel of John

Fourth and goal on the one-yard line. All the fans in the stadium are on their feet. The quarterback takes the ball, takes a small step back and then lunges into the end zone. Touchdown! The crowd erupts into a frenzy. But wait a minute. Who is that guy in the front row behind the end zone? It's the ever-faithful sign-waver! And what is on his sign? You guessed it—JOHN 3:16. No football game is complete without the most popular verse in the Bible waving around in the stands.

No other verse seems to summarize the message of the Bible like John 3:16. Likewise, no book of the Bible points to Jesus quite like the Gospel of John. The book has no other significant purpose other than simply to point to Christ. When we want to share the gospel with a friend, we give him a copy of the Gospel of John. No other writings introduce us to Jesus like John.

"I am the good shepherd; and I know My sheep, and am known by My own. As the Father knows Me, even so I know the Father; and I lay down My life for the sheep. And other sheep I have which are not of this fold; them also I must bring, and they will hear My voice; and there will be one flock and one shepherd." Shown here is a third-century depiction of The Good Shepherd from the catacombs of Saint Callixtus.

Through the centuries theologians have discussed the profound truths of Scripture, the indescribable attributes of God and the intricacies of salvation, sanctification and end times. But Karl Barth, a well-known twentieth-century theologian, is reported to have said that the most profound truth he ever learned was "Jesus loves me, this I know / For the Bible tells me so." While we would not refer to Barth as a guide in other areas (some of his theology is, well, messed up), he understood the central truth of Scripture which is also the core message of John, that God, in Jesus Christ, has shown His love to us, and that by believing in Him we might have eternal life.

General Information

Author and Context

John was a fisherman by trade and his work was hard labor. He was a man of humility. He follows without delay when John the Baptist points him to Jesus. He rarely even mentions his own name in his own Gospel. He was one of the "pillars of the church" and Paul regarded him highly (Gal. 2:9).

A possible "co-author" to John's Gospel states in John 21:24, 25 a brief postscript added later, that his testimony is true. This writer places his stamp of certification to the authenticity of the account.

We understand that Jesus worked more intimately with an inner group within the twelve, namely, Peter, James and John. This Gospel reveals that within that special group Jesus had an even more unique relationship with John, who calls himself "the one whom Jesus loved."

This title suggests an intimacy that Jesus apparently did not have with anyone else. In 13:23 the disciple is "leaning on Jesus' bosom," a position of closeness while fellowshipping over a meal. It is while Jesus is hanging on the cross, however, that we observe the depth of the relationship between this disciple and his Lord. First, the fact that John was even at the foot of the cross reveals that he had a profound love for Jesus and would not abandon Him as did the others. He was the only disciple to witness the death of Christ. Second, Jesus, in the agony of His execution, turns His thoughts to His mother. He is concerned for her welfare. Instead of entrusting her to the care of the most likely candidate, a family member, He turns to John, the disciple whom He loved and says, "Behold your mother!" Jesus desired to hand her over to the care of the one He trusted and loved the most, the Apostle John.

Significance

In the ancient world a soldier's shield often contained a distinguishing sign which identified him with the land for which he fought. Likewise, a signet ring contained a special mark which pointed to the identity and authority of the owner. The word used for "sign" in these two instances is the Greek word *semeia*, one of the most characteristic words in the Gospel of John. When Jesus breaks what we call the "laws of nature" and performs a miracle, John calls it a *semeia*, a sign. But a sign of what? It was a sign of His identity as the Son of God.

John states at the end of his account that "Jesus did many other signs in the presence of His disciples, which are not written in this book" (20:30). So why did John choose to record certain events and leave out others? Was he ignorant of these other events? Certainly not. He clearly was including instances in the life of Jesus which most boldly proclaimed His identity.

John does not beat around the bush concerning the purpose of his book. "But these things are written that you may believe that Jesus is the Christ, the Son of God, and that believing you may have eternal life" (20:31). The Gospel of John centers on a series of signs, or miracles, which point to Jesus as the Messiah, the anointed and promised One of Israel. The purpose of reading about these signs is not to simply respond with a "Wow, that's cool!" Rather, the book challenges readers to believe upon this Jesus and receive eternal life as a result.

Setting

Attempting to determine when and to whom a book was written can be a bit tricky when the writing took place 2,000 years ago. Liberal scholarship of the late nineteenth and early twentieth centuries concluded that it was not even the Apostle John who wrote the Gospel that bears his name and that it was most likely written sometime in the middle of the second century.

In 1920, a landmark discovery in Egypt changed all of this. A man named Benard Grenfell discovered the oldest known manuscript fragment of the New Testament, called The Rylands papyrus. Dating back to A.D. 125, it contains portions of John 18, causing most scholars to return to a much earlier date for the Gospel of John's writing. Some early church fathers point to a date sometime around A.D. 90. Still other scholars view the evidence and determine that it was a date before A.D. 70.

Now we turn to the question of the audience. To whom was John writing? Matthew addresses his Gospel to a Jewish audience, and Mark writes to the church in Rome. Luke's target audience is a much broader Gentile group. John, however, seems to have no specific target audience. He is writing his account of the good news, and it is addressed to the whole world.

The Sea of Galilee, or Lake Kinneret, is a 13 x 7 mile fresh-water lake located in the northern portion of Israel. The Sea of Galilee is notorious for storms that can turn smooth waters to large white caps and swells in just a few minutes.

Worldview

I remember a grammar school teacher who played a fun game with us. She would take four items and place them on the table in the shape of a square. Three of the objects would have something in common (three pieces of fruit for example) and the fourth would be entirely different (a wrench). We would sing a song, "Which of these four is doing its own thing, which of these four are kind of the same?" As first or second graders, we had fun figuring out which of the four items was the odd ball.

THE EAGLE

The high soaring eagle has been the traditional symbol for St. John the Evangelist because of his "soaring" witness to Jesus' divine nature. The eagle shown here is from the Book of Kells, a harmony of the four Evangelists that is the greatest of a group of manuscripts produced from the late sixth century through the early ninth century in Celtic monasteries. The name "Book of Kells" is derived from the Abbey of Kells in Kells, County Meath, in Ireland, where it was kept for much of the medieval period. The Abbey of Kells was founded in the early ninth century, at the time of the Viking invasions, by monks from the monastery at Iona—a missionary centre for the Columban community founded by Saint Columcille in the middle of the sixth century. When repeated Viking raids made Iona too dangerous, the majority of the community removed to Kells. Most believe that the Book of Kells was begun at Iona and finished at Kells.

The symbols for the four Evangelists—the eagle, the winged lion, the winged man and the winged ox—are lifted from Ezekiel's vision of four living creatures: "As for the likeness of their faces, each had the face of a man; each of the four had the face of a lion on the right side, each of the four had the face of an ox on the left side, and each of the four had the face of an eagle" (Ezekiel 1:10).

In studying the four Gospels, John is the odd ball. He is the one "doing his own thing." His account of the life of Jesus Christ is markedly different from the other three. For this reason Matthew, Mark and Luke are called the "synoptic Gospels" (literally, "seeing together"). John omits a large amount of material found in the synoptics, and some of this material is surprisingly important: the temptation of Jesus, Jesus' transfiguration and the account of the institution of the Lord's Supper. John does not mention any examples of Jesus casting out demons. The Sermon on the Mount and the Lord's Prayer are not in John's Gospel. And the use of narrative parables, a significant part of Jesus' teaching ministry in the synoptic Gospels, is absent in John, the fourth Gospel.

Conversely, John includes a considerable amount of material not found in Matthew, Mark or Luke. All of the events recorded in John 2–4 (including the miraculous transformation of water into wine at the wedding in Cana, the dialogue with Nicodemus, and the episode with the Samaritan woman) are not in Matthew, Mark or Luke. John mentions prior visits to Jerusalem before Passion Week, whereas the other Gospels do not. The resurrection of Lazarus and the extended discourse in John 13–17 are not in the first three Gospel accounts. All of this is to point out the extent to which the Gospel of John is distinctive from the other three. John, inspired by the Holy Spirit, clearly demonstrates his purpose for writing (20:31) by carefully choosing the events that communicate his intent, which is to reveal Jesus as the Christ, the Son of God. He even writes in that same context that "truly Jesus did many other signs in the presence of His disciples, which are not written in this book." John was not unfamiliar with those events. He simply chooses to mention some and not others according to his purposes.

As mentioned earlier, the Gospel of John centers on a series of signs, or miracles. John structures his book around seven such signs which each point to a different aspect of Jesus' person and work. While John does not

Chart 1: THE SEVEN SIGNS OF THE GOSPEL OF JOHN

	MIRACLE	REFERENCE	APPLICATION
1	Transformation of water into wine	John 2:1–12	The New Birth[1]
2	Healing of the nobleman's son	4:46–54	Our healing and nobility in Christ
3	Healing of the lame at the pool of Bethesda	5:1–17	Our healing and ability to live the Christian life
4	Feeding of the thousands	6:1–13	Nourishment in the faith
5	Walking on the water and calming the disciples	6:16–21	Our fears calmed by Christ
6	Healing of the blind man	9:1–41	Our new sight in Christ and our commission to preach to the spiritually blind
7	Resurrection of Lazarus	11:1–45	Resurrection of the believer from physical death to eternal life

always state explicitly the broader application of each sign, they seem to follow a logical progression. Chart 1 shows each sign with a suggested application.

In these seven signs John takes us from new birth in Christ to the final resurrection. But he does not simply provide his audience with the wonder of the miracle. Coupled with the sign is a teaching which relates to the miracle recorded. In each sign John prepares the reader for the teaching which follows. Chart 2 shows how John relates the teachings of Jesus to the signs He performed.

When we read John's Gospel carefully, considering each sign and its attendant meaning, we are led, with Thomas, to bow in faith and worship, acknowledging Jesus as Lord. It almost seems as though John wants us to view them as rungs in a ladder which lead us upward through life, leading and pointing to Christ the whole way. Let's dig a little deeper into each of the signs in order to understand the gospel the way John intended.

The miracle of the transformation of the water into wine at the wedding in Cana is not only the first miracle in John; it is also the first of all the miracles Jesus performs. It marks the beginning of Jesus' public ministry and speaks volumes about Who Jesus is. The conversation Jesus has with His mother before the miracle reveals that Jesus Himself saw this miracle as monumental. It marks a key transition in the history of God's redemptive plan. The clay jars filled with water hark back to the ceremonial washings in the Old Testament. Wine symbolizes eternal life in the Kingdom of God.

More significant than the symbolism of the miracle itself, however, is what exactly Jesus is saying about Himself in this sign. Jesus is proclaiming that He is the fulfillment of the Old Testament prophesies and foreshadowing concerning the Messiah.

Chart 2: THE SEVEN MIRACLES AND THEIR ATTENDANT TEACHINGS

	MIRACLE	REFERENCE	TEACHING
1	Transformation of water into wine	John 3	Necessity of the New Birth
2	Healing of the nobleman's son	John 5:19–30	Life in Christ
3	Healing of the lame at the pool of Bethesda	John 5:19–30	Life in Christ
4	Feeding of the thousands	6:27–40	Jesus as the Bread of Life
5	Walking on the water and calming the disciples		No particular teaching in the context of this miracle
6	Healing of the blind man	John 9:35-41	Spiritual blindess
7	Resurrection of Lazarus	John 11:25-26, 12:23-26	Jesus as the Resurrection and Life

He is boldly stating that He is the Son of God and He has come to grant eternal life to His people. In 2:11 John writes, "This beginning of signs Jesus did in Cana of Galilee, and manifested His glory; and His disciples believed in Him." In 1:1, 14 he had already stated that Jesus was the divine logos, the Word of God, and that He had become flesh in order to dwell among us. John is making it crystal clear to his readers that Jesus is not simply a man who taught some great truths and performed miraculous signs. John is communicating that Jesus is God.

Even before the recording of this first miracle, John prepares his audience for this profound truth in the prologue (1:1–18). Whereas the other Gospels begin their record of the life of Jesus with His birth, John introduces Christ, not from his birth, but from "the beginning" as the Word Who as Deity is the Creator Himself (1:1–3). God has stepped out of heaven and taken upon Himself human flesh in order that he might take away our sins as the spotless, sacrificial Lamb (1:29). One has to wonder what the guests who were invited to the wedding at Cana would have thought if they knew that they were going to an event during which God, in human form, would actively make His entrance into the world of Man and proclaim his mission to bring eternal life to sinful humanity.

As mentioned before John does not leave his readers in the dark as to the meaning and application of the signs Jesus performed. In John 3 we encounter a Pharisee who comes to Jesus by night to inquire about His teaching. In this familiar passage Jesus relates

to him the necessity of being born again (3:3). So the gospel is not just about the proclamation of the truth about Christ; it is also a call to repent and be born again. When Nicodemus does not understand Jesus' words about being born of "water and the Spirit" (3:5) Jesus rebukes this teacher of Israel for not grasping His teaching and perhaps calling to mind Old Testament passages in which water and spirit are linked (Isa. 32:15; 44:3; Ezek. 36:25–27). These passages refer to God pouring out His Spirit at the end of the age. The point is that John prepares the reader for the teaching of Christ by first presenting him with the sign which points to the identity of Christ.

We will consider the second and third signs together. The second sign John records is the healing of the Nobleman's son. He states that the boy was actually at the point of death (4:47). Jesus, without even seeing the boy proclaims that he is well. As the eternal Logos spoke the worlds into existence, He speaks the boy's healing, and he is healed.

In the third sign Jesus heals a man who had been lame for 38 years. At the command to take up his bed and walk the man is cured. This emphasis on the power of the word of Jesus prepares the reader for the teaching which follows.

Throughout the rest of chapter five John records Jesus' teaching on life in the Son. He states that the one who hears the word He is preaching and believes in Him will have everlasting life (5:24). Regarding Jesus' identity, John emphasizes Jesus' equality with the Father (5:17, 19, 21, 23, 26). John communicates that Jesus' healing comes from none other than God Himself. Thus far, we have seen Jesus perform three miracles, and we have noted John's record of the teaching of Christ that accompanies the signs. We turn now to the fourth miracle.

The fourth miracle, the feeding of the thousands, is one of the most well-known of Jesus' miracles. The disciples wondered how they were going to feed all of these people who had been following Jesus. He takes five barley loaves and two fish, gives thanks and distributes enough to feed them all. There are even twelve baskets of leftovers! The next day, knowing that the miracle of the previous day was still fresh on their minds, Jesus tells the crowd not to labor for the food which perishes, but rather labor "for the food which endures to everlasting life" (6:27).

He goes on to make a contrast between the bread Moses gave and Himself as the "Bread of Life" (6:35). This is the first of the seven "I am" sayings in the Gospel of John, all of which hark back to Exodus 3:14. In this passage Moses is arguing with God that he is not able to confront Pharaoh. When Moses protests that the children of Israel will not even know the name of the God who is bringing about this redemption, God says to Moses, "I AM WHO I AM," and Moses is to tell them that "I AM" has sent him. These "I am" sayings in John clearly look back to the statement in Exodus and reveal that John is equating Jesus with Yahweh in the Old Testament. In other words, Jesus is boldly asserting His own deity.

Not only is John clearly pointing to the Godhood of Jesus, he is showing how this God has come to feed His people. The miracle sets the stage for the teaching that Jesus has come to grant us food that will cause us to never hunger again. In fact, the one who eats this bread, says Jesus, will live forever (6:51).

The fifth sign John records, Jesus walking on the sea and calming the disciples, seems to have no immediate teaching attending it, so we come now to the sixth, the healing of the man who had been blind since birth. Jesus refers to Himself as the "light of the world" (9:5), and then He proceeds to heal the man. The teaching which accompanies this sign is found in 9:35–41. After the Pharisees excommunicate the healed man, Jesus seeks him out and asks him if he believes in the Son of God. The man believes and worships Jesus. At no time does Jesus refuse the man's worship, another clear sign of His claim to deity. Finally, Jesus ends up engaging the Pharisees concerning the whole event, addressing true blindness and true sight.

Jesus uses the sign and the accompanying teaching to point out that His followers are those who have true vision in the form of faith. Jesus states that His mission in coming into the world was that "those who do not see may see, and that those who see may be made blind" (9:39). The Pharisees with whom Jesus was speaking lacked the humility to admit that they were sinners and in need of a Savior. Jesus is teaching not only that He is God and that He has the ability to give them eternal life, but also that we must acknowledge our position as sinners.

The final sign John uses to proclaim the truth about Jesus is the resurrection of Lazarus. Even before the miracle, John records that Jesus is teaching about

"This is the message which we have heard from Him and declare to you, that God is light and in Him is no darkness at all. If we say that we have fellowship with Him, and walk in darkness, we lie and do not practice the truth. But if we walk in the light as He is in the light, we have fellowship with one another, and the blood of Jesus Christ His Son cleanses us from all sin" (I John 1:5–7).

Himself as the "resurrection and the life" and that the one who believes in Him shall never die (11:25–26). In this instance John records some of the teaching beforehand, preparing the reader for the sign to come. Finally, Jesus speaks forth the word and Lazarus comes out of the tomb.

The rest of the teaching that accompanies this sign is found in 12:23–26. Here Jesus uses the image of a grain of wheat to explain His own work. The growth comes after the death. Likewise, He is hinting at the future resurrection of believers. John has brought the reader from the new birth to the resurrection, all the while unveiling the true identity of Jesus.

As if writing of these seven signs and the teachings which follow were not enough, John chooses seven miracles that have an even deeper significance. A clear connection exists between these actions which Jesus performs and actions of God in the Old Testament. The miracles Jesus performs involve saving, healing, feeding, calming, opening eyes and raising from the dead. These are all deeds done by God and recorded in the Old Testament. Chart 3 shows the connection.

How could John shout it any louder? Jesus is God! He was not a mere man who did some good deeds, taught some great truths and then was martyred for his views. He claimed to be the true and living God. Too often modern man wants to portray Jesus as a really nice guy who went about doing good. "He was a wonderful moral teacher," it is said, "and we can learn much from him, but the idea that he is God is an idea that subsequent generations invented." Reasoning like this, however, poses a serious problem. Jesus clearly claimed to be God. How could a man be a good moral teacher if the heart of his teaching is a lie? If his own teaching concerning his own identity is a lie, then how can we possibly label this man as good?

In Part 2 of his book *Mere Christianity,* C.S. Lewis argues that there are really only three choices regarding Jesus' claim to be God. He was either a liar, a lunatic or He was indeed Lord. When each of these three is examined, it becomes clear that the only logical choice is to acknowledge His deity—Lord!.

If Jesus were a liar, He would not have died for a lie. He set His sights on the cross, and He never wavered in his resolve to obey His Father. No one dies for something they know is a lie.

Some might contend that Jesus claimed to be God and truly thought He was God, but that He was mistaken or actually crazy—after all, He died on the cross holding this belief. But the lunatic theory simply does not fit with the picture we see of Jesus in the Gospels. He is level-headed, astute, informed, loving and sober. This is not the description of a crazy person.

The third choice is that Jesus is indeed who He Himself claimed to be: God. It is the only choice that makes sense of the facts. It is the choice that John proclaims in his Gospel. But John does not stop there. His Gospel reveals that the Spirit has a distinct role and identity as well, thus bringing us to a fuller view of the Triune God.

Jesus not only is endowed with the Spirit, He grants the fullness of the Spirit to those who serve Him (3:34). Jesus sends the Spirit (15:26). In His Farewell Discourse Jesus refers to the Spirit as the *parakletos,* a term which reveals the Spirit's role as Comforter and Guide. The Spirit descends from heaven and rests upon Jesus (1:32). Jesus explains that one must be born of the Spirit in order to inherit eternal life (3:5). It is the Spirit who gives life (6:63). The Spirit was to come after Jesus departed (7:38–39). He is described as the "Spirit of truth" (14:17), and when Jesus states the Spirit will come to them, He says He will come to them (14:15–18). It is the Spirit who will teach all things and bring to remembrance the things Jesus taught (14:26). The Spirit also proceeds from the Father (15:26) and comes to convict and guide (16:7–15). At the end of the Gospel John records that Jesus breathes on them and tells them to "receive the Holy Spirit" (20:22).

These functions of the Holy Spirit cumulatively bring us to the conclusion that the Holy Spirit is indeed God. He descends from heaven, is necessarily present in salvation, gives life, comes after Jesus leaves, exemplifies and teaches truth, convicts of sin, and guides the believer. These are all functions of God Himself. The Gospel of John is therefore a very trinitarian Gospel. He presents a rich vision of the Trinity and the identity and role of each member of the Godhead.

In addition, unique to John's Gospel is a series of sharp contrasts: light vs. dark (1:4–9), love vs. hatred (15:17, 18), from above vs. from below (8:23), life vs. death (6:57–58), truth vs. falsehood (8:32–47). John states at the end of the book that his primary purpose

Chart 3: **JESUS' MIRACLES AND THE CONNECTION WITH GOD IN THE OLD TESTAMENT**

	JESUS' SIGN	GOD IN THE OLD TESTAMENT	REFERENCE
1	Water to Wine–Signifying the newbirth or the wine of salvation	"My shield and the horn of my salvation."	Ps. 18:2
		The image of the great banquet that will celebrate God's salvation.	Isa. 25:6–9
2 & 3	Healing	"I wound and I heal."	Deut. 32:39
		"And by His stripes we are healed."	Isa. 53:5
		"Come let us return to the Lord; for He has torn, but He will heal us."	Hosea 6:1
4	Feeding	The giving of manna to the children of Israel in the wilderness.	Ex. 16
		The feeding of the 100	2 Kings 4:42–44
5	Calming	"He restores my soul . . . I will fear no evil."	Ps. 23:2, 4
6	Opening blind eyes	While there is no specific instance of God healing a blind person in the Old Testament, it is clearly a function God performs, and Jesus' healings clearly hark back to promises that God would heal: "The eyes of the blind shall be opened."	Isa. 35:5
7	Raising from the dead	The Shunamite's son is raised from the dead	2 Kings 4:32–37

This mosaic, c. 500–526, depicts Jesus feeding the five thousand as recorded in John 6: "And Jesus took the loaves, and when He had given thanks He distributed them to the disciples, and the disciples to those sitting down; and likewise of the fish, as much as they wanted. So when they were filled, He said to His disciples, 'Gather up the fragments that remain, so that nothing is lost.' Therefore they gathered them up, and filled twelve baskets with the fragments of the five barley loaves which were left over by those who had eaten."

in writing is to reveal Jesus as the Son of God and that by believing in Him we might have eternal life (20:31). These sharp contrasts drive home the point that John is presenting a choice to his readers: either acknowledge who Jesus is and believe in Him or realize that you are rejecting God Himself. Jesus is light (1:7), and those who believe in Him have the light and are granted the privilege of becoming the children of God (1:12), while those who reject Him continue in darkness. The Gospel of John is easily divided into three main sections.

PROLOGUE: CHAPTER 1
BOOK OF SIGNS: CHAPTERS 2–11
BOOK OF PASSION: CHAPTERS 12–21

—Bruce Etter

For Further Reading

Calvin, John. *Harmony of Matthew, Mark, Luke, John 1–11* (Calvin's Commentaries). Grand Rapids: Baker Book House, 1933.

Carson, D.A. *The Gospel According to John* (The Pillar New Testament Commentary). Grand Rapids: Eerdmans, 1991.

Veritas Press Bible Cards: Gospels. Lancaster, Pa.: Veritas Press. 107, 110, 113, 118.

Session I: Prelude

A Question to Consider

What do you think is the most fascinating miracle Jesus performed? Why do you find it so interesting? What do you think was Jesus' purpose in doing this miracle?

From the General Information above answer the following questions:

1. What was John doing before and after receiving the calling from Jesus?
2. How does John refer to himself in his Gospel? What significance does this have?
3. In the Gospel of John what are "signs?" What significance do they have?
4. What does John say is his purpose in writing his account of Jesus?
5. What evidence do we have that John was not written later in the second century, as some scholars contend?
6. Name the seven signs of John with their references.
7. What accompanies the miracles John records?
8. Why is Jesus the Lord, and not a liar or a lunatic? Why can't He just be a great moral teacher?

Reading Assignment:
John 1–11

Christ is the door. He is like a shut door to keep out thieves and robbers. The shutting of the door secures the house—and what greater security has the church of God than the wisdom, power and goodness of Jesus standing between it and all its enemies? And Christ is like an open door to welcome our admission into the flock of God and into the heavenly kingdom.

Session II: Discussion

John 1-11

A Question to Consider

Consider the founders of the world's major religions: Abraham/Moses, Jesus, Buddha, Mohammed, and Krishna. Who did they claim to be? Who do their followers say they are? How do they compare with Jesus regarding their claims and how they are perceived today?[3]

Discuss or list short answers to the following questions:

Text Analysis

1. What specific claims does Jesus make about Himself in these passages? Look for five of the seven[4] "I am" sayings. (6:27–35, 8:12, 9:5, 10:7–17, 11:25–26)
2. In the context of these passages, what aspect of the metaphor is Jesus stressing in each one (i.e., what is this image teaching us about Jesus)?
3. In the context of these passages does Jesus leave any room for the option that He may be "one of many" in these different areas? In other words, is it possible that Jesus is saying that there could be other sources of eternal life, other "doors" or other "shepherds?"
4. Do you see any overlap between what Jesus is teaching in these "I am" sayings and in the signs? Do you see Jesus stressing some of the same things in the "I am" sayings that He emphasized in the signs?

Cultural Analysis

1. What is the general attitude in our culture about the exclusive claims Jesus makes?
2. How is this attitude manifest in our culture?

Summa

Write an essay or discuss this question, integrating what you have learned from the material above.

Compare the claims of Jesus with the claims of the founders of other world religions. What makes Him unique?

Session III: Recitation

John 1-11

Comprehension Questions

Answer the following questions for factual recall:

1. According to 1:1–3 did Jesus have a beginning? How does the text explain this?
2. According to 1:14 what did Jesus do?
3. What does Jesus do during His first recorded trip to the Temple in John?
4. With whom does Jesus speak in chapter three and what is the topic of their conversation?
5. In chapter 4 Jesus has a conversation with another person. Who is this person, and what do they discuss?
6. Why do many of Jesus' disciples turn away from Him? Who does not leave?
7. What family members do not believe in Jesus?
8. How does Jesus deal with the woman caught in adultery?
9. What is the reaction of the Pharisees to Jesus' raising Lazarus from the dead?

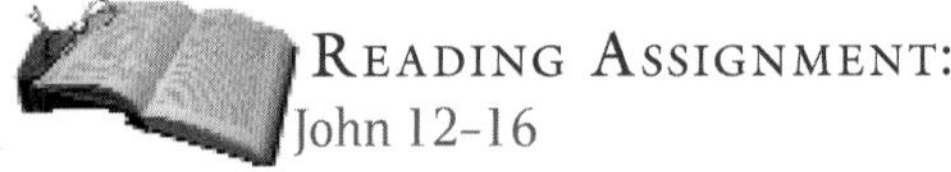

Reading Assignment:
John 12-16

Session IV: Discussion

John 12-16

A Question to Consider

Who or what is the Holy Spirit? How would you explain the Holy Spirit to a Muslim or a Buddhist or anyone who is not familiar with the Christian faith?

Discuss or list short answers to the following questions:

Text Analysis

1. List some conclusions concerning the Holy Spirit that can be drawn from 14:15–18. What other "jobs" does the Holy Spirit have?
2. What is the context of Jesus' teaching on the Holy Spirit in John 16?
3. What can we learn from simply understanding the heart of Jesus' teaching (Christ's coming and dying as a sacrifice for sinners) and the context (Jesus going away) in which He discusses the Holy Spirit?

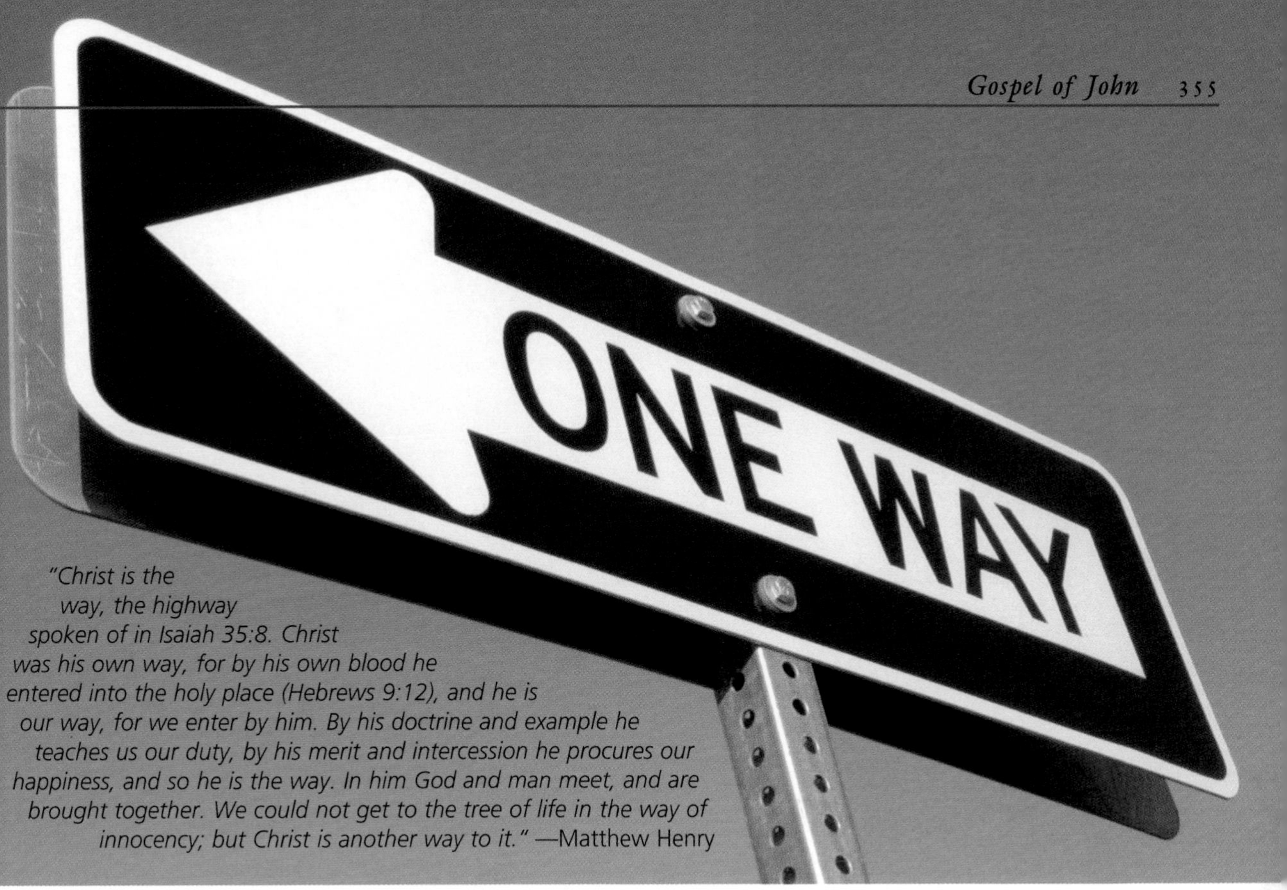

"Christ is the way, the highway spoken of in Isaiah 35:8. Christ was his own way, for by his own blood he entered into the holy place (Hebrews 9:12), and he is our way, for we enter by him. By his doctrine and example he teaches us our duty, by his merit and intercession he procures our happiness, and so he is the way. In him God and man meet, and are brought together. We could not get to the tree of life in the way of innocency; but Christ is another way to it." —Matthew Henry

Cultural Analysis

1. How does our culture generally understand the Holy Spirit?
2. How do some contemporary churches today mistakenly view the Holy Spirit? (On what person of the Trinity do they focus, and how do they connect the Holy Spirit with emotion?)
3. What might be the danger of this unbalanced stress on the Spirit?

Biblical Analysis

1. What more do we learn about the Spirit from Ephesians 1:13–14?
2. How does this compare to the work of the Holy Spirit in the Old Testament?

Summa

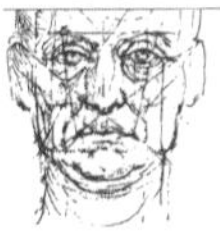

Write an essay or discuss this question, integrating what you have learned from the material above.

How would you explain to an unbeliever the Holy Spirit in terms of His person (who He is) and work (what He does)?

Reading Assignment:

John 17–21

Session V: Recitation

John 12–21

Comprehension Questions

Answer the following questions for factual recall:

1. What is the real purpose of the expensive spikenard which is poured on Jesus?
2. What does Isaiah have to do with the unbelief of those who rejected Jesus?
3. What great act of humility does Jesus perform in chapter 13? When and where does this event take place?
4. What did Jesus say His followers would be able to do as a result of His going to the Father?
5. For whom is Jesus praying in John 17?
6. How does Jesus respond to the high priest when He is asked about His disciples and His doctrine concerning the setting in which His teaching was done?
7. What specific prophecies does John mention while Jesus is enduring His crucifixion?
8. Who addresses Mary Magdalene at the empty tomb?
9. Who receives restoration at the end of the Gospel? Why?

SESSION VI: EVALUATION

Grammar

All tests and quizzes are to be taken with an open Bible and an open book. Answer each of the following questions in complete sentences (2 points per answer).

1. Explain the importance of the word *sign* in the Gospel of John.
2. Approximately when and to whom was the Gospel of John written?
3. List the seven signs of John.
4. In the Gospel of John what is the relationship between the sign and Jesus' teaching?
5. What is the purpose of John? State specifically why he wrote this Gospel.
6. Give a basic outline of John.
7. What does the Holy Spirit do?

Logic

Demonstrate your understanding of the worldview set forth in John. Answer two of the following four questions in complete sentences; your answer should be a paragraph or so (10 points per answer).

1. Why are Lord, liar or lunatic the only choices for us when we consider Jesus' true identity?
2. How does Jesus relate His first sign, transforming the water into wine, to a specific teaching. Explain.
3. How does Jesus relate the sign of the feeding of the thousands to a specific teaching? Explain.
4. What deeper truth was Jesus communicating when He raised Lazarus from the dead?

Lateral Thinking

Answer one of the following questions. These questions will require more substantial answers (16 points).

1. Using only the Gospel of John, respond to the Jehovah's Witness view that Jesus is a created being and not God.
2. Respond to the notion that the Holy Spirit is a force, not a person. Explain how the Gospel of John is trinitarian.

OPTIONAL SESSION: ACTIVITY

Who Do You Say Jesus Is?

Invite an individual from another faith to come and share his views about his own religion. Also ask him to share his specific views about the deity of Jesus.

Here are some questions that students might ask the visitor:

1. What does your religion teach about Jesus? Who was He, and what did He do?
2. How does your religion define sin?
3. How does your religion define righteousness? What is the source of righteousness or law in your religion?
4. Does your religion teach that people need to be saved?

ENDNOTES

1 Some scholars also see this miracle as symbolizing the transformation of order into the new, i.e., Jesus as the full expression of what was only a shadow in the Old Testament.

2 *This endnote appears only in the teacher's edition.*

3 Websites providing helpful information in this area can be found at Links 1and 2 for this chapter at www.VeritasPress.com/OmniLinks.

4 We have not yet read the last two in the reading assignments.

The Merry Adventures of Robin Hood

Robin Hood & his Merry Men entertaining Richard the Lionheart in Sherwood Forest by Daniel Maclise (1806–1870). Maclise was born in Cork, Ireland, and studied there before going to London to study at the Royal Academy Schools. He was offered the presidency of the academy there in 1866, but he declined.

The stories surrounding Robin Hood are both myth and history—the tales of a legendary character surrounded by the bravest and the strongest and the best men of all England, lurking in Sherwood Forest, abiding more closely to the law than the lawmakers themselves.

Take from the rich, give to the poor. This is the moral the western world draws from Robin Hood, and story after story tries to imitate and expand on this theme.

At first, western stories imitated this moral closely. Movie screen computer hackers, outlaws, lone cowboys, would take wealth from those that could spare it and give it to those that needed it. But that story is now morphing. No longer do the heroes of modern tales simply give the money to the poor (except rarely). They keep it. They have been wronged themselves; they are the poor. They take the wealth and then keep the wealth. The rich can spare it, and our heroes need it. Or they just want it.

But regardless of how well we imitate him, Robin Hood is the model for most every American hero. He is the upright cowboy who fights all the corruption in whatever town he blows into. The sheriff is not strong enough to handle the evil himself, or he is part of the problem. This upright cowboy leads jail breaks when innocent people are locked up, and he'll even rob the bank when the money belongs somewhere else. People love a good outlaw, but in recent times that has been shifting. They still love a good outlaw. But now they love a bad outlaw too. They love any outlaw. Mobsters, gunfighters, renegades and assassins—those are the heroes of our society. And Robin Hood would have hated all of them.

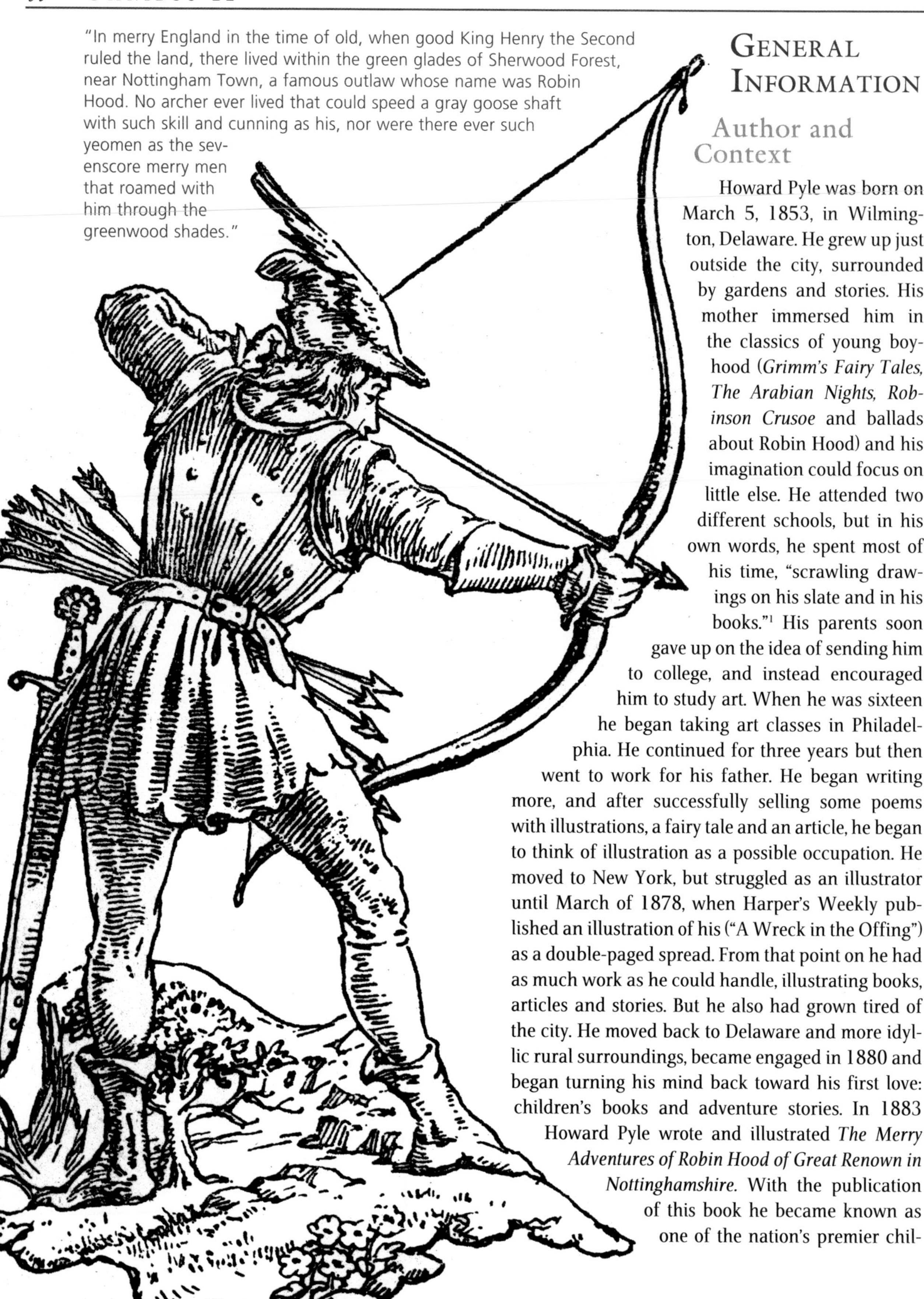

"In merry England in the time of old, when good King Henry the Second ruled the land, there lived within the green glades of Sherwood Forest, near Nottingham Town, a famous outlaw whose name was Robin Hood. No archer ever lived that could speed a gray goose shaft with such skill and cunning as his, nor were there ever such yeomen as the sev-enscore merry men that roamed with him through the greenwood shades."

General Information

Author and Context

Howard Pyle was born on March 5, 1853, in Wilmington, Delaware. He grew up just outside the city, surrounded by gardens and stories. His mother immersed him in the classics of young boyhood (*Grimm's Fairy Tales, The Arabian Nights, Robinson Crusoe* and ballads about Robin Hood) and his imagination could focus on little else. He attended two different schools, but in his own words, he spent most of his time, "scrawling drawings on his slate and in his books."[1] His parents soon gave up on the idea of sending him to college, and instead encouraged him to study art. When he was sixteen he began taking art classes in Philadelphia. He continued for three years but then went to work for his father. He began writing more, and after successfully selling some poems with illustrations, a fairy tale and an article, he began to think of illustration as a possible occupation. He moved to New York, but struggled as an illustrator until March of 1878, when Harper's Weekly published an illustration of his ("A Wreck in the Offing") as a double-paged spread. From that point on he had as much work as he could handle, illustrating books, articles and stories. But he also had grown tired of the city. He moved back to Delaware and more idyllic rural surroundings, became engaged in 1880 and began turning his mind back toward his first love: children's books and adventure stories. In 1883 Howard Pyle wrote and illustrated *The Merry Adventures of Robin Hood of Great Renown in Nottinghamshire.* With the publication of this book he became known as one of the nation's premier children's writers and illustrators. He moved on to other projects (*Otto of the Silver Hand, Men of Iron, The Garden Behind the Moon* and others) and also began teaching art at Drexel University in 1894. Eventually, he quit Drexel and began the Howard Pyle School of Art in 1900 with only twelve students accepted in the first year out of hundreds of applicants. Two of the most famous of his eventual students included a young N.C. Wyeth and Maxfield Parrish, both of whom would go on to have a great impact on American illustration and art. These artists and others who followed after them, as well as after Pyle, are said to belong to the Brandywine tradition, after the region of the country where Pyle lived and taught.

Pyle died abroad in 1911, but the mark he left on American art and storytelling appears to be permanent. *The Merry Adventures of Robin Hood* may be the best example of his dual talent and of why he had such influence.

Significance

Howard Pyle's *Robin Hood* has affected our culture in a number of ways. His style of illustration and writing both influenced storytelling and art in our culture. But then there is the significance of the stories themselves and of Robin Hood himself. The story of Robin Hood dressing as a beggar and Little John dressing as a Friar, of Robin Hood traveling to the great tournament in London, of his kindness to Sir Richard of the Lea—these things have their own significance. Pyle's story is far more potent, because it was one of the primary channels for the communication of the hero Robin Hood into our contemporary culture. Today's children may only know of Robin Hood through Walt Disney's fox, but without Pyle there may not have been a fox, or an Errol Flynn in green tights, or Kevin Costner as Robin Hood, Prince of Thieves. Pyle wrote in a way that makes his readers feel as if they are reading the original legends, as if they are listening to the stories told by some broad yeomen straddling a bench at the Blue Boar Inn with his thighs all wrapped in Lincoln green and some good October brew in his belly. Pyle took the legends and stories surrounding an outlaw hero who died in December of 1247, and he brought them near. He brought them near enough for modern children to feel their texture and walk in the sprawling woods of the thirteenth century. He did that for children at the turn of the nineteenth century and for any other child who has read him since. The fact that stories about Robin Hood still crop up regularly in popular and trite culture around us today testifies to two things. First, Robin Hood's life was potent in a way that few others are and still influences our concepts of goodness today. Second, we owe Pyle our gratitude for connecting our culture more closely to the story of Robin of Sherwood Forest. In his writing and art there will always be an avenue to sense the texture and substance of the stories about the outlaw when we all grow weary of the animated fox.

Main Characters

The Merry Adventures of Robin Hood are just that, a collection of adventure stories that frequently involve different characters and different circumstances. But at the same time, we have a band of regulars. Many men join with Robin in Sherwood, but only a few pop up throughout the course of multiple adventures. There is, of course, Robin Hood himself. He is an outlaw and a gentleman. He is the greatest archer in all of England and lives by poaching deer in Sherwood Forest. His right hand man is John Little, affectionately renamed Little John by Will Stutely because of his seven-foot height and broad shoulders. Will Stutely is the wiley woodsman most often left in command in Robin's absence. Will Scarlet is Robin's nephew, not as large as Little John but the strongest of the band and prone to dress prettily (all in scarlet and smelling a rose when Robin found him). Sir Richard of the Lea is a nobleman of high rank who comes to have a profound loyalty to Robin, and Allan a Dale is the minstrel with the silvery voice (made a rooster folk-singer by Disney). Friar Tuck is the well known and thick-bodied chaplain of the band. There are many others, but these are those that are both the most memorable and most essential characters to the various adventures. The villains are a hodge-podge of wealthy churchmen, civil officials using their positions for themselves instead of defending the weak and private citizens and who who gouge the general populace and take advantage of the poor.

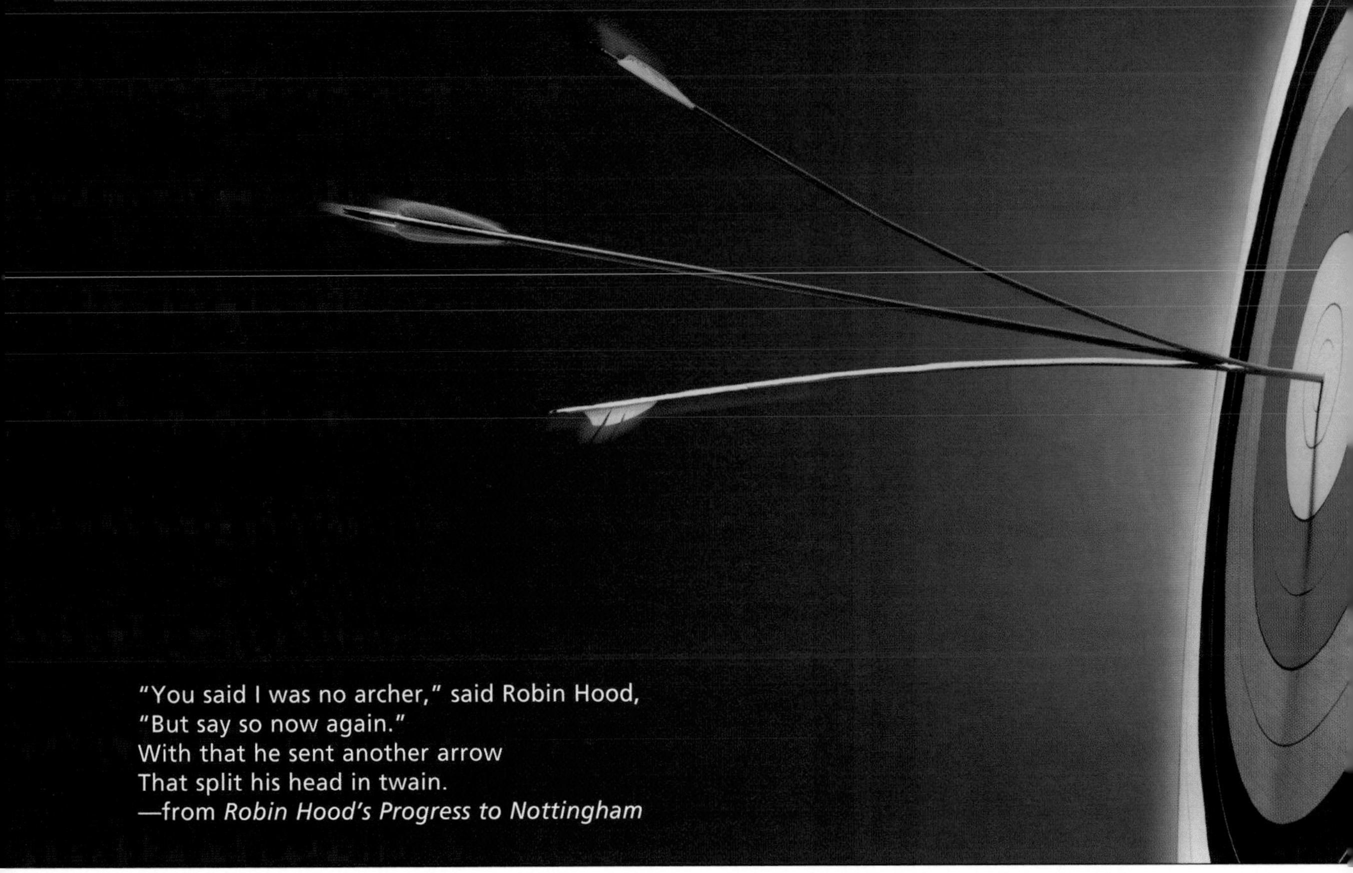

"You said I was no archer," said Robin Hood,
"But say so now again."
With that he sent another arrow
That split his head in twain.
—from *Robin Hood's Progress to Nottingham*

Summary and Setting

There is no central plotline, no fundamental conflict that *Robin Hood* hinges on. These are adventures, but they are still coherent and maintain consistent themes and meanings; and there is a general flow to Robin Hood's life. He begins his career as an outlaw at the age of eighteen on his way to an archery tournament. A forester mocks him, questioning his skill. When Robin takes the man's challenge and drops the largest buck in a herd of deer in the distance, the man grows angry and threatens him for killing one of the king's deer. He then shoots at Robin's back while Robin walks away. Robin shoots back and kills the man. From that point on he is an outlaw, but throughout his initial Sherwood career, he kills only one other man. That man is Guy of Gisbourne, a heinous and bloodthirsty outlaw sent by the sheriff to hunt down Robin Hood. Other men condemned for poaching, or in the case of Will Scarlet, accidental death, gather around Robin Hood, usually through amusing encounters in which Robin or one of his men is bested by some newcomer in a bout of quarterstaffs, which are long wooden poles used as weapons.

Three kings rule during the life of Robin Hood. The first is Henry II, the second is Richard of the Lion's Heart, and the third is King John. Robin is tolerated by Henry II until he bests the king's archers in a London tournament, and then he is hunted ruthlessly by King Harry (who had promised Queen Eleanor that Robin would have safe passage for forty days). The Sheriff of Nottingham and the Bishop of Hereford both play major roles in attempting to capture and execute Robin and his men. When Henry II dies, Richard comes to the throne and, while touring the country, dresses himself and his men as friars and enters Sherwood Forest. There he discovers the true nobility and loyalty of Robin Hood. When he reveals himself, Robin and his men fall to their knees as loyal subjects and Richard pardons them. Most of the outlaws are made royal rangers of the forest ,while Robin himself and some of the others are taken into the king's service. Richard comes to love Robin, makes him an earl and takes him off to the wars with him.

But when Richard dies, Robin returns to Sherwood and has no desire to leave, despite King John's prohibition. The Sheriff of Nottingham and others come once more to hunt him, and the sheriff and many men are killed. Robin grows ill, and travels to his cousin (a prioress at a nunnery[2]) for help. Though Robin's favor with Richard gained her the position she holds, she fears King John, and instead of opening a lesser vein in Robin's arm, she opens an artery, locks the room, and lets him bleed to death.

So Robin lived under three kings, an outlaw in the eyes of two, but a nobleman in the eyes of Richard of the Lion's Heart.

Worldview

Robin Hood was a man after God's own heart. He loved and served the weak. He loved those beneath him and gave them his own life. He was not a man of blood throughout most of his life and did not become one until he was made an earl and fought alongside Richard of the Lion's Heart. The character Pyle describes for us in Robin Hood understands what it means to be an aristocrat, a nobleman and a leader, far more so than the leaders of the church, the aristocracy or King Henry himself. Robin Hood is an informal nobleman, more noble than those in England with the proper pedigree.

So what does it mean to be an outlaw? Outside of what law? If you are outlawed, then you are banned. You are not allowed. You are against the rules. But maybe you *should* be against the rules. Or maybe you're in favor of the rules, but those with the authority to enforce them refuse to, or they manipulate and distort them to their own purpose.

No Christian should be an outlaw if the laws do not demand immorality and if they are justly enforced. But is a Christian allowed to defend himself against an assault from a policeman (or forest ranger)? Or must he simply allow himself to be killed? If he does defend himself and kills the policeman or ranger, and the local magistrate wants to hang him, then would it be wrong for him to hide in a national park and survive by poaching deer? If he does, then he has begun to live outside the law of man. But is he outside the law of God?

In Adam, all of our lives and laws are flawed and corrupt. They are less than perfect, and yet we remain obligated to them. We are in covenant to abide by the law of the land. But in God, we have greater obligations. We may not harm the weak. We must love others better than ourselves. We must love the Lord our God with everything we have. But the magistrates are in covenant as well. They are nevertheless held to the law, and even if they change it, or choose to ignore it, it still binds them, as does the Law of God.

In the story of Robin Hood, the Sheriff of Nottingham, the Bishop of Hereford, the fat churchmen and even King Henry himself were all outlaws in that they broke their oaths, violated covenant with their subjects and otherwise considered themselves above or *outside* the law. And "outside the law" is simply a long way of saying *outlaw*. Robin Hood submitted to the law where he could, but when the king's officials tried to kill him, forcing him into the wood, where is the evil in living on the king's deer? When a thief robs and persecutes the poor, is it wrong to rob the thief and buy grain for the widows? King or not, can you break a covenant of safe passage? Where Robin Hood dwells outside the law, he sets an example of righteousness for those who say they dwell within it. Robin Hood is what a king and a nobleman should be.

Sir Richard of the Lea

In the story of Sir Richard of the Lea, Robin shows his full character. He sets out to find adventure, but instead he finds a knight, poor and sorrowful. The knight is Sir Richard, and Robin brings him into Sherwood to cheer him and see if he can assist him. Elsewhere Little John has captured the wealthy Bishop of Hereford and also brings him to dine in the forest.

Robin demonstrates his worth in how he deals with the knight. Though he is simply an outlaw and a commoner, he takes responsibility for whomever he finds around him, whether their blood is blue or red. Sir Richard's story moves him. His son Henry was made a knight and went to his first tournament. Sir Henry rode well and defeated every knight he jousted, but at the end, jousting with a powerful knight, both lances shattered and a splinter killed his opponent. Despite the law, Sir Henry was blamed and the dead knight's powerful friends used their influence at court to take all of Sir Richard's wealth in exchange for his son's life. Contracts were broken, laws were manipulated, and no matter how much Sir

Richard paid, the ransomers demanded more. Finally Sir Richard pawned his castle and estate to the Prior of Emmet, a wealthy and corrupt church official. Sir Richard must default on his payment and the prior will seize all of his lands in exchange for no more than a pittance.

Robin sees the injustice and looks to make things right where the sheriff, the Lords and even the king will not. He takes five hundred golden pounds from the Bishop of Hereford (an official in the same church as the prior), and he gives it to Sir Richard to pay his debt. Sir Richard will only accept it as a loan, but when he leaves, Robin gives him more, placing a gold chain around the knight's neck as befits the man's station and Robin's men kneel and bind golden spurs to the man's heels.

Robin is the king. He is the one who rights wrong, and who returns men to their proper stations. He is not merely the servant of the poor common people and the protector of widows. He is also the protector of knights and noblemen. He is the protector of true law. He desires nothing for himself, and only justice for others. In another story we learn of his strong distaste for false beggars and lazy men so it is not simply wealth or poverty that brings his like or dislike. It is righteousness and justice, falsehood and injustice. If a man is poor but lazy he does not gain anything from Robin. If a man has been wronged, even a high born nobleman like Sir Richard of the Lea, then he has all the aid and protection that Robin Hood can give him.

The story of Sir Richard ends with even more emphasis on Robin's kingliness. Sir Richard swears him fealty, and in a later adventure, reveals to King Richard himself, that his loyalty to Robin is more primary than his loyalty to the king. Robin is the one who sustained him, who filled the role of protector that a king should have, and remade him a knight.

But despite Robin's assumption of authority he remains a loyal subject to the crown. He is loyal to Henry II and Queen Eleanor, although he flees Henry's men. And he is then loyal to Richard when he assumes the throne, proclaiming his fealty to Richard in the presence of the king when he believes him to be only a monk.

Richard of the Lion's Heart recognizes that Robin is noble and the real governor of the region despite the sheriff and then makes him an earl. He is not making Robin Hood into something new. He is making official what Robin already

King John is known through history as a failure—he failed to hold onto his land in France, failed to hold on to his crown and ended up having the Magna Carta imposed on him. His image is that of a lecherous greedy coward. Some have pointed to his administrative skills to try to paint him in a better light, but with the legends of Robin Hood so popular, how could he ever hope to look good?

is. The lone upright cowboy gets a badge and can no longer work against or outside the system. He must work to defend the system against those who abuse it from within.

In many ways, Robin Hood is King David. Both were outlaws, both were betrayed by their kings to some extent and lived outside the law while remaining loyal to the crown. Both gathered mighty men around themselves and loved music. Both sought to see righteousness throughout the land, and neither would dare assault the person of the king, even when declared his enemy. David ate the showbread. Robin ate the deer. Both had times when they fell into folly. David committed adultery and lost his sons because of it. Robin tried to remove his badge and once more become an outlaw when circumstances did not necessitate it as they once had, and he died for it. But both are nevertheless men that Christian men and women should look to as examples of godly boldness, mercy, leadership and righteousness.

The examples of both men should be worrisome to modern Christians. When do we become outlaws in response to governors at war with their people and with the laws themselves? When do we poach deer in the National Parks or hide from the authorities in caves? When do we start robbing the rich and giving to the poor?

The life of Robin Hood, as Pyle tells it, is an example to us but it is still complicated. We are bound to our laws and to our rulers, but in Adam they are imperfect and can become enemies just as a father can become hostile to his own children. We are bound to these authorities, but we are more profoundly bound to Christ. What would He have us do? When would He have us become outlaws in order to better obey the law and His law? These are all questions that may seem ridiculous in our time, but they are important in all times.

Christians must always be a submissive and unrebellious people; that is something that should never change. This means we should be outlaws when that makes us *more* submissive, not less. King David and Robin Hood would have been less submissive to God had they befriended the wickedness around them. Yet in both cases, they were not the ones to step outside the law. Where they stood they were righteous, and the law stepped outside of them.

—*N. D. Wilson*

For Further Reading

Green, Roger Lancelyn. *The Adventures of Robin Hood.* New York: Penguin, 1994.

Session I: Prelude

A Question to Consider

What do you think is appealing about the story of a good outlaw?

From the General Information above answer the following questions.

1. Should Christians ever be rebels? How so?
2. What made Robin Hood kingly?
3. How well do modern stories of men living outside the law (books and movies) imitate the story Howard Pyle tells us about Robin Hood?
4. Think of a number of figures from history, literature or Scripture and discuss which one Robin Hood most resembles.
5. In what ways should Christian men want to imitate Robin Hood, and in what ways should they not?
6. Is it possible that Christian men and women could find themselves as far outside modern American law as Robin was outside of old England's?

Reading Assignment:
Prologue & Part I

Session II: Discussion

Prologue & Part I

A Question to Consider

How does pride cause us to stumble?

Discuss or list short answers to the following questions:

Text Analysis

1. In Robin's encounter with the foresters, is he being prideful?
2. How do we see pride in Robin's first encounter with Little John? How is this pride dealt with?

3. What kind of man is the Tinker?
4. What motivates the Sheriff to hold the archery contest? What is he counting on for his trap to work?
5. Why does Robin want to lie low while the Sheriff's men are searching for them? What does the rest of the band think about this?
6. What does it finally take to motivate Robin to come out of hiding? What does this show about Robin?

Cultural Analysis

1. Is pride considered a sin in our culture?
2. How do sports stars in our culture show pride? What about movie stars and rock stars?
3. Does our culture ever call something pride when it is not?

Biblical Analysis

1. What does Scripture say about the prideful (Ps. 94)?
2. Look at Matthew 26:57–68. How does what Christ is accused of relate to pride? What's different about Christ's pride?

SUMMA

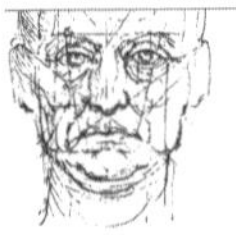

Write an essay or discuss this question, integrating what you have learned from the material above.

How can you tell if you are a proud person?

READING ASSIGNMENT:

Part II

N.C. (Newell Convers) Wyeth (1882–1945), is one of the most celebrated illustrators in the history of art. Wyeth grew up on a farm near Walden Pond, where he developed a love of nature. He was accepted in 1902 to the Howard Pyle School of Art in Wilmington, Delaware. Under Pyle's tutelage, Wyeth's innate talent blossomed. Within a year he had his first illustration published, and it was a cover for a 1903 issue of *The Saturday Evening Post.* Wyeth graduated from the Pyle School of Art in 1904 and by 1911 had established what would become a quite successful association with the publisher Charles Scribner's Sons. Above is one of his classic works of Robin Hood which was painted for Scribner's. N.C. Wyeth also is the father (and grandfather) of several other important American artists—Andrew, Henriette and Jamie Wyeth.

Session III: Activity

Part II

Archery Contest and Cudgel Battle

Games constitute a large portion of the action in *Robin Hood.* From a certain perspective this could be seen as frivolous. However, it has been suggested that, instead of the label *homo sapiens* (Latin for "thinking man"), we might better be described as *homo ludens* ("playing man") or *homo ridens* ("laughingman"). It's certainly true that we learn a lot from playing. Games can be a microcosm of human conflict that teach us how to deal with and enjoy both adverse and lucky situations. In that spirit, organize a combination Archery Contest and Cudgel Battle.

For the Archery Contest you'll need bows, arrows and targets. The middle circle of the target is worth ten points, with each subsequent circle worth one point less, making the outer circle worth one point. If an arrow hits the line, the shooter receives the higher point. Shoot from a distance of about 15 paces (if you are having trouble hitting the target from there, you might move the line closer). Each archer shoots three arrows per turn. There will be three rounds. At the end of the first round the archer with the lowest score will be dropped. The same goes for the second round. In the third round the outer four circles of the target will be counted as zero; only the middle six circles will be scored. The archer with the highest score at the end of the third round wins the Locksley Award.

For the Cudgel Battle your best bet for an authentic weapon is to cut yourself a good staff of ground oak. Barring this, wooden broom handles serve quite well. Those with less of a taste for stinging knuckles might want to consider lighter wooden dowels (or wearing hockey or lacrosse gloves). Section off a space approximately 20 feet by 20 feet and mark the boundaries. You will need judges. They will be responsible to watch for boundary transgressions (fouls) and to keep track of points earned by contact. Each player is allowed two fouls. On the third they forfeit the match. Contact with the opponent's body is assigned points as follows: feet (one point), shins and arms (two points), thighs (three points), torso (four points). Contact with the head will also be counted a foul. Contestants face off two at a time for three two-minute rounds. Points are tallied and the loser is eliminated. For added safety a lacrosse helmet and pads work well. Using the pads might free the players to compete with more tenacity.

If you are in a setting with boys and girls and want to crown a champion of both groups, have the girls compete in archery and the boys do the cudgel. Afterward you can throw a banquet or a Sherwood Forest Picnic in honor of your champions.

Reading Assignment:
Part III

Session IV: Recitation

Parts I–III

Comprehension Questions

Answer the following questions for factual recall:

1. What does Robin do to fall afoul of the law?
2. How does Robin avoid being arrested by the Tinker?
3. Why does the Sheriff of Nottingham decide to hold a shooting match?
4. What does the Sheriff decide after Will Stutely's rescue? Why does he decide this?
5. What reason does Robin give for taking the Sheriff's money after the feast?
6. Why is Robin reluctant to let Little John go to the Fair in Nottingham?

7. Previously, Robin gave a rationale for robbing the Sheriff of a large sum of money, but when Little John steals the Sheriff's silver, Robin makes him give it back. Why? What is Robin's rationale behind stealing?
8. Why does Robin want to watch Little John take a "drubbing" from Arthur a Bland?
9. What does Robin find out about the stranger in scarlet that surprises him?
10. What is Robin's plan to trick the Miller? How does it go wrong?
11. What two sorts of events are repeated throughout these last three chapters?

READING ASSIGNMENT:
Part IV

SESSION V: DISCUSSION
Part IV

A Question to Consider

What is the proper place of celebration?

Discuss or list short answers to the following questions:

Text Analysis

1. So far Robin and his men have been feasting, pulling tricks and playing games. How does Allan a Dale pose a problem for them?
2. What gets Robin and his men back into the spirit of feasting after Allan tells his story? Whom do they need for the plan to work?
3. What's strange about the Friar that Robin comes across?
4. As the band sets out to Ellen o' the Dale and Sir Stephen's wedding, they enjoy the sights of the countryside. What is Robin's remark at this point? What does he mean by quoting Little John's song?
5. When the Bishop asks Robin to play the harp, what is Robin's response and what does he mean by it? How does this fit in with celebration?
6. What is the effect on Friar Tuck of the happenings at the wedding? What do we learn about the feasting in Sherwood after the wedding?

Cultural Analysis

1. Eating and drinking are two aspects of celebration that come up again and again in *Robin Hood.* Does American culture celebrate through eating and drinking?
2. What is our culture's view of entertainment? Is there a difference between entertainment and celebration?

Biblical Analysis

1. Reflect on Psalm 104:14–15. For what are the three things listed in verse 15 given? What is important about the context that verse 14 gives us?
2. One way that we give thanks to God is by tithing. Look at Deuteronomy 14:22–26. What are some of the different ways of tithing which this passage describes? What is the purpose of tithing here?
3. Read Matthew 11:18–19 and John 2:1–11. What is Christ bringing in His ministry?

SUMMA

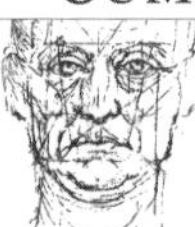

Write an essay or discuss this question, integrating what you have learned from the material above.

What is the proper place of celebration?

READING ASSIGNMENT:
Part V

SESSION VI: WRITING
Part V

Create a ballad

Amongst activities like feasting, reveling and game playing in *Robin Hood* we find ballad singing. Ballads. are quite simply poems or songs which tell a story. Think of the song *The Battle of New Orleans* or even the Beatles' *Rocky Raccoon.* Ballads were often used to commemorate heroic deeds or tragic deaths. In fact, Homer Pyle's stories about Robin Hood are drawn mostly from folk ballads lauding the outlaw. Your task in this assignment will be to compose a short ballad in classic ballad form.

Your subject matter will be taken from any of the stories we have covered thus far. There are several

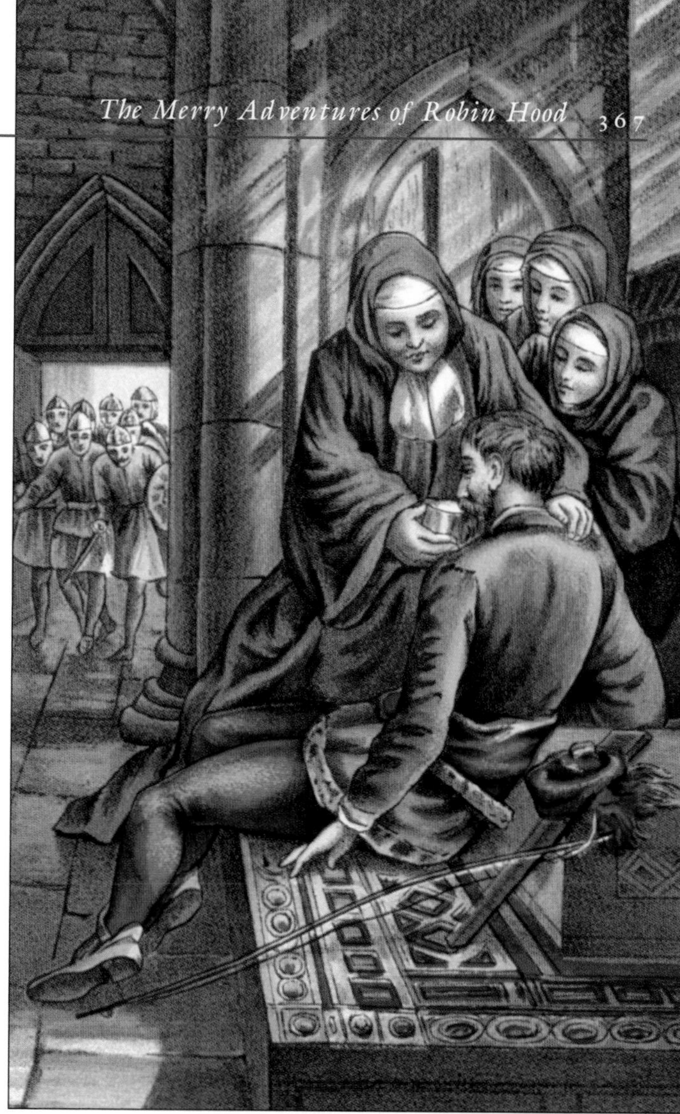

"The early gray of the coming morn was just beginning to lighten the black sky toward the eastward when Little John and six more of the band came rapidly across the open toward the nunnery. They saw no one, for the sisters were all hidden away from sight, having been frightened by Little John's words. Up the stone stair they ran, and a great sound of weeping was presently heard. After a while this ceased, and then came the scuffling and shuffling of men's feet as they carried a heavy weight down the steep and winding stairs. So they went forth from the nunnery, and, as they passed through the doors thereof, a great, loud sound of wailing arose from the glade that lay all dark in the dawning, as though many men, hidden in the shadows, had lifted up their voices in sorrow." Robin is pictured here being attended by the nuns.

form requirements which your ballad must follow. You must tell your story in four stanzas of four lines each. Lines two and four of each stanza must rhyme. You must include a refrain of two lines which will be repeated at the end of each stanza.

Your ballad must also be written in ballad meter. *Ballad meter* is composed of iambs. An iamb is made up of two syllables in which the second syllable is stressed. Thus, the rhythm is *da DUM.* Words like *giraffe* and *invent* are examples of iambs. One iamb can also be called an iambic foot. In iambic poetry we measure each line by the number of iambs. If we have four iambs (or iambic feet) in a line, we say that line is written in iambic *tetra*meter. If we have three iambs, we call that iambic *tri*meter. In ballad meter we alternate iambic tetrameter with iambic trimeter. Here's an example of four lines in ballad meter from Sir Walter Scott's *Brignall Banks.*[3]

O Brignall banks are wild and fair,
And Greta woods are green,
And you may gather garlands there,
Would grace a summer queen:

Lines one and three of each of your stanzas will be in iambic tetrameter and lines two and four will be in iambic trimeter. The refrain will be one line of iambic tetrameter followed by a line of iambic trimeter.

As you can see, this sort of meter has a strong singsong rhythm, which is the point.

Reading Assignment:
Part VI

Session VII: Discussion
Part VI

A Question to Consider

Is it proper to deceive deceitful people? Can we trick the wicked?

Discuss or list short answers to the following questions:

Text Analysis

1. Little John's helping the three maids is funny, but is there anything else going on there that sets the stage for events that come later?
2. How are the monks who confront Little John hypocrites? What is Little John's first reaction to them? How does he change this?
3. Why does Little John have the Brothers pray? How does Little John get their money from them?
4. What does the beggar do after Robin promises he

will not take anything but the beggar's clothes? What do we learn about Robin's standards for stealing from his response to this?
5. How does Robin's trickery with the beggars go? What can we draw from this?
6. What do we know about the Corn Engrosser before Robin begins to travel with him? How does Robin's deceit work this time?

Cultural Analysis

1. What does our culture tend to say about Christians and hypocrisy?
2. How would our culture receive Christ's exhortation to be "wise as serpents and harmless as doves?"

Biblical Analysis

1. Read Joshua 2 and the genealogy of Christ in Matthew 1:5. Does Rahab use deceit? Is she judged for it?
2. Read Genesis 3:14–15 and Judges 4. What is the relationship between these two passages? Is Jael right or wrong?
3. In Matthew 12:13–17 the Pharisees come to Christ to try to deceive him. What happens?

SUMMA

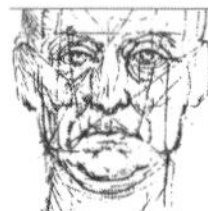

Write an essay or discuss this question, integrating what you have learned from the material above.

Is it proper to deceive deceitful people? Can we trick the wicked?

READING ASSIGNMENT:
Part VII

SESSION VIII: RECITATION

Parts IV-VII

Comprehension Questions

Answer the following questions for factual recall:

1. What reason does Allan a Dale have to be melancholy?
2. Why does Robin need to find the Curtal Friar of Fountain Abbey?
3. After Robin takes his dunking from the Friar, what two things does Robin notice about him that don't quite seem hermit-like?
4. What deal does Robin make with the Bishop before the wedding begins? How does the Bishop pay for his wager?
5. What is Sir Richard of Lea's predicament?
6. Robin attempts to cancel Sir Richard's debt and allow him to keep the money as a gift. Why doesn't he?
7. When the two friars tell Little John they have no money, Little John urges them to pray to Saint Dunstan. What happens when they do?
8. When Robin approaches the four beggars, what is funny about the description of them realizing that someone is coming?
9. What are the terms of the agreement between Queen Eleanor and King Henry at the archery match in Finsbury Fields?
10. How does the Bishop convince King Henry to break his promise of a forty-day pardon to Robin and his men? What does Sir Robert Lee do when he does?

READING ASSIGNMENT:
Part VIII & Epilogue

SESSION IX: DISCUSSION

Part VIII & Epilogue

A Question to Consider

How should we react to authority? What if the authority is an unworthy one?

Discuss or list short answers to the following questions:

Text Analysis

1. What kind of a man is Guy of Gisbourne? What kind of an authority would ally itself with someone like Guy?
2. What is the obvious hypocrisy that the Sheriff displays in convicting all three of the boys for killing one deer when he has hired Guy of Gisbourne?
3. How does King Richard compare to some of the other authority figures we've seen so far? What makes him different?

4. How does Robin behave differently in King Richard's presence?
5. When Robin comes back to Sherwood Forest, how is he changed?

Cultural Analysis

1. The abortion issue is probably the issue that most often tempts Christians to civil disobedience. Should we take action against abortion?
2. The men and women of the Sixties tried very hard to teach us to question authority. But what happens when *their* children grow up?

Biblical Analysis

1. Read 1 Samuel 24. Why is David troubled? What is the main point of David's speech to Saul?
2. Read Luke 20:1–19. Why won't Christ tell the religious "authorities" by what authority He is acting? How does His parable offend them?

Summa

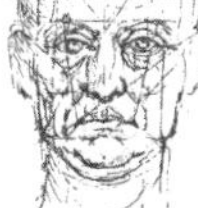

Write an essay or discuss this question, integrating what you have learned from the material above.

How should we react to authority? What if the authority is an unworthy one?

Optional Session A: Evaluation

All tests and quizzes are to be given with an open book and a Bible available.

Grammar

Answer each of the following questions in complete sentences. Some answers may be longer than others. (2 points per answer)

1. How is Robin outlawed in the beginning of the book?
2. When Will Stutely is captured by the Sheriff, how do Robin and his men rescue him?
3. How does Little John end up living at the Sheriff's house?
4. How does Little John come upon the Tanner of Blyth, and what happens when he confronts him?
5. What is Sir Richard of the Lea's story? How does he resolve his conflict with the Prior of Emmet?
6. How does Little John end up about to be hung? How is he saved?
7. How does Robin come to his end?

Logic

Choose two out of the following three questions to answer in a paragraph or two. (10 points per answer)

1. What is Robin Hood's view of authority?
2. How do Robin and his men treat celebration?
3. How are Robin's original outlawry and his eventual demise tied together?

Lateral Thinking

Answer one of the following questions. These questions will require more substantial answers. (16 points per answer)

1. Think about the heroes you've encountered in your readings in the Omnibus program. How is Robin a different kind of hero?
2. Contrast Robin with King David. We've already talked about similarities. What sets them apart?

Optional Session B: Activity

Meeting other Robin Hoods

For many years Robin Hood has been a favorite character in American film and literature. Like many heroes of his age, however, many legends and stories exist concerning Robin Hood. These tales have been put together in different ways to tell different stories. These stories have spawned movies which are retellings and include additional stories. We think Pyle's version is best suited for you, but here are a few others to examine for fun:

> *The Adventures of Robin Hood* retold by Roger Lancelyn Green. (You might want to read this to your little brother, but if you are mean to him after reading it, beware—especially if he owns any arrows.)

Robin has also inspired a number of movies. If you view these, as always, take care to get parental permission. Also try to determine and jot down some notes on how the movie was different from Pyle's book. Where did it fall short? Where did it improve on Pyle? Among the best are:

The Adventures of Robin Hood (1938). This version is the masterpiece by which all other Sherwood Forrest movies are inspired. It stars Errol Flynn and Olivia de Havilland.

Robin Hood: Prince of Thieves (1991). This is the tale retold with some modern twists. It stars Kevin Costner, Mary Elizabeth Mastrantonio and Morgan Freeman as a Muslim who, just to prove that we are super-egalitarian, turns out to be more Christian than the Christians (still, it is hard not to like Morgan Freeman in any role he plays).

Robin Hood (1973). This animated Disney classic is great viewing for all ages. This classical movie is filled with the voices of Peter Ustinov, who plays "that good for nothing John" who is trying to steal the throne from Richard the Lionhearted, and it echoes with the folksy country ballads of Roger Miller.

Endnotes

1 Pitz, Henry. *The Brandywine Tradition.* Boston: Houghton Mifflin, 1969.

2 A nunnery is an abbey for women, and a prioress is like an abbot, the ruler of the nunnery.

3 Scott, Sir Walter. *Brignall Banks* from the Oxford Book of English Verse.

"Bury me where my arrow falls . . ." Just outside the gatehouse of Kirklees Priory a gravestone was found bearing a partial inscription "here lies Robard Hude . . ." Could this really be the final resting place of the famous archer?

A Midsummer Night's Dream

It's a beautiful day, and you're hiking in the woods with friends and family. Then, suddenly, things start to go wrong. Night comes early and a fog rolls in. You become separated from the group. Your two remaining friends glance over at you, scream in terror and run away into the darkness. You start hearing voices. Suddenly, up ahead on the trail you see a large mirror hanging from a branch. To your horror you see that your face is gone, replaced by a donkey's head! Then, of course, you wake up. You breathe a sigh of relief—it was all a dream.

Later that day, you're a fly on a wall, eavesdropping on other people's lives. You see them love, cry, laugh and fight for a noble cause. You almost become them, living inside their lives. Time seems to slow down as you become completely absorbed in the action. Finally, the battle is won, the fortune made, the conflict resolved and the guy and girl live happily ever after. The lights come up, and you unfold yourself from your chair, brushing popcorn off your lap. As you walk out of the theater, blinking in the bright sunlight of a Saturday afternoon, it's almost like waking up from another dream. Time has kept on ticking past while you've been losing yourself in days and months and years made of only lights and shadows.

How can such unreal, insubstantial things have any importance? What can they teach us about real love, real loyalty, real faith and real faithlessness? Can these experiences of the imagination give us more truth than mere "cool reason?" Shakespeare invites us to step into his dream-story to find out.

General Information

Author and Context

Shakespeare lived during a time of great growth and turmoil in England, a time of Protestant-Catholic conflict, the colonization of the Americas and the defeat of the Spanish Armada. It was a time of exploration, growing wealth, new inventions and political change, all of which contributed to the "English Renaissance" of art and learning under the long reign of Elizabeth I (1558-1603).

Some scholars have doubted that William Shakespeare really wrote the works credited to him, but their theories have not become mainstream. What we do know about Shakespeare's life has been pieced together from church and legal records as well as

Arthur Rackham's vision of the wedding scene from *A Midsummer Night's Dream* scattered references by his contemporaries. He was born in Stratford-upon-Avon in April of 1564, the son of a glove-maker, and he probably attended the local grammar school. He was first mentioned as a London actor in 1592, when an older playwright called him "an upstart Crow" and a "Johannes factotum" (jack-of-all-trades). After a two-year interlude when theaters were closed due to plague, he joined a popular company called "Lord Chamberlain's Men," acting as well as writing. *A Midsummer Night's Dream* was written around this time (c. 1595), one of his later "early" comedies. He eventually became part owner of his theater company, and King James I became its patron, inspiring the company to change its name to "The King's Men" in 1603. Shakespeare retired to his hometown in 1611 as one of its wealthiest citizens and died on April 23, 1616. The epitaph he wrote for himself concluded with this bit of doggerel or crudely fashioned verse: "Blest be the man that spares these stones, But cursed be he that moves my bones."

William Shakespeare

Significance

A Midsummer Night's Dream has long been a favorite Shakespeare play, perhaps because it is short, light, funny and fantastical. Though not performed in its original version for a long time after the mid-1600s, it was revived in the Victorian era with extravagant productions including dozens of actors, music, dancing and ornate costumes. Henry Purcell wrote an opera version called *The Fairy Queen*, and Felix Mendelssohn wrote a well-known musical accompaniment. It inspired Rudyard Kipling to write his great children's story *Puck of Pook's Hill*. Numerous film interpretations have been made, and the play has become an essential part of a theater director's résumé.

A few famous lines are Lysander's lament that "the course of true love never did run smooth" (Act 1, scene 1), Helena's bitter assertion that "Love looks not with the eyes, but with the mind; And therefore is wing'd Cupid painted blind" (1.1) and Theseus's bemused comment that "The lunatic, the lover, and the poet, are of imagination all compact" (5.1). In these and other passages, the play gives a complex and classic representation of the struggle between emotion and reason.

The play has also helped preserve and popularize folktale images of fairies and other fantasy characters, both as gauzy, butterfly-winged women and as wild tricksters like Puck, bringing such images and stories into the mainstream of Western literature. Modern fantasy would not be the same without *A Midsummer Night's Dream*. As one critic said in 1908, "even today it is not easy to shake off the inherited impression that the fairies are only what Shakespeare shows them to be. . . . He invested them with a delicate and graceful fancy that has held the popular imagination ever since."[1]

Main Characters

Theseus, the duke of Athens, and Hippolyta, his bride-to-be, have few actual lines, but very important roles. Together, they represent nobility, order and reason in the midst of chaos—their wedding story "frames" the play, giving it weight and stability.

The four lovers get much more stage time, but they still tend to be caricatures rather than characters. Lysander is a roses-and-chocolates sort of fellow who has won Hermia's love (1.1) despite the resistance of her father. The short, spunky Hermia defies her father Egeus's command to marry Demetrius and is willing to elope with Lysander. Helena is perhaps the most interesting of the four, following Demetrius despite his cruel treatment of her, betraying her friends in a pitiful attempt to get his attention and constantly doubting herself when he finally falls in love with her. Demetrius himself is far from lovable. It is no accident that he is the only character who remains forever under the influence of the fairies' magical love-potion—he needs it.

The fairy characters—Puck, Oberon and Titania—express the wildness and unpredictability of nature and emotion. The argument between Oberon and Titania, resolved through trickery and magic, mirrors and becomes entangled with the conflicts of the human lovers.

The craftsmen, particularly Bottom, provide a good deal of comic relief as they enthusiastically work on their silly performance of the tragic Pyramus and Thisbe story. They do have an important role, though, because their play mirrors the main story. Through them, Shakespeare pokes fun at serious lovers' tragedies and invites us not to take his play too seriously, either.

Summary and Setting

The story takes place in and around Athens under the rule of Theseus (c. thirteenth century B.C.), but the play does not depend much on this setting. Instead, Shakespeare combines ingredients from various times and places for his mixed-up, dreamlike play. Such incongruity and anachronism is a well-known habit of Shakespeare. Greek gods are thrown together with fairies from later European legends; nuns exist before Christ was born (e.g., 1.1); ancient Greeks refer to St. Valentine's Day (4.1). All this adds to the story's confused, dreamlike feel.

The play opens with Theseus and Hippolyta's approaching marriage. We find that Hermia loves Lysander, but her father wants her to marry Demetrius, who has recently abandoned Helena. Hermia and Lysander plan to elope the next night, but they tell Helena, who then tells Demetrius. The four end up in the forest outside of Athens, along with Bottom and the craftsmen, who are rehearsing a play for the wedding, and the fairy-rulers Titania and Oberon, who are arguing over the custody of a young orphan boy. Trying to get his way, Oberon sends Puck to use a magical flower to make Titania fall in love with the first thing she sees. He also tells Puck to enchant Demetrius to love Helena. Puck mistakenly puts the spell on both Lysander and Demetrius, and they abandon Hermia and fall in love with Helena, who thinks they are mocking her. Puck then makes Titania fall in love with Bottom, whom he has enchanted with a donkey's head. Eventually the confusion is happily sorted out, and the lovers return to Athens to be married, after which they watch the craftsmen's hilarious attempt to perform their tragedy.

Worldview

Christians have often been suspicious of magic, even when it appears in literature. This understandable attitude has its roots in Israel's law, which forbade any kind of witchcraft (Deut. 18:10–14; Lev. 19:6) and which was reaffirmed in the New Testament when newly converted Christians burned their books of magic (Acts 19:19). Furthermore, the only supernatural creatures the Bible talks about are angels or demons, so Christians often don't know what do with stories about fairies, elves and hobgoblins.

What are we to make of this? As you've learned from reading stories like J.R.R. Tolkien's *Lord of the Rings* and C.S. Lewis's *Chronicles of Narnia,* magic (understood a certain way) can be a rich inspiration for Christian literature. It expresses the key doctrine that the world is personal and poetic, not mechanical. After all, it is a world created out of nothing, only by a word. It is a world governed by a faithful covenant and upheld by God's power (Heb. 1:3; Col. 1:17). It is a world where miracles happen: languages are mysteriously mixed up, oceans are parted, iron floats on water, a virgin gives birth, water is changed into wine and the dead are raised to life. In this sense the Bible is full of magic.

Magic in literature also makes us see in a new light the things that we think we know already. Lewis describes Christ's atonement in terms of the Deep Magic of Aslan and the Emperor-over-the-Sea. Tolkien describes the artistry and skill of the elves in terms of magic. Sauron's ring becomes a symbol of selfishness, excessive ambition and the corrupting desire for unlimited power. We know that those things are evil when we start the book, but actually

Appalled by the weaver's awful acting, Puck gives Nick Bottom an ass-head. When Bottom strolls out of the woods to give his lines from the play "Pyramus and Thisbe," his friends run from him in fear. Bottom is unaware of the new appearance and walks through the woods singing.

seeing them at work in the story adds a whole new dimension. Christian literature can rightly use the categories of good magic and bad magic rather than avoiding magic altogether.

The world of *A Midsummer Night's Dream* is very much a world governed by magic—so much so that some conservative Christians have criticized it for having elements of paganism. The whole plot hangs on Oberon's spells, and the fairies are the ones really making things happen, both creating new conflicts and solving existing ones. But the magic, although it temporarily mixes things up, eventually works for good, overcoming Egeus's unreasonableness and Demetrius's cruelty and unfaithfulness, bringing happiness to the four lovers.

In the meantime, though, the magic can be a frightening thing. It seems uncontrollable, almost taking on a life of its own. It brings confusion that causes Helena and Hermia very real anguish and almost draws Demetrius and Lysander into a deadly duel. It causes the beautiful, noble Titania to fall in love with the foolish, monstrous Bottom, and she is forced to give up her orphan boy to Oberon, breaking her word to the boy's mother. So although things turn out peacefully and happily (except perhaps for Titania!), we are reminded that magic is a dangerous and untamed thing, not to be trifled with.

In all of this, the Christian God is seemingly nowhere to be found, which is understandable, given the play's setting in ancient Greece. But even the Greek gods are pushed to the background. This world seems to belong to the fairies, who influence human affairs as well as the workings of nature (2.1; 2.2; 3.2; 5.2). But they themselves cannot always predict or control what will happen, for they are part of the world as well. They even get caught up in their own squabbles and conflicts, just like the Greek gods. Puck seems to think that "fate o'er-rules" our intentions (3.2). Hermia shares this belief in fate, saying that true love is destined always to be "cross'd" (1.1), and responds with a stoic patience. It is a world of extremes—chaos and unpredictability on the one hand and certain destiny on the other.

Even so, we can still trace God in this pagan environment. Remember that Shakespeare is a Christian. This must color our interpretation, because the author's deep beliefs will leave some mark on the story and give it new meanings. With this in mind, we can see traces of the Triune God in both the play of the fairies and the final, seemingly fated outcome. Remember that the God of the Bible is not a Zeus (as in Homer), but He is not a motionless, distant ideal either (as in Plato). He is involved in the world, appearing as a character in the story, even seeming to change His mind over time (e.g., Ex. 32:14). Perhaps more shockingly, He is a God who plays. He tricks people, tests them and leads them briefly astray. At the risk of being irreverent, He is sometimes very Puckish. Remember when He commanded Abraham to sacrifice Isaac, but provided a ram at the last minute? How could He do that? Did he enjoy the drama? Didn't He know that human sacrifice is serious? What about when He allowed Job to be stripped of everything he had? When He allowed Shadrach and his friends to be thrown into the fiery furnace, only to let them walk around in the flames, laughing?

This very real aspect of God can and should be frightening in a healthy way. As Lewis noted in the Narnia books, He is not "tame." Like Shakespeare's magic, and the fairies who use it, He is neither predictable nor safe. This could lead us to despair and the wrong kind of fear, except that we also know He is sovereign and has promised to save His people. Sometimes when things happen to us that don't seem to make sense, we can feel a bit like Hermia or Helena, feeling deserted or mocked by everyone, lost in the woods. However, despite the tricks and tests, despite the seeming confusion and chaos that we sometimes find ourselves in, we know that He can and will work all things out for good (Rom. 8:28). As in the play, the whole thing will someday seem like just a bad dream (Rom. 8:18; 1 Cor. 13:12).

The craftsmen's play-within-the-play reminds us that the play itself has an author (Shakespeare) and is also itself a play-within-a-play, shaped within the master plot of God's divine purpose. God is the master author. But to the rationalist, who thinks that logic and natural law are the only things worth considering, all stories and poetry are "shadows" or an insane man's talk (see 5.1). Because the rationalist cannot appreciate stories, he can never understand the great Story of the gospel that God is telling in the world. Those who know the great Storyteller, however, can know and appreciate the very real power of believing storytellers as shapers of the world. These faithful tellers of tales bear the image of God partly by imitating His story in writing their own.

If God is the author, then even things that seem chaotic and harmful still glorify Him. The world can only go upside-down if it is possible to be right-side-up to begin with. If everything is crazy, then "crazy" has no meaning. If magic makes no sense, there still must be such a thing as sense. The same assumption also makes comedy and laughter possible. We laugh at things that don't seem to match up—things we think are *incongruous.* When Groucho Marx said, "One morning I shot an elephant in my pajamas. How he got into my pajamas, I'll never know," two different incongruities, or mismatches, are at work—an ambiguous meaning and a bizarre image. But this only works if there is such a thing as real meaning and ordinary images. Bottom's mistakes are similar: "I'll speak in a monstrous little voice;" "we may rehearse more obscenely and courageously" (1.2). Again, such mismatches can have meaning only against a true reality where things really do match up. A purely irrational and unpredictable world can't be funny—it would be boring randomness, like static on the radio. You could say that humor, just like our ability to perceive something "wrong" or fallen about the world, only holds up if it is supported by Eden on one side and heaven on the other. There has to be a right for us to know that something is wrong.

Having looked at what the play says about God and the world, where then do the characters stand? How do they begin, how do they end up, and do they change for better or worse during the course of the story? Have they been redeemed and saved, or are they still lost? Why do they make the choices they do?

As we have seen, the play is framed by the wedding story of Theseus and Hippolyta. They are calm, collected and certain. Hippolyta is a no-nonsense woman who takes life a bit too seriously; she can't enjoy the craftsmen's sincere but absurd play, because she values perfection too much. Theseus is more open, but he still sides rigidly with law and order, supporting Egeus in spite of Helena's moving emotional appeals. Egeus and Demetrius both emphasize their "rights" and "privileges" against the love of Hermia and Lysander. The only appeal that Egeus, Demetrius and Theseus make is to the brute force of human authority and human laws—there is no higher moral ground.

At first glance, we might see this opening conflict as one between pure law and pure emotion. The love of Lysander and Hermia is being repressed by authorities who prize classical Greek ideals of law, order and reason to the exclusion of everything else. This is not the case at all. As the scene goes on, we see that Demetrius and Egeus merely hide behind reason and law to enforce their own irrational whims. Lysander is Demetrius's equal, and Egeus has no real reason to prefer one to the other (1.1). Furthermore, Demetrius has just dropped Helena after making her believe he loved her; he is thus a "spotted and inconstant man," controlled by his whims and unable keep his own promises.

The beginning of the play, then, portrays conflict brought about by people trying to impose their desires by pretending to have law and reason on their side. The lovers, who appear to be emotional rebels, actually have a perfectly reasonable case that brings even Theseus up short. The play thus begins with a fallen environment where authority has been taken over by irrationality, refusing to give true justice. A father is provoking his child (cf. Eph. 6:4), and a ruler, instead of punishing the evildoer (Rom. 13:3–4), is about to force Hermia into an unjust dilemma. Not submitting to the law of God or even the law of their own gods, men give themselves ultimate authority. Egeus asks Theseus to uphold the "ancient privilege of Athens" which gives fathers the power of life and death over their children, treating them like property (1.1). Theseus backs him up, saying that Hermia should view her father "as a god". Forget about the world getting mixed up by the fairies—the world of *A Midsummer Night's Dream* is upside-down from the very beginning.

It only becomes clearer that human "reason" is not what we think. It is a flawed tool that is not a sure way to happiness or truth. We often can't tell what is truly rational, and we often use "reason" merely to justify our irrational desires. All of the characters under the influence of the love potion claim that they are acting rationally. Lysander insists to Helena, "The will of man is by his reason sway'd; And reason says you are the worthier maid" (2.2). Titania claims to be enthralled by Bottom's virtue (3.1), to which Bottom replies, "Methinks, mistress, you should have little reason for that: and yet, to say the truth, reason and love keep little company together now-a-days." The intoxicated Titania then praises foolish Bottom as "wise."

We can thus read the play as partly a criticism of

Puck, or Robin Goodfellow, is "a shrewd and knavish sprite" in the service of Oberon. Oberon sends him to get the flower "love-in-idleness" and put it in the eyes of a youth "in Athenian garments," but he gives it to the wrong person. Yet Puck takes sadistic delight in the confusion caused by his mistakes.

the Greeks. Human reason cannot ultimately be reasonable. It cannot, by itself, find truth and create happiness. Shakespeare hints that it needs a healthy dose of magic now and then to keep it honest. This is not to say that reason is useless or nonexistent—we couldn't say human reason is "faulty" or "limited" if we didn't have some idea of true Reason, the Logos of God. However, reason isn't everything. It must be redeemed by the magic of grace and love. It is a gift we are to use in order to love God and our neighbor better; it is not itself the ultimate standard or final good. As Theseus says, love, poetry and magic, even if they sometimes seem crazy, can apprehend "more than cool reason" (5.1). Was God strict and "reasonable" when he loved us and gave His Son for us, though we were still rebels? Of course not—extravagant grace and love fulfilled and overwhelmed the law.

Based upon this, we might be tempted to think that the play exalts love and emotion over reason. Shakespeare does use his magic to symbolize the mystery of love. Near the beginning, Egeus complains that Lysander has "bewitch'd" Hermia, and the metaphor is appropriate. The main use of magic in the play is to make people fall in or out of love. It is love and magic that save Demetrius from his own unfaithfulness, solving the play's main dilemma.

Nevertheless, love and emotion clearly get their share of Shakespeare's criticism as well. We saw earlier that there is good and bad magic—so also there is good and bad love. Dante makes a similar point in his structuring of Hell, Purgatory and Heaven—there is perfect love, defective love (laziness) and perverted love (greed, lust, etc.). Good love loves what is noble and is faithful to it, while bad love has an inappropriate object or is constantly unfaithful. Shakespeare's characters in this play are always thinking about keeping or breaking promises. Demetrius's love for Hermia is defective because he has been unfaithful. His love prevents him from keeping his promises, and his right love must be restored by magic. Titania's love for Bottom, brought on by Oberon's magic, is similarly inappropriate and disturbing even if it is humorous. We need both reasonable love and loving reason. As Bottom says, the two must "keep . . . company together" (3.1).

Remember that the Greek philosophers stood for reason and order, and Athens has always been the symbol of Greece. You may be familiar with Aeschylus's *Oresteia* trilogy (remember from *Omnibus I?*). In *The Eumenides*, the last play of his trilogy, Aeschylus seeks to establish a new and reasonable system of justice and order in the polis, a shelter from the chaos of the world. Shakespeare deals with the same theme on a lighter note, contrasting the wild, natural fairy world of rural England with the ordered city of the Greeks. It turns out both places have things to teach one another. The Greek city cannot solve the dilemma of the lovers, instead threatening them with unreasonable punishment. They have to escape from it into the forest in order to solve their problems. However, they cannot remain there long. They must return to the city to be married, founding a new order based on the old one but grown wiser from its journey outside. If we see the forest as an Eden-like place touched by the Fall, and the city as a failed attempt at human order, we could see the final marriage scene as a picture of the Eden-city of Revelation where Christ and his bride are joined forever (Rev. 21:2).

—*Jared Miller*

For Further Reading

Briggs, Katharine. *The Anatomy of Puck: An Examination of Fairy Beliefs among Shakespeare's Contemporaries and Successors.* London: Routledge & Paul, 1959.[2]

Halio, Jay. *A Midsummer Night's Dream.* Shakespeare in Performance Series. Manchester: Manchester University Press, 2003.[3]

Scott, Mark, ed. *Shakespeare for Students.* Farmington Hills, Mich.: Thomson Gale, 1992.[4]

Spielvogel, Jackson J. *Western Civilization.* Seventh Edition. Belmont, Calif.: Thomson Wadsworth, 2009. 477–481.

Session I: Prelude

A Question to Consider

What is love?

From the General Information above, answer the following questions:

1. What are our main sources for information about Shakespeare's life?
2. The most famous lines from *A Midsummer Night's Dream* deal with what main theme?
3. How can the idea of "magic" contribute to Christian literature?
4. What attribute does God share with the fairies in the play? In what major way does He differ from them?
5. What basic assumption do we need for both the concept of "wrongness" and the concept of humor to have meaning?
6. Many people assume this play is *just* about order, law and reason against chaos, mischief and emotion. Why is this interpretation too simplistic?
7. How do the two main locations in the play (Athens and the forest) relate to the play's main theme(s)?

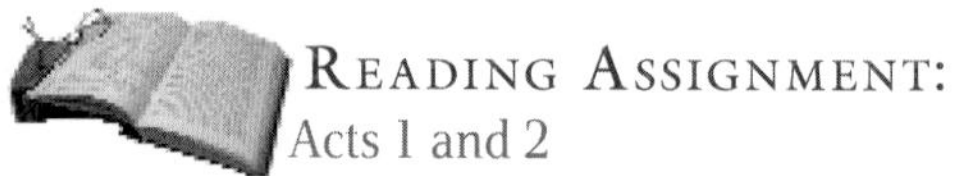

READING ASSIGNMENT: Acts 1 and 2

Session II: Writing

Acts 1 and 2

Progymnasmata

As we have learned, the *progymnasmata* were composition exercises used by ancient rhetoricians to sharpen various key skills needed by an educated and eloquent person. For this assignment, choose one of the following exercises. It will be due at the beginning of Session IV.

Choice 1: Defense or Attack of a Law

One of these progymnasmata was called a *Defense or Attack of a Law*. In this exercise a student defends a certain law or a proposed one. A *Defense of a Law* has six parts. Classical rhetoricians devised several main approaches for evaluating laws. After a short introduction, in which the student should state the law and his position on it, the first section is *Legality*. In this section, the writer compares the law under consideration with other laws (precedents) to check its consistency. For example, in modern America, Congress must make sure the laws it passes are consistent with the Constitution, which is officially the highest law in America. The writer might also refer to similar laws in other countries as examples, even though they are not binding. The second section is called *Justice*. This goes beyond current laws to appeal to a universal sense of what is right or just. Referencing God (or in the case of the Greeks, gods) helps here to establish a framework of justice that is above the law. One could also appeal to common sense, tradition or custom in this section. The third section is called *Expediency*. This judges whether the law will have good practical effects on the country and includes an examination of the law's probable consequences. You should first consider whether those consequences are desirable, then compare intended consequences versus possible consequences in order to ensure that the law is an appropriate way to achieve the intended effect. Fourth, an argument can be made from *Practicability*. In this section one can argue that a law is practical (or if attacking the law, impractical). This might cause someone to say that the law would be more trouble than it is worth, or that it would be easy to implement and would have a wonderful effect on society. The fifth section is *Decency*. This section explores whether the proposed law is polite and whether it complies with the precepts of morality. After this, the *Consequences* are considered. This means that one would have to consider what the result of passing the proposed law would be. Finally, a *Conclusion* summarizes the argument.

The opening conflict of A Midsummer Night's Dream *depends on a law in Athens which gives fathers absolute control over the lives of their children. Suppose you are an ancient Athenian discussing this law. Using the above framework, both defend and attack the law, allowing about 350–500 words for the defense and the same for the attack. In both arguments, you must at some point appeal to the idea of "love" to support your case.*

As much as possible, try to put yourself in the context of ancient Athens. For the section on legality, remember that, when Greece was ruled by kings and tyrants, laws did not have the same importance in this context so it may be difficult to find material for this section. You can thus make reference to other laws, like the Code of Hammurabi and the Mosaic Law of Israel. Remember that you will be able to appeal to common sense, decency, traditions and customs in the section on justice.

Introduction
- State the law and your own position

I. Legality
- Compare the law with other laws

II. Justice
- Appeal to a universal sense of what is just

Theseus and Hippolyta, shown here during their combative courtship, are Shakespeare's personification of civilization and order. They appear only at the beginning and at the end of the play. As the action moves to the forest, civilization recedes into the background, to reappear only when order is restored in Act 5.

III. Expediency
- Evaluate the practical effects of the law
- Examine the law's probable consequences

IV. Practicability
- Argue that the law is practical (or impractical)

V. Decency
- Argue on the grounds of politeness and morality

VI. Consequences
- Discuss the result if the law is passed

Conclusion

CHOICE 2: COMMONPLACE

Another of the *progymnasmata* is called a *commonplace.* It is an exercise in which you consider a general virtue or vice, expanding on or "amplifying" its goodness or badness. It has six parts. The first part is called the *Contrary,* in which the virtue or vice is contrasted with its opposing vice or virtue, thus highlighting its essential aspects and its goodness or badness. For instance, if you are writing a commonplace on faithfulness, you might start with a *Contrary* contrasting faithlessness with fidelity in order to show how wicked faithlessness is. The second part is called a *Comparison.* In it you compare this virtue or vice to a similar one, in order to highlight how much better or worse the other is. For example, if you want to condemn deceitfulness, you might compare it to sloth. In this *Comparison,* you want to show that, even though sloth is wicked, compared to deceit, which uses the mind to mislead others for ill, sloth is the lesser sin. The third section is called a *Proverb.* This section introduces a relevant proverb or common-sense idea that condemns the vice or praises the virtue. The book of Proverbs contains a wealth of these kind of statements. The fourth section is called a *Digression.* In the *Digression,* you describe and condemn the type of person who has the vice (or praise the person of virtue). This description should be one that demonstrates how ugly this sin is. The fifth section is called a *Refutation.* This is a response to the objection that this vice deserves more pity than condemnation (e.g., "they can't help it"). Finally, in the sixth part, called *Useful Topics,* use the elements of "Defense or Attack of a Law" in order to evaluate the virtue or vice. For example, if the vice is cowardice, you could talk about legality (laws against deserting from the army), justice (universal values of selflessness and sacrifice rather than self-interest), expediency (a nation of cowards will not survive) and practicability (many examples show that people can and do choose bravery over cowardice).

Shakespeare lived during the reign of Queen Elizabeth I, whose coat of arms is pictured above. The Latin inscription *semper eadem,* meaning "always the same," could easily characterize her stable personality as a ruler. Elizabeth was the daughter of King Henry VIII. She never married and had no children. She reigned for forty-four years and died in 1603. She was succeeded by James I.

Using this general outline, write a commonplace amplifying the vice of fickleness (unfaithfulness) in the context of romantic love. Length: 500–700 words.

I. Contrary
- Contrast the vice or virtue with it opposite

II. Comparison
- Compare the vice or virtue to a similar trait

III. Proverb
- Introduce a relevant idea or saying that supports your argument

IV. Digression
- Describe the kind of person who has this trait
- Use this example to illustrate the trait's desirability or sinfulness

V. Refutation
- Respond to possible objections

VI. Other Topics & Conclusion
- Evaluate the trait according to its legality, justice, expediency, practicability, decency and consequences
- Conclude by restating your position

Reading Assignment:
Act 3

Session III: Activity
Act 3

Debate

This session is intended to sharpen your logical and rhetorical skills in the context of literature. A basic formal debate is structured around a statement called a *resolution*. One side affirms the resolution and is called the *affirmative;* the other side denies it and is called the *negative*. The order of speaking is as follows:

1. First affirmative opening: introduction, proof of resolution
2. First negative opening: introduction, refutation of resolution
3. Second affirmative opening: additional proofs (*not* a response)
4. Second negative opening: additional refutations (*not* a response)

In this first half of the debate, both sides present only their own arguments; they do not specifically respond to the other side. That is reserved for the second-half rebuttals. At this point there is a brief intermission as each side evaluates the other side's arguments and plans rebuttals.

5. First negative rebuttal
6. First affirmative rebuttal
7. Second negative rebuttal
8. Second affirmative rebuttaL

Each team should assign students to the following roles:

1. Prover: develops the opening arguments and anticipates rebuttals.
2. Stater: delivers the introduction, which lays out the basic issue at stake, explains the team's position and outlines the major arguments. It may be combined with opening speakers.
3. Opening speaker: delivers the opening arguments.
4. Rebuttal speaker: delivers the rebuttals.
5. Scribe/advisor: takes notes on other side's arguments and prepares for rebuttals. Offers input to provers as well.

Some of these roles may be combined; others may have multiple students filling them. Each speech may be allotted about five minutes. Note that the affirmative has the advantage, because it both begins and ends the debate. The debaters should speak from notes instead of reading a written speech. It is wise to anticipate opposing arguments, since there is little time to prepare for the rebuttals.

Choose one of the following resolutions for debate. If time permits, six small teams could debate all three topics over two class periods. For individual students with no debating opponents, write out what you would say as a "position paper" for each phase of the debate (or for selected phases).

Resolution 1.

Lysander and Hermia are justified in disobeying Theseus and Egeus by trying to elope.

Resolution 2.

Oberon was right to use magic on Titania in order to get the orphan boy from her.

Resolution 3.

The fairies and magic in the play are an edifying expression of the Christian worldview.

Reading Assignment:
Act 4

Session IV: Discussion
Acts 1-4

A Question to Consider

Why do people marry?

Discuss or list short answers to the following questions:

Text Analysis

1. What is the subject of the very first lines of the play? Why does it begin with this topic?
2. Why does Egeus not approve of Lysander?
3. Why is this ironic in light of Lysander's argument

against Demetrius in 1.1?

4. Look at the many passages in the play that refer to promises and faithfulness. (Pick a few from the following scenes: 1.1; 2.1; 2.2; 3.2; 4.1. There are also some in Act 5 if you've read ahead.) Overall, do they give an optimistic or pessimistic view of people's ability to keep their promises?

Cultural Analysis

1. How does our secular culture view marriage?
2. Who defines marriage in our society?
3. Why would two nonbelievers marry in our culture?
4. Do we think of romance and marriage as connected?

Biblical Analysis

1. What are the biblical reasons for marriage (Song of Sol. 1:2; Prov. 5:18; Eccles. 9:9; Mal. 2:15; Eph. 5:25-31; 1 Cor. 7:9; and Ex. 20:14)?
2. How does the Bible define marriage (Prov. 2:17; Mal. 2:14; Gen. 1:27; Matt. 5:32)?
3. How should one decide whom to marry?
4. What is the biblical relationship of romance to marriage (Prov. 5:18–19; Song of Sol. 3:5; Eph. 5:25-31)?
5. Why is marriage an important biblical symbol (Eph. 5:25-31; Rev. 21:2)?

Summa

Write an essay or discuss this question, integrating what you have learned from the material above.

Describe how romance should exist alongside commitment in Christian marriage, and contrast this with the secular view. Does *A Midsummer Night's Dream* support the Christian idea? Why or why not?

Reading Assignment:
Act 5

Session V: Discussion

Act 5

A Question to Consider

How do fiction and imagination relate to "real life"?

Discuss or list short answers to the following questions:

Text Analysis

1. What does Helena mean when she says, "Love looks not with the eyes, but with the mind"? What does she mean by "mind"—reason or imagination? Which (according to her) perceives reality correctly—the eyes or the mind?
2. In light of the above question, along with Helena's phrase "light as tales" and Theseus's speech, fiction appears to be similar to what vice?
3. Theseus lumps together "the lunatic, the lover, and the poet". According to him, what tendency do they all share? How could you criticize his comparison?
4. Describe the craftsmen's discussion at the beginning of 3.1. What are their assumptions about theater? Their audience? Why is this so funny?
5. What is the actual reaction to their play?
6. Why would Shakespeare devote a long scene to the craftsmen's play when the main action of his play is already over? What comment, if any, might he be making on his own play?
7. What does Puck say about the play (and theater in general) in his final speech? Relate it to the craftsmen's prologues to their play. Do you agree with Puck?

Cultural Analysis

1. Fiction has a wider audience today than ever before. What is the main reason we view or read stories (outside of school)—entertainment or edification?
2. Can a story ever be "just a story" (or in Puck's words, just a bunch of insubstantial "shadows")? Will stories always communicate some value-system or idea of the good?

Biblical Analysis

1. Is fiction a "lie" or deception and thus not edifying for Christians? Is truth found only in nonfiction?
2. What are some examples of fiction, storytelling and symbol in the Bible? Metaphors can also be thought of as a type of fiction, because they say something "is" what it "is not." (Look at the following passages if you need a nudge: Psalm 26:7; Psalm 106; Acts 7:1–53; 2 Samuel 12:1–13; Eze-

kiel 17:1–10; Matthew 13 and John 1:29.)

3. Does the Bible give any precedent for stories as pure entertainment? Does fiction always have to have some edification (Phil. 4:8; Gal. 5:13; 1 Cor. 6:12)?
4. Fiction requires us to imagine what other people's lives are like, putting ourselves in their shoes. Relate this to the Second Greatest Commandment (Matt. 22:39).
5. Helena says that love looks with the imagination, not with the literal eyes. Is this how God loved us when we were still sinners? How might Christian charity (sacrificial love) be considered "imaginative" or "creative" love? How is this different from the "imaginative love" in the play (Ezek. 16:1–14; Rom. 5:8; Eph. 5:25–27)?

DON'T BE SUCH AN ASINUS

In *A Midsummer Night's Dream,* a fairy turns a character's head into the head of an ass. Many of us grow up calling a donkey a *donkey* and feel a bit uncomfortable calling it an *ass.* This is quite reasonable, once we explore the origins of the word. It comes down to us from the Latin *asinus,* meaning "donkey." An insult frequently found in older literature is to call someone an *ass.* This may simply mean they are foolish and dull-witted, like an ass (donkey). Unfortunately, in more recent times (and especially in America), calling someone by this name usually means they are a buttocks, not a donkey. Where did this embarrassing (not to mention vulgar) confusion arise?

The confusion is explained by the fact that this one term actually descends from *two* words, not just one. Another word for "buttocks" in English was *arse* (and this is still in common usage in Britain). This word has undergone a change in pronunciation over the past few centuries, dropping the *r* so that it sounds very similar to *ass* (the donkey). Interestingly, Shakespeare gives us a comedic clue that the two words were at least beginning to merge in his day. What is the name of the character whose head is changed into that of an ass? Bottom!

Summa

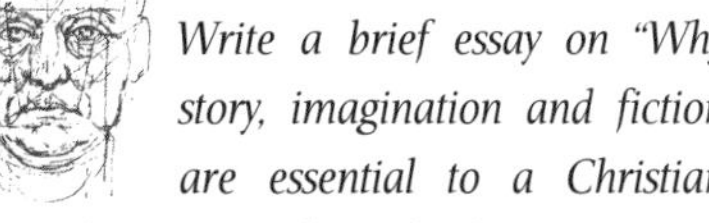

Write a brief essay on "Why story, imagination and fiction are essential to a Christian worldview." Briefly apply what you write to A Midsummer Night's Dream.

What aspects of the play are edifying for Christians? What aspects are not?

Session VI: Recitation

Comprehension Questions

Answer the following questions for factual recall:

1. Summarize the main points of Shakespeare's life.
2. Summarize the cultural significance of *A Midsummer Night's Dream.*
3. The play opens with preparations for what event? Why?
4. Why do Lysander and Hermia have to elope?
5. Why are Oberon and Titania at odds?
6. How does Oberon win the argument?
7. What mistake does Puck make with the love potion?
8. What event takes up most of Act 5, scene 1?

Conceptual Questions

Answer the following in a few sentences:

1. What role do magic and fairies play, from a Christian perspective?
2. Describe the ideas of love and commitment in the play.
3. What does the play say about the nature of fiction and imagination?

"Through the house give glimmering light / By the dead and drowsy fire; / Every elf and fairy sprite / Hop as light as bird from briar, / And this ditty after me / Sing, and dance it trippingly." Oberon and Titania make their way to bless the marriages in this painting by London artist and poet William Blake (1757–1827).

Optional Session A: Activity

Art and Design in Theater: Creating a Scene

In this activity, choose a scene from the play and then design some aspect of a production of that scene: set, costumes and major props, or technical aspects. Choose one of the options below and include the elements listed. Regardless of which type of design is chosen, write a brief "Creative Vision Statement" which explains what aspect of the play you are designing, summarizing the major aspects of your design and showing how the design will reinforce, clarify and amplify the play's themes in that particular scene and in the play as a whole. Please be aware that the cliché design of *A Midsummer Night's Dream* was created by the Victorians, and it has been so successful that we have come to think of it as the *only* way to "do" fairies or forests or Greek cities. Try to break out of this model and be creative, either completely updating your production, or putting a new twist on a traditional-style production.

Choice 1: Set Design

This option requires artistic sense and technical know-how, as well as hands-on construction work, if you will actually build a set. This activity involves several elements:

1. Decide the setting (time and place) for the play. Shakespeare used ancient Athens, but you might decide to use, for example, present-day New York (the forest being Central Park, of course!).
2. Choose your scene. The basic setting will be either "forest" or "Athens," but you will still need to customize it for the action of a particular scene. Choose one with potential for a challenging design. If you choose 5.1, for example, you'll have to design two sets—the Athens set and the play-within-the-play set.
3. Decide on the stage layout. A stage doesn't have to be a framed box in front of the audience. You are free to work with designs that use circular or semicircular stages, or layouts that mingle parts of the "stage" with the audience.
4. Make rough sketches. Do several of these to try out various ideas. Save them and turn them in with your final materials.
5. Make the final drawing. Use color and plenty of detail.
6. Optional: Construct a model. Time, energy and instructor permitting, build a model stage based on your drawing.
7. Optional: Construct a full-size set. Again, resources permitting, you can realize your full design life-size. It makes sense to do this if the class or theater club will actually use it for a performance.

8. Optional: Design a poster to advertise your "production" of the play.

Choice 2: Costume Design

In a real production, the costume designer would work closely with the director and set designer to ensure consistency. For this assignment, you are on your own. Choose three characters (at least one human and one fairy) and design their costumes and any main props or accessories they may have (e.g., a scepter for Oberon). This assignment includes several elements:

1. Decide on the setting (time and place) for the play. As with the set design, you can go with Shakespeare's ancient Athens or with another setting such as present-day New York. This choice will drastically affect your designs, so choose carefully.
2. Choose your scenes. If one or more of your characters appears in various scenes at different times, then you'll need to choose which scene you'll design for. For example, Theseus will have a different costume in 1.1 (in Athens) than in 4.1 (hunting in the forest).
3. Create rough sketches. Do several of these to try out various ideas. Save them and turn them in with your final materials.
4. Do the final drawings. Use color and plenty of detail.
5. Optional: Make a small-size version. Time, energy and instructor permitting, make a one-quarter to one-sixth scale costume based on one of your drawings.
6. Optional: Make a full-size costume. Again, resources permitting, you can realize one or more designs life-size. It makes sense to do this if the class or theater club will actually use it for a performance.
7. Optional: Design a poster to advertise your "production" of the play.

Choice 3: Technical Design

Technical design may be a good option for students who are more interested in engineering than in art. Still, it requires good artistic sense. Choose one interesting (and long) scene and work out the following elements:

1. Blocking.
   The blocking of a play describes in detail the physical movements of the actors around the stage. Normally the director and actors would decide this. It is important that it look natural and work well within the constraints of the stage. You'll have to make a rough stage design to really know how the blocking will go. Make an annotated version of the scene that includes your blocking directions.
2. Lighting.
   There's much more to lighting than just making sure the audience can see the actors. Many options are available that affect the look and feel of the production. Students may do extra reading and research on the options and technology available. The color and intensity of the lights can set the mood. Harsher and softer lights draw attention to the actors and set, "focusing" the audience's attention. Sideways lights can set off shapes more dramatically. Lights can move or flash for special effects. Lights can even be fitted with plates having cutout patterns (called *gobos*) which project shapes onto the stage to help with the setting (e.g., a branch/leaf design with a green light can help create the forest setting). Create a detailed list of light changes and effects tied to line cues from the play.
3. Sound Effects.
   Try to think of additional sounds beyond those mentioned in the text of the play such as music or the baying of Theseus's hounds; there is lots of room to be creative. For example, create a sound effect that is played whenever the magical love-juice is used on someone, or a melody that accompanies the entry and exit of fairies. Make a CD of sounds with numbered tracks that are tied to cues in the scene.
4. Special Effects.
   These are called for explicitly in some scenes (as when Puck makes a fog come down to separate Demetrius and Lysander), but again, you should be inspired to add creative effects of your own. For one example, you could have some fairies "fly" on or off the stage. Make sure you describe the effect in detail, as well as what mechanical means you plan to use to accomplish it.

Optional Session B: Activity

View a Live Performance or Film Version

Merely reading a play is like hearing someone describe ice cream instead of actually getting to taste it. So, if you have the opportunity at some point in the school year (preferably during or after reading the original play), see a live performance of *A Midsummer Night's Dream.* Be prepared beforehand with questions and topics to think about and jot down some notes about the performance during scene changes and intermissions. If that option is not available, you could take time to view a film version, pausing a few minutes at appropriate breaks to make notes.[5]

The classic film adaptation is the black and white 1935 version, directed by William Dieterle and Max Rheinhardt and featuring a star-studded cast including Olivia de Havilland, Mickey Rooney and James Cagney. The setting is fairly traditional, though the script has been somewhat altered from the original. Another popular version came out in 1999 (directed by Michael Hoffman; PG-13), which stars Kevin Kline, Michelle Pfeiffer, Stanley Tucci, Rupert Everett, Calista Flockhart, Christian Bale and Sophie Marceau, among others. The script is shortened and the setting is changed to circa 1900 Italy. Other TV or live filmed versions exist, but the ones listed are probably the biggest-budget and best-known adaptations.

Following are a few suggested questions and topics to have in mind before viewing a production. They may also be used as a starting point for a discussion or short essay after viewing the production.

1. Directing. The director approves and coordinates all aspects of the play, though most directors will not micromanage the acting and design. The director is responsible also for any changes to the original script (many directors have cut, added to and rearranged Shakespeare's texts). The overall look and feel, as well as the emphasizing of themes, is up to the director. In the production you see, evaluate the various choices the director made. What changes were made to the text? Why? Were they effective? Was the setting changed to a different time or place than ancient Athens? How does that setting add to this production's interpretation of the play? What is the overall look and feel? What themes do you think were emphasized?
2. Design. This very broad aspect of play and film production includes sets, lighting, costumes, makeup, sounds, special effects and props. In a good production, all these aspects of the play (or film) will be chosen carefully to support the general artistic vision of the director. (One director put on *A Midsummer Night's Dream* in a stage that looked like a large white box—hopefully the production you see won't be quite that extreme.) Design is the most prominent, noticeable aspect of a production that distinguishes it from others and expresses a unique "take" on the story. For example, should the forest outside of Athens be dark, overgrown and menacing, or should it be light and airy like a park? Assess the design of the production you view, asking yourself whether each element is effective in communicating a particular vision or interpretation of the play.
3. Acting. It is always surprising how much the delivery of a line can change its meaning. Before you view a production, read through the play once more (remember, it's a short play!) and imagine how the lines might be delivered by actors—sadly, angrily, sarcastically and so on. Choose a few of your favorite lines and imagine in detail how they "ought" to be delivered. Practice delivering them a few times in front of a mirror. When you see a production, compare renditions. Was it as you expected? Was it better or worse? Why did the actors choose the deliveries they did?

Endnotes

1 Sedgwick, Frank. *Sources and Analogues for Shakespeare's 'A Midsummer Night's Dream.'* New York: Duffield, 1908. 35.

2 An overview of the fairy background of the play, with special attention to Puck. This is one of several books Briggs has written on fairies and Celtic folklore.

3 This is an overview of various productions of the play, mostly twentieth-century ones. It is useful for understanding the translation of a play from text to production.

4 Introductory criticism of several Shakespeare plays. As a secular text, some aspects should of course be approached with discretion.

5 It is always advisable to preview films before showing them.

Secondary Books

Second Semester

Winning His Spurs: A Tale of the Crusades

Jonathan Edwards entered Yale College at age thirteen and graduated at age seventeen. He served as a minister at age nineteen, and after returning to Yale at age twenty he passed the examination for a Master of Arts degree. In an age characterized by a lowering of expectations and standards, we marvel at such maturity and responsibility. There was a time, however, when a boy was expected to behave like a man at age thirteen. There was a time when a thirteen-year-old boy was expected to be skilled at something other than playing video games. Unfortunately, we live in an age characterized by low expectations for our youth. We rarely envision our teenage boys taking on such responsibilities or taking up five small stones and slaying a giant.

Winning His Spurs takes us back to a time when a young boy was challenged to behave like a man. We are encouraged to rethink the expectations we have of our youth. As we observe the life of Cuthbert, the main character, we get a glimpse of the bravery and courage that a young boy can have. As we enter into the events surrounding the crusade to recapture the Holy Land, we see the action through the eyes of a valiant boy, and we are forced to reexamine our own lives. If we view literature and history as an opportunity to explore our own hearts, *Winning His Spurs* is a call for men to stand up and face life's challenges with renewed vigor and courage.

General Information

Significance

In an age so characterized by technology and "looking forward," history is not always at the top of the list of exciting things to do. A good dose of Henty, however, can cure this ailment. There is nothing stale in his adventurous stories as he takes the reader into a time period by means of a fictional youth and walks through the historical events of that day.

In *Winning His Spurs,* the hero, Cuthbert, goes off to fight in the Third Crusade against the Muslims who are occupying Jerusalem. As the true events of history unfold, we are able to learn of the character traits that should exemplify our youth. He is bold, courageous, wise and dedicated to his leader and cause. The fictional character Cuthbert interacts with real historical figures like King Richard,

A bronze cross worn by crusaders during the eleventh century.

King Philip, Saladin and Robin Hood.

Henty has the uncommon ability to educate the reader about real history, while at the same time teaching the reader about real character. While we are learning about the events of the Third Crusade, we are challenged to live a life more like that of Cuthbert. There is a marked difference between reading a dry history book on the one hand, and reading a novel that takes the reader into the very midst of the culture and the events as they occur on the other.

Jacques de Molay, Master of the Knights Templar (c.1243–1314).

Main Characters

Henty's books contain both fictional and historical figures. Among the fictional characters is Cuthbert, the young hero of the book. His father is a Norman, and his mother is Saxon. Cuthbert, therefore, signifies the unity of two peoples between whom there was much enmity in the time period of the novel. The Normans were Scandinavians (by way of France) who conquered the Saxons in 1066. Cnut is Cuthbert's impetuous yet valiant friend who accompanies him in his travels and adventures. Early in the book Cuthbert wins the favor of the Earl of Evesham, who takes him along as his page on the crusade. Of course, no novel about knights and crusades would be complete without a damsel in distress. Our damsel in this novel is the fair Lady Margaret.

The fictional characters interact with individuals who actually participated in the real historical events. Among these, the most important are Richard the Lion-Hearted, king of England; Philip, the king of France; and Saladin, the leader of the Muslim forces who opposed the crusaders. There is also John, the brother of Richard, who attempted to take the throne away from his own kin while Richard was away fighting to free the Holy Land (for more about King John see the chapter on *Robin Hood*).

Summary and Setting

Cuthbert is a fifteen-year-old boy whose life does not seem to be especially exciting. As the novel opens, he is sitting on a wall as a casual observer to the hustle and bustle as group after group of armed men enter the castle of the Earl of Evesham. His life changes drastically, however, as he soon finds himself embroiled in a dispute between the earl and the Baron of Wortham. The clash between the two nobles comes to a head as Margaret, daughter of the earl, is kidnapped by thugs hired by the baron. Cuthbert catches the attention of the earl when he rescues the daughter and aids in the attack against the castle of the baron. We quickly learn what may have been going through the mind of this fifteen-year-old boy as he sat on that wall at the beginning of the book: when the earl then asks him what he can do to repay him for his bravery, Cuthbert responds, "At present I need nothing, but should the time come when you may go to the wars, I would fain ride with you as your page, in the hope of some day winning my spurs also in the field."

The historical background of *Winning His Spurs* is the Third Crusade of the late twelfth century. Muslims had taken the holy city of Jerusalem, and Christians were inspired to recapture the city and the Holy Sepulcher (i.e., Christ's Tomb). Cuthbert accompanies the Earl of Evesham as they venture out for the Holy Land. King Richard the Lion-Hearted leads the English forces, and Philip leads the French troops. While the Christians win a significant victory at Acre, they are unable to reclaim Jerusalem due to the strength and number of the Muslim forces under Saladin, their leader.

Along the way Cuthbert encounters perils of many kinds, but in the end the young boy returns home a man. He displays courage in the face of danger at every turn as he stands up to men who are older and stronger. He experiences kidnapping and injury and nearly dies on more than one occasion.

He is noticed by and receives the praise of men of the highest rank. In the end he returns to England as a knight and an earl. He has won his spurs, and he even gets the girl.

Worldview

Have you ever wondered what sets you apart from everyone else? What makes you different? What is unique about you among the millions of people your age? Everyone wants to believe that there is something special that distinguishes him or her from the crowd. "Surely," we think to ourselves, "there is something I can do that makes me exceptional."

Imagine yourself living in the year 1188. There are no cars, no computers and no electricity. There is no middle class, and if you are not part of the wealthy nobility you are likely to be very poor. Life is tough. There is, however, one sure way to distinguish yourself, at the same time obtaining eternal favor from God, and that is to leave your friends and family and take up arms to fight the Turks in the Holy Land. You are told that, if you will fight in the crusade, you will be absolved from your sin. You are convinced that the best way to advance God's kingdom is by force. You are galvanized to action by the convincing arguments of your spiritual leaders—so off you go.

"The few, the proud, the Marines!" I remember seeing the commercials as a teenage boy and dreaming of the glory of fighting for my country. I would dream of returning home decked out in my military attire after having fought in a foreign land and freeing some people from Communist aggression. I would think of the honor I would receive and how proud my parents would be. Similarly, in the mind of a young boy living in the twelfth century, nothing would have consumed his thoughts like the glory of becoming a true knight. He dreamt of rescuing the lady from the dragon and fighting for the honor of his people.

In his books Henty does not seek to defend the accepted views of the society of that day. Rather, he is writing to give an example of what a young boy of high character might have looked like in that particular time. We must, therefore, give a critique of some of the aspects of the crusade mentality, while at the same time also taking a look at the particular character traits of the fictional young hero Henty places before us.

How are we to understand and interpret our Christian brothers of this era? Do we dismiss them as crazy? Misguided? First, we must understand that there had developed a strong sense of the sanctity of certain locations, like the tomb of Christ. The place itself was considered to be holy, and the frustration of not even being able to visit because of Muslim occupation was great. Second, there was a belief that the ultimate experience as a Christian would be to travel where Christ lived and to experience His passion where He knew it. The Stations of the Cross developed as a result of not being able to actually go to the Holy Land. The idea was that, if we cannot be in Jerusalem, we will bring Jerusalem to the people. So priests would set up pretend "stations" which represented different events of Christ's death, and worshipers would then pray through these stations, thus experiencing the passion of Christ. All of this is to say that there was an intense motivation to recapture Jerusalem and force the heathen to convert, thinking that this would be the most effective means of advancing the kingdom of God.

The Reformers sought to correct some of this thinking by presenting a more biblical view of the cultural mandate. The idea is that we do not spread the gospel by force, but rather by infiltrating our faith into every aspect of our culture. The command in Genesis 1:26–28 and Psalm 8:5–8 that we exercise dominion is understood to extend to the entire culture in which we live. Christians should be seeking to see Christ recognized as King and Lord in every area of life. In the workplace, in the arts and in our schools we proclaim the Lordship of Christ. The expectation and hope is that as God regenerates hearts,

Florine, the duke of Burgundy's daughter, courageously fights alongside her fiance, the prince of Denmark.

those individuals will bring their sphere of influence under the dominion of Christ.

Both of these approaches recognize that we are at war. The crusade mentality, however, uses lesser weapons, like swords instead of the more powerful weapon of the preaching of the gospel (Rom. 1:16).

Henty does not express approval or disapproval of the medieval mindset. He is seeking to reveal the character of a young man who happens to be living in that particular culture and participating in those specific events. He sets up several contrasts to Cuthbert's character so that the reader can make the comparisons from different angles. The idea is that the reader can then see what traits like courage and loyalty look like in various circumstances, and he is then encouraged to live out these godly qualities in real life.

A few examples from the book will suffice to show how Henty develops this theme throughout. The first clear example is the contrast between Cuthbert and the page of King Philip of France. En route to the Holy Land there is a minor conflict between the two pages, and so the respective monarchs decide to allow the boys to fight it out. Cuthbert defeats his older and larger opponent and thus wins the favor of the king. He is prepared to move on with the mission of traveling to the Holy Land, but the embarrassed and humiliated French page seeks revenge, and Cuthbert is injured severely as a result. In the end Cuthbert is forced to kill the page in self-defense. Henty is clearly setting up a comparison of the praiseworthy character of Cuthbert versus the deplorable actions of the other page. Even though Cuthbert is younger and less experienced, he is a boy of higher character. He fights for what is right and is prepared to move on afterward. "Choose to be more like Cuthbert in these kinds of situations," says Henty.

The second example brings the matter to a whole new level. Throughout the story Henty reveals bits and pieces of the character of King Richard himself. He portrays the king as an impulsive man in his marriage to the princess of Berengaria, as an impatient man as he sets sail prematurely for Sicily, as a violent and merciless man as he has all the defenders of Acre massacred, and as a divisive man as he is not even able to get along with the other Christian leaders of the crusade.

Cuthbert, on the other hand, displays the opposite of all of these qualities at one point or another. He shows patience and self-control when the Austrians use a parade to denigrate the English, whereas Cnut, his faithful yet impetuous companion, reacts impulsively and almost gets Cuthbert killed. He shows compassion and rescues the daughter of the earl at one stage in the book and a traveler who is attacked by wolves at another. Finally, in contrast to the divisiveness of the king, he acts as a source of unity. He brings the woodsmen and the earl, bitter enemies, together to fight against the wicked Baron of Wortham. This is a sort of foreshadowing of the fact that Normans and Saxons would fight together on the battlefield against the Muslims.

A third contrast is between Cuthbert and Rudolph, the illegitimate Earl of Evesham. When Cuthbert returns from the crusade he learns that Rudolph had been given the title of earl by John, the brother of Richard. As Cuthbert fights to claim what is rightfully his, the title of earl, Rudolph seeks to marry Margaret, the lady given to Cuthbert by her father, the original Earl of Evesham. In addition, Rudolph kidnaps Cuthbert's mother in an act of cowardice. Cuthbert, on the other hand, shows nothing but respect and honor for women. He honors his mother by obeying her in the beginning of the book, and by protecting her near the end. He rescues the Lady Margaret from the hands of her captors, and he patiently awaits her hand in marriage until the time is right.

In addition to the contrasts between our hero and others of lesser character, we see a particular biblical principle worked out in his life. In the parable of the unjust steward, Jesus teaches that when we are faithful in smaller things we are given charge over greater things (Luke 16). In the beginning of the book we see that Cuthbert is faithful and courageous as a fifteen-year-old boy. He comes to the aid of the earl and helps in defeating the baron. He is satisfied to serve as the page of the earl and earn the right to greater honor. He stands up to the wicked French page as his reputation as a man of valor increases. He rescues the princess of Berengaria and displays great maturity as he counsels her to seek to mitigate the anger of the king concerning the matter. All of these events lead up to his becoming a knight and eventually the earl of Evesham. He was faithful in the relatively small encounters in his life, and it led to the bestowal of great honor upon him.

Another theme we see in *Winning His Spurs* is the idea that character is not something that should be expected from adults only. Young people can display maturity beyond their years when faced with particular challenges. We see Henty stressing that Cuthbert is accomplishing these tasks *as a teenager.* In the very first sentence of the book he is described as a "lad of some fifteen years." We know from the beginning that we are dealing with a boy, not a grown man. In the fight with the French page, Henty stresses that Cuthbert's opponent is older and bigger than he. When Cuthbert is recognized on the battlefield, others acknowledge that he seems so young to be in the position he is in. He gains for himself a reputation for having distinguished himself at such a young age. When he returns to England as a knight and an earl, Henty reminds the reader that he is still a man of only eighteen years. His point is clear. He is calling young men to emulate the behavior of the hero. He is setting forth a larger-than-life example. While a real Cuthbert may not exist, he is the standard to shoot for.

We see this theme in Scripture as well. We are not allowed to see any sins of Joseph, the brother who was sold into slavery. We only see how he responded with maturity and love. He is the example to follow in times when we are wronged by others. David's youthfulness is stressed when he is chosen to be the king of Israel. Daniel displays unusual confidence and wisdom as he stands up to the Babylonians, yet he is only a youth. Mary is probably a teenager when visited by the angel to announce her role in the redemption of the world, and she responds with faith in God's plan. Finally, Paul counsels Timothy to not allow others to look down upon him because he is a young pastor. Rather, he encourages him to be an example in word and conduct.

A final theme that we see developed in the book is the reality of ethnic tension and a right response to it. From the beginning we are brought into twelfth-century England, where there existed hostility between the Saxons and their Norman conquerors.

Cuthbert is a symbol of unity in this ethnic tension, in that his father is Norman and his mother is Saxon. We see this inclination for unity when Cuthbert rescues the princess of Berengaria and makes one request of her. He asks her to do her best to calm the anger of King Richard against the French. Cuthbert himself had cause to be bitter towards the French after the incident with King Philip's page, but instead he displays maturity in doing what is best for all in the situation.

In contrast to King Richard, who offends the French and the Austrians, Cuthbert works to bring about the best for the common good. He is the only one in his age group who speaks other languages, a sign of maturity.

Our culture is in great need of considering the themes Henty addresses. Many young people in our culture lack direction, and they have few models of true courage. We have lost a sense of chivalry and a drive to fight for the honor of God and country. May the youth in our day rise to the challenge Henty presents that we focus on the responsibilities God has placed before us. Too often we strive for "greater" responsibilities, not realizing that when we are faithful in the small things, God will bless us with greater authority.

—*Bruce Etter*

For Further Reading

Kuiper, B. K. *The Church in History.* Grand Rapids: Eerdmans, 1966. 116–122.

Potter, William. *The Boy's Guide to the Historical Adventures of G. A. Henty.* San Antonio: The Vision Forum, Inc., 2003.

Spielvogel, Jackson J. *Western Civilization.* Seventh Edition. Belmont, Calif.: Thomson Wadsworth, 2009. 294–301.

Veritas Press History Cards: Middle Ages, Renaissance and Reformation. Lancaster, Pa.: Veritas Press. 15.

Session I: Prelude

A Question to Consider

Would you be willing to die fighting for your faith? Should Christians fight for the honor of their religion?

From the General Information above, answer the following questions:

1. What is the historical setting of the novel? Who are the main historical figures involved?
2. What was Henty's two-fold purpose in these kinds of novels?
3. What motivated men to fight in the Crusades?
4. What does Cuthbert's age have to do with the point of the novel?
5. What was the final result of the Third Crusade?
6. What role does John, the brother of King Richard, play?
7. What rewards does Cuthbert gain as a result of his accomplishments?

Reading Assignment:
Chapters 1–4

Session II: Discussion

Chapters 1–4

A Question to Consider

Were the Crusades a just war?

Discuss or list short answers to the following questions:

Text Analysis

1. What was Cuthbert's attitude about fighting in the crusade? What does this reveal about the general attitude of Christians in the twelfth century concerning the crusade?
2. Why did Richard decide to "take up the cross" and go to war against the Muslims? In what sense did he view the crusade as a just war?
3. What was the view of the Earl of Evesham? What does this reveal?

4. In chapter four, Cuthbert hears from Father Francis about the crusade. Make a list of the pros and cons of the war according to the priest.

Cultural Analysis

1. What is the general attitude about war in our society?
2. How does the culture view the Crusades? Would it be considered a just war in the minds of anyone?
3. How does the culture link the Crusades to modern Christianity?

Biblical Analysis

1. What are some general issues concerning war addressed in the Bible (Num. 1:2–4; Deut. 20:1–12; Ps. 127:1)?
2. What does the Bible say about the general principles which were the motivating force behind the Crusades (Prov. 17:17; John 15:13)?
3. Is there biblical justification for any of the reasons given by the crusaders (Judg. 11 and 12)?

SUMMA

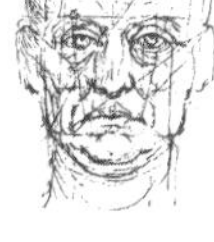

Write an essay or discuss this question, integrating what you have learned from the material above.

Among the primary individuals involved in the beginning of the book, do any have a biblical view of the crusade? Discuss the views of Cuthbert, King Richard, Father Francis and the Earl of Evesham.

READING ASSIGNMENT:

Chapters 5–8

Richard the Lion-Hearted and Saladin at the Battle of Arsuf.

Session III: Recitation

Chapters 1-8

Comprehension Questions

Answer the following questions for factual recall:

1. Who is Sir Walter, and with whom does he have a dispute?
2. Who is Margaret, and what significance does she have in the story?
3. Who is Gurth? Why does Cuthbert visit him?
4. What was Cuthbert's response when the earl asked what he could do to repay him for rescuing his daughter?
5. What does Father Francis tell Cuthbert about the past hundred years concerning the struggle for the Holy Land?
6. How does Henty describe King Richard?
7. What is Cuthbert's first test of physical strength? Why was it such a significant challenge?
8. What tragedy does Cuthbert experience in chapter 7?
9. What character flaws in King Richard do we see in chapter 8?

Reading Assignment:

Chapters 9-12

A statue of King Richard that stands outside Parliament in London.

Session IV: Discussion
Chapters 9-12

A Question to Consider

What differentiates courage from foolhardiness?

Discuss or list short answers to the following questions:

Text Analysis

1. What happens to the Princess Berengaria in chapter 9?
2. What does Cuthbert tell the princess when he rescues her?
3. What is the response of the princess?
4. What two rash decisions does King Richard make in chapters 10 and 11?
5. What accolade does Cuthbert receive as a result of his bravery in chapter 12?

Cultural Analysis

1. What is the general perception of "spontaneity" in our culture?
2. How might the king's decisions in these chapters be viewed by our culture?

Biblical Analysis

1. What does the Bible say about foolish behavior as it relates to this section of the book (Prov. 10:8 and 28:26)?
2. What specific applications can be made with respect to Cuthbert and King Richard from the principles of foolishness that we considered in Proverbs 10:8 and 28:26?
3, How might the point of the Parable of the Talents in Matthew 25 apply to Cuthbert?

Summa

Write an essay or discuss this question, integrating what you have learned from the material above.

If you had to name one specific area, what is it that differentiates between courage and foolhardiness?

Reading Assignment:
Chapters 13-17

Session V: Recitation
Chapters 9-17

Comprehension Questions

Answer the following questions for factual recall:

1. Who was at the head of planning the abduction of the Princess Berengaria?
2. What is the result of the attack on the group in chapter 10?
3. Who is the leader of the Saracens?
4. What additional promotion does Cuthbert receive in chapter 11?
5. What common tactic employed by the Saracens almost take the life of King Richard in chapter 12?
6. Who dies in chapter 16? What is his final request?
7. Meanwhile, what is going on back in England?
8. What is the outcome of Richard's campaign in Palestine?

Reading Assignment:
Chapters 18-20

Session VI: Activity
Chapters 18-20

Crusade Route

Print out the map provided in the teacher's edition. Record the route taken by the English crusaders to the Holy Land either by drawing a line or numbering the places in order. After you are done, you can color your map if you like. Answer the following questions:

1. Approximately how many miles did King Richard and his men travel to arrive at their destination?
2. Was most of the journey by land or by sea?
3. When the Christians took Acre, how close were they to Jerusalem, the Holy City?

Reading Assignment:
Chapters 21-23

Fontevraud Abbey in Anjou, France, contains the tomb of King Richard, his parents and his sister Joan.

SESSION VII: DISCUSSION

Chapters 21–23

A Question to Consider

How is Islam different from Christianity? Are there similarities? Research the specific differences.

Discuss or list short answers to the following questions:

Text Analysis

1. How much does Henty discuss the details of Islam?
2. What are the Muslim forces called in the book?
3. What is the general impression of Islam that Henty leaves with the reader?
4. What negative, yet truthful, portrayal does Henty give of Muslims?

Cultural Analysis

1. How does our culture view Islam?
2. How is the Muslim view of salvation evaluated by the culture?

Biblical Analysis

1. What is the biblical response to Allah?
2. What is the Biblical view of salvation?
3. State what the Bible says about the following beliefs of Islam: there is only one God; Mohammed is the "seal" of the prophets (this is the idea that Mohammed is the last prophet and there are no more to come); the idea that the Koran was delivered to mankind via the angel Gabriel.

SUMMA

Write an essay or discuss this question, integrating what you have learned from the material above.

What do Muslims believe about God, Jesus, sin and salvation? Are these views biblical at all?

READING ASSIGNMENT:
Chapters 23–26

SESSION VIII: RECITATION

Chapters 18–26

Comprehension Questions

Answer the following questions for factual recall:

1. Richard is accused of killing whom? What is Cuthbert's response to the accusation?
2. With whom does Cuthbert stay for a month's time on his way back to England?
3. John, the brother of King Richard, tries to gain support from what two leaders?
4. Who is given the title of Earl of Evesham by John?
5. What kind of person is Rudolph? How do we know this?
6. What famous character does Cuthbert meet in chapter 25?
7. Who accompanies Cuthbert in his search for the

king? Where do they find him?

8. What comes of the king's trial? What happens to John and Rudolph?

Part of the ruins of Krak des Chevaliers, a castle famous for having served as the headquarters of the Knights Hospitaller in Syria during the Crusades.

Session IX: Debate

A Just Crusade

In an effort to enhance rhetorical skills, organize a debate in which students argue whether or not the Crusades meet the criteria to be considered a just war.

Depending on the class size, a student from each side must play a role by giving an opening speech, a rebuttal speech or a concluding speech. For the individual student, choose a side and write out a defense of one side of the debate.

1. A competent authority must declare the war.
2. The war must have a just cause.
3. The force used in the war must be proportional to the cause.
4. All peaceful means of settling the dispute must have been exhausted before the war is declared.
5. The goal of the war must be a just and equitable peace.

Optional Session A: Activity

Crusades Chart

Research all the major crusades and make a chart stating the date, individuals involved, events and results of each crusade.[1]

Optional Session B: Evaluation

All tests and quizzes are to be given with an open book and a Bible available.

Grammar

Answer each of the following questions in complete sentences. Some answers may be longer than others (2 points per answer).

1. List the main historical figures in the book.
2. What is the historical setting of the book?
3. What "promotions" does Cuthbert receive by the end of the story?
4. What two ethnic groups resided in England during this time?
5. What request does the Earl of Evesham make as he is dying?

6. Who attempts to take the throne of England while Richard is away fighting?
7. What is the result of the crusade?

Logic

Answer the following question in complete sentences; your answer should be a paragraph or so. Answer two of the three questions (10 points per answer).

1. How does the principle of the Parable of the Talents in Matthew 25 apply to the life of Cuthbert? How would it apply to you?
2. What is the significance of Cuthbert's treatment and view of women?
3. Discuss the good and bad character traits of King Richard. How did each help and/or hurt the cause?

Lateral Thinking

Answer one of the following questions. These questions will require more substantial answers (16 points per answer).

1. Were the Crusades just wars? Give a reasoned argument for your position. Discuss the difference between a just war and a justly fought war.
2. Compare and contrast the character of Cuthbert with that of his trusty companion Cnut.

ENDNOTE

1 Answers and resources can be found at Links 1and 2 for this chapter at www.VeritasPress.com/OmniLinks.

THE TWO TOWERS

When you travel, what do you notice most? Is it the new places you get to know or the scenery there? Is it the cost of the travel? Perhaps it is the homesickness. Some look forward to any trip with intense longing, counting the days until they get to go. Others want nothing more than to get back home again because none of the pillows in the motels are anything like the one back home. And in keeping with the theme of the books we are reading, some might even call their home pillow, "My precious."

Hrum, Hoom. Very odd indeed! Do not be hasty, that is my motto . . .. Root and twig, very odd!

Whenever we travel, one of the necessary consequences of it is *separation.* When we go somewhere—whether it is off to summer camp, or to see our grandparents, or off to fight against orcs—it is not usually possible for everyone we know to go with us. And if they did, we wouldn't call it "a trip" but rather something like a mass migration. When we travel, we always leave some friends at home. In addition there are many times that some of our friends are traveling at the same time we are, but they are going somewhere else. We are in the airport in Minneapolis while they are somewhere in the air over Texas. As we think about those we love as we travel, we often wonder, "I wonder what they are doing *now*."

In *The Two Towers,* the fellowship of the Ring has separated and scattered, and we follow their separate adventures through this book. There are powers at work for good far above the set plans of that faithful company, and these powers have used the attack of the orcs and the temporary failure of Boromir to accomplish what probably would not have been done by the fellowship voluntarily—the scattering of the fellowship of the Ring. And throughout this book, all the characters can ask themselves, "I wonder what they are doing now." "How are Frodo and Sam doing?" "I wonder where Merry and Pippin are."

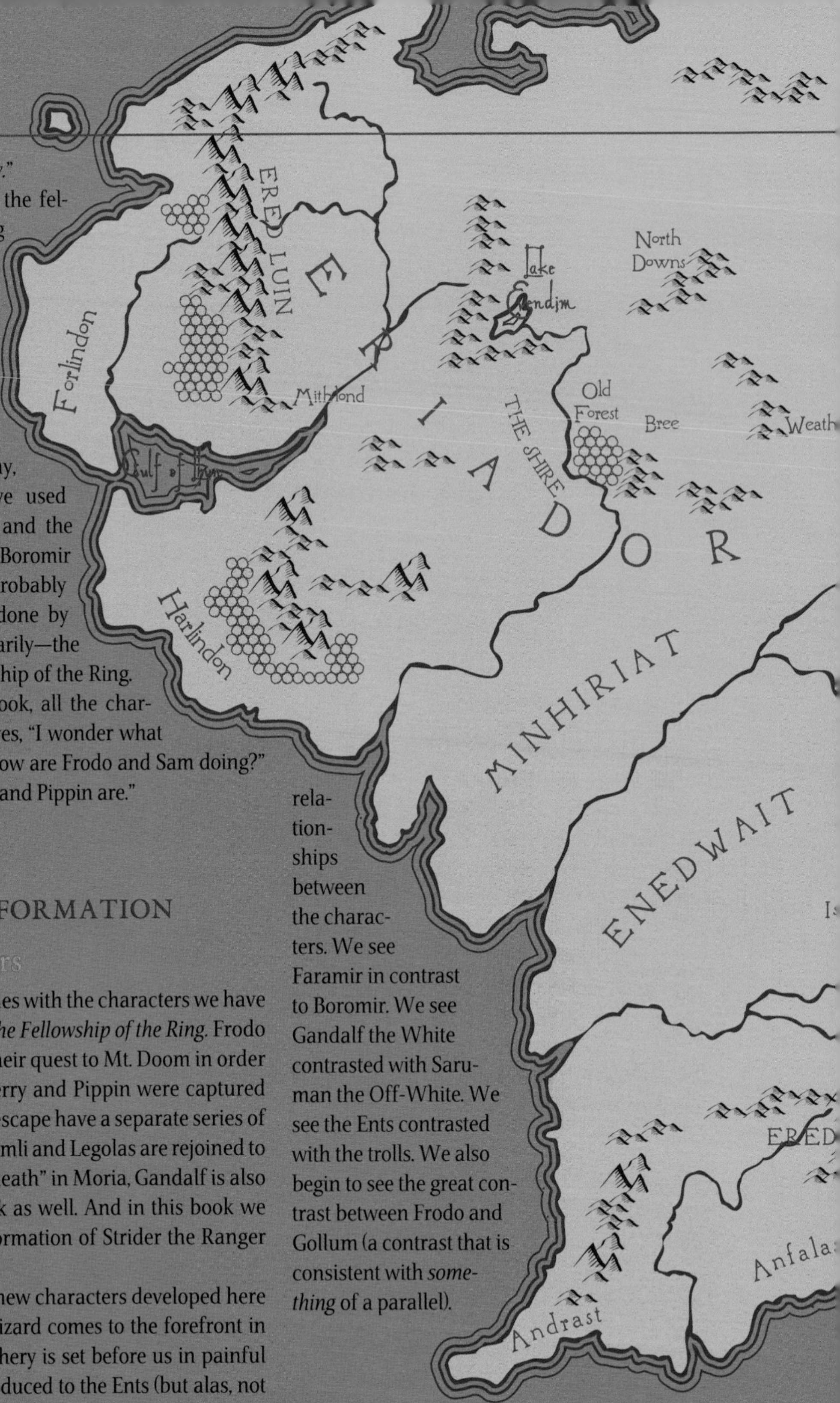

General Information

Main Characters

The Two Towers continues with the characters we have been introduced to in *The Fellowship of the Ring.* Frodo and Sam continue on their quest to Mt. Doom in order to destroy the Ring. Merry and Pippin were captured by orcs, and after their escape have a separate series of adventures. Aragorn, Gimli and Legolas are rejoined to them, and despite his "death" in Moria, Gandalf is also a character in this book as well. And in this book we begin to see the transformation of Strider the Ranger into Aragorn the King.

But there are some new characters developed here as well. Saruman the wizard comes to the forefront in this book, and his treachery is set before us in painful detail. We are also introduced to the Ents (but alas, not to the Entwives), and to Treebeard (also called Fangorn) who is chief among the Ents. Faramir, brother of Boromir, comes into this book as one of the noblest (and humblest) warriors in all Middle-earth. Of course, we cannot forget Theoden and the Riders of Rohan.

It is also in this book that we start to see many of the relationships between the characters. We see Faramir in contrast to Boromir. We see Gandalf the White contrasted with Saruman the Off-White. We see the Ents contrasted with the trolls. We also begin to see the great contrast between Frodo and Gollum (a contrast that is consistent with *something* of a parallel).

Summary and Setting

The setting of Middle-earth is, of course, the same as in *The Fellowship of the Ring.* But in *The Two Towers* we follow the separate adventures of the members of the

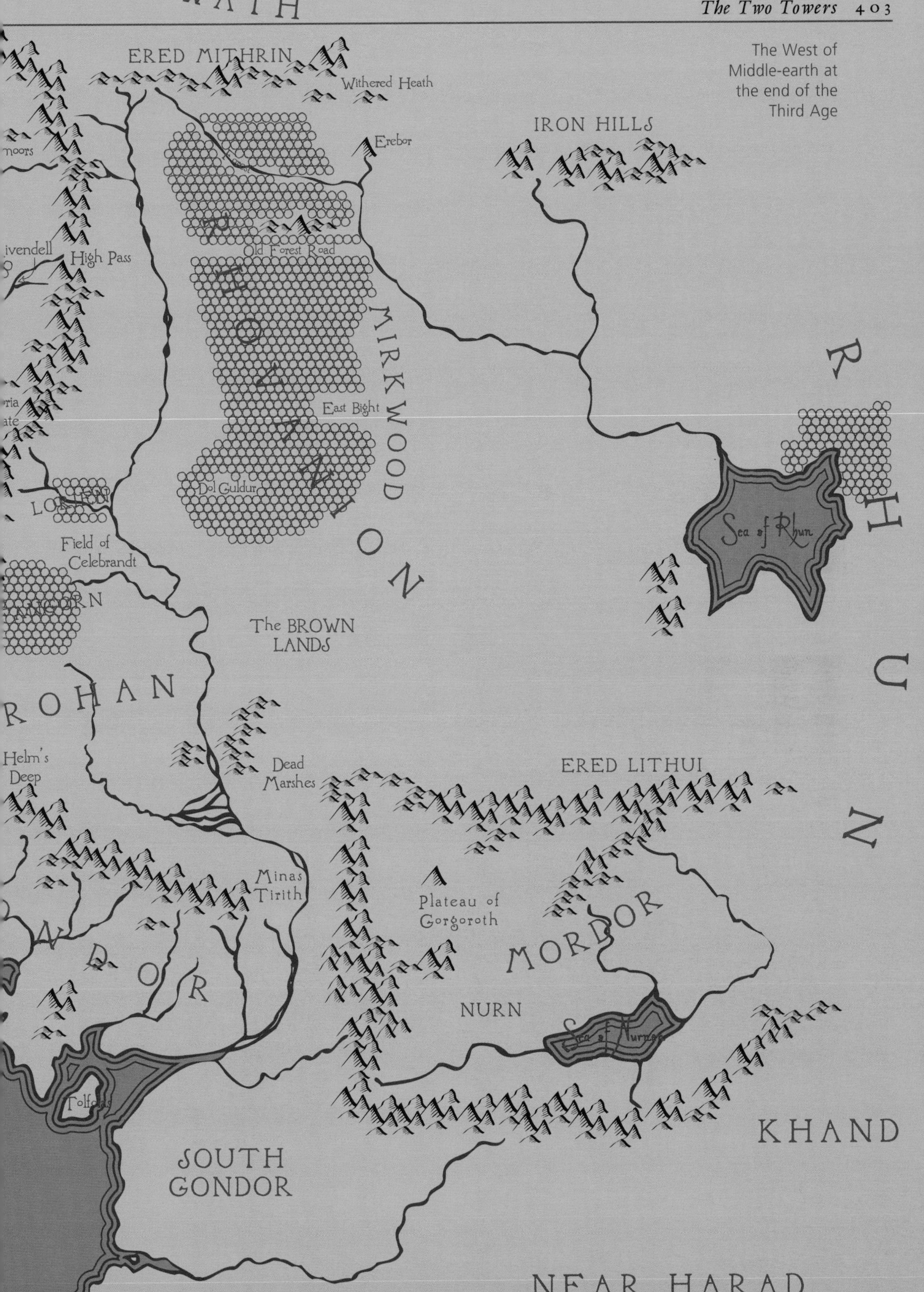
FORODWATH
The West of Middle-earth at the end of the Third Age
ERED MITHRIN
Withered Heath
IRON HILLS
Erebor
Old Forest Road
High Pass
RHOVANION
MIRKWOOD
East Bight
Dol Guldur
Field of Celebrandt
The BROWN LANDS
ROHAN
Helm's Deep
Dead Marshes
ERED LITHUI
Minas Tirith
Plateau of Gorgoroth
MORDOR
NURN
Sea of Rhun
RHUN
Sea of Nurnen
KHAND
SOUTH GONDOR
Tolfalas
NEAR HARAD

broken fellowship of the Ring. Boromir falls in battle, and Merry and Pippin are captured by orcs. Aragorn, Legolas, and Gimli pursue their captors, and finally catch up with them. But by that time, Merry and Pippin have made their escape into the forest, where they meet up with the Ents, an event highly significant in the coming fall of Saruman. Gandalf returns as Gandalf the White, and we are introduced to the Riders of Rohan as Gandalf is used to bring their king, Theoden, back from a dishonorable (and enchanted) old age. And of course, Frodo and Sam make their way into Mordor (where the shadows lie) in order to attempt the destruction of the Ring. They are trailed by Gollum, who is driven by a hunger for "his precious." This book contains one of the great battle scenes in all Middle-earth, the great battle at Helm's Deep.

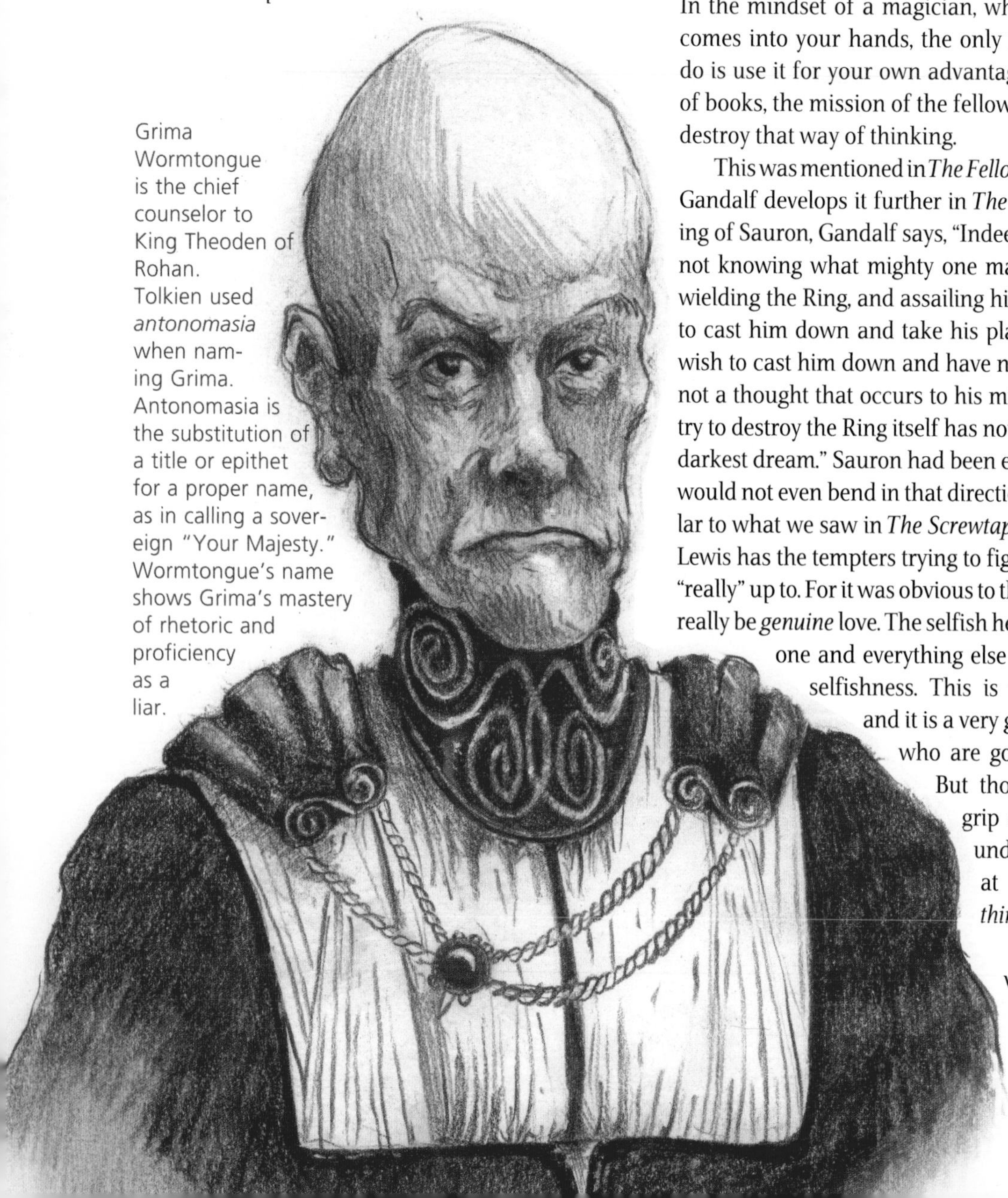

Grima Wormtongue is the chief counselor to King Theoden of Rohan. Tolkien used *antonomasia* when naming Grima. Antonomasia is the substitution of a title or epithet for a proper name, as in calling a sovereign "Your Majesty." Wormtongue's name shows Grima's mastery of rhetoric and proficiency as a liar.

Worldview

The story told throughout *The Lord of the Rings* is one sustained story, and so we should not look for a dramatic shift in the theme from book to book. *The Two Towers,* like *The Fellowship of the Ring,* is about the same basic conflict between humble and noble self-sacrifice on the one hand, and a hungry grasping after power on the other. For that reason, we need to reinforce some of the themes already treated, and then we will be able to look at some aspects of this story that stand out from what has gone before.

On the subject of magic, J.R.R. Tolkien continues to show precisely how evil magic is. As we have already noted, this evil is manifested in a desire to manipulate matter in such a way as to gain power over others. In the mindset of a magician, whenever such power comes into your hands, the only reasonable thing to do is use it for your own advantage. But in this series of books, the mission of the fellowship is to reject and destroy that way of thinking.

This was mentioned in *The Fellowship of the Ring,* but Gandalf develops it further in *The Two Towers.* Speaking of Sauron, Gandalf says, "Indeed he is in great fear, not knowing what mighty one may suddenly appear, wielding the Ring, and assailing him with war, seeking to cast him down and take his place. That we should wish to cast him down and have no one in his place is not a thought that occurs to his mind. That we should try to destroy the Ring itself has not yet entered into his darkest dream." Sauron had been evil so long, his mind would not even bend in that direction. This is very similar to what we saw in *The Screwtape Letters,* where C.S. Lewis has the tempters trying to figure out what God is "really" up to. For it was obvious to them that it could not really be *genuine* love. The selfish heart measures everyone and everything else in terms of its own selfishness. This is what Sauron does, and it is a very great mistake. Those who are good understand sin. But those who are in the grip of sin do not really understand goodness at all—although they *think* they do.

This emphasis is very important. In this book, we do

not have just a bare assertion that these people over here are "good" and that those others are "bad." The categories of good and evil are not just arbitrarily assigned. Tolkien shows us on every page (as his plot unfolds) how one group rejects magic and grasping after power, and how Sauron lusts for power, and how that lust is his undoing. Books that treat good and evil superficially do it by simply assigning "the roles." This group is considered to be bad and that group is good in much the same way that a pick-up basketball game at a local city park is between shirts and skins. But Tolkien's treatment of this is profound, and extends into every step that every character in the book takes. Is this character part of the heroic attempt to destroy the Ring? Or is this character trying to impede (for whatever reason) the destruction of the Ring?

We noted in the essay on *The Fellowship of the Ring* that "Tolkien hated things that clanked and smoked." This antipathy comes out in his treatment of Saruman in this book. Treebeard said this of Saruman: "And he got more and more like that; his face, as I remember it—I have not seen it for many a day—became like windows in a stone wall: windows with shutters inside . . . He has a mind of metal and wheels." Saruman loved the kind of machinery that would give him power, and this kind of perverse "industrialism" went hand in hand with his lust for magical tools. And as he loved in this way, he became more and more distant—and less personal. His face, and his eyes, began to close up inside, away from growing things. At the same time, he developed orcs that could abide the sunlight—the Uruk-Hai. "Are they Men he has ruined, or has he blended the races of Orcs and Men? That would be a black evil!" Saruman is clever, but in Tolkien's mind he was too clever by half, and his "wisdom" has gotten detached from the world of living things.

The Riders of Rohan are Tolkien's brilliant recasting of ancient Anglo-Saxon society: what would Anglo-Saxons have been like with horses instead of ships? They are a noble people, but in Tolkien's world, this kind of evaluation is always qualified. When Aragorn speaks of them, he tempers his comments. "'I have been among them,' answered Aragorn. 'They are proud and willful, but they are true-hearted, generous in thought and deed; bold but not cruel; wise but unlearned; writing no books but singing many songs, after the manner of the children of Men before the Dark Years." Because they are "proud and willful," it is possible to manipulate them, which has happened through Wormtongue's lying counsel to King Theoden. Thus it is that a noble people are not preparing for war with Sauron and Saruman, although it should have been obvious that war was necessary and inevitable.

This relates to another important element in the story. Although Tolkien knows how to paint villains who are as villainous as it gets (Nazgûl, orcs, Balrogs), he also knows that evil can be soothing and very seductive. When Saruman spoke, the effect was devastating. "Mostly they remembered only that it was a delight to hear the voice speaking, all that it said seemed wise and reasonable, and desire awoke in them by swift agreement to seem wise themselves." The voice of Saruman was extremely seductive. Part of that enticement was the desire to impress, the desire to "seem wise themselves," to be included in the "in group" that could leave all the old scruples behind. The pressure to go this way seemed at the moment like wisdom, like growing up.

For another example, King Theoden came under the influence of false counsel from Grima Wormtongue for a time, but when Gandalf brought him to his senses, he saw it all for what it was. Theoden had *been* bewitched, and then when he was brought out of it, Grima tried to tell him he was actually heading *into* bewitchment. But Theoden was free of it by this point. "'If this is bewitchment,' said Theoden, 'it seems to me more wholesome than your whisperings. Your leechcraft ere long would have had me walking on all fours like a beast.'" The same thing happened to Prince Rilian in *The Silver Chair*. The Green Lady told him that, when he was strapped in the silver chair, he was under a deep enchantment, but that was actually the only time when he wasn't under a deep enchantment.

The Bible tells us that the devil is the father of lies, and when he lies he speaks so fluently because it is his native language. And one of the most effective ways to lie is to accuse those who are good of being the cause of all the trouble. Before Theoden is brought back to his right mind, this is how he sees the arrival of Gandalf to his hall. "But truth to tell your welcome is doubtful here, Master Gandalf. You have ever been a herald of woe. Troubles follow you like crows, and ever the oftener the worse." In other words, whenever there s trouble, Gandalf has to be *somewhere* around. The mplication is that Gandalf is the cause of the trouble. But this is like thinking that wet streets cause rain, or firemen cause fires. After all, we always see them together. In the Bible, when King Ahab causes a drought by turning his nation to idolatry, when he finally meets the prophet of God who brought the judgment, how does he greet him? Ahab says that *Elijah* is the one who troubles Israel (1 Kings 18:17). But Gandalf sees through this same trick in his reply. "Yet in two ways may a man come with evil tidings. He may be a worker of evil; or he may be such as leaves well alone, and comes only to bring aid in time of need."

Something very similar happens in the confrontation with Saruman. He is a proud and haughty wizard. So what does he do? He accuses *Gandalf* of being proud and haughty. The best defense is a good offense. All this trouble could have been avoided if Gandalf had only been willing to *listen.* "I endeavored to advise you for your own good, but you scarcely listened. You are proud and do not love advice, having indeed a store of your own wisdom . . . ." Saruman thinks that Gandalf is the one with the problem. Saruman would not listen to advice, and so he accuses Gandalf of not listening to advice. Saruman was proud, so he accuses Gandalf of being proud. In *The Two Towers* we see that one of the central weapons of those who are evil is the weapon of the lie. And the lies are usually not stupid lies—they are told for a reason, and that reason is that they work. There are people out there who would think that Gandalf was actually proud, and that Saruman was humble.

But though he lies, he has not completely convinced himself. By this point in the story, although Saruman has fallen, he is not past the point of no return. Gandalf invites him to come down from his tower—to use the biblical word, to repent. "A shadow passed over Saruman's face; then it went deathly white. Before he could conceal it, they saw through the mask the anguish of a mind in doubt, loathing to stay and dreading to leave its refuge. For a second he hesitated, and no one breathed. Then he spoke, and his voice was shrill and cold. Pride and hate were conquering him." Fangorn had seen the shutters going up behind Saruman's eyes earlier, but it is not until this point that the shutters finally slam completely shut.

Evil devours, and when the evil is

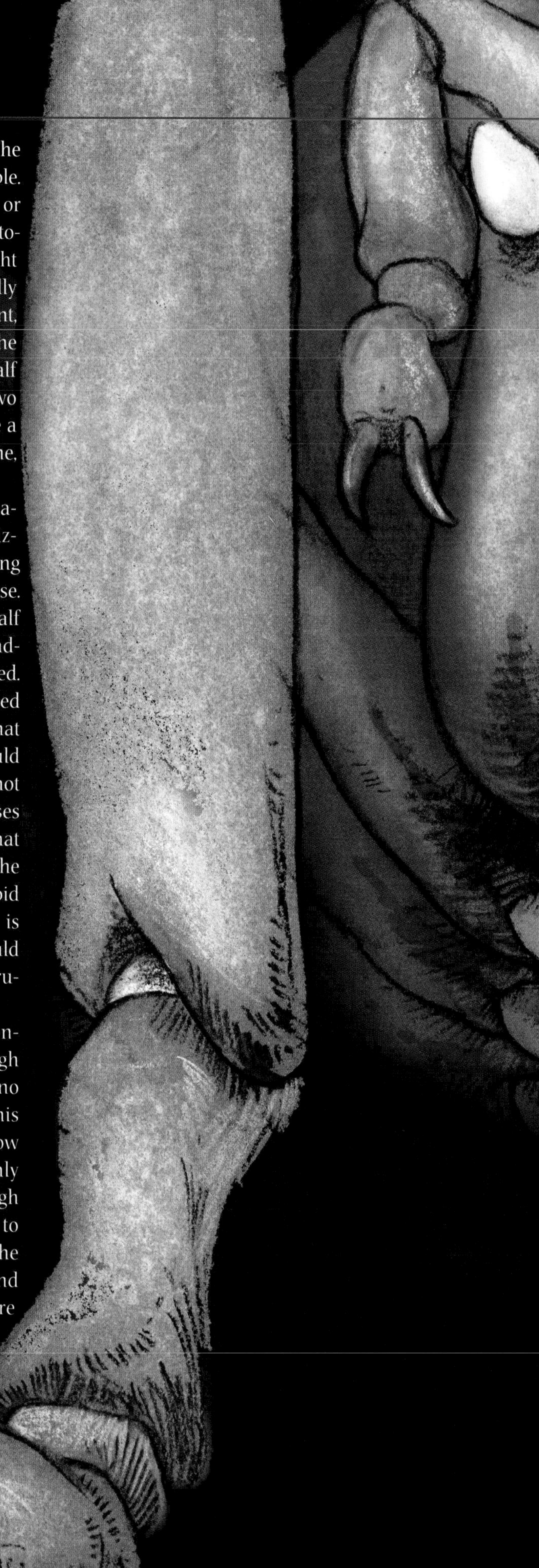

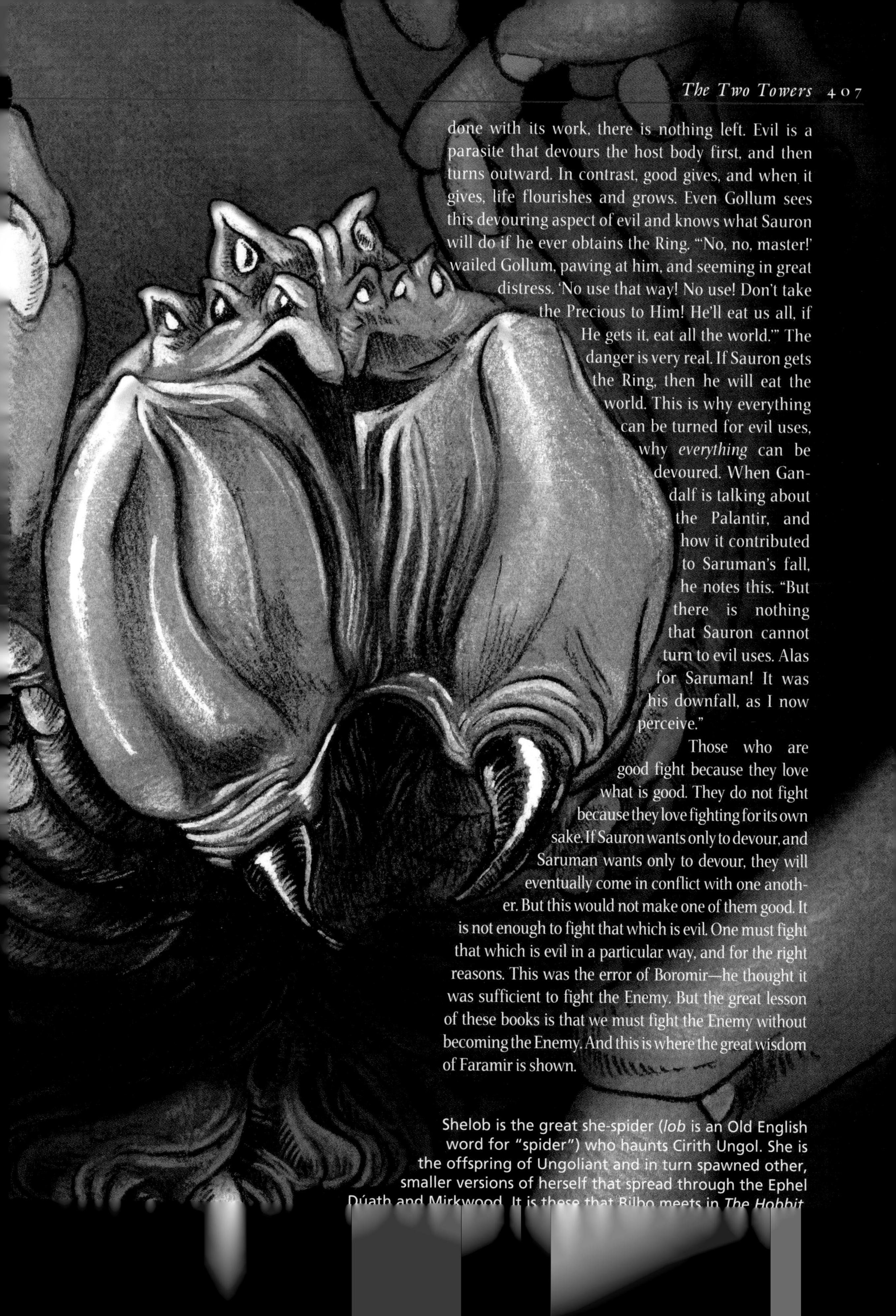

done with its work, there is nothing left. Evil is a parasite that devours the host body first, and then turns outward. In contrast, good gives, and when it gives, life flourishes and grows. Even Gollum sees this devouring aspect of evil and knows what Sauron will do if he ever obtains the Ring. "'No, no, master!' wailed Gollum, pawing at him, and seeming in great distress. 'No use that way! No use! Don't take the Precious to Him! He'll eat us all, if He gets it, eat all the world.'" The danger is very real. If Sauron gets the Ring, then he will eat the world. This is why everything can be turned for evil uses, why *everything* can be devoured. When Gandalf is talking about the Palantir, and how it contributed to Saruman's fall, he notes this. "But there is nothing that Sauron cannot turn to evil uses. Alas for Saruman! It was his downfall, as I now perceive."

Those who are good fight because they love what is good. They do not fight because they love fighting for its own sake. If Sauron wants only to devour, and Saruman wants only to devour, they will eventually come in conflict with one another. But this would not make one of them good. It is not enough to fight that which is evil. One must fight that which is evil in a particular way, and for the right reasons. This was the error of Boromir—he thought it was sufficient to fight the Enemy. But the great lesson of these books is that we must fight the Enemy without becoming the Enemy. And this is where the great wisdom of Faramir is shown.

Shelob is the great she-spider (*lob* is an Old English word for "spider") who haunts Cirith Ungol. She is the offspring of Ungoliant and in turn spawned other, smaller versions of herself that spread through the Ephel Dúath and Mirkwood. It is these that Bilbo meets in *The Hobbit*

> War must be, while we defend our lives against a destroyer who would devour all; but I do not love the bright sword for its sharpness, nor the arrow for its swiftness, nor the warrior for his glory. I love only that which they defend: the city of the Men of Numenor; and I would have her loved for her memory, her ancientry, her beauty, and her present wisdom. Not feared, save as men may fear the dignity of a man, old and wise (Book IV, chap. 5).

Love bestows, and sacrifices, and honors, and does not devour. That which is evil calls for others to sacrifice on its behalf. That which is good reverses this and is willing to face great evil simply because it is the right thing to do. As Aragorn puts it, "There are some things that it is better to begin than to refuse, even though the end may be dark." This is part of the order of the world and is why the raw power and force of evil has trouble prevailing against the good. When a great leader of those who are good falls, there will always be someone smaller to step into his place. Aragorn says, "When the great fall, the less must lead."

Tolkien's vision at this point is extraordinarily biblical. Not only does the fellowship engage to destroy the Ring, contrary to every expectation of Sauron, they also do it by entrusting the Ring to a hobbit. If they were going to destroy the Ring (odd enough though that is), why wouldn't they muster the greatest army possible to fight their way to Mt. Doom? The answer is that the least will become the greatest. Talking about the death of Boromir, Gandalf says this about Merry and Pippin: "But he escaped in the end. I am glad. It was not in vain that the young hobbits came with us, if only for Boromir's sake. But that is not the only part they have to play. They were brought to Fangorn, and their coming was like the falling of small stones that starts an avalanche in the mountains."

This is very true of Merry and Pippin in *The Two Towers,* and we shall see the climax of this truth with Frodo and Sam in the next book. The coming of the hobbits is a parable for Middle-earth, and for our own time as well. He who has ears to hear, let him hear.

—Douglas Wilson

For Further Reading

Carpenter, Humphrey, ed. *The Letters of J.R.R. Tolkien.* New York: Houghton Mifflin, 1981.

Carpenter, Humphrey. *Tolkien.* New York: Ballantine Books, 1977.

Newsom, William Chad. *Talking of Dragons.* Ross-shire, Scotland: Christian Focus Publications, 2005.

Peters, Thomas. *The Christian Imagination.* San Francisco: Ignatius Press, 2000.

Tolkien, J.R.R. *The Silmarillion.* New York: Houghton Mifflin, 1977.

Arwen Undomiel took after her foremother, Luthien Tinuviel—the most beautiful of the children of Elves and Men and who was the first elf to marry a human and become mortal.The Peredhil (half-elves), who were the descendants of Luthien, could choose to become mortal, and Arwen did so to be with Aragorn.

Session I: Prelude

A Question to Consider

How does the plot line of the story in *The Lord of the Rings* reveal character?

From the General Information above answer the following questions:

1. Why does Sauron not guess what his enemies are up to?
2. Who is the "industrialist" in this book?
3. Who are the Riders of Rohan?
4. How did Wormtongue effectively lie about Gandalf?
5. What was the effect of Saruman's speech?

Reading Assignment:
Book III, Chapters 1–2

Session II: Discussion

Book III, Chapters 1–2

A Question to Consider

Should we fear evil?

Discuss or list short answers to the following questions:

Text Analysis

1. At the beginning of the book where are Frodo and Sam headed? What does this tell us about their "fear" of evil?
2. Aragorn discovers slain orcs from a different tribe. What does this reveal? What does this tell us about unity in the camp of evil?
3. What is the relationship of orcs to day and night? What is Tolkien saying about evil?

Cultural Analysis

1. What do we see in our culture that reveals the popular view concerning the fear of evil?
2. What assurance does the culture have in the struggle with evil?

Biblical Analysis

1. What was Jesus' attitude toward evil? (Mark 5: 1–20 ; Luke 8:26–39; 1 Cor. 15; Ps. 110)
2. What does Paul teach us about evil in Ephesians 6?
3. What does Scripture teach our attitude toward evil should be in light of the final outcome in the end? (Rev. 19–22)

Summa

Write an essay or discuss this question, integrating what you have learned from the material above.

How do you explain your view of evil to an unbeliever?

Reading Assignment:
Book III, Chapters 4–6

Session III: Recitation

Book III, Chapters 1–6

Comprehension Questions

Answer the following questions for factual recall:

1. What exactly is going on at the very beginning of the book? Where are Frodo and Sam in relation to the Fellowship, and what is Aragorn doing?
2. What happens to Boromir? What confession does he make?
3. What is Aragorn's theory as to why the two hobbits separated from the group? Is he correct?
4. In chapter two how does Aragorn know that the hobbits are still alive?
5. Who is Saruman? Whose side is he on?
6. What strange but friendly creature do Merry and Pippin meet up with in chapter 4?
7. As they continue their search for the hobbits, what clue do Aragorn and Gimli find indicating that they are still alive?
8. How does Gandalf explain his rebirth? What is his new name?
9. As Gandalf and the others march toward Isengard, whom are they going to see? What comes of the visit?

Reading Assignment:
Book III, Chapters 7–8

SESSION IV: DISCUSSION
Book III, Chapters 3–6

A Question to Consider

What are the marks of a true friend?

Discuss or list short answers to the following questions:

Text Analysis

1. When Pippin has the dream that he is surrounded by orcs, to whom does he call? What significance might this have in relation to friendship?
2. What are Pippin's thoughts about having been asked to come along on the journey? What can we learn about friendship from Pippin?
3. What do we learn about friendship from the Ents?
4. What lessons of friendship can we learn from Gandalf in this section?

Cultural Analysis

1. What commonly defines a friend in our society?
2. What can we say about the longevity of friendships in our culture?

Biblical Analysis

1. Who in *The Lord of the Rings* trilogy comes to mind when reading the following passages about friendship: Proverbs 12:26, 22:24–25, 17:17, 13:20, 18:24?
2. How is Christ the ultimate example of a friend? (John 15:13; Phil. 2:1–8)

SUMMA

Write an essay or discuss this question, integrating what you have learned from the material above.

What are the key attributes of a true friend in the following individuals: Gandalf, Sam, Frodo and Pippin?

READING ASSIGNMENT:
Book III, Chapters 9–11

SESSION V: RECITATION
Book III, Chapters 7–11

Comprehension Questions

Answer the following questions for factual recall:

1. At the battle in Helm's Deep, whose appearance causes the orcs to shudder in fear and to retreat?
2. Who appears soon after him?
3. After a brief rest the group travels to Isengard to confront Saruman. How has Isengard changed?
4. Who is at Isengard when they arrive? What are they doing?
5. How had the Ents contributed to the fight?
6. When Gandalf confronts Saruman and Wormtongue what does Worm-tongue do in anger?

The Uruk-hai first appear about the year 2475 of the Third Age, when they destroy Osgiliath. They are a new, larger breed of Orcs that can withstand the light of the sun, and some say they are the result of crossbreeding between Orcs and Men.

7. What power does the palantir have? Who briefly succumbs to its evil?
8. What does Gandalf hope will be the result of Pippin's mistake?

READING ASSIGNMENT:
Book IV, Chapter 1

SESSION VI: WRITING

Book III, Chapter 4–Book IV, Chapter 1

The Extent of the Evil

Read the following quotations and answer the questions with brief essays.

BOOK III, CHAPTER 4:

> "Pippin looked behind. The number of the Ents had grown—or what was happening? Where the dim bare slopes that they had crossed should lie, he thought he saw groves of trees. But they were moving! Could it be that the trees of Fangorn were awake, and the forest was rising, marching over the hills to war?"

Is there a connection between this quote and Romans 8:19–23?

BOOK III, CHAPTER 5:

> "The Dark Lord has Nine. But we have One, mightier than they: the White Rider. He has passed through the fire and the abyss, and they shall fear him. We will go where he leads."

What does this quote reveal about Aragorn's view of Gandalf?

BOOK IV, CHAPTER 1:

> "Yess, wretched we are, precious," Gollum whined. "Misery misery! Hobbits won't kill us, nice hobbits."
> "No, we won't," said Frodo. "But we won't let you go, either. You're full of wickedness and mischief. . . ."

What does this quote tell us about Gollum?

READING ASSIGNMENT:
Book IV, Chapters 2–3

SESSION VII: CREATIVE WRITING

The Lost Chapter

Character, character, character. Personality interests readers first, not plot. A great plot with boring characters will always produce a weak story. Interesting characters with a weak plot will hook our attention, at least for a while.

How does an author create a believable character in a story, even a fantasy story? The great writers always tell us that the best characters are always grounded in some one real person. That person will be twisted and exaggerated in various ways, but it always seems to start with that real person who has caught the interest of the writer. Look around you. Are there people, whether you like them or not, whom you find interesting and offbeat? Those people are seeds for story characters. Maybe it's an odd uncle or a friend's sister or a store clerk. Study that person and find out their pattern, what makes them interesting.

Most often, we find people most interesting who are mixes of wants and reactions, mixes of good and bad, mixes of ugly and beautiful. Readers do not believe characters that are too good or too bad. We have to have aspects of the person to both love and hate, whether it's a hero or a villain. A villain that is completely evil is pretty boring and unbelievable; the same goes for a pristine, perfect hero. We start to yawn. They are not real, because we know how real people operate. We're all a mix of good and bad.

Tolkien's character, Gollum, stands as one of the great personalities of the trilogy. We know him and hate him well. It seems as if he takes up actual space and time; we could touch him. Gollum is a painful mix of two people clearly pulling in opposite directions. But Tolkien's other characters also stand out. Frodo and Sam are heroes, but they have interesting flaws, too, alongside their admirable traits. If they weren't flawed, we wouldn't find them interesting at all.

Write a one or two page episode based on information from Tolkien's characters.

1. Before writing, make two lists for each character. For each, list their good and quirky traits alongside their less-than-stellar faults.

2. Select a prominent character from Tolkien's work and think about writing a brief scene that takes place about a month before that person is called into their place in the story. For example, imagine Gollum as a hobbit before he started degenerating, before he ever found the Ring. Imagine him having a disagreement with his sister—a completely made-up new character. Or similarly, imagine Sam getting into a bit of a disagreement with Frodo a month before Frodo finds out about the Ring.
3. Have the scene's disagreement come about because of one of the character's weaker traits, though he or she doesn't admit it.
4. The goal of the scene should be to persuade the reader to find one of the characters particularly quirky and interesting. Think of that person in your life who stands out as interesting. Make a list of things that real person does that draws interest and then create the same or similar things for your fictional character to do.
5. Be sure to show us good traits and bad traits in each of your characters, but make sure we're drawn to one or both. Make the good traits outweigh the bad traits.
6. Don't allow your characters just to talk. Have them doing something. Character is best revealed through action, especially action where two people disagree about what to do.

For today's session, start making up your characters, listing their attributes and starting your story. We will be come back to this and finish our stories in Session XII.

READING ASSIGNMENT:
Book IV, Chapters 4–6

SESSION VIII: DISCUSSION

Book IV, Chapters 1–6

A Question to Consider

Is it ever right for the state to take a life?

Discuss or list short answers to the following questions:

Text Analysis

1. In *The Fellowship of the Ring* what was Frodo's attitude concerning Gollum's life? What was Gandalf's opinion?
2. What was Gandalf's reason for saying this? What did he know or suspect to be true about Gollum that Frodo did not see?
3. How has Frodo changed his position on this issue by the time we come to *The Two Towers?* Why do you think he takes this new position?

Cultural Analysis

1. What is the general attitude toward capital punishment in our culture? What is the underlying belief of this view?
2. Where does the culture see an inconsistency in the evangelical view of abortion and capital punishment?

Biblical Analysis

1. What is the biblical support for capital punishment? (Gen. 9:6; Rom. 13)
2. Is Gandalf's view of capital punishment unbiblical?
3. What is the Christian response to the argument that evangelicals are inconsistent in their view of abortion and capital punishment?

SUMMA

Write an essay or discuss this question, integrating what you have learned from the material above.

Is the state *required* to take life?

READING ASSIGNMENT:
Book IV, Chapters 7–8

Session IX: Recitation

Book IV, Chapters 1–7

Comprehension Questions

Answer the following questions for factual recall:

1. What is the only food keeping the hobbits alive?
2. Who joins the hobbits soon after they finish eating? What is he doing? What ensues?
3. What creature keeps flying over the hobbits?
4. What does Frodo learn as he listens to Gollum speaking to himself in his sleep?
5. What are the Mûmak?
6. What prophecy does Faramir remember?
7. How does Faramir learn of his brother's treachery?

8. What do the hobbits spot as they approach the Southward Road?

Reading Assignment:

Book IV, Chapters 9–10

Session X: Discussion

Book IV, Chapters 7–10

A Question to Consider

Why do some people give up so easily while others are so persistent?

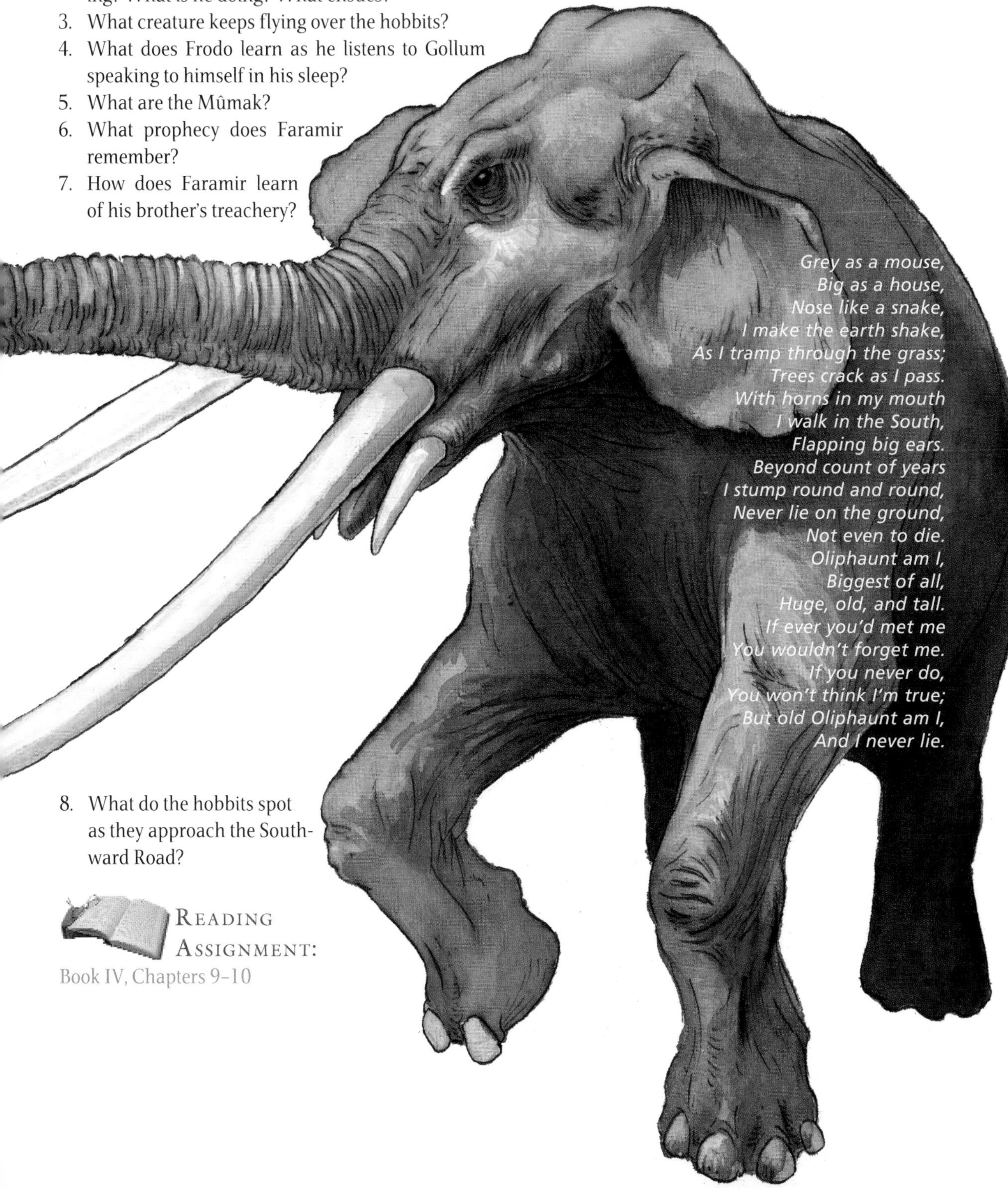

Grey as a mouse,
Big as a house,
Nose like a snake,
I make the earth shake,
As I tramp through the grass;
Trees crack as I pass.
With horns in my mouth
I walk in the South,
Flapping big ears.
Beyond count of years
I stump round and round,
Never lie on the ground,
Not even to die.
Oliphaunt am I,
Biggest of all,
Huge, old, and tall.
If ever you'd met me
You wouldn't forget me.
If you never do,
You won't think I'm true;
But old Oliphaunt am I,
And I never lie.

Discuss or list short answers to the following questions:

Text Analysis

1. At the end of book IV, chapter 7 Frodo exclaims to Sam, "They cannot conquer forever!" Discuss what this tells us about his resolve.
2. What does Sam assume about the mission when he believes Frodo to be dead? What does this reveal about Sam's sense of purpose in this mission?

Cultural Analysis

1. How has the culture romanticized this sense of purpose?
2. How would most people answer the question as to why some give up and others seem to persist?

Biblical Analysis

1. What can we observe in Scripture relating to the issue of persistence to the end in accomplishing a goal (Prov. 3:5, 6; Acts 15:36; Rom. 1:13; Matt. 10:5-15; 16:21; 26:17-19)?
2. What do these individuals have in common concerning the nature of their vision for the future (Rom. 15:20; 2 Cor. 11:24-29; Phil. 3:14)?

Summa

Write an essay or discuss this question, integrating what you have learned from the material above.

How do we account for the fact that there are individuals who are persistent, yet ungodly?

Reading Assignment:
Book IV, Chapters 9–10

Session XI: Recitation

Book IV, Chapters 8–10

Comprehension Questions

Answer the following questions for factual recall:

1. As the hobbits sleep on the stairs of Cirith Ungol, Sam awakens. What does he find Gollum doing?
2. Gollum later leads them into a cave which he claims is the entrance to a tunnel. What do they expect to encounter? What do they actually encounter in the cave?
3. What is the phial of Galadriel? How does Frodo use it?
4. How does Frodo get through the cobwebs?
5. What is the result of the spider's poison upon Frodo? How does Sam respond?
6. What thoughts come to Sam as he is thinking about the "death" of Frodo?
7. Sam takes the Ring from Frodo and puts it on. What special power does he have that we did not know about before? What does Sam learn as he listens in on their conversation?
8. How does *The Two Towers* end?

Optional Activity

Once you have read *The Two Towers* (preferably several times), it may be safe to watch Peter Jackson's rendition of it in film. When you are watching the movie, keep a note pad handy to jot down any places where the movie and the book diverge. When you are done, go back through your list and see how many of your discrepancies you can prove, and how many are just interpretive questions.

Session XII: Creative Writing

The Lost Chapter, Part 2

We return now to the assignment we began in Session VII. Pick up where you left off and complete the story. When you're done, go back through and look for sentences and descriptions that don't do much work; they just seem to lie there, not grabbing our attention. Cut those out or trim them down. Your writing should include only that which is necessary. When you think you're done, read it out loud to someone and get their suggestions. Always be teachable. Go back and make things clear that your "audience" says they didn't get. Go back and cut out parts where their interest lagged. Then try reading it again to someone else.

Optional Session: Evaluation

Grammar

Answer each of the following questions in complete sentences. (2 points per answer)

1. At the beginning of *The Two Towers* what is the state of the Fellowship?
2. What is an Ent? What significant contribution do the Ents make?
3. What crucial mistake does Wormtongue make?
4. What is a Nazgûl? How are they used by Sauron?
5. What is the prophecy that causes much curiosity in Faramir?
6. Who is Shelob? What happens in Shelob's Lair?
7. What does Sam learn by listening to the orcs? Where are we at the end?

Logic

Demonstrate your understanding of the worldview set forth in The Two Towers. *Answer two of the following three questions in complete sentences; your answer should be a paragraph or so. (10 points per answer)*

1. Tolkien chooses to keep Frodo entirely absent from Book III, directing our attention instead to the wanderings of Merry, Pippin and Aragorn's group. Why do you think the main protagonist of the novel does not appear in Book III at all?
2. Considering their histories, how might Saruman and Sauron represent two different types of evil?
3. How does Frodo's opinion change concerning what should be done about Gollum's sordid past?

Shadowfax the Great is the finest horse in Rohan and the greatest of all horses at the end of the Third Age. A descendant of a horse tamed by the first king of Rohan, Shadowfax is of a breed of horses brought to Middle-earth from the Undying Lands by the valar Orome. Shadowfax's beautiful coat appears silver during the day, and shadowy gray at night, he can run great distances without tiring and is the only free horse in Middle-earth who is able to endure the terror of the Nazgûl.

Lateral Thinking

Answer one of the following questions. These questions will require more substantial answers. (16 points each)

1. Answer the questions below about the following quotation: *"I did not give you leave to go," said Gandalf sternly. "I have not finished. You have become a fool, Saruman, and yet pitiable. You might still have turned away from folly and evil, and have been of service. But you choose to stay and gnaw the ends of your own plots."* Did Gandalf fear evil? What should be our attitude toward evil? How do Gandalf's words echo the teaching of the book of Proverbs concerning foolishness? (Prov. 1:7; 3:35; 10:8; 12:15)
2. What can we learn from Frodo's change of heart concerning Gollum?

Henry V

How do you feel when your father tells you to do something? And is it the same feeling you have when your little sister tries to boss you around? What is the difference?

Authority is often defined as "the right to be obeyed," but it's probably easier to think about authority as a voice. Whenever you listen to one voice and ignore others, then that voice has authority. Authority belongs to the voice that stops an argument, the voice that makes a final decision, the voice that tells you what to do, the voice that belongs to the person who can punish you. In every situation, there is a voice of authority: the voice of your mother telling you to come inside when all your friends are telling you to stay out a bit longer; the voice of a teacher telling you to stop chatting with the other students and get to work; the voice of a husband who tells his wife to ignore what her friends are saying and listen to him. Many today listen to an "inner voice," the voice of their own thoughts. Ultimately, for Christians, authority is the voice of God speaking in the Scriptures.

Authority is an enormous problem in the modern world, especially in modern America. Many years ago, Robert Nisbet wrote a book about today's world called *The Twilight of Authority*. He said that modern people are confused about authority, and we have only become more confused since Nisbet wrote. The problem is not that modern people don't recognize authority. We do, however much we might say

Henry borrows a cloak and disguises himself to wander among the common soldiers at night to bolster his people, not with a passionate speech as a divinely appointed king, but as a master politician working the crowd.

that we are free to choose whatever we want. The problem is that we modern people have a hard time explaining why we listen to one voice rather than another. There are so many voices telling us what to do—voices in popular music, voices from movies, voices from the television news, voices from advertising—and we have a hard time figuring out which voice is the true voice of authority. We can't tell the difference between the angry shouts of the baseball team managers and the deciding voice of the umpire. In the end, we simply choose to listen to one of the many voices, which is to say that we pretend to be our own authority.

Authority is always two-sided. On the one hand, the person with authority has to possess something that gives his voice greater power than other voices. But on the other hand, the voice of authority has to be *heard.* If no one believes that the umpire's voice is decisive, then the umpire's authority is not really authority. This is the double problem of modern authority. From the side of the ruler, we wonder, "What gives authority to a particular voice? Why should one voice stand out from the others? Does one man's voice have authority because he's got a bigger gun? Or does his voice have authority because he has gone through a ceremony of inauguration?" From the side of those ruled, we wonder, "How can we tell who speaks with authority? Does he wear a special uniform? What makes us obey *this* voice rather than *that* one?"

Authority was much simpler in the medieval world. Authority flowed from the top. Medieval people heard God's voice as the ultimate authority. When God spoke in His word or through His church, all debate and discussion had to stop. In politics, medievals believed that God had given authority to certain people. They believed the Pope had the authority of Christ, because Jesus had told Peter that he had the keys of the kingdom, and emperors or kings had authority from God as well. The big debate in the medieval world was whether the king received his authority directly from God or whether he had authority through the Pope. But no one doubted that he had to listen to the voice of the king. And he had to listen because the king's voice was the voice of God.

Medieval nations symbolized the fact that the king's authority came from God through various ceremonies, rituals and signs. Kings were anointed, just as Jesus had been anointed with the Spirit. Because of his anointing, the king was seen as an image of "Christ." Because of the anointing, the king was holy. He could not be touched, and an attack on the king was an attack on God. Above all, because of his anointing, the king's voice was a voice of authority.

Henry V is the last of a series of four plays written by Shakespeare on English history. Through these four plays, Shakespeare dramatizes the change from the medieval to the modern world and especially from medieval to modern views of political authority. *Henry V* takes place in a world where the royal anointing no longer has the authority it had in the medieval world. Shakespeare raises the question, "If a king does not have his authority from God, and if this authority is not made visible in a public ceremony, why should we listen to his voice?" If the king can't be rec-

Shakespeare's plays concerning the monarchy during the time of the Wars of the Roses, commonly called the *tetrarchy,* demonstrate the Bard's own political shrewdness.

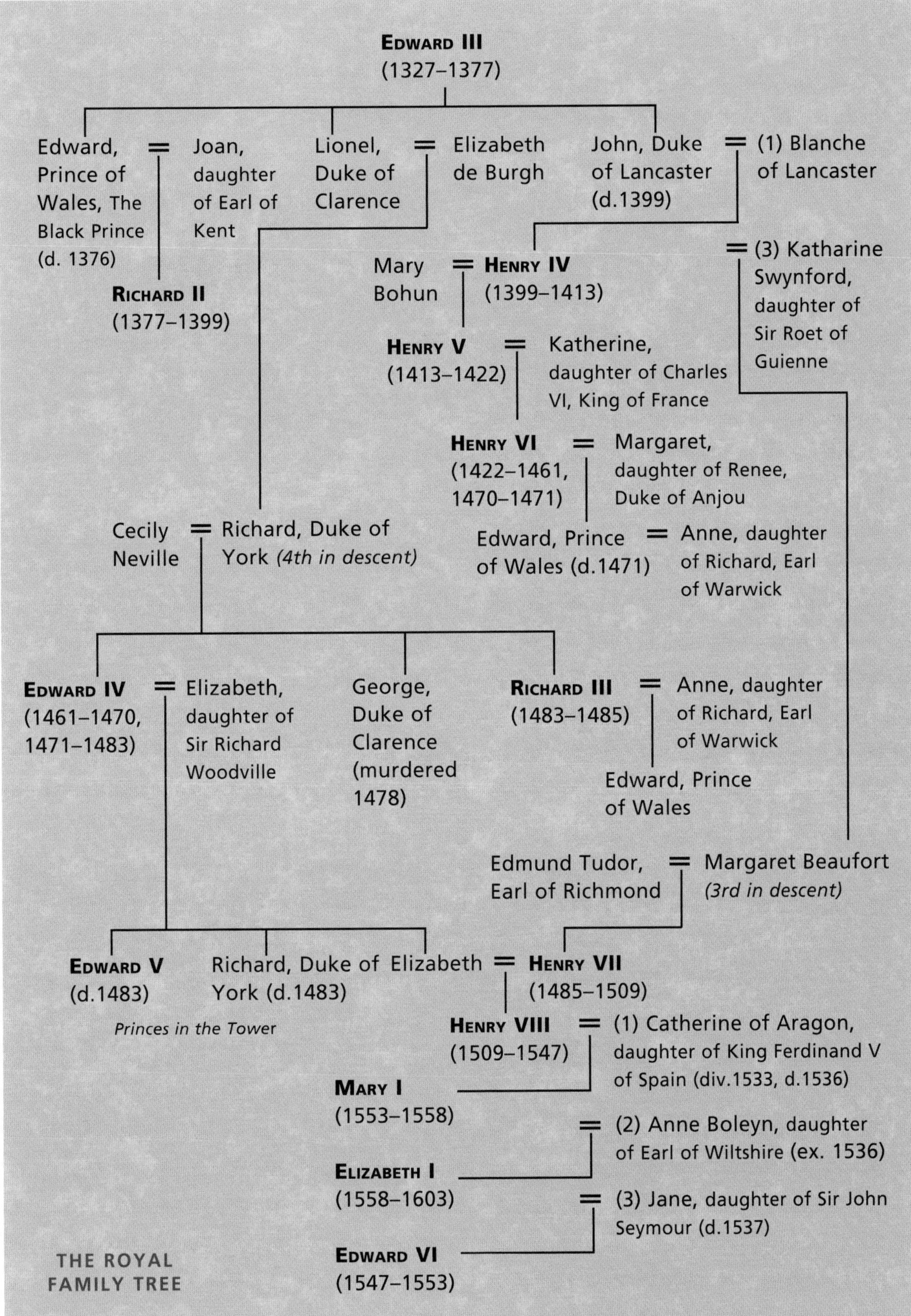
EDWARD III
(1327–1377)
Edward, Prince of Wales, The Black Prince (d. 1376)
=
Joan, daughter of Earl of Kent
Lionel, Duke of Clarence
=
Elizabeth de Burgh
John, Duke of Lancaster (d.1399)
=
(1) Blanche of Lancaster
= (3) Katharine Swynford, daughter of Sir Roet of Guienne
RICHARD II
(1377–1399)
Mary Bohun
=
HENRY IV
(1399–1413)
HENRY V
(1413–1422)
=
Katherine, daughter of Charles VI, King of France
HENRY VI
(1422–1461, 1470–1471)
=
Margaret, daughter of Renee, Duke of Anjou
Cecily Neville
=
Richard, Duke of York *(4th in descent)*
Edward, Prince of Wales (d.1471)
=
Anne, daughter of Richard, Earl of Warwick
EDWARD IV
(1461–1470, 1471–1483)
=
Elizabeth, daughter of Sir Richard Woodville
George, Duke of Clarence (murdered 1478)
RICHARD III
(1483–1485)
=
Anne, daughter of Richard, Earl of Warwick
Edward, Prince of Wales
Edmund Tudor, Earl of Richmond
=
Margaret Beaufort *(3rd in descent)*
EDWARD V
(d.1483)
Richard, Duke of York (d.1483)
Princes in the Tower
Elizabeth
=
HENRY VII
(1485–1509)
HENRY VIII
(1509–1547)
=
(1) Catherine of Aragon, daughter of King Ferdinand V of Spain (div.1533, d.1536)
MARY I
(1553–1558)
=
(2) Anne Boleyn, daughter of Earl of Wiltshire (ex. 1536)
ELIZABETH I
(1558–1603)
=
(3) Jane, daughter of Sir John Seymour (d.1537)
EDWARD VI
(1547–1553)
THE ROYAL FAMILY TREE

ognized by his anointing, what makes us listen to his voice rather than that of another? What is the basis of politics in a world where the royal anointing no longer carries the power it did for the Middle Ages? Shakespeare's answers to that question are as important now as they were when he first wrote the play.

General Information

Author and Context

Shakespeare (in my view, not Edward de Vere or Francis Bacon) wrote *Henry V* around 1600, in the last years of the reign of Elizabeth I. It is the final play in a *tetrology,* a group of four plays that hang together chronologically and thematically. The plays in this tetrology are *Richard II, Henry IV, Parts I and II,* and *Henry V.* Shakespeare wrote another tetrology on English history: *Henry VI, Parts I, II* and *III,* and *Richard III.* Overall, these eight plays tell the story of the English monarchy during the Hundred Years' War and the Wars of the Roses, and of the rise of the Tudor dynasty, the dynasty of Elizabeth I.

Henry V takes place during the Hundred Years' War, which lasted from 1337 to 1453. This war involved England and France in a struggle over control of the French monarchy. It began during the reign of Edward III (1327–1377), who claimed that he should be the king of France because his mother, Isabella, was a French princess. His son, Edward the Black Prince, was killed fighting in France the year before his father died. Richard II, son of the Black Prince, succeeded Edward III, but other branches of the family also wanted the English throne and were willing to fight for it.

Richard II (1377–1399) was only ten years old when he became king. As he grew up, various parts of Edward III's family started fighting for power. Things came to a head when Richard sent his cousin, Henry Bolingbroke, into exile. Two years later, Henry returned to England, overthrew Richard and became King Henry IV (1399–1413). Shakespeare's *Richard II* begins with Henry Bolingbroke's exile and tells the story of Bolingbroke's revolt. That play ends with the death of Richard II.

The other branches of Edward's family were not happy that Henry had become king. Various powerful families, especially the Mortimers and the Percies, attempted to overthrow him. Shakespeare's play *Henry IV,* Part I ends with the battle of Shrewsbury, where Bolingbroke's son, Prince Hal (the future Henry V), kills Henry Percy (Hotspur) and ends the Percy rebellion. By the time Henry V (1413–1422) came to the throne, the competitors for the throne were defeated, and Henry could turn his attention back to Edward III's dream of taking over France. Shakespeare's *Henry V* tells the story of Henry's French campaigns, which took place between 1415 and 1420.

When Henry V died prematurely, his son, Henry VI (1422–1461/1470–1471), ascended the throne as king of England and France. During his lifetime, England lost the French throne, and the Wars of the Roses began between two branches of Edward III's family, known as the houses of Lancaster and York. The civil wars ended when Henry Tudor, who had ancestors from both of the warring families, defeated King Richard III at Bosworth Field. Henry Tudor became Henry VII (1485–1509) and inaugurated the dynasty that included Henry VIII, Edward VI, Mary I and Elizabeth I.

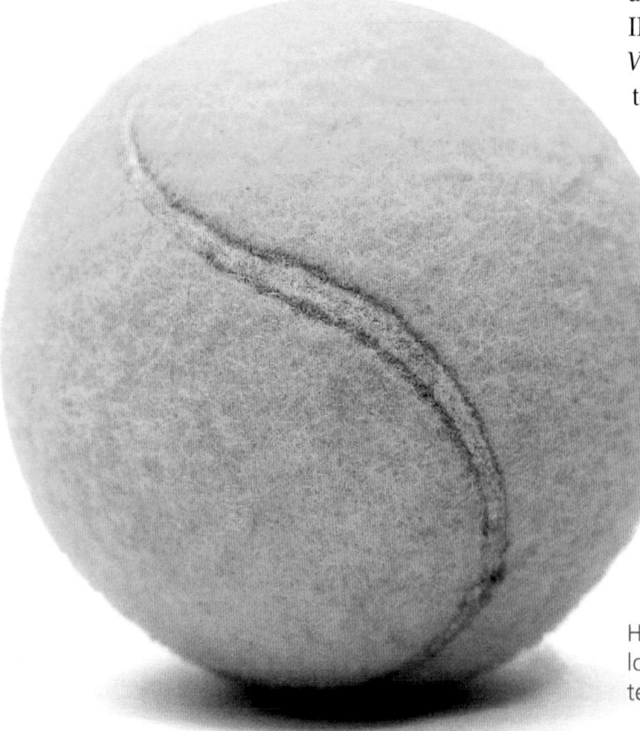

Henry's carefully crafted portrayal of himself as a loafer fooled even his opponents, who sent him tennis balls to mock his youthful indiscretions.

Significance

Henry V has long been one of Shakespeare's most popular history plays. The events depicted in the play were important for the first Elizabethan audiences, since Shakespeare was telling the story of the origins of the Tudor dynasty, which was still ruling Britain. On the surface, the play is a hymn to England, telling the story of one of England's great kings and one of its greatest military triumphs at the battle of Agincourt. Because of this, the play has been trundled out periodically whenever England needs an injection of patriotic fervor. The actor Laurence Olivier read Henry's speech before the battle of Harfleur ("Once more unto the breach, dear friends, once more, or close the wall up with our English dead!") on British radio in 1942 when England was fighting Nazi Germany. Throughout World War II, Olivier, then serving in the British military, gave pep talks that ended with the same speech, and in 1944 Olivier produced and starred in a film version of the play.

More recently (in 1989), Kenneth Branagh filmed the play, which is more pessimistic about British conquests. Branagh's war scenes are bloody and muddy, wholly unlike the clean heroism of Olivier's battles. Instead of highlighting the patriotic aspects of the play, the film emphasizes the futility and costs of the war. Branagh's film was *Henry V* for the generation disillusioned by the American war in Vietnam and the British war in the Falkland Islands (1982).

From its first production in the early seventeenth century, *Henry V* has been produced to explore issues of patriotism, warfare, imperialism, justice and the meaning of political authority.

Main Characters

Henry V dominates the play. No one else in the play has nearly as many lines, and none of the other characters are as well-developed. All the other characters are important only in relation to him. The characters divide into various groups: Henry is surrounded by a crowd of nobles who serve as his war counsel and as his soldiers in the French invasion. A number of characters (Pistol, Bardolph, Nym) are old friends from his youth. The French characters are divided into the members of the royal family and the nobles.

There are some memorable minor characters, such as the Welsh captain Llewellyn (also called Fluellen) and Pistol, one of Henry's old drinking partners. The French Prince, called the Dauphin, is a comically proud young man, whose skill does not match his boasting. Katherine, the French princess whom Henry eventually marries, has a couple of charming scenes.

One important character is not a character in the story at all. In this play, Shakespeare uses a *Chorus* to introduce each act, a device popular in ancient Greek and Roman plays. Shakespeare's Chorus is a single man, rather than a group, and his role is to introduce the scenes, set the context, and give background. The Chorus has definite opinions about Henry, but it's important to notice that his opinions are not necessarily the same as Shakespeare's.

Summary and Setting

As noted above, *Henry V* focuses on Henry's French campaign. Act 1 describes the preparations for that campaign. The play begins with a secretive meeting between two clergymen, the Archbishop of Canterbury and the Bishop of Ely, who are plotting to win Henry's support for the church in a struggle with the House of Commons. During a war council in the following scene, Canterbury and Ely tell the nobles that, according to law, Henry has a right to the French crown. An ambassador from France brings a message from the French prince, the Dauphin, along with a gift, a box of tennis balls, which the Dauphin uses to remind Henry of his playful youth.

Act 2 alternates between scenes in Eastcheap, London, where Henry's boyhood companion, Sir John Falstaff, is dying, and scenes of preparation for war. Henry exposes a conspiracy among several noblemen. Acts 3–4 dramatize the French campaign, including the battle for the city of Harfleur and the decisive battle of Agincourt. Along the way, Shakespeare includes a scene where soldiers from various parts of the United Kingdom (Ireland, Scotland, Wales, England) argue among themselves; one where Princess Katherine of France learns some English from a lady-in-waiting; and Henry's visit to his troops on the night before Agincourt, which ends with a soliloquy about kingship.

The play ends with a scene in the French court, where Henry woos Katherine and the French sign a peace accord with England that grants Henry's son the right to wear the French crown. The Chorus closes the play by reminding the audience that Henry VI "lost

ENGLISH LONGBOW

Henry V's ragtag army that engaged the French in the famous battle at Agincourt was largely made up of yeoman conscripts wielding the famous English "longbow." According to one authority the longbow was the "national weapon of the English army" from the thirteenth until the sixteenth century, was instrumental in the English victories over France (including Agincourt) in the Hundred Years' War, and in England's replacing France as the foremost military power in late medieval Europe. "The longbow was the machine gun of the Middle Ages: accurate, deadly, possessed of a long-range and rapid rate of fire, the flight of its missiles was likened to a storm. Cheap and simple enough for the yeoman to own and master, it made him superior to a knight on the field of battle."

The longbow was so named for its length—the bow was the height of the archer, between five and six feet tall. Usually made out of staves of yew wood (single long pieces of a strong, yet flexible hardwood) the bow had a "draw weight" of up to 90 pounds and could accurately propel three-foot-long arrows against targets up to two hundred yards away. Its closest competitor, the continental crossbow, was no match for the longbow in accuracy or range. A well trained English military bowman could shoot ten to twelve arrows a minute.

There is a continuing dispute over exactly how much of a factor the longbow was in Henry's great Agincourt victory. Some say that the longbow was the key to victory, others that the rain and mud, Henry's choice of battle location and the valor of Henry's weary troops won the day.

France and made his England bleed."

Worldview

Shakespeare's Richard II is every inch a medieval king. He believes to the bottom of his heart that he has been chosen by God to be England's king. He sees himself as a Christ figure, a holy man because of crown and oil. He believes that God will protect him from all "Judases" who seek to betray him. In the middle of the play, when Henry Bolingbroke returns to England and threatens to overthrow the king, Richard tells the Earl of Northumberland the origins and meaning of his kingship:

> Because we thought ourself thy lawful king:
> And if we be, how dare thy joints forget
> To pay their awful duty to our presence?
> If we be not, show us the hand of God
> That hath dismissed us from our
> stewardship;
> For well we know, no hand of blood and bone
> Can gripe the sacred handle of our sceptre,
> Unless he do profane, steal, or usurp.
> And though you think that all, as you
> have done,
> Have torn their souls by turning them
> from us,
> And we are barren and bereft of friends;
> Yet know, my master, God omnipotent,
> Is mustering in his clouds on our behalf
> Armies of pestilence; and they shall strike
> Your children yet unborn and unbegot,
> That lift your vassal hands against my head
> And threat the glory of my precious crown
> (*Richard II*, Act 3, scene 3).

Since God has made him king, no human, "no hand of blood and bone," can seize his power from him. Anyone who attempts to seize the crown is guilty of profaning, stealing and usurping the throne, and God will send armies of pestilence to punish the usurpers. God made the king. Only God can unmake him. Ultimately, however, *Richard II* tells about the overthrow of a lawful monarch, a king who bears God's authority. Threatened by Bolingbroke, Richard agrees to resign the crown.

But how can this be? If God made him king, how can he un-king himself? Just as importantly, how can Bolingbroke have any authority as king? Henry can't say that everyone should obey his voice because he has a royal anointing, for he has just overthrown a man with a royal anointing. He can't say that the people should listen to him because God gave him the kingdom, because he's just taken the kingdom for himself. Throughout the Middle Ages, the ceremony of royal anointing gave the king authority. Once Henry has attacked the anointed king, what basis is there for his own authority?

Henry V is well aware of the dilemma. As he prays on the night before the battle of Agincourt, Henry admits to God that his English crown is not securely on his head:

> Not to-day, O Lord,
> O, not to-day, think not upon the fault
> My father made in compassing the crown!
> I Richard's body have interred anew;
> And on it have bestow'd more contrite tears
> Than from it issued forced drops of blood:
> Five hundred poor I have in yearly pay,
> Who twice a-day their wither'd hands hold up
> Toward heaven, to pardon blood; and I have built
> Two chantries, where the sad and solemn priests
> Sing still for Richard's soul. More will I do;
> Though all that I can do is nothing worth,
> Since that my penitence comes after all,
> Imploring pardon (Act 4, scene 1).

Henry realizes that he got the crown of England at the expense of Richard's blood. He has done all he knows to do to appease God's anger for that, but in the end his only hope is that God will overlook his father's fault—at least until the battle is over.

Henry not only recognizes that his own claim to England's throne is stained, but he also raises questions about the power of ceremony itself. Can ceremony actually confer authority? Can ceremony give a king a voice that his subjects will hear? Henry thinks not:

> O hard condition,
> Twin-born with greatness, subject to the breath
> Of every fool, whose sense no more can feel
> But his own wringing! What infinite
>   heart's-ease
> Must kings neglect, that private men enjoy!
> And what have kings, that privates have
>   not too,
> Save ceremony, save general ceremony?
> And what art thou, thou idle ceremony? . . .
> Art thou aught else but place, degree and form,
> Creating awe and fear in other men?
> Wherein thou art less happy being fear'd
> Than they in fearing.
> What drink'st thou oft, instead of homage sweet,
> But poison'd flattery? O, be sick, great greatness,
> And bid thy ceremony give thee cure!
> Think'st thou the fiery fever will go out
> With titles blown from adulation?
> Will it give place to flexure and low bending?
> Canst thou, when thou command'st the
>   beggar's knee,
> Command the health of it? (Act 4, scene 1)

"Twin-born." The king was born once as a man, and born again as king in the ceremony of coronation. But what does this ceremony get him? Because of the ceremony, people must bow and scrape and flatter the king. But ceremony does not give the king any power to cure the sick, to make his country strong and prosperous. In the end, for Henry, the ceremony of anointing simply means the king cannot sleep at night.

The difference between medieval and modern conceptions of authority is captured by the contrast between *Richard II* and *Henry V*. These plays show the difference between medieval and modern politics. And the focal point is the question of ceremony. If ceremonies are not effective, what is the basis of authority?

One answer to this question becomes plain when we consider *Henry V* in connection with the two parts of *Henry IV*. Although these two latter plays are named for Henry V's father, Henry, as Prince Hal, is really the main character. During these plays, however, he is not a very princely young man. He spends his time with lowlife characters like Sir John Falstaff, Pistol and Bardolph, drinking late into the night in seedy taverns and sometimes joining his friends in illegal capers.

This gives us one part of Shakespeare's answer to the question about authority. Henry V cannot point to his royal anointing or to any other ceremony as a basis for his authority. He can't make his men listen to him because he has authority from God, since his father got his authority by his own power. He can't make men obey him by claiming to be high above them. Realizing this, Henry establishes authority among his men by coming down to their level. The time he spent in taverns as a youth was time well spent, because it taught him how to socialize with commoners. It gave him the "common touch." In terms of modern politics, Henry V is a democratic politician. His authority rests on his ability to gain and retain popularity—and notice that the word *popularity* comes from the Latin word *populus,* meaning "people."

Several scenes in the play bring this out clearly. During the night before the battle of Agincourt, Henry goes wandering about the camp, talking to and encouraging his men. The Chorus captures the tone of this visit. His men are cold and fearful, until Henry appears:

> For forth he goes and visits all his host.
> Bids them good morrow with a modest smile
> And calls them brothers, friends and
> countrymen.
> Upon his royal face there is no note
> How dread an army hath enrounded him;
> Nor doth he dedicate one jot of colour
> Unto the weary and all-watched night,
> But freshly looks and over-bears attaint
> With cheerful semblance and sweet majesty;
> That every wretch, pining and pale before,
> Beholding him, plucks comfort from his looks:
> A largess universal like the sun
> His liberal eye doth give to every one,
> Thawing cold fear, that mean and gentle all,
> Behold, as may unworthiness define,
> A little touch of Harry in the night
> (Act 4, Prologue).

According to medieval legend, a king could heal with a touch. Henry has no such power, but because he treats his men as equals, he brings them strength and evokes love from them. He is like a warming and brightening sun in the dark night before the battle.

Act 4, scene 1 shows this even more dramatically. Henry puts off his royal robes, dons the clothing of a common soldier, and goes out among his men in disguise. He talks with them, argues with them and is even challenged to a duel. But his ability to go undetected among his men shows again that he gains authority and evokes the loyalty of his men by becoming one of them. Far and away the most famous speech in *Henry V* is his rousing pep talk before the battle of Agincourt, often memorized by English and American schoolchildren (Act 4, scene 3). Henry fights with his men in common "fellowship" with them, and together they form a "band of brothers," a "happy few." Harry the king, he predicts, will be only one among the heroes remembered for the battle. Henry is able to lead his soldiers to victory not because he stands Godlike above them; he leads his men because he stands among them.

Though this "democratic" impulse is not as explicitly Christian as Richard II's medieval view of kingship, there is a profound Christian principle at work. Henry exercises his kingship not by lording it over his men, but by taking their position and acting as their servant. He puts aside his glory, takes on the form of a slave, and tabernacles among them.

Another side to Henry V's vision of authority, however, is more disturbing. In fact, Shakespeare's portrayal of Henry is disturbing from the beginning. In his first soliloquy in *Henry IV, Part I,* Henry explains to the audience why he spends time in the tavern associating with men like Falstaff:

> I know you all, and will awhile uphold
> The unyok'd humour of your idleness.
> Yet herein will I imitate the sun,
> Who doth permit the base contagious clouds
> To smother up his beauty from the world,
> That, when he please again to lie himself,
> Being wanted, he may be more wond'red at
> By breaking through the foul and ugly mists
> Of vapours that did seem to strangle him.

> If all the year were playing holidays,
> To sport would be as tedious as to work;
> But when they seldom come, they wish'd-for
> come,
> And nothing pleaseth but rare accidents.
> So, when this loose behaviour I throw off
> And pay the debt I never promised,
> By how much better than my word I am,
> By so much shall I falsify men's hopes;
> And, like bright metal on a sullen ground,
> My reformation, glitt'ring o'er my fault,
> Shall show more goodly and attract more eyes
> Than that which hath no foil to set it off.
> I'll so offend to make offence a skill,
> Redeeming time when men think least I will
> (*Henry IV, Part I,* Act 1, scene 2).

Hal considers his tavern friends "base contagious clouds," while he is the sun. The sun is more brilliant and dramatic when it comes out from behind a dark cloud. That is why he spends so much time with Falstaff and the others. When he becomes king, he plans to burst out from among his friends and astonish everyone with his reformation. He is using his friends in order to establish his own power in the future. Henry is not interested in changing his character; he wants to make it *appear* that he has changed his character.

Henry creates a dramatic entrance so that everyone will be awed and will think of him as a ruler. He tries to establish political authority on the basis of drama. replacing the ceremony of divine anointing with a display. This is the transition in authority between the Middle Ages and the modern world: it is a transition from ceremony to spectacle. In Henry's world, authority has ceased to be *theological;* it has become *theatrical.*

Spectacle, keeping up appearances, creating dramatic scenes—these are inherent to modern, democratic views of authority. A democratic ruler can maintain authority only as long as he is popular. But a good ruler is always going to make decisions that many of his people will dislike.[1] How can a ruler make difficult but unpopular decisions when he has to make sure that people like him? Another Shakespearean character, Coriolanus, recognizes this dilemma when he asks why rulers who have "gentry, title, wisdom" should have to conform to "the yea and no of general ignorance"? (*Coriolanus,* Act 3, scene 1). Politicians, who have to wait upon the approval of "general ignorance," can maintain their power only by tickling the ears and dazzling the eyes of their electors.

Henry managed the symbols and portrayals of power at his disposal, winning over the people by stagecraft rather than appealing to divine authority. This is common in contemporary politics, as image consultants spin their magic to make somebodies out of nobodies.

If they want to gain and maintain power, they have little choice but to go theatrical.

Henry's effort to root his authority in spectacle and drama affects the whole political system. Ceremonies teach standards of life. An anointed king may not actually submit to God and may not be very Christlike. But the anointing is a reminder that he is called to be Christlike. The anointing is a constant reminder of the kind of king he is *supposed* to be. The ceremony offers a standard that a king has to measure up to and a standard by which he may be judged. If a king proves a tyrant, it is possible to say he has betrayed his kingship and violated his sacred anointing. And a king who betrays his anointing has lost his authority; his voice is no longer heard as the voice of God.

But in a democratic system, what standards is a ruler supposed to live up to? Even if a ruler changes his policies fifty times in two years, we cannot say he has failed to live up to his office so long as he remains popular—precisely because his whole calling, his office, is to remain popular. If a ruler becomes a tyrant but still remains popular, we have no basis for saying he has violated his office. If a ruler says "Yes" today and "No" tomorrow but remains popular, we have no grounds for saying that his voice has lost authority.

Already in the seventeenth century, Shakespeare recognized that the West had seen a profound change in the character of political authority, and he would not be surprised to learn that politicians gain and maintain authority today by producing glitzy TV ads, surrounding themselves with celebrities, maintaining an impression of being "cool." Shakespeare was one of the early prophets of the modern crisis of authority.

Henry V gives us a portrait of a Christian king who is beginning to operate on non-Christian principles of authority. *Henry V* does not give us any solutions to the dilemma. For Christians, however, the answer should be obvious: If the crisis has come because we have excluded God from our notions of political authority, the solution is to return to Paul's declaration, that the powers that be are ordained of God. The solution is to recognize that the ultimate voice of authority is the voice of God and that our voices have authority only from Him.

—*Peter J. Leithart*

For Further Reading

Alvis, John E. "Spectacle Supplanting Ceremony: Shakespeare's Henry Monmouth," in John E. Alvis and Thomas G. West, eds., *Shakespeare as Political Thinker.* Wilmington, Del.: ISI Books, 2000.

Brennan, Anthony. *Henry V.* New York: Twayne Publishers, 1992.

Leithart, Peter J. *Brightest Heaven of Invention: A Christian Guide to Six Shakespeare Plays.* Moscow, Idaho: Canon Press, 1996.

Saccio, Peter. *Shakespeare's English Kings.* Oxford: Oxford University Press, 2000.

Veritas Press History Cards: Middle Ages, Renaissance and Reformation. Lancaster, Pa.: Veritas Press. 20.

Session I: Prelude

A Question to Consider

What is the basis for authority? Why should we listen to one voice more than others?

From the General Information above, answer the following questions:

1. What was the Hundred Years' War about?
2. What is a tetrology? What are the two tetrologies Shakespeare wrote about English history?
3. Who was Henry Bolingbroke? What did he do?
4. How has this play been interpreted in the past?
5. What does Richard II say about the power of ceremony?
6. Why are the commoners important in *Henry V?*

Optional Activities

Watch Kenneth Branagh's film version of *Henry V.* Summarize the story of the play from watching the movie. If you can find it, also watch Laurence Olivier's film version of the play. How does Olivier's film differ from Branagh's?

Do research on the real Henry V. (Peter Saccio's *Shakespeare's English Kings* is a good source.) What kind of upbringing did Henry V have? What kind of king was he?

Do research on medieval warfare and on the battle of Agincourt in particular. What happened in the battle? Why did the English have such an advantage over the French?[3]

READING ASSIGNMENT:

Henry V, Acts 1–2

SESSION II: DISCUSSION

Henry V, Acts 1–2

A Question to Consider

How does Henry V attempt to establish his authority over his kingdom and his nobles? What is Shakespeare showing us about political authority in the modern world?

Discuss or list short answers to the following questions:

Text Analysis

1. What kind of men are the churchmen in Act 1, scene 1? What does this say about the church's ability to support Henry's authority?

WARS OF THE ROSES

Henry V was involved in the early stages of the Wars of the Roses, in which two royal houses descended from King Edward III, Lancaster and York, laid claims to the English throne. The name "Wars of the Roses" came from the badges adopted by the two royal houses, the Red Rose of Lancaster and the White Rose of York.

The rift between Lancaster and York developed after Henry Bolingbroke, Duke of Lancaster, overthrew his cousin, King Richard II in 1399. Although his claim to the throne was weak, Bolingbroke's bold move succeeded largely because of Richard II's unpopularity, and the Duke ruled as Henry IV until his death in 1413. The one conspiracy during his son Henry V's reign was probably connected to the festering conflict. Richard, Earl of Cambridge (and descendent of Edward III) was executed in 1415 for treason before the English campaign leading to the Battle of Agincourt in France.

The Wars heated up during Henry VI's weak reign. Powerful nobles with private armies of knights and feudal retainers lined up on both sides, and personal vendettas stoked much of the action. From 1459 through 1471 fourteen major battles were fought across much of England. Towton, the biggest battle, killed over 20,000 men, still the largest single day's loss of life on English soil. Decapitated heads of several leading nobles were prominently displayed on the gates of York city by both sides. When Edward IV was restored in 1471, an uneasy peace reigned until his death in 1483. Lancastrian Henry Tudor (Henry VII) defeated Richard III of York at the famous battle of Bosworth Field in 1485, effectively ending the wars. He reunited the two royal houses by marrying Elizabeth of York and merging the rival symbols into a new emblem: the red and white Tudor Rose.

SAINT CRISPIN

One of the greatest speeches in all of Shakespeare's plays is the "St. Crispin's Day" speech by Henry V just before the Battle of Agincourt. In the traditional church calendar the feast day honoring St. Crispin is October 25. Interestingly, St. Crispin was neither a great king nor a great warrior.

He was a shoemaker.

Did you ever think about how important everyday things like shoes are? Sometimes we get the wrong picture about God's world and think that only "great" or "famous" things or people are important. That's not what God thinks. The church in history has sometimes recognized this in the past. Crispin is the patron saint of shoemakers, tanners, leatherworkers and saddle makers. Among other things the honoring of Crispin, the shoemaker, implies an understanding in the early church that Jesus has redeemed the whole creation and that we are to do everything we do, including everyday work like making shoes as well as evangelism, to the honor and glory of God. There should be no "sacred/secular" distinction.

Crispin (also known as Crispinius and Crepinus) was born into a noble Roman family in the third century A.D. Although historical details are sketchy, apparently Crispin and his brother, Crispian (or Crepinianus, also a saint) fled persecution for their Christian faith, ending up in the ancient town of Soissons (northeast of Paris, France). There they preached the gospel to the Gauls and made shoes to support themselves and give to the poor. The success of their ministry came to the attention of Rictus Varus, governor of Belgic Gaul and a staunch enemy of the gospel. He had the faithful brothers tortured, then beheaded around A.D. 286. In the sixth century a church was built in Soissons to honor the brothers.

2. What is the argument of Canterbury and Ely in the war council? Is it convincing? Why do they present the argument the way they do?
3. What does the Dauphin send to Henry? Why does he send this particular gift?
4. How does Henry react? Is he playing a role in this scene?
5. How does Henry trap the conspirators in Act 2, scene 2? What does he plan to do with them? What does this say about Henry's authority as a king?

Cultural Analysis

1. Many have said that America faces a crisis of authority. What are the signs of this crisis? Think of conditions in schools, in families and in the political sphere.
2. During past presidential elections, candidates have surrounded themselves with movie stars, rock singers, and sports personalities. In light of *Henry V*, what does that tell you?
3. Stjepan G. Mestrovic, a professor of sociology at Texas A&M, argues in his book *The Post-Emotional Society* that "Western societies are entering a new phase of development in which synthetic, quasi-emotions become the basis for widespread manipulation by self, others, and the culture industry as a whole." In the political sphere, he refers to President Bill Clinton's ability to politically survive various scandals as an example of post-emotionalism: "Clinton's 'I feel your pain' line is not something most people notice, or remember, for they tend

to react as he does, with a false empathy where compassion would have been more appropriate. In this book, I refer to Clinton as the post-emotional President." How does Mestrovic's thesis apply to Henry V?

Biblical Analysis

1. How are kings made kings in Scripture? Look at 1 Samuel 9–10, 16. From where does the authority of a king come?
2. Find some passages in Samuel that talk about the king's "anointing." What effect does the anointing have on the king? What effect does it have on the king's subjects?

Summa

Write an essay or discuss this question, integrating what you have learned from the material above.

Write a brief constitution for a Christian society. Explain how the rulers of the society will be chosen and how their authority will be expressed.

Reading Assignment:
Henry V, Acts 3–4

Session III: Discussion

Henry V, Acts 3–4

A Question to Consider

What is a ceremony? Why do we have ceremonies? Do ceremonies actually *do* anything? What is the connection between ceremony and authority?

Discuss or list short answers to the following questions:

Text Analysis

1. What is going on in Act 3, scene 3? Who are the characters? What does this scene tell you about Henry's Britain?
2. Why does Shakespeare include the scene with Katherine and her lady in Act 3, scene 5? Why does this scene focus on language?
3. Why does Henry describe ceremony as an "idol" in Act 4, scene 1?
4. According to Henry, what does ceremony accomplish?
5. Why is it said the commoner has a better life than a king?

Cultural Analysis

1. What are some of the common ceremonies in our culture? How do people view them? Do we think ceremonies are important? Would things be different if we took ceremonies more seriously?
2. The English anthropologist Mary Douglas has written, "One of the great problems of our day is the lack of commitment to common symbols. If this were all, there would be little to say. If it were merely a matter of our fragmentation into small groups, each committed to its proper symbolic forms, the case would be simple to understand. But more mysterious is a wide-spread, explicit rejection of rituals as such. Ritual is become a bad word signifying empty conformity" (*Natural Symbols*, p. 1). Where is Douglas's statement evident by the rejection of ritual in our churches and culture?

Biblical Analysis

1. Read through Genesis 17, which describes the institution of circumcision. What does circumcision do to a circumcised person? Look also at Romans 6. What does Paul teach about baptism there?
2. Study one of the rituals in Leviticus 1–5 and summarize the main elements of that ritual: the animals involved, what's done with the different parts of the animal, the different movements and actions. What does it all mean?
3. It has been said that when something is important, human beings turn it into a ceremony. Is that a biblical concept? Why do humans act that way?

Summa

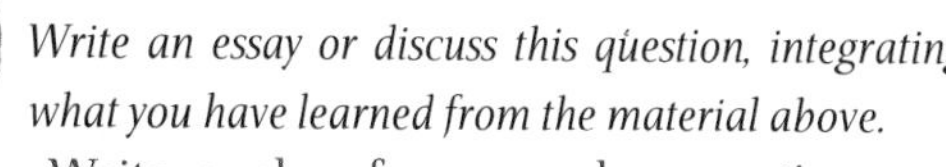

Write an essay or discuss this question, integrating what you have learned from the material above.

Write a plan for a royal coronation ceremony. Remember to list the people involved, where the coronation takes place, where the participants stand,the material elements used (e.g., crown, oil, robe). In a separate essay, explain why you put the ceremony together the way you did.

Reading Assignment:
Henry V, Act 5

SESSION IV: RECITATION

Henry V, Act 5

Comprehension Questions

Answer the following questions for factual recall:

1. What is the Chorus's opening speech about?
2. According to Mistress Quickly, why does Falstaff die?
3. What happens to Bardolph? Why is this important?
4. What does Henry do on the night before the battle of Agincourt?
5. What is the atmosphere in the French camp before Agincourt?
6. How does Henry motivate his men to fight?
7. What happens to the boys who are guarding the English soldiers' baggage? What does Henry do in response?
8. What happens between Henry V and Williams?
9. What does Llewellyn do to Pistol at the end of the play?
10. What is the point of the Duke of Burgundy's speech in Act 5, scene 2?

SESSION V: ACTIVITY

Drama

Acting out a scene or delivering a speech is exceedingly important for students of Shakespeare. Shakespeare gets into the bones when it is delivered out loud and all the wonderful rhythms and sounds roll across the tongue. It is also helpful for students to have to figure out what kind of character they are playing and how they can embody that character in a performance. If there is time for more elaborate performance, students can investigate questions of staging and gesture. All of this takes Shakespeare out of the book and onto the stage, where he belongs.-

Optional Activity

PUBLIC SPEAKING

Memorize the St. Crispin's Day speech or have an oratory contest with it. The winner of the contest will be the one who can memorize the most of it in 20 minutes or the one who gives the most stirring rendition of it. (If you ever become a sports coach, it is good to have this speech memorized, because it can translate into a really nice pep talk before a game.)

This day is called the feast of Crispian.
He that outlives this day and comes safe home,
Will stand a tip-toe when the day is nam'd,
And rouse him at the name of Crispian.
He that shall live this day, and see old age,
Will yearly on the vigil feast his neighbours,
And say "Tomorrow is Saint Crispian."
Then will he strip his sleeve and show his scars,
And say "These wounds I had on Crispin's day."
Old men forget: yet all shall be forgot,
But he'll remember with advantages
What feats he did that day: then shall our names,
Familiar in his mouth as household words
Harry the king, Bedford and Exeter,
Warwick and Talbot, Salisbury and Gloucester,
Be in their flowing cups freshly remember'd.
This story shall the good man teach his son,
And Crispin Crispian shall ne'er go by,
From this day to the ending of the world,
But we in it shall be remember'd;
We few, we happy few, we band of brothers;
For he today that sheds his blood with me
Shall be my brother; be he ne'er so vile,
This day shall gentle his condition:
And gentlemen in England now a-bed
Shall think themselves accurs'd they were not here,
And hold their manhoods cheap whiles any speaks
That fought with us upon Saint Crispin's day.

SESSION VI: ACTIVITY

Debating the Authorship of Shakespeare's Plays

For a couple of centuries, various writers have disputed the authorship of Shakespeare's plays, arguing that someone other than the actor William Shakespeare was responsible for the plays. The most important debate is between "Stratfordians," who claim that William Shakespeare of Stratford wrote the plays under his name, and "Oxfordians," who claim that the plays were written by Edward de Vere, the Earl of Oxford. Organize a debate between Stratfordians and Oxfordians.

To prepare for the debate, take some time to read and think through the arguments at the websites provided at Links 4–6 for this chapter at www.VeritasPress.com/OmniLinks.

Also read these preliminary thoughts: On September 25, 1987, American University in Washington, D.C., sponsored a moot court in the Metropolitan Memorial United Methodist Church. Presiding over the court were three Supreme Court justices: Harry Blackmun, William Brennan and John Paul Stevens. More than one thousand people turned out to hear Peter Jaszi and James Boyle debate the authorship of Shakespeare's plays. Jaszi argued that Edward de Vere, seventeenth Earl of Oxford, had written the plays, while Boyle argued for the Stratfordian burgher and actor William Shakespeare. All three justices concluded that the Oxford case was unproven, though the de Vere Society Newsletter later complained that Brennan was more a witness for the Stratfordians than an impartial judge.

The Oxfordian view dates back to the early part of this century, to an English schoolmaster named Thomas Looney, whose book *Shakespeare 'Identified'* was published in 1920 and republished in 1948. Looney was not the first to doubt the standard account of the playwright's life; in the mid-nineteenth century, a rather pitiable woman from Hartford, Connecticut, Delia Bacon, published a book on the philosophy of Shakespeare's plays in which she argued that Francis Bacon, whom she eventually claimed as a forebearer, had written the plays. She received grudging aid from Emerson, Hawthorne and Carlyle, though none believed her account. She believed that the evidence could be found in Shakespeare's grave, and she stole into Holy Trinity in Stratford late one night and poked around Shakespeare's grave in an unsuccessful search for confirmation of her theory.

The story of the "quest for the historical Shakespeare" is a fascinating one, and understandable in some sense. Shakespeare is without question the premier poet and writer in the English language, and English has become in this last century a worldwide language. He was recently selected in a British poll as the "man of the millennium." Despite his stature, however, comparatively little about William Shakespeare is known, and what we know makes him seem so prosaic, so normal, that it does not seem to fit the wonderful poetry of the plays and sonnets.

Shakespeare's support of the Tudor monarchy was evident in his plays and was very pleasing to Elizabeth I.

Optional Activity

Search the local theaters for a performance of *Henry V.* In many cities smaller theatrical groups present Shakespeare's plays.

Optional Session: Evaluation

Grammar

All tests and quizzes are to be taken with an open Bible and an open book. Answer each of the following questions in complete sentences. Some answers may be longer than others (2 points per answer).

1. How did Henry IV become king?
2. How did Henry V spend his youth? Why?
3. What was the Hundred Years' War about?
4. What is Henry's purpose in invading France?
5. What happened at the battle of Agincourt?
6. What happened during the reign of Henry VI?

Logic

Answer two of the following four questions in complete sentences. Your answer should be a paragraph or so (10 points per answer).

1. What does Henry V do to secure his authority as king?
2. Explain Henry's meditation on ceremony and its importance in the play.
3. Does Shakespeare portray Henry V favorably or unfavorably?

Lateral Thinking

Answer one of the following questions. These questions will require more substantial answers (16 points per answer).

1. The Oresteian trilogy describes the change from a monarchical political system to a democratic one. Discuss the similarities and differences between Aeschylus's plays and Shakespeare's tetrology.
2. Compare and contrast Henry's qualities as king with Shakespeare's Julius Caesar or Sophocles' Oedipus.

Endnotes

1 At the time of this writing, the once-popular British Prime Minister Tony Blair is under attack from all sides because of his support for the war in Iraq.

2 *This endnote appears only in the teacher's edition.*

3 There are many websites available for this research. On Agincourt see, for example, Link 2 for this chapter at www.VeritasPress.com/OmniLinks. On medieval warfare in general, see Link 3.

Richard III

If a sentence were a hamburger, then what would the meat be? Is the meat the "meaning" of the sentence? And are decorative embellishments like the condiments? Are style and rhetoric *optional?* How many things can we take away and still have a "hamburger"? And is a sentence like a hamburger at all?

Rhetoric, the study of how to communicate persuasively in speech and writing, is an ancient art. It was one of the main courses of study in ancient schools, along with grammar and logic. During the days of the Roman Empire, learning rhetoric was a path to power and prestige. Augustine, the great church father of North Africa, was trained as a rhetorician and was climbing the ladder of Roman society when God called him to a very different sort of speech-making in the pulpit at Hippo.

According to the Roman author Quintilian, rhetoric is "the good man speaking well." For Romans like Cicero, skill in speaking and persuading was essential to the life of a political leader. As Cicero writes in his treatise *On Invention,* "There is a scientific system of politics which includes many important departments. One of these departments—a large and important one—is eloquence based on the rules of art, which they call rhetoric . . .. Therefore we will classify oratorical ability as a part of political science."

Not everyone in the ancient world was a fan of rhetoric. In Plato's dialogue *Gorgias,* Socrates challenges the Sophists of Athens, who emphasized rhetorical ability, arguing that rhetoric could be used by ignorant people. Plato thinks rhetoric, the art of speaking and being persuasive, is very different from philosophy, the pure and unadorned search for Truth. In the modern world, the suspicions about rhetoric have become even more pronounced. In his *Essay Concerning Human Understanding* (1689), one of the most important books of the early modern period, John Locke argues that rhetoric is nothing more than a way to prettify falsehoods: "if we would speak of Things as they are, we must allow, that all the Art of Rhetorick, besides Order and Clearness, all the artificial and figurative application of Words Eloquence hath invented, are for nothing else but to insinuate wrong *Ideas*, move the Passions, and thereby mislead the Judgment; and so indeed are perfect cheats." For Plato and Locke, rhetoric is the condiment on the burger that makes the meat taste better. Philosophers don't care for spices. They want to be fed. They want just the meat itself. Hold the mustard.

Today, many writers tell us that we live in a "postmodern" era. One of the clearest signs of this new period of thinking is the revival of rhetoric. Many people today still hold to something like Locke's

Maybe a sentence *could* be a burger, but what if a burger was a king? Would the lying Richard III be a Whopper and Henry VII be a Big Mac? And if Henry VII was a Big Mac, what would that make Henry VIII?

or Plato's suspicions about rhetoric, but "postmodern" thinkers say that we can't help but use rhetoric. When they say this, they have a couple of things in mind. First, they say we use rhetoric because we are always using literary devices like metaphors, similes and comparisons. Locke says that rhetoric "misleads the Judgment," but of course rhetoric is not an incompetent guide dog that leads us down a wrong path. It doesn't *really* lead anything at all. Locke's statement assumes a metaphor, a comparison in which words are like Daniel Boone, leading people down a trail toward their goal. For postmoderns, we always want the meat to have *some* flavor. We may not put spices on our food, but when we don't, it's because we want the food to have a particular flavor, a "natural" flavor. Philosophers speak and write in pictures just like everyone else. They just pretend not to.

Second, we are always using rhetoric because every time we open our mouths we are trying to convince someone of something. We may avoid using rhetorical tricks; but a speech without rhetorical trickery is trying to persuade by avoiding trickery. Take Locke's argument against rhetoric above. He is trying to *persuade* his readers that he is right, and he does this by calling rhetoric an "artificial" way of speaking that "misleads" into something "wrong." Who wants something "artificial" when you can have something "natural"? Rhetoricians don't lie outright, but they "insinuate," a word that implies cunning and trickery. Locke uses rhetoric to attack rhetoric. He chooses words that make rhetoric sound cheap (artificial) and even dangerous. It's impossible to do otherwise. The alternative would be for Locke to present an argument *without* making any effort to persuade. Locke could argue against rhetoric by using words that made rhetoric seem cuddly and warm, but that wouldn't persuade anyone. If Locke did this, there would be no point in arguing in the first place.

Oddly, the postmodern thinkers who say that we can't avoid using rhetoric also accept much of Plato's and Locke's negative pictures of rhetoric. They often say that rhetoric is an act of violence. They assume that people should be completely free to determine for themselves what they think is true or false, good or bad. Everyone should be free to make up his own mind about whether abortion is good or evil. If a prolifer tries to *persuade* someone to defend unborn babies, he's attacking that person's freedom, his ability to make his mind up for himself. Rhetoric is unavoidable, but all rhetoric, all attempts at persuasion, are acts of violence They are all attempts to control another person. All rhetoric is tyranny, but we cannot escape this tyranny. We just have to live with it. Violence and tyranny are bad, but unfortunately they are the only game in town.

Christians should be aware that our language is full of pictures, metaphors and similes. We shouldn't pretend that it's not. God is the world's best poet and storyteller, and the Bible is one of the great books of story and poetry. But Christians have to reject the postmodern view that all rhetoric is violence or tyranny. God speaks to us in rhetorical forms, seeking to persuade us, but He doesn't persuade us by being a tyrant. When we are persuaded by the Word of God, we are truly free. God brings a new game to town—a game of loving persuasion that liberates rather than enslaves.

Like many of Shakespeare's political plays, *Richard III* shows how rhetoric can be used for political purposes, often for *evil* political purposes. Richard III is a king who uses rhetoric to gain power and then begins to exercise tyrannical power over England. For Richard III, rhetoric is all tied up with violence and tyranny. But that is not the only game in town. There is also the rhetoric of divine judgment, of prophecy. Richard is a tyrant, but by the end of the play, tyranny is ended. If Shakespeare does not directly or finally resolve the postmodern dilemma concerning rhetoric, he provides in *Richard III* a laboratory where we can test and explore the relations of rhetoric, violence and tyranny.

General Information

Author and Context

Richard III became king at the end of the Wars of the Roses, and the origins of this series of civil wars go back to the reign of Richard II. Henry Bolingbroke overthrew Richard II, grandson of King Edward III, and reigned as King Henry IV. He was followed by Henry V, who was, in turn, succeeded by his son, Henry VI (for more, see the essay on *Henry V* in this volume). Henry VI (reigned 1422–1461; 1470–1471) was crowned king as an infant, but even when he grew up he was an ineffectual ruler. Early in his reign, the policies of the Royal Protector, Somerset, led to the loss of most of England's French holdings

This engraving of the bard is from the cover of a 1623 collection titled *Mr. William Shakespeares Comedies, Histories, & Tragedies. Published according to the True Originall Copies.*

which were won during the wars of Henry V. Because of the way Henry IV had become king, his line had always been suspect. Shakespeare depicts Henry VI as a good king—genuinely pious and just. For many English noblemen, however, his reign was a disaster. During the last decades of his reign, another line of the family of Edward III, led initially by Richard, Duke of York, pressed its case for the throne of England. The family and followers of Richard were known as the "Yorkists," while the followers of Henry VI were known as the "Lancastrians." The Yorkists were represented by the White Rose, the Lancastrians by the Red.[1]

Intermittent war began in 1455, and Edward IV, son of Richard of York, took the throne in 1461 after a victory over the Lancastrians at Mortimer Cross. The Lancastrians did not give up, and Edward was forced to flee England in 1470. During the next year, Henry VI returned to the throne, after having spent the previous decade languishing in the Tower of London as Edward's prisoner. Edward returned in 1471, defeated the Lancastrians at Tewkesbury and executed Henry VI. Edward returned to the throne. All this has already happened when Shakespeare's play opens.

It appeared that the civil war was over, and Edward set out to reform the royal finances and establish firmer control over Wales and Scotland. But Edward also gained the reputation for gluttony and lust, and created strife within his own family by marrying the widow Elizabeth Woodville. Her family was already of noble status, but Elizabeth's elevation to queen encouraged the Woodvilles' ambitions. Besides, the Woodvilles had previously supported the Lancastrian side during the Wars of the Roses. Edward's brothers, Richard, Duke of Gloucester (later Richard III), and George, Duke of Clarence ("Clarence" in Shakespeare's play), nurtured a settled hostility to Elizabeth's family. Richard was convinced, for instance, that the Woodvilles were behind Clarence's execution in February 1478.

Edward IV died in April 1483, and a few days later his son was proclaimed King Edward V, though he was not publicly crowned. In June of the same year, Richard Gloucester, who had served as Protector for the young prince, became king, with his wife Anne taking her role as queen. According to the legend, Richard had long been aiming to take the throne from his brother or after his brother and between April and June of 1483 systematically eliminated all rivals. It is true that Richard plotted and murdered his way to the throne, spreading rumors about Edward's children. It is also true that Richard usurped the throne. But it is doubtful that he was as monstrous as Shakespeare makes him out to be. Peter Saccio suggests that he was governed more by fear of conspiracy from Elizabeth Woodville's relatives, who had been joined by some of Richard's former allies.[2] Whatever his long-term designs, Richard did take the throne, and Edward V and his brother Richard were mysteriously murdered in the Tower of London. Shakespeare's play focuses largely on this period in 1483, when Richard plotted to take the throne from his young nephew. Once on the throne, Richard reigned for less than two years before being defeated by Henry Tudor, later Henry VII, at the battle of Bosworth Field in 1485.

Shakespeare always takes liberties with historical facts, but with *Richard III* the gap between drama and history is wider than usual. Contrary to Shakespeare's portrayal, Richard was probably not a hunchback or physically deformed in any way; he did not seduce Lady Anne in the presence of her father-in-law's corpse, as is depicted in 1.2; he did not have his brother Clarence murdered, but instead pled for the king to spare him; his real hostilities were directed against Edward's queen Elizabeth and her family (see 1.3), not against Edward himself. Shakespeare did not invent the legend of the monstrous Richard. He found it all in his main source for English history, the *Chronicles* of Raphael Holinshed, and Holinshed drew his portrait of Richard directly from Sir Thomas More's *History of King Richard III* (1557; an excerpt from More's work is cited in the study guides below). But Shakespeare makes this legend of Richard popular.

Significance

Richard III is the final play in a tetrology, a series of four plays that covers the English civil war known as the Wars of the Roses. The first three plays in the series are the three parts of Henry VI. This tetrology was written before Shakespeare's other English tetrology (*Richard II, Henry IV, Parts 1* and *2*, and *Henry V*), but the events in *Henry VI—Richard III* follow the events of *Richard II—Henry V*. Thus, the actual sequence of kings is: Richard II, Henry IV, Henry V, Henry VI, Edward IV (about whom Shakespeare did not write a play) and Richard III. *Richard III* thus, in a sense, forms the climax of Shakespeare's plays on English history.

Shakespeare wrote *Richard III* in the late 1590s, during the reign of Elizabeth I, the granddaughter of Henry VII. For Shakespeare himself, the play was a turning point in his career, the first of his great tragic plays. Richard himself was the first of Shakespeare's great villains and has become a proverbial murderous tyrant. For Elizabethan audiences, the story of Richard III was fairly recent history, and it was important because it

A description of Henry VII from *The Anglia Historia:* "His body was slender but well built and strong; his height above the average. His appearance was remarkably attractive and his face was cheerful, especially when speaking; his eyes were small and blue, his teeth few, poor and blackish; his hair was thin and white; his complexion sallow."

told the story of the Tudor dynasty of which Elizabeth I was a part. Throughout the centuries, Shakespeare's portrayal has been popularly accepted as historically accurate, despite repeated attempts by historians to defend Richard's reputation. Richard's defenders even have their own "Richard III Society" complete with its own web site.[3] Still, the legend of a monstrous, deformed Richard lingers on. The pen may be mightier than the sword, but poets, it appears, wield mightier pens than historians.

Near the beginning of Al Pacino's 1996 film *Looking for Richard,* Pacino stalks the streets of New York looking for someone who can recall something about the play. He is largely unsuccessful. Despite a few famous moments and lines ("Now is the winter of our discontent"; "My horse! My horse!"), the play is not well known, certainly not as well known as Shakespeare's later great tragedies or many of his comedies. This is partly due to the play's complex political situation and the large cast of characters (see below). Still, the play is a favorite of actors, who can sink their teeth deeply into the complexities of Richard's character. And the play has been a subject of several films. James Keane's 1912 film version is the oldest surviving American feature film. In 1954, Laurence Olivier starred in another film version, and more recently Ian McKellan starred as a modernized fascist Richard III in a significantly edited version of the play.

Main Characters

Next to Hamlet, Richard III is the largest role in Shakespeare. Dominant as he is in the action, however, Richard is surrounded by a large number of other characters. It is difficult to keep track of them all, especially since several have the same name (Edward is the king, he has a son Edward, and Edward was also the name of Henry VI's son; Queen Elizabeth has a daughter named Elizabeth). To make sense of the play, it is important to sit down for a few minutes first to figure out who is who. A helpful reference is the Royal Family Tree, which appears in the chapter on *Henry V.*

The characters can be classified by family connection and by alliances. First, there is the royal family itself. At the beginning of the play, Edward IV is king, with Elizabeth his queen. They have two sons, Edward and Richard. His two brothers, Richard, Duke of Gloucester, and George (known as "Clarence"), are important members of the royal court. His mother, the widow of Richard, Duke of York, is still alive. Queen Elizabeth's family is not strictly part of the royal family but are important noblemen nonetheless. Apart from Elizabeth herself, the most important member of her family is the Earl of Rivers.

Another group of characters comes from a previous generation of the royal family. Queen Margaret, the widow of Henry VI, is still alive in the play and is a ghostly reminder of the unfinished business of the past. Her daughter-in-law, Lady Anne, had been married to Henry VI's son Edward and during the play marries Richard of Gloucester. This group of characters also includes several ghosts—including Henry VI and Prince Edward—who appear to Richard toward the end of the play.

Second, there are groups of characters formed by political alliance rather than blood. "Richmond," the future Henry VII, leads a company of noblemen. Among the nobles allied at one time or another with Richard of Gloucester (Richard III) are Hastings, Lord Stanley, the Earl of Derby (known as "Derby" in the play), Buckingham and Norfolk. Richard also has a company of henchmen at hand to carry out murders and such.

Summary and Setting

The plot of *Richard III* traces Richard's relentless drive to take the throne of England and his elimination of all rivals and obstacles that stand in his way. *Richard III* is off and running from the first scene. The play begins with a long speech from Richard directed to the audience, where he reveals his intention to set his brother, the king, against his brother, the Duke of Clarence, in order to gain the crown. He woos Lady Anne, the widow of Edward Prince of Wales, whom Richard has had killed, but Queen Margaret, Henry VI's widow, shows up to curse the king, Richard, and Queen Elizabeth. Two of Richard's brutal assistants kill Clarence and then dump the corpse in a barrel of wine in the Tower of London. Richard has eliminated one rival, and he is ready to strike as soon as Edward IV is out of the way.

During a conference where Edward is attempting to establish peace between various nobles, Richard appears to inform everyone that Clarence is dead.

Soon after, Edward himself dies of natural causes, and Richard takes over the role of "Protector," caring for Edward's sons and basically running the government. When Edward's son, Prince Edward, arrives in London, he is sent to the Tower, along with his brother, Richard. Meanwhile, Richard turns against his former ally Hastings, accusing him of treason and sending him away to be beheaded. To neutralize the power of Edward's sons, Richard starts a rumor that they are bastards and plots to eliminate Clarence's children as well. Without legitimate heirs to the throne, Richard accepts the crown. One of his first acts as king is to send Tyrrel to kill the princes in the tower.

Knowing they are ruled by a butcher, the Bishop of Ely joins with Buckingham and Henry of Richmond (the future Henry VII) to mount an attack on Richard and remove him from the throne. Richard has Buckingham executed. As he sleeps on the night before joining battle with Richmond, Richard dreams that he sees a parade of his victims tormenting him. The same ghosts visit Richmond and offer him encouragement. At Bosworth Field, the two armies meet, and Richard puts up a tremendous fight. At the last, however, he is defeated and ends the play screaming pathetically for help: "A horse! A horse! My kingdom for a horse!" The play ends with Richmond's coronation as Henry VII and the end of England's bloody period of civil war.

Worldview

For Shakespeare, as for many writers since Plato, political order is closely related to the order of the soul. A man who cannot govern his own desires and hungers cannot govern a kingdom well. In order to rule well, a king must seek the interests of his nation above his own interests, and that means he has to "deny himself," as Jesus taught. Henry VI was such a king, at least in Shakespeare's depiction. Shakespeare scholar Harold Goddard has observed that Henry VI is the most neglected of Shakespeare's kings, yet he was among the best: "Henry was a simple and sincere, a morally courageous and genuinely religious man and king. He is the only one of Shakespeare's kings whose public and private personalities are identical."[4]

Richard III appears (as Richard Gloucester) in the plays about Henry VI. By the end of the *Henry VI* trilogy, it is clear that Richard is a very different sort of man than Henry. As is clear from a long soliloquy in Act 3, Richard is greedy for the throne, ambitious, relentless and unscrupulous (3.2). Richard's character is all here: his physical deformities, which prevent him from pursuing the ladies; his ambition for the crown; his ability to change shape and color as necessary to suit his purposes; his willingness to hack away anyone who stands between him and the achievement of his desires. He is clearly a man without any restraint of appetite. His soul is in chaos, and he is going to create chaos in England as well. He does not govern his soul; he will not govern a country either.

This is the Richard who opens the play bearing his name. The themes of Shakespeare's *Richard III* are nicely captured by a comparison of speeches at the beginning and end of the play. Unusually for Shakespeare, the title character is onstage at the beginning of the play and introduces himself before any other characters comment on him or the events (1.1). In the 1995 film production of *Richard III* starring Ian McKellan (who also played "Gandalf" in Peter Jackson's film version of *The Lord of the Rings*) in the title role, the first lines of this speech are spoken before nobles gathered to celebrate the accession of Edward IV to the throne following the death of Henry VI. The lines work wonderfully as a political speech. Like Claudius's speech at the beginning of *Hamlet,* it expresses the feeling of relieved endurance, the sense of "bruised but unbowed" that comes at the end of a long contest or battle. War has packed up the trumpets and taken up the lute; he has put his steeds to pasture and is instead chasing a lady around her chamber.

The speech is well-designed for public consumption, showing Richard to be as slick a political operator as any politician of the "information age." His first lines express the change of political climate in terms of a change of seasons: the "winter of our discontent" is turned into "glorious summer" because Edward has taken the throne. But we know from the remainder of the speech that Richard himself doesn't know how to stop fighting, as even War himself does. He cannot hope "to strut before a wanton ambling nymph" since he is a disfigured hunchback with a withered arm and bad teeth. Now that the war is over, he will have to content himself with "plots" and "inductions dangerous," by which he will "set my brother Clarence and the king/ In deadly hate the one against the other." He cannot rest from war. If he cannot fight on the battlefield he will set land mines all around Edward's court and wait for the explosions. In the light of the remainder of the speech, the first line takes on a different color. It appears to stand alone, implying that Richard considers Edward IV's reign to be the "winter of our discontent." Surely, Richard himself is discontented because his brother reigns and he doesn't. And he means to be content.

In Shakespeare's stage version, however, Richard enters the stage and delivers this speech *"solus,"* alone. Still, Richard has an audience, the actual theater audience watching the play. To the characters in the play itself, this speech is private. Even in this setting, Richard is revealed as a character with a gift for rhetoric. He is attempting to win over the theater audience with his honesty about his villainy, his devilishly clever plots against his brother and the king, his ability to act a part. This self-revealing speech at the beginning of the play sets our expectations for the remainder of the production, and we expect Richard to be a bad guy who is very good at being bad and very good at pretending to be good. He wants to make us enjoy watching him being bad; and he succeeds.

Winter is the season mentioned at the beginning of the play. Summer is the season invoked at the end. At the beginning of Act 5, Richmond, the future Henry VII, first appears in the play. He encourages his followers, who have suffered under Richard's murderous tyranny, with promises of new life. Richard thought of Edward's reign as a "winter," but his own reign was the one that brought a chill to England. Richmond, however, actually does bring a promise of renewal, of order, of prosperity, of "summer fields and fruitful vines." In the closing speech of the play, Richmond describes the renewal of England after the horrible butchery of the Wars of the Roses (5.5). Again, Richmond speaks of prosperity and happiness, a union of the divided houses of York and Lancaster, smiling, fair prosperous days. After the sacrificial division of England, she will be raised again and reunited. The overall arc of the play, then, is from winter to summer, from division to reunion, from butchery to resurrection. Richmond comes, according to Marjorie Garber, as "a Christian ruler

In *Richard III* the Duke of Gloucester has Edward V and his younger brother Richard placed in the Tower of London to "protect" them. After getting the crown, Richard decides that he must kill the young princes, and most historians believe he probably did order their deaths. In 1674 workmen remodelling the Tower dug up a box containing two small human skeletons. These bones were later put in an urn and interred in Westminster Abbey, as they were thought to belong to the two princes.

CATESBY: . . . *His horse is slain, and all on foot he fights,*
Seeking for Richmond in the throat of death.
Rescue, fair lord, or else the day is lost!
KING RICHARD: *A horse! a horse! my kingdom for a horse!*

In the 1995 film *Richard III* adaptated by and starring Sir Ian McKellen the action transpires in a 1930s fascist version of England. Famous buildings are relocated and their uses reassigned in this imaginary Britain, and the play's famous line—"My kingdom for a horse!" gets a whole new twist when Richard's jeep is stuck in the mud during the final battle and he calls for any transportation—*even a horse.*

who defeats . . . the energetic anarchy of Antichrist, the devil Richard."[5] Under Richard, the chaos of the king's soul stretches out to encompass the whole land; under Richmond, order is restored.

But the arc of the story is different for Richard himself. He proves himself a superior rhetorician, stage director and actor throughout the early parts of the play. Richard's gift for persuasion is stunningly successful in his seduction of Lady Anne, the widow of Edward the Prince of Wales, whom Richard has murdered (1.2). He proves to be good even at a role that he claims he is ill-suited to play—the role of lover (1.1). He is much more suited to play the role of Vice and to play it effectively (3.1). Morality plays in the Middle Ages often included an allegorical character known as "Vice," a semi-comic villain, often the Devil's assistant, who takes delight in causing disorder just because he likes disorder. Richard has the same childlike delight in chaos. Other characters are more direct; they don't see Richard as the Devil's assistant, but as the Devil himself. Various characters describe him as a "fiend," a "devil" and a "hell-hound."

His favorite pose, however, is that of a simple, straightforward, honest, childishly innocent man. Like the philosophical heirs of Plato, he uses his rhetoric to pretend that he is not using rhetoric. As Garber points out, he likes to disguise himself as a man incapable of wearing disguises. One of his favorite tricks is to describe himself as an innocent "child," too soft to handle the challenges of politics (1.3). Garber recognizes that there are biblical themes in the background:

> When Buckingham urges him to go after the young Princes and separate them from the

> Queen's relations, Richard replies, 'I, as a child/ Will go by thy direction.' His is a malign parody of the biblical injunction 'and a little child shall lead them' (Isaiah 11:6), as well as of the instruction of Jesus: 'Suffer the little children to come unto me, and forbid them not: for of such is the kingdom of God.' But Richard is not Christ but Antichrist[6]

Richard *pretends* to be an innocent child. He is a *Herod*, murdering innocent children. There is a lesson in this: beware of anyone who insists on telling you how open, honest and straightforward they are. They are not any of these things, and they are wanting to sell you something that's not worth a fraction of what they are asking.

Richard even uses his deformity and ugliness to good advantage. Sigmund Freud, the founder of psychoanalysis, saw in Richard a universal human impulse to compensate for early slights and disadvantages: "Richard is an enormous magnification of something we find in ourselves as well. We all think we have reason to reproach Nature and our destiny for congenital and infantile disadvantages; we all demand reparation for early wounds." But, as Garber shrewdly points out, while this is Richard's claim, he really is using his "congenital disadvantages" to his own advantage. She adds, "for Shakespeare's Richard self-pity is only a tool, a guise, and a ploy."[7] He is the first professional victim, using his deformities to worm his way to power.

The audience knows from the first scene that Richard is playing a part and directing the action for his own benefit. We know that he is not what he seems. But many of the characters in the play are not aware of his chicanery—at least not at first. Some characters, such as Queen Margaret, know that he's a "devil" and a "fiend" from the beginning. As the play goes on, other characters become increasingly aware of what Richard is doing. They begin to see through the mask of innocence and recognize the villain underneath. His rhetorical mask starts slipping off. This is evident in the language that Shakespeare gives him. At the beginning of the play, Richard is poetic and witty, but once he has become king his jokes are tired and strained, and he becomes less poetic. His imagination has been focused too long on his plots and inductions, and it begins to dry up.

Other characters see the change. While Richard was stunningly successful in wooing Lady Anne, his later attempt to arrange for his marriage to Princess Elizabeth (daughter of Edward IV) is unsuccessful. Buckingham plays dumb when Richard, now crowned, hints that the king's son, "young Edward," is a threat that must be removed (4.2). As Garber says, "The play is not proceeding as King Richard intends, and Buckingham refuses to take direction."[8] Richard's ability to rule by rhetoric and theatrical skill has declined significantly. This is in part because Richard's reign, like Macbeth's, leads his nation into a period of chaos and disorder. As always in Shakespeare, the reign of a villain upsets both natural and social order. As Richard contemplates what to do with the princes, sons of the dead king, he turns to his page for advice. Garber points out the double irony of this situation: "a child advises a king, and aids in the assassination of children."[9] Like Macbeth, Richard wades so far into blood that there is no turning back.

The most telling sign of disorder is the collapse of language, the failure of Richard's rhetorical strategies. Richard is confused (4.4) and eventually declines into nonsensical babbling (5.5). As he dreams of a progression of the ghosts of those he has murdered, Richard suddenly starts from his slumber and jabbers out a choppy speech (5.3). Lacking any supporters, he is reduced to self-love: Richard loves Richard, a godlike isolation that is underscored by his repeated uses of the biblical name for God, "I am." But his isolation has not brought unity or peace to his soul. His isolation splits him into two, into the murderer that he wants to escape and the fearful child who wants to escape.

It is difficult to imagine two speeches more different than Richard's opening lines and this late soliloquy. The assured, self-conscious villain of Act 1 has turned a scared rabbit, frightened now of himself. At the beginning, he was in control, stage-managing plots and inductions dangerous for his own purposes. He has realized through the course of the play that he is not in control. When ghosts start appearing, Richard learns that there's more in heaven and earth than he realized. There are powers greater than his political manipulations.

From early in the play, it is clear that Richard is eventually going to fall into the holes he is digging for

The Duke of Clarence had plotted against his brother Edward IV and was imprisoned in the Tower of London for his treason. He was executed February 18, 1478, and tradition has it that he was drowned in a butt of Malmsey wine as in *Richard III*. Though this story may have started as a joke due to the duke's reputation as a heavy drinker, the fumes from an open butt could knock a man unconscious, and at almost ninety gallons, a butt is large enough to drown in.

others. High above all the plotting and cunning that Richard can muster is a deeper cunning and a larger plot, and in this plot of divine vengeance Richard is destined for destruction. When Richard's murderers come to kill his brother Clarence, Clarence reminds them that "the great King of kings/ Hath in the table of his law commanded/ That thou shalt do no murder" (1.4) and warns them that God will avenge him. The citizens discussing the effects of Richard's reign decide to "leave it all to God" (2.3).

The most dramatic statement about God's justice and vengeance comes from Queen Margaret, the widow of Henry VI, who pronounces curses against Queen Elizabeth and Richard (1.3) that essentially lay out the plot of the whole play. As a representative of the older, departing generation, Margaret's role is similar to that of the ghost of King Hamlet, a reminder that the crimes of the past have not been sorted out. Margaret is a prophetess, as a number of the characters recognize (3.3; 5.1.), and her premonitions are buttressed by various omens, dreams and portents throughout the play. Clarence dreams of drowning after Richard knocks him from a ship; Stanley dreams that a boar—Richard's sign—will attack. Omens are ignored, with predictable consequences. As Garber points out, "The cadences of Margaret's language deliberately recall the biblical rhythms of *lex talionis*, the law of retaliation . . .. Margaret's sonorous demand, 'Edward thy son, that now is Prince of Wales, For Edward my son, that was Prince of Wales,' emphasizes the degree of similarity and repetition involved in this conflict between Lancaster and York"[10] Richard may attempt to escape the consequences of his actions, may attempt to cover his tracks with yet another murder, yet another plot, but there is something beyond Richard's power controlling the course of events. Call it Fortune. Call it Justice. Call it God. It is the "more" that Richard failed to reckon with.

Richard is skillful in using rhetoric to manipulate and to create chaos that he later pretends to fix. He uses rhetoric to advance his tyranny. His murders are just an extension of the way he talks. But the play makes clear that the violent rhetoric of Richard does not have the last word. There is a God in heaven distributing rewards and punishments, doing justice. Those who seek to trap with false rhetoric will eventually find themselves in those very traps.

—Peter J. Leithart

For Further Reading

Garber, Marjorie. *Shakespeare After All.* New York: Pantheon, 2004. 131–159.

Goddard, Harold. *The Meaning of Shakespeare.* Chicago: University of Chicago Press, 1951. Vol. 1, 35–40.

Saccio, Peter. *Shakespeare's English Kings.* Oxford: Oxford University Press, 1977.

Session I: Prelude

A Question To Consider

What is rhetoric? Is rhetoric good or bad?

From the General Information above answer the following questions:

1. Summarize the background to the Wars of the Roses.
2. Is Shakespeare's portrayal of Richard III historically accurate? Where did he get his information?
3. What is Richard's opening speech about?
4. How does Richmond's speech at the end of the play relate to Richard's at the beginning?
5. What is Richard's state of mind at the end of the play? How can you tell?
6. What are the signs that Richard's kingdom is falling apart?
7. Why is Queen Margaret important in the play?

Reading Assignment:
Act 1

Session II: Discussion

Act 1

A Question to Consider

What is the point of rhetoric in political life? Should politicians aim at "rhetoric" or at "substance"?

Discuss or list short answers to the following questions:

Text Analysis

1. What is Richard trying to convince the audience of in his opening speech?
2. How does Richard use language to persuade the audience to take his side?
3. Why does Edward want to imprison and kill Clarence?
4. Whom does Richard blame for Clarence's troubles?
5. How does he use language to convince Lady Anne to marry him?
6. How does Queen Margaret's manner of speech differ from Richard's?
7. Describe Clarence's dream. What does it have to do with the plot?
8. How does Clarence attempt to persuade the murderers not to kill him?

Culture Analysis

1. Analyze the following statement, which appeared in a letter to the editor of the *Chicago Tribune:* "Impoverished students deserve solutions, not rhetoric."
2. The late French philosopher Jacques Derrida writes this: "Rhetoric, as such, depends on conditions that are not rhetorical. In rhetoric and speaking, the same sentence may have enormous effects or have no effects at all, depending on conditions that are not verbal or rhetorical. I think a self-conscious, trained teacher of rhetoric should teach precisely what are called 'pragmatics'; that is, the effects of rhetoric don't depend only on the way you utter words, the way you use tropes, the way you compose. They depend on certain situations: political situations, economical situations" ("On Rhetoric and Composition: A Conversation" [1990]). What does Derrida mean? Is this true? How can this statement be applied to *Richard III*?
3. In Plato's dialogue, *Gorgias,* Socrates argues with Gorgias about rhetoric. Toward the end of the dialogue, Socrates concludes, "The rhetorician need not know the truth about things; he has only to discover some way of persuading the ignorant that he has more knowledge than those who know," and "In my opinion, then, Gorgias, it [i.e., rhetoric] is a certain pursuit that is not artful but belongs to a soul that is skilled at guessing, courageous, and terribly clever by nature at associating with human beings; and I call its chief point flattery." What does Socrates mean? Do you agree?

Biblical Analysis

1. In 1 Corinthians 2:4, Paul writes that "my speech and my preaching were not with persuasive words of human wisdom, but in demonstration of the Spirit and of power." Is Paul rejecting rhetoric?
2. Look up Exodus 4:10 and Jeremiah 1:6. What do these passages teach about the persuasive power of words? How do these passages illumine issues concerning rhetoric?

3. What relevance do Psalm 19 and John 1:1–14 have for our understanding of rhetoric?

SUMMA

Write an essay or discuss this question, integrating what you have learned from the material above. What is the biblical view of rhetoric?

READING ASSIGNMENT:
Acts 2–3

SESSION III: DISCUSSION

Acts 2–3

A Question to Consider:

What is tyranny? How should we respond to tyranny?

Discuss or list short answers to the following questions:

Text Analysis

1. What is Edward attempting to do at the beginning of Act 2? What does this say about Edward's qualities as a king?
2. Why are Queen Elizabeth and the Duchess of York so distraught when the king dies?
3. What are the three citizens discussing in Act 2, scene 3?
4. How does Richard treat the young Prince Edward? Why?
5. What does Richard do with Hastings? Why?
6. How does Richard react when Buckingham insists that he take the crown? Why?

Culture Analysis

1. In his *Second Treatise on Civil Government,* John Locke defines tyranny as follows: "As usurpation is the exercise of power, which another hath a right to; so tyranny is the exercise of power beyond right, which no body can have a right to. And this is making use of the power any one has in his hands, not for the good of those who are under it, but for his own private separate advantage. When the governor, however entitled, makes not the law, but his will, the rule; and his commands and actions are not directed to the preservation of the properties of his people, but the satisfaction of his own ambition, revenge, covetousness, or any other irregular passion" (chap. 18). Explain this definition of tyranny in your own words. Give some examples of tyranny in the world today—whether in political life, in the church or in other areas.
2. The American War for Independence was a response to the tyranny of the English king, but some Americans after the war feared that Ameri-

Shakespeare's play casts Richard III in the role of one of history's most evil villains—a characterization that is quite understandable when one realizes that Elizabeth was a descendant of the Earl of Richmond, who defeated Richard and started the Tudor dynasty.

cans would become tyrants of each other. On November 22, 1787, the *New York Journal* printed an anti-Federalist article by a writer known as "Cato." The writer criticized the new Federal Constitution under consideration by the Constitutional Convention. He wrote, "It is a duty you owe likewise to your own reputation, for you have a great name to lose; you are characterized as cautious, prudent and jealous in politics; whence is it therefore, that you are about to precipitate yourselves into a sea of uncertainty, and adopt a system so vague, and which has discarded so many of your valuable rights. Is it because you do not believe that an American can be a tyrant? If this be the case you rest on a weak basis; Americans are like other men in similar situations, when the manners and opinions of the community are changed by the causes I mentioned before, and your political compact inexplicit, your posterity will find that great power connected with ambition, luxury, and flattery, will as readily produce a Caesar, Caligula, Nero, and Domitian in America, as the same causes did in the Roman empire." What is his argument about tyranny? Was he right about the danger of tyranny?

Biblical Analysis

1. Examine Romans 13:1–7. What powers do political rulers have? Is there any limit on those powers? Look also at Psalm 2.
2. Proverbs contains many statements about the relationship between tyranny and personal lack of self restraint. According to 16:32, 25:28 and 11:10–11, what is that relationship?

Summa

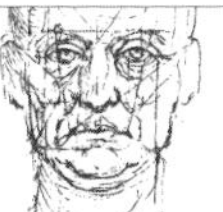

Write an essay or discuss this question, integrating what you have learned from the material above.

What is the root of tyranny? How does *Richard III* illustrate this?

Reading Assignment:

Acts 4–5

Session IV: Recitation

Acts 4–5

Comprehension Questions

Answer the following questions for factual recall:

1. What do the murderers do with Clarence's body after they kill him?
2. Who is the Duchess of York? What is her relationship to Richard?
3. Richard claims to be under attack by sorcery. From whom?
4. Who kills the princes in the tower?
5. Whom does Richard want to marry in Act 4? Why?
6. Whose ghosts appear to Richard during the night?
7. What are Richard's final lines in the play?

Session V: Activity

Option 1

Memorize one of the famous speeches of the play, such as the opening soliloquy by Richard; deliver your speech before your classmates in a speech contest or before your family.

Now is the winter of our discontent
Made glorious summer by this sun of York;
And all the clouds that lour'd upon our house
In the deep bosom of the ocean buried.
Now are our brows bound with victorious
wreaths;
Our bruised arms hung up for monuments;
Our stern alarums changed to merry meetings,
Our dreadful marches to delightful measures.
Grim-visaged war hath smooth'd his wrinkled
front;
And now, instead of mounting barded steeds
To fright the souls of fearful adversaries,
He capers nimbly in a lady's chamber
To the lascivious pleasing of a lute.
But I, that am not shaped for sportive tricks,
Nor made to court an amorous looking-glass;
I, that am rudely stamp'd, and want love's majesty
To strut before a wanton ambling nymph;
I, that am curtail'd of this fair proportion,
Cheated of feature by dissembling nature,

Deformed, unfinish'd, sent before my time
Into this breathing world, scarce half made up,
And that so lamely and unfashionable
That dogs bark at me as I halt by them;
Why, I, in this weak piping time of peace,
Have no delight to pass away the time,
Unless to spy my shadow in the sun
And descant on mine own deformity:
And therefore, since I cannot prove a lover,
To entertain these fair well-spoken days,
I am determined to prove a villain
And hate the idle pleasures of these days.
Plots have I laid, inductions dangerous,
By drunken prophecies, libels and dreams,
To set my brother Clarence and the king
In deadly hate the one against the other:
And if King Edward be as true and just
As I am subtle, false and treacherous,
This day should Clarence closely be mew'd up,
About a prophecy, which says that 'G'
Of Edward's heirs the murderer shall be.
Dive, thoughts, down to my soul: here
Clarence comes.

Option 2

Prepare a scene from the play, either as a readers' theater or as a production of the scene.

Option 3

Thomas More wrote a history of Richard III.[11] Read the following excerpt and answer the questions:

> "Richarde the third sonne, of whom we nowe entreate, was in witte and courage egall with either of them, in bodye and prowesse farre vnder them bot, little of stature, ill fetured of limmes, croke backed, his left shoulder much higher then his right, hard fauoured of visage, and suche as is in states called warlye, in other menne otherwise, he was malicious, wrathfull, enuious, and from afore his birth, euer frowarde. It is for trouth reported, that the Duches his mother had so muche a doe in her travaile, that shee coulde not bee deliuered of hym uncutte: and that hee came into the worlde with the feete forwarde, as menne bee borne outwarde, and (as the fame runneth) also not vntothed, whither menne of hatred reporte aboue the trouthe, or elles that nature chaunged her course in hys beginninge, whiche in the course of his lyfe many thinges vnnaturallye committed. None euill captaine was hee in the warre, as to whiche his disposicion was more metely then for peace. Sundrye victories hadde hee, and sommetime ouerthrowes, but neuer in defaulte as for his owne parsone, either of hardinesse or polytike order, free was he called of dyspence, and sommewhat aboue hys power liberall, with large giftes hee get him vnstedfaste frendshippe, for whiche hee was fain to pil and spoyle in other places, and get him stedfast hatred. Hee was close and secrete, a deepe dissimuler, lowlye, of counteynaunce, arrogant of heart, outwardly coumpinable where he inwardely hated, not letting to kisse whome hee thoughte to kyll: dispitious and cruell, not for euill will alway, but after for ambicion, and either for the suretie or encrease of his estate. Frende and foo was muche what indifferent, where his advauntage grew, he spared no man deathe, whose life withstoode his purpose. He slewe with his owne handes king Henry the sixt, being prisoner in the Tower, as menne constantly saye, and that without commaundemente or knoweledge of the king, whiche woulde vndoubtedly yf he had entended that thinge, haue appointed that boocherly office, to some other than his owne borne brother."
>
> Richard the III son, of whom we now entreat, was in wit and courage equal with either of them in body and prowess far under both, little of stature, ill featured of visage, and such as in states called warlye, in other men otherwise, he was malicious, wrathful, envious, and from afore his birth, ever froward. It is for truth reported, that the Duchess his mother had so much ado in her trivale, that she could not be deliveded of him uncut: and that he came into the world wit the feet forward, as men of hatred report about the truth, of else that nature changed he course in his beginning, which in the course of his life

many things unnaturally committed. None evil captain was he in the war, as to which his disposition was more metely then for peace. Sundry victories had he, and sometimes overthrows but never in default as for his own person, either of hardiness or politic order, free was he called of dispence and somewhat about his power liberal, with large gifts he get him steadfast hatred. He was close and secret, a deep dissimilar, lowly, of countenance, arrogant of heart, outwardly compinable where he was inwardly hated, not letting to kiss whom he thought to kill: dispiteous and cruel, not for evil will always, but after for ambition, and either for the surety or increase of his estate. Friend and foe were much what indifferent, where his advantage grew, he spared no man death, whose life withstood his purpose. He slew with his own hands King Henry VI, being prisoner in the Tower [of London] as men constantly say, and that without commandment or knowledge of the king, which would have undoubtedly if he had intended that thing, have appointed boocherly office, to some other than his own brother.

1. Compare More's description of Richard to Shakespeare's.
2. More was a lawyer and author, most famous for his book *Utopia.* He served as Lord Chancellor of England under Henry VIII, but Henry executed him when he refused to agree that the English king was the head of the English church. Why would a man such as More have written this description of Richard?

Session VI: Review or Evaluation

Grammar

Answer each of the following questions in complete sentences. Some answers may be longer than others. (2 points each)

1. How did the Wars of the Rose begin?
2. Why were Elizabethans interested in the story of Richard III?
3. Who is Queen Margaret? What does she say?

THE GLOBE

Shakespeare's plays were performed at other theaters during the his life, but the Globe Theatre was where his best known plays, including *Richard III,* were originally produced. The Globe was built in 1598 on the banks of the Thames river in the "sporting district"—a disreputable region that hosted bear-baiting, cock-fighting and ignominious taverns outside the jurisdiction of London's officials. It burned down in 1613, was reopened in 1614, but then was levelled in 1644 by Cromwell's round heads to construct tenement housing on the site. The exact dimensions of the theater are a source of great speculation, but in Shakespeare's *Henry V* it is called "this wooden O." So it was probably a round—or at least octagonal— building, and many believe it was 100 feet wide and three stories tall. Being an open-air theater, productions at the Globe were given during the mid-afternoon. Unlike productions of Shakespeare's plays today, in the bard's day plays were put on without any background scenery. The rebuilt Globe or, "Shakespeare's Globe Theatre" opened in 1997 and hosts plays every summer.

4. Who were the Woodvilles, and why does Richard hate them?
5. Whom does Richard marry? Why is this surprising?
6. Whom has Clarence killed? Why?
7. What does Richard do to get rid of Edward IV's sons?

Logic

Answer the following questions in complete sentences. Your answer should be a paragraph or so. Answer two of the three questions. (10 points each)

1. How does Richard III use rhetoric to advance his goals? Give two examples.
2. Discuss two events in the play that illustrate Richard's tyranny.
3. In *Henry VI,* Part 3, Richard describes himself as a "chameleon." What does he mean by that? Give two examples that illustrate this quality of his character.

Lateral Thinking

Answer one of the following questions. These questions will require more substantial answers. (16 points each)

1. Compare and contrast the character Richard III with the character Macbeth.
2. Is Richard III more like Julius Caesar or like the conspirators Brutus and Cassius? Explain your answer.

Optional Session: Activity[12]

Looking For Richard

Watch selected portions of Al Pacino's *Looking For Richard.* The film is fascinating. It is not a film of the play as such, but a documentary about a production *of Richard III.*

Endnotes

1 This symbolism is carried on in Lancaster, Pennsylvania (the home of Veritas Press and Veritas Academy) and nearby York, Pennsylvania. These two cities have numerous contests that are still called the War of Roses. So, in one small way the Wars of the Roses continue today.

2 Saccio, Peter. *Shakespeare's English Kings.* Oxford: Oxford University Press, 1977. 169–178.

3 The Richard III Society website can be found at Link 1 for this chapter at www.VeritasPress.com/OmniLinks.

4 Goddard, Harold. *The Meaning of Shakespeare.* Chicago: University of Chicago Press, 1951, vol. 1. 28–32.

5 Garber, Marjorie. *Shakespeare After All.* New York: Pantheon, 2004. 159.

6 Ibid., p. 140.

7 Ibid., p. 137.

8 Ibid., p. 146.

9 Ibid., p. 153.

10 Ibid., pp. 148–149.

11 The full text is available at Link 2 for this chapter at www.VeritasPress.com/OmniLinks.

12 Teachers or parents will want to view the film themselves first, to ensure that it is suitable for the students.

Ephesians

He made known to me the mystery . . . that the Gentiles should be fellow heirs, of the same body . . .

Why do people like to read mysteries? Some enjoy puzzles and like the challenge of figuring out whodunit. Others like the suspense and excitement that comes with not knowing what is going to happen next. Some mystery writers develop habits, so that all their stories are basically the same. "Franklin W. Dixon," the collective name given to the various authors of the Hardy Boys series, was this kind of mystery writer. Anyone who has read more than two Hardy Boys books knows that the stories are similar. It will turn out that Frank and Joe are working on the same case as their father, the famed detective Fenton Hardy; that Chet's most recent hobby will be useful in solving the case; and that the boys will be captured late in the book and the criminals will confess everything just before the boys escape to get help. People read this kind of mystery because it is comfortable and familiar. "There Chet goes again," we think. And we smile. Or puke.

God is the greatest of all mystery writers, writing the greatest of all mysteries. His mystery is not just in a book (though it is); His mystery is worked out in history. That is what Paul is writing about in Ephesians. He uses the word *mystery* six times. At the beginning of the book, he writes that God has "made known to us the mystery of His will" (Eph. 1:9). Paul's work as an apostle is all tied up with the mystery. Through a "revelation," God "made known to me the mystery" (3:3), and he writes so that his readers "may understand my knowledge in the mystery of Christ" (3:4). When Paul preaches about Jesus to the Gentiles, God brings to light *"the fellowship of the mystery, which from the beginning of the ages has been hidden in God who created all things"* (3:9). Paul goes around the Mediterranean, telling people whodunit and why.

Paul says that Christ's relationship to the church is like a husband's relationship to his bride and concludes by saying, *"This is a great mystery, but I speak concerning Christ and the church"* (5:32). Near the end of the book, he urges the Ephesians to pray for him, so that *"utterance may be given to me, that I may open my mouth boldly to make known the mystery of the gospel"* (6:19).

For Paul, a "mystery" is a secret, something hidden. A mystery is something that we cannot speak about in public. When we know a mystery, we have to hold our tongues and be silent. That's how Paul sees the Old Testament—God is telling a story in history, but the real point and direction of the story is still secret. God's secret is a secret only for a time. It won't be a secret forever. The mystery is revealed in Jesus, and the gospel is about the unveiling of this mystery. When Paul preaches the gospel, he is telling the secret things of God, he is uncovering treasures hidden from before the foundations of the world.

What is the mystery that God has kept secret for so long? For starters, it's a big mystery, a mystery that has to do with God's purpose for *"all things . . . which are in heaven and which are on earth"* (1:10). It's a cosmic mystery. The word *cosmic* comes from the Greek word *cosmos,* which means "world." Something is cosmic if it involves the whole creation. God's secret is the secret of the universe.

Paul also says that the mystery has to do with the way God has dealt with Jews and Gentiles. The mystery "in other generations was not made known to the sons of men, as it has now been revealed to His holy apostles and prophets in the Spirit," and he explains that this new revelation is "that the Gentiles are fellow heirs and fellow members of the body, and fellow partakers of the promise in Christ Jesus through the gospel" (3:5-6). The secret is about what God intends to do with the human race, why He chose Israel only to (apparently) reject Israel, what He intends to do with the vast throng of humanity that was not a part of Israel.

Ephesians is one of the greatest summaries of Paul's teaching and preaching. And it is about the greatest mystery story ever.

General Information

Author and Context

Though many writers today do not believe that Paul wrote Ephesians, they are wrong. He did. Paul knew the Ephesian church quite well. He first visited the church during his third missionary journey and spent three years there (Acts 20:31). During his stay, his preaching provoked riots in the city. Demetrius, a silversmith of Ephesus, complained that Paul was attacking the Ephesian goddess Artemis, and Demetrius was able to stir the city into a frenzy (Acts 19:21–41). After the riot, Paul left the city (Acts 20:1), and traveled in Macedonia and Greece. Before heading back to Jerusalem, however, he stopped again in Ephesus to address the elders of the church and say goodbye (Acts 21:17–38).

Paul calls himself the "prisoner of Christ Jesus" (Eph. 3:1), and toward the end of the letter he calls himself "an ambassador in chains" (6:20). Paul thus wrote the letter to the Ephesians during an imprisonment. Paul was imprisoned various times and in various places, so we can't be certain when he wrote the letter or where he was when he wrote it. Marcus Barth writes, "Assuming that Paul was executed in Rome in A.D. 63, after spending two years in a Caesarean prison and two in Rome (partly in prison)—choices for the origins of Ephesians come down to Rome and the years 61–63, or to Caesarea two or three years earlier." Barth thinks that "Rome, about [A.D.] 62, is the best guess for the origin."[1] If Barth is right, then Ephesians was written shortly before Paul's death. He may already have known he was going to die. In Ephesians (along with Colossians and Philippians), we have one of Paul's last statements of his gospel.

Significance

With many of Paul's letters, it is fairly easy to see why Paul wrote the letter. The Corinthian church was divided and full of strife, and Paul wrote to tell them to behave themselves. Galatians was written to win the Galatian Christians back from the Judaizing heresy. Many of Paul's letters are addressed directly to a congregation, and they often deal with specific problems in those congregations (cf. 1–2 Corinthians and Galatians). In those letters, the recipients are mentioned right at the beginning.

But the purpose of Ephesians is not clear from the letter itself, and many of the manuscripts of Ephesians do not contain the phrase "at Ephesus" in 1:1. The letter doesn't seem as personal as some of Paul's other letters. Paul does not greet any members of the Ephesian church (see the greetings in Romans 16), even though Paul had spent years in their city.

This doesn't mean that the letter has no connection to Ephesus. It probably was written to the region of Ephesus, but it wasn't necessarily addressed to the church in Ephesus that Paul knew and worked with. Mark Horne writes, "It is likely then that Ephesians was written to be circularized to the congregations in the region of Ephesus. It is a letter written 'to whom it may concern,' the saints in general whom Paul has never met and whose particular circumstances Paul may be unaware of."[2] As Horne says, "Ephesians is as close as we will come to a theological tract written by Paul. Its form indicates that it is more likely than any-thing else the Apostle has written to be a generic 'Introduction to Pauline Theology' or 'Systematic Theology 101.'" Even more than Romans, which is often taken as a summary of Paul's teaching as a whole, Ephesians is a letter that captures the heart of Paul's beliefs and ministry.

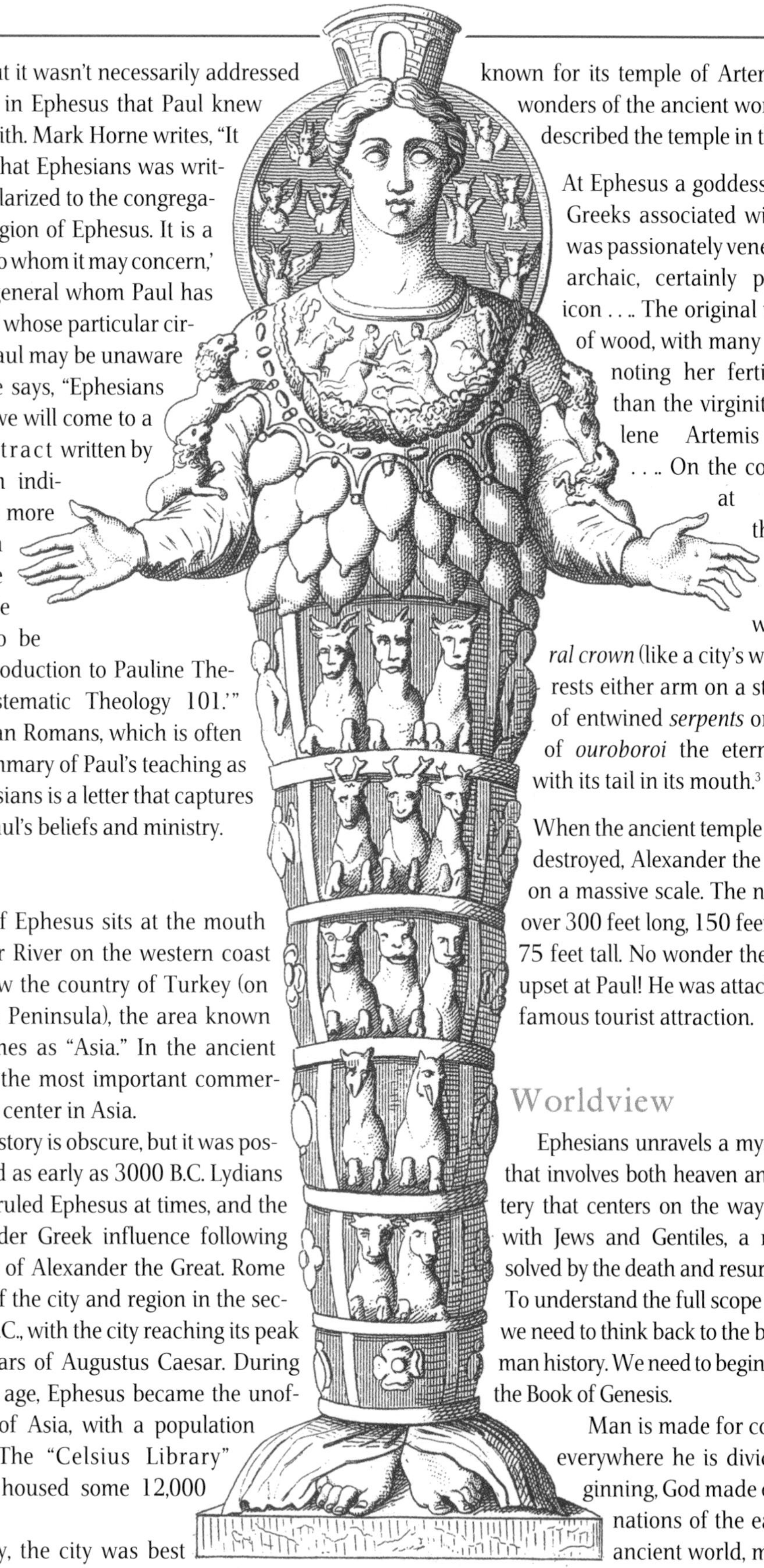

Setting

The city of Ephesus sits at the mouth of the Cayster River on the western coast of what is now the country of Turkey (on the Anatolian Peninsula), the area known in biblical times as "Asia." In the ancient world, it was the most important commercial and trade center in Asia.

Its early history is obscure, but it was possibly inhabited as early as 3000 B.C. Lydians and Persians ruled Ephesus at times, and the city came under Greek influence following the conquests of Alexander the Great. Rome took control of the city and region in the second century B.C., with the city reaching its peak during the years of Augustus Caesar. During the Augustan age, Ephesus became the unofficial capital of Asia, with a population of 225,000. The "Celsius Library" of Ephesus housed some 12,000 scrolls.

Religiously, the city was best known for its temple of Artemis, one of the wonders of the ancient world. One source described the temple in this way:

> At Ephesus a goddess whom the Greeks associated with Artemis was passionately venerated in an archaic, certainly pre-Hellenic icon . . .. The original was carved of wood, with many breasts denoting her fertility, rather than the virginity that Hellene Artemis assumed . . .. On the coins minted at Ephesus, the many-breasted goddess wears a *mural crown* (like a city's walls) . . .. She rests either arm on a staff formed of entwined *serpents* or of a stack of *ouroboroi* the eternal serpent with its tail in its mouth.[3]

When the ancient temple of Artemis was destroyed, Alexander the Great rebuilt it on a massive scale. The new temple was over 300 feet long, 150 feet wide and over 75 feet tall. No wonder the Ephesians got upset at Paul! He was attacking their most famous tourist attraction.

Worldview

Ephesians unravels a mystery, a mystery that involves both heaven and earth, a mystery that centers on the way God has dealt with Jews and Gentiles, a mystery that is solved by the death and resurrection of Jesus. To understand the full scope of that mystery, we need to think back to the beginning of human history. We need to begin, as always, with the Book of Genesis.

Man is made for communion, but everywhere he is divided. In the beginning, God made of one blood all nations of the earth. Yet in the ancient world, men were divided: Greeks despised barbarians and slaves; Romans considered non-Romans to be inferior; men such as Aristotle considered women to be defective and inferior males, and Aristotle believed that some people were naturally slaves. In some ways, racism, hostility to people of different colors and physical features, is a modern development. But certain kinds of racism existed in the ancient world.

But the division of the human race was not merely a result of human bigotry and sin. God Himself divided the race. He scattered the nations at Babel, confusing their languages so that they could not cooperate in their rebellion against Him (Gen. 11). Soon after Babel, he chose one nation among those scattered nations and lived among them (Gen. 12). He gave them the Torah, the Law of Moses, which distinguished them from the other nations. Israel was cut off from the Gentiles. As soon as Yahweh commanded Abraham to cut his body and the bodies of his sons with circumcision, the body of the human race was also cut in two. On the one side is the "circumcision;" on the other side is the "uncircumcision."

Dividing a living thing in two is a sure-fire way to kill it. (Don't try it on your little sister or your uppity housecat; trust me.) Throughout the Old Testament, the body of the human race was a corpse lying out on the earth, divided between Israel and the nations, Jew and Gentile. The human race was dead and was waiting for a resurrection.

It appeared that God had everything under control. He had selected one nation out of all the nations of the earth to be His special possession, His holy nation. Israel was supposed to be the people that would reverse the sin of Adam by worshiping God and Him alone; they were supposed to reverse the sin of Cain by living with their brothers in harmony; they were supposed to remain unstained by the world and not intermarry with idolatrous Gentiles. By living this way, they were supposed to be the model of how all men and women everywhere were supposed to live.

But Israel failed. Israel indulged in idol worship almost from the beginning—constructing a golden calf at Sinai and later worshiping the Baals. Instead of living as a single people, Israel quickly divided into northern and southern kingdoms. They adopted pagan customs and ways of life. Instead of being a model of how to live faithfully before God, they became a mirror image of the Gentile world. Paul is talking specifically about Jews (he uses the pronoun we) when he writes that "we all once conducted ourselves in the lusts of our flesh, fulfilling the desires of the flesh and of the mind, and were by nature children of wrath, just as the others" (Eph. 2:3).

By the time Jesus came, the Jews had made things even worse. Instead of realizing that the human race could not stay divided into two forever, and instead of being humbled by their history of idolatry and apostasy, many Jews had become proud. They believed that Jews could be alive all on their own. Many Jews behaved as if they were the Green Knight's head, which you have already read about, cheerfully talking and blinking after it had been cut off from the body. They thought God favored them and them alone, and that they didn't need the Gentiles to keep on living.

This gets us to the mystery that Paul is talking about in Ephesians. The mystery is twofold. First, what in the world was God doing with Israel? Why would he choose a special people only to let them slip away into idolatry? Had he lost control of the situation? Second, what was he doing with Gentiles? Did he intend to leave them out in the cold? Are the Gentiles going to be "second class" citizens in the human race that God is preparing?

Paul answers these questions directly or indirectly in the first half of Ephesians. He begins with a long sentence blessing God for His work in Jesus the Messiah (1:3–14). This whole section is a long prayer of praise and blessing to God. What does Paul bless God for? Three things: he blesses God for making a plan, for making a plan that centers on Jesus and for fulfilling that plan through Jesus.

First, the plan. This is one of the great passages in Scripture about "predestination," the belief that God has decided who will be saved and who will not be saved before they have done anything at all. Paul says that God chose His people long before His people even existed to be chosen. He chose them "before the foundation of the world" (1:4), before the first stone of the house of creation was laid. God "chose us" (1:4), and Paul even uses the word *predestined* (1:5). Besides, God "works all things after the counsel of His will" (1:11). He not only chooses who will be saved and who will not, but also works out how "all things" will happen. He is in absolute control of every thing that has been made and every event that occurs in history. God doesn't look ahead to see what people will do and then make a decision about how to treat them. He chooses what He is going to do, and then He works "all things" to achieve what He has chosen.

What does this have to do with the mystery? It means that the division of the human race and the failure of Israel are not out of God's control. What God intends to do with the human race, with the cosmos, is what God has always intended to do. He didn't start revising the chapters of His mystery story halfway through. He is still writing the same story He planned from the beginning, before creation ever existed.

Second, Jesus. In this passage, Paul writes again and again that Jesus, the Son of God in human flesh, is at the center of God's mystery story. Through Jesus, sinners have forgiveness and redemption (1:7). Because Jesus shed His blood for us, we are saved from wrath and hell and the death of our sins (cf. 2:8–10). The "mystery of God's will" looks forward to the gathering together of all things in Christ (1:9–10). Jesus has been raised up to the heavenly places far above all authorities and powers (1:20–23). Whatever God is up to, whatever He is keeping quiet about throughout the Old Testament, is now revealed in Jesus.

Jesus, of course, does not work alone in any of this. God the Father chooses, predestines, works all things in and through and for the sake of Jesus, and it is also through Jesus that we receive the Holy Spirit as a "guarantee" of our future inheritance (1:13–14). All

"When He ascended on high, / He led captivity captive, / And gave gifts to men." (Now this, "He ascended"—what does it mean but that He also first descended into the lower parts of the earth? He who descended is also the One who ascended far above all the heavens, that He might fill all things.) (Eph. 4:8–10) Christians have disagreed vehemently about this verse over the centuries. Some believe that it asserts Christ's descent into hell and His rescuing of the Old Testament saints. Some believers think that the Old Testament saints waited in Hades, sort of a holding cell in hell, until the time of the Resurrection. This artistic representation sets forth this view. Other Christians believe that the "captivity" that Christ led "captive" was the demonic spirit over whose kingdom Christ triumphed in the Cross and Resurrection.

three persons of the Triune God are at work to fulfill the plan—the Father originating, the Son accomplishing, the Spirit completing.

What Jesus does, He does for us. God has chosen us "in Him," that is, in Jesus (1:4). God never thought of us for even a moment without also thinking about Jesus. God the Father's goal in choosing us in Jesus also involves Jesus. Jesus is the Son, and we are predestined "to adoption as sons by Jesus Christ" (1:5). Adam was created to be God's son but was estranged from his father and never achieved the kingship that God intended to give him. Jesus is the true Son, the Last Adam, Who has been given a throne (1:21–23). And because we are in Jesus, we are also given thrones in heavenly places (2:7).

Third, the fulfillment of the plan in Jesus. As Paul explains later in Ephesians 2, one of the main things "summed up" in Christ is the human race. Though Gentiles have long been afar off and excluded from the commonwealth of Israel and "strangers from the covenants of promise" (2:12–13), Jesus unites Gentiles and Jews into "one new man from the two, thus making peace" (2:15). As a result, Gentiles are no longer strangers and aliens, but rather fellow citizens with the Jews, part of the one new humanity that God has brought into being. What is the secret of God's work in dividing Jews from Gentiles? The secret is Jesus. God divided Jews from Gentiles in order to reunite them through the death and resurrection of Jesus (2:16).

But God, who is rich in mercy, because of His great love with which He loved us, even when we were dead in trespasses, made us alive together with Christ (by grace you have been saved) . . . (Eph 2:4–5)

The conclusion of the first two chapters of Ephesians is that God has now, in Jesus and through the Spirit, unified the divided human race, revealing the secret that had been hidden, His plan for the human race that He laid out from the beginning. Paul begins in chapter 3 to apply this teaching. Because you have been made "one new man" in Jesus, he begins, you should live in a way that manifests that truth. But he interrupts himself in chapter 3 with a discussion of his own role in the unveiling of the mystery. As noted above, he sees his own apostolic preaching and teaching to the Gentiles as an unveiling of the secret things of God. In 3:6, Paul gets the closest he ever does to defining what the mystery is: The secret is that the Gentiles are completely equal to the Jews, that there is no difference, that all those who trust in Jesus are united as a new human race in Jesus.

Paul picks up the thread of his discussion at the beginning of chapter 4 and urges the Ephesians to "walk worthy of the calling with which you have been called" (4:1). What calling? The calling to unity, the calling to live as the human race was created to live—

worshiping God, loving one another, resisting the evil men and forces that stand against God. Paul reinforces the unity that Christians have by listing seven of the "ones" that define the church (4:4–6). Pastors, teachers and other leaders of the church are given to the church to enable her to grow up into the fullness of their unity in Christ, and not be divided from one another or from their head.

Beginning in Ephesians 4:17, Paul exhorts the Ephesians to change particular aspects of their lives. They are to "put off" old habits the way one takes off a set of worn clothes, and to "put on" new habits, which are the habits of Christ. Paul is telling the Ephesians, in very specific terms, how they are to live out the reality of what God has planned for them *in* Christ and accomplished for them *through* Christ. God's plan in Christ is to form a human race that does not "walk as the rest of the Gentiles walk" (4:17). Instead of a race full of ignorance and darkness, God intends to form a race that lives in truth (4:17–24). In place of a race full of wrath and anger, God intends to form a new humanity characterized by patience and longsuffering (4:26–27). Instead of a human race dominated by greed and theft, God will form a hard-working and generous people (4:28). Instead of using words to kill and tear apart, the new humanity in Jesus will use words that edify and build up (4:29). The new race will not be filled with immorality or impurity or greed and will be free of "filthiness" and "foolish talking" (5:3–4). The new humanity will not be filled with wine and drunkenness but with songs and psalms of joy (5:18–19). In short, once God puts the divided carcass of humanity back together in His Son, the human race will begin to *live.*

For Paul, God's plan also involves the transformation of family life. In place of the disordered marriage of Adam, who turned into an attacker of his sinful bride (Gen. 3), Paul envisions marriages that manifest the mutual love and mutual submission of Christ and His church (5:22–33). God's plan in Christ is to renew husbands as loving heads of their wives, and wives as loving, submissive helpers to their husbands. He calls fathers to raise their children in the way of the Lord and instructs children to obey their parents (6:1–3).

Paul is not naïve about the world. He announces that in Christ a divided human race has been reunited. But he also knows that the human race remains, until the final judgment, divided between those who are in Christ and those who are outside, between Christians and "Gentiles" (4:17). He knows that Christians will have to battle against the world and against spiritual powers, and he urges his readers to prepare themselves for this battle (6:10–20). The most serious enemies of the church are not human beings, but "principalities and powers." Spiritual powers, demons and Satan foolishly hope to prevent God's mystery from reaching the last chapter. These powers also can get embodied in political structures and cultural habits. A nation that gives constitutional permission to women to abort their babies, for example, cooperates with the principalities and powers. Though Christians fight principalities and powers and spiritual forces, we are also often opposed by and have to oppose other people. Paul is not talking about a battle that takes place in the air. He's talking about a battle that takes place on earth. The battle is much bigger than it looks. But it is taking place *here.*

Though the mystery was not made known to earlier generations (3:5), what God does through Jesus is consistent with what He's done throughout history. Every time God divided something in the Old Testament, He always put it back together again, even better than before. Israelites cut sacrificial animals in pieces for sacrifice, but then the fire transformed the animal into a new, unified cloud of smoke that could go up to God. The Tabernacle was ripped in pieces after the battle of Aphek (1 Sam. 4–6), but then God put it back together in the Temple, which was even better than the Tabernacle. Israel was torn into the northern and southern kingdoms, but then God knit them back together during the Babylonian exile and promised them they would be stronger than ever.

Long before Abraham, God showed how He was going to work with man. Adam started as one man, but God put him into a deep sleep and tore him in two. From the rib He took from Adam, God created Eve. There was a separation, but the separation led to a greater unity because Adam and Eve became one flesh (Gen. 2).

If this is what God did to Adam, and if this is what God did to Israel, surely this is what God would do with the whole human race. He scattered the nations at Babel, but surely He meant to gather them again. He ripped the human race in two by the cutting of circumcision, but surely He meant to bring together Jew and Gentile into one new man.

The elegant Celsius Library in Ephesus was built as a memorial to the Roman governor Gaius Julius Celsus Polemaeanus. His son, Consul Gaius Julius Aquila buried his father there in a lead-lined sarcophagus. The library's vast collection of books rivaled those of the libraries at Pergamon and Alexandria. At his own death, Aquila bequeathed 25,000 denarii for the library's upkeep.

The gospel in the New Testament announces that this is precisely what God has done, and no book of the New Testament makes this point more clearly than Ephesians. When Paul preaches the gospel, he announces to people that they can be united to God through the death and resurrection of Jesus. That is at the heart of the gospel. But right next to that, Paul also announces to people that they can be united to each other. In reconciling men to Himself, God also reconciled men to each other. That is the resurrection of the corpse of the human race.

God created humanity for communion, with Him and with each other. Through the mysterious process of tearing and reuniting, God has achieved that goal. In the death and resurrection of Christ Jesus, those who believe can draw near to God. In Christ Jesus, they can draw near to each other. That is the great secret that Paul reveals in Ephesians, the secret of world history. The secret of God.

—Peter J. Leithart

For Further Reading

Veritas Press Bible Cards: Acts through Revelation. Lancaster, Pa.: Veritas Press. 149.

Wright, Tom. *Paul for Everyone: The Prison Letters.* Louisville: Westminster/John Knox, 2004.

Session I: Prelude

A Question to Consider

Does God control everything? Are human beings really free in any sense?

From the General Information above, answer the following questions:

1. What does Paul mean by a "mystery"?
2. Describe Paul's activities in Ephesus.
3. What was Ephesus famous for in the ancient world?
4. Who was the letter to the Ephesians first sent to? How do we know?
5. Where was Paul when he wrote this letter?
6. What is God's plan for the human race?

Reading Assignment:

Ephesians 1–2

Session II: Discussion

Ephesians 1–2

A Question to Consider

Who decides who gets saved and who doesn't? Is our salvation God's choice or ours?

Discuss or list short answers to the following questions:

Text Analysis

1. What did God choose us for? What is He intending to do with us?
2. How does Paul describe the condition of people outside of Christ?
3. What kind of power is available to those who believe?
4. Explain the connection between "works" and "workmanship" in Ephesians 2:9–10. (How does the description of us as "workmanship" point to the fact that our works do not save us?)
5. What does it mean to say that the Spirit is the "pledge" of our inheritance?

Cultural Analysis

1. Cicero wrote (*On Fate*, 28), "If it is your fate to recover from this illness, you will recover, regardless of whether or not you call the doctor. Likewise, if it is your fate not to recover from this illness, you will not recover, regardless of whether or not you call the doctor. And one or the other is your fate. Therefore it is pointless to call the doctor." (By the way, Cicero did not agree with this argument.) How would you respond as a Christian to this? How is fate different from predestination? Is it?
2. Horoscopes are very popular today. If you search for "horoscope" on the Web, you'll get millions of hits. What is a horoscope? What kind of worldview is behind the uses of horoscopes? How would you analyze this as a Christian?

Biblical Analysis

1. Is Paul's teaching on election new (choose three of the following verses to look up: Ps. 33:10; Isa. 14:27; 43:13; Job 9:12; 23:13; Dan. 4:35)?
2. Many Gentiles were saved in the Old Testament (Melchizedek, Jethro, Rahab, Ruth, etc.). How can Paul say that Gentiles were *"without Christ, being aliens from the commonwealth of Israel . . . having no hope and without God in the world"* (2:12)?

Summa

Write an essay or discuss this question, integrating what you have learned from the material above.

If God controls all things, are human beings free at all?

Reading Assignment:

Ephesians 3–4

Husbands, love your wives, just as Christ also loved the church and gave Himself for her, that He might sanctify and cleanse her with the washing of water by the word, that He might present her to Himself a glorious church, not having spot or wrinkle or any such thing, but that she should be holy and without blemish. So husbands ought to love their own wives as their own bodies...(Eph. 5:25–28)

SESSION III: DISCUSSION

Ephesians 2–4

A Question to Consider

Is the human race supposed to be divided or unified? In what ways?

Discuss or list short answers to the following questions:

Text Analysis

1. How does Paul use the words "circumcision" and "uncircumcision" in Ephesians 2:11? How is this different from his use of the term in Romans 2:28–29; Philippians 3:2–3? To whom is he referring in each case?
2. How did the cross help to reunite the human race?
3. What kind of house is Paul talking about in Ephesians 2?
4. What does Paul mean by "one baptism" in Ephesians 4:5?

Cultural Analysis

1. *Racism* is a common term in our day. What does the word mean? As a Christian, what do you think of racism?
2. Charles Darwin wrote, "I do not believe it is possible to describe or paint the difference of savage and civilized man. It is the difference between a wild and tame animal." And, "At some future period, not very distant as measured by centuries, the civilized races of man will almost certainly exterminate and replace the savage races throughout the world."[4] Are these racist statements? Why or why not?
3. The United Nations Charter of 1945 states that one of the principal aims of that institution is to "to practice tolerance and live together in peace with one another as good neighbours." What do you think of this goal? Has the United Nations successfully achieved this goal?

Biblical Analysis

1. Compare Isaiah 59:15–21 with Ephesians 6:10–20. What does the comparison tell you? What does this imply about the "armor of God"?
2. Paul spends most of Ephesians talking about the unity of Jew and Gentile in Christ, yet he ends with an exhortation to put on armor. Is this a contradic-

tion? Why or why not?
3. Some Christians have used Genesis 9:20–27 to show that blacks—supposedly the descendants of Ham—were condemned to be slaves. Is that a valid interpretation of the passage?

Summa

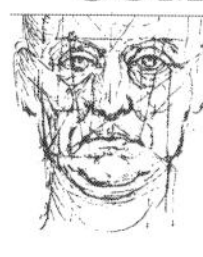

Write an essay or discuss this question, integrating what you have learned from the material above.

Does God want the human race united? How?

Reading Assignment:

Ephesians 5–6

I, therefore, the prisoner of the Lord, beseech you to walk worthy of the calling with which you were called, with all lowliness and gentleness, with longsuffering, bearing with one another in love, endeavoring to keep the unity of the Spirit in the bond of peace. (Eph. 4:1–3)

Session IV: Recitation

Ephesians 1–6

Book Overview

Answer the following questions for factual recall:

1. What does Paul pray for in chapter 1?
2. Where is Jesus exalted?
3. How are people saved from death in sin?
4. What does Paul pray for at the end of chapter 3?
5. What gifts does Christ give to His church?
6. How is the church like a body?
7. How are husbands supposed to love their wives?
8. What does Paul tell slaves to do?
9. List three pieces of the armor of God.

Session V: Activity

In Christ

1. List all the verses where Paul uses the phrase "in Christ" throughout Ephesians. Summarize the various things that we receive "in Christ."
2. List the exhortations in Ephesians 4–6, and classify them according to the Ten Commandments.

Session VI: Activity

Unity in the Church

Paul teaches in Ephesians that one of God's central goals in sending Jesus into the world was to unify the human race, and he emphasizes as strongly as he can that the church is that unified race, combining Jews and Gentiles. Here are several possible activities to determine how well the church is living up to that calling:

1. Interview your own pastor or pastors, asking them how much contact they have with Christians and pastors from other churches. Ask the pastors how they think church unity should be pursued. *Caution: Students need to be careful not to come off as "know-it-alls" to their pastors.*
2. Take a survey of local pastors. Here are some possible questions:

   • Does your church pray for other churches in town?

- Do you ever meet with pastors who are not in your denomination?
- What does your church do to recognize the unity of the body of Christ outside of your own denomination?
- What are the biggest hindrances to unity in the body of Christ in your opinion?

Once the survey questions are formulated, call or interview in person area pastors and then compile the results. *Caution: Again, students must be careful not to leave the impression that they know the pastors' business better than the pastors.*

3. If you are in a class situation that includes students from various denominations, conduct a mock "dialogue" among various denominations. Choose a topic that divides the church (e.g., predestination, justification by faith, infant baptism), and take opposing positions. (Of course, this works best if students actually have opposing positions!) Ask them to come up with a statement that lays out areas of agreement as well as areas of disagreement on the topic.

Optional Session: Evaluation

Grammar

Answer each of the following questions in complete sentences. Some answers may be longer than others. (2 points per answer)

1. Where was Paul when he wrote Ephesians?
2. What happened when Paul visited the Ephesians?
3. What does "predestination" mean?
4. How, according to Paul, are Jews and Gentiles reunited?
5. What does Paul mean by "mystery"?

Logic

Answer the following questions in complete sentences. Your answers should be a paragraph or so. Answer two of the questions. (10 points per answer)

1. Explain the relationship of God's control and human freedom. Are they contradictory?
2. How was the human race divided in the Old Testament? How did God reunite it?
3. How does God expect the new human race to live? Give specific examples.

Lateral Thinking

Answer each of the following questions in complete sentences. These questions require more substantial answers. (16 points per answer)

1. Review the history of the world in Genesis and the history of Israel in 1 & 2 Kings. How does Paul's gospel address the problems that arise in those books?
2. According to Virgil's *Aeneid,* Rome has been given imperial power forever (*imperium sine fine*), to rule other peoples with justice. Paul's letter to the Ephesians also talks about a ruler, Jesus, who rules a "nation" made up of peoples from every tribe and tongue. How are the Roman and Christian ideals different?

Endnotes

1 Barth, Marcus. *Anchor Bible: Ephesians.* Garden City, N.Y.: Doubleday, 1974. Vol. 1, 51.

2 Mark Horne, unpublished lectures on Ephesians, delivered at Dabney Center, a ministry of Auburn Avenue Presbyterian Church, Monroe, Louisiana, 2005.

3 According to an article on the Wikipedia online encyclopedia, found at Link 1 for this chapter at www.VeritasPress.com/OmniLinks.

4 Quoted in Joe Conley, "Is Darwinism Racist? Creationists and the Louisiana Darwin-Racism Controversy."

The Return of the King

When you were little, did you ever plant seeds in an egg carton? The first time you did this, it was perhaps all that your mother or your kindergarten teacher could do to keep you from digging them up every day to see how they were doing.

Even the smallest child knows that a seed is supposed to turn into something else entirely. The problem that small children have with the process is not the transformation, but with the idea of *gradual* transformation. Because of impatience, a small child does not want to wait for gradual transformations. But in fact, God created the world in such a way that gradual transformations are so commonplace that we often don't even see them or recognize them. Sudden transformations catch our eye, and we call them miracles. When Jesus made wine out of water in the miracle at Cana, He did it suddenly, and the people who saw Him do it noticed what happened because it was so unusual. But God changes water into wine all the time—all the wine in the world used to be water—but because the transformation is slow and involves water falling out of the sky, soaking into the dirt, getting sucked into roots, being shaped into tasty globules called grapes, being picked off the vine, smashed into a glorious paste and eventually bottled, we call it the work of "nature."

Why a photograph of a homely hobbit hole while our heroes are struggling in the dark War of the Ring? The Shire, with its green hills, clean rivers and lovely woodlands—whose inhabitants indulge in its unspoiled pleasures—represents all that is good in Middle-earth. It is this goodness that is the true heart of the cause in the fight against the evil of Mordor.

One of the marks of a person who is educated to think like a Christian is the fact that he or she has learned to notice these gradual transformations. He does not take them for granted. Nor does he see them and mistakenly attribute them to some kind of impersonal "natural law." Our task, as we finish reading *The Lord of the Rings,* is to see how J.R.R. Tolkien reflected this Christian wisdom so ably—because *The Return of the King* is all about gradual transformations, which are no less complete for all that when they are done.

General Information

Main Characters

The Return of the King continues with the characters we have been introduced to in the earlier books, with just a few important developments. We still have Frodo and Sam on the way to Mount Doom. Merry and Pippin are still with us, as are Aragorn, Gimli, Legolas and Gandalf. Gollum assumes a much more important role in this last book.

The most important new character is Denethor, the father of Boromir and Faramir. He is a steward of Gondor and has been a noble adversary of the growing power of Sauron—but unfortunately he has a weakness that Sauron is able to exploit successfully. We also come to know Eowyn far better than we did before this book. As the tale concludes, she comes to the point of noble despair and is restored in a very interesting way.

Summary and Setting

The culminating book of *The Lord of the Rings* is set in Middle-earth, as are the others. In this last book, the great armies of Middle-earth form up for their great confrontation. Gondor is under siege, and the Riders of Rohan go to their aid. Aragorn goes to their aid by a different route, through the Paths of the Dead. Sauron, the evil threat to all that is good, has mustered his forces and is on the march. And while these armies are marching and fighting, the final outcome of all things depends on the two hobbits making their way to Mount Doom, where the Ring of Power was first forged and which is the only place it can be destroyed. As they come to that place, how J.R.R. Tolkien managed to write such a satisfying surprise, in such a predictable place, is one of the great achievements of his book.

Worldview

Throughout these books, we have noted a recurring pattern. The wicked seize after power, while the righteous are willing to deny themselves and relinquish it. This is not only the divide between righteousness and unrighteousness, it is also the division between magic and black technology on the one hand, and craftsmanship and art on the other. And so we have seen that all the wicked characters in these books lust after the Ring and all the righteous are those who want to see it destroyed. And so it looks as though the unrighteous will win (because they are willing to grab what they want) and the righteous will throw away a perfectly good opportunity to destroy the bad guys (because they decide to destroy the Ring).

But to use a truth you might have learned from *The Lion, the Witch and the Wardrobe,* there is always a deeper magic. The Bible teaches that those who humble themselves will be exalted (James 4:10). The one who wants to become great must become the servant of all (Mark 9:35). Jesus Christ went to the cross, which really was a shameful death, and He did it for the joy that was set before Him (Heb. 12:2). And this is the deeper magic. Death is followed by resurrection. This is God's consistent pattern for victory. The advance of God's kingdom is a series of triumphs that were cleverly disguised as disasters. Middle-earth may seem like a very different world, but because this pattern is seen and honored, we can tell that fundamentally it is the same world—it is God's world.

J.R.R. Tolkien had a word to describe an aspect of this pattern, and that word was *eucatastrophe.* The word *catastrophe* indicates the intensity of the kind of ending he had in mind, but the prefix eu means good or blessed. In this sense, the resurrection of Jesus after He had been dead for three days was a *eucatastrophe.* Learning that your teacher changed your grade from a 92 to a 94 is not a eucatastrophe. In Middle-earth, just when everything seems absolutely hopeless, and the good guys go on doing their duty, simply because it is their duty, at that moment, everything turns right.

"'Gandalf! I thought you were dead! But then I thought I was dead myself. Is everything sad going to come untrue? What's happened to the world?' 'A great Shadow has departed,' said Gandalf . . ."

But there is another important aspect of this. It is not as though the righteous are threatened, and then at the last moment deliverance comes, and so everybody goes back to exactly the place where they were before. No, the long and slow process of coming to the point where everything seems hopeless, followed by this eucatastrophic and climactic deliverance, is a process that completely transforms the characters who go through it. When Jesus comes back from the dead, He is recognizably the same person (Jesus of Nazareth), but at the same time He is also transformed by His conquest of death (He is the Lord of glory). In Christian stories, this element of continuity and transformation is reflected in the characters. And so this is the kind of thing (in varying degrees) that happens to virtually ever major character in *The Lord of the Rings.*

J.R.R. Tolkien guides us slowly and imperceptibly to this place. For example, look at how Aragorn speaks when we first meet him in Bree. "'Well,' said Strider, 'with Sam's permission we will call that settled. Strider shall be your guide.'" Compare this with his kingly speech in the last book. "Between us there can be no word of giving or taking, nor of reward; for we are brethren. In happy hour did Eorl ride from the North, and never has any league of peoples been more blessed, so that neither has ever failed the other . . ." Early in the story, Strider's appearance and speech is homely. By the end of the books, his bearing, demeanor and speech are overwhelmingly kingly. Aragorn does not just become the king; he is transformed in the course of the story and he *becomes king.*

Consider who is transformed in the course of these books and the "death" that each undergoes in the course of this transformation. Like his son Boromir, this is something that Denethor does not understand—for him death is the end. Because he does not understand the great death and resurrection pattern, he sees by his art the deliverance of his own city and yet does not recognize it. Thinking that he has greater wisdom than Gandalf, he misses the deepest wisdom of all. "And even now the wind of thy hope cheats thee and wafts up Anduin a fleet with black sails. The West has failed. It is time for all to depart who would not be slaves." Gandalf says later that although

The Lieutenant of the Tower of Barad-dûr was of the race of the Black Numenoreans. He "entered the service of the Dark Tower when it first rose again," which some say refers to Sauron's return during the Second Age. Others assert that he entered Sauron's service when the Dark Lord rebuilt Barad-dûr in 2951 of the Third Age—68 years before the War of the Ring.

. . . as the sweet influence of the herb stole about the chamber it seemed to those who stood by that a keen wind blew through the window, and it bore no scent, but was an air wholly fresh and clean and young, as if it had not before been breathed by any living thing and came new-made from snowy mountains high beneath a dome of stars, or from shores of silver far away washed by seas of foam.

Denethor was "too great to be subdued to the will of the Dark Power, he saw nonetheless only those things which that Power permitted him to see." And the thing he missed was this great theme of transformation.

Those who are transformed include Gandalf the Grey, who becomes Gandalf the White—after his "death" in Moria. Aragorn is transformed from a solitary Ranger into a great king—after his "death" of riding through the paths of the dead. Frodo is transformed to such an extent that he cannot settle again in the Shire. Sam can live contentedly in the Shire, but he has been transformed in a different way. Both Frodo and Sam were brought back from the brink of death at Mount Doom. Merry and Pippin are not *as* transformed, but the changes are still marked, and they are changes that come from life after death. In all this, sacrifices are made on behalf of others, as Frodo put it. "It must often be so, Sam, when things are in danger: some one has to give them up, lose them, so that others may keep them." But on the other side of sacrifice is great joy—joy that cannot be touched by any of the troubles of Middle-earth. Sam has this realization when he looks up at the sky in Mordor and sees a star. "For like a shaft, clear and cold, the thought pierced him that in the end the Shadow was only a small and passing thing: there was light and high beauty for ever beyond its reach." Ultimate goodness is out of evil's reach. But then in another sense, in Christian stories, goodness comes down to where evil *can* reach it. Death therefore comes to do its work, and in that work death is tricked. Goodness is transformed into a higher and deeper good. And this is something that those who traffic in magic can never understand—until it is too late.

> And far away, as Frodo put on the Ring and claimed it for his own, even in Sammath Naur the very heart of his realm, the Power in Barad-dûr was shaken, and the Tower trembled from its foundations to its proud and bitter crown. The Dark Lord was suddenly aware of him, and his Eye piercing all shadows looked across the plain to the door that he had made; and the magnitude of his own folly was revealed to him in a blinding flash, and all the devices of his enemies were at last laid bare. Then his wrath blazed in consuming flame, but his fear rose like a vast black smoke to choke him. For he knew his deadly peril and the thread upon which his doom now hung.

Frodo succumbs to the power of the Ring at the very last moment, and he does this for several reasons. The first is seen in the quotation above—it is a dramatic reason. Tolkien does not want Sauron to be absolutely blind-sided. He wants Sauron to have some notion that he might be defeated before he actually is—it is necessary to have Sauron know before he falls that he is in danger. Tolkien did something similar when he tells us earlier that Aragorn had revealed himself to Sauron through the Palantir. "'Yes, Master Gimli, he saw me, but in other guise than you see me here. If that will aid him, then I have done ill. But I do not think so. To know that I lived and walked the earth was a blow to his heart, I deem; for he knew it not till now.'"

The other reason that Frodo fails at the very end is to show that evil is resisted by mortals and not by super-humans. "'I have come,' he said. 'But I do not choose now to do what I came to do. I will not do this deed. The Ring is mine!' And suddenly, as he set it on his finger, he vanished from Sam's sight." Frodo fails, but then, when he does, the mercy he had earlier shown to Gollum comes back to deliver him. And even Sam, who had resisted Frodo's earlier kindness to Gollum had eventually shown that same mercy to Gollum himself. And this mercy was used at the end to make a decision for Frodo that he was no longer strong enough to make himself. "Yes," said Frodo. "But do you remember Gandalf's words: *Even Gollum may have something yet to do?* But for him, Sam, I could not have destroyed the Ring. The Quest would have been in vain, even at the bitter end. So let us forgive him!"

There are a few other important elements to consider in this book. One of them is the fact that it is possible to enter into conflict and war with a clean conscience. "And then all the host of Rohan burst into song, and they sang as they slew, for the joy of battle was on them, and the sound of their singing that was fair and terrible came even to the City." A few pages later, Eomer shows the same exhilaration of battle when he mistakenly thinks that Aragorn's ships belong to the enemy. "These staves he spoke, yet he laughed as he said them. For once more lust of battle was on him; and he was still unscathed, and he was young, and he was king: the lord of a fell people. And lo! even as he laughed at despair he looked out again on the black ships, and he lifted up his sword to defy them." As Christians we know that we are not to be bloodthirsty for the sake of entertainment. But although this sentiment of Eomer's is not something we are used to, it would have been recognized by the warrior psalmist of Israel (Ps. 58: 10; 68:1, 23; 144:1).

One last lesson of this

Frodo and Sam are the only ones of the Fellowship to see the black, immeasurably strong, tower of Barad-dûr as they travel toward Mount Doom, and Tolkien only gives the reader the faintest glimpse as he writes: ". . . rising black, blacker and darker than the vast shades amid which it stood, the cruel pinnacles and iron crown of the topmost tower of Barad-dûr . . ."

great book needs to be emphasized. After all the great battles have been fought, the great deeds done, the great legends established and the great songs composed, Tolkien has the Halflings return to the Shire. And there, in the Shire, they discover that the wickedness they have been fighting has come to their home in a petty and vindictive form. The lesson here is that it is not enough to fight the great evils. The applications of the noblest battles are worthless unless we are courageous enough to extend them.

The scouring of the Shire is a deeply satisfying conclusion to *The Lord of the Rings* for several reasons. The first is that the idea of a homecoming in which everything is put right is a formula that people have loved since Homer wrote the *Odyssey.* But secondly, the great battle has been fought. Now the task is to apply the fruits of that victory. We as Christians know that Jesus has defeated Satan in His death and resurrection. Our task is to apply that victory where we live and put the Shire to rights. Gandalf says this to the hobbits: "'I am not coming to the Shire. You must settle its affairs yourselves; that is what you have been trained for.'"

It is very interesting to note the form in which evil comes to the Shire. For Tolkien, hobbits represent the ordinary working folk. His picture of the evil they must confront is very interesting indeed—he shows us evil in the form of petty bureaucracy and rule-making. The hobbits don't come back to the Shire to find a mayor with red eyes dressed in ominous black, with lightning bolts coming from his finger-tips. They come back to petty oppression and Rules. As Hob put it, "It's all these 'gatherers' and 'sharers', I reckon, going round counting and measuring and taking off to storage. They do more gathering than sharing, and we never see most of the stuff again." It is important to note that Tolkien represents the returning hobbits as free, and not as scofflaws.

The returning hobbits know what true law is. They know what freedom is. And Tolkien makes it as plain as anything that we need to learn what they knew. As Sam said to the gatekeeper, "If hobbits of the Shire are to be kept out in the wet on a night like this, I'll tear down your notice when I find it."

When they find a place to sleep, they find other things as well. "In the upper rooms were little rows of hard beds, and on every wall there was a notice and a list of Rules. Pippin tore them down." "'All right, all right!' said Sam. 'That's quite enough. I don't want to hear no more. No welcome, no beer, no smoke, and a lot of rules and orc-talk instead.'"

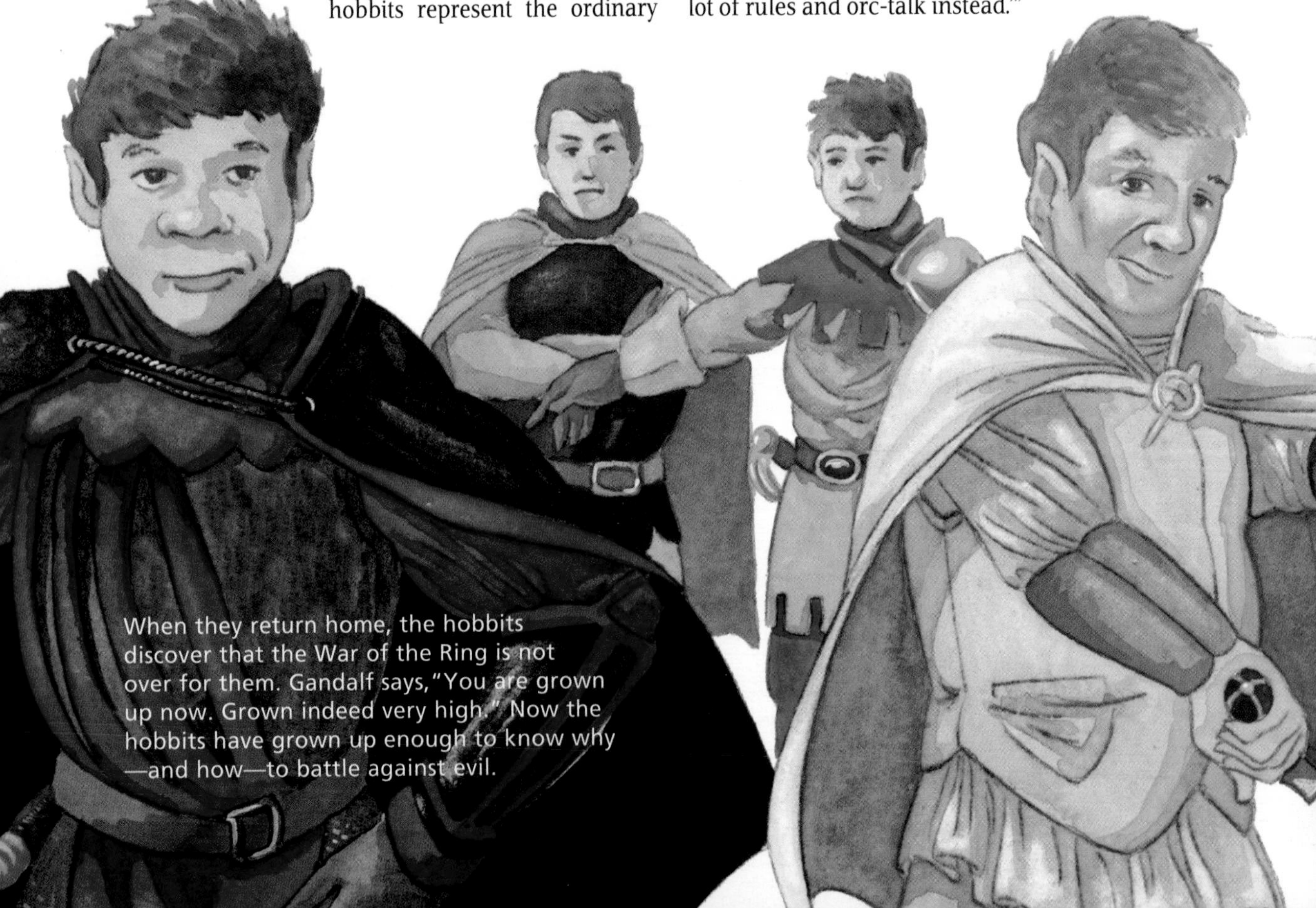

When they return home, the hobbits discover that the War of the Ring is not over for them. Gandalf says, "You are grown up now. Grown indeed very high." Now the hobbits have grown up enough to know why—and how—to battle against evil.

"'If I hear *not allowed* much oftener,' said Sam, 'I'm going to get angry.'"

Genuine evil has come to the Shire, and real damage is done. And just as it was resisted in Mordor and before the gates of Minas Tirith and in the siege of Orthanc and in the desperate battle at Helm's Deep, so must it be resisted in the Shire. Saruman has come to the Shire in order to maliciously strike back at the hobbits, and so he must be resisted there as well. But this resistance is closer to home, and it shows at the last what all the fighting is *over.* The point of *freedom* is not so that the word freedom can float over our heads and light up the sky. The point of freedom is to enjoy a pint of beer and a pipe, to tend the garden, to read stories to your little ones (including this one) and to enjoy your supper. At least this is how Samwise Gamgee sees it.

> And he went on, and there was yellow light, and fire within; and the evening meal was ready, and he was expected. And Rose drew him in, and set him in his chair, and put little Elanor upon his lap. He drew a deep breath. "Well, I'm back," he said.

—Douglas Wilson

Further Reading

Carpenter, Humphrey, ed. *The Letters of J.R.R. Tolkien.* New York: Houghton Mifflin, 1981.

Carpenter, Humphrey. *Tolkien.* New York: Ballantine Books, 1977.

Newsom, William Chad. *Talking of Dragons.* Ross-shire, Scotland: Christian Focus Publications, 2005.

Peters, Thomas. *The Christian Imagination.* San Francisco: Ignatius Press, 2000.

Tolkien, J.R.R. *The Silmarillion.* New York: Houghton Mifflin, 1977.

WHATEVER HAPPENS TO . . .?

Even though the six appendices at the end of *The Return of the King* are not assigned reading, you will do well not to ignore them. The histories, chronologies, family trees, calendars and explanations about the languages of Middle-earth help round out the whole experience of reading the *Ring* trilogy.

Have you wondered about the earlier lives of the characters? In the appendices you can learn of the death of Aragorn's father by an orcish arrow and of Aragorn spending his youth at Rivendell. It is here that Aragorn and Arwen first meet, pledging their love to one another. We learn of the earlier association between Aragorn and Denethor and why Denethor is suspicious of Gandalf, as well as an explanation of why Faramir is not Denethor's favorite son.

The appendices also tell us of the earlier, dark deeds of Sauron and of Saruman's gradual taking over of Isengard. We also can read about the beginnings of the Dwarves and the history of Khazad-dûm. From the very detailed chronology of the events of *The Hobbit* and *The Lord of the Rings* you may discover all about the travels of Gollum and of Gandalf that are merely hinted at in the stories themselves.

Are you curious about what becomes of the hobbits after the events in the story? The appendices tell of marriages, children and political accomplishments. Also, if you skip reading the appendices, you will miss how Legolas and Gimli cause a final end to the Fellowship of the Ring in Middle-earth. And you will forever be wondering.

In spite of what is presented in the movie version of *The Return of the King,* Aragorn was *not* the undisputed heir to the throne of Gondor. Long ago an ancestor of Aragorn tried to claim the throne, but Gondor's nobles ruled that his claim wasn't legitimate, because the family did not descend directly from Isildur's brother, Anárion. Thus the rule of Gondor was placed under the Stewardship for about a thousand years. When Aragorn was put forward as king, Denethor believed that Gandalf was trying to be in charge through establishing a puppet king: *"But I say to thee, Gandalf Mithrandir, I will not be thy tool! I am Steward of the House of Anárion. I will not step down to be the dotard chamberlain of an upstart. Even were his claim proved to me, still he comes but of the line of Isildur. I will not bow to such a one, last of a ragged house long bereft of lordship and dignity."*

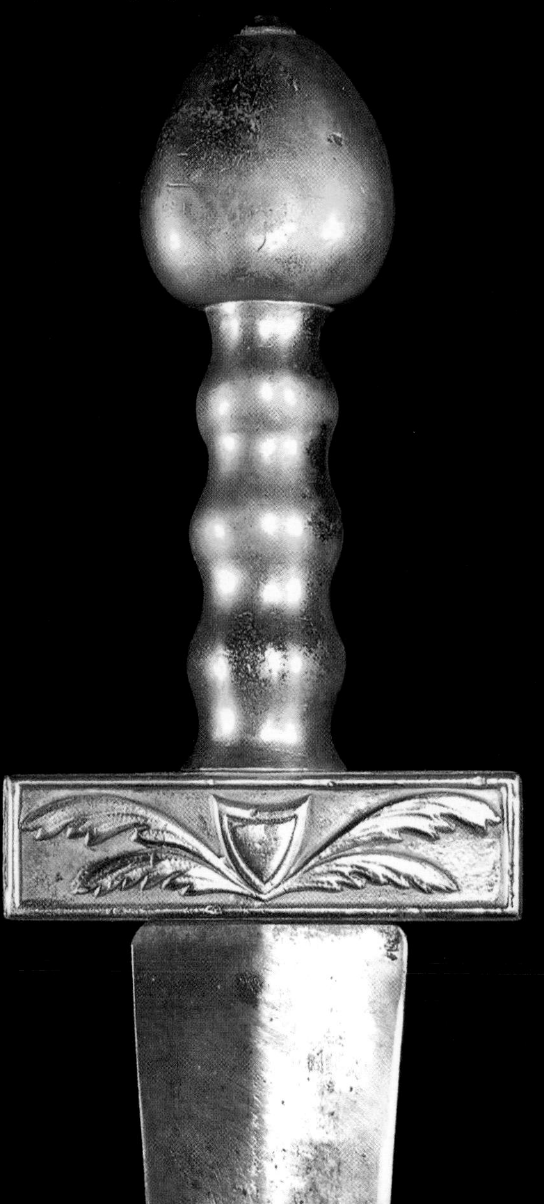

Session I: Prelude

A Question to Consider

What is a eucatastrophe? In what way is this a biblical pattern? How does it play out in *The Lord of the Rings?*

From the General Information above answer the following questions:

1. What distinction between good and evil becomes increasingly clear in the final book?
2. What is the difference between Aragorn's speech in *The Fellowship of the Ring* and his speech in *The Return of the King?*
3. How do the main characters "die?"
4. What happens after each of these characters reaches the point of death?
5. Why is Gollum still alive at the end of the book?
6. Why is the scouring of the Shire such a satisfying end for the story?

Reading Assignment:
Book V, Chapters 1–3

Session II: Discussion

Book V, Chapters 1–3

A Question to Consider

What happens when we shirk our calling?

Discuss or list short answers to the following questions:

Text Analysis

1. What is the result of Aragorn looking into the palantir?
2. As discussed in the worldview essay, Aragorn undergoes a transformation (a sort of resurrection) as he is becoming king. Where does he go that serves as a symbol of his "death?"
3. What happens at the Stone of Erech?
4. What does all this tell us about Aragorn and his identity and calling?

Cultural Analysis

1. How might our culture's individualism affect its view of calling?

2. How would the idea of shirking a calling be interpreted in our culture?

Biblical Analysis

1. What specific command did God give to Jonah? What was his immediate response (Jonah 1:1–3)?
2. What was God's response? What did the men on the ship decide to do (Jonah 1:7–16)?
3. What happens to Jonah (Jonah 1:17–2:10)?
4. What conclusions can be drawn from Jonah about shirking our calling?

Summa

Write an essay or discuss this question, integrating what you have learned from the material above.

Compare and contrast Aragorn and Jonah regarding their response to their calling. How do we know what our calling is?

Reading Assignment:
Book V, Chapters 4–6

Session III: Recitation

Book V, Chapters 1–6

Comprehension Questions

Answer the following questions for factual recall:

1. Where in the story does *The Return of the King* begin?
2. Why are they traveling at night?
3. As Gandalf and Pippin approach, Denethor is staring into his lap. What is he holding?
4. What is the history of the Paths of the Dead?
5. What new position does Merry attain?
6. Why does Denethor oppose sending the Ring with Frodo?
7. During the siege of Gondor, the Enemy shoots fiery missiles into the first ring of the city. What are these missiles?
8. Who are the Woses?

Reading Assignment:
Book V, Chapters 7–8

Session IV: Discussion

Book V, Chapters 7–8

A Question to Consider

How would you describe a great leader? What is he like? What does he do? What characterizes a poor leader?

Beregond, son of Baranor, Guard in the Third Company of the Citadel, who is assigned to instruct Pippin in the passwords of Minas Tirith. Beregond helped save the life of Faramir and was promoted to the Captain of the Guard, called the White Company.

Discuss or list short answers to the following questions:

Text Analysis

1. What happens to Denethor after the battle at Minas Tirith? Why does he do what he does?
2. How does Tolkien contrast the leadership of Theoden, Gandalf and Aragorn with that of Denethor?
3. What does Aragorn do after the battle?
4. Who is assigned as interim leader of Gondor? By whom?
5. What does Aragorn discover when he enters the city disguised? How does he respond?
6. What basic lessons of leadership can we learn from Aragorn in this section?

Cultural Analysis

1. Think of recent leaders in our culture who have been popular. What are they like?
2. Can you think of any recent leaders like Aragorn? Gandalf?
3. List the qualities of the man whom you would label as the greatest leader of your time.

Biblical Analysis

1. Complete chart 1 by listing the characteristics of a godly leader and, by logical implication, the characteristics of an ungodly leader that the Scriptures show us.
2. Name other men in Scripture whose lives could be examined to glean characteristics of good and bad leadership (Gen. 11–25; Deut.; 1, 2 Sam.; Psalms; 2 Kings 22; Acts and Epistles; The Gospels; 1 Kings 11–14; 1 Kings 16–22; 2 Chron. 21; 2 Kings 21).

SUMMA

Write an essay or discuss this question, integrating what you have learned from the material above.
Describe the profile of an ideal leader.

READING ASSIGNMENT:
Book V, Chapters 9–10

SESSION V: ACTIVITY

Book V, Chapter 9

Songs in *The Lord of the Rings*

Songs play an important role in the *Rings Trilogy*. There are more than 120 songs throughout the entire story, and Tolkien uses them to create images which otherwise would have been difficult to create.

In book V, chapter 9, Legolas recounts how Aragorn led the Company and all of the Dead to the River Anduin

Chart 1: LEADERS IN SCRIPTURE

SCRIPTURE PASSAGE	CHARACTERISTIC OF A GODLY LEADER	CHARACTERISTIC OF AN UNGODLY LEADER
Num. 14:8; Josh. 23:9–11		
Num. 13:28–33; 14:9		
Num. 32:10–12		
Deut. 3:28; Josh. 21:43–45		
Josh. 1:6–9		
Josh. 1:8; 8: 34–35		
Josh. 22:5; 24:16; Judg. 2:7		

and how the Dead swept through the invading Enemy, causing sailors to throw themselves overboard. In the midst of telling his incredible story he pauses and sings a song describing the land of Lebennin.

Answer the following questions about the song and then take a stab at writing your own.

1. Exactly where in recounting his story does Legolas pause to sing the song?
2. What effect does this pause in the story have? What images does the reader see that he would not have seen otherwise?
3. What deeper image is created in the mind of the reader?

Activity A

Choose a place in the story up to this point where there is no song. Insert a song of your own composing. Be sure to make it as Tolkienesque as possible. Read (or, if you dare, sing) the songs in class and see if your classmates know where the song fits.

Activity B

Choose a song in the text up to this point. Analyze it with the following questions:

1. Where does the song fit in the context of the *Ring Trilogy?*
2. What effect does it have on the reader?
3. What does it add to the story?
4. What would be missing without it?
5. What deeper images are aroused by the song?
6. Who is the composer/singer, and why is this significant at this point in the story?

Finally, try to find a familiar hymn or psalm that might be an appropriate tune for the song. Sing away!

READING ASSIGNMENT:
Book VI, Chapter 1–2

SESSION VI: RECITATION

Book V, Chapter 7–Book VI, Chapter 2

Comprehension Questions

Answer the following questions for factual recall:

1. In book V, chapter 7, *The Pyre of Denethor,* Denethor has gone mad. What happens when he faces Gandalf?
2. What does the Steward then tell Gandalf?
3. How does Denethor die? What does he take with him?
4. What restrains Aragorn from claiming the throne?
5. What mutual agreement do Aragorn, Eomer and Imrahil reach regarding their leadership?
6. How does Aragorn end up spending that night? Why? How does he do it?
7. What is Gandalf's opinion as to the likelihood of victory against the enemy?
8. As the Company reach the Black Gate who greets them there? What is he like?
9. The story returns to Frodo and Sam in *The Tower of Cirith Ungol.* What thoughts go through Sam's mind when he is tempted by the power of the Ring?

READING ASSIGNMENT:
Book VI, Chapters 3–4

SESSION VII: DISCUSSION

Book V, Chapters 9–10

A Question to Consider

Should wars be fought when there is little or no hope of victory?

Discuss or list short answers to the following questions:

Text Analysis

1. In book V, chapter 9 what does Gandalf suggest concerning war with Mordor?
2. What does Gandalf hope Sauron will think when they attack? What is his strategy?
3. What does Gandalf say concerning their hope of final victory?

Cultural Analysis

1. Discuss what the popular opinion of our culture would be concerning entering into a war. What questions usually arise?
2. How has the culture adopted the general view of pragmatism when it comes to the issue of war?

3. Was there a time in our history when this was different?

Biblical Analysis

1. Did God ever lead Israel into a battle that seemed from a human perspective most likely to end in defeat (Num. 13:31; Josh. 1)?
2. Do these instances in Scripture apply to us today?
3. How might Proverbs 14:34 steer us away from basing decisions to go to war on popularity or the likelihood of victory?

Summa

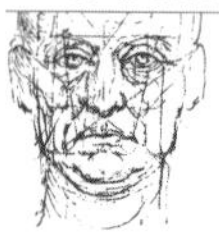

Write an essay or discuss this question, integrating what you have learned from the material above.

Do you agree or disagree with Gandalf's approach to the question of whether a nation should go to war when there is little or no hope of victory? Why? How about the other leaders with Gandalf? How do they weigh in and what insight do they provide?

Reading Assignment:

Book VI, Chapter 5

Ghan-buri-Ghan, chieftain of the Druedain, and one of his people. The Druedain live in the Druadan Forest in Gondor, are short and broad with flat faces, dark eyes, wispy beards, and they only wear grass skirts. They are also known as the Wild Men, and the Rohirrim call them the Woses. On March 13, 3019, Ghan-buri-Ghan shows King Theoden of Rohan a secret way through the Stonewain Valley to the Pelennor Fields.

Session VIII: Activity

Book VI, Chapters 1–5

Languages in *The Lord of the Rings*

As a linguist Tolkien learned over a dozen languages and actually invented several languages which appear in *The Lord of the Rings.*[1]

Answer the following questions and then do the translation exercise below:

1. Why do you think Tolkien found it necessary to invent languages for his trilogy?
2. Why do you think there are sections when the speakers in the story speak their native languages (book VI, chaps. 1, 4, 5)?

3. How does Tolkien incorporate language into the power of the Ring?

Tolkien did not see the need to create complete languages that were able to be spoken. It would have been a tremendous task to invent vocabulary for an entire language. Our work here, therefore, must be limited to transliteration—taking the letters of one language to form words in another language.

Choose a phrase from this section in the book and transliterate it into the Elvish tongue using the alphabet below. Vowels in this language are similar to Hebrew vowel points in that they are marks placed above the consonants.

a = ∴	b = pɒ
c (ts) = ƅ	c (ch) = q
d = pɔ	e = ´
f = ƅ	g = ɯq
g (j) = cq	h = λ
h (x) = d	i = ˙
j (y) = ɑ	j (zh) = cd
k = q	l = ꞇ
m = m	n = mɔ
o = ˆ	p = p
r = ɣ	s = 6 or ?
s (sh) = d	t = p
u = ˀ	v = bɒ
w = ɒ	z = ɛ or ʒ

Reading Assignment:
Book VI, Chapter 6

Session IX: Recitation

Book VI, Chapters 1–6

Comprehension Questions

Answer the following questions for factual recall:

1. What does Sam do when Frodo completely gives out?
2. Who suddenly shows up?
3. How does Gollum get the Ring from Frodo?
4. How do the hobbits exit Mount Doom?
5. In the ceremony with Aragorn what gift does Frodo give to Sam?
6. What does Gandalf explain about the new reckoning of time?
7. What is Aragorn's new name? Whom does he wed?
8. What does Treebeard do that distresses Gandalf? Why did Treebeard do this?
9. What is the name of Bilbo's collection of books? What significance do they have?

Reading Assignment:
Book VI, Chapters 7–9

Session X: Discussion

Book VI, Chapter 9

A Question to Consider

What will heaven be like?

Text Analysis

1. Why do Bilbo and Frodo sail off into the West?
2. Who lives in the Undying Lands?[2]
3. What description of this land does Tolkien give?[3]
4. What seems to be the meaning of this land? Why all the mystery?

Cultural Analysis

1. Before discussing the culture's view of what heaven is like, we must determine if the culture even accepts its existence. Does our culture even believe in heaven?
2. How might we account for different levels of belief in heaven among the nations?
3. What do people generally believe heaven is like?

Biblical Analysis

1. What does the Bible say about heaven (Acts 7:49; Heb. 4:9; Rev. 7:16–17)?
2. Why do you think the Bible is vague in its descriptions of heaven (1 Cor. 15)?
3. How is Tolkien's handling of "heaven" like or unlike what we read in the Bible?
4. What value is there in having only a general idea of heaven?

SUMMA

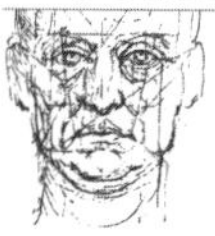

Write an essay or discuss this question, integrating what you have learned from the material above.
How does Tolkien create the same sense of wonder about heaven as the Bible does? How is this effective?

Optional Activity

Once you have read *The Return of the King* (preferably several times), it may be safe to watch Peter Jackson's rendition of it in film. When you are watching the movie, keep a note pad handy to jot down any places where the movie and the book diverge. When you are done, go back through your list and see how many of your discrepancies you can prove and how many are just interpretive questions.

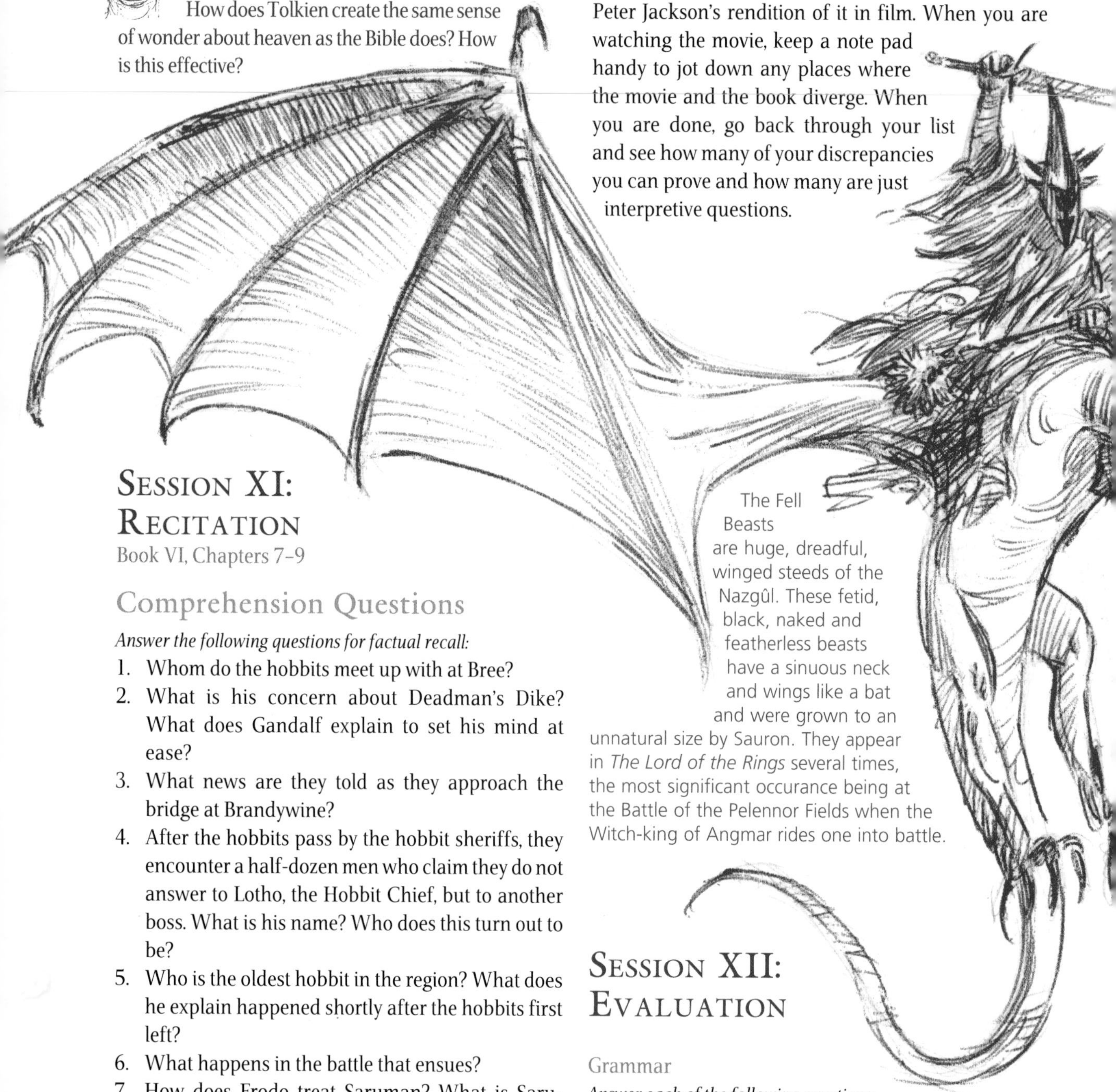

The Fell Beasts are huge, dreadful, winged steeds of the Nazgûl. These fetid, black, naked and featherless beasts have a sinuous neck and wings like a bat and were grown to an unnatural size by Sauron. They appear in *The Lord of the Rings* several times, the most significant occurance being at the Battle of the Pelennor Fields when the Witch-king of Angmar rides one into battle.

SESSION XI: RECITATION

Book VI, Chapters 7–9

Comprehension Questions

Answer the following questions for factual recall:

1. Whom do the hobbits meet up with at Bree?
2. What is his concern about Deadman's Dike? What does Gandalf explain to set his mind at ease?
3. What news are they told as they approach the bridge at Brandywine?
4. After the hobbits pass by the hobbit sheriffs, they encounter a half-dozen men who claim they do not answer to Lotho, the Hobbit Chief, but to another boss. What is his name? Who does this turn out to be?
5. Who is the oldest hobbit in the region? What does he explain happened shortly after the hobbits first left?
6. What happens in the battle that ensues?
7. How does Frodo treat Saruman? What is Saruman's response to this treatment?
8. Whom does Sam marry?
9. Whom do Frodo and the others meet as they enter the Woody End? What are they wearing?

SESSION XII: EVALUATION

Grammar

Answer each of the following questions in complete sentences. (2 points per answer)

1. What is the name of the major city of Gondor?
2. What oath had the Men of the Mountains made? What was the result of the breaking of the oath?

3. What happened to Denethor before he died? How did he die?
4. What unique, kingly power does Aragorn learn he possesses?
5. What thoughts come to Sam's mind when he puts on the Ring?
6. At Mount Doom how does Gollum get the Ring from Frodo?
7. Now that the Third Age of Middle-earth is over, what new age has come?

Logic

Demonstrate your understanding of the worldview set forth in The Return of the King. *Answer the following questions in complete sentences; your answer should be a paragraph or so. Answer two of the three questions. (10 points per answer)*

1. In *The Lord of the Rings* there are several pairs of characters who act as doubles for each other. When we look at their lives we often see two divergent paths of behavior. King Theoden and Lord Denethor are one such pair. How does Tolkien show us the comparison in their lives and deaths? Include the connection to Psalm 1 in your answer.
2. In the face of battle different men behave in different ways. Compare the response of Denethor during the siege of Gondor and Gandalf's words just before the final battle. How do we see the character of each man in the heat of war?
3. How do the following words of Gandalf come true? "Even Gollum may have something yet to do." How is this ending ironic? How do Jesus' words in Mark 8:34–38 apply?

Lateral Thinking

Answer one of the following questions. These questions will require more substantial answers. (15 points each)

1. How might Aragorn be conceived of as a symbol of Christ? What similarities are there between the two?
2. How do Gandalf's words concerning the fighting of a war with little or no chance of victory represent a wise balance? Explain why you agree or disagree.

Optional Session: Activity

Book IV, Chapters 2–3

Drawing a Timeline

Using the timeline in the appendix in the back of *The Return of the King* or from other resources, draw a timeline and plot the following events in the history of Middle-earth. Be sure to divide the time into the different ages of Middle-earth.

1. The Great Battle–the Host of Valinor break Thangorodrim and overthrow Morgoth
2. Migration of dwarves to Moria
3. Sauron begins to stir again in Middle-earth.
4. Sauron chooses Mordor as a stronghold.
5. The beginning of the forging of the Rings
6. The completion of the Rings
7. Sauron fights with the elves, and the Rings are hidden.
8. Sauron is driven from Eriador, and there is a long time of peace.
9. The attack on Gondor by Sauron
10. The end of the Second Age
11. Evil grows as orcs increase in the Misty Mountains.
12. The Great Plague ravishes Gondor.
13. Nazgûl gather at Mordor. A Balrog appears in Moria and the elves flee.
14. Gandalf's journey to Dol Guldur
15. The White Council is formed, and Deagol finds the One Ring.
16. Smeagol hides in the Misty Mountains.
17. Sauron populates Moria with his creatures.
18. Rohan and Gondor are attacked. Gandalf comes to the aid of the Shire-folk.
19. War of the dwarves and the orcs
20. Gandalf learns of Sauron's plan to gather the Rings.
21. Birth of Bilbo Baggins
22. Birth of Aragorn

23. Bilbo finds the Ring.
24. Gollum begins his search for the Ring's thief.
25. Sauron begins the rebuilding of Barad-dûr.
26. Bilbo's farewell feast
27. The Company of the Ring leaves Rivendell.
28. Frodo and the Dead Marshes
29. Frodo and Sam enter Shelob's Lair.
30. Downfall of Barad-dûr and the passing of Sauron

Questions About the "Chief Days"

1. How long after the fall of Barad-dûr is the funeral of King Theoden?
2. When does Saruman head towards the Shire?
3. What two events occur on September 22 of that year?
4. How does the Third Age end?
5. What office does Sam end up holding?

Endnotes

1 Information on these languages can be accessed in the appendix of some versions of the *Trilogy*, in Ruth S. Noel's *The Languages of Middle-earth*, or found on various websites like the one at Link 1 for this chapter at www.VeritasPress.com/OmniLinks.

2 This information can be researched online or in *The Silmarillion* 23. This question and the next may be considered as optional, since the answers are not found in *The Return of the King*.

3 This information can be researched online. This question may be considered as optional, since the answer is not found in *The Return of the King*.

Appendix I: Reading Schedule

Semester 1

	PRIMARY	RATING*	SECONDARY	RATING
Week 1	The Church History	4.6.0	The Hobbit	3.1.6
Week 2	The Church History	4.6.0	The Hobbit	3.1.6
Week 3	The Church History	4.6.0	The Fellowship of the Ring	3.1.6
Week 4	The Church History	4.6.0	The Fellowship of the Ring	3.1.6
Week 5	Confessions	5.3.2	The Fellowship of the Ring	3.1.6
Week 6	Confessions	5.3.2	The Fellowship of the Ring	3.1.6
Week 7	Confessions	5.3.2	The Nine Tailors	1.0.9
Week 8	On the Incarnation	8.2.0	The Nine Tailors	1.0.9
Week 9	On the Incarnation	8.2.0	The Nine Tailors	1.0.9
Week 10	The Creeds	9.1.0	The Dragon and the Raven	1.6.3
Week 11	The Ecclesiastical History	3.6.1	The Dragon and the Raven	1.6.3
Week 12	The Ecclesiastical History	3.6.1	The Gospel of John	7.2.1
Week 13	The Ecclesiastical History	3.6.1	The Gospel of John	7.2.1
Week 14	The Rule of St. Benedict	7.2.1	The Merry Adventures of Robin Hood	1.3.6
Week 15	Beowulf	2.2.6	The Merry Adventures of Robin Hood	1.3.6
Week 16	Beowulf	2.2.6	The Merry Adventures of Robin Hood	1.3.6
Week 17	Beowulf	2.2.6	A Midsummer Night's Dream	3.1.6
Week 18	The Song of Roland	2.4.4	A Midsummer Night's Dream	3.1.6
Week 19	FINALS			

Semester 2

	PRIMARY	RATING	SECONDARY	RATING
Week 1	The Song of Roland	2.4.4	Winning His Spurs	1.6.3
Week 2	The History of the Kings of Britain	2.8.0	Winning His Spurs	1.6.3
Week 3	The History of the Kings of Britain	2.8.0	Winning His Spurs	1.6.3
Week 4	The History of the Kings of Britain	2.8.0	The Two Towers	3.1.6
Week 5	The History of the Kings of Britain	2.8.0	The Two Towers	3.1.6
Week 6	Macbeth	2.3.5	The Two Towers	3.1.6
Week 7	Macbeth	2.3.5	The Two Towers	3.1.6
Week 8	Sir Gawain and the Green Knight	2.3.5	Henry V	2.3.5
Week 9	Sir Gawain and the Green Knight	2.3.5	Henry V	2.3.5
Week 10	The Divine Comedy: Inferno	4.2.4	Richard III	2.3.5
Week 11	The Divine Comedy: Inferno	4.2.4	Richard III	2.3.5
Week 12	The Divine Comedy: Inferno	4.2.4	Ephesians	9.0.1
Week 13	The Canterbury Tales (Selected Tales)	2.2.6	Ephesians	9.0.1
Week 14	The Canterbury Tales (Selected Tales)	2.2.6	The Return of the King	3.1.6
Week 15	The Bondage of the Will	7.3.0	The Return of the King	3.1.6
Week 16	The Bondage of the Will	7.3.0	The Return of the King	3.1.6
Week 17	The Bondage of the Will	7.3.0	The Return of the King	3.1.6
Week 18	FINALS			

**The books are weighted in the following order: Theology, History and Literature*

Appendix II: Timeline

Do you yourselves know that you are saved through faith in Christ, not through anything you have done or ever will do, but simply through your faith in Christ's finished work on Calvary's cross—as He died in space and time, in history?
—Francis Schaeffer

HISTORY

47–44 B.C. Reign of Julius Caesar

31 B.C.–A.D. 14 Reign of Augustus

A.D. 14–37 Reign of Tiberius

A.D. 37–54 Reign of Caligula

A.D. 41–54 Reign of Claudius

LITERATURE

THEOLOGY

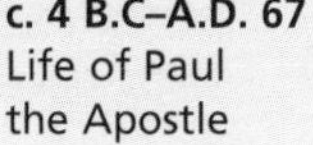

c. 4 B.C–A.D. 67 Life of Paul the Apostle

c. A.D. 10–100 Life of John the Apostle

c. A.D. 30 Crucifixion, Resurrection and Ascension of Christ

Paul at Ephesus

. . . and fear fell on them all, and the name of the Lord Jesus was magnified. And many who had believed came confessing and telling their deeds. Also, many of those who had practiced magic brought their books together and burned them in the sight of all. And they counted up the value of them, and it totaled fifty thousand pieces of silver. So the word of the Lord grew mightily and prevailed. (Acts 19:17–20)

HISTORY

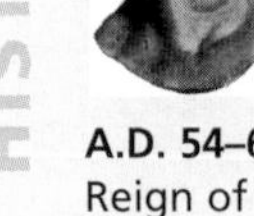

A.D. 54–68 Reign of Nero

A.D. 68–69 Reign of Galba

A.D. 69 Reign of Otho

A.D. 69 Reign of Vitellius

A.D. 69–79 Reign of Vespasian

A.D. 70 Destruction of Jerusalem

A.D. 79–8 Reign of Titus

LITERATURE

THEOLOGY

c. A.D. 62 *Letter to the Ephesians* Paul

c. A.D. 63 *Gospel of John*

A.D. 100 — A.D. 200 — A.D. 300

A.D. 81–96
Reign of
Domitian

A.D. 98–116
Reign of
Trajan

A.D. 193–211
Reign of
Severus

A.D. 249–251
Reign of
Decius

c. A.D. 260–339
Life of Eusebius

A.D. 284–305
Reign of
Diocletian

A.D. 286
Split of the
Roman Empire

c. A.D. 297–373
Life of
Athanasius

A.D. 306–337
Reign of
Constantine

Eusebius Sophronius Hieronymus—or Saint Jerome—is best known as the translator of the Bible from Greek and Hebrew into Latin. Jerome's edition, the Vulgate, is still the official biblical text of the Roman Catholic Church. Jerome was born around A.D. 340 in modern-day Bosnia to Christian parents but was not baptized until about 360, when he went to Rome to pursue his rhetorical and philosophical studies. He spent some time in the desert as an ascetic before being ordained a bishop around 379. One of the most learned of the western Fathers, in the Roman Catholic Church he is recognized as the patron saint of librarians and translators.

HISTORY

A.D. 308–324 Reign of Licinius

A.D. 313 Constantine and the Edict of Milan

c. A.D. 325 *History of the Church* Eusebius

THEOLOGY

c. A.D. 320 *On the Incarnation* Athanasius

A.D. 325 First Council of Nicea

c. A.D. 340–397 Life of Saint Ambrose

c. A.D. 360–435 Life of Pelagius

A.D. 367 Closing of the Canon

A.D. 386 St. Augustine Converts to Christianity

A.D. 400

A.D. 500

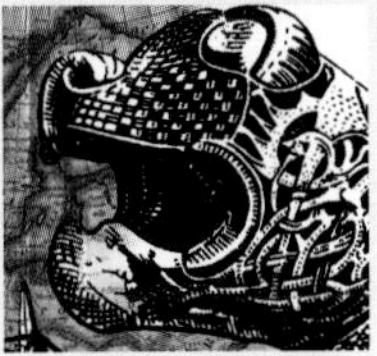

c. A.D. 400–1000
Barbarian Invasion and Vikings

A.D. 476
End of the Western Roman Empire

A.D. 527–565
Justinian the Great

A.D. 570–632
Mohammed and Islam

c. A.D. 398
Confessions
Augustine

A.D. 405
St. Jerome Completes the Vulgate

A.D. 451
The Council of Chalcedon

A.D. 480–543
Life of St. Benedict

A.D. 600

A.D. 700

HISTORY

A.D. 673–735 Life of Bede

A.D. 714–814 Charles Martel, Pepin the Sh
and Charlemagne

LITERATURE

THEOLOGY

c. A.D. 540 *Rule of St. Benedict*

A.D. 540 St. Benedict and Monasticism

A.D. 590–604 Pope Gregory (the Great)

A.D. 597 Augustine arrives in England

A.D. 800

A.D. 900

1000

c. A.D. 731 *Ecclesiastical History* Bede

August 15, 778 Battle of Roncevaux Pass

A.D. 871–901 Alfred the Great

A.D. 962–973 Otto I and the Holy Roman Empire

1054 The East/West Schism

1066 William the Conqueror and the Battle of Hastings

c. 1090–1155 Life of Geoffrey of Monmouth

c. A.D. 750 *Beowulf*

c. 1050 *The Song of Roland*

1100 | 1200 | 1300

HISTORY

1095–c. 1250 The Crusades

c. 1138 *History of the Kings of Britain* Geoffrey of Monmouth

1215 The Magna Carta

1254–1324 Marco Polo

c. 1300–1517 The Renaissance

1301 Black Guelfs come to power in Florence and Dante is exiled

LITERATURE

1265–1321 Life of Dante Alighieri

c. 1320 *The Divin Comedy: Inferno* Dante

1182–1224 St. Francis of Assisi

1225–1274 St. Thomas Aquinas

1400

1337–1453 The Hundred Years War, The Black Death, and Joan of Arc

1394–1460 Prince Henry the Navigator

1413–1422 Reign of Henry V

1453 The Fall of Constantinople to Mohammed II

1456 Gutenberg Prints the Bible

1340–1400 Life of Geoffrey Chaucer

c. 1380 *Sir Gawain and the Green Knight*

c. 1385–1400 *Canterbury Tales* Chaucer

1376–1417 The Great Papal Schism

c. 1380 John Wycliffe and John Huss

1500

HISTORY

1483–1485
Reign of Richard III

1492
Columbus Sails to the New World

1513–1538
Cortez, de Soto, de Leon, and Coronado, the Spanish Explorers

1519–1522
Magellan Circumnavigates the Earth

LITERATURE

THEOLOGY

1478
The Inquisition

1483–1546
Life of Martin Luther

1509–1564
John Calvin

1517
Martin Luther Begins the Reformation

September 1524
Erasmus writes his *Diatribe*

December 1525
Bondage of the Will Luther

1564–1616 Life of William Shakespeare

c. 1593 *Richard III* Shakespeare

c. 1596 *A Midsummer Night's Dream* Shakespeare

1525 Ulrich Zwingli and the Anabaptists

1534 The Act of Supremacy

1536 Calvin's *Institutes*

1545–1563 The Council of Trent

1560 John Knox and the Reformation in Scotland

1600 1700 1800 1900

HISTORY

1832–1902 Life of G.A. Henty

1882 *Winning His Spurs* Henty

1885 *The Dragon and the Raven* Henty

LITERATURE

c. 1599 *Henry V* Shakespeare

c. 1606 *MacBeth* Shakespeare

1853–1911 Life of Howard Pyle

1883 *Robin Hood* Pyle

1892–1973 Life of J.R.R. Tolkien

1893–1957 Life of Dorothy L. Sayers

1934 *The Nine Tailors* Sayers

THEOLOGY

John Ronald Reuel Tolkien (January 3, 1892–September 2, 1973) is the author of *The Hobbit* and *The Lord of the Rings.* He worked as reader in English language at Leeds from 1920 to 1925, as professor of Anglo-Saxon language at Oxford from 1925 to 1945, and of English language and literature, also at Oxford, from 1945 to 1959. He was a strongly committed Christian and a close friend of C. S. Lewis. Tolkien never expected his fictional stories to become popular, but he was persuaded by a former student to publish *The Hobbit* in 1937. *The Hobbit* was popular enough for the publisher to ask for a sequel. Tolkien spent more than ten years writing *The Lord of the Rings* and its appendices. Tolkien continued to work on the history of Middle-earth until his death.

1937 *The Hobbit* Tolkien

1954 *Fellowship of the Ring* Tolkien

1955 *The Two Towers* Tolkien

1955 *Return of the King* Tolkien

INDEX

SELECT ILLUSTRATION CREDITS

NED BUSTARD: **95, 101, 165, 182, 185, 190, 193, 221, 289, 301, 401, 402, 461, 491.** *More of Ned's work can be seen at www.WorldsEndImages.com.*

MATTHEW CLARK: **98, 103, 123, 124, 127, 129, 133, 138, 201, 227, 232, 245, 258, 290, 296, 297, 302, 303, 305, 311, 374, 404, 406, 410, 417, 463, 465, 466, 469, 472.** *More of Matthew's work can be seen at www.DrawingMatthewClark.com.*

HEIJIN ESTHER KIM: **316.** *Esther can be reached at heijin.kim@gordon.edu*

JUDITH HUNT: **130, 149, 196, 234, 238, 293, 298, 299, 313, 319, 340, 408, 415, 440, 464, 474.** *More of Judith's work can be seen at www.huntjudith.com.*

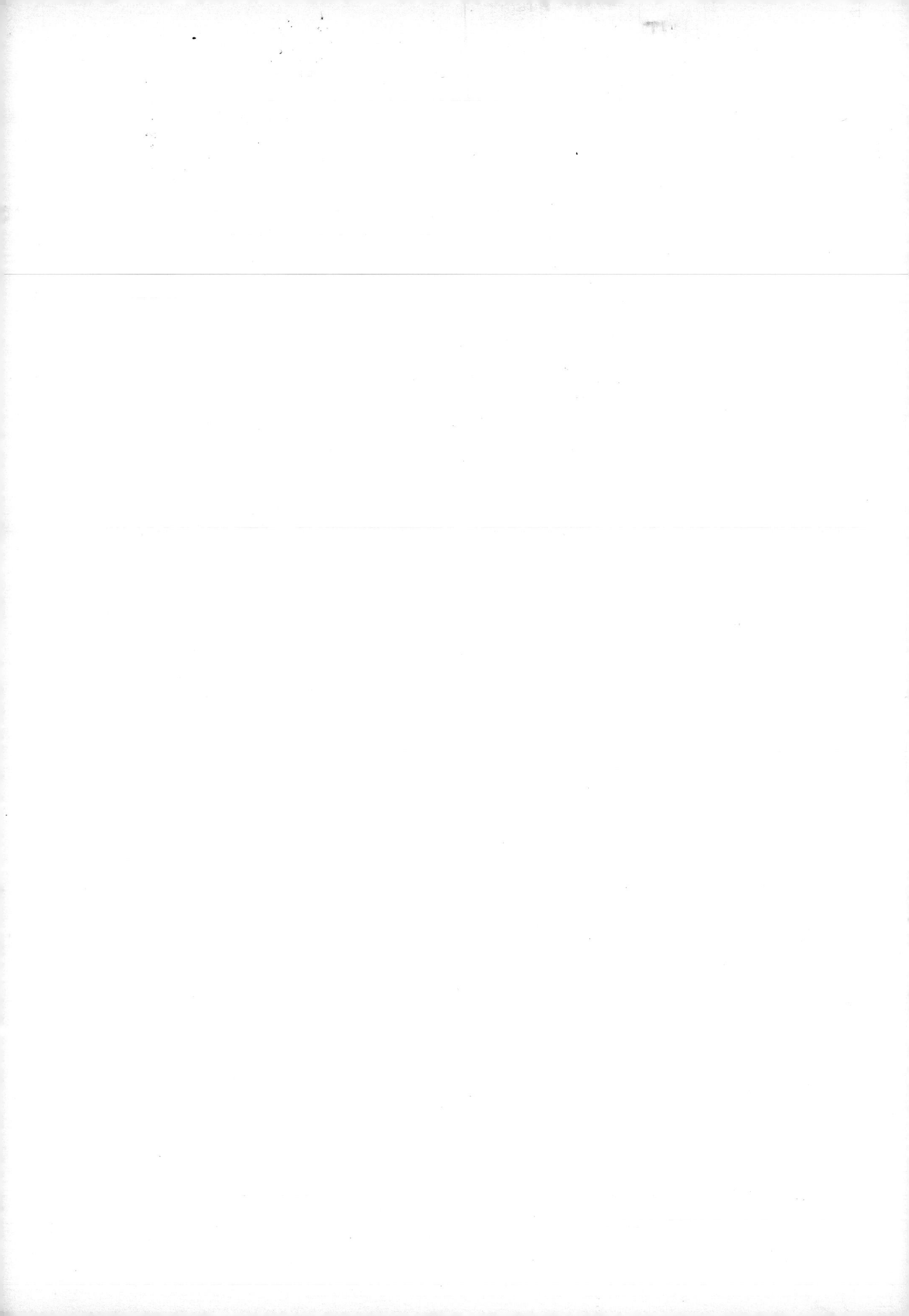